Real Estate and Taxation in Singapore

Real Estate
and Taxation in
Singapore

Tay Hong Beng · Leung Yew Kwong · See Wei Hwa

 World Scientific

NEW JERSEY · LONDON · SINGAPORE · BEIJING · SHANGHAI · HONG KONG · TAIPEI · CHENNAI · TOKYO

Published by

World Scientific Publishing Co. Pte. Ltd.

5 Toh Tuck Link, Singapore 596224

USA office: 27 Warren Street, Suite 401-402, Hackensack, NJ 07601

UK office: 57 Shelton Street, Covent Garden, London WC2H 9HE

Library of Congress Control Number: 2022944873

British Library Cataloguing-in-Publication Data
A catalogue record for this book is available from the British Library.

ISBN 978-981-122-649-6 (hardcover)
ISBN 978-981-122-652-6 (ebook for institutions)
ISBN 978-981-122-653-3 (ebook for individuals)

For any available supplementary material, please visit
https://www.worldscientific.com/worldscibooks/10.1142/11997#t=suppl

Desk Editor: Thaheera Althaf

Typeset by Stallion Press
Email: enquiries@stallionpress.com

Printed in Singapore

Preface

We have chosen the theme of Singapore real estate and tax for this book, for a couple of reasons. Firstly, real estate is highly sought after in land scarce Singapore and the topic has always generated strong interest. Secondly, it is noted that all the major taxes in Singapore, i.e. income tax, property tax, stamp duty and GST, may be applicable at various stages of the property ownership cycle, i.e. from the acquisition of the property, to its ownership and eventually the disposal of the property. This book will help the reader to navigate through the various tax issues encountered in the course of the ownership of a property.

Furthermore, in Singapore, fiscal tools have increasingly been used to curb or moderate the exuberance of the property market, especially the residential property market, and in the past, have been used to stimulate property development and ownership. This book will help the reader to appreciate the significance and impact of the various fiscal tools which have been introduced in Singapore over the years. As each property market cycle ebbed, some fiscal tools may have been dismantled or tweaked but the remnant features of some of these tools may still be observed. We will discuss some of these features.

Just as tax law can be quite complex, the structural framework governing the property market can also be complex. Some of the intricacies pertaining to the property market (e.g. the Master Plan and its land use zones, the land betterment charge system, the machinations of the Planning Act) have been grafted into the design of the tax system. Hence, a layer of complex tax rules may intersect with another layer of complex property market rules, which in turn gives rise to complicated tax law governing the Singapore real estate sector.

For example, in respect of stamp duty, the five land-use zones of "Residential", "Commercial and Residential", "Residential/Institution", "Residential with Commercial at 1st Storey" and "White" in the Master Plan promulgated under the Planning Act, have been used to identify properties for the levy of the additional buyer's stamp duty (ABSD) and the additional conveyance duty (ACD) under the Stamp Duties Act. However, the delineation of the precise land uses permissible within each of these zones for land-use planning purposes under the Planning Act, may not render those zones with the precise qualities for the seamless application of the taxes which are imposed to target the speculative demand of residential properties.

In this book, we will discuss the pertinent features of the Singapore property market where they intersect with the workings of the tax system. The views expressed in the book are wholly ours and they do not represent those of any organisation.

Tay Hong Beng
Leung Yew Kwong
See Wei Hwa

1 May 2022

Acknowledgement

The relevant Singapore legislation provisions are subject to copyright and are reproduced in the book with the permission of the Attorney-General's Chambers of Singapore ("AGC"). Readers of the book may consult the Singapore Statutes Online at https://sso.agc.gov.sg for the latest version of the relevant legislation provisions

Extracts from the cases reported in the Singapore Law Reports (Reissue) (1965–2009) and the Singapore Law Reports (2010-present) are reproduced with permission from the Singapore Academy of Law. All rights reserved. No portion of the cases may be used or reproduced without the prior written consent of the Singapore Academy of Law.

Contents

Preface   v
Acknowledgement   vii

Chapter 1 Takings and Givings: Transformational Role in Real
           Estate Landscape   1

1. Introduction   1
2. "Takings"   4
    2.1. Compulsory land acquisition   4
    2.2. En bloc or collective sales   31
    2.3. Transformation of Kampong Glam   47
3. "Givings"   52
    3.1. Rejuvenational role of the extension of state land leases   52
    3.2. Contest of space underground   56
    3.3. Repeal of rent control   58
    3.4. COVID-19 (Temporary Measures) Act   61

Chapter 2 Property Market Cycles: Fiscal and Macroprudential
           Measures   69

1. Introduction   69
2. Macroprudential Policy Instruments   73
3. Fiscal Measures   74
    3.1. Property tax   74
    3.2. Income tax   76

3.3. Stamp duty 78
3.4. Development charge 99

Chapter 3 Master Plan: From Blueprint to Guide 101

1. Introduction 101
2. Master Plan 103
   2.1. Long term plan 106
   2.2. The current 2019 Master Plan 108
   2.3. Master Plan zones 111
   2.4. Planning permission 121
3. Land Betterment Charge 126
   3.1. Chargeable consent 129
   3.2. Rates of land betterment charge 131
4. Development Charge 136
   4.1. Development ceiling 139
   4.2. Development baseline 140
   4.3. Development charge exemption 148
   4.4. Development charge table 150
   4.5. Section 39 valuation 164
   4.6. History of development charge 168
5. Differential Premium 173
   5.1. "Topping up" premium 181
6. Extension Charges under the Residential Property Act 182

Chapter 4 Real Estate Developers: A Much Regulated Sector 187

1. Introduction 187
2. Stamp Duty 189
   2.1. Additional Buyer's Stamp Duty 189
   2.2. En bloc purchase 192
   2.3. Conveyance directions 195
   2.4. Additional conveyance duty 199
   2.5. Mixed-use developments 199

3. Income Tax   200
    3.1. Time of recognition of income   201
    3.2. Deduction of costs   209
    3.3. Diminution in value   213
    3.4. Timing of deduction   218
    3.5. The single project concession   221
    3.6. Developer may hold investment properties   221
    3.7   Change of intention from trading stock to investment   223
4. Goods and Services Tax   236
5. Property Tax   238

Chapter 5 Property Investment: Deriving Long-Term Recurrent
           Income   243

1. Introduction   243
2. Income Tax   245
    2.1. Basis of taxation of rental income   245
    2.2. Deductions of outgoings and expenses   255
    2.3. Capital allowances   299
3. Goods and Services Tax   311
4. Property Tax   312
    4.1. Annual value   314
    4.2. Property tax rebates   326
5. Stamp Duty   328
    5.1. Lease vs licence   328
    5.2. Lease duty   330
    5.3. Revision of rent during the term of the lease   336

Chapter 6 Acquisition and Disposal of Real Estate: Asset Sale
           Transactions   341

1. Introduction   341
2. Acquisition of Real Estate in Singapore   342
    2.1. Buyer's stamp duty   343
    2.2. Additional buyer's stamp duty   351

2.3.	Goods and Services Tax	357
2.4.	Qualifying certificate and clearance certificate issued under the Residential Property Act	357
2.5.	Rules for new housing loans	364
3.	Disposal of Real Estate in Singapore	372
3.1.	Seller's stamp duty	372
3.2.	Income tax	378
3.3.	Goods and Services Tax	390

Chapter 7 Acquisition and Disposal of Real Estate Holding Entities: Equity Sale Transactions — 393

1.	Introduction	393
2.	ACD: An Added Complexity	394
2.1.	Introduction of the ACD regime	395
2.2.	Overview of the ACD regime	398
2.3.	ACDB and ACDS	399
2.4.	Fundamental concepts of ACD	400
2.5.	ACD rates	410
2.6.	Anti-avoidance provisions	411
3.	Stamp Duty	414
3.1.	Advancement of the duty point from the transfer instrument to the sale and purchase agreement	414
3.2.	Remission of stamp duty payable in respect of the sale and purchase agreement	415
3.3.	Stamp duty on deferred consideration and earn-outs	417
3.4.	Stamp duty and partnership interests	419
3.5.	Relief from stamp duty	422
4.	Income Tax	422
4.1.	Badges of trade test	422
4.2.	Safe harbour rule	423
4.3.	Singapore-sourced or foreign-sourced?	426
4.4.	Other income tax related issues	427
5.	Goods and Services Tax	428
6.	Property Tax	429

7. Due Diligence Work 430
8. Tax Warranties and Indemnities 431
   8.1. Tax warranties 431
   8.2. Disclosure letter 434
   8.3. Tax indemnity 437

Chapter 8 Singapore Real Estate Investment Trusts: 20 Years of
           Phenomenal Growth 439

1. Introduction 439
2. S-REITs: An Overview of the Key Milestones 441
   2.1. The initial years 444
   2.2. Internationalization of S-REITs 447
   2.3. REIT exchange traded funds and futures: The next
       engine of growth 450
   2.4. Ongoing mergers and consolidations 452
   2.5. Increasing focus on environmental and sustainability
       factors 453
3. Key Events Leading to the Listing of the First S-REIT 454
4. The S-REIT Advantage 456
   4.1. Real estate companies 456
   4.2. Investors 458
5. S-REITs: Growing the Real Estate Portfolio 459
   5.1. Acquisition of yield-accretive assets 459
   5.2. Asset enhancement initiatives 461
   5.3. Mergers and consolidations 461
6. Typical Structure of S-REITs 466
   6.1. S-REIT 467
   6.2. Sponsor 469
   6.3. Unitholders 470
   6.4. Trustee 471
   6.5. S-REIT manager 471
   6.6. Property manager 478
7. Code on Collective Investment Scheme for Property Funds 478
   7.1. Permissible investments 480

7.2. Limitation on sources of other revenue   481
7.3. Restriction on development activities   482
7.4. Limitations on borrowings and leverage   483
7.5. Valuation of the underlying real estate assets   487
8. Income Taxation of S-REITs, Approved Sub-Trusts and
   Approved REIT Exchange Traded Funds   488
   8.1. Income tax transparency treatment   491
9. Income Tax Treatment of Trustee   499
10. Income Tax Treatment of Unitholders   500
   10.1. Types of distribution   500
   10.2. Profile of unitholders   501
   10.3. Distributions out of specified income accorded with
          tax transparency treatment   501
   10.4. Distributions out of income subject to tax in the
          hands of trustee (i.e. where tax transparency does
          not apply)   503
   10.5. Distributions out of non-taxable amounts (e.g. capital
          gains or tax exempt income)   504
   10.6. Summary table   504
11. Income Tax Exemption of Foreign-Sourced Income   504
   11.1. Automatic tax exemption under section 13(8)   506
   11.2. Tax exemption under section 13(12)   507
12. Other Taxes   509
   12.1. Goods and Services Tax (GST)   509
   12.2. Stamp duty   512

Chapter 9 Business Trusts: An Alternative to REITs?   517

1. Introduction   517
2. Business Trusts: An Overview of the Key Milestones   520
   2.1. Listing of the first real estate focused business trust   520
   2.2. Largest IPO of a business trust and first merger between
         business trusts   522
   2.3. Proliferation of hospitality trusts   522
   2.4. Other observations   524

3. Business Trusts: Key Features   526
   3.1. What is a business trust   526
   3.2. Registration under the Business Trusts Act   528
   3.3. Registered business trusts vs S-REITs vs companies   529
   3.4. Other unique features pertaining to business trusts   533
4. Typical Structure of Registered Business Trusts   535
   4.1. Registered business trust   536
   4.2. Sponsor   537
   4.3. Trustee-manager   538
   4.4. Unitholders   541
5. Taxation of Registered Business Trusts   541
   5.1. Income tax   541
   5.2. Goods and Services Tax   546
   5.3. Stamp duty   547

Chapter 10 Private Real Estate Funds: A Platform to Enhance
           Value   549

1. Introduction   549
2. Fund Platforms of Singapore Real Estate Developers   550
3. Fund Management Ecosystem in Singapore   554
   3.1. Types of fund vehicles   556
   3.2. Common features of fund management arrangements   565
4. Typical Fund Structures   566
   4.1. Fund vehicles constituted as companies   567
   4.2. Fund vehicles constituted as limited partnerships   567
   4.3. Fund vehicles constituted as trusts   568
   4.4. Fund vehicles constituted as VCCs   569
5. Private Equity Real Estate Funds   570
   5.1. Overview   570
   5.2. Private equity funds   572
   5.3. Private equity real estate funds   573
   5.4. Private equity real estate funds vs REITs vs listed real
       estate companies   576
   5.5. Offer of securities   576

6. Fund Management 578
  6.1. Licensed fund management companies 579
  6.2. Registered fund management companies 579
  6.3. Other exempt fund management companies 582
7. Taxation of Fund Management Companies and Fund Vehicles 585
  7.1. Taxation of fund management companies 586
  7.2. Taxation of fund vehicles 588

Epilogue: Looking into the Future 605
Postscript 609
Authors' Biography 611
Index 613

CHAPTER 1

Takings and Givings: Transformational Role in Real Estate Landscape

1. Introduction

The vibrancy and diversity of the real estate landscape in Singapore owe a great deal to various land use policy and legislative initiatives which have been implemented in the course of our post-independence history.

At different times in the history of Singapore, certain tenets of property ownership or historic legacies had to be dismantled or modified for the development exigencies or to unleash the development energies of the land economy. In this chapter, we will discuss the transformational roles of a mix of land use policy and legislative initiatives which underpin the real estate landscape in Singapore. These initiatives may be classified as "takings" (which involve the expropriation of property or contractual rights of certain sectors with compensatory payments) and "givings"[1] (which may involve the award or conferment of rights to certain sectors frequently with consideration payments from those sectors).

A case of "physical giving" involves the allocation of "Housing and Development Board" (HDB) flats under the "Build-To-Order" (BTO) scheme, with attractive architecture and good locations such as those at

---

[1] See Abraham Bell and Gideon Parchomovsky, 'Givings', (2001) 111 *Yale Law Journal* 547. The term 'givings' was used as the logical opposite of 'takings' where the State exercises its power to expropriate the property interests of a person. The authors discussed three varieties of 'givings', namely 'physical giving', 'regulatory giving' and 'derivative giving'.

Duxton, Dawson and Boon Keng estates and the forthcoming Greater Southern Waterfront[2]. The windfall benefit or "lottery effect"[3] for the fortunate purchasers of those flats may be seen from the substantial gains[4] they make where they later sell the flats after satisfying the minimum occupation period. The phenomenon of "regulatory giving" arises whenever the Government, in the exercise of its regulatory powers, enhances the value of certain properties, e.g. where a higher-value use and/or greater intensity of development is allotted to land under the Master Plan. The existing owners which are affected may in turn monetize the enhanced capability of their land, either through resale or redevelopment. Finally, there is "derivative giving" where for example, the establishment or re-allocation of certain schools in the Bishan and Bukit Timah areas, enhances the values of residential properties in the neighborhood.

"Takings" and "givings" may be seen as two sides of the same coin. There may be a need for a "taking" (e.g. the compulsory acquisition of the Pearls Centre near the Outram Park MRT station) for there to be a subsequent "giving" (which may involve the re-parcellation and sale of the land around the MRT station). The most direct reciprocity in a "taking" and "giving" scenario, is perhaps in the "Selective En bloc Redevelopment Scheme" (SERS) where aging HDB flats are acquired under the Land Acquisition Act and the lessees of those flats are offered new replacement flats at reasonable prices on a priority basis in HDB BTO projects[5]. In the case of the 34-year old Rochor Centre (comprising 567 HDB flats and 187 shops), it was demolished

---

[2] There is social imperative for the inclusion of HDB estates in choice locations in order to keep the Singapore society egalitarian and inclusive and that some of the prime residential locations should reflect the diversity of the Singapore society: see 'Ensure the low-income group can live in 'choice' public estates,' *The Sunday Times*, 6 December 2020.

[3] See 'HDB 'lottery' conundrum: analysts weigh in on ways to mitigate it,' *The Business Times*, 3 December 2020, and 'Bigger subsidies, clawbacks being weighed to counter the HDB lottery effect' *The Business Times*, 25 May 2021 on various suggestions to mitigate the 'lottery' effect such as shorter leases, longer minimum occupation periods, sell-back to HDB and taxes or levies. Each of the suggestions has its trade-off. On 27 October 2021, the Government announced the prime location public housing (PLH) model to keep public housing in prime locations affordable, accessible and inclusive for Singaporeans. The Rochor BTO flats are to be the first to come under the PLH model.

[4] In 2019 and 2020 respectively, there were 64 and 82 HDB flats which were sold for at least $1 million.

[5] In Ting Xu and Wei Gong, 'Taking as giving, appropriation as access: transfers of land development rights and China's recent experiments,' (2013) 64 *Northern Ireland Legal Quarterly* 411, the authors in reading through the 'community lens', postulated that taking could be giving and appropriation could also provide access. For a discussion of some of the perceived criteria for SERS, see 'Will your HDB flat be put up for SERS,' *EdgeProp*, 20 September 2021.

to make way for the southern stretch of the North–South Corridor. Any remnant land may then be put to more profitable use. The HDB flat owners who had to vacate the site, were paid market values of their old flats, and were assured of new replacement HDB flats at BTO prices, near Kallang MRT station. It was a win–win proposition in the continuous renewal of the Singapore built environment[6].

Together, the "takings" and "givings" work as enablers to transform the real estate development scene in Singapore. Both "takings" and "givings" may be seen as public intervention measures and there are three broad approaches in such measures in the property market with different levels of public intervention, namely (i) direct public intervention; (ii) regulatory measures; and (iii) market incentives[7]. A form of direct public intervention in "taking" and "giving" are the compulsory acquisition of land and the development of HDB BTO[8] flats for allocation to eligible buyers, respectively. A form of regulatory measure in "taking" and "giving", are the control of rent of properties and its subsequent decontrol respectively. A form of market incentive in "takings" and "givings" will be the use of tax or plot ratio incentives respectively, in discouraging or facilitating the behavior of the market players. In this chapter, the following "takings" and "givings" are discussed:

- Takings
  - (a) the regime of compulsory land acquisition[9];
  - (b) the regime of *en bloc* sales; and
  - (c) the repossession of Istana Kampong Glam and the transformation of the Kampong Glam area.
- Givings
  - (a) the rejuvenational role of the extension of State land leases before their expiry date;

---

[6] See 'Rochor Centre case: Compensation relook?,' *The Straits Times*, 18 January 2012.

[7] Gill-Chin Lim, 'Land markets and public policy: A conceptual framework,' *Habitat International* 11(1) (1987), 23–27. The three approaches stated by the author have some broad correspondence with 'physical giving', 'regulatory giving' and 'derivative giving' postulated by Abraham Bell and Gideon Parchomovsky.

[8] 'BTO' is the acronym for Build-To-Order flats which are sold directly by the Housing and Development Board.

[9] Compulsory acquisition of land is frequently referred to as 'eminent domain' and 'takings' in the United States: see Kim, Lee and Somin, *Eminent Domain: A Comparative Perspective* (Cambridge University Press, 2017) and George Skouras, *Takings Law and the Supreme Court* (Peter Lang Publisher, 1998).

(b)   the expansion of the use of subterranean space;

(c)   the repeal of rent control; and

(d)   the rental relief during the COVID-19 outbreak in 2020.

2. "Takings"

2.1. Compulsory land acquisition

In the early post-independence days, when there was a great need for accelerated development of affordable housing and infrastructure, the Government had resorted to the greater use of the powers under the Land Acquisition Act. At that time, large tracts of land in Singapore were still occupied by disused or under-used rubber estates, cemeteries and squattered farm land[10].

Besides the resort to compulsory acquisition powers for affordable public housing[11] and infrastructural development for roads, mass rapid transit, airports, etc., the powers were also used for the assembly of suitably sized plots of land for sale to and development by the private sector. For example, many small plots which accommodated shophouses were acquired and amalgamated to accommodate the modern buildings with larger footprints. Compulsory acquisition has also been resorted to where:

(a)   there was a need for comprehensive development of an area close to Government infrastructural works. For example, the Pearls Centre, a mixed development of retail and residential units together with a cinema, was acquired in 2012 under the Land Acquisition Act[12] for the construction of underground tunnels for Outram MRT and also to

---

[10] See Lim Chin Joo, 'Compulsory acquisition in Singapore,' (1968) 10 *Malayan Law Review* 1.

[11] See Stephen Yeh, *Households and Housing* (1984), Department of Statistics Census Monograph No. 4, on the Singapore housing situation in 1980, the tracing of the growth in the housing stock from 1970 to 1980 and the projection of housing needs and demand for the period from 1980 to 1990, and also John Humphrey, *Geographic Analysis of Singapore's Population* (1985), Department of Statistics Census Monograph No. 5.

[12] In a press release, 'Pearls Centre Owners and Tenants Accept Government's Compensation,' by the Singapore Land Authority on 25 April 2013, it was reported the 241 (out of 243) or 99.2% of the Pearls Centre owners have accepted the Government's compensation package comprising the statutory compensation and an ex-gratia payment. The remaining two owners have requested for an extension of time for them to respond to the offer of the compensation package.

pave the way for a future comprehensive development of the Outram MRT station area. The entire Outram area (comprising also the area formerly occupied by the Outram Park public housing) will no doubt provide a number of sites under the Government Land Sales program for competitive bidding in future[13]; and

(b) public safety requires such acquisition: The 5-storey Hock Kee House at the corner of Geylang Road and Paya Lebar Road was acquired in 2005, as its structure was considered unsafe with the commencement of deep excavation works required for the construction of the Circle Line[14]. In April 2021, a 4-storey mixed use building at Nos. 68–74 Thomson Road situated opposite United Square, was also acquired as the building was considered not strong enough to withstand the excavation works for the North-South Corridor tunnel nearby[15].

Of course, the exercise of the compulsory acquisition powers requires political will and general public support. As Dr Liu Thai Ker stated[16]:

To develop a city, a government needs to have ample land. We are fortunate that the Singapore government had the strong support of citizens for acquiring land for public development. The ability to acquire land for development is one of the key reasons Singapore has managed to become a highly liveable city in a relatively short time. In order to gain public support for land acquisition, there must be a clear urban plan explaining every parcel of acquired land will be used for, and the government should keep to such commitments. Furthermore, landowners should always be properly compensated according to the prevailing market value of the acquired land.

---

[13] Former Head of Civil Service, Mr Ngiam Tong Dow referred to the Government policy of acquiring private properties within a certain radius of a MRT system, so that small lots could be consolidated and tendered out publicly for comprehensive development, in Zhang Zhibin (ed.), *Dynamics of the Singapore Success Story: Insights by Ngiam Tong Dow* (Cengage Asia Pte Ltd, 2011), p. 151.

[14] See S. Jayakumar, *Governing: A Singapore Perspective* (Straits Times Press, 2020), pp. 126–128.

[15] See 'Thomson Road building next to North-South Corridor tunnel to be demolished for safety reasons', *The Straits Times,* 16 April 2021.

[16] *Key Factors for Successful Urbanisation: Singapore's Experience*, CLC Insights, Issue No. 54, February 2020, published by the Centre of Liveable Cities. Dr Liu was formerly Chief Executive Officer and Chief Planner of the Urban Redevelopment Authority.

In Singapore, the policy to use the compulsory powers of the State to undertake further development for economic growth is a deliberate one. This can be seen from the non-adoption of Article 13 of the Malaysian Constitution in the formulation of the Singapore Constitution at the time of independence from Malaysia in 1965[17]. Article 13 of the Malaysian Constitution reads as follows:

1. No person shall be deprived of property save in accordance with law.
2. No law shall provide for the compulsory acquisition or use of the property without adequate compensation.

The then Minister for Law, Mr E. W. Barker provided the rationale for the non-adoption of Article 13 as follows[18]:

Clause 13 — We have specifically set out to exclude. The reason is quite simple. This [the Malaysian] Constitution was drawn up by five eminent jurists from five of the major Commonwealth countries for the old Federation of Malaya. It is, in form, modelled upon a similar provision in the Constitution of the Republic of India. Since the passage of that section in the Indian Constitution, amendments have had to be introduced because land reforms were not possible, if the strict tenor of the words were to be complied with. In other words, in clause 2, once we spell out that no law shall provide for the compulsory acquisition or use of property without adequate compensation, we open the door for litigation and ultimately for adjudication by the Court on what is or is not adequate compensation.

... It very often happens, as it did in the case of the development of the Jurong industrial site, that when public funds have been expended in considerable amounts for the development of roads, services, harbours, the adjacent land appreciates in value. And when it became necessary to acquire parts of the adjacent land for future expansion of the estate itself or for ancillary services such as schools, hospitals, and so on, we had to pay the owner under our present acquisition laws the enhanced value of

---

[17] S 6 of the Republic of Singapore Independence Act, No. 9 of 1965, also provided specifically that 'Article 13 [of the Malaysian constitution] shall cease to have effect.'

[18] *Singapore Parliamentary Debates, Official Report*, 22 December 1965, vol. 24, cols 435–436.

the land, a value to which he himself had contributed nothing and which was, in fact, created wholly by the expenditure of State funds .... Whilst we were still in Malaysia, we had sought to get Article 13 excluded in its application to us, but, in the nature of things, these matters took a very long time for any decision to be made or for some reason or other no decision was made. Now the jurisdiction again reverts to this House and it is our intention that the Land Acquisition Bill shall be proceeded with and Article 13 excluded.

Earlier when Singapore was still part of Malaysia, the Land Acquisition (Amendment No. 2) Bill 1964 was tabled in the Singapore Legislative Assembly on 10 June 1964. The Bill was sent to the Select Committee but was withdrawn on advice by the State Advocate General in view of the operation of the Article 13 of the Malaysian Constitution. The then Minister for Law, Mr E. W. Barker explained the withdrawal as follows[19]:

> The State Advocate-General's Chambers have looked into these matters and have advised that, in order to remove any doubts on the validity of this new legislation, it will be necessary for the Malaysian Parliament to exempt such a Bill from the operation of Article 13 of the Constitution ....
>
> Representation will be made to the Central Government for such an exemption provision to be passed in Parliament in order that these projects can be carried out in Singapore without any uncertainty about the constitutional validity of the formula for compensation.

After Singapore became independent, the Constitutional Commission appointed in 1966 to look into the issue of protecting minority rights, recommended the provision of a constitutional safeguard for property, which was similar to the provisions of Article 13 of the Malaysian Constitution, and the proposed provision was as follows:

1. No person shall be deprived of property save in accordance with law.
2. No law shall provide for the compulsory acquisition or use of property except for a public purpose or a purpose useful or beneficial to the public and except upon just terms.

---

[19] *Singapore Legislative Assembly Debates, Official Report*, 16 June 1965, vol. 23, col. 812.

Such a constitutional safeguard was however not adopted in the Singapore Constitution. In explaining the background to such non-adoption, Mr K. Shanmugam, then Minister for Foreign Affairs and Minister of Law in delivering the keynote address at the Rule of Law Symposium 2012 said[20]:

> Property rights are fundamental to a market economy. We respect that, and the ordinary law of the land recognises and gives effect to property rights. But, differently from other countries, we made a conscious decision, when we gained independence, not to enshrine the right of property in the *Constitution*. We also gave the Government wide powers to acquire land for development.
>
> We had several reasons for doing this. Singapore is a small country. Land is scarce. We could not leave its use and allocation purely in private hands. To pursue economic growth, the Government had to actively optimise the use of land. The Government also had another goal — the social and political goal of universal homeownership. To do this, the Government had to acquire land for public housing. The Government's approach at that time was not consistent with market principles, or received wisdom on the sanctity of private landed property. But they were certainly aimed at the public good.
>
> In many countries, the extensive powers of acquisition that we have had been abused for private gain. But in Singapore we have used those powers for good. As a result of the Government's policies, about 85% of Singaporeans today live in public housing. Homeownership is around 90%. We are a property-owning democracy. Citizens have a home to call their own, a real stake in their country.

Nevertheless, a challenge against compulsory acquisition was made in *Eng Foong Ho v Attorney-General*[21] on the ground that the principle of equal protection in Article 12 of the Singapore Constitution was breached. In that case, a Chinese temple which was close to the new Bartley Mass Rapid Transit (MRT) station was acquired, whereas the nearby Ramakrishna Mission and the Bartley Christian Church were not acquired. In that case, the Urban

---

[20] K. Shanmugam, 'The rule of law in Singapore,' [2012] *Singapore Journal of Legal Studies* 357.

[21] [2008] 3 SLR(R) 437. Cited by the Court of Appeal in *Syed Suhail bin Syed Zin v Attorney-General* [2021] 1 SLR 809, where the 'deliberate and arbitrary' test was mentioned in evaluating whether there is discrimination in an executive action.

Redevelopment Authority (URA) explained that the temple adjoined State land, which offered the opportunity for the amalgamation of the temple and State land for the optimization of land use, whereas the Ramakrishna Mission was under study for conservation and was eventually *gazetted* for conservation and the site of the church did not offer the opportunity for the amalgamation with the adjoining land. There was no deliberate and arbitrary discrimination against the Chinese temple and the challenge was dismissed by the courts. Nevertheless, it has to be noted that the compulsory acquisitions of properties used for religious worship have to be handled with sensitivity[22].

The approach of the Government in respect of land use is communitarian[23]. As was explained by the then Prime Minister, Mr Lee Kuan Yew in his address at the opening of the Singapore Academy of Law on 31 August 1990[24]:

> The basic difference in our approach springs from our traditional Asian value system which places the interests of the community over and above that of the individual.
>
> In English doctrine, the rights of the individual must be the paramount consideration. We shook ourselves free from the confines of English norms which did not accord with customs and values of the Singapore society.
>
> … We also put communitarian interests over those of the individual, when sea-front land is acquired for reclamation by cancelling the right of individual sea-front owners to compensation for loss of sea frontage[25].
>
> And in acquiring fire-sites we pay compensation as without vacant possession even though the premises had been vacated because of the fire[26].

In a later interview on 31 August 2012, Mr Lee in reply to a question posed by Dr Liu Thai Ker, said[27]:

---

[22] See S. Jayakumar, *Governing: A Singapore Perspective* (Straits Times Press, 2020), pp. 124–126.

[23] See 'Land Law and Public Housing' in Connie Carter, *Eyes on the Prize — Law and Economic Development in Singapore* (Kluwer Law International, 2002).

[24] (1990) 2 SAcLJ 155.

[25] This was achieved through the legislative amendment of the Foreshores Act.

[26] This refers to the former 'fire site' provisions in the Land Acquisition Act where land which was acquired after a fire, could be compensated at one-third of the vacant land value.

[27] *Urban Solutions,* Issue 2, February 2013, p. 10 published by Centre of Liveable Cities.

Dr Liu: I feel that land acquisition is an example of our very creative, farsighted, unconventional legal system, which is one of the key factors to our success story. What would you say about that?

Mr Lee: I anticipated these problems. At the low point [in the property market], people gave up on Singapore and said, "this place is going down the drain" and property prices went down. So I pushed this legislation through. It's probably because of my legal background that I wanted to get the legality of what we were doing properly entrenched, so that it cannot be varied and changed for fickle reasons.

2.1.1. *Public purpose*

The procedure of the compulsory acquisition involves the publication of a *Gazette* notification of the acquisition of the relevant land lots. In this respect, section 5(1) of the Land Acquisition Act provides that:

Whenever any particular land is needed —

(a) for any public purpose;
(b) by any person, corporation or statutory board, for any work or an undertaking which, in the opinion of the Minister, is of public benefit or of public utility or in the public interest; or
(c) for any residential, commercial or industrial purposes,

the President, may by notification published in the *Gazette*, declare the land to be required for the purpose specified in the notification.

The statutory language in section 5(1)(c), i.e. "for any residential, commercial or industrial purposes" in contradistinction with that in section 5(1)(a), i.e. "for any public purpose", seems to suggest that land may be acquired for "residential, commercial or industrial purposes" which may not be a public purpose[28]. However, the purpose of section 5(1)(c) was explained by the then Prime Minister, Mr Lee Kuan Yew, during the Second Reading of the Land Acquisition (Amendment No 2) Bill 1964, as follows[29]:

---

[28] In the Report of the Housing Committee 1947, (1948) Government Printing Office, the Committee stated that it was at least doubtful whether the acquisition of land for housing was acquisition for a 'public purpose' within the meaning of the Land Acquisition Ordinance.

[29] *Singapore Parliamentary Debates, Official Report*, 10 June 1964, vol. 23, col. 26. The 1964 Bill was sent to the Select Committee but was withdrawn on the advice of the State Advocate-General that the validity

The Explanatory Statement of the Bill sets out the contents of the Bill. Section 5 of the principal Ordinance which provided for the acquisition of land for public purposes has been redrafted to define specifically and enlarge the meaning of "public purposes".

This redraft, which is more specific, follows the Federal Land Acquisition Act and is considered desirable in view of the increasing tempo of public development and the need to acquire land for a variety of public purposes, including residential development by the Housing and Development Board, industrial development by the Economic Development Board, as well as urban renewal of the City as envisaged in the next few years.

In *Teng Fuh Holdings Pte Ltd v Collector of Land Revenue*, Andrew Phang J (as he then was), held that the purpose in section 5(1)(c) was also to be a "public purpose", even where the land acquired were later to be resold to private developers. The learned judge after citing the above-mentioned passage of the Parliamentary speech of the Prime Minister, said[30]:

> The above passage appears to support the interpretation I have taken to the effect that whilst the legislative intention behind s 5(1) of the Act in general and s 5(1)(c) in particular is indeed broad, any acquisitions pursuant thereto (including s 5(1)(c)) would still be regarded as serving the "public purpose" ... This might conceivably include the acquisition of land for resale to private developers. Arguably, such a purpose might not have fallen within the rubric of "public purpose" under s 5(1)(a) in the *traditional* sense of the term but would probably be considered to do so now. I refer, in particular, to the phrase, "*enlarge the meaning of* 'public purposes'" [emphasis added], in the quotation in the preceding paragraph. This particular legislative amendment was in fact ultimately incorporated into the present Act[31].

---

of the provisions may be called into question on the basis that they may be in breach of Article 13 of the Federal Constitution, at the time when Singapore was still part of Malaysia. The provisions were reintroduced in the Land Acquisition (Amendment) Bill 1966.

[30] [2006] 3 SLR(R) 507 at [52].

[31] In the controversial US Supreme Court case of *Kelo v City of London*, (2005) 545 US 1, it was held that the use of eminent domain powers to enable an urban redevelopment plan featuring a mix of private uses met the 'public purpose' test as the redevelopment would increase the city's tax base and would bring general economic benefits to the community.

Indeed, the release of land for private enterprise development has been a key plank of urban renewal strategy from the early days. As Mr Alan Choe explained[32]:

The release of land for private enterprise in an urban renewal area must be based on a competitive system. This could be done by accepting the highest price for the land without regard to design or accepting the best design scheme without regard to land price. Both these systems have short-comings. The best alternative is by competition for use of the land on lease based on the best design, land price and economic proposition submitted. This would suggest a happy compromise enabling fulfilment of broad objectives. Extreme care and judgement should, therefore, be exercised in drawing up the terms and conditions of the competition.

In order to accommodate considerations of good design schemes for strategic Government Land Sales sites the dual-envelope Concept and Price tender system, was introduced in 1997[33]. Under the dual-envelope system, the "first envelope" contains the design schemes of the competitive bidders. Only those bidders with qualifying designs in their "first envelopes", will have their "second envelopes" opened as well. The site is then awarded to the tenderer who has submitted the highest bid amongst those with qualifying designs[34]. In the case of the award of the land for the two integrated resorts to Marina Bay Sands and Resorts World Sentosa, the prices of the land were however fixed and the bidders therefore competed on the basis of

---

[32] See Alan Choe, 'Urban renewal' in Ooi Jin-Bee and Chiang Hai Ding (eds.), *Modern Singapore* (University of Singapore Press, 1969), p. 168. Mr Choe was then Head of the Urban Renewal Department in the Housing & Development Board. The Urban Renewal Department later became the Urban Redevelopment Authority in 1974 and Mr Choe was its first General Manager.

[33] See *Land Framework of Singapore: Building a Sound Land Administration and Management System*, Urban Systems Studies series (Centre of Liveable Cities, 2018), p. 45. With the advent of the Singapore Green Plan 2030, the provision of a centralized cooling system to improve the overall energy efficiency of development has become a factor for consideration of the concept in the dual envelope system: see 'URA extends Jalan Anak Bukit site's tender deadline to June 29', *The Business Times,* 6 April 2021.

[34] In 2019, URA modified the dual-envelope system for the two sites: a White site at Kampong Bugis and a hotel site at River Valley Road released under the 2H2019 Government Land Sales (GLS) program. Under the modified system, a tenderer with a shortlisted concept proposal could be offered the option to top up its bid price to match the highest bid price amongst the shortlisted concept proposals. This option will only be offered selectively to only one or two exceptionally outstanding proposals, *The Edge,* 16 December 2019.

the merits of their designs and concepts[35]. The criteria for evaluating the tenders for the sites of the integrated resorts included: (a) tourism appeal and contribution, (b) architectural concept and design, (c) quantum of development investment and (d) strength of the consortium and partners[36].

Where the Government were to acquire land even for general development, such general development would be a public purpose. With regard to the Government's decision of a public purpose, Chua J in *Galstaun and another v Attorney-General*, stated[37]:

> Government is the proper authority for deciding what a public purpose is. When the Government declares that a purpose is a public purpose, it must be presumed that the Government is in possession of facts which induce the Government to declare that the purpose is a public purpose.

In acquiring land, the purpose for which the land is proposed to be acquired is stated in the *Gazette* notification. In this regard, the then Minister for Law Mr E. W. Barker stated in Parliament in response to a question on land acquisition[38]:

> When Government acquires land, the purpose for doing so is always stated. Where private land is required for a specific development, i.e. road widening, Mass Rapid Transit, school development, defence or Housing and Development Board purposes, the Gazette Notification under section 5 of the Land Acquisition Act will always as a matter of policy specifically state so. However, for cases where development is of general nature, i.e.

---

[35] See 'Marina Bay IR land price fixed at $1.2b,' *The Business Times*, 5–6 November 2005. The land prices for the integrated resort sites at Marina Bay and Sentosa, were fixed at S$1.2 billion and S$600,000 respectively.

[36] See S. Jayakumar, *Be at the Table or Be on the Menu: A Singapore Memoir* (Straits Times Press, 2015), p. 170.

[37] [1979–1980] SLR 589 at [9].

[38] *Singapore Parliamentary Debates, Official Report,* 9 December 1986, col. 899. In the cases of the compulsory acquisition of the Jurong Country Club and the Raffles Country Club, the purpose was for the proposed Kuala Lumpur–Singapore High Speed Rail (HSR) project and *for general development.* Although the HSR project was formally abandoned on 1 January 2021, the 143-hectare Raffles Country Club site is still needed for the Cross Island Line's western depot and the integrated train-testing center and the 67-hectare Jurong Country Club site will be used for mixed-use development comprising offices, hotels, retails and residences: 'HSR termination will not affect overall plans for Jurong: Ong [Ye Kung],' *The Straits Times*, 5 January 2021.

for clearance of dilapidated structure under the Garden City Programme, for sprucing up land within the water catchment boundaries where urbanisation will not be allowed or for clearance of remnant squatters, the public purpose under section 5 in the Gazette Notification will then be stated as "General Development". In the majority of cases, the acquisitions are for specific purposes.

Section 5(3) of the Land Acquisition Act provides that the *Gazette* notification is "conclusive evidence" that the land is needed for the purposes specified in the section 5(1) notification. However, the Court of Appeal in *Teng Fuh Holdings Ltd v Collector of Land Revenue,* where the acquired land was not developed for the specified purpose for more than 20 years, stated[39]:

> We are of the view that when the allegation of bad faith is founded on a very substantial period of inaction, an explanation should be given. Prolonged inaction, if not explained, could constitute an arguable case or a *prima facie* case of reasonable suspicion that the land was not needed for general redevelopment when it was acquired in 1983.

Nevertheless, substantial latitude and flexibility is given to the government authorities in the exercise of the compulsory acquisition powers. In this regard, Andrew Phang J (as he then was) in *Teng Fuh Holdings Ltd v Collector of Land Revenue* said[40]:

> In my view, and viewing the matter from the particular perspective of land acquisition in the Singapore context, it is imperative that a balance be found in the tension between ensuring that the purposes of the [Land Acquisition] Act and ensuring the public benefit are achieved on the one hand and ensuring that there is no abuse of power on the other. In this regard, it is important to note that the Act was promulgated not only for public benefit but also because land is an extremely scarce and therefore valuable resource in the Singapore context These are in fact inextricably related reasons. This being the case, it is clear why much more latitude and flexibility is given to government authorities. As a corollary, it is not the

---

[39] [2007] 2 SLR(R) 568 at [38].

[40] [2006] 3 SLR 507 at [36].

task of the courts to sit as makers of policy. This would in fact be the very antithesis of what the courts ought to do. But latitude and flexibility stops where abuse of power begins.

For all practical purposes, the owner would have little right to object to the compulsory acquisition. In this regard, the Court in *Lim Kim Som v Sheriffa Taibah bte Abdul Rahman* stated[41]:

> The owner of land has no right to object to the acquisition.... There is no way an owner of the subject land can object to the acquisition and there is no way he can take steps to prevent the progress of the machinery of acquisition. His only interest .... is how much he would get as compensation for the acquisition of his land.

Nevertheless, from time to time, the statutory language in the Land Acquisition Act had to be ironed out. In the past, statutory boards undertook some compulsory acquisition work themselves and had some of their officers appointed as Collectors of Land Revenue for that purpose[42]. The statutes which created those statutory boards, had language which in some instances[43], seemed to suggest that the statutory boards had first to attempt acquisition by private treaty before resorting to compulsory acquisition. In *United Engineers Ltd v Collector of Land Revenue*[44], Lai Kew Chai J in construing the then relevant provisions of the Port of Singapore Authority Act said:

---

[41] [1994] 1 SLR(R) 233 at [44]. This case concerned a contract for the sale of a property which was discharged due to frustration as the property concerned was subject to compulsory acquisition under the Land Acquisition Act, after the contract was entered into. See also *Liten Logistics Services Pte Ltd v ORG Powell Packaging Pte Ltd and Another Appeal*, [2013] SGCA 42.

[42] The compulsory acquisition work was subsequently consolidated within the Land Office (which later became the Singapore Land Authority in 2001) in the late 1980s. This follows from the establishment of a committee in 1987 chaired by Permanent Secretary Ngiam Tong Dow to review land acquisition policies and to establish tighter checks and balances. The establishment of the committee followed the suicide of the then Minister for National Development, Mr Teh Cheang Wan who was being investigated for accepting two bribes. As the then Prime Minister, Mr Lee Kuan Yew said: 'In one case, it was to allow a development company to retain part of its land which had been earmarked for compulsory government acquisition, and in the other to assist a developer in the purchase of state land for private development,': see *Land Acquisition and Resettlement: Securing Resources for Development* (Centre of Liveable Cities, 2014), pp. 38–39.

[43] Specifically, the statutory text had the words 'and cannot be acquired by agreement'.

[44] [1981–1982] SLR(R) 540.

[22] I am accordingly satisfied that plainly the words in the subsection are merely words descriptive of a state of affairs and are not intended to prescribe a condition precedent which the Port of Singapore Authority has to comply.

[23] Read in this light, the Port of Singapore Authority under the subsection has to satisfy the President of the Republic of Singapore that the land it requires for its purposes is not available for acquisition by private treaty. If the President thinks fit, compulsory acquisition will be ordered. It is exclusively a matter between the Port of Singapore Authority and the President in the course of public administration. Seeing that the subsection and the Land Acquisition Act is not dealing with the same subject of compulsory acquisition and are not in conflict, it must obviously follow that neither the maxim *generalia specialibus non derogant* (general things do not derogate from special things) nor the other maxim *generalibus specialia derogant* (special things derogate from general things) is of any relevance in these proceedings. This is the true, natural and reasonable construction which does not do violence to the scheme of compulsory acquisition of land in Singapore for public purposes.

Following that case, the Statutes (Miscellaneous Amendments) Act 1983[45] was enacted to remove any doubt that any compulsory acquisition of land for the relevant statutory boards may be made without prior negotiations with the landowner. The Explanatory Statement to the Statutes (Miscellaneous Amendments) Bill 1982[46] stated as follows:

This Bill seeks to amend the provisions of the Acts specified in the Schedule so as to remove any doubt that any compulsory acquisition of land for the purposes of the statutory bodies established by those Acts can be made without prior negotiations with the landowner.

The Bill further provides that no previous compulsory acquisition will be questioned on the ground that there had been no prior negotiations with the landowner and also for the dismissal of any pending action in respect of any such matter. It confirms a High Court decision on this point and puts an end to all further litigation on the matter.

[45] No. 7 of 1983.
[46] No. 25 of 1982.

With the coming into operation of the Statutes (Miscellaneous Amendments) Act 1983, the words "and cannot be acquired by agreement" in the Port of Singapore Authority Act, the Economic Development Board Act, the Jurong Town Corporation Act, the Public Utilities Act, the Housing and Development Act, the Preservation of Monuments Act, the Urban Redevelopment Act and the National University of Singapore Act, were deleted.

In Singapore, the Cabinet oversees each compulsory acquisition proposal by the Government with robust procedures[47]. As the then Deputy Prime Minister and Minister for Law, Professor S Jayakumar said in the Parliamentary debate on the Land Acquisition (Amendment) Bill 2007, on 11 April 2007[48]:

> ...all proposals for land acquisition are carefully considered. Government agencies that initiate acquisition must provide full justifications on why the acquisition is necessary. They would also have to ensure that prior approval is obtained for the intended use before requests for acquisition can be considered. For major acquisitions, the proposals will also have to be presented to a Ministerial committee comprising the Minister for Law, Minister for National Development and which sometimes can include other Ministers like the Minister for Transport if it concerns land acquisition related to MRT or major expressway development. Finally, every proposal for land acquisition must be submitted to Cabinet for approval.

Such a robust procedure has been put in place, as compulsory land expropriation may be abused to benefit particular individuals or groups of

---

[47] Jianlin Chen, 'Curbing Rent-Seeking and Inefficiency with Broad Takings Powers and Under Compensation: The Case of Singapore from a Givings Perspective,' (2010) 19 *Pacific Rim Law & Policy Journal* 1. In 2011, the Singapore Land Authority established a Land Acquisition Inter-Agency Committee, chaired by a senior official of the Ministry of Law and attended by key development and user agencies. The Committee allows agencies to examine alternatives to acquisition more closely and to discuss the timing, management and announcement of the proposed acquisition: *Land Acquisition and Resettlement: Securing Resources for Development,* (Centre for Liveable Cities, 2014), p. 38. See also S. Jayakumar, *Governing: A Singapore Perspective* (Straits Times Press, 2020), pp. 123–124.

[48] *Singapore Parliamentary Debates, Official Report,* 11 April 2007, vol. 83, cols. 377 and 378.

individuals[49]. As was explained by former Permanent Secretary Mr Ngiam Tong Dow, "A Land Acquisition Act is a very powerful tool, and in the wrong hands, it can be easily abused. Acquisition can easily degenerate into expropriation, where corrupt officials in the name of the State turf out peasants with little or no compensation and resell the land to hungry developers for a high premium, pocketing, as alleged in the press report, the difference for themselves"[50].

2.1.2. Compensation under the Land Acquisition Act

Before 2007, the compensation awarded for properties compulsorily acquired under the provisions of Land Acquisition Act generally tended to be much lower than the market values of those properties prevailing at the time of the acquisition. This was on account of various statutory features in the Land Acquisition Act then in force, some of which are discussed below[51]:

(a)   The compensation was pegged at the market value as at stipulated statutory dates or that as at the time of acquisition, whichever was lower. For acquisitions made before 30 November 1987, the statutory date for the valuation of compensation awards was 30 November 1973. Where property values were stable or were on the downtrend, the "statutory date" mechanism for determining the compensation did not give rise to low compensation awards for the dispossessed owners. For example, land values from 1973 to 1979 were generally on the downtrend. Consequently, properties which were acquired from 1974 to 1979, were paid compensation based on their values at the time of acquisition, as they were lower than those as at 30 November 1973. However, where the property market was on the uptrend, e.g. during the period from 1980

---

[49] Margaret Hanson, 'Legalized rent-seeking: Eminent domain in Kazakhstan,' (2017) 50 Cornell International Law Journal 15 and Mina Manuchehri, 'Large-scale land acquisitions and applying a gender lens to supply chain reform,' (2016) 25 Washington International Law Journal 365.

[50] Ngiam Tong Dow, 'Individual rights and public interest in development: Singapore's experience,' a speech given by the former Head of Civil Service at the Singapore Academy of Law on 31 January 2007, in the Lunchtime Talk with Expert Series. The speech is reproduced in Chapter 21 of Zhang Zhibin (ed.), Dynamics of the Singapore Success Story: Insights by Ngiam Tong Dow (Cengage Asia Pte Ltd, 2011).

[51] See Lydia Sng, 'Singapore's Land Acquisition Act — Third World to First World,' in The Evolution of Singapore Real Estate: Journey to the Past and Future, 1940–2016 (Knight Frank Pte Ltd, 2015).

to 1987, the property values as at the time of acquisition were generally higher than those as at 30 November 1973, the statutory date. Hence, the dispossessed owners were only compensated at property values prevailing in 1973, which were below those at the time of acquisition. For acquisitions made during the period from (i) 30 November 1987 to 17 January 1993 (ii) 18 January 1993 to 26 September 1995, and (iii) after 27 September 1995, the statutory dates for the purposes of valuation for compensation were 1 January 1986, 1 January 1992 and 1 January 1995 respectively.

The harshness of such compensation at market values as at the statutory dates was mitigated in the case of property owners who were eligible for *ex gratia* compensation. In 1982 when the scheme of *ex gratia* compensation started, it was to top up the compensation to the market values of owner-occupied residential properties as at the date of acquisition, subject to maximum total compensation of $600,000[52]. The then Minister of Law, Mr E. W. Barker explained the need for the *ex gratia* compensation in Parliament as follows[53]:

> From 1974 to early 1979, the open market value of land was lower than the 1973 level. It was only with the escalation of property prices after 1979 that compensation awards have generally been paid at the November 1973 values. This disparity between the compensation awards under the [Land Acquisition] Act and the open market value as at the date of acquisition has widened, and Government is aware that compensation under the Act to owner-occupiers of dwelling houses or flats may be inadequate to allow such owner-occupiers to obtain suitable alternative accommodation. To provide relief in such instances, Members are aware of Government's recent decision to make *ex gratia* payment in addition to compensation payable under the Act. The relief payment together with the acquisition award or the

---

[52] Later increased to $1.8 million in 1995: see *Land Office Annual Report 1995*. Nevertheless, the owners whose properties have been compulsorily acquired, have no legal entitlement to the *ex-gratia* compensation: see *Ahmad Kasim bin Adam (suing as Administrator of the Estate of Adam bin Haji Anwar, deceased) v Singapore Land Authority and others* [2020] 4 SLR 1447.

[53] Budget FY 83, Committee of Supply debate on 17 March 1983, *Singapore Parliamentary Debates, Official Report*. See S. Jayakumar, *Governing: A Singapore Perspective* (Straits Times Press, 2020), pp. 121–122, on the roles of Ministers S. Jayakumar, S. Dhanabalan and Mah Bow Tan, in the institution of the scheme of *ex-gratia* payments.

Appeals Board award, if any, would be up to the market value of the acquired property as at the date of *Gazette* notification for acquisition, or $600,000 whichever is less. This ceiling of $600,000 should enable owner-occupiers of dwelling properties whose land is acquired to buy an average semi-detached house or medium-sized flat. Further, this ex-gratia payment takes retrospective effect from 1st January 1981.

However, where the market value of the property as at the statutory date exceeded $600,000, there would be no *ex gratia* compensation. Non owner-occupiers were also not eligible for the *ex gratia* compensation. Apparently, such owners were considered to have the resources to cushion the adverse impact of the compulsory acquisition. The amount of $600,000 would have provided for the purchase of at least a semi-detached house in the 1980s. Quite obviously, the *ex gratia* compensation was to enable the affected owners to purchase replacement homes. In 1996 when 700 properties were acquired for the construction of the MRT North East Line, the *ex gratia* compensation was extended to owners of shophouses. Owners who have multiple properties were also eligible for the *ex gratia* compensation, provided that the acquired property was owner-occupied. Property owners who have purchased their properties at a time of higher prices, may have faced financial hardship where the prevailing market values at the time of compulsory acquisition, for their properties were much lower. In such cases, the compensation moneys may not be sufficient for those owners to repay their mortgage loans. Since 1998, *ex gratia* compensation has been extended on a case-by-case basis to owners who suffered severe hardship, taking into account the purchase price, owner-occupational status and the age and health of the owners[54]. With compensation presently pegged at market values prevailing at the date of acquisition, there has been relatively lesser need to resort to *ex gratia* compensation.

(b)   The compensation was pegged at the market value based on the existing use or the continued use in accordance with the Master Plan, whichever is the lower. The policy reason for this statutory provision

---

[54] Bryan Chew *et al.*, 'Compulsory acquisition of land in Singapore — A fair regime?' (2010) 22 *Singapore Academy of Law Journal* 166 at 176–177.

for compensation was explained by the then Minister for Law, Mr E. W. Barker at the second reading of the Land Acquisition (Amendment) Bill 1973, as follows:

> This will obviate the argument that is sometimes made where land has been zoned for a restrictive use, as for example, 'public open space', that the land has got considerable potential for development for residential or other purposes. In future, such arguments based on the hypothetical consideration that a future change of zoning or use will be granted by the Planning Department will not be taken into consideration in determining the compensation payable upon acquisition. Thus, land zoned 'Agriculture', 'Rural', 'Green Belt' or 'Unclassified' at the time of acquisition, will be valued as such.

Compensation on the basis of the hypothetical potential value of the land acquired would have been prohibitive in the early days of national development. The following observation was made by the Housing Committee in 1947 with regard to the costs of compensation[55]:

> The existing compensation clauses would probably make land costs prohibitive. At present land is, in practice in the Courts, valued with regard to any hypothetical potential use, and fantastic valuations are arrived at which result in public improvements being abandoned. This practice is out of date and the Colony [Land Acquisition] Ordinance (for the present purpose at any rate) should follow English Law, under which compensation is based on the land's present use and without regard being had to hypothetical development values.

Generally, this statutory provision did not work to the detriment of many properties, as the existing uses of most properties were generally in conformity with the uses allowed under the Master Plan. However, for properties where their existing use provided a lower value than that under the Master Plan use, the owners would only be compensated at the value based on their existing use, although the property could have been redeveloped the property to a "higher" use based on the zoning in the Master Plan.

---

[55] *Report of the Housing Committee* (Government Printing Office, 1948), p. 14.

(c) The so-called "7-year rule" where the statutory compensation would exclude any increase in value of the acquired property over the past 7 years on account of the provision of public amenities. The rationale for this rule was explained by the then Minister for Law and National Development Mr E. W. Barker at the second reading of the Land Acquisition Bill 1966 as follows:

> ... the assessment of compensation provisions have been re-drafted on the basis of two principles enunciated by the Prime Minister in December 1963. Firstly, that no landowner should benefit from development which has taken place at public expense and, secondly, the price paid on acquisition of land for public purposes should not be higher than what the land would have been worth had the Government not carried out development generally in the area ....

Although the principle underpinning the rule was clear, the discounting of the valuation to disregard the increase that may have arisen on account of the construction of public infrastructure and amenities, was subject to uncertainties and subjectivities. This was because all the properties in the neighbourhood of the properties acquired, would have similarly benefitted from the public infrastructure and no reference could therefore be made to sales of properties in the neighbourhood which were "untouched" by the public infrastructure, for an objective measure of the "unearned increment". Further, any reduction in the compensation for the acquired property on account of the 7-year rule, would have meant that the owner would not be able to re-enter the property market for a similar property, with the reduced compensation. He would hence be put at a disadvantage *vis-à-vis* other property owners on account of his property being compulsorily acquired.

(d) There were the "fire site" provisions in the then sections 33(2) and 33(3) of the Land Acquisition Act, where land acquired *after* a fire could be compensated at the lower of (i) one-third the vacant site value (as the land would be vacant after the fire, although it may have been occupied by squatters or ground tenants before the fire) or (ii) the value of the land on the basis that it was actually encumbered with squatters or ground tenants before the fire. Frequently, the extent of the encumbrance before the fire may not be determined with certainty, after the fire has occurred, in which case the one-third vacant land value cap would nevertheless have applied. The one-third vacant site land value was arrived on the assumption that the value of the site which would have been vacant after the fire would be about 3 times that of the land which was encumbered with squatters before the fire. With the one-third vacant land value cap for compensation, a land owner would not get a windfall gain, from a compensation award made after the fire. It is to be noted that the compensation was paid to the land owner whose land has been acquired. The squatters or ground tenants who were displaced by the fire, had to be resettled by the Government.

During the times where there were many squatters in Singapore and when the Control of Rent Act was still in force, there could be two possible basis of the compensation award under the Land Acquisition Act, i.e. (i) valuation on an encumbered basis which was lower where the landowner was unable to deliver vacant possession of the acquired land (on account of the squatters or statutory tenants on the land) and the Government had to resettle the squatters or statutory tenants[56] or (ii) valuation on a vacant possession basis which was higher where the landowners was able to deliver vacant possession of the acquired land. As was explained by the then Minister of Law, Professor S Jayakumar in Parliament on 15 April 1999[57]:

> As for Lot 53 which was acquired under the Land Acquisition Act, the normal process is for Land Office to make a compensation award based on vacant possession, in which case the issue of resettlement will not arise. However, if the landowner does not deliver vacant possession, an award on an encumbered basis will be made instead, in which case the occupiers of the property will be cleared under the existing resettlement policy.

---

[56] Farmers who were resettled were not only given priority in the allocation of new HDB flats, but were also paid compensation for their fruit trees, pig pens and other structures. This gave rise to some farmers putting in place overnight, fruit saplings and cementing of floors, in order to claim more compensation: see Simon Tay (ed.), *A Mandarin and the Making of Public Policy: Reflections by Ngiam Tong Dow* (NUS Press, 2006), p. 103.

[57] *Singapore Parliamentary Debates, Official Report,* 15 April 1999, col. 1182 where the Minister was explaining the basis of compensation in relation to the acquisition of the property next to the Istana Kampong Glam.

The rationale of the "fire site" provisions was explained by the then Prime Minister Mr Lee Kuan Yew at a Committee hearing on the pricing of land for the development of HDB flats, as follows[58]:

When fires took place to get rid of squatters, to stop fires and prevent owners from profiting from accidental fires, we passed a special provision — which I did personally in this House in 1961 after the Bukit Ho Swee fire — so we could acquire the land as if it had been squattered and so the state would pay for the land that was unencumbered as if it were encumbered.

Lord Wilberforce in the Privy Council case of *Robinson & Co Ltd v Collector of Land Revenue*[59] concerning the compensation for the Robinsons department store fire site at Raffles Place[60], commented on the policy of the "fire site" provisions as follows:

There appears to be no doubt as to the 'mischief' which this provision was designed to meet, a mischief exemplified by the consequences of a previous devastation by fire at Bukit Ho Swee. This was that landowners, whose land was occupied by squatters or tenants, might be fortuitously enriched by the removal of these persons in consequence of the devastation, if they were able to claim compensation on a vacant possession value. To accept this would not only be unfair to the public as taxpayers but would be an incentive to arson. The provisos clearly have the object of preventing fortuitous enrichment of this kind by requiring the land to be valued as if the squatters or tenants were still there.

The year 2007 saw a momentous but welcome departure from the earlier compensation regime under the Land Acquisition Act where the statutory award was frequently not based on the market value of the acquired land prevailing at the time of acquisition. With effect from 12 February 2007, the compensation is based on the market value of the acquired land as at the date

---

[58] *The Straits Times*, 22 March 1985.

[59] [1979–1980] SLR(R) 483 at [12].

[60] The Robinsons department store fire site at Raffles Place after its acquisition by the State, was subsequently sold to the private sector. The site is now part of the development known as One Raffles Place.

of the publication of the section 5 *Gazette* notification of the acquisition[61]. In providing the factual backdrop for the departure at the second reading of the Land Acquisition (Amendment) Bill 2007, the then Deputy Prime Minister and Minister for Law, Professor S. Jayakumar said[62]:

> Singapore today has become more developed and urbanised. Land acquisitions now affect far more people than those carried out in the 1970s and 1980s. Today, many more Singaporeans own private properties. It is often that Singaporeans sink a major portion of their life savings and future earnings into their property.
>
> ... Over the years, we have sought to cushion the impact of this approach by periodically updating the statutory date and also through *ex gratia* payments. However, after reviewing the [Land Acquisition] Act, we have decided that these provisions are no longer appropriate in the current context. We are therefore amending the Act to provide for compensation at the prevailing market value.

Although there should be less grievances now that the compensation is based on the market value of the acquired land as at the date of the *Gazette* notification, affected property owners may nevertheless perceive unfairness in the following scenarios:

(a)   The actual compulsory acquisition of land for the public purpose may be preceded by public announcements on intended requisition of the

---

[61]   S 33(1)(a)(ii) of the Land Acquisition Act 1966. S 33(1)(a)(i) provides for the compensation to be at the market value of a s 3 notification that a property is likely to be acquired if it is followed by a s 5 notification within 6 months of the s 3 notification. In practice, the s 3 notification procedure is not adopted by the Collector of Land Revenue. Since the coming into operation of the Land Acquisition (Amendment) Act 2015, No. 12 of 2015, on 8 May 2015, airspace and subterranean space may be acquired without acquiring the land itself. The basis for the compensation for such acquisition is provided in s 33(1A) of the Act.

[62]   *Singapore Parliamentary Debates, Official Report*, 11 April 2007, vol. 83, col. 501. The move towards 'fair market value' compensation of acquired properties as at the date of compulsory acquisition also took into account the advent of Free Trade Agreements that Singapore has with various countries, which often provide for expropriation at fair value: see Wenhua Shan, *The Legal Protection of Foreign Investment* (Hart Publishing, 2012), pp. 593–616 on 'Singapore' as reported by Jean Ho, and Loretta Malintoppi and Charis Tan (ed.), *Investment Protection in Southeast Asia* (Brill Nijhoff Publisher, 2017), pp. 297–340 on 'Singapore' as reported by Charis Tan and Kate Lan where it is noted that it is commonly provided in the bilateral investment treaties that expropriation or measures having the effect of expropriation is prohibited unless the measures are taken for: (a) a public purpose (b) on a non-discriminatory basis; (c) in accordance with the State's laws; and (d) against prompt, adequate and effective compensation. See also S. Jayakumar, *Governing: A Singapore Perspective* (Straits Times Press, 2020), p. 122.

land. For example, future land requirements for road expansion may be indicated by way of road lines in the road line plans[63] of the Land Transport Authority or land may be rezoned in the Master Plan for the intended public purpose. Such public announcements may serve to depress the market value (and consequently any compensation under the Land Acquisition Act) of the land ahead of the compulsory acquisition.

In this regard in *Ng Boo Tan v Collector of Land Revenue*[64], the Court of Appeal in a majority judgment held that no element of any loss of value caused by the process of acquisition (in that case caused by the indication of road lines on the land to be acquired) is to be compensated. In that case, the evidence indicated that the apartments suffered a drop of 40% in the market value where the road lines affecting the property were taken into account[65].

In a case where part of the car park (with an area of 200 m^2 and zoned "Road" in the Master Plan) of the Faith Assembly of God Church at Kim Keat was compulsorily acquired for the road-widening, a nominal compensation of $1 was awarded under the Land Acquisition Act on the basis that no one would buy a piece of land zoned "Road". The basis of a $1 nominal compensation for land that is zoned "Road" in the Master

---

[63] As indicated on the website of the Land Transport Authority (LTA), the portions of land which are required as road reserve are indicated on the Road Line Plan. These portions of land are to be set aside when development takes place on the subject lots or when road construction/improvement is carried out by the LTA, whichever is the earlier. Where the lots are developed, the land required as road reserve shall be surrendered to the State, but the area of the surrendered land may be used for the computation of the plot ratio of the development. See *Yeo Yoke Mui v Ng Liang Poh*, [1999] 2 SLR(R) 701 for a case where a property was affected by a 'road proposal' as indicated in the Road Interpretation Plan issued by the Land Transport Authority.

[64] [2002] 2 SLR(R) 633.

[65] In the dissenting judgment, Chao Hick Tin JA set out the severe consequences of the non-application of the reverse or negative *Pointe Gourde* principle (where the depressant effect of public announcements on the market value of the land acquired is not disregarded) at [82], 'The consequences of holding that the negative *Pointe Gourde* principle can have no place under our [Land Acquisition] Act could be very severe. It could lead to the acquired property being compensated perhaps even nominally. Let me explain. As is often the case, a public scheme is announced before the lands affected are actually acquired. It could be six months, or a year or two before the acquisition. It could even be very much longer, as in the present case. ... If the negative *Pointe Gourde* principle is held not to be applicable, no one would thereafter touch it. ... Conceivably, the land could, as a result, have no significant market value at the time of acquisition.' In a commentary on the case, 'Is there any *Pointe*,' [2003] *Singapore Journal of Legal Studies* 262, Professor Tan Sook Yee found the technical and policy reasons of the grounds given in the dissenting judgment of Chao Hick Tin JA, 'extremely persuasive'.

Plan was explained by Ms Indranee Rajah[66] on 11 April 2007 at the debate at the second reading of the Land Acquisition (Amendment) Bill 2007:

> The problem arises in this way. In many cases, land was purchased, let us say, back in the 60s or 70s. The way the Planning Department provided for roads in the event of redevelopment was that if you had a piece of land, they provide for a road widening line. The land would still be zoned residential, commercial or mixed used with a road widening line running through it, so that whoever bought it would know that, in the event of redevelopment, it would be set back and a road would run through it.
>
> What happens somewhere along the way is that the Planning Department changed the practice. And instead of drawing road widening lines, they zoned the strip of land for "road". The moment it is zoned as "road", then any potential buyer, looking at it, is going to give it a zero value for that strip. And in the context of land acquisition, because in land acquisition, zoning is one of the factors we have to take into account in determining compensation, and we must look at the market value just before the land is acquired. If there is a strip of land there which is zoned for road, that basically means that that strip is worth zero. And for compensation purposes, we have got to exclude the value of that strip of land.

However in the Kim Keat case, an *ex gratia* compensation of $64,000 was also awarded "to correct the unintended effect of designating road lines to road zones in the Master Plan", as the rezoning of the acquired land to "Road" in the Master Plan was to reflect the planning intent for the area and there was no intention to change the compensation approach for land that was designed as roads through a change in zoning under the Master Plan[67].

(b) There are other situations where the statutory compensation will only be a nominal $1. Some of such situations was set out by the then Senior

---

[66] The speech by Ms Rajah was not made in her Ministerial capacity but in her capacity as a Member of Parliament as she has yet to assume political office at that time.

[67] See letter from the Singapore Land Authority published in *The Straits Times* on 22 May 2004 and Bryan Chew *et al.*, 'Compulsory acquisition of land in Singapore — A fair regime?' (2010) 22 *Singapore Academy of Law Journal* 166 at 181.

Parliamentary Secretary to the Minister for Law, Associate Professor Ho Peng Kee[68]:

> Sir, as a general rule, the Government does not acquire land for $1. However, there are some special circumstances where it does so. These are:
>
> (a) firstly, where the land is that part of a site that has been set aside for public purposes such as roads or drainage reserves, as required under the planning approval given for the development of the site[69];
>
> (b) secondly, where the land is an odd piece which cannot be developed on its own and is designated for road or drainage reserves, such as backlanes, spray corners and public access roads; or
>
> (c) thirdly, where the land has been sub-leased by the owner for a long tenure like 999 years. In such a case, the sub-lessee would be paid the full statutory compensation. The owner is paid only the compensation for his nominal reversionary interest in the land, that is, the residual interest at the end of the sub-lease.

Another situation where the statutory compensation may be nominal $1 is where a small piece of land may be acquired and the betterment[70] conferred on the remaining land retained by the owner, far outweighs the value of the land acquired, on account of the infrastructure (such as a MRT station) to be built. This was explained by the then Senior Minister of State for Law, Associate Professor Ho Peng Kee in respect of the *Chuan Park* case[71]:

---

[68] *Singapore Parliamentary Reports, Official Report*, 7 November 1996, vol. 66, cols. 861–862. Although the Parliamentary statement was made before 2007 (i.e. before the Land Acquisition Act was amended to provide for compensation based on market value at the time of acquisition of the land), the situations set out in the statement where a nominal compensation of $1 is awarded, still hold true after the 2007 legislative amendments.

[69] In such situations, the 'Gross Floor Areas' (GFA) attributable to the part of the site which has been set aside, is frequently allotted to the part of the development site retained by the owner, such that the GFA that may be built on the retained development site, is not smaller that the GFA that may have been built on the entire development site: see the grounds of decision of *Singapore Investments (Pte) Ltd v The Collector of Land Revenue* AB 2013.036, for an example, although in the case the statutory compensation for the acquired land was $155,000.

[70] S 33(1)(b) of the Land Acquisition Act provides that such betterment may be taken into account in assessing the compensation to be awarded to the owner whose land is acquired.

[71] *Singapore Parliamentary Reports, Official Report*, 15 August 2003, cols. 2461–2462.

For the Chuan Park situation, it is entirely different, based on the provisions of the Land Acquisition Act. There is a provision in the Land Acquisition Act which takes into account any increase in value going to the owner whose land has been acquired and who has got remaining land. In other words, for Chuan Park, in fact, only 0.6% of the land was acquired out of the entire piece of land and the benefit to the owner arising from the proximity of the MRT station has been estimated at about $18 million. So there is this set-off provision in the Land Acquisition Act. Hence, based on this set-off provision, a $1 nominal compensation will be given to Chuan Park owners. Chuan Park owners have appealed. I think we should leave it to the Land Appeals Board to decide on this case.

(c) It is to be noted that compensation under the Land Acquisition Act may take into account the potential value of the acquired land for uses which are permissible under the prevailing Master Plan, as provided in section 33(5)(e) of the Land Acquisition Act which reads as follows:

the market value of the acquired land shall be deemed not to exceed the price which a *bona fide* purchase might reasonably be willing to pay, after taking into account the zoning and density[72] requirements and any other restrictions imposed by or under the Planning Act 1998 as at the date of acquisition and any restrictive covenants in the title of the acquired land, and no account shall be taken of any potential value of the land for any other use more intensive than that permitted by or under the Planning Act 1998 as at the date of acquisition.

---

[72] The word 'density' in s 33(5)(e) refers to the former use of density control in the Master Plan for the purpose of development control. The present measurement for development control is 'gross plot ratio' (GPR) which governs the 'gross floor area' (GFA) which may be constructed for a site. For example, a development site of 1000m² with a GPR of 1.036 in the Master Plan can accommodate a building with a GFA of 1,036 m². When GPR was substituted as a development control measure in the 1980s, the factor of 0.0056 was used to convert density control measures. For example, where the prescribed density of a site was 185 persons per hectare in the Master Plan, the equivalent GPR was 1.036 (185 × 0.0056). Hence, we have rather odd number as GPR for many pieces of land (e.g. 1.036 rather than 1.0). The conversion factor was arrived at with the assumption of 1 person having a floor area allowance of 40 m² with a neutral of common area of 40%, giving a GFA of 56 m² (1.4 × 40 m²) for 1 person. Hence density control of 1 person per hectare would translate to a GFA of 56 m² for 10,000 m² of land or giving the conversion factor of 0.0056 (56/10,000). The conversion factor of 0.0056 is stated in rule 7(1) of the Planning (Development Charges) Rules, Cap. 232, R5.

However, the potential value has to be supported by objective evidence. For example, there may be potential for *en bloc* sales at increased prices for an intensity permitted under the Master Plan. However, such potential is likely to be disregarded as speculative unless there is evidence which points strongly to an *en bloc* sale being imminent with confirmed price offers or where there is sales evidence of units within the development at higher prices in anticipation of the *en bloc* sale[73].

Even where there is provisional permission granted by the Chief Planner for a "higher-value" use, it is to be disregarded for the purpose of determining the compensation unless the owner has the more definite written permission granted under the section 14(4) of the Planning Act[74], as section 33(5)(e) of the Land Acquisition Act provides that "no account shall be taken of any potential value of the land for any other use more intensive than that permitted by or under the Planning Act as at the date of acquisition".

Compensation for land which is acquired may be awarded to a "person interested" which is defined in section 2 of the Land Acquisition Act as "every person claiming an interest in compensation to be made on account of the acquisition of land under this Act, but does not include a tenant by the month or at will". While it is usually the owner of the acquired property who is awarded compensation under the Land Acquisition Act, a lessee or sub-lessee who is not a monthly tenant or a tenant by will, may pursuant to section 10 of the Land Acquisition Act also make representations to the Collector of Land Revenue in any inquiry. The Collector may then decide on the facts of the case, whether to make a compensation award to the lessee or sub-lessee as the case may be. The basis of the claim of any lessee or sub-lessee will be the loss of "profit rent", where the sitting lessee or sub-lessee

---

[73] See *Swee Hong Investment Pte Ltd v Collector of Land Revenue*, [2004] 1 SLR(R) 664. Although that case concerned the former version of s 33(5)(e) of the Land Acquisition Act which provided for compensation to be at the lower of (i) the existing use value or (ii) the Master Plan use value, it is likely that unless there is actual evidence of sales of units within the development at higher prices in anticipation of *en bloc* sale, claims for any potential for *en bloc* sale are likely to be considered speculative, even though the potential nature and intensity of development may be envisaged in the prevailing Master Plan.

[74] See *Collector of Land Revenue v Mustaq Ahmad s/o Mustafa*, [2002] 1 SLR(R) 413. The *Mustafa* case was discussed in the grounds of decision of the Land Acquisition Appeals Board in *Singapore Investments Pte Ltd v The Collector of Land Revenue* AB 2013.036, which are available on the Ministry of Law website.

is paying a contractual rent for the acquired property, which is lower than its prevailing market rent. To that extent that the lessee or sub-lessee enjoys a "profit rent" (being the difference between the prevailing rent and the contractual rent for the period before the contractual rent is revised to the prevailing rent), the Collector may then decide to make an compensation award to the lessee or sub-lessee. Whether there is a "profit rent" or not in a particular case, is a question of fact. Where the lessee's existing contracted rent is at or above the prevailing market rent, there will be no award of compensation for profit rent[75].

Nowadays, many of the compulsory acquisition exercises undertaken are to implement the HDB's "Selective En-bloc Redevelopment Scheme" (SERS). SERS as the name suggests, is undertaken by HDB on a selective basis, where old HDB apartment blocks situated on sites with high redevelopment potential, are compulsorily acquired. The total compensation package for SERS is generally attractive, where the individual flat owners are compensated with the market value for their flats under the Land Acquisition Act and are resettled in new HDB flats which are offered to the flat owners for purchase at attractive prices. The land affected by SERS is then more intensively redeveloped by HDB in accordance with modern standards. In this way, entire precincts of the HDB estate are redeveloped.

2.2. En bloc or collective sales[76]

While an *en bloc* sale may amount to a "taking" from the perspective of the minority owners who are "dragged along" in the sale of their homes, it is a "giving" from the perspective of the majority owners who seek to realize substantial gains from the sale of their homes. This is another illustration of the proverbial two sides of the same coin.

---

[75] See *YCH Distripark Ltd v Collector of Land Revenue*, [2020] 2 SLR 733, where the Land Acquisition Appeals Board made a nil compensation award for the sub-lessee, as it decided that there was no profit rent enjoyed by the sub-lessee. The grounds of decision of the Appeals Board is available on the Ministry of Law website.

[76] Ter Kah Leng, 'A man's home is [not] his castle: En bloc collective sales in Singapore,' (2008) 20 *Singapore Academy of Law Journal* 49 and 'En bloc sales in Singapore: Critical development in the law,' (2009) 21 *Singapore Academy of Law Journal* 485, Teo Keang Sood, 'Collective sales in Singapore: Selected issues,' (2010) 22 *Singapore Academy of Law Journal* 485, Chen Jianlin, 'China's "Ding Zi Hu", US's Kelo and Singapore's en-bloc process: A new model for economic development from a givings perspective,' (2008) 24 *Journal of Land Use* 107.

Given the substantial Government ownership of development land, the contribution of land supply for development has been made substantially by the Government since the first sale of land in 1967 under the Urban Renewal program. The contribution by privately-held land into the market for development land was insignificant by comparison. Things began to change more significantly with the release of the first of the 55 non-statutory "Development Guide Plans" (DGPs) in 1994[77]. The forward-looking DGPs indicated enhanced development intensities intended for various sites without conferring any statutory rights on the land owners. The statutory rights of land owners were then governed by the prevailing statutory Master Plan[78]. Nevertheless, the indications in the DGPs were sufficient to ignite expectations with respect to the enhanced development intensities. "The land-use planning density bonus gave rise to attractive land value enhancement possibilities that triggered a string of what have been called *en bloc* or collective sales. In such a sale, owners of fragmented interests in land responded to the DGP inducement of private gains by banding together to sell their combined sites for redevelopment collectively[79]."

Under the regime of *en bloc* or collective sales in Singapore, the majority owners in a strata-titled development may "drag along" the minority owners in a sale of all the strata units in a development subject to certain statutory conditions[80]. The regime is borne out of the Government policy to facilitate a redevelopment of older developments by private enterprise

---

[77] The 55 DGPs which covered the whole of Singapore were released over a period of years as and when the preparation of each DGP was completed. The DGPs were later adopted to form the statutory Master Plan in 1998. According to Pan Tien Chor, then Executive Director of Investment Sales at Jones Lang Wootton, the first collective sale happened earlier in 1979/1980 when five owners of bungalows at Anderson Road with a total site area of about 1 hectare, sold their properties together, and the site was subsequently developed into '18 Anderson': see Pan Tien Chor, 'What it takes for collective sales,' *The Business Times*, 29 May 1996.

[78] It was not until the coming into operation of the 1998 Master Plan (incorporating the 55 DGPs) that the prescriptions of the Master Plan were delinked from the historic statutory land use entitlements captured by the new concept of development baseline.

[79] Lum Sau Kim, Sim Loo Lee and Lai Choo Malone-Lee, 'Market-led policy measures for urban redevelopment in Singapore,' *Land Use Policy* 21 (2004), 1–19 at 2.

[80] In Edward SW Ti, 'Towards Fairly Apportioning Sale Proceeds in a Collective Sale of Strata Property', (2020) 43 *University of New South Wales Law Journal* 1494, it has been pointed that other jurisdictions have similar statutory provisions which enable supermajorities to sell strata developments, e.g. Dubai (75% majority), Japan (80% majority), New Zealand (75% majority), Hong Kong (80% or 90% majority) and some Canadian provinces (75% or 80% majority).

as "there is public interest in intensifying developments and rejuvenating older developments"[81]. Chan Sek Keong CJ in delivering the judgment of the Court of Appeal in *Ng Swee Lang and another v Sassoon Samuel Bernard and others*, set out the policy on collective sales as follows[82]:

> ... It is a statutory construct to give effect to the Government's policy to facilitate urban renewal by enabling old apartment blocks to the redeveloped by the private sector. Initially, a collective sale could take place only if the subsidiary proprietors of all the lots in the subject property consented to the sale. However, due to rapid changes in the economic and environmental landscape of Singapore, the Government decided to modify its policy on collective sales by relaxing the strict statutory conditions applicable to such sales. At the second reading of the Land Titles (Strata)(Amendment) Bill 1999 ... to enact these changes, the Minister of State for Law said ...:
>
> > I had informed this House on 19th November last year [i.e. 1997] that [the] Government would be attending the law to make it easier for *en bloc* sales to take place. The current position is that a single owner, for whatever reasons, can oppose and thwart a sale. [The] Government has received many appeals and feedback from frustrated owners whose desires to sell their flats or condominiums *en bloc* have been so thwarted. As a result, these buildings cannot take advantage of enhanced plot ratios to realise their full development potential, which would have created many more housing units in prime 999-year leasehold or freehold areas for Singapore. A secondary benefit is that these developments, especially in the older ones, could have been rejuvenated through the *en bloc* process.
> >
> > I said that the law would be amended to remove the need for unanimous consent ...[I]n land-scarce Singapore, such an approach was even more imperative as it would make available more prime land for higher-intensity development to build more quality housing in Singapore .... I highlighted the fact that safeguards would be put in place to protect the interests of the minority owners.

---

[81] *Per* Mr K. Shanmugam, Minister for Law at the second reading of the Land Titles (Strata) (Amendment) Bill 2010.

[82] [2008] 2 SLR 597 at [5].

For such a regime of collective sales to work, there need to be the following accompanying factors:

(a) The bestowal of an increased development intensity and/or a more lucrative land use under the Master Plan upon the properties affected, which would give rise to a premium for the redevelopment potential;

(b) The willingness of the State to issue a fresh 99-year lease for the redevelopment in the case of those properties on 99-year leasehold tenures where the remaining term of the leases is significantly less than 99 years; and

(c) An economic climate where developers may expect to develop and sell their redeveloped units within the prescribed 5-year framework, without having to pay the prohibitive additional buyer's stamp duty.

In Singapore where public infrastructure is continually improved and upgraded to cater to the increased population and economic activities, the Master Plan promulgated under the Planning Act has to provide for more intensive use of land[83]. For the purposes of planning for infrastructure needs, the Government has published the White Paper, "A Sustainable Population for a Dynamic Singapore", together with a "Land Use Plan to Support Singapore's Future Population: A Sustainable Population for a Dynamic Singapore" in January 2013, setting out the planning parameter of a 6.9 million population by 2030[84].

Since 1998, the Master Plan has been designed as forward-looking instrument and it indicates the longer term land use intentions. Yet such land-use indications or "givings" could give rise to windfalls to the owners of the affected properties. For example, in the 1985 Master Plan, the Walshe Road area has a plot ratio of 1.036 with a maximum allowable height of two storeys and had two-storey houses situated on large sites. Under the Tanglin "Development Guide Plan" (DGP) which later became part of the 1998 Master Plan, the plot ratio was raised to 1.6 and the height control was

---

[83] Nevertheless, for specific sites which are subject to *en bloc* sales, the Land Transport Authority may require a pre-application feasibility study in assessing the impact of the potential new development on the surrounding road infrastructure and the supportable number of dwelling units in the new development.

[84] See '6.9m population figure not a forecast or target: Khaw [Boon Wan],' *The Business Times*, 2–3 February 2013.

revised to 10 storeys[85]. Such an indication in the DGP by the stroke of the pen of the planner, saw the rise of land values in that area. The owners of the detached houses (which could be redeveloped for more intensive use) sold the properties to developers who redeveloped the combined sites into high-rise luxury apartment developments.

These land value increases from such statutory "givings" are captured for the public coffers by way of the development charge levied under the Planning Act, since replaced by the land betterment charge under the Land Betterment Charge Act. "If the sudden windfall gain brought about by the stroke of a pen is not partially creamed off ..., it may lead to accusations of unfair treatment and enrichment"[86].

The enactment of the Strata Titles (Amendment) Act in 1999 to pave the way for *en bloc* sales without the unanimous consent of all the subsidiary proprietors within the strata-titled development, may be seen as a "taking" insofar as far as the minority owners (who do not agree with the *en bloc* sale) in the development are concerned[87]. In *Lo Pui Sang v Mamata Kapildev Dave* concerning the collective sale of the Horizon Towers, Choo Han Teck J in rejecting the submission that the *en bloc* regime in the Land Titles (Strata) Act is in breach of the equal protection clause in Article 12 of the Singapore Constitution said[88]:

> ... the omission of a provision in our Constitution that would have ensured a fundamental right to own property was a deliberate omission given the scarcity of land in Singapore and as such, the court must recognise that there is no such fundamental right under our Constitution. The Land Acquisition Act (Cap. 152, 1985 Rev Ed) in fact allows the government to acquire any land in Singapore for specific purposes so long as it provides due compensation.

In the contest in the built environment, minority interests have frequently to be sub-ordinated to the public or greater good. There have

---

[85] Lum Sau Kim, Sim Loo Lee and Lai Choo Malone-Lee, 'Market-led policy measures for urban redevelopment in Singapore,' *Land Use Policy* 21 (2004).

[86] Leung Yew Kwong, *Development Land and Development Charge in Singapore* (Butterworths, 1987), p. 126.

[87] See Sim Loo Lee, Lum Sau Kim, Lai Choo Malone-Lee, 'Property rights, collective sales and government intervention: averting a tragedy of the anticommons,' *Habitat International* 26 (2002), 457–470 where the *en bloc* sales involving Kim Lin Manson at Grange Road/Jalan Arnap were examined.

[88] [2008] 4 SLR(R) 754 at [7].

been a number of ways of doing it: using the compulsory land acquisition powers of the State or using market forces as in *en bloc* sales facilitated by the Land Titles (Strata) Act[89]. In explaining how a single owner may thwart an *en bloc* sale, the then Minister of State for Law, Associate Professor Ho Peng Kee at the second reading of the Land Titles (Strata)(Amendment) Bill 1998 said[90]:

> The current position is that a single owner, for whatever reason, can oppose and thwart the sale. Government has received many appeals and feedback from frustrated owners whose desires to sell their flats or condominiums *en bloc* have been so thwarted. As a result, these buildings cannot take advantage of enhanced plot ratios to realise their full development potential, which would have created many more housing units in prime 999-year leasehold or freehold areas for Singaporeans. A secondary benefit is that these developments, especially the older ones, could have been rejuvenated through the *en bloc* process.

For the workings of the *en bloc* sale regime, a consent level has to be established. This was explained by the then Minister of Law, Professor S Jayakumar at the third reading of the Bill on 4 May 1999 where the Select Committee Report presented to Parliament on 19 April 1999 was discussed[91]:

> The Select Committee has decided to keep the present approach in the Bill, i.e., the 90% consent level for developments less than 10 years and 80% for developments 10 years or older. Ultimately, it should be left to market forces and conditions which will determine if an *en bloc* sale is economically viable. The 90%/80% level linked to the 10 years age of the development was considered a reasonable criterion. The consent level should be pegged to the age of the development as it is more likely that older developments will be sub-optimally utilised and have higher repair bills.

---

[89] 'The view taken by the Ministry of Law is that a strata title holder holds property as a tenant-in-common with his neighbours. In other words, proprietary ownership in properties governed by the [Land Titles (Strata) Act] is a *communitarian* enterprise rather than an individual right': Tang Hang Wu, 'The Legal Representation of the Singaporean Home and the Influence of the Common Law,' (2007) HKLJ 81, 89.

[90] *Singapore Parliamentary Reports, Official Report*, 31 July 1998.

[91] *Singapore Parliamentary Reports, Official Report*, 19 April 1999.

The "consent level" was initially set at consent from subsidiary proprietors with not less than 90% of the share values for developments which are less than 10 years old[92]. In respect of developments which are at least 10 years old, the consent level was set at consent from subsidiary properties with not less than 80% of the share values. In the 2007 legislative amendment of the Land Titles (Strata) Act, an additional condition (i.e. 90% or 80% of the total area of lots, excluding any accessory lot) was added. For developments which are less than 10 years old, the subsidiary proprietors who consent to the collective sale, must therefore have not less than 90% of the share values and not less than 90% of the total area of all the lots (excluding the area of any accessory lot), with similar legislative amendments made for developments which are at least 10 years old. This legislative amendment was to address the issues concerning mixed-used developments where commercial units have a greater share value compared with residential units having the same floor area. With this legislative amendment, the subsidiary proprietors of commercial units with their greater share values, cannot push through an *en bloc* sale without "buying in" the vast majority of the subsidiary proprietors of the residential units as well.

The Land Titles (Strata) (Amendment) Act 1999[93] which set out the statutory framework for the *en bloc* sale of strata-titled properties first came into operation on 11 October 1999[94]. For the *en bloc* sale to be economically

---

[92] The age of the development is measured from the date of issue of the latest 'Temporary Occupation Permit' (TOP) on completion of the development and if there is no TOP, the date of issue of the Certificate of Statutory Completion as provided in s 84A of the Land Titles (Strata) Act. In *Kok Chong Weng and others v Wiener Robert Lorenz and others (Ankerite Pte Ltd)*, [2009] 2 SLR(R) 709 which concerned the former HUDC Gillman Heights development (now the site of The Interlace) where there was no TOP issued, the Court of Appeal held that the oversight of the legislative draftsman should not be allowed to frustrate the primary legislative purpose or intent of the Act and considered the age of the development by reference to the 'date when the building authority would have regarded the development as being completed and fit or ready for occupation'. The case was referred to by Chief Justice Sundaresh Menon in the 25th Singapore Law Review Annual Lecture in 2013, to illustrate the purposive interpretation of statutes.

[93] Act 21 of 1999.

[94] Land Titles (Strata) (Amendment) Act (Commencement) Notification 1999, S 445/99. The *en bloc* sale of Goldenhill Condominium at Lorong Chuan was reportedly the first case heard by the Strata Titles Board under the new statutory framework: see 'Goldenhill set to be first case to go before Strata Titles Board,' *The Business Times*, 5 November 1999.

viable, the price of the development site has to rise to a level that is attractive for the majority (be it 90% or 80% as the case may be) to want to sell their units. The majority will only want to embark on the process of an *en bloc* sale where the prices at which they could get in an *en bloc* sale is at a premium above what each of them could otherwise get by selling their units individually in the market.

Objections may be made to a proposed *en bloc* sale where the subsidiary proprietor would incur a "financial loss" on account of the proposed sale, as provided under section 84A(7) of the Land Titles (Strata) Act. A subsidiary proprietor may incur a financial loss where for example, the sale proceeds apportioned to his unit, is insufficient to cover the costs of his earlier acquisition and any seller's stamp duty he may have to pay on account of his holding of the unit for less than 3 years. Objections may also be made on the ground that the transaction is not in good faith, under section 84A(9)(a)(i) which reads as follows:

> the transaction is not in good faith after taking into account only the following factors:
>
> (A) the sale price;
> (B) the method of distributing the sale proceeds; and
> (C) the relationship of the purchaser to any of the subsidiary proprietors.

2.2.1. *Distribution of en bloc proceeds*

In this section, we propose to discuss only the method of distributing the sale proceeds as provided in section 84A(9)(a)(i)(B) of the Land Titles (Strata) Act. A number of cases have gone before the courts on this issue. In practice, the sale proceeds may be apportioned amongst the subsidiary proprietors of the strata lots in accordance with the strata areas, share values or valuations of the strata lots or a combination of any two or all of those factors.

The Singapore Institute of Surveyors and Valuers has pointed out that the following methods are commonly used in the distribution or apportionment of the total sale proceeds from an *en bloc* sale, among subsidiary proprietors[95]:

(a) Based purely on share value
This method may be used when the units are of the same or similar strata/floor areas with the same or similar share values.

(b) Based purely on strata/floor area
This method may be used when all the units are of the same or similar strata area or the unit value rates are similar for various sizes.

(c) Based on combination of share value and strata/floor area
This method may be where there are wide differences in the share value and/or strata/floor areas among the various units.

(d) Based on valuation
This method may be used when the general attributes of the property are to be considered.

The terms "share value" and "strata area" need some explanation. The "share values" of the units in a strata-titled development are assigned by the developer. Under section 11(1) of the Building Maintenance and Strata Management Act, the developer is not to sell any unit in a development unless a schedule of strata units showing the proposed share values to be allotted to the various units in the development, has been filed and accepted by the Commissioner of Buildings. When the developer applies for the strata titles of the units in the development, he has also to indicate the share values of the various units in the development[96]. As provided under section 30(2) of the Land Titles (Strata) Act, the share value of a lot shall determine:

(a) the voting rights of the subsidiary proprietors;
(b) the quantum of the undivided share of each subsidiary proprietors in the common property; and

---

[95] Para 5.4.2 of Valuation Guidelines for Collective Sales under the Land Titles (Strata) Act, available on the Institute's website. In para 5.4.3 of the Guidelines, it is also pointed out that there are other combinations of the methods set out in para 5.4.2

[96] S 9(2)(a) of the Land Titles (Strata) Act.

(c) the amount of contributions levied by a management corporation on the subsidiary proprietors of all the lots in a subdivided building.

When the concept of share values to be assigned to individual strata lots was first conceived, it was obviously to facilitate the operation of the maintenance and upkeep of the estate of the development, rather than for the distribution of the sale proceeds from an *en bloc* sale. The subsidiary proprietor of a strata lot with a larger share value will have to make a greater contribution towards the maintenance of the common property. Nevertheless, the subsidiary proprietors will also own the common property of the development as tenants-in-common in terms of the proportions or ratios indicated by their share values[97]. This is provided under section 13(1) of the Land Titles (Strata) Act which reads as follows:

On registration of the strata title application the Registrar shall enter a memorial in the land-register on the volume and folio of the parcel to the effect that a subsidiary strata land-register has been created, and thereupon the common property shall be held by the subsidiary proprietors as tenants-in-common proportional to their respective share value and for the same term and tenure as their respective lots are held by them.

With the share values conferring the statutory rights with respect of the common property, it is little wonder that the share value of a strata lot has become a factor for the apportionment and distribution of the sale proceeds for any *en bloc* sale.

The Commissioner of Buildings has provided guidelines on the assignment of share values[98]. Under those guidelines, strata units in a wholly

---

[97] In *Management Corporation Strata Title Plan No. 2297 v Seasons Park Pte Ltd*, [2005] 2 SLR(R) 613, Chao Hick Tin JA in delivering the judgment of the Court of Appeal, said at [12], 'Under the [Land Titles (Strata)] Act, the subsidiary proprietors of individual units in a private development, like the condominium here, own the common property as tenants-in-common.'

[98] *Guidelines for Filing Schedule of Share Values under the Building Management and Strata Management Act*, Version 1.1. (May 2008), available on the website of the Building Control Authority. For the earlier guidelines issued by the Commissioner of Buildings, see *Guidelines for Allotment of Share Value Entitlements* [1981] 2 MLJ lxiii which superseded the earlier guidelines issued on 1 December 1979 and reproduced in [1980] 1 MLJ lxxxvi, and the booklet, *What you need to know about the Share Value of your property*, jointly published by the Building and Construction Authority, the Real Estate Developers' Association of Singapore, the Singapore Institute of Surveyors and Valuers and the Association of Property & Facility Managers in August 2001. Before 1979, it seems that there were no guidelines and developers were left

residential development will be assigned share values which are based on floor area groupings of 50 m² intervals as follows:

Floor Area (m²)	Share Value in Whole Number
50 and below	5
51 to 100	6
101 to 150	7
151 to 200	8
201 to 250	9
251 to 300	10
and so on	

The strata area of a unit which will include areas such as ledges and is calculated from the middle of the structural walls, is generally not much greater than the usable floor area. However, void areas such as the air space above the first storey ceiling height (such as those in found living areas which have high ceilings) are also counted as part of the strata area. Such void areas within the strata area are not usable floor area, and generally do not fetch the same value as usable floor area[99].

The schedule of strata areas with corresponding share values gives some recognition that the larger strata lots would generally accommodate a larger number of occupants and would generally have a greater demand in respect of the services for the common property.

Where the development is a single-use non-residential one comprising wholly shops or offices or warehouses, etc, the share values of the strata lots will correspond to the floor areas of the strata lots.

Quite obviously, where the units in a development are similar in terms of their uses, sizes and share values, there may be less controversy over how the sale proceeds from the *en bloc* sale are to be apportioned and

---

to allot share values which they considered to be fair and reasonable for the principal purpose of the levy of maintenance charges on the subsidiary proprietors: see Edward SW Ti, 'Towards Fairly Apportioning Sale Proceeds in a Collective Sale of Strata Property', (2020) 43 *University of New South Wales Law Review* 1494.

[99] In *Cheok Doris v Commissioner of Stamp Duties* [2010] 4 SLR 397, the facts concerned the buyer rescinding the contract when she discovered that the strata area of the building comprised 22% void area.

distributed among the subsidiary proprietors, as the sale proceeds in such cases are mostly divided equally among the subsidiary proprietors. As may be expected, greater disagreements are likely to occur in the case of mixed-use developments comprising retail and residential units. The differences between the values of retail and residential units may be so large that the owners are unable to agree to any basis of apportionment of the sale proceeds such that the threshold consent level may not even be reached for the launch of an *en bloc* sale.

Even where the threshold consent level is reached, there have been cases where the disputes on the method of apportionment of the sale proceeds have reached the courts. In such cases, the strata areas and/or share values of units within the developments, had varied significantly and the subsidiary proprietors had differing views on the method of the apportionment of the sale proceeds. Some of the subsidiary proprietors may consider that the sale proceeds should be apportioned according to the market values of their respective strata lots. Other subsidiary proprietors may consider that the market values of the individual strata lots (which may vary according to the height, physical orientation and condition) do not provide a fair basis for the apportionment of the sale proceeds, as the developer is essentially buying the land for the purpose of redevelopment. In practice, a compromise on the method of apportionment has to be reached amongst the subsidiary proprietors, in order that the *en bloc* sale may proceed.

In *Deorukhkar Sameer Vinay and Others v Quek Chin Kheam*[100], the apportionment method with respect to the sale proceeds of the residential development known as the Albracca situated at No. 1 Meyer Place where the strata areas and share values of the various residential units varied significantly, was examined. The development comprised a 10-storey residential building with 11 units of varying sizes. There were five apartment units and six maisonette units with strata areas ranging from 154 to 369 m². The seven larger units within the development had share values of 6 each, while the remaining four smaller units had share values of four each, giving a total share value of 58 for the entire development.

---

[100] [2018] SGHC 171.

—

In that case, the "collective sale committee" (CSC) has adopted an apportionment method which gave equal weightage to the share value, strata area and current market value, of the units. In other words, the apportionment was based on 1/3 share value, 1/3 strata area and 1/3 current market value. This apportionment method gave smaller variations of the premium between the smallest and the largest units, with the largest premium (i.e. the difference between the apportioned sale prices minus the market value had the unit been sold separately in the market and not in an *en bloc* sale) was 73% and the lowest premium of 58%, the difference being 15 percentage points. The CSC has adopted this method after comparing a method based on 50% share value and 50% strata area, which gave a larger difference in the premium of 23 percentage points. In deciding that the CSC had acted in good faith, Tan Siong Thye J said at [92]:

> ... based on Savills' valuation figures and the sale price of $69,119,000, I find that the MOA [Method of Apportionment] of 1/3 [Share Value] — 1/3 [Strata Area] — 1/3 [Current Market Value] was indeed the fairest MOA. It resulted in the narrowest band of premium different. It also evened out the differences between share value, strata area and current market value such that none of the owners was significantly favoured or disadvantaged.

In the earlier case of *Dynamic Investments Pte Ltd v Lee Chee Kian Silas and others*[101], which concerned the apportionment of the sale proceeds of the residential development known as Holland Hill Mansions, the High Court has held that the adoption of 50% "Strata Area" (SA) and 50% "Share Value" (SV) by the sales committee was in good faith[102]. In that case, there were 118 apartment units of varying sizes with the smallest strata area being 57 m² and the largest being 642 square metres. Their shares values ranged from 3 to 6. As the allocated share values of the various units were not in proportion to the strata areas, an apportionment based solely on share values

---

[101] [2008] 1 SLR(R) 729.

[102] In Lim Lan Yuan, 'Collective sales and related valuation issues: a Singapore case study,' *Journal of Property Investment & Finance* 28(2) (2010), 140–149, the author cited a case where the Strata Titles Board was satisfied that an apportionment of the sale proceeds based on a weightage of 70% strata area and 30% share value, was in good faith on the facts of that case.

would result the smallest unit receiving sale proceeds which would be half of that allocable to the largest unit. On the other hand, if the apportionment was to be made solely on the basis of the strata area, the largest unit would receive sale proceeds which would be 11 times that allocable to the smallest unit. In deciding the sales committee had acted in good faith in adopting the 50% Strata Area and 50% Share Value method of apportionment, Andrew Ang J said at [33]:

> The SA-SV method serves as a compromise between the two methods. The SISV Guidelines point out that this method "would even out the differences in strata areas and share values where there are big discrepancies in both among the various units". It is therefore not surprising that all five groups of property agents who made representations to the [sales committee] recommended the SA-SV method. In the result, this was the method adopted in the collective sale agreement signed by the subsidiary proprietors holding between them more than 80% of the share value. It represented the fairest of the three methods under discussion, serving to moderate the extremes which either of the other two methods would have led to.

Yeo Sok Hoon and others v Tan Thiam Chye and another[103] concerned a 12-storey commercial building known as The Realty Centre situated at Enggor Street. The building had 32 office units of four sizes, three retail units on the ground floor and a food and beverage unit at the top floor, giving a total of 36 units. However, despite the variation in terms of size and use, each of the 36 units had a share value of 1. There were two contending methods of apportionment of the sales proceeds in that case. One method was based on a ratio of 70% valuation, 20% share value and 10% strata area. The other method was a two-tier one where the sale proceeds were first to be paid out on the basis of the market value of the 36 individual units, with the balance of the sale proceeds (which represent the premium on account of the *en bloc* sale) to be distributed amongst the 36 subsidiary properties in equal shares. In balancing the two methods of apportionment, the concept of premium variance test was adopted, as set out in [17] of that case:

---

[103] [2020] 5 SLR 1042.

The underlying principle behind the [premium variance test] is to narrow the premium variance so as to ensure that all owners gain near-similar premiums from this collective sale. A large premium variance would suggest that certain units are obtaining far more premium from the sale price than the other units, which may make it inequitable to these other units. In short, a large premium variance suggests that certain units are enjoying an advantage at the expense of others. It is a good indicator of whether the [Method of Apportionment] chosen is fair.

On the facts of the case, the method based on the ratio of 70% valuation, 20% share value and 10% strata area, was found to give a much smaller premium variance, which indicated that the method was fair and equitable and was properly adopted by the CSC.

2.2.2. *Voluntary Early Redevelopment Scheme*

The public housing version of *en bloc* sales in the "Voluntary Early Redevelopment Scheme" (VERS), was announced by the Prime Minister at his 2018 National Day Rally, but the implementation details have yet to be announced. It is not envisaged that VERS may be initiated at will by the HDB flat owners. Eligible HDB precincts will first have to be identified by HDB and the flat owners may then be able to initiate the process of HDB buying back entire apartment blocks for redevelopment. VERS also affords the opportunity for the renewal of the built environment within old HDB estates, with infrastructure and lifestyle amenities seen in the newer HDB estates.

Basically, VERS is to address the issue of "lease decay" as HDB flats approach the end of their 99-year leasehold tenure[104]. As the implementation of VERS is only expected in about 20 years' time when the older HDB flats have about 30 years left in their leasehold tenure, the details of VERS (including the compensation package for the HDB flat owners) are still being worked out carefully.

---

[104] See 'Will you still love your HDB flat when it's over 64?' *The Straits Times*, 12 April 2017, and 'Owners worry older HDB flats a depreciating asset,' *The Sunday Times*, 15 April 2018.

"Selective En-bloc Redevelopment Scheme" (SERS), with its generous compensation and resettlement package, has earlier been initiated by the Government, where HDB blocks with greater redevelopment potential are compulsorily acquired. As not all HDB flats will be eligible for SERS, they will in the normal course of events, eventually revert to the State at their end of their 99-year leasehold tenure. Yet as HDB flat owners perceive their flats as their largest investments, the eventuality of "losing" their flats upon expiry of the leasehold tenure is somewhat unimaginable. The simultaneous expiry of the leasehold tenures of apartment blocks in entire precincts, also poses resettlement issues for the Government. Yet the automatic renewal of leases, on payment by the HDB flat owners of some lump sum or recurrent consideration, may not be tenable as aging flats have finite physical lives. There is also the issue of perpetuating home ownership within families who have existing homes with such automatic renewal of leases. The Government has also to cater to the housing needs of future generations who may not have the benefit of the inheritance of HDB flats. In the implementation of VERS, the issues that the Government has to consider, include the following:

(a) even though the compensation package under VERS is not expected to be as generous as that for SERS since the VERS sites are those which has lesser redevelopment potential, the compensation package may still represent some bounty granted to the HDB flat owners affected, and VERS has to be implemented in a fiscally-sustainable manner, without burdening the future generations;

(b) the process of selecting the HDB precincts for VERS and staging the redevelopment for the precincts and towns affected, in conjunction with the other HDB programs such as the Home Improvement Programs;

(c) the minimum percentage of votes required of the HDB flat owners within a precinct before VERS may be triggered and the alternative arrangements for those owners who do not have the financial resources to purchase replacement HDB flats. The current 80% threshold consent level for *en bloc* sales under the Land Titles (Strata) Act may provide some guide.

We will no doubt, see announcements of the implementation details of VERS in the years ahead.

2.3. Transformation of Kampong Glam

Unlike the other land policy and legislative initiatives discussed earlier which affect the whole of Singapore, the 1999 legislative amendment of the Sultan Hussain Ordinance[105] has a more limited geographical impact as it only affected the Kampong Glam area roughly bounded by Beach Road, Jalan Sultan, Victoria Street and Ophir Road. Nevertheless, we propose to discuss the case of Kampong Glam as its history goes back to the founding days of modern Singapore in the 19th century and it also shows how a statutory framework has earlier inhibited development in the Kampong Glam area.

Today, the Kampong Glam area exists as a conservation area with the Malay Heritage Centre (which was the site of the former Istana Kampong Glam) and the neighboring Sultan Mosque as its central attractions. In contrast, on the east side of Jalan Sultan we see HDB flats and the commercial buildings which were first built in the 1960s and 1970s[106] under the urban renewal program.

The Kampong Glam conservation area[107] could have met with the same development fate as the east side of Jalan Sultan, had it not been for the existence of the Sultan Hussain Ordinance[108]. The Ordinance was enacted in 1904 to cater for the financial needs of the descendants of Sultan Hussain who had earlier entered into the treaty with the East India Company which paved the way for the founding of modern Singapore. At the founding of Singapore, Sultan Hussain was allotted the area of Kampong Glam for the occupation of his family. Upon his death, Sultan Iskandar Ali Shah (Sultan Ali) inherited the estate and upon the death of Sultan Ali, the estate passed to

---

[105] Sultan Hussain (Amendment) Act 1999, Act 23 of 1999.

[106] The area east of Jalan Sultan comprising 90 acres, was indicated as Precinct North 1 in the Central Area urban renewal plan and was slated for early redevelopment: see Alan Choe, 'Urban renewal,' in Ooi Jin-Bee and Chiang Hai Ding (eds.), *Modern Singapore* (University of Singapore, 1969). See also *Urban Redevelopment: From Urban Squalor to Global City* (Centre of Liveable Cities, 2016), p. 22.

[107] The Kampong Glam area was indicated as Precinct North 4 with its 33 acres, in the Central Area urban renewal plan: see Alan Choe, 'Urban renewal,' in Ooi Jin-Bee and Chiang Hai Ding (eds.), *Modern Singapore* (University of Singapore, 1969).

[108] The Ordinance was amended in 1999 to provide compensation for the occupants of the Istana Kampong Glam and allowed for greater investment in the Kampong Glam area. For a background of the Ordinance, see Kwa Chong Guan, 'Origins of the Sultan Hussain Ordinance 1904,' in Kevin YL Tan and Michael Hor (eds.), *Encounters with Singapore Legal History* (Singapore Journal of Legal Studies (publisher), 2003).

Tunku Alum. Upon the death of Tunku Alum, there was litigation amongst the descendants. In *Tunku Mahmoud bin Sultan Ali and Others v Tunku Ali bin Tunku Allum and Others*[109], the Straits Settlements Court of Appeal in 1897 held that Sultan Hussain only had a life interest in Kampong Glam as the Sultan of Johore. His son Sultan Ali also took a life interest as Sultan of Johore and upon the death of Sultan Ali, Tunku Allum in turn took a life interest having sufficiently answered the description of "heirs and successor" of Sultan Ali. The Court held that upon the death of Tunku Allum, there was "no one to answer the description of his heir and successor and accordingly there was no one in existence who was entitled in law to the property either for life or absolutely". The land reverted as Crown property. The colonial government however felt obliged to provide financially for the descendants of Sultan Hussain and enacted the Sultan Hussain Ordinance, to so provide for the descendants from the revenue collected from the properties in the Kampong Glam Estate. Under the Sultan Hussain Ordinance, an annual sum of $750 was to be paid to the descendants of Sultan Hussain. Where the lands in Kampong Glam Estate were to yield a net annual revenue exceeding $750, a further sum not exceeding 90% of the excess over $750, was to be paid to the descendants.

With the statutory framework of the Sultan Hussain Ordinance operating over the State lands in Kampong Glam Estate[110], they could not possibly have been redeveloped in the way that the area east of Jalan Sultan was redeveloped in the 1960s and 1970s[111]. In a sense, the Kampong Glam Estate was then frozen in its own history. The amounts of payment made to the beneficiaries under the Sultan Hussain Ordinance and the number of beneficiaries were reported by the then Finance Minister, Dr Goh Keng Swee in Parliament[112]:

---

[109] (1898–1899) 5 SSLR 96. See Kwa Chong Guan, 'Reflections on Sultan Hussein in Singapore's history,' in Zainul Abidin Rasheed, Wan Hussin Zoohri and Norshahril Saat (eds.), *Beyond Centennial: Perspectives on Malays*, Chapter 41 (World Scientific Publishing Co Pte Ltd, 2020), pp. 695–703, for a brief history on the dispute.

[110] In the *URA Manual for Kampong Glam Conservation Area*, July 1988, it was stated that the Kampong Glam Historic District covers an area of approximately 9 hectares of land with about 65% under fragmented private ownership while the remaining 35% are government-owned.

[111] That area presently has Textile Centre, Golden Sultan Plaza, City Gate and HDB developments.

[112] *Singapore Parliamentary Debates, Official Report*, 18 December 1967, col. 775.

So in the administration of the properties under the Sultan Hussain Ordinance, provision is made for an annual payment to be made to the family and descendants of the late Sultan and throughout the years the net revenue has been paid out to the descendants and this amounted to $63,379.99 in 1964. In 1965 it was $60,422.28. In 1966 it came to $61,005.85. There are now 23 beneficiaries and all payments are made in accordance with the provisions of the law.

By 1999, the number of beneficiaries had risen to 79 but the annual amount to be distributed to them had reduced to $29,231. The then Minister for Law, Professor S. Jayakumar explained in Parliament as follows[113]:

Therefore, the Kampong Glam Estate including the former Istana has been State Land since 1897. The British Government then enacted the Sultan Hussain Ordinance in 1904. The intention of the Ordinance was to take care of the financial needs of the family at that time of the late Sultan Hussain who were described by the then British Governor as "very improvident people". The Ordinance provided for annual payment of monies to the family of the late Sultan Hussain pegged to the income derived from the Kampong Glam Estate. These payments were not intended to be in perpetuity but were intended to be made only to "the family of the late Sultan Hussain" at the time the Ordinance was enacted. Nevertheless, for historical reasons, annual payments were continued to be made by subsequent Governments all these 100-odd years. This has led to a very unsatisfactory situation. Firstly, while the number of beneficiaries has steadily increased, the payments are getting smaller as the income from which the payments are made has diminished. Secondly, in future the payments would become even smaller over time as the number of beneficiaries increases.

As may be seen over time, the scheme under the Sultan Hussain Ordinance did not even work to the benefit of the beneficiaries, as the annual payments continued to diminish, which was not unexpected. This is because where 90% of the revenue from the Kampong Glam Estate continued to be distributed to the descendants, this was little incentive for

---

[113] *Singapore Parliamentary Debates, Official Report*, 15 April 1999, col. 1183.

third parties to invest in the infrastructure and conservation of the Kampong Glam Estate as the substantial amount of any increase in revenue would go to the beneficiaries. A win-win solution had to be found, which provides for the rejuvenation of Kampong Glam and equitably for the descendants of Sultan Hussain as well. This was done with the coming into operation of the Sultan Hussain (Amendment) Act 1999. At the second reading of the Sultan Hussain (Amendment) Bill 1999 on 6 July 1999, Professor S. Jayakumar said[114]:

> The Sultan Hussain Ordinance was enacted to take care of the financial needs of the late Sultan Hussain's family at that time. Since then, the number of beneficiaries has steadily increased and the payments have been diminishing as the income from which the payments were made declined. The individual payments would become even smaller over time if the number of beneficiaries increases. The Government had therefore decided to implement a new scheme that would work to the advantage of the beneficiaries. Under this scheme, the Government will increase the amount of payment from the current level of $29,231 per annum to $350,000 per annum, which is more than 10 times the current annual payment. This revised sum will be maintained for a fixed period of 30 years, starting from this year. In addition, the Government will offer any beneficiary the option of receiving a lump sum payment up-front instead. The lump sum would be equivalent to the present value of the 30-year payment stream. From the beneficiaries' point of view, this would work out to be more advantageous than the current system of receiving a dwindling annual sum indefinitely.
>
> The Land Office has informed all the beneficiaries of the proposed new scheme. So far, an overwhelming majority of 64 beneficiaries or 81% have informed the Land Office that they wish to opt for lump sum payment. When the amendments to the Ordinance come into force, payments can be made to the beneficiaries who have opted for a lump sum payment under the new scheme.
>
> Sir, turning to the actual provisions of the Bill, new section 4A enables the establishment of the proposed new payment scheme.

---

[114] *Singapore Parliamentary Debates, Official Report*, 6 July 1999, col. 1704. See also S. Jayakumar, *Governing: A Singapore Perspective* (Straits Times Press, 2020), pp. 128–129.

The proposed scheme will apply to members of the family of the late Sultan Hussain who, before 4th May 1999, were receiving an annuity under the Ordinance.

New section 4A provides that sections 3 and 4 of the main Ordinance shall cease to have effect on the day the new scheme is established. What this means, Sir, is that the existing scheme of payments will cease upon the establishment of the new improved scheme.

Under paragraph 4(4) of the Sultan Hussain (New Scheme for Payment of Annuity or Commuted Gratuity) Regulations[115], where a beneficiary opted for a lump sum gratuity payment instead of the annual payments, the commuted gratuity would be the net present value of the future stream of annuities payable. The discount rate to be used in arriving at the net present value was determined by the Minister. It was reported that the revised payment and resettlement benefits would cost the Government some $7.5 million[116].

While what is stated above may be stated clinically, what is the perspective of the occupants of those who had to vacate Istana Kampong Glam under the new scheme? A perspective of the erstwhile occupants of Istana Kampong Glam was provided by Ms Hidayah Amin[117]:

Leaving the Istana
December 1999 was the fateful date when the descendants of the Sultan had to leave their 160-year old palace. Istana Kampong Gelam was once crowded with about 200 descendants of Sultan Hussein. To accommodate the increasing number of descendants, members of the royal family had to build annexes made of tin and plywood and turn the gardens into parking lots. ...

Interestingly, Tengku Sri Indra[118] opined that "one of the best things that happens to the royal family of Singapore is when the government took away the palace" as it "made people who live in the Royal Istana realise that there is a bigger world outside there ... they realise that they have to

---

[115] Cap. 382, RG 1.
[116] '80% accept lump sum offer,' *The Straits Times*, 7 July 1999.
[117] Hidayah Amin, *Leluhur Singapore's Kampong Gelam* (Helang Books, 2019), p. 80. The author herself was born in Gedung Kuning, the Yellow Mansion at Sultan Gate, just outside the Istana Kampong Glam.
[118] Tengku Sri Indra is a direct descendant of Sultan Hussain.

pay electricity bills which they did not have to pay ... But now, they realise the only way to survive is to make out a living, to be a rich[119] earner, raise children and educate them and compete in the present world.

As may be seen, what may be a "taking", may also be a "giving". They are two sides of the same coin.

3. "Givings"

In the real estate scene, Singapore has harnessed the development energies of the private sector and has continually reviewed land use policies to facilitate the unleashing of those energies. The "givings" from those policies, are discussed here. In some of the givings, there are direct consideration payments received by the State; for example, where it receives a differential premium for the lifting or amendment of title restrictions in State leases, since replaced by the land betterment charge under the Land Betterment Charge Act. In other givings, there may not be direct consideration payments, for example where land is allocated for value-enhancing uses (such as for the relocation of good schools), such that property values in the neighborhood are uplifted. Nevertheless, there may be collateral payments in the form enhanced property tax or development charge (since replaced by the land betterment charge under the Land Betterment Charge Act) when surrounding land is redeveloped subsequently.

3.1. Rejuvenational role of the extension of State land leases

The alienation of State land is now generally by way of a lease of a term not exceeding 99 years. This is as provided in rule 10 of the State Lands Rules[120] which reads as follows:

> The title ordinarily to be issued shall be a lease for a term not exceeding 99 years, except that where land is not capable of independent development and is required for development with the aplicant's land, the title to be issued may be the same as that of the applicant's land.

---

[119] The word 'rich' appears in the original text of the book. It may be a typographical error. The correct word may be 'wage'.

[120] Cap. 314, R1.

■

The practice of issuing titles longer than those of 99-year leaseholds was discontinued in 1947 and the policy of having leaseholds with terms not exceeding 99 years, is to safeguard future planning and land allocation[121]. The use of the public leasehold system to recapture land value at the time of lease modification and lease renewal has also been practised in other jurisdictions[122].

A summary of the history of the land tenure system in the early days of Singapore is provided in the *Singapore Annual Report 1958*, where the following is stated[123]:

> After the founding of Singapore in 1819 and prior to the Treaty of 2nd August 1824, which ceded Singapore to the East India Company, the uncertain tenure of the East India Company precluded the issue of permanent titles. From 1826 leases were granted for periods of 999 years, but in 1838 leases for terms up to 99 years were substituted as a common title for land within the narrow limits of the town. Land in the country was also obtainable on short term leases as laid down by the Indian Act XVI of 1839, but these were considered insufficiently secure to encourage proper cultivation and from 1845 onwards grants in freehold were made for such land. Insufficient allowance was made for the town's expansion, and many areas now in the most crowded parts of the city are held under these freehold titles originally intended to be purely agricultural land.
>
> Singapore was transferred to the control of the Colonial Office in 1867, and the titles for land, both in town and country thereafter were mainly leases for terms of 99 or 999 years. In 1886 the Crown Lands Ordinance introduced a statutory form of title — the present statutory land grant,

---

[121] 'Alienation and Sale of State Land,' paper by Pang Boon Yong, Director (Alienation), Ministry of Law, in the Real Estate Developers' Association of Singapore Seminar, *Land & Property Laws in Singapore*, 13 October 2000. The US Government has also carved out 99-year leaseholds out of their freehold land at King's Road and Grange Road, for sale to developers for development. At the end of the 99-year tenure, the land will revert to the US Government. More recently, Far East Organization has done the same for a few of its developments, e.g. the Shore Residences at the corner of Amber Road and Mountbatten Road, with its 103-year lease.

[122] See Yu-Hung Hong, 'Policy dilemma of capturing land value under the Hong Kong public leasehold system,' and Yu-Hung Hong and Steven Bourassa, 'Rethinking the future roles of public leasehold,' in Steven Bourassa and Yu-Hung Hong (eds.), *Leasing Public Land: Policy Debates and International Experiences* (Lincoln Institute of Land Policy, 2003)and Steven Bourassa, Max Neuttze and Ann Louise Strong, 'Assessing betterment under a public premium leasehold system: principles and practice in Canberra,' *Journal of Property Research* 14 (1997), 49–68.

[123] Government Printing Office, 1959 at pp. 116–117. See also James Lornie, 'Land tenure,' in Walter Makepeace *et al.* (eds.), *One Hundred Years of Singapore* (Oxford University Press, 1991).

which is a grant in perpetuity, subject to quit rent and subject also the various conditions. This statutory land grant until recently continued to be the usual form of title issued; but the present policy is to restrict the issue of grants in perpetuity, substituting as far as possible leases for terms not exceeding 99 years. ...

The issue of grants in fee simple is restricted to special cases. With increasing development in all areas of the island and the great rise in land values in the years between the two world wars, there was a tendency for the small fruit and vegetable growers to be driven off the land. As a counter-measure, the Government [has issued] permits, renewable annually, for the temporary occupation of Crown land. This has had a marked effect in keeping the small cultivators on the land. A further and more recent development is that, in order to induce greater investment and more permanent improvement on the land, approval has been given to the issue of agricultural leases of 30 or 60 years on favourable terms.

With leasehold tenures, the remaining term of the leases will diminish with the effluxion of time. Land with short remaining terms will not be attractive for redevelopment as the ultimate buyers of the redeveloped properties, will demand a long period of ownership. In such economics of redevelopment, some of the leases may need to be "topped up" or "upgraded" to fresh 99 years, in order that the real estate fabric is continually rejuvenated.

The Government has been "topping up" or "upgrading" some of leases to fresh 99-year terms on payment of a "topping up" premium. This is usually done when the owner secures a written permission to redevelop the leasehold properties. For example, the Keppel Group upgraded its leases at its former Telok Blangah shipyard, for redevelopment into Corals at Keppel Bay, Caribbean at Keppel Bay and Reflections at Keppel Bay[124]. When the former Shing Kwang House and ICB Building at Shenton Way were to be redeveloped into the SGX Centre, their leases were "topped up" to a fresh 99-year lease[125]. At that time, it was reported that the Land Office (which later became the Singapore Land Authority) was reviewing its lease renewal policy. It was reported that the official position was that "the main objective of the review is to promote urban renewal in an orderly manner and address

---

[124] 'Harbourside Project — Group may save $600m in land premiums,' *The Straits Times*, 7 November 1998.
[125] 'Govt studying whether to top up leases,' *The Business Times*, 23 October 2000.

potential problems such as physical deterioration of buildings"[126]. Quite obviously, the extension of the terms of the lease, cannot be granted on demand from the existing lessees[127]. The Government will also have to balance the benefits of the extension of the lease against the long term plans for the area in which the leasehold property concerned is situated. Where for example the leasehold property is situated within an area of surrounding State land and there may be larger plans for redevelopment, the lease may not be renewed or extended and may be allowed to run out. In the case of more urgent need for land, the leasehold properties may even be compulsorily acquired, as in the case of Pearls Centre in the Outram MRT area. Generally, extension of leases may be considered where[128]:

(a) development/redevelopment of the land is very substantial and would not be feasible/possible unless the tenure is upgraded, e.g. in the development of buildings in the central business district following substantial upgrading of allowable development intensity by Urban Redevelopment Authority (URA);

(b) it is the government's desire/objective to see the land developed/ redeveloped and there is no adverse implications on future development potential of adjoining lands, e.g. in the Hillview and Tanjong Rhu areas where the land has been rezoned from industrial use to residential use; and

(c) the area is not affected by public development/redevelopment scheme to justify compulsory acquisition to achieve the development/ redevelopment.

Certainly, the extension of State leases has helped in the rejuvenation of the urban fabric. One needs only look at the stretch of Shenton Way from Lau Pat Sat to AXA Tower, to see how new buildings have replaced the old, in this urban renewal[129].

---

[126] 'Lease renewal policy now under review,' *The Straits Times*, 24 October 2000.

[127] '60% of lease top-up bids approved since 2007,' *The Business Times*, 21 June 2010

[128] Pang Boon Young, Director (Alienation), Ministry of Law, 'Alienation and Sale of State Land' in the Real Estate Developers' Association of Singapore seminar, *Land & Property Laws in Singapore*, 13 October 2000.

[129] The exception in that stretch of Shenton Way is Shenton House situated at No. 3 Shenton Way, which is strata-titled. It seems that the subsidiary proprietors of Shenton House, are unable to agree on an equitable method of apportionment of the sale proceeds for an *en bloc* sale to proceed.

The renewal of leases has been extended to strata-titled developments owned by multiple subsidiary proprietors. In late 2004, we saw the *en bloc* sale of the aging Eng Cheong Tower (since redeveloped into Southbank) at North Bridge Road. It was the first *en bloc* sale involving a leasehold property[130]. At the time of *en bloc* sale, the remaining term of the 99-year leasehold tenure, was only of 65 years. Normally, a developer would not acquire such a leasehold property for redevelopment, as new residential units with such leaseholds would be virtually unsaleable. What made the *en bloc* sale possible, was the in-principle approval from the Singapore Land Authority to refresh the lease into a new 99-year lease on payment of a "topping-up" or upgrading premium.

3.2. Contest of space underground

Reclamation of land from the sea has been undertaken in Singapore since the 19th century[131] and has added substantial land for Singapore's development. In more recent years, we have seen the reclamation of the Marina Square area and the Marina Bay Financial District[132] which expanded the city area[133]. The sale of land in those areas has added dynamism to the Singapore property market. In 2013 when the Government released the White Paper on Population with a 6.9 million population as a basis for future planning, it also released a

---

[130] 'Eng Cheong set to be first 99-year *en bloc* sale,' *The Business Times*, 17 November 2004 and 'Eng Cheong a good collective sale model,' *The Business Times*, 11 January 2005. The pioneering case of Eng Cheong Tower, was followed by the *en bloc* sales of many 99-year leasehold estates: see '*En bloc* for privatized HUDC apartments?' *The Business Times*, 30 November 2004.

[131] The Telok Ayer Reclamation started with the creation of land on which now stands Cecil Street and Robinson Road was completed by 1890 at a cost of $300,000. With the reclamation, 'a wide extent of valuable building land secured in a direction where the town had become most congested [and] a direct road has been opened of the docks, and a steam tramway brings them in close connexion with the commercial quarters of Singapore': *Annual Report of the Straits Settlements*, 1890, pp. 5–6, and cited in Goh Chor Boon, *Technology and Entrepot Colonialism in Singapore, 1819–1940* (ISEAS Publishing, 2013), p. 110.

[132] See 'Development of Marina Bay,' in *Urban Redevelopment: From Urban Squalor to Global City* (Centre of Liveable Cities, 2016), pp. 89–93. This sideway expansion of the central business district followed the earlier expansion into Shenton Way recovered from the sea in the Telok Ayer Reclamation project: see Lee Kheng Chye, 'Shenton Way development scheme on Crown Land,' in *The Evolution of Singapore Real Estate — Journey to the Past and Future: 1940–2015* (Knight Frank Pte Ltd, 2015), pp. 34–37.

[133] Under s 5 of the Foreshores Act, the President may by proclamation published in the *Gazette*, declare any land formed from the reclamation of the foreshore or from the sea, as State land.

Land Use Plan indicating that 5,200 hectares of land (chiefly around Tuas and Pulau Tekong) would be reclaimed by 2030[134].

As may be seen, in the growth of physical infrastructure, Singapore has gone sideways and upwards. It is only natural that the exploitation of land downwards will grow in pace. In 2013, when the 2014 Master Plan was being prepared, Minister Khaw Boon Wan was reported as considering the drawing up of an underground equivalent of the Master Plan in the *Business Times* on 4 September 2013. He was reported to have stated in a post titled "Exploiting Exciting Possibilities Underground":

> In parallel, we are thinking of the possibility of developing an underground equivalent of the Master Plan to see how practical underground plans can complement the above ground Master Plan to make our city even more exciting and liveable.

In this regard, the URA has commissioned a benchmarking study of 10 cities to bring together good international practices in relation to the use of subterranean space[135].

To facilitate the greater use of subterranean space, the State Lands Act was amended in 2015 by inserting section 3B. The opening words of section 3B(1), "To avoid doubt, it is declared that for all purposes ....", were intended for the provisions in section 3B to have retroactive effect, and to make it clear that any subterranean space below 30 metres from the Singapore Height Datum[136] is State land. As stated in the Explanatory Statement to the State Lands (Amendment) Bill 2015[137]:

---

[134] See 'Plan to grow space for rising population,' *The Straits Times*, 1 February 2013. The reclamation has not been without issues with Malaysia: see Cheong Koon Hean, Tommy Koh and Lionel Yee, *Malaysia and Singapore: the Land Reclamation Case — From Dispute to Settlement* (Centre of International Law, Straits Times Press and Institute of Policy Studies, 2013); Tommy Koh and Jolene Lin, *The Land Reclamation Case: Thoughts and Reflections* (2006) 19 SYBIL 1 and Kadir Mohamad, 'The land reclamation by Singapore in the Straits of Johor,' in *Malaysia Singapore Fifty Years of Contentions 1965–2015*, Chapter Six (The Other Press, 2015).

[135] Stephen Hamnett and Belinda Yuen, *Planning Singapore; The Experimental City* (Routledge, 2019), p. 221. Of course, JTC Corporation has earlier pioneered underground oil storage in its Jurong Rock Cavern project: see 'Pushing Limits-Underground', *The Business Times*, 18 November 2008.

[136] 'The Singapore Height Datum (SHD) corresponds to the mean sea level established historically and it also the datum point on which the Reduced Level calculations used by surveyors in Singapore are based': see Elaine Chew, 'digging deep into the ownership of underground space — Recent changes in respect of subterranean land use,' [2017] *Singapore Journal of Legal Studies* 1.

[137] Bill No. 6/2015. Section 3B(1) has been renumbered as section 9(1) in the 2020 Revised Edition of the State Lands Act 1920.

First, the new section 3B clarifies the law on ownership of the subsoil below the surface of any land of which a person is an owner. The new section 3B(1) declares that for all purposes, any land that is the surface of any defined parcel of the earth includes only so much of the subterranean space below the land as is reasonably necessary for the use and enjoyment of the land. This is defined to mean such depth of subterranean space as is specified in the State title for that land. However, if no such depth is specified in the State title, the land includes subterranean space to −30.000 metres from the Singapore Height Datum.

At the same time, the Land Acquisition Act was also amended to enable the State to acquire subterranean space or airspace, without necessarily having to acquire the surface land as well[138]. Later in the same year, in a declaration under section 5 of the Land Acquisition Act, subterranean space between 2.2 m from Singapore Height Datum (top level) and 12.1 m from Singapore Height Datum (bottom level), of some lots in Mukim 27, was acquired[139]. In the years to come, we will no doubt see greater use of the subterranean space.

3.3. Repeal of rent control

The repeal of Control of Rent Act with the coming into operation of the Control of Rent (Abolition) Act 2001 on 1 April 2001 may be seen as a "giving", as the lifting of rent control gave rise to substantial enhancement in value in respect of the properties affected. The repeal of rent control has seen the refurbishment of shophouses and the substantial enhancement in their values, as the rents in such properties are now subject to market forces and not artificially depressed by the rent control regime.

The Control of Rent Act had earlier applied to all premises built or completed on or before 7 September 1947, regardless of the nature of the use of the premises (i.e. whether they were used for residential purposes or otherwise). It was imposed after World War II, when there was a substantial escalation of rents due to the acute shortage of accommodation.

---

[138] The Land Acquisition (Amendment) Bill 2015, No. 7/2015 introduced the provisions for the amendment of s 5.

[139] Government *Gazette*, 5 June 2015.

However, as the Act did not apply to premises built or completed after 7 September 1947, the construction of new buildings was not discouraged. As the Act constrained the amount of rents that may be charged for the occupation of the rent-controlled properties, it led to a rundown of the physical fabric of those buildings as the owners would not spend much money to maintain them. Yet the Act which was meant to protect the interests of tenants when there was a general shortage of accommodation, could not have been repealed earlier when such shortage was still acute. The premature repeal of the Control of Rent Act before sufficient alternative accommodation became available on the market, may see the eviction of the affected tenants which may not have been acceptable socially.

Hence, the decontrol of rents was done in stages as there had to be sufficient alternative accommodation in the stock of properties for the statutory tenants, who may have to vacate the decontrolled premises as they may not be able to afford the rents when recalibrated to market levels, once the rents of the premises were free from control.

The first step was to decontrol premises in a certain geographical area. This was done with the enactment of the Controlled Premises (Special Provisions) Act which came into operation in 1970 and which has since been repealed. A "designated development area" which encompassed the areas around Robinson Road, Cecil Street, Raffles Place and Market Street, was delineated for the purpose, under the Act. The "designated development area" had the shape of a shoe on the map of the area, and the area subsequently became popularly known as the Golden Shoe area[140]. Under the Controlled Premises (Special Provisions) Act, owners of rent-controlled premises in the designated development area, could recover possession of their premises where they had approved development plans.

---

[140] See Chua Beng Huat, *The Golden Shoe: Building Singapore's Financial District* (Urban Redevelopment Authority, 1989), and 'Case study 1: Decisive state intervention — The Golden Shoe Financial District,' in *Urban Redevelopment: From Urban Squalor to Global City* (Centre of Liveable Cities, 2016), pp. 59–60. As the Government also built a multi-storey car park and hawker center building at Market Street and named it Golden Shoe Car Park (since demolished in 2018 for the redevelopment into a commercial building named CapitaSpring), some have associated the name 'Golden Shoe' with the building there. Round about the same time, a stretch of Beach Road was promoted as the 'Golden Mile' where land was put up for public tender for the purposes of development. The buildings known as Golden Mile Complex and Golden Mile Towers amongst others were erected there. The preface 'Golden' for both Golden Shoe and Golden Mile at that time, was to signal the promise that those areas may bring for the redevelopment of the city.

The tenants and other occupiers who were in occupation of the premises may be evicted on payment of reasonable compensation, under the heads of compensation provided in the Act. Any dispute on the quantum of the compensation would be determined by the Tenants Compensation Board which was established under the Act. This mechanism was necessary as statutory tenants may also be extortionate in their negotiations with the owners for compensation. The Act enabled the redevelopment of many of the controlled premises in the Golden Shoe area into new commercial buildings, as it provided for a mechanism for the owners to evict the tenants on payment of reasonable compensation. This first step on decontrol was manageable as the statutory tenants that may be affected were limited to those in the designated development area and they were paid some compensation by the property owners. This initiative at decontrol came at a time when Singapore was in the initial years of independence and the economy was still fragile and in need of investment. Technically, more "designated development areas" could have been declared under the Act to enable other areas to be developed but this never came to pass.

The next step in decontrol came 10 years later in 1980, after Singapore has made significant progress in the construction of HDB housing to alleviate the acute shortage of residential accommodation. Domestic premises (i.e. those which were used as dwelling houses) were decontrolled with the coming into operation of the Control of Rent (Exemption) Notification 1980[141] on 24 October 1980. Where the domestic premises on or after 24 October 1980 had not been occupied by the owner or let to a tenant, they were exempt from the provisions of the Control of Rent Act. Further where domestic premises which were owned by a body corporate, had been occupied by or let to its director or employee, they were also so exempt from the provisions of the Control of Rent Act. In other words, it was not a blanket decontrol of domestic premises. Where the domestic premises were occupied by statutory tenants before the coming into operation of the 1980 Notification and were still occupied by those tenants, the domestic premises continued to be subject to the Control of Rent Act. This reservation under the 1980 Notification, was obviously to prevent the mass eviction of such

---

[141] S 290/1980.

tenants by the owners. However, premises which were not so occupied, were to be free from rent control thenceforth.

Later with the Control of Rent (Exemption) (Consolidation) Notification 1988[142], non-domestic premises were also decontrolled on similar conditions where they were satisfied on or after 7 October 1988. Nevertheless, in respect of premises which continued to let to statutory tenants after those dates (i.e. 24 October 1980 or 7 October 1988 as the case may be), they remain subject to the Control of Rent Act.

It was only with the repeal of the Control of Rent Act on 1 April 2001, that those premises which remained subject to the Control of Rent Act (as the conditions in the 1980 and 1988 Notifications were not satisfied), were alleviated from the shackles of rent control such that free market forces could operate in respect of those premises, which comprises mainly shophouses. The operation of free market forces in respect of those shophouses has seen investment and refurbishment of those premises and today each of those refurbished shophouses is frequently a multi-million dollar asset, and they add to a diversity of asset classes in Singapore.

3.4. COVID-19 (Temporary Measures) Act

The early part of the year 2020 saw the outbreak of COVID-19 in Singapore. The Government enacted the COVID-19 (Temporary Measures) Act 2020[143] to deal with various issues as the pandemic affected all sectors of the economy. In this section, we will only discuss the "giving" of the rental relief to tenants. The landlords may perceive the rental relief accorded under the Act as a "taking". However, as the rental relief is perceived as a one-off intervention in the rental market, it is not expected to fundamentally affect the investment ecomomics in non-residential properties. What may be transformational for such investment are the behaviors brought about by COVID-19: working remotely from home and changes in requirements for logistical facilities for supply chains. Nevertheless, as the Act still represents

[142] Cap. 58, 1990 ed, N4 (repealed).
[143] Act No. 14 of 2020. The COVID-19 (Temporary Measures) Bill 2020, No. 19/2020 was introduced in Parliament as an Urgent Bill on 7 April 2020 and was passed by Parliament and assented to by the President on the same day.

an unprecedented statutory intervention in the market forces affecting non-residential properties, the workings of the Act are discussed here.

One aspect of Act pertains to the mandatory transfer of the benefit of the property tax remission received by landlords to their tenants. In essence, an owner of a property pays over the sum of property tax which he otherwise has to pay to the Government, to his tenant, or he may use the sum to set-off against the rents due from his tenant. It is a monetary relief given to the tenants to help them meet the challenges that they encountered during the outbreak in 2020[144].

The relief however does not change the long-term fundamental workings of the property market. Nevertheless, this is the first time that the Government has directly intervened in making it mandatory for the owner who has been given a property tax reduction, to transfer the benefit of the tax reduction to his tenant. Part 6 of the Act which deals with the passing on of the benefit of the property tax remission came into operation on 22 April 2020[145].

Under section 29(2) of the Act, the owner of a property must pass on the benefit of the property tax remission given under the Property Tax (Non-Residential Property) (Remission) Order 2020[146] to the prescribed tenant. It is to be noted that the property tax remission under the Property Tax Act is given to the owner of the properties. There is nothing in the Property Tax Act, which empowers the Minster to impose a condition that the remission will only be given to the owner, if he were to pass on the benefit of the property tax remission, to his tenant. Hence, Part 6 of the COVID-19 (Temporary Measures) Act has to be enacted to provide the statutory power to compel the owner to pass on the benefit of the property tax remission that he has received, to his tenant.

Briefly, the property tax remission was given under the Property Tax (Non-Residential Properties) (Remission) Order 2020. There were three

---

[144] See 'Govt aware of risk that rental help may prolong exit of unviable businesses: Shanmugam,' *The Business Times*, 6–7 June 2020.

[145] COVID-19 (Temporary Measures) Act (Commencement No. 3) Notification 2020, S 310/2020.

[146] S 155/2020 which was published on 10 March 2020 as amended by Property Tax (Commercial Properties) (Remission)(Amendment) Order 2020, S 305/2020, which was published on 20 April 2020 which enhanced the rates of property tax remission given under the original Order. This Order is made under s 6(8) of the Property Tax Act. See also IRAS e-Tax Guide, *Property Tax Rebate for Non-Residential Properties in 2020*, Fifth edition, 29 December 2020.

rates of remission, i.e. 100%, 60% and 30% for non-residential properties with no remission for residential properties. The 100% remission[147] of the property tax for the entire year 2020 was given for properties which are most affected by the COVID-19 outbreak (such as hotels, service apartments, foreign workers' dormitories, MICE facilities, shops, restaurants, amusement centers, sports and recreation buildings, cinemas, theatres, premises of tourist attraction). The lowest rate of 30% remission for the year 2020, was given for owners of buildings, such as office buildings, factory and warehouse buildings. The intermediate rate of remission of 60% was only given to the owners of two properties, i.e. the integrated resorts at Marina Bay Sands and Resort Worlds at Sentosa, each of which is assessed with a single annual value. It would seem that the 60% remission was a blended rate which reflected the perception that while parts of the integrated resorts (i.e. hotels, shops, MICE premises[148] and theme park) would otherwise qualify for 100% remission if those parts were standalone properties, there may be greater sensitivity to accord 100% remission for the casino component within those properties. However, the actual reason for the intermediate remission rate of 60% was not publicly announced.

Section 29(2) of the COVID-19 (Temporary Measures) Act provided that the owner must pass the benefit of the reduction in property tax to the "prescribed lessee" or "prescribed licensee", where a property (in whole or part) was leased or licensed to them, "for any part of the period to which the prescribed remission relates". The remission under the Property Tax (Non-Residential Properties) (Remission) Order 2020, was for the entire year of 2020.

The detailed rules pertaining to the passing on of the benefit of the property tax reductions received by owners to the "prescribed lessees" and "prescribed licensees" are set out in the COVID-19 (Temporary Measures)

---

[147] A remission of 100% effectively means that no property tax was payable for the year 2020.

[148] MICE is the acronym for 'meetings, incentive travel, conventions and exhibitions'. Three MICE premises are specifically named in the Property Tax (Non-Residential Properties) (Remission) Order 2020, i.e. Suntec Singapore Convention and Exhibition Centre, Singapore Expo and Changi Exhibition Centre, as they are each assessed with the individual annual values. The Raffles City Convention Centre was also given 100% remission, as part of the function rooms of Fairmont Hotel. The two other convention premises at Marina Bay Sands and Resort Worlds at Sentosa, are part of the integrated resorts (which include casino components) which are assessed with single annual values and were given an overall 'blended' remission rate of 60%.

(Transfer of Benefit of Property Tax Remission) Regulations 2020[149]. A "prescribed lessee" is "a specified lessee of the property or any part of the property at any time in the period between 3 April 2020 and 31 December 2020 (both dates inclusive)"[150]. The term "specified lessee" in regulation 4(1) is in turn defined in regulation 2(1) as "the lessee who enters into a lease agreement with the owner for the whole or any part of the property for a purpose other than accommodation at the property or part of the property". Examples of "purposes other than accommodation at the properties" are given at paragraph 9.6(b) of the IRAS e-Tax Guide, *Property Tax Rebate for Non-Residential Properties in 2020*[151], as hotels, serviced apartments and workers' dormitory. Hence according to the IRAS guide, tenants at hotels, serviced apartments and workers' dormitory using parts of those properties for accommodation, were not "prescribed lessees" and were not entitled to the transfer of the benefit of the property tax remission from their landlords.

A sub-tenant who had a lease agreement with the head tenant, but not with the owner of the property, was also not a "prescribed lessee" and was accordingly not entitled to the transfer of the benefit of the property tax remission.

Short-term lessees who had lease agreements with the owners of properties, were entitled to the benefit, as there was no specification of any minimum period of the lease for the qualifying "prescribed lessee", unlike that for "prescribed licensee" which was defined in regulation 2(1) as "a licensee who enters into a license agreement with the owner for the whole or any part of the property (a) for an initial period of at least 12 months, and not including any period of extension or renewal that may be provided under the license; and (b) for a purpose other than accommodation at the property or part of the property".

As may be seen, the qualifying licensee had to have a license agreement for an initial period of at least 12 months. This was meant to exclude short-

---

[149] S 375/2020 which came into operation on 13 May 2020.

[150] Reg 4(1) read with the definition of 'specified lessee' in reg. 2(1) of the COVID-19 (Temporary Measures) (Transfer of Benefit of Property Tax Remission) Regulations 2020, S 375/2020. The Regulations were amended to take into account circumstances encountered in their implementation: see COVID-19 (Temporary Measures) (Transfer of Benefit of Property Tax Remission) (Amendment) Regulations 2020, S 1019/2020, gazette on 18 December 2020.

[151] Fifth edition, 29 December 2020.

term licensees such as drivers who parked their vehicles at a carpark on hourly parking charges, advertisers who put up their advertisements at the premises of an owner, licensees of co-working spaces, etc. Such short-term licensees were not as adversely affected by the COVID-19 outbreak and in any case, the charges during that period would have been adjusted according to market conditions, and the licensees would have had cognizance of those charges when entering into the short-term license agreements.

However, tenants were entitled to the benefit of the property tax reductions received by the owner. So long as the property was let to the tenant at any time during the period from 3 April 2020 to 31 December 2020, the tenant was entitled to the benefit of the property tax reduction for his period of the lease within the year of 2020. If the property has been leased to the tenant for the entire year of 2020, the tenant was entitled to the benefit for the full year as the property is leased to him "for the period to which the prescribed remission relates" within the meaning of section 29(2) of the COVID-19 (Temporary Measures) Act 2020.

Elaborate rules were set out in the COVID-19 (Temporary Measures) (Transfer of Benefit of Property Tax Remission) Regulations 2020, on the computation of the benefit to be transferred to the tenant. Where the tenant occupied the entire property or unit which had been assessed with an annual value, the identification of the amount of benefit to be transferred to the tenant, was a simple task. The entire remission received by the owner was to be transferred to the tenant who was in occupation for the entire year of 2020.

Where the property or unit occupied by a tenant was part of a larger property or unit which had been assessed with a single annual value, the owner would have had to apportion the benefit of the property tax remission amongst the various tenants[152].

What started out as the transfer of the benefit of property tax remission to the tenant, soon developed into a rental relief framework when it was apparent that some tenants needed greater assistance. In view of the severe economic fallout from the COVID-19 outbreak, the Government proposed legislative amendments to the COVID-19 (Temporary Measures) Act 2020,

---

[152] Reg 7 of the COVID-19 (Temporary Measures) (Transfer of Benefit of Property Tax Remission) Rules 2020, S 375/2020.

just two months after its enactment. On 5 June 2020, the COVID-19 (Temporary Measures) (Amendment) Bill[153] was introduced in Parliament as an Urgent Bill, and was enacted on the same day[154].

Earlier on 3 June 2020, the Ministry of Law in a press release entitled "New Rental Relief Framework for SMEs" in relation to the proposed legislative amendments, the following additional rental relief measures were announced for tenants which are small and medium enterprises (SMEs):

(a) Government cash grants of approximately 0.8 month of rent for qualifying commercial properties and approximately 0.64 month of rent for industrial and office properties. This cash grant together with the transfer of the benefit of the property tax remission, took the rental relief to approximately 2 months of rent relief for qualifying commercial properties and 1 month of rent for industrial and office properties.[155] The Inland Revenue Authority of Singapore has been assigned the function of disbursing cash grants to mitigate rental costs[156]; and

(b) Additional rental waiver to be borne by landlords, amounting to an additional 2 months' waiver of the base rent for qualifying commercial properties and 1 month for industrial and office properties[157]. Individual owners who were landlords of lower-value non-residential properties may however halve the rental waiver made available to their tenants[158]. A valuation review panel has also been established to adjudicate on the disputes between the landlords and tenants with respect to the rental waivers[159].

---

[153] Bill 28/2020.

[154] The COVID-19 (Temporary Measures) (Amendment) Act 2020, (Act No. 29 of 2020), except sections 7, 8(f), 15 and 16, came into operation on 20 June 2020: see COVID-19 (Temporary Measures) (Amendment) Act 2020 (Commencement) Notification 2020, S 475/2020.

[155] Section 19H of the COVID-19 (Temporary Measures) Act read with regulations 10 and 11 of the COVID-19 (Temporary Measures)(Rental and Related Measures) Regulations 2020, S 664/2020.

[156] Inland Revenue Authority of Singapore (Assignment of Functions) (No. 2) Notification 2020, S 64/2020 which came into operation on 30 July 2020. The notices of cash grant were sent to the eligible owners of non-residential properties in mid-August 2020.

[157] Section 19J of the COVID-19 (Temporary Measures) Act read with regulations 12 and 13 of the COVID-19 (Temporary Measures) (Rental and Related Measures) Regulations 2020, S 664/2020.

[158] COVID-19 (Temporary Measures) (Rental and Related Measures) Regulations 2020, S 664/2020 which came into operation on 31 July 2020.

[159] COVID-19 (Temporary Measures) (Valuation Review Panel) Regulations 2020, S 553/2020 which came into operation on 15 July 2020.

At the second reading of the COVID-19 (Temporary Measures) (Amendment) Bill on 5 June 2020, the Minister for Law, Mr K. Shanmugam explained the need to intervene as follows:

> In my speech then [when the COVID-19 (Temporary Measures) Bill was moved in an urgent just under two months ago], I explained why intervention was needed. The economic shock was unprecedented in magnitude (in terms of the impact), and the speed at which this impact was felt.
>
> I also set out the principles for such intervention. The starting point is always that the sanctity of contract is fundamental. It's a key aspect of the rule of law, and we do not lightly intervene. But sanctity of contract cannot be an absolute. I said that intervention is needed when the core interests of our people are at stake, and there is a need to safeguard the fundamental integrity of the economic structure for common good. Such intervention has to be reasonable and of generally limited duration.

In providing a context to the novel statutory interventions in the COVID-19 (Temporary Measures) Act, Minister K. Shanmugam in an interview with the television channel CNBC on 7 April 2020 said[160]:

> You're looking at economic devastation. Businesses destroyed, people's lives ruined, and in such a situation, you don't talk contract. You talk equity, you talk justice, you talk about what is the right thing to do.

The year 2020 was indeed an *annus horribilis* which needed unprecedented statutory interventions[161].

---

[160] As reported on the Ministry of Law website, accessed 14 August 2020.

[161] With respect to relief given to qualifying small medium enterprises for the period of Phase 2 (Heightened Alert) from 16 May to 13 June 2021, the half-month rental relief cash payouts were given directly by the Government to qualifying tenants in privately-owned commercial properties, without involving the landlords in the process. In addition, with the coming into operation of the COVID-19 (Temporary Measures) (Amendment No. 4) Act 2021 (Act 26 of 2021) and the COVID-19 (Temporary Measures) (Rental Waiver Due to COVID-19 Event in 2021) Regulations 2021 (S 751/2021), landlords of non-residential properties were required to provide two weeks of rental relief to qualifying tenants to mitigate the impact of COVID-19 measures occurring during the period from 5 August 2021 to 18 August 2021.

CHAPTER 2

Property Market Cycles: Fiscal and Macroprudential Measures

1. Introduction

From time to time, governments have been faced with the need to moderate the escalation of property prices. In the 1950s, during the preparation of the first Master Plan[1], there were concerns of speculation in property prices ahead of the adoption of the Master Plan in 1958, as for the first time there would be a statutory blueprint regulating the land use in Singapore. The government then commissioned a report with regard to the control of land prices. A report was duly presented to the then Minister for Local Government, Lands and Housing, Inche Abdul Hamid bin Haji Jumat on 7 October 1955[2]. The Report recommended a Land Purchases Control scheme where the purchases of real estate, were to be subject to the consent of the Minister. This recommendation was however not implemented[3].

In post-independence Singapore, the cyclical manifestations of the property market could also be seen from time to time. Fiscal instruments and macroprudential measures have been used to moderate the excesses of property cycles in Singapore. It is perhaps appropriate to trace the history of

---

[1] The Master Plan is a statutory plan which indicates the permissible land use and development intensity for land in Singapore. See Chapter 3 for further details.

[2] JFN Murray, *A Report on Control of Land Prices, Valuation and Compulsory Acquisition of Land* (Government Printing Office, October 1955).

[3] The recommendation was probably too drastic and would have created a bureaucracy, if it was implemented.

the property market cycles since independence and the fiscal responses to the swings in the property market.

After independence and following the British announcement in 1967 on its planned withdrawal of its armed forces from Singapore[4], the property market sentiments were dim. The property market began to improve from 1969[5] and there was a setback in 1971 when most of the British forces finally withdrew from Singapore and with President Richard Nixon's announcement in August 1971 of the suspension of the convertibility of the US dollar to gold. In 1972 however, the Singapore economy experienced a double-digit growth and the property market turned sharply upwards. Property prices especially residential ones continued its sharp growth into 1973, until the Government announcement in September 1973 on the restriction of the purchase of residential properties by foreigners[6]. This was followed by a period of depressed property prices from 1974 to 1978. The property market recovered in 1979 and experienced a boom from 1979 to mid-1981, which was again followed by a period of depressed property prices[7]. The recession of 1985 and 1986 due to a combination of a slowdown in global demand and high domestic operating costs, was a turning point in Singapore's economic development[8]. The Government convened an Economic Committee in April

---

[4] The British withdrawal from the 'east of Suez' is often cited as a turning point which marked the end of the British Empire. As the British 'retreated' from the east of Suez, it was increasingly drawn towards integration with the European Economic Community (i.e. the predecessor of the current European Union), which it joined in 1973. The British eventually voted to leave the European Union in a referendum held in June 2016, and officially left the European Union in 2020 after a number of delays to its exit (colloquially termed as 'Brexit').

[5] Tan Ling Ling, *A Study of Land Values in Singapore*, October 1970, Economic Development Division, Ministry of Finance (MOF).

[6] The Residential Property Act was enacted on this Government policy. See 'The Residential Property Act: Citizenship and its entitlements,' *CLC Insights,* Issue No. 58, July 2020, published by the Centre of Liveable Cities. In many countries, various measures have been introduced to curb excessive residential property price increases from the effects of foreign-buying: see Edward SW Ti, *Politics and Policy: Chinese money and its impact on the Regulation of Residential Property on the West,* (2013) 83 Conv 371.

[7] See 'Property price changes in Singapore in the last decade,' *Economic Survey of Singapore, Third Quarter 1983* (Ministry of Trade and Industry), pp. 12–14 and Ng Hui Meng, 'Private Residential property market and the macroeconomy,' *Economic Survey of Singapore, First Quarter 2002* (Ministry of Trade and Industry), pp. 53–71.

[8] See Cheah Hock Beng, 'The downturn in the Singapore economy: Problems, prospects and possibilities for recovery,' in Lim Joo-Jock (ed.), *Southeast Asian Affairs 1986* (Singapore Institute of Southeast Asian Studies, 1986) and reproduced in Daljit Singh and Malcolm Cook, *Turning Points and Transitions: Selections from Southeast Asian Affairs 1974–2018* (ISEAS Publishing, 2018). The 1985 recession coincided with historic shutdown of the Singapore Stock Exchange for 3 days in November 1985 to forestall panic dumping of shares following the voluntary request by Pan-Electric Industries Ltd to suspend the trading of its shares in both the Singapore Stock Exchange and the Kuala Lumpur Stock Exchange, upon a default

1985 in connection with the sharp downturn in the economy. The Economic Committee chaired by the then Minister of State for Trade and Industry, Mr Lee Hsien Loong, published its Report in February 1986, where the following comments were made in respect of the real estate sector[9]:

> The effects of the downturn of the property market are not confined to the construction industry. Given the extent of the linkages between the property market and the rest of the economy, a total collapse of the property market would have serious repercussions on the whole economy. In particular, any further drastic decline in property prices could affect the integrity of the banking system.
>
> The property glut will take time to be absorbed. In the meantime, the government should avoid doing anything to aggravate the situation, such as by selling further parcels of land[10], or letting out its vacant properties at rock bottom prices. *Should there be further drastic falls in property prices, the government's priority should be to insulate the banking system and the rest of the economy from the possible repercussions.* The Property Market Consultative Committee under the Ministry of Finance is studying the problems in detail, and will produce more specific recommendations on how to solve them. (Emphasis added)

As has been pointed out by the 1986 Economic Committee, the stability in the property market is inter-linked with that of the financial sector and

---

of the loan repayment, which added to the economic plight. A director of the company, Mr Tan Koon Swan, a prominent Malaysian politician was subsequently prosecuted: see Monetary Authority of Singapore, *Case Study on Pan-Electric Crisis*, MAS Staff Paper No. 32, June 2004; N. Anparasan, *White-collar Crime in Singapore: Then and Now*, (2009) 21 SAcLJ 16 and '1985: Pan-El capped watershed year for S'pore,' *The Business Times*, 27 May 2015.

9 Report of the Economic Committee, *The Singapore Economy: New Directions*, (Ministry of Trade and Industry, February 1986), p. 201.

10 When property prices were escalating, however, the Government has added land supply to the market, to cool the property market: see 'Govt bumps up land supply to cool market,' *The Business Times*, 22–23 May 2010. The Government through the Government Land Sales (GLS) program, has also used the supply of development sites, to help moderate the property market excesses. The joint statement issued by the Ministry of National Development (MND), MOF and MAS on 19 February 2010 on the introduction of seller's stamp duty for example, also mentioned that there was adequate supply of housing units in the pipeline. However, as the gestation period for the supply of new homes constructed by housing developers, is somewhat long, the contribution of the supply side alone, does not adequately address the immediate situation of escalating prices in the property market. See 'Balancing act with constant fine-tuning,' *The Business Times*, 7 October 2010, on the various public and private housing market rule changes made during the period from 1980 to 2010.

the rest of the economy, whether the prices are rapidly rising or falling. This was also echoed in a paper by the Monetary Authority of Singapore (MAS), three decades later as follows[11]:

> In Singapore, property market stability is closely linked to macroeconomic and financial stability. Property is the largest component of household wealth, representing about half of the total household assets. Mortgage loans account for some three-quarters of total household liabilities, and property-related loans form a substantial portion of banks' loan books. As a result, adverse developments in the property market could have serious implications for households, the banking system and the broader economy. Therefore, when property prices rose rapidly shortly after the Global Financial Crisis, the Singapore authorities decided to introduce a series of measures to promote a more stable and sustainable property market.

The contagion risks that unsustainably high and rising property prices have on the broader economy was also highlighted in the document, *MAS' Approach to Macroprudential Policy* as follows[12]:

> Cross-sectional systemic risks arise from the interconnectedness or linkages among financial institutions as well as between financial institutions and other economic actors. Such linkages can be in the form of direct lending or trading exposures. They can also be indirect, arising from common membership of payment, clearing and settlement systems or holding common exposure to similar assets.
>
> These interconnections can serve as contagion channels through which shocks propagate across the financial system and the broader economy. For example, when a financial institution defaults on its obligations, other financial institutions with significant exposures to that financial institution would suffer financial losses (real or accounting markdowns) and could also come under stress. Another example is where distressed market participants conduct fire-sales of assets into illiquid markets. This could drive down market prices of these assets and force others to mark down

---

[11] Wong Nai Seng *et al.*, Using macroprudential tools to address systemic risks in the property sector in Singapore,' *SEACEN Financial Stability Journal* 27 (2015) 4. See also 'List best practices for use of macro-prudential policies in housing market,' *The Business Times*, 14 October 2020.

[12] Published by the MAS in January 2019, see p. 4.

the values of their holdings; thereby leading to spiraling impact on other seemingly less-connected market participants. Failing financial institutions could also impact households and corporates that rely on them for credit and other financial services.

... In the property market for example, unsustainably high and rising property prices could presage a subsequent sharp correction that would significantly impact households and banks, given their high exposure to property. Over the medium-term, property prices and credit trends should be aligned with broader economic fundamentals. Accordingly, the use of macroprudential tools in the sector pre-empts destabilising effects arising from volatility in prices and credit.

Given the contagion risks, it is little wonder that the Government would monitor the movements of property prices closely and that the housing market is highly regulated both in terms of macroprudential and fiscal policies.

2. Macroprudential Policy Instruments

Macroprudential policy is concerned with the stability of the financial system as a whole. In Singapore, such policy has historically a significant focus on the private residential property market, given the importance of residential properties for household balance sheets and banks' loan portfolios[13].

The demand for private residential property is dependent on price and interest rates (or cost of borrowing). Rising income, confidence factor, appreciating stock value (wealth effect), as well as population growth would also increase housing demand. In addition, investment demand of residential property is a function of expectations of future price increase. Speculations in a rising market could result in private residential property prices getting out of line with underlying fundamentals and lead to a property market bubble[14].

To prevent the property market bubble from developing, the range of available instruments in the macroprudential toolkit include the loan-to-value (LTV)

---

[13] See *Macroprudential Policies in Singapore*, at the MAS website.

[14] 'Residential property prices and national income,' *Economic Survey of Singapore, First Quarter 2001* (Ministry of Trade and Industry, p. 49). See 'Why rising mortgage debt alarms policymakers' *The Straits Times*, 8 December 2021.

ratios[15], debt service-to-income (DSTI) ratios[16], higher risk weights on mortgage loans in the calculation of capital-asset ratios of the financial institutions and larger loan loss provisions on mortgage loans by the financial institutions[17]. In addition, the risk profiles of borrowers may also be monitored, e.g. the share of borrowers taking up multiple housing loans, the average tenure of new housing loans. The use of interest rates in moderating the exuberance of the property market is generally not used as interest rates will impact businesses as well[18].

3. Fiscal Measures

3.1. Property tax

In respect of fiscal measures, the early ones adopted in Singapore related to property tax. When economic prospects were dim following the separation of Singapore from Malaysia in August 1965, Singapore embarked on a scheme of urban renewal in order to provide the infrastructure for its economic development and to encourage investment so as to pump prime the economy.

---

[15] The LTV limit was reduced on 20 February 2010, from 90% to 80% for all housing loans provided by financial institutions regulated by the MAS, at the same time that the seller's stamp duty (SSD) was re-introduced. On 6 July 2018, there were further reductions in the LTV limits by 5 percentage points. For the first housing loan for individual borrowers with loan tenure of 30 years or less, the LTV limit was reduced from 80% to 75%. For the third housing loan for the individual borrower, it can go as low as 15%. For non-individual borrowers, the LTV limit was reduced from 20% to 15% for all housing loans. See *United Overseas Bank Ltd v Lippo Marine Collection Pte Ltd* [2021] SGHC 283 on MAS Notice 632 prescribing the LTV limit.

[16] Generally referred to as Total Debt Servicing Ratio (TDSR) in Singapore: see *Guidelines on the Application of Total Debt Servicing Ratio for Property Loans under MAS Notices 645, 1115, 831 and 128* (MAS, June 2013). With TDSR, a borrower's monthly instalments for all debt servicing must not exceed 60% of his gross monthly income. During the COVID-19 outbreak period, the MAS clarified that TDSR will not apply for individuals in the cases of: (a) deferment of mortgage repayments (for residential, commercial or industrial properties); (b) refinancing of owner-occupied residential mortgages; (c) mortgage equity withdrawal loans if the LTV ratio does not exceed 50%; and (d) unsecured credit facilities such as credit cards and personal loans: see MAS media release on 7 April 2020. See also J. J. Woo, 'Singapore's policy style: Statutory boards as policymaking units,' *Journal of Asian Public Policy* 8 (2015), 120–133, where the role of MAS in policy making in avoiding a property bubble and in fostering long term stability in the property market, is discussed.

[17] See L. Zhang and E. Zoli, *Leaning Against the Wind: Macroprudential Policy in Asia*, IMF Working Paper (2014), p. 6, and the *Report on Financial Stability Review* by the Macroprudential Surveillance Department of the MAS, and its update on the Private Residential Property Market, published in November 2017.

[18] See 'Property cycles hard to predict,' *The Straits Times*, 11 November 2019, where the comments of the Finance Minister Tharman Shanmugaratnam at a forum to gather feedback for the Economic Strategies, on the use of the interest rates was reported.

The first Urban Renewal Sale of Sites[19] was launched in 1967. The then prevailing property tax rate was 36% per annum. However, in respect of the sites sold in the first three Urban Renewal Sales of Sites program conducted in 1967, 1968 and 1969, respectively, the applicable property tax rate was reduced to 12% per annum for a period of 20 years, to encourage real estate developments[20].

When residential property prices escalated in the early 1970s culminating in the Government announcement on 10 September 1973 restricting the purchase of residential properties by persons who were not Singapore citizens, a property tax surcharge of 10% per annum was imposed from 1 January 1974[21], on the annual value of residential properties which were acquired by non-citizens before September 1973 and continued to be owned by them. The surcharge was to add to the costs of the holding of residential properties by the non-citizens.

During the economic recession in 1985/1986[22], the Property Market Consultative Committee reporting to the Minister of Finance, recommended an interim 30% rebate of the property tax from 1 July 1985 to 31 December 1986[23], when the then prevailing property tax rate was 23%. The recommendation was accepted and implemented and a property

---

[19] The Urban Renewal Sales of Sites program was conducted by the Urban Renewal Department of the Housing and Development Board, before the establishment of the Urban Redevelopment Authority of Singapore in 1974. The program was the precursor of the present Government Land Sales (GLS) Program. There were 13, 14 and 19 sites sold under the First, Second and Third Sale of Sites Program, respectively. Some of the buildings erected on the sites which are still in existence are the People's Park Complex, Shenton House, International Plaza and Peace Centre: see *Chronicle of Sale Sites* (Urban Redevelopment Authority, 1983). The GLS program was also used to moderate the swings of the housing market, by increasing land supply where prices were escalating and by decreasing land supply where the housing market was in the doldrums.

[20] Leung Yew Kwong and See Wei Hwa, *Property Tax in Singapore*, Third Edition (Lexis Nexis, 2015), p. 44. Alan Choe who was in charge of urban renewed then, had pushed for a property tax rate of 20% for a period of 5 to 6 years and was pleasantly surprised with the government's decision on a concessionary property tax rate of 12% for 20 years: see 'The Government Land Sales Programme: Turning Plans into Reality, Urban System Studies (2021, Centre of Livable Cities), p. 17.

[21] The Property Tax (Surcharge) Act was enacted for the purpose, and it was only repealed from 1 July 2006 via the Property Tax (Surcharge) (Abolition) Act 2007, Act 8 of 2007.

[22] In *Industrial & Commercial Bank Ltd v Li Soon Development Pte Ltd*, [1993] 3 SLR(R) 581, Chao Hick Tin J (as he then was) noted at [57]: 'On the evidence before me, the plain truth of the matter is that between 1985 and 1986 property prices in Singapore were sliding. Recession hit Singapore in 1985.'

[23] See *Action Plan for the Property Sector: Report of the Property Market Consultative Committee* (MOF, February 1986), p. 5.

tax rebate of 30% was given for commercial and industrial properties from 1 July 1985. The rebate was subsequently increased to 50% from 1 July 1986 and the concession period was extended to 31 December 1988[24]. The property tax rate was eventually reduced to the present 10% and over the years the collection of property tax has declined, in relative terms against the other taxes like income tax and goods and services tax.

From time to time, property tax rebates have been provided to property owners during periods of downturn in the economy, such as during the Asian financial crisis from 1998 and the Severe Acute Respiratory Syndrome (SARS) outbreak in 2003[25]. The rebates which effectively reduced the property tax payable were to provide relief to the property owners during challenging economic times. More recently during the COVID-19 outbreak in 2020, property tax rebates were also given to provide relief to business owners. However in this most recent episode, property owners who were given the property tax rebates, had to pass on the benefit to their qualifying tenants, with the coming into operation of the COVID-19 (Temporary Measures) Act 2020[26] and the COVID-19 (Temporary Measures) (Transfer of Benefit of Property Tax Remission) Regulations 2020[27].

3.2. Income tax

Income tax was used for the first time as a property market cooling measure in 1996, when the Government on 14 May 1996 announced both income tax and stamp duty measures which came into operation the next day on 15 May 1996, in an attempt to curb the rapid escalation of property prices[28].

The Income Tax Act was amended in order to subject the gains on the disposal of real property and shares of "land rich"[29] companies to income

---

[24] See Leung Yew Kwong and See Wei Hwa, *Property Tax in Singapore*, Third Edition (LexisNexis, 2015), pp. 15–17.

[25] For more details on property tax rebates, see Leung Yew Kwong and See Wei Hwa, *Property Tax in Singapore*, Third Edition (LexisNexis, 2015), at pp. 42–44.

[26] Act 14 of 2020.

[27] S 375/2020.

[28] See Liu Hern Kuan *et al.*, *Annotated Statutes of Singapore Volume 9(2)* (Butterworths Asia, 2000), pp. 485–500.

[29] The term 'land rich' is used in Australia tax legislation in reference to companies whose assets are substantially in real property. The term is not generally used in Singapore tax legislation.

tax, where the holding period of such assets was 3 years or less[30]. However, with the onset of the Asian financial crisis during the last quarter of the following year, property speculation effectively died out. The provisions on the taxation of short-term gains were eventually repealed in 2002[31].

However, not all the statutory provisions introduced for the May 1996 property market cooling measures were repealed. What still remains today is section 45D of the Income Tax Act, which imposes an obligation on the buyer and his lawyers in the case of the purchase of property, to withhold an amount from the purchase price, which is payable to a non-resident vendor whose gains arising from the disposal is subject to tax as a trading gain under section 10(1)(a) of the Act[32]. This "withholding tax" feature of the measures where the sum withheld by the buyer is paid over to the Comptroller of Income Tax, is still considered necessary as a tax collection mechanism where the non-resident vendor would otherwise be out of reach, in so far as the Comptroller is concerned.

In the latest series of property market cooling measures implemented by the Government from 2010, the income tax measure for taxing the gains from the disposal of properties within a minimum holding period, has not been re-introduced. This may be because the income tax measure is considered less potent in curbing the escalation of property prices, as it will only bite where the taxpayer has made a gain from a disposal of property, and the tax is only a fraction of the actual gains. The income tax measures do not increase the initial costs of acquisition and the subsequent costs of disposal of the property, and hence do not have the immediate potency to help curb speculative demand. It is perhaps for that reason, that we see

---

[30] Sections 10F and 10G were inserted by the Income Tax (Amendment) Act 1996, Act 23 of 1996, to deem such gains as 'gains of an income nature' falling within the provisions of s 10(1)(g) of the Income Tax Act. However, that did not mean that where the holding period was longer than 3 years, the disposal gains were not taxable. Whether the disposal gains in respect of longer holding periods were subject to tax, was still subject to the applicable general principles governing s 10(1)(a) and s 10(1)(g) of the Income Tax Act.

[31] See Income Tax (Amendment) Act 2002, Act 37 of 2002.

[32] Under the common law, the location of the source of the gain from the disposal of immovable property is at the location where the immovable property is situated: *Liquidator, Rhodesia Metals Limited v Commissioner of Taxes*, [1940] AC 774. The withholding tax mechanism in s 45D is merely a tax collection mechanism. Where the non-resident does not make any gain which may be subject to tax, or where his tax on any gain is less than the amount of tax withheld, the non-resident may still file a tax return so that any amount withheld which may be in excess of the tax properly payable, may be refunded to him.

the stamp duty measures playing the primary role in the recent cooling measures, as far as fiscal ones are concerned.

3.3. Stamp duty

Stamp duty was first used as a fiscal measure for property market cooling purposes in 1996[33]. On 14 May 1996, the Government announced stamp duty and income tax measures which came into operation the next day[34]. The stamp duty measure took the form of the seller's stamp duty (SSD) where the seller had to pay the SSD if he were to resell a residential property within 3 years of its acquisition. The SSD is in addition, to the buyer's stamp duty (BSD) which has to be paid by the buyer. An important change which was also made is that the stamp duty (whether SSD or BSD) has to be paid on the contract instrument instead of the transfer instrument, for all transactions involving immovable property[35]. Consequently, the buyer has to pay the BSD earlier and will need to have the cash resources to pay the BSD at the contract stage, as there would not be sufficient time to make the application to the Central Provident Fund Board for the disbursement of funds for the payment of the BSD. Each sub-purchaser (if any) of the property will also have to pay BSD on his contract. Before the change in the duty point where BSD was paid on the transfer instruments, a sub-purchaser who on-sold the property before the transfer stage, did not suffer the incidence of the BSD as there was no transfer of the property to the sub-purchaser[36].

However, with the onset of the Asian financial crisis in the last quarter of 1997 and where the local property market was also adversely affected, the

---

[33] The incidence of stamp duty on the buyer of a property has always been a feature of the stamp duty instrument, as a tax. See 'Have property cooling measures lost their punch?' *The Business Times*, 16–17 May 2020 where the property market cooling measures for the last 25 years from 1996 were discussed.

[34] See Chen Jianlin, Tools for immediate regulatory tax implementation: Subsidiary legislation v legislation by press release,' [2015] *Singapore Journal of Legal Studies* 1, for a discussion on the implementation of tax measures without the immediate backing of tax legislation.

[35] This is effected by way of a legislative amendment of s 22 of the Stamp Duties Act. See *Commissioner of Stamp Duties v Sinpex Investments Pte Ltd (formerly known as Interocean Properties Pte Ltd)*, [1993] 1 SLR(R) 577 for a case relating to the situation before the 1996 legislative amendment of the Stamp Duties Act.

[36] When the property market speculation was rampant, purchasers of properties may buy a property and soon thereafter re-sell the properties at a profit, without having had to proceed to the transfer stage, which may be some 2 months after the contract is executed.

SSD was suspended from 19 November 1997[37] and eventually repealed in 2005[38]. Nevertheless, even with the repeal of the SSD in 2005, the provision in the Stamp Duties Act pertaining to the advancement of the "duty point" from the transfer instrument to the contract instrument, brought about by the 1996 property market cooling measures, remains to this date[39]. In other words, the incidence of the stamp duty with respect to immovable property transactions, has remained on the executed contract instrument, and has not reverted to the transfer instrument, which was generally the situation before the 1996 legislative amendment.

The prevailing BSD rates are as follows:

Consideration/Market Value (whichever higher)	BSD Rates	
	For Residential Property	For Non-Residential Property
First S$180,000	1%	1%
Next S$180,000	2%	2%
Next S$640,000	3%	3%
Exceeding S$1 million	4%	

3.3.1. *Seller's stamp duty*

The stamp duty instrument again plays its major role in the more recent measures for property market cooling[40]. With the low interest rate environment following the Global Financial crisis in 2008/2009, there emerged a rapid escalation of property prices especially in the housing

---

[37] Stamp Duties (Seller's Duty) Remission Order 1998, S 11/1998.

[38] Stamp Duties (Amendment No. 2) Act 2005, Act 39 of 2005.

[39] In income tax, the withholding tax mechanism in s 45D of the Income Tax Act brought about by the 1996 measure, also remains in the statute book to this date, even where income tax measures with respect to the property market cooling have been repealed.

[40] See Deng Yongheng and Joe Gyouko, *Singapore's Cooling Measures and its Housing Market: Overview and Analysis* (Institute of Real Estate Studies, National University of Singapore, 30 July 2017). For a study on behavorial responses to the seller's stamp duty, see Tam, Eddy HF, *Behavioural Response To Time Notches in Transaction Tax: Evidence from Stamp Duty in Hong Kong and Singapore* (Centre for Business Taxation Working Paper, Oxford, 2018).

market. This led to the re-introduction of the SSD on 20 February 2010[41]. The SSD is computed on the sale price (and not on the gains from the disposal of property) where the owner of the property sells the property within the prescribed holding period. Therefore, even where the owner does not make a profit on the resale of his property, he would still have to pay the SSD if he were to resell the property within the prescribed holding period. Speculators who do not have holding power may therefore be deterred by the SSD.

As the statutory provisions for the imposition of the SSD earlier introduced in 1996, have been repealed in 2005, legislative amendments had to be made to the Stamp Duties Act to implement the SSD in 2010. The Stamp Duties (Amendment) Bill 2010 was tabled in Parliament by way of an "Urgent Bill" on 12 March 2010 and was passed on the same day[42].

Sections 22A, 22B and 22C which were inserted by the 2010 legislative amendments for the imposition of the SSD, enable the implementation details of the SSD to be prescribed by way of subsidiary legislation. With the empowering provisions in the main Act, particular categories of properties may be targeted for the application of SSD, with various lengths of the minimum holding period and at various rates of duties, by way of subsidiary legislation.

The Stamp Duties (Section 22A) Order 2010[43] was duly *gazetted*, and had retrospective operation from 20 February 2010. Under the Order, SSD at the same amount of the buyer's stamp duty was imposed where residential property was resold within the minimum holding period of 1 year. As would be seen subsequently, the features of the SSD (whether in terms

---

[41] See joint media statement issued on 19 February 2010 by the MND, MOF and MAS. The SSD instrument is not peculiar to Singapore. Hong Kong also introduced a stamp duty where a residential property is resold within 24 months called 'special stamp duty', on 20 November 2010. Earlier, the Singapore Government had attempted to rein in the property market by putting a stop to the interest absorption scheme where developers in order to stimulate demand, would absorb the interest payments payable by the purchasers on the bank loans, until the completion of the property under development. The Singapore Government also announced the resumption of land sales in the following year: see 'Govt reins in property market,' *The Straits Times*, 15 September 2009. The MAS also warned that if economic growth proves to be weaker than expected, property buyers could suffer losses as the market corrects and prices fall. Even if the economic recovery stays on course, property buyers could see a rise in interest rates: see 'MAS flags two risks to property buyers,' *The Straits Times*, 10 November 2009.

[42] Act 6 of 2010.

[43] S 209/2010.

of the categories of property affected, the amount of SSD or the specified holding period) may be tweaked as required, to target particular categories of immovable property with calibrated amounts of SSD and specified holding periods. Even where SSD is to be removed, only the subsidiary legislation needs to be repealed. The empowering provisions in the main Act will remain in place, such that the SSD may be re-introduced in future should the need arises and there will be no necessity to go to Parliament to enact an amendment of the main Act for that purpose. The then Minister for Finance, Mr Tharman Shanmugaratnam said as much at the second reading of the Stamp Duties (Amendment) Bill 2010 on 12 March 2010[44]:

> A seller's stamp duty is part of the range of policy instruments that the Government may use from time to time to pre-empt or mitigate property market bubbles. However, the process of introducing and repealing provisions in the Stamp Duties Act each time we have to introduce, vary or remove a seller's stamp duty is not efficient, especially when we have to respond in a timely and calibrated fashion to changes in the property market cycle.
>
> The Amendment Bill will therefore introduce general provisions on a seller's stamp duty and allow the Government to introduce, vary or remove the seller's stamp duty via a Ministerial Order.
>
> ...
>
> The amendments to the Stamp Duties Act will as I have mentioned provide the Government with the policy flexibility to introduce future stamp duty changes where necessary in response to changing conditions in the property market. The Government however does not intend to change the seller's stamp duty liberally. Any future change to the seller's stamp duty will be a carefully considered decision, taking into account all prevailing and projected factors at the time.

As subsequent events indicate, the SSD is not a very potent measure at a time when prices are escalating rapidly as it only bites at the point of sale of the property. SSD does not add to the initial costs of acquisition of the property, and therefore does not immediately help to curb demand. Those

---

[44] *Singapore Parliamentary Debates, Official Report*, 12 March 2010. When the Stamp Duties (Amendment) Act 2010 was enacted, it was deemed to have come into operation on 20 February 2010.

who expect prices to escalate and have the holding power, would envisage that they could always wait out the statutory holding period, to avoid the incidence of SSD[45].

The Government in introducing the property market cooling measures, obviously does not intend to crash the market[46]. Measures were adopted incrementally to cool the market when it was observed that the situation did not improve. As was stated in the joint statement issued by the Ministry of National Development (MND), the Ministry of Finance (MOF) and the MAS on 19 February 2010:

> Therefore, the Government has decided to introduce calibrated measures now to temper sentiments and pre-empt a property bubble from forming. We will tighten the supply of credit to the housing market to encourage greater financial prudence among property purchasers. The Government prefers to take small steps early, rather than be forced to impose more drastic measures after a bubble has formed.

After the re-introduction of the SSD in February 2010, the prices in the property market nevertheless escalated much faster than desired, and the Government had to make further changes to the SSD on 30 August 2010, just 6 months after the re-introduction of the SSD. The prescribed holding period was extended from 1 to 3 years. The rate of the SSD was however on a reducing scale, with SSD being at the same rate as the BSD if the property was resold within the first year of acquisition, decreasing to two-thirds of the rate for resales within the second year and one-third of the rate for resales within the third year[47].

---

[45] In Deng Yongheng, Tu Yong and Zhang Yangjiang, *Explicit Measures of Impacts of Transaction Taxes as Market Cooling Measure: Evidence from Seller's Stamp Duty from Housing Market*, Working Paper, Institute of Real Estate & Urban Studies (National University of Singapore, 2019), a finding was that SSD has a weak impact on curbing market booms.

[46] See 'Property cycles hard to predict,' *The Straits Times*, 11 November 2009, where Finance Minister Tharman Shanmugaratnam was reported as saying, 'Property cycles are hard to predict, but the Government will try to avoid boom-bust cycle. We will keep our eyes on the ball and use all the tools at our disposal, but in a calibrated fashion,' at a forum to gather feedback for the Economic Strategies Committee.

[47] Article 3(ba) of the First Schedule to the Stamp Duties Act and the Stamp Duties (Section 22A) (Amendment) Order 2010, S 473/2010.

However, with low borrowing costs and excess liquidity globally, there was little sign that the escalation of residential property prices was abating[48]. Another 4½ months after the August 2010 measures, the Government had to enhance the features of the SSD. On 14 January 2011, the specified holding period for residential properties was extended from 3 years to 4 years and the rates of SSD were enhanced significantly, starting with 16% of the amount of the consideration or value of the resold properties within the first year, decreasing to 4% in the fourth year[49]. The SSD was further extended to industrial properties from 12 January 2013[50], when it was found that the speculative demand for residential properties was partly diverted or has spilled over to industrial properties.

About 4 years later, on 10 March 2017 and around mid-day[51], the Government announced the reduction of the specified holding period for residential properties from 4 to 3 years, with the SSD rate reduced by 4 percentage points for each of the 3 years of the specified holding period, i.e. the SSD will be reduced to 12% for a resale within the first year, decreasing to 8% in the second year and to 4% in the third year. The reason given in the joint press release of MOF, MND and MAS on 10 March 2017, was that "the number of property sales within the 4-year window has fallen significantly over the years since this measure was introduced". The changes were to take effect the next day[52].

The moderation of the features of the SSD was perhaps meant as a "sweetener", as a new stamp duty measure, i.e. the Additional Conveyance Duty (ACD), was announced at the same time. After all, the SSD features could afford to be recalibrated at that time, as after the many rounds of cooling measures from February 2010, there seemed to be little opportunities for a quick resale of properties for profit.

---

[48] See 'The hazy mix of cooling measures, excess liquidity and real demand,' *The Business Times*, 27–28 November 2010.

[49] Article 3(bb) of the First Schedule to the Stamp Duties Act and the Stamp Duties (Section 22A) (Amendment) Order 2011, S 15/2011.

[50] Articles 3(bd) and 3(be) of the First Schedule to the Stamp Duties Act.

[51] This is in contrast with the general practice of announcing tax measures after the closing of the stock market. The latest round of enhancement of the rates of the additional buyer's stamp duty was announced just before midnight on 15 December 2021. This move was obviously to prevent sellers and buyers from rushing to agree to the issue of an option to purchase before the enhanced ABSD rates came into operation on 16 December 2021.

[52] Joint Press Release on Measures relating to Residential Property by the MND, MOF and MAS, 10 March 2017. The Stamp Duties (Section 22A) (Amendment) Order 2017, S 83/2017, was made to effect the SSD changes.

With the ACD, the acquisition or disposal of equity interests of residential property holding entities would in certain circumstances, be subject to substantial stamp duties as if the underlying residential properties were acquired or disposed directly. However, the man-in-the-street would have little experience with such indirect transactions of properties through shares of the entity that owns the properties, and the announcement of the ACD made little impact on the general public. Instead, the 10 March 2017 announcement was perceived as a signal that the Government would be relaxing the cooling measures. On the same day, the shares of the major real estate developers listed on the Singapore Exchange, went up from 1.46% to 8.10%. The FTSE ST Real Estate Holding and Development Index was up 3.8%. The next day, there was greater prominence given to the SSD changes than the introduction of the ACD in the press[53].

There was a perception that the Government was easing the cooling measures with the 10 March 2017 announcement. The article, "Singapore property market: Getting ready for the upturn", published in *The Business Times* about a month later on 21 April 2017, with the following analysis, reflected the prevailing mood:

> ... Macroprudential policies have entered into an easing cycle. Since February 2010, Singapore policymakers have implemented seven rounds of property cooling measures, utilizing a broad mix of credit-based and fiscal measures. Taken together, they were extremely effective in curbing speculative demand and price pressures in the property market.
>
> Yet, the government's intervention is not one-sided. Policymakers in Singapore have a strong track record of actively reviewing property legislation, and history shows that an excessive correction in prices is as zealously guarded against as a housing bubble.
>
> During 1997, 2001 and 2008, policymakers implemented loosening measures after property price declines ranging from 8 per cent to 16 per cent. Today, with private property prices already declining by close to 12 per cent from its peak, we have entered an easing cycle in macroprudential policies. In March this year, the government made modest revisions to the seller stamp duty and total debt servicing ratio. These calibrated

---

[53] See 'Stamp Duty tweak may give market a fillip,' *The Straits Times*, 11 March 2017, and 'Surprise tweaks in property cooling measures seen signaling further unwinding,' and 'Singapore property market finally sees slight easing — and a new stamp duty,' *The Business Times*, 11–12 March 2017.

adjustments were not meant to have a significant impact on the property market, but sent a clear signal that the government stands ready to support the housing market where necessary.

With the 10 March 2017 announcement, the Singapore residential property market was to see a rebound[54] and a feverish pace of *en bloc* sales[55] thenceforth. However, the 10 April 2017 relaxation of the specified holding period for SSD from 4 to 3 years, did not seem to be intended as a signal for the easing of the cooling measures. After all, the additional buyer's stamp duty (ABSD) which is the more potent property cooling measure which adds to the immediate cost of acquisition was still in place then.

It may have been considered that the reduction of the specified holding period from 4 to 3 years for the SSD, was hardly able to fuel demand. After all, the SSD still bites where a resale takes place within 3 years of the purchase of the property. But it seems that the residential property market was waiting for the signal for a relaxation of property market measures, to burst out of the doldrums. The 10 April 2017 announcement provided that signal. This episode shows how difficult it is to assess beforehand, whether policy instruments will yield the desired outcomes as it is difficult to predict the cognition and choices of the people to whom the policy is intended for[56].

The increase in property price after the 10 April 2017 announcement went unabated. Repeated government warnings did not curb the property price increases and the increasing prices that developers were paying for land[57].

---

[54] 'Property prices inflecting, on track to double by 2030,' *The Business Times*, 26 April 2017, and 'The property market — is it a-turnin'? *The Business Times*, 30 September–1 October 2017.

[55] 'Windfall gains from *en bloc* fever are likely to be capped,' *The Business Times*, 12 September 2017, 'Is optimism in the Singapore property market justified,' *The Business Times*, 15 September 2017 and 'Land Sales: When flour is costlier than bread,' *The Business Times*, 24 October 2017. In the MAS, *Financial Stability Review*, November 2017, 'Box P: Update on the private residential property market,' at p. 100, MAS warned: 'The development of the *en bloc* and GLS sites will more than double the total number of units available for sale in the near term. Over the medium term as these projects are progressively completed, the private housing stock will grow. If it is not matched by increased occupation demand, it will add to the existing vacancies that are already elevated and weigh on rentals and property prices.'

[56] See generally David Low (ed.), *Behavioural Economics and Policy Design* (World Scientific Publishing Co Pte Ltd, 2012).

[57] 'Repeated warnings on property market exuberance may have muted impact,' *The Business Times*, 6 December 2017 and 'Singapore govt's housing market warning may fall on deaf ears,' *The Business Times*, 23–24 December 2017.

The Government then announced further ABSD measures on 6 July 2018[58]. Had it not been for the cooling measures, there may have been greater pain with the outbreak of COVID-19 global pandemic in 2020, some one and a half years later[59].

3.3.1.1. Mechanics of the SSD[60]

The SSD impacts residential and industrial properties where the resale of the properties occurs within the specified holding period of 3 years[61]. For the computation of the specified holding period, the dates of acquisition and disposal are taken to be the date when the sale and purchase agreement for the acquisition or disposal is executed, or the date of exercise of the option pertaining to the acquisition or disposal, as the case may be[62]. In the case of properties which were rezoned to Master Plan zones and/ or granted permitted uses affected by SSD after the date of their acquisition, the date of "acquisition" will be reset to the date of rezoning or grant of permitted use, as the case may be for the purpose of computing the specified holding period for the purposes of SSD[63].

The rate of SSD to be computed on the amount of the consideration in respect of the sale of the property, is 12%, 8% and 4% for residential properties where the resale occurs in the first, second and third year of the specified holding period, respectively. In respect of industrial properties, the corresponding rates of SSD are 15%, 10% and 5%[64]. The higher rates of SSD for industrial properties compared with those for residential properties, are not the result of any deliberate policy to tackle greater speculative demand for industrial properties. Rather, the comparatively lower SSD

---

[58] A year after the introduction of the enhanced ABSD measures, there was no sign of the relaxation of those measures: see 'Singapore not relaxing property cooling measures soon, says MAS chief,' *The Business Times*, 28 June 2019.

[59] 'Cooling measures may have spared property market greater pain,' *The Straits Times*, 24 April 2020.

[60] See IRAS e-Tax Guide, *Imposition of Stamp Duty on Sellers for Sale or Disposal of Residential Property*, Seventh Edition, 15 September 2011.

[61] Para 9 of the Stamp Duties (Section 22A) Order 2010, S 209/2010.

[62] S 22A(12)(a) of the Stamp Duties Act.

[63] S 22A(13)(f) of the Stamp Duties Act and para 8(3) of the Stamp Duties (Section 22A) Order, S 209/2010.

[64] Article 3(bg) of the First Schedule to the Stamp Duties Act.

rates for residential properties were a consequence of the reduction of the specified holding period for residential properties from 4 to 3 years with effect from 11 March 2017, when the SSD rates of 16%, 12%, 8% and 4% for resales within the first, second, third and fourth year of the specified holding period, became 12%, 8% and 4% for resales within the first, second and third years of the specified holding period. The slightly higher rates of SSD for industrial properties were not adjusted to be in line with those for residential properties.

As to what are "residential properties" and "industrial properties" affected by the SSD, they are to be determined according to the zones in the Master Plan as well as the permitted uses for a property, under the Planning Act. There are various Master Plan zones that may accommodate residential development and a range of developments which may be industrial in character.

For the purposes of SSD, "residential properties" are those properties with any of the five Master Plan zones of "Residential", "Commercial and Residential", "Residential/Institution", "Residential with Commercial at 1st Storey" and "White"[65] ("the Master Plan zones limb") as well as those with permitted use for solely residential purposes or for mixed purposes, one of which is residential, under the Planning Act[66] ("the permitted use limb").

"Industrial properties" are those properties with any of the six Master Plan zones of "Business Park", "Business Park — White", "Business 1", "Business 1 — White", "Business 2" and "Business 2 — White"[67] ("the Master Plan zones limb"), as well as the following 17 permitted uses ("the permitted use limb") as set out in the Schedule to the Stamp Duties (Section 22A) Order 2010[68]:

1 General industrial building
2 Light industrial building
3 Special industrial building
4 Any other factory, including food factory
5 Business park
6 Call center

---

[65] Para 8(1)(b)(i) of the Stamp Duties (Section 22A) Order 2010, S 209/2010.
[66] Para 8(1)(b)(ii) of the Stamp Duties (Section 22A) Order 2010, S 209/2010.
[67] Para 8(1)(a)(i) of the Stamp Duties (Section 22A) Order 2010, S 209/2010.
[68] S 209/2010.

7 E-business
    8 Food catering
    9 Industrial training
  10 Laboratory
  11 Laundry
  12 Media activities
  13 Motor vehicle showroom
  14 Science park
  15 Showroom
  16 Warehouse
  17 Any other use of an industrial nature.

There is a need to go down to the details of "permitted uses" for the classification of industrial properties in the legislation, as some buildings situated in the six Master Plan zones, may have been subdivided into strata lots and sold and the permitted uses of the various strata units within the buildings may differ. Given the width of the nature of uses that may be permitted in the six Master Plan zones and not all the permissible uses within those zones fall within the policy intent for the imposition of SSD, there was the need to specify the nature of uses that fall within the scope of SSD in the legislation.

The resale of "residential properties" and "industrial properties" within the specified holding period of 3 years, will attract SSD at the relevant rates.

3.3.2. *Additional buyer's stamp duty*

After the introduction of SSD and when residential property prices did not show any sign of abating sufficiently, the Government introduced a new stamp duty measure, i.e. the ABSD for the first time, from 8 December 2011[69].

The Government is determined to rein in the escalation of residential property prices. In this regard, the Deputy Prime Minister, Mr Tharman

---

[69] MAS empirical work shows that tax measures (i.e. SSD and ABSD) had a larger impact on property transactions and prices than the lending (i.e. LTV and TDSR requirements) and land supply measures: MAS, *MAS' Approach to Macroprudential Policy*, January 2019 at 'Box Item 2: Effectiveness of macroprudential policies on the property market' at p. 22.

Shanmugaratnam, was quoted to have said the following during the 10th anniversary luncheon of the Credit Counselling Singapore[70]:

> We have seen correction in both private property prices and HDB resale prices over the last 4–5 quarters, but there is some distance to go in achieving a meaningful correction after the sharp run-up in prices in recent years.
>
> If we do not get a meaningful reversal after each upswing, property prices will run ahead of the growth of household incomes over the long term, which we should avoid.

The ABSD[71] which is payable in addition to the BSD[72], basically increases the costs of acquisition of a residential property. The amount of ABSD payable, is calibrated to the profile of the buyer (i.e. whether he is a Singapore citizen, permanent resident and on the number of residential properties he already owns). The Singapore citizen buying his first residential property does not have to pay any ABSD. Quite obviously, the ABSD is not to deter the Government's mission of encouraging home ownership amongst its citizenry. Unlike the SSD, which is calibrated against the length of the holding period, the ABSD has to be calibrated to cater to the social objectives of encouraging home ownership by citizens.

A remission of the ABSD may be given in the case where a developer purchases a property for the purpose of housing development[73]. The rationale for such remission is that the developer is adding to the housing supply, which would have the effect of moderating price increases. One of the main conditions for the remission is that the developer has to complete the housing development and sell all units of housing accommodation in

---

[70] See 'Tharman: Home prices correction not there yet,' *The Business Times*, 29 October 2014.

[71] The detailed rates of the ABSD are specified in Article 3(bf) and Article 3(bh) of the First Schedule to the Stamp Duties Act. For the 5-year period from 2017 to 2021, the average annual amount of ABSD collected from Singapore citizens buying a second residential property was around $244 million. The annual amount of ABSD collected from Singapore citizens buying a third and subsequent residential property for the same period was around $106 million: Parliamentary reply by Minister Lawrence Wong on 14 February 2022.

[72] The detailed rates of BSD are specified in Article 3(a) of the First Schedule to the Stamp Duties Act.

[73] Stamp Duties (Housing Developers) (Remission of ABSD) Rules 2013, S 362/2013 and Stamp Duties (Non-Licensed Housing Developers) (Remission of ABSD) Rules 2015, S 764/2015.

the development within the stipulated period of 5 years in the case of a housing developer licensed under the Housing Developers (Control and Licensing) Act[74] and 3 years in the case of a developer who is not required to be licensed under the said Act.

The rates of ABSD may be adjusted nimbly by way of subsidiary legislation, as the situation may require.

Another calibration of the ABSD was announced on 5 July 2018[75]. In a joint statement issued that day by the MOF, MND and MAS, the status of the private housing market was given as follows:

> After declining gradually for close to 4 years, private residential prices began rising in 3Q 2017. Prices have increased sharply by 9.1% over the past year. Demand for private residential property has also seen a strong recovery, as transaction volumes continue to rise.
>
> The sharp increase in prices, if left unchecked, could run ahead of economic fundamentals and raise the risk of a destabilising correction later, especially with rising interest rates and the strong pipeline of housing supply.
>
> The Government has therefore decided to raise ABSD rates and tighten LTV limits for residential property purchases.

From 6 July 2018, the ABSD rate is increased by 5 percentage points for all individuals, other than the Singapore citizen and permanent resident buying their first residential property in Singapore where the ABSD rate remains at 0% and 5%, respectively. For entities, the ABSD rate is increased by 10 percentage points.

A non-remittable ABSD of 5% was introduced for housing developers purchasing residential properties for development. The developers would also be faced with a 25% remittable ABSD, provided they were able to complete

---

[74] Cap. 130. A housing developer of more than 4 units in a development is required to be licensed under the Act. See *Asia Development Pte Ltd v Commissioner of Stamp Duties*, [2018] SGHC 41, *Re Asia Development Pte Ltd*, [2019] 3 SLR 713 and *Asia Development Pte Ltd v Attorney-General*, [2020] 1 SLR 886 where a developer applied for an extension of time to complete and sell the units in a housing development. Developers have cut prices to clear their stock of housing units in order to avoid the ABSD: see 'Rational Pricing Responses of Developers to Policy Shocks': Evidence from Singapore', Diao Mi, Fan Yi and Sing Tien Foo, Institute of Real Estate & Urban Studies Woking Paper Series 2020, 7 March 2020, and 'To beat ABSD, 38 Jervois developer launches fire sale to clear units', *The Business Times*, 3 June 2020.

[75] After the ABSD was first introduced on 8 December 2011, the ABSD rates were increased on 12 January 2013.

and sell all the units in the housing development within the stipulated period[76]. Basically the housing developer was faced with a stamp duty costs of nearly 9% of the price it pays for the residential development property (i.e. BSD of nearly 4% and ABSD of 5%), even where it managed to complete and sell all the housing developments within the stipulated period and does not have to pay the 25% remittable ABSD. The ABSD rates for acquisition of residential property by entities for the period from 6 July 2018 to 15 December 2021, are as follows:

Purchaser	ABSD Rate (from 6 July 2018 to 15 December 2021)
Entities (which are housing developers)	30% comprising the following: • 25% remission is available subject to meeting conditions; and • 5% (non-remittable)
Entities[77] (which are not housing developers)	25%

Transitional provisions were however introduced in the case of options to purchase granted on or before 5 July 2018 but were exercised after 5 July 2018. For such cases, the increase in ABSD which came into force on 6 July 2018 were remitted[78].

---

[76] See Stamp Duties (Amendment of First Schedule) (No. 2) Notification 2018, S 452/2018. The ABSD mechanism is such that ABSD of 30% is imposed on a housing developer under paragraph (x) of Article 3(bf) of the First Schedule to the Stamp Duties Act, and a remission of the ABSD to the extent of 25%, is provided to the housing developer under rule 3(1A)(c) of the Stamp Duties (Housing Developers) (Remission of ABSD) Rules and rule 3(1A)(c) of the Stamp Duties (Non-licensed Housing Developers) (Remission of ABSD) Rules.

[77] In *Zhao Hui Fang v Commissioner of Stamp Duties* [2017] 4 SLR 945, it was held that the transfer of a residential property to a charitable trust was not liable to ABSD as Article 3(2)(d) of the First Schedule to the Stamp Duties Act stated that where a reference is made to a grantee, transferee or lessee who holds the residential property on trust, the reference is to the beneficial owner. It was held that neither the factual beneficiaries of the charitable trust nor the trustees nor the public were the beneficial owners of the property in that case, and that the beneficial interest in a chartable purpose trust is simply 'in suspense' and not extant. The effect of *Zhao Hui Fang* has since been overtaken, with the implementation of ABSD (Trust) on 9 May 2022.

[78] Stamp Duties (Instruments on or before 5 July 2018) (Remission) Rules 2018, S 453/2018. There were other situations where remission of the increase in ABSD were given. For example, in the case where a tender for a development site under the Government Land Sales was made before 6 July 2018 and the award of the site was made after 6 July 2018: see 'CapitaLand and CDL team again — this time for Sengkang mixed development,' *The Business Times*, 17 August 2018 where the site was on a dual-envelope (price and concept) State tender.

The new measures both in terms of their timing and magnitude, seemed to have caught many industry players by surprise[79]. Before 6 July 2018, there were however some indications that property market cooling measures may be enhanced. The Managing Director of the MAS at the media briefing of the MAS annual report on 4 July 2018 a day before the new measures were announced, noted the euphoria in the Singapore property market and stated that that the Government was closely monitoring developments in the residential market and remained committed to ensuring a sustainable market[80].

While some industry players lamented the increases in the ABSD[81], there were also those who acknowledged that there were potential hazards both from the demand and supply sides in the property market and accepted the measures as prudent and necessary[82].

One has to realize and accept that the Government's greater constituency is the Singapore citizenry and a stable and sustainable residential property is of prime importance to the Government. The Government's commitment to minimize exuberance and prevent bubbles from developing, in the residential property market was again emphasized by the Minister for National Development, Mr Lawrence Wong at the REDAS annual dinner on 15 November 2018 where he is reported to have said, "Let me be very clear that government cannot and will not take a hands-off attitude to the property cycle. So there should not be any surprise when we intervene in the market, because that is our approach and attitude"[83]. The latest round of ABSD rate enhancements came into operation on 16 December 2021, to cool the property market. The ABSD rate for entities which are not housing developments has been increased to 35%. For housing developers, the 35%

---

[79] See 'Property players reel from sudden measures,' *The Straits Times*, 6 July 2018 and 'Property curbs: Ahead of the curve but too much?' *The Business Times*, 6 July 2018. The Real Estate Developers' Association of Singapore, issued a statement on 6 July 2018 arguing that the property market was in the early stages of a recovery and the recovery was in line with economic fundamentals: see 'No rationale for tough cooling measures: Redas,' *The Business Times*, 7–8 July 2018.

[80] 'MAS warning of 'euphoria' puts Singapore property market on notice,' *The Business Times*, 5 July 2018.

[81] Some of these developers have just replenished their land bank before 6 July 2018 as they were clearing their stock of completed residential units with relative ease in the last 12 months before then.

[82] See 'ABSD hike: Pre-emptive but prudent,' editorial in *The Straits Times*, 12 July 2018 and Benjamin Cher, 'Unexpected property cooling measures a necessary pain for longer-term stability,' *The Edge Singapore*, 16 July 2018.

[83] 'Govt 'can't be hands off about the property cycle,' *The Business Times*, 16 November 2018 and 'July curbs to prevent bubbles, says Lawrence Wong,' *The Straits Times*, 16 November 2018.

ABSD may be remitted subject to conditions, but they are subject to an additional 5% ABSD which is not remittable.

With the COVID-19 outbreak and in view of the suspension of construction works during the circuit breaker period and the slow resumption of construction works thereafter, the 5-year period provided for the completion of housing development before any clawback of the ABSD remission, has been extended by a year. On the other hand, the concurrent 5-year period provided for the sale of all the residential units has been extended by only 6 months, taking into account that it is possible to sell a residential unit even before the completion of the unit. The difference in the periods of extension indicates that while the Government is sympathetic to the delay in the construction works in view of the COVID-19 situation, it is less so towards a delay in the sale of residential units by developers. The rationale for the ABSD remission accorded to developers is still very much for them to sell the units to stabilize the market prices.

The extended periods however only apply to residential properties acquired by developers for development on or before 1 June 2020 and where the expiry of the 5-year period occurs on or after 1 February 2020[84]. In other words, those developers who acquire their residential development properties after 1 June 2020 and who will be aware of the COVID-19 challenges, will not benefit from the extension of the 5-year period.

There is a similar extension of the prescribed period for non-licensed housing developers (i.e. housing developers building 4 units or less residential units on a site) before any ABSD clawback takes place[85], from 3 years to (a) 4 years for the completion of the housing development; and (b) 3 years and 6 months for the sale of the all the residential units in the development.

---

[84] A 6-month extension was first given under the Stamp Duties (Housing Developers) (Remission of ABSD) (Amendment) Rules 2020, S 367/2020 which were published on 6 May 2020 and deemed to have come into operation on 1 February 2020. The Rules also provide for the extension of the timeline for the developer to commence development from 2 years from the date of execution of the agreement to purchase the residential development site, to 2 years and 6 months from such date. A further 6-month extension was later given under the Stamp Duties (Housing Developers) (Remission of ABSD) (Amendment No. 2) Rules 2020, S 876/2020 which were published on 9 October 2020 but are deemed to have come into operation on 1 August 2020.

[85] The extension was also given in two tranches of 6 months, first under the Stamp Duties (Non-Licensed Housing Developers)(Remission of ABSD) (Amendment) Rules 2020, S 368/2020 which are deemed to have come into operation on 1 February 2020 and later under the Stamp Duties (Non-Licensed Housing Developers) (Remission of ABSD) (Amendment No. 2) Rules 2020 S 877/2020 which are deemed to have come into operation on 1 August 2020.

3.3.2.1. Mechanics of ABSD

ABSD is charged on documents in respect of "residential property" under the head of charge specified in Article 3(bh) of the First Schedule to the Stamp Duties Act. "Residential property" that is subject to ABSD is defined in paragraph 1 in Article 3 of the First Schedule, as follows:

> "Residential property" means in the case of paragraph (bf) or (bh) of this Article, any immovable property that is either —
>
> (i) zoned or situated on land that is zoned in any of the following manners under the Master Plan:
>
>   (A) "Residential";
>   (B) "Commercial and Residential";
>   (C) "Residential/Institution";
>   (D) "Residential with Commercial at 1st Storey";
>   (E) "White"; or
>
> (ii) permitted under the Planning Act 1998 to be used for solely residential purposes or for mixed purposes, one of which is residential.

With the words "immovable property zoned or situated on land that is zoned" in paragraph (i) of the above definition, the practice of the Commissioner of Stamp Duties is that where vacant land or land with *all* of the buildings and improvements situated thereon are being acquired, one looks at the Master Plan zone of the property (and not at its permitted use) to determine if the property to be acquired is "residential property". If the Master Plan zone of the property is one of the 5 zones listed in the definition, the property is by definition, "residential property". However, where parts of the built-up property are acquired (i.e. where the building has been subdivided into strata lots) such that the acquisition is not of the land with all of its buildings and improvements situated thereon, one looks at the permitted use of those parts of the built-up property or strata lots under the Planning Act, to determine if the property to be acquired is "residential property" falling under paragraph (ii) of the above definition.

However in view of the word "or" which appears between paragraphs (i) and (ii) of the definition of "residential property" as may be seen above, it may be argued that a property qualifies as "residential property" if it answers to the descriptions in paragraph (i) *or* (ii) of the definition. Hence, there is some uncertainty of the stamp duty treatment with respect to a property (which is to be acquired with the entire building situated on the land) which is not situated on land with one of the 5 stipulated Master Plan zones (for example it may be zoned Commercial) and hence does not fall under paragraph (i) of the definition, but parts of the property may be permitted to be used for residential purposes under the Planning Act, which answer to the description in paragraph (ii) of the definition. In such situations, it may be argued that those parts of the property permitted to be used for residential purposes, may still be considered as "residential property" falling under paragraph (ii) of the definition, despite the fact that the building is not situated on land with any one of the 5 stipulated Master Plan zones specified in paragraph (i) of the definition. Hence it is prudent to write to the Commissioner for a confirmation of the ABSD does not apply in such situations.

Where vacant land or land with all of the buildings or improvements situated thereon are acquired and it falls under any of the 5 stipulated Master Plan zones, the part of the property attributable to residential purpose for the computation of the ABSD is provided in the table at paragraph 2A in Article 3 of the First Schedule to the Stamp Duties Act, and it is as follows:

White	100% of gross floor area
Residential	100% of the gross floor area
Residential/ Institution	100% of the gross floor area
Commercial and Residential	60% of the gross floor area
Residential with commercial on the 1st storey	Total gross floor area less the minimum gross floor area which must be set aside for commercial uses under the Master Plan

However in respect of land with any of the above-mentioned 5 Master Plan zones, where there is any requirement by the Government agencies to set aside a certain amount of the gross floor area for non-residential purposes, it may be possible to get the approval of the Commissioner of Stamp Duties, to exclude that gross floor area, from the ABSD computation. For example, some "White" sites offered for sale by the Government, may come with a minimum requirement for retail or office space. In that case, the successful tenderer may seek the Commissioner's approval to exclude the gross floor area pertaining to the non-residential use from the ABSD computation. For example in the case of the "White" site at Marina View which was tendered out in September 2021 under the GLS program, ABSD was not to be computed in respect of the tender price in respect of the minimum requirment of 25.6% of total GFA used for hotel and hotel-related purposes.

3.3.3. *Additional conveyance duty*

With the introduction of ABSD on the *direct* acquisition of residential property, there was greater inducement for the *indirect* acquisition of residential property through the acquisition of shares of companies that own residential property, where the assets of such companies comprise mainly residential properties. The imposition of the additional conveyance duty (ACD) under sections 23, 23A, 23B and 23C of the Stamp Duties Act in respect of the acquisition and disposal of "equity interest" in "property holding entities" from 11 March 2017, has increased the transaction costs for such acquisitions and disposals.

Such *indirect* acquisition may have been used in the past, as the stamp duty charged for the acquisition of company shares is at the rate of 0.2% of the consideration of the shares whereas that charged for the acquisition of immovable property is much higher, at rates up to 4% of the consideration for the immovable property[86]. The acquirer of the company shares, will end up owning the target company and indirectly owning all of the properties that the company directly or indirectly owns. Quite obviously, if the acquirer is only interested in certain (and not all of the) properties owned by the company, he will not acquire shares of the company. When the acquirer acquires the target company, he will also essentially acquire the legacy issues that come with the company. For example, the target company may have

---

[86] One such case was in *Andermatt Investments Pte Ltd v Comptroller of Income Tax*, [1995] 2 SLR(R) 866 where the acquisition of the shares of the company owning the immovable property and the subsequent liquidation of the company such that the immovable property may be distributed *in specie* to the shareholders, while saving on stamp duty, suffered from the disallowance of tax deduction on the interest expense relating to the loan earlier taken for the acquisition of the shares. Since 6 August 2018, the highest marginal rate for stamp duty has been increased to 4% for any tranche of the consideration for the purchase of the residential property above $1 million.

acquired its properties a long time ago at lower market prices. If the acquirer were to cause the target company to subsequently sell those properties, the target company may end up with a substantial amount of income tax on the gains from such sale, as the taxable gains are computed on the profits based on the historic cost of the properties.

In any case, to "level the playing field" in respect of the stamp duty payable for such acquisition of the shares of a property-owning company where the acquired company is subsequently liquidated with the immovable property distributed *in specie* to the shareholders of the liquidated company, Article 3(h) was earlier inserted into the First Schedule of the Stamp Duties Act in 2002[87] to impose the *ad valorem* stamp duty on such distribution as if it were a conveyance on sale. However, where there was no intention to liquidate the company and distribute the immovable properties *in specie* to the shareholders, the duty under Article 3(h) is not triggered and *ad valorem* stamp duty for the acquisition of the shares of the company remains comparatively lower at 0.2%.

With the imposition of ABSD, the stamp duty applicable for the *direct* acquisition for residential property becomes even higher, while the stamp duty for the acquisition of shares of a company remains at the rate of 0.2% of the consideration or value for the shares. To put the stamp duty impact on the direct and indirect acquisitions of residential property on par, the Government introduced the ACD[88]. The details of the ACD will be discussed in Chapter 7 on real estate holding entities.

3.3.4. *Advancement of the duty point from the transfer instrument to the sale and purchase agreement*

With the introduction of ACD, an amendment[89] was also made to section 22(1)(b) by the Stamp Duties (Amendment) Act 2017, such that the sale and purchase agreement instead of the transfer instrument with respect of the shares of a property holding entity (PHE), became the chargeable instrument.

---

[87] Stamp Duties (Amendment) Act 2002, Act No. 38 of 2002.

[88] See IRAS e-Tax Guide, *Additional Conveyance Duties (ACD) on Residential Property Holding Entities,* Third Edition, 5 July 2018 and Vincent Ooi, *The New Additional Conveyance Duties Regimes in the Stamp Duties Act,* (2018) 30 SAcLJ 119 and *Stamp Duty Issues in Singapore Corporate Practice* (2018) 30 SAcLJ 949.

[89] The words 'and stock or shares' were deleted from s 22(1)(b).

Briefly, a PHE is an entity which is "rich" in residential properties, i.e. the value of their residential properties (owned directly or indirectly) represents 50% or more of the total value of all the tangible assets of the entity.

The amendment of section 22(1)(b) however had the effect of advancing the incidence of stamp duty to the contract or agreement, not only for ACD cases, but for non-ACD cases as well. In other words, the incidence for all share transactions was advanced, such that the chargeable instrument is the contract or agreement, whereas before 11 March 2017, the chargeable instrument with respect to share transactions, was the transfer instrument.

However, since 11 April 2018, the stamp duty on the contract or agreement for non-ACD cases has been remitted under rule 2 of the Stamp Duties (Agreements for Sale of Equity Interests) (Remission) Rules 2018[90]. With this remission, the chargeable instrument for share transactions for non-ACD cases, effectively reverts to the transfer instrument.

The amendment of section 22(1)(b) in the Stamp Duties (Amendment) Act 2017, has at least one other inadvertent effect. By advancing the incidence of the duty to the sale and purchase agreement for share transactions, the acquisition and disposal of shares listed on the Singapore Exchange, also became subject to stamp duty, where a contract or agreement is entered into in respect of a transaction involving the sale and purchase of shares listed on the Singapore Exchange. Such a sale and purchase agreement may be entered into between the vendor and the purchaser, in respect of a married deal involving listed shares.

Before the amendment of s 22(1)(b), in respect of share transactions, the chargeable instrument was the transfer instrument, and not the sale and purchase agreement. There is generally no transfer instrument with respect to shares listed on the Singapore Exchange, as the legal owner of the shares is the Central Depository (Pte) Ltd and the settlement of the transaction is by way of book entries. Hence, the execution of a transfer instrument[91] is not required and no stamp duty is therefore chargeable in respect of transactions of shares listed on the Singapore Exchange.

---

[90] S 201/2018.

[91] In *The Enterprise III Fund Ltd and others v OUE Lippo Healthcare Limited*, [2019] 2 SLR 524, the Court of Appeal noted at [98] that 'transfers of [scripless] shares are made by way of book-entry in the Depository Register and not by way of an instrument of transfer'.

The statutory protection given to the book-entry system under section 81SM(2) of the Securities and Futures Act[92] is also instructive in this regard. That provision reads as follows:

> A transfer of securities by the Depository by way of book-entry to a depositor under this Part shall be valid and shall not be challenged in any Court on the ground that the transfer is not accompanied by a proper instrument of transfer or that otherwise the transfer is not made in writing.

With the enactment of the Stamp Duties (Agreements for Sale of Equity Interests) (Remission) Rules 2018[93], the stamp duty on the contract or agreement for the sale of any book-entry securities, has since been remitted from 11 April 2018[94]. The remission also applies to ACD in the case where the equity interest to be acquired, is that of an entity listed on the Singapore Exchange, which is a PHE. Such remission reflects the policy that ACD is not to be charged on any contract or agreement pertaining to shares of companies listed on the Singapore Exchange, even where the companies are PHEs. It is also to be noted that where equity interests of a listed entity are acquired, the investor is essentially acquiring the business of the listed entity rather than underlying residential properties *per se*.

3.4. Development charge

With the coming into operation of the Land Betterment Charge Act, the land betterment charge has replaced the development charge (DC)[95]. Despite the change in nomenclature, the land betterment charge insofar as it pertains to the grant of planning permission under the Planning Act, operates very much in the same manner as the DC. In this section, we will briefly discuss the DC as it operated under the Planning Act in relation to the property

---

[92] Cap. 289.

[93] S 201/2018.

[94] Under rule 3 of the Stamp Duties (Agreements for Sale of Equity Interests) (Remission) Rules 2018, S 201/2018.

[95] The Land Betterment Charge Act (No. 11 of 2021) was passed by Parliament on 10 May 2021, but has yet to come into operation. See Chapter 3 for further details on the land betterment charge and the DC.

cycle, as it will shed light on the manner in which the new land betterment charge will operate.

While the DC was not normally seen as a fiscal measure to moderate the excesses of the swings in the property market, it had the effect of a built-in stabilizer of sorts for the property market. When developers paid higher prices for land whether under the Government Land Sales program or in *en bloc* sales, the rates in the DC Table for the ensuing half year would also have increased in tandem with the prices of previous half year. This meant that the DC payable in the ensuing half year for development sites where the planning permission gave an enhancement in land value beyond that of the Development Baseline, would also increase. Such increase in the DC may have acted as a dampener on the bid prices for land in the subsequent period[96]. However, as may be seen in the more recent spate of land value increases during the period from April 2017 to July 2018[97], the DC instrument alone was not sufficiently potent to arrest the price increases. It was the introduction of hefty increases in the ABSD on 6 July 2018 and 16 December 2021, which brought the feverish increases in residential property prices to a halt.

---

[96] See 'Impact of hike in DC rates,' *The Business Times*, 5 March 2018.

[97] The period also saw an increase in the number of *en bloc* sales, with 35 residential deals at $10 billion in 2018, 27 deals at $8.13 billion in 2017 and 3 deals at $1 billion in 2016, compared to the all-time record of $21.8 billion in the 2005–2007 cycle: see 'Blockbuster year for selling *en bloc* last year,' *The Sunday Times*, 10 February 2019.

CHAPTER 3

Master Plan:
From Blueprint to Guide

1. Introduction

The tax system rides on the nomenclature in the Master Plan and the provisions of the Planning Act[1] for various purposes. For example, in respect of stamp duty, five Master Plan zones[2] where residential development may be undertaken have been designated for the incidence of the additional buyer's stamp duty (ABSD), additional conveyance duty (ACD) and the seller's stamp duty (SSD) and six Master Plan zones[3] where industrial/warehouse development may be undertaken have been designated for the incidence of SSD. In respect of Goods and Services Tax (GST) the supply of land zoned "Residential" has been designated as an exempt supply[4]. In respect of income tax, "industrial land" has been defined as "any land zoned for the purpose of "Business 1" and "Business 2" (other than "Business 1 White" and "Business 2 White") under the Master Plan, for the purpose of the land intensification allowance[5].

The Planning Act[6] also sets out the procedure for the application of written permission for development of land. The approved use granted by

---

[1] Chapter 232, Singapore Statutes.

[2] Namely 'Residential', 'Commercial and Residential', 'Residential/Institutional', 'Residential with Commercial at 1st Storey' and 'White'.

[3] Namely 'Business Park', 'Business Park — White', 'Business 1 (B1)', 'Business 1 — White', 'Business 2 (B2)', and 'Business 2 — White'.

[4] Para 2 of Part I of the Fourth Schedule to the Goods and Services Tax Act.

[5] S 18C(12) of the Income Tax Act.

[6] In *Borissik Svetlana v Urban Redevelopment Authority*, [2009] 4 SLR(R) 92, the High Court noted at [38] that as the Planning Act with its long title being an 'Act to provide for the planning and improvement of

the written permission under section 14 of the Planning Act, is frequently used to define the nature of the use of land and buildings, for tax purposes. For example, during the COVID-19 outbreak, non-residential properties qualified for remission of 30%, 60% or 100% of property tax for the year 2020, depending on the permitted use of buildings. The permitted use was determined according to: (a) the use granted by the written permission under section 14 of the Planning Act, (b) the use permitted under a notification issued under section 21(6) of the Planning Act; or (c) the actual use of the property on 1 February 1960 to the extent that it has not been put to any other use subsequently[7]. Hence, it is useful to understand the workings of the Master Plan and the provisions of the Planning Act as they underpin the framework of the relevant taxes.

In addition, a land betterment charge (LBC) may be imposed under the Land Betterment Charge Act[8] in certain circumstances where planning approval is given for the development of a property. It will be useful to understand the existing development charge (DC) system and the method of DC computation as the workings of the new LBC largely follow those of DC, in this respect. Under the LBC Act, where the development land is the subject of a State lease and a varying of the restrictive covenant in the lease is required for the development of the land, LBC (which is to replace the differential premium (DP) in this respect) may also be payable. The nature and method of computation of DP is also discussed in this chapter, as the workings of the new LBC largely follow those of DP. With the coming into operation of the LBC Act, the new LBC is to replace both DC and DP.

Finally for completeness, the extension charge imposed under section 31(5A) of the Residential Property Act, for an extension of the project completion period, will also be discussed in this chapter, as the extension charge may affect the economics of the entire development.

Singapore and for the imposition of development charges on the development of land and for purposes connected therewith', it is 'only to be expected that the Urban Redevelopment Authority (URA) will develop its planning policies and guidelines over time and amend them as and when required.'

[7] Para 2(3) of the Property Tax (Commercial Properties)(Remission) Order 2020, S 155/2020, as amended by the Property Tax (Commercial Properties) (Remission) (Amendment) Order 2020, S 305/2020, where the subsidiary legislation has been renamed Property Tax (Non-Residential Properties) (Remission) Order 2020, to better reflect the nature of the properties granted property tax remission.

[8] Act 11 of 2021 which was passed by Parliament 10 May 2021 but has yet to come into operation at the time of writing.

2. Master Plan

The Master Plan which is the statutory land use plan promulgated under the provisions of the Planning Act, governs the nature of land use and the intensity for developments in respect of land in Singapore. The first Master Plan was submitted to and approved by the Governor in Council on 5 August 1958 under the provisions of the Singapore Improvement Ordinance[9]. At that stage, the Master Plan may have been seen as a blueprint for the future development of Singapore.

The Master Plan which now comes under the Planning Act, includes the approved maps and written statement[10], and is reviewed and amended at least once every 5 years[11] to accommodate changing land use needs and demands. The specifications of the Master Plan then guide the Chief Planner in his day-to-day development control work. In *Tay Theng Khoon v Lee Kim Tah (Pte) Ltd*[12], Lai Kew Chai J in delivering the judgment of the Court of Appeal summarized the workings of the Master Plan as follows:

> [30] ... The master plan, together with the written statement, is a town-planning tool by which the Government through the planning authorities seeks to control the development of land in Singapore. The master plan and written statement were first approved in 1958 under the Singapore Improvement Trust Ordinance, which Ordinance was repealed by what is now the Planning Act. Broadly, these two instruments set out what the planning authorities see as the desired way in which lands in Singapore should be used. The master plan and written statement are subject to periodical reviews under the Act, no doubt to take account of the fast changing social and economic conditions and needs of the country.

---

9   Cap. 259, 1955 Edition of the Singapore Ordinances. The planning provisions of the Singapore Improvement Ordinance were subsequently subsumed under the Planning Ordinance: see Singapore Legislative Assembly, *Official Report of the Select Committee on the Planning Bill*, 27 November 1958, which was debated by the Legislative Assembly on 26 January 1959. The 1958 Master Plan envisioned the then population of about 1.5 million would grow to 2 million over a 20-year planning period. For a discussion of rudimentary attempts at urban planning in the early 1900s, see Brenda SA Yeoh, *Contesting Space: Power Relations and the Urban Built Environment in Colonial Singapore* (Oxford University Press, 1996), pp. 160–168.
10 S 6 of the Planning Act. The maps and Written Statement of the 2019 Master Plan are available on the URA website, www.ura.gov.sg.
11 S 8(1) of the Planning Act.
12 [1992] 1 SLR(R) 409.

[31] The planning authorities (the "competent authority" appointed under s 3 of the Act) go about controlling land uses by the granting and withholding of planning permissions, and the imposition of conditions in the granting of such permissions. In the exercise of their powers and functions, they are backed by legislation. It is provided by s 10 of the Act that no person shall develop or sub-divide any land without the written permission of the competent authority. It is further provided by sub-s (5) of that section that in considering any application for permission to develop or sub-divide land, the competent authority shall act in conformity with the provisions of the master plan. As is well said by a writer, Leung Yew Kwong in his book *Development Land and Development Charge in Singapore*, development control achieves its objective by its largely negative, policing, function of refusing planning permission for a development.

[32] As development control came into existence after the country had already undergone substantial development, it is not surprising that it does not seek to alter existing land uses by any positive action, such as by the forced elimination of existing non-conforming uses. Rather, it does so by controlling future development, by controlling proposed uses, using the master plan as a guide. The master plan is merely a guide, albeit a powerful guide backed by legislation, by which the competent authority exercises planning control of future development by the means indicated above.

In respect of more positive action in land use planning, the Government has a tool in the Government Land Sales (GLS) program, which enables it to play a more "activist" role in molding the built environment. By putting land for sale at strategic locations and at various times, with detailed specifications of permissible uses and design, the Government has been able to better steer the achievement of planned land uses in Singapore. The Government has also taken positive action in master-planning entire greenfield sites such as those in the Suntec City[13], Marina Bay[14] and one-north[15] areas, as well

---

[13] Choy Chan Pong and Phua Shi Hui, *Master Developer Projects in Singapore: Lessons from Suntec City and Marina Bay Financial District* (Centre of Liveable Cities, 2018).

[14] See Lee Kah-Wee, 'Planning as state-effect: Calculation, historicity and imagination at Marina Bay, Singapore,' *Planning Theory & Practice* 19(4) (2018), 477–495.

[15] See *One-north: Fostering Research, Innovation and Entrepreneurship*, Urban Systems Studies series (Centre of Liveable Cities, 2018).

as in the use of subterranean space[16]. In the implementation of the GLS program, the following key operational factors in the partnering of the private enterprise have contributed tremendously to its success[17]:

(a) Ensuring transparency and integrity;

(b) Understanding market needs;

(c) Using flexible pragmatic approach to achieve development objectives;

(d) Providing incentives for the private sector;

(e) Cultivating trust and a common purpose with the private sector; and

(f) Creating a platform for innovation and design excellence.

Before the advent of statutory land use controls in Singapore, there were some controls in private hands where some developers and landowners resorted to imposing private restrictive covenants on the nature and intensity of use of the land that they have subdivided and built upon, in order to preserve the exclusiveness of their developments. For example, some of the restrictive covenants that may be seen in some of the old land titles for land in the "Good Class Bungalow"[18] areas, provided that only a single detached house may be erected on the land lot. With the advent of statutory land use controls, owners of the land lots have been able to apply to court for the discharge of some of these private covenants where they are not consistent with the intentions of the Master Plan. The situation in Singapore mirrors that in England and Wales. In this regard, Lord Wilson in *Peninsula Securities Ltd v Dunnes Stores (Bangor) Ltd*[19], pointed to the situation in England and Wales:

---

[16] The coming into operation of the State Lands (Amendment) Act 2015 (Act 11 of 2015) on 8 May 2015 which clarified that surface landowners own the underground space up to 30 m under the Singapore Height Datum, facilitates the Government long-term planning for the development and use of the underground space: see Elaine Chew, 'Digging deep into the ownership of underground space — Recent changes in respect of subterranean land use,' *Singapore Journal of Legal Studies* 1 (2017) and 'Going underground — Singapore's new frontier,' *The Straits Times*, 2 May 2019.

[17] *Urban Redevelopment: From Urban Squalor to Global City*, Urban Systems Studies series (Centre of Liveable Cities, 2016), pp. 52–57. See also *The Government Land Sales Programme: Turning Plans into Reality*, Urban Systems Studies series (Centre of Liveable Cities, 2021).

[18] The term 'Good Class Bungalow' is frequently referred to by its acronym, 'GCB' in common parlance. The term was first used in the early land use plans of the Planning Department, in designating areas reserved for the development of detached houses with a minimum plot size of 1,400m². The locations of the 39 GCB areas are indicated in the non-statutory special and detailed control plans (SDCP) available on the URA website, www.ura.gov.sg. The SDCP support the Master Plan, in respect of the Competent Authority's development control work.

[19] [2020] 3 WLR 521 at [55].

In its report entitled "Making Land Work: Easements, Covenants and Profits À Prendre" (2011) (Law Com No. 327), [2011] EWLC 327, the Law Commission of England and Wales explained the background to section 84 as follows:

7.3 In the 19th century, and well into the 20th, land was sold off from large estates so as to facilitate urban expansion, but frequently subject to extensive restrictive covenants. These covenants had an important social function in the era before public planning control and often served to preserve the amenity of an area, controlling building and land use and ensuring consistent development. ... However, social needs change over time ... Landowners and developers may wish to discharge, or at least modify, covenants on the basis that they are no longer serving a useful purpose but their presence on the title to the land is impeding a change of use or a development.

2.1. Long term plan

Upstream from the statutory Master Plan, is the Long Term Plan, formerly known as the Concept Plan[20]. The Long Term Plan has no statutory force and is the broad-brush long-term strategic land use and transportation plan prepared by Urban Redevelopment Authority (URA) to guide optimal land use and allocation and the evaluation of major long-term proposals for the next 40–50 years. The Long Term Plan, reviewed every 10 years, sets the strategic context for the preparation of the Master Plan, but unlike the Master Plan, does not provide the specific details such as zoning and plot ratio, affecting individual plots of land[21]. The latest Long-Term Plan Review in 2021 was launched by the Minister for National Development, Mr Desmond Lee on 17 July 2021 with its emphasis on "planning for optionality and resilience for future Singapore"[22].

The 1971 Concept Plan was the first concept plan prepared in Singapore under the State and City Planning Project with the assistance of the United

---

[20] A copy of the Concept Plan is available on the website of URA, www.ura.gov.sg.

[21] See 'Concept plan, the future of directions for planning,' PLANEWS 14 (April 1993).

[22] See URA website on the article 'Adapting to a Disrupted World' written by URA CEO Lim Eng Hwee and published on 7 July 2021.

Nations Development Program[23]. It guided urban development (and conceptualized the Marina Bay area as an extension of the central business district), the development of HDB[24] new towns and key infrastructure, such as expressways and the relocation of the civilian international airport from Paya Lebar to Changi, and seeded the idea of the mass rapid transit network to alleviate traffic congestion in the city.

Following from the 1971 Concept Plan was the 1991 Concept Plan which had its vision as "Towards a Unique Tropical City of Excellence" based on a projected population[25] by year X, and it was also the backdrop of "The Next Lap"[26]. In the book of the same name which set out the aspirations of the Government, it is stated at page 16:

> In Singapore, we live in an urban environment. We want a city that is pleasant to work and live in a city of beauty, character and grace. To achieve this, we need variety in our physical landscape. In our master plan, green space, the hills, the sea, beaches and rivers are carefully woven into the urban landscape[27]. It is a city we will be proud to call home.

One of the key strategies of the 1991 Concept Plan was the decentralization of commercial activities to reduce congestion in the CBD and to create job centres in the suburban areas where most of the population live. Land was

---

[23] Alan Choe, 'The early years of nation-building: Reflections on Singapore's urban history,' in Heng Chye Kiang (ed.), *50 Years of Urban Planning in Singapore* (World Scientific Publishing Co Pte Ltd, 2017) and *Singapore, Unlimited* (Centre of Liveable Cities, 2020).

[24] The Housing and Development Board (HDB) public housing program is a key national policy in Singapore and is underpinned by the values of accessibility, inclusivity and diversity: see Indranee Rajah, 'Striking a balance in building HDB flats in prime locations', *The Straits Times* 11 June 2021 and *The Business Times* 12–13 June 2021.

[25] In the 2013 Population White Paper, it was projected that the population would reach 6.5–6.9 million by 2030. In 2020 General Election, the projected population was a political issue. Dr Liu Thai Ker, one-time Chief Planner clarified that the 10 million population number was a planning parameter and not a target for Singapore: *The Sunday Times*, 18 July 2020.

[26] 'The Next Lap' as a term has been coined for the phase after the passing on of the baton of premiership from Mr Lee Kuan Yew to Mr Goh Chok Tong on 28 November 1990. The book *The Next Lap* was published for the Government by *Times Editions Pte Ltd* in 1991. See also 'Concept plan, the future of directions for planning,' *PLANEWS* 14 (1993) and *Challenges and Reforms in Urban Governance: Insights from the development experience of China and Singapore* (Centre of Liveable Cities, 2016), pp. 96–112.

[27] The idea of waterfront living was promoted in the 1991 Concept Plan and land at Tanjong Rhu, Robertson Quay and Bayshore Road was subsequently sold under the GLS program, for waterfront condominium housing projects: *The Government Land Sales Programme: Turning Plans into Reality*, Urban System Studies series, (Centre of Liveable City, 2021), pp 48–49,

tendered out under the GLS program in Tampines regional centre and the city fringe areas like Bugis and Novena where commercial buildings were erected[28]. The 1991 Concept Plan also suggested the amalgamation of the seven separate lands into Jurong Island for industrial use.

Following from the 1991 Concept Plan was the 2001 Concept Plan with its vision of "Towards a thriving world-class city in the 21st century" and a focus on enhancing Singapore's natural and built identity. With the "Identity Plan" under the 2001 Concept Plan, there was to be greater focus on the retention and reinforcement of the character of four thematic clusters: (a) "old world charm" cluster comprising Balestier, Tanjong Katong, Jalan Besar, Joo Chiat and East Coast Road; (b) "urban villages" cluster comprising Anak Bukit, Jalan Leban, Thomson Village, Springleaf and Coronation areas; (c) "rustic cloves" cluster comprising Punggol, Coney Island, Changi Village, Pasir Ris and Pulau Ubin; and (d) "South Ridges" cluster with its natural parks along the ridges and its panoramic views. The "Parks and Waterbodies Plan" under the 2001 Concept Plan was to bring the original garden city concept to the next phase of a "city in a garden"[29].

The latest concept plan is the 2011 one[30] which continues to lay out the land use strategies to sustain economic growth, develop a congestion-free city and provide for a high-quality living environment. As may be envisaged, the preparation of each Concept Plan "involved many Ministries and agencies and provided a whole-of-government platform to make strategic decisions on the long-term deployment of land"[31].

2.2. The current 2019 Master Plan

The current Master Plan which is in operation and which implements the strategies of the Long Term Plan, is the 2019 Master Plan which together

---

[28] *The Government Land Sales Programme: Turning Plans into Reality,* Urban System Studies series, (Centre of Liveable City, 2021), pp 46–47.

[29] Nicholas Wong, 'Urban planning in Singapore — Its past & challenges ahead,' in *The Evolution of Singapore Real Estate — Journey to the Pass and Future: 1940–2015* (Knight Frank Pte Ltd, 2015), pp. 168–179.

[30] The public consultation on the Long Term Plan Review (LTPR) for the 2021 Long Term Plan, commenced in July 2021.

[31] Ng Lang, 'Planning to overcome the constraints of scarcity,' in Heng Chye Kiang (ed.), *50 Years of Urban Planning in Singapore* (World Scientific Publishing Co Pte Ltd, 2017), p 73.

with the Written Statement are statutory documents[32]. Quite obviously, the 2019 Master Plan is not an entirely fresh land use plan, as compared with the earlier 2014 Master Plan. Much of the provisions in the 2014 Master Plan were carried forward to the 2019 Master Plan as the actual land uses on the ground have been in place for some time and they cannot and are not envisaged to be changed overnight. Nevertheless, there are new features with each Master Plan. For example, in the 2014 Master Plan,

(a) the three new Identity Nodes, i.e. Holland Village, Jalan Kayu and Serangoon Gardens, with their "quaint charm and distinctive low-rise village atmosphere with a wide range of cafes, bars and eateries"[33], were identified as heritage sites for preservation;

(b) the three areas at Marina South, Kampong Bugis[34] and Holland Village[35], were identified as districts which will provide new homes in pedestrian-oriented developments; and

(c) more than 70 buildings have also been identified for conservation.

As stated in paragraph 8.1 of the Written Statement to the Master Plan, the competent authority may allow for incentive plot ratio. With the 2019 Master

---

[32] Under the Planning (Master Plan) Rules, Cap. 232, R1, the draft 2019 Master Plan was advertised as required under rule 4 and was available for inspection during the month-long period from 27 March 2019 to 25 April 2019: see notice of advertisement under rule 4 by the Chief Planner, first published in the Government *Gazette*, Electronic Edition on 27 March 2019. Under rule 5, every objection or representation concerning any proposal for amendment to the Master Plan must be accompanied by a statement of the reasons or explanations for the objection or representation. By way of a notice under rule 7(a) of the Planning (Master Plan) Rules, R1, the Master Plan 2019 and its Written Statement took effect on 18 November 2019: see *Gazette* Notification No. 3281 of 29 November 2019.

[33] See 'High hopes for low-rise village,' *The Straits Times*, 23 November 2013. Changi Village and Tanjong Katong were earlier identified as identity nodes, since the concept was introduced by URA in 2002.

[34] URA has announced that the precinct at Kampong Bugis will be made available for sale to a master developer. The single developer will have to propose an integrated master plan to achieve the planning outcomes of (a) car-lite residential precinct with comprehensive network of pedestrian walkways and cycling paths, (b) community building with public spaces and (c) sustainable district level systems to enhance storm water treatment and the attractiveness of the environment: see URA website.

[35] A 2.3 hectare site comprising the open car park at Holland Village was launched for sale under the GLS scheme in late 2017 under the dual-envelope concept (or Concept and Price Revenue tender) where those bids with qualifying concepts are first short-listed, and the site is then awarded to the highest bidder amongst the short-listed bidders. The site has two areas: one for residential development where a strata-titled development was allowed and another for mixed-use development where no strata subdivision was allowed. The site was eventually awarded to Far East Organization which submitted the highest bid, amongst five bidders which were short-listed out of the initial 15. This exercise attracted multiple bids with various concepts from the same bidders, e.g. the Far East Organization submitted three bids, and there were two bids each from Guocoland, Perennial and Pontiac Land.

Plan, a CBD Incentive Scheme has been proposed (replacing the bonus plot ratio scheme introduced in 1989) where a plot ratio increase of between 25% and 30% is given for the conversion of office buildings (which are at least 20 years old) to hotels and residential apartments or mixed-used developments. However, there are minimum plot-size requirements for the incentive[36]. This scheme which came into effect from the date of gazette notification of the 2019 Master Plan, applies to the area at Anson Road, Cecil Street, Shenton Way, Robinson Road and Tanjong Pagar and its objective is to bring vibrancy to the area as a place to live and play, besides as a place for work[37].

The other incentive proposed with the 2019 Master Plan and which came into effect on 27 March 2019, is the Strategic Development Incentive (SDI) scheme where owners of adjacent commercial or mixed-use (but not predominantly residential) developments in "strategic" areas (especially those in the Orchard, CBD and Marina Centre areas) may together submit development proposals for increased plot ratio and flexibility in land use and building height[38]. Under the SDI scheme, it has been reported that URA has offered the owners of three adjoining buildings at Orchard Road (i.e. Midpoint Orchard, Orchard OG and Faber House) a higher plot ratio and redevelopment into hotel/serviced apartments if the three sites were to be redeveloped together[39]. Other proposals in the 2019 Master Plan include:

(a) the Greater Southern Waterfront which will see the transformation of the area along a 30 km stretch from Pasir Panjang to Marina East (including

---

[36] See 'PIL Building fails to get URA nod to tap CBD Incentive Scheme because of its site area,' *The Business Times*, 24 September 2020, where it is reported that the PIL Building at Cecil Street with a site area of 1,812m² did not meet the minimum plot-size requirement of 2,000m² for a non-corner site in the Cecil Street locale to benefit from the scheme. See 'International Plaza fails to get URA's nod for CBD Incentive Scheme', *The Business Times*, 1 November 2021, where it is reported that International Plaza already has a good mix of uses (including a significant residential component) and an existing gross plot ratio of 19.24, the outline application for the proposed redevelopment under the CBD incentive scheme was turned down.

[37] URA Circular, *Rejuvenation Incentives for Strategic Areas: Central Business District (CBD) Incentive Scheme*, of 27 March 2019. See also 'URA's draft Master Plan 2019: Make Singapore's CBD great,' *The Sunday Times*, 7 April 2019. The incentive is necessary as the CBD plots are mostly privately owned, unlike the Marina Bay area comprising mainly greenfield reclaimed land owned by the State, where the plots are sold with the planned mix of residential, commercial and entertainment facilities to provide the area with vibrancy.

[38] URA Circular, *Rejuvenation Incentive for Strategic Areas: Strategic Development Incentive (SDI) Scheme*, of 27 March 2019. See also 'New incentive schemes welcome boosts for CBD; will developers bite?' *The Business Times* editorial, 5 April 2019.

[39] See *The Straits Times*, 21 December 2019. However, it seems that the owners of the three buildings are going their separate ways, with Midpoint Orchard going for an en-bloc sale and Faber House to be redeveloped into a 18-storey, 250-room hotel with a bank and food & beverage outlets: see *The Sunday Times*, 20 February 2022.

Pulau Brani), to an area of desired location for urban living with the decantation of the port westwards to Tuas and the expiry of the lease for the Keppel Club, and the rejuvenation of the Pasir Panjang Power District (which comprises two former power station buildings and oil tanks)[40]; and

(b) the aerotroplis around the Changi International Airport with the addition of Terminal 5 with access to the Tanah Merah Ferry Terminal, with new recreational and tourism possibilities.

Besides the quinquennial revisions of the Master Plan, *ad hoc* amendments to the Master Plan may also be made[41], to facilitate changes to land uses and their development intensity. These changes may require rezoning of the land, changes to the plot ratio, designation of conservation areas and changes to the Master Plan written statement[42]. The Master Plan is also supported by specific and detailed control plans (SDCPs), which are non-statutory control plans providing guidelines and controls for specific areas of development and are used for processing development applications[43].

2.3. Master Plan zones

Land parcels in Singapore are assigned various land use prescriptions or "zones" as prescribed in the Master Plan[44]. Each land parcel may be used in accordance with the conditions of its designated zone. We will discuss those zones insofar as they are material in relation to the tax issues.

---

[40] The Greater Southern Waterfront project was first mentioned by Prime Minister Lee Hsien Loong at the 2013 National Day Rally, and also at the 2019 National Day Rally where he mentioned that there would be 9,000 housing units (both public and private) to be built on the Keppel Club site and a NTUC resort along the lines of Downtown East at Pasir Ris, would also be built on Pulau Brani after the PSA Brani Terminal has been decanted from the island. See also 'Wanted: Bold ideas for new waterfront,' editorial in *The Straits Times*, 29 October 2018.

[41] S 8(2) of the Planning Act.

[42] S 8(3) of the Planning Act.

[43] The SDCPs may be accessed from the URA website.

[44] The interpretations of the 31 land use zones in the Master Plan, are stated in Table 1 of the Written Statement to the 2019 Master Plan. The nomenclature of the zones has been updated from time to time, in keeping with changing needs and requirements. The earlier nomenclature of zones such as Green Belt, Principal Business Offices and Stores, Rural Centre and Settlement, Main Shopping and Light Shopping which were used in the 1958 Master Plan and in some cases up to the early 1990s, are no longer used. See Edward Ti, *An Overlooked Overriding Interest in Singapore's Torrens System*, [2018] 28 Conv 280, where it was suggested relevant information from the Master Plan be reflected in the Certificate of Title of the land concerned.

2.3.1. *Residential zones*

The main zones in the Master Plan that allow residential development are "Residential", "Residential with Commercial at 1st Storey", "Commercial and Residential", "Residential/Institution" and "White". The planning intention of the "Residential" zone is indicated in Table 1 of the Written Statement to the 2019 Master Plan as follows:

> The areas zoned "Residential" are used or intended to be used mainly for residential development. The developments in this zone are subject to controls on building form and building height as determined by the competent authority. The quantum of all ancillary or non-residential uses needed for support or management of a residential estate such as a condominium development are to be determined by the competent authority according to the scale of the residential development.

The development of serviced apartments may be allowed on land zoned "Residential" subject to evaluation, by the competent authority. Where land is approved for the development of serviced apartments, the land retains its "Residential" zone, there being no separate land use zone for serviced apartments in the Master Plan[45]. This is unlike the situation with hotels, where the land approved for hotel development has generally to be zoned or rezoned to "Hotel" in the Master Plan.

2.3.2. *"White" sites*

URA introduced the concept of "White Site" in the mid-1990s to provide developers with greater flexibility in terms of development options on land parcels sold under the GLS scheme[46]. In the Written Statement of the

---

[45] Serviced apartments are inevitably caught by the ABSD and ACD measures targeted at 'residential property', in view of their 'Residential' zone. An application for remission from ABSD and ACD may then have to be made, where serviced apartments are involved in a transaction. Remission of ABSD and ACD may be given by the authorities, as serviced apartments which are generally required to be constituted under as single title, are akin to hotels and are not considered to be the target of the property cooling measures.

[46] See Ong Seow Eng *et al.*, 'Strategic considerations in land use planning: The case of white sites in Singapore,' *Journal of Property Research* 235 (2004) 21, and Seow Kah Peng, 'The impact of the new Master Plan on property development in Singapore,' paper given in the seminar held by the Real Estate Developers' Association of Singapore on 18 May 1999 with respect to the theme, *Update on Property*

2019 Master Plan, the use of sites zoned "White" is stated as "mainly for commercial, hotel, residential, sports & recreation and other compatible uses, or a combination of two or more such uses as a mixed development". If developers were to change the type, mix or quantum of uses within the permissible parameters under the terms of the State lease for "White Sites" during the lease period, no land betterment charge (formerly known as differential premium) is levied[47]. In *United Lifestyle Holdings Pte Ltd v Oakwell Engineering Ltd*[48], Lee Sieu Kin JC (as he then was) has likened the "White" zone to a sort of "wild card" which the developer could wield, in giving him the required flexibility in the use of the land.

In the early "White Sites" sold under the GLS scheme, the developers had greater flexibility on the uses they could adopt for the sites. However, the actual mix of uses adopted by developers for particular sites, sometimes did not turn out according to what may have been envisaged by the urban planners, especially with the benefit of hindsight[49].

In the later "White Sites", URA has generally stipulated certain quantum of the gross floor area (GFA) is for a particular use, in order to realize longer-term planning intentions for the area. For example, the "White Site" situated at Central Boulevard between One Raffles Quay and Asia Square and sold in 2016, had stipulations of a *minimum* GFA of 10,000m² for the office component, and a *maximum* GFA of 5,000 m² for shops, restaurants and outdoor refreshment areas, with the remaining GFA to be used for additional office, commercial school, hotel, serviced apartments and/or residential uses. In respect of the "White Site" where Asia Square Tower 2 is situated, the earlier URA conditions of tender were for a maximum permissible GFA

Development Laws in Singapore. The first two White Site zones introduced in 1995 through the GLS program are now the site of Manulife Tower at the corner of Cross Street and Telok Ayer Street and the IOI Plaza at the corner of Middle Road and Prinsep Street.

[47] See *The Government Land Sales Programme: Turning Plans into Reality,* Urban Systems Studies, (Centre of Liveable Cities, 2021), p 113.

[48] [2002] 1 SLR(R) 726 at [11].

[49] For example, the China Square 'white site' sold in 1995 which was developed into office buildings, food and beverage outlets, with the conservation shophouses, was later considered to lack vibrancy after office hours, as it did not have a residential component. On the other hand, the 'white site' at Marina Boulevard sold in 2002, was developed by the developer into a residential development known as The Sail@Marina Bay with a small retail component, and it was later considered by the urban planners that some office component in that development situated at the Marina Bay area, would have been desirable: see *Working with Markets: Harnessing Market Forces and Private Sector for Development* (Centre of Liveable Cities, 2017), pp. 56–57.

of 113,580m², with at least 60% of the maximum GFA for office use, at least 25% of the maximum GFA for hotel use, and the remaining 15% could be developed for additional office, hotel or other permitted uses such as retail, residential, entertainment or recreational uses[50]. In respect of the "White Site" situated at Marina View which was awarded under the GLS scheme on 29 September 2021 on the basis of a sole bid by the IOI Properties group, the stipulated use was for at least 25.6% of the total GFA to be for hotel and hotel-related purposes and not more than 74.4% of the total GFA was for residential purposes (including serviced apartments).

As residential use is permissible on a site which is zoned "White", an owner of such a site, would be able to develop at least a residential component on the site. Even where the site is already developed for non-residential uses, the owner of the entire development would have the flexibility of demolishing the existing non-residential development on the sites, for redevelopment with a residential component. As sites zoned "White" may be used for residential development, they are the subject matter for the regimes of SSD, ABSD[51] and ACD[52], which are fiscal measures to moderate the price rises in the residential property market.

2.3.3. "Business 1", "Business 2", "Business 1 — White" and "Business 2 — White zones"

The four zones of "Business 1" (or B1), "Business 2" (or B2), "Business 1 — White" and "Business 2 — White"[53] in the Master Plan, have been used in the stamp duty legislation for the prescription of the levy of the SSD for industrial properties. Where a property situated within any of such land use zones is disposed of, within the specified holding period of 3 years[54], the seller has to pay the SSD. The SSD came into operation on 12 January 2013 to curb speculation in the industrial property market[55].

---

[50] *Daisho Development Singapore Pte Ltd v Architects 61 Pte Ltd*, [2020] SGHC 16 at [6]. The Westin Singapore presently stands on the site.

[51] See definition of 'residential property' in Article 3 of the First Schedule to the Stamp Duties Act.

[52] See Stamp Duties (Section 23) Order 2017, S 100/2017.

[53] The other zones prescribed are 'Business Park' and 'Business Park — White' which are discussed in the next section of this chapter.

[54] Paras 8(1)(a) and 9(a) of the Stamp Duties (Section 22A) Order, S 209/2010, as amended.

[55] See IRAS e-Tax Guide, *Stamp Duty: Seller's Stamp Duty on Industrial Properties*, 11 February 2013.

Those four zones were first introduced in the 2003 Master Plan which came into operation on 1 December 2003. The B1 and B2 zones are primarily for industrial and warehouse uses, and they replaced the nomenclature of Warehouse, Light Industry and General Industry zones as used in the earlier Master Plans. The then new zones were formulated using an impact-based zoning approach, as is explained in the URA Circular of 10 December 2003 as follows:

> This approach allows industrialists to vary or change the uses according to changing business conditions without the need to rezone the site. This means that businesses can have mixed-use developments under one roof or within the same site. Under this approach, businesses will be grouped to their impact on the environment....
>
> Business uses which impose nuisance buffers no greater than 50 metres can be allowed within the B1 zones, whereas all business uses, including B1 uses and those which impose nuisance buffer more than 50 metres and health and safety buffers, will be allowed within the B2 zone.

As may be seen, the B1 use is differentiated from the B2 use, on the basis of the environmental impact of the activities which may be conducted within land in such zones. B2 uses which entail pollutive industrial activities are to be located farther away from other areas such as residential areas.

Quite obviously, ancillary uses have to be allowed within the B1 and B2 zones. For example, there will be a need to have ancillary office space which is used in conjunction with the B1 and B2 uses within the building[56]. As provided in rule 3(3) of the Planning (Use Classes) Rules[57], "a use which is

---

[56] In *Green v Britten & Gilson*, [1904] 1 KB 350, Mathew LJ in deciding that a store may be ancillary to the business of a shop, said at p. 357, 'No doubt there are many cases to which that word ['ancillary'] can properly be applied, as where the store is subsidiary, subordinate, or appurtenant to the business carried on in the shop.' However, see *RBC Properties Pte Ltd v Defu Furniture Pte Ltd*, [2015] 1 SLR 997 where on the facts, the showroom use was considered an independent use, rather than an ancillary use. See also *Straits Colonies Pte Ltd v SMRT Alpha Pte Ltd*, [2018] 2 SLR 441, where URA refused an application for the use of a shop unit within the Kallang Wave Mall as 'restaurant cum pub' as such use was considered to cause disamenity to the surrounding areas, and instead first granted planning permission for 'restaurant with ancillary bar' for 3 years and on appeal granted planning permission for 'restaurant with ancillary bar and ancillary live entertainment' for a year, subject to review. The limited period of the planning permission allows URA to test the use. Should there be legitimate complaints that the permitted use causes disturbance to the area, the planning permission may then be allowed to lapse.

[57] Cap. 232, R2.

ordinarily incidental to and included in any use specified in the Schedule is not excluded from that use as an incident thereto merely by reason of its specification in the Schedule as a separate use". In other words, whereas for example an office use falls under use class II of the Planning (Use Classes) Rules[58], that does not preclude an office use which is ordinarily incidental to the use of a light industrial building (use class VII) from being included in use class VII. Such ancillary use (within a use class) will not require planning permission, whereas change of use from one use class to another will require planning permission.

In any planning permission given, the competent authority is careful to state clearly that a use may be ancillary to the main use, where the intention is for such ancillary use, especially following from *Tan Boon Liat & Co (S) Pte Ltd v Attorney General*[59]. In that case, the specification of the use of the office and stores as ancillary to the use of factories may have been inadvertently omitted in the written permission, when it was granted by the competent authority for a 15-storey flatted factory with offices and stores. After the written permission was granted, the competent authority wrote to the developer to remind him that the offices and stores as stated in the 1971 written permission were meant specifically as associated uses to the flatted factories and that the offices and stores should not be rented out separately as offices and stores. The construction of the building on the site known as Tan Boon Liat Building was completed in August 1976. The developer then sought a declaration from the High Court that the office and storage uses as stated in the 1971 written permission were not ancillary or connected with the use of a unit as factory. Chua J in deciding in favor of the developer said at [17]:

> There is no ambiguity in the terms of the 1971 written permission. Given its natural meaning it is obvious that the developed project can be used for any of the usages specified: as factory, as office or as store; or a combination of these usages. It is to be noted that none of the three conditions imposed pursuant to s 9(5) [now s 14(4)(a) of the Planning Act] relates to the restrictive use of factory, office and store as interpreted by the defendant.

---

[58] Cap. 232, R2.

[59] [1989] 1 SLR(R) 389.

It appears to me that the competent authority had impliedly approved the use of office or store separately in the building. The competent authority's desire to impose restrictions on such uses was an afterthought. It was only in August 1975, after almost four years from the date of the 1971 written permission, that the competent authority made reference to the 1971 written permission in these terms: 'to remind you that offices and stores as stated in the written permission are meant specifically as associated uses to the flatted factory and should not, therefore, be leased or rented out separately as offices or stores.'

The quantum of permitted ancillary uses in both B1 and B2 zones is not to exceed 40% of the total floor area. The types of B1 or B2 uses as the case may be, and the ancillary uses that may be allowed are subject to the evaluation of the competent authority and other relevant authorities[60]. The types of ancillary uses that may be permitted, may quite obviously change over time. For example, the start-up company, honestbee, was allowed to incorporate a retail operation as part of the B1 ancillary use in an industrial building at Boon Leat Terrace. An URA spokesman in responding to queries, was reported to have said, "With business structures and requirements evolving, we recognize the need to provide flexibility for business to co-locate ancillary uses that support their core industrial activities, and to pilot new business ideas. With support from Enterprise Singapore, we allowed ancillary retail uses for honestbee to pilot new technologies and innovation for their business in an industrial premise"[61].

The "Business 1 — White" and "Business 2 — White" zones were also introduced in the 2003 Master Plan on a pilot basis for sites considered suitable for the inclusion of shop, restaurant, residential and association uses in addition to the Business uses. In this regard, the URA circular of 10 December 2003, stated as follows:

Together with the implementation of the new Business zones, URA is also introducing new Business 1 — White and Business 2 — White zones on pilot basis in the Master Plan 2003. These zones aim to provide

---

[60] See 'Written Statement of the 2019 Master Plan.

[61] See 'Honestbee gets nod to pilot new industrial space concept', *The Business Times*, 4 February 2019.

greater flexibility to businessmen by allowing uses permitted within the White zone to be integrated with the developments on such sites. These uses can include shops, restaurants, residences and association uses. On such sites zoned Business 1 — White or Business 2 — White, developments that meet the minimum gross plot ratio (GPR) as indicated in the Master Plan 2003 for the Business uses will be given an additional GPR (also stipulated in the Master Plan 2003) for the White uses. The new Business — White zone will be first introduced at a pilot area at Kallang Avenue.

2.3.4. *"Business Park"* and *"Business Park — White"* zones

The Business Park zones are also subject to the regime of the SSD[62]. They were introduced into the Master Plan in the 1990s to better integrate manufacturing with knowledge-intensive activities, where a flexibility of the usage of floor space is needed to accommodate the needs of modern businesses. The following two main features distinguish Business Parks from industrial estates[63]:

(1) the range of permitted uses that are generally non-production in nature but are characteristic of high-technology and research-oriented industries; and

(2) the emphasis on landscaping, quality building designs and provision of amenity facilities to reflect the importance placed by companies on the image of the Business Park and the welfare of their employees.

As was stated by a senior government planner[64]:

> Another characteristic in business park development is the flexibility in the usage of floor space. A modern business is usually structured to achieve an integration of their various business functions within a single building. This "total business" concept centres on a high value-added

---

[62] Para 8(1)(a) of the Stamp Duties (section 22A) Order 2010, S 209/2010.

[63] See *Guidelines for Business Park Development* (URA, February 1993), p. 2.

[64] Mr John Keung (then Assistant Chief Planner in the Planning Department, which was merged with URA with the coming into operation of the Urban Redevelopment Authority (Amendment) Act 1989), in his paper 'Physical Planning in Singapore: Strategic Directions' at the Planning Seminar of the Singapore Institute of Planners on 29 April 1989.

product would involve co-locating a firm's product design, product development, engineering, production, marketing, distribution, servicing and other support activities. The conventional office and light industrial space become indistinguishable. Flexibility on the usage of floor space is, therefore, needed to accommodate these modern businesses.

However, business parks were already conceived and master-planned by the Jurong Town Corporation (JTC), even before the introduction of the Business Park zone in the Master Plan. In 1980, JTC released a plan to "prepare for new industrial landscapes and infrastructure that were conducive to the higher value industries, as the economy moved into a capital and technology intensive phase of industrialization"[65].

The plans for Singapore Science Park[66] at South Buona Vista and the International Business Park at Jurong East, were conceived or implemented in the 1980s[67]. Today, the locations of the Business Park clusters are at the International Business Park (in Jurong East), one-north (at North Buona Vista where businesses in biomedical sciences in Biopolis, infocomm technology in Fusionpolis and media industries in Mediapolis commingled)[68], Science Parks I, II and III (at South Buona Vista)[69], Mapletree Business City (at Pasir

---

[65] *Industrial Infrastructure: Growing in Tandem with the Economy* (Centre of Liveable Cities, 2013), p. 14.

[66] The Science Park is a more specialized type of business park.

[67] See 'High-tech business park,' *The Straits Times*, 12 November 1988 on JTC's implementation of the International Business Park and the findings of the study mission to business parks in the United States, Japan, United Kingdom and France, comprising officials from JTC, the Ministry of National Development, Economic Development Board and the then Planning Department. See also Francis Koh *et al.*, 'An analytical framework of science parks and technology districts with an application to Singapore,' *Journal of Business Venturing* (2005) Vol 20, pp 217–239.

[68] See 'Shaping a work-live-learn-play knowledge landscape' on the 200-hectare one-north development at North Buona Vista,' *Industrial Infrastructure: Growing in Tandem with the Economy* (Centre of Liveable Cities, 2013), pp. 21–22.

[69] Science Parks I (30 hectares) and II (25 hectares) which consist of mostly standalone buildings and which began operations in 1982 and 1993 respectively, have a plot ratio of 1.2 in the 2014 Master Plan, as against the greater plot ratios in Mapletree Business City (plot ratio 2.8) and in the 200-hectare one-North development. There have been calls for an increase in the plot ratios for Science Parks I and II, such that new high-specification premises may be built which may offer connectivity, amenities and opportunities for 'placemaking' for new economy companies. 'Placemaking' refers to the multi-faceted approach to the planning, design and management of public spaces: see 'CapitaLand gains big canvas for S'pore redevelopments from ASB purchase,' *The Business Times*, 23 September 2019. The acronym 'ASB' refers to 'Ascendas Singbridge'. CapitaLand Development and Ascendas REIT have formed a joint venture to develop a life science, innovation campus at Science Park Drive: See, 'Ascendas Reit, CLD in JV to redevelop 1 Science Park Drive,' *The Business Times*, 16 Nov 2021, where the CEO of CapitaLand Development is reported to have said, 'As the master developer, owner and operator of Singapore Science Park (SSP1), we have been steadily unlocking the precinct, potential through redevelopment and land intensification initiatives.'

Panjang/Alexandra Roads), Changi Business Park, Clean Tech Park (at Jalan Bahar/Nanyang Avenue in Jurong West)[70] and the Seletar Aerospace Park[71]. Other tech-themed business parks include the Jurong Innovation District and the Punggol Digital Hub[72].

The Business Park zone caters to non-pollutive industries and businesses engaged in high-tech, research and development and other non-production-related functions of manufacturing, located in park-like environment. The Business Park — White zone was introduced in 2001 to provide greater flexibility by combining commercial activities and other compatible uses (as represented by the White component) within industrial developments[73].

As may be seen from the changes to the Business Park zones from the 1990s, the Government has been progressively revising industrial land policies to cater to the changing business models and needs of industrialists and businesses. Nevertheless, the industrial use landscape keeps evolving. The Committee on the Future Economy (CFE) in its Report published in February 2017, pointed to the increasing "servicisation" of industrial activities. The CFE Subcommittee on the Future City made the Recommendation SC4.3: "Provide more flexibility for mixed-use and innovative work arrangements", calling for district-level flexibility in land use. The Recommendation was as follows[74]:

> The increasing 'servicisation' of industrial activities, where companies integrate service-type headquarter function with production facilities, is blurring the lines between services and manufacturing. We should provide more flexibility to integrate industrial with other uses to allow businesses to better tap on horizontal and vertical synergies across the different sectors and catalyse new innovations. For example, this can be achieved

---

[70] See 'A living laboratory for clean industries,' *Industrial Infrastructure: Growing in Tandem with the Economy* (Centre of Liveable Cities, 2013), pp. 22–23.

[71] See 'An integrated park for aerospace industries' in *Industrial Infrastructure: Growing in Tandem with the Economy* (Centre of Liveable Cities, 2013), p. 24.

[72] See 'First batch of firms to set up shop at Punggol digital hub', *The Straits Times* 29 July 2021.

[73] See URA Circular *New Business Park-White zone and Relaxation of DC Guidelines for Business Park, Industrial and Warehouse Developments*, 15 January 2001 and the URA letter 'Government does adjust land-use policies' published in *The Business Times* on 22 February 2017.

[74] See 'Shaping business parks, mixed-used clusters for Industry 4.0,' *The Business Times*, 28 September 2017.

by having complementary uses like medical technology firms and hospitals close to each other, or siting different functions like R&D, production, office and retail together. Such district-level flexibility would also allow developers to change uses within the district to meet the needs of ever-evolving business models.

2.4. Planning permission

The written permission (WP) granted for the development of land under section 14(4) of the Planning Act is frequently used as the reference point for the determination of the nature of the permitted use of the land for tax purposes[75]. Hence, a knowledge of the procedure for the application for the grant of WP is useful in the understanding of the taxes which use such a reference point.

As is well known, the Planning Act regulates the carrying out of any development of land in Singapore. Section 12(1) of the Planning Act prohibits the carrying out of any development of land without planning permission. The word "development" is defined widely in section 3(1) of the Planning Act to mean "the carrying out of any building, engineering, mining, earthworks or other operations in, on, over or under land, or the making of any material change in the use of any building or land". Despite the width of the definition of the word "development", it has been necessary to amend the definition from time to time, in view of changes in the real estate landscape. For example, in order to combat the disamenities caused by the use of dwelling-houses for short term accommodation, section 3(3)(d) and the Fourth Schedule were inserted by the Planning (Amendment) Act 2017[76]. Under the provisions introduced in 2017, the use of a dwelling-house to provide short term accommodation for less than 3 consecutive months in return for the payment of rent or other form of consideration, constitutes "development" which will require planning permission[77].

---

[75] See for example, Stamp Duties (Section 23) Order 2017, S 100/2017. For income tax purposes, the written permission is also an important piece of evidence to support any change of intention of a property from being an investment property to trading stock, especially where the written permission is issued with the payment of LBC.

[76] Act 7 of 2017.

[77] See *Public Prosecutor v Su Jiqing Joel*, [2021] 3 SLR 1232 where hefty fines were imposed on the unlawful provision of short-term accommodation in dwelling-houses.

In pursuance of the conservation of heritage buildings and areas, section 12(2) of the Planning Act also prohibits the carrying out of any works within a conservation area without conservation permission. In *Public Prosecutor v Project Lifestyle Pte Ltd*[78], where a hefty fine was imposed in a case involving a material change of use of premises in the Kampong Glam Conservation Area from a restaurant to a bar without planning permission, See Kee Oon JC (as he then was) said at [9]:

> It is important to bear in mind that conservation is not merely aimed at preserving our historical and cultural heritage in the form of bricks and mortar. The focus has to be about "preserving certain characteristics and appearance of conservation areas".

In compliance with the provisions of the Planning Act, a person intending to carry out any works or any material change of use of premises, has to apply for planning permission. A person intending to apply for WP, may first apply to the competent authority for preliminary advice on a matter relating to the development of his land[79]. This pre-application consultation services (PACS) procedure provides for consultations on the application of development guidelines on the development proposals for specific sites, before detailed plans are finalized. The preliminary advice given by the competent authority however does not constitute an in-principle approval of the proposed development and does not authorize the development of the site in question[80].

Proposals involving departures from the Master Plan planning parameters (i.e. land use, gross plot ratio, building and storey height) do not fall within the scope of PACS. Such proposals are to be submitted as an outline application for planning assessment[81] where the competent authority will consider the parameters relating to land use, intensity, type, form and height of the proposed development[82]. A potential purchaser

---

[78] [2015] SGHC 251.

[79] S 12B(1) of the Planning Act. URA has introduced a pre-application consultation services (PACS) from 5 February 2018: see URA Circular, *New Pre-Application Consultation Services (PACS)*, 5 February 2018.

[80] S 12B(2) of the Planning Act.

[81] S 18(1) of the Planning Act.

[82] S 18(2) of the Planning Act.

of a property intending to redevelop the property, may use the outline permission mechanism, to test the receptiveness of the competent authority with respect to his development plans before committing to a purchase of the property.

The outline permission granted by the competent authority will constitute in-principle approval of the proposed development but does not authorize the development of the site in question[83]. The outline permission has a life of 6 months unless otherwise specified or directed by the competent authority[84]. The outline permission lapses upon expiry of the validity period. Formal application for the WP, together with the proposal/ sketch plans, has to be endorsed by the owner of the property. Where the applicant has exercised an option to purchase the land, the application must be accompanied by a letter of consent from the owner or the owner's solicitors[85]. Upon the formal application, the competent authority may grant WP under section 14(4) of the Planning Act.

The section 14(4) WP may be unconditional or subject to conditions. For example, the WP may be subject to the condition that it is granted for a period of specified number of years. In situations where the WP is only limited to a specified number of years, it is to afford the opportunity for the competent authority to observe if the permitted use would create disamenities in the area. If so, the WP may not be renewed. The competent authority may instead of granting a WP under section 14(4), first grant a provisional permission under section 17(1), subject to conditions[86]. The provisional permission may allow the applicant to carry out some preliminary works, while attempting to comply with the conditions. Where the competent authority is satisfied that all the conditions have been complied with, it will then grant a final permission under section 17(4)

---

[83] S 18(3) of the Planning Act.

[84] S 18(4) of the Planning Act.

[85] Rule 3(3) of the Planning (Development) Rules 2008, S 113/2008.

[86] Section 17(1) of the Planning Act. The provisional permission may be extended by the competent authority where there are good reasons to do so: see *Innovative Corporate Pte Ltd v Ow Chun Ming and Clydesbuilt (Holland Link) Pte Ltd*, [2020] 2 SLR 943 at [8] where the provisional permission was extended three times with each extension of 6 months' validity, before written permission was obtained. Such extensions of the provisional permissions were envisaged in rule 17 of the Planning (Development Charges) Rules, Cap. 232, R5, which provided for the use of the appropriate DC Table corresponding to the date of the provisional permission or its extension, in computing the DC.

which is deemed to be a WP under section 14(4). Where an application for WP is refused by the competent authority, or where WP or provisional permission is granted by the competent authority subject to conditions, the applicant who is aggrieved by the decision of the competent authority, may appeal to the Minister[87].

The provisional permission as may be seen from its name, does not have the certainty of the WP. In *Collector of Land Revenue v Mustaq Ahmad s/o Mustafa*, the Court of Appeal in refusing to take into account the provisional permission in determining the compensation award under the Land Acquisition Act, stated[88]:

> The provisional approval granted to Mustaq cannot be equated with written permission to develop the site. If provisional permission for a proposed plan is to be taken into account for the purpose of determining the market value of an acquired property, it will be necessary to evaluate whether or not it is likely that written permission will eventually be granted after the submission of building plans, and whether or not the written permission may include restrictions, which have to be taken into account. Such speculation is unnecessary and undesirable.

Besides the section 14(4) WP which may be used for the purposes of determining the permitted use of a property, the authorized use of a property under a notice made under section 21(6) of the Planning Act or the existing use of a building as at 1 February 1960, have also been used as the references on the permitted use of a property, in tax legislation[89]. Hence, it is useful to discuss the concepts of authorized use under a section 21(6) notification and the 1960 existing use.

In the Planning Act, the Minister has powers under section 21(6) to authorize any development, by notification in the *Gazette*, without the

---

[87] S 22 of the Planning Act, Cap. 232. See also *Borissik Svetlana v Urban Redevelopment Authority* [2009] 4 SLR(R) 92. In that case, the owners on being refused written permission by the URA to build a replacement detached house upon the demolition of their semi-detached house, applied to the High Court for a mandatory order to quash the decision of the URA. The High Court in rejecting the application, accepted the proposition that courts should not interfere with issues of planning permission which involve interrelated considerations of fact, law, degree and policy which are better dealt with by an appeal to the Minister under a procedure provided in the Planning Act. For the UK position, see Simon Payne, *Planning Conditions — Enforcement and Variation*, [1993] Conv 119.

[88] [2002] 1 SLR(R) 413 at [10].

[89] See for example, the Stamp Duties (Section 22A) Order 2010, S 209/2010 as amended, in respect of SSD.

requirement for the issue of a section 14(4) WP. Essentially, a development authorized by a section 21(6) Notification is "deemed authorized without express WP"[90]. The section 21(6) Notification is usually made for relatively minor types of development, where the development may be proceeded with after the plans for the development or use of a property have been lodged with the competent authority. Such a simplified procedure allows for a nimble development and use of the property and at the same time frees up the resources of the competent authority which may otherwise have to deployed in the processing of an application for a section 14(4) WP. For example, the Planning (Development of Land Authorization for Medical Clinics) Notification Order 2014[91] was *gazetted* under the powers in section 21(6). Under the Notification, the use of a shop may be changed to that of a medical clinic without the need for a section 14(4) WP, subject to the condition *inter alia,* that the aggregate of the shop's floor area and the total floor area used for medical clinics in the building, does not exceed 1,000m² or 20% of the building's commercial floor area, whichever is the lower. More recently, the Planning (Enterprise District — Lodgment Authorization) Notification 2020[92] was *gazetted* to implement a relatively more liberal land use control environment for the Jurong Innovation District[93] and the Punggol Digital District. Of course in respect of those two districts, the fact that the government agency of Jurong Town Corporation is the master lessee and land-use planner, may have facilitated the adoption of a more

---

[90] The term 'deemed authorized without express written permission' is used in the LBC Act to refer to 'a development authorized by notification in the *Gazette* made under section 21(6) of the Planning Act 1998': see s 2(1) of the Act.

[91] S 836/2014 which came into operation on 23 December 2014. The other s 21(6) Notifications include Planning (Development of Land Authorization) Notification (Cap. 232, N1), Planning (Development of Land Authorization for Housing and Development Board and Jurong Town Corporation) Notification (Cap. 232, N2), Planning (Development of Land — Lodgment Authorization) Notification (Cap. 232, N3), Planning (Changes in Use — Lodgment Authorization) Notification (Cap. 232, N5), Planning (Development of Land Authorization for National Parks Board) Notification (Cap. 232, N8), Planning (Child Care Centre — Authorization) Notification (Cap. 232, N10), Planning (Child Care Center — Change in Use Lodgment Authorization) Notification 2005 (S 137/2005), Planning (Covered Pedestrian Linkways Authorization) Notification 2014 (S 773/2014), Planning (Development of Land Authorization for Applicable State Property) Notification 2015 (S 411/2015) and Planning (Development of Land Authorization for Last Approved Use) Notification 2017 (S 231/2017) and the Planning (Development of Land for Agricultural Use — Lodgment Authorization) Notification 2019 (S 637/2019).

[92] S 881/2020.

[93] The Hyundai Motor Group Innovation Centre amongst others, is located within the Jurong Innovation District which has seen substantial new investments in innovative technology: see 'Jurong Innovation District has S$420m new investments,' *The Business Times*, 21 October 2020.

liberal control mechanism by the competent authority under the Planning Act. It is to be noted even where certain developments may come under the simplified procedure of section 21(6), the competent authority may audit a case to ensure that the terms of the section 21(6) Notification have been complied with in that case.

Turning finally to the "1960 existing use" as a reference to the permitted use of a building, this reference came about as the predecessor of the Planning Act, i.e. the Planning Ordinance 1960, first came into operation on 1 February 1960 to regulate the use of land and buildings. Before that date, there was generally no statutory control of the use of a building. Consequently, the use to which a building was put as at that date of 1 February 1960, has been accepted as the "existing use" of the building, for which no section 14(4) WP is required[94].

3. Land Betterment Charge

At the time of writing this chapter, the Land Betterment Charge Act[95] has been passed by Parliament but has yet to come into operation. The development charge (DC), the temporary development levy (TDL)[96] and the differential premium (DP) were to be replaced by the land betterment charge (LBC). As it is a matter of time before the LBC Act comes into operation, we have written this chapter in the context as if the LBC Act has already come into operation and the LBC has replaced the DC, DP and TDL.

The grant of planning permission may trigger the levy of the LBC under the LBC Act. The LBC replaces the existing taxes known as the DC and

---

[94] See the definition of the term 'existing use' in rule 2 the Planning (Use Classes) Rules, Cap. 232, R2. In some instances, approval for the 'existing use' may have been given under the Singapore Improvement Ordinance, since repealed: see *Chuan Hoe Engineering Pte Ltd v Public Prosecutor*, [1996] 3 SLR(R) 200.

[95] Act 11 of 2021.

[96] TDL was first introduced in December 2003 as a 'time based' levy pegged to the period of permission, to help reduce the start-up cost for businesses which would otherwise have to pay the full DC. It was imposed under Part VA of the Planning Act when any planning permission or conservation permission was given for a specified period of 10 years of less. Under the Planning (Temporary Development Levy) Rules (Cap 232, R9), TDL was calculated as a percentage of the applicable DC. The percentage ranged from 3.8% (where the specified period of the planning or conservation permission was for one year) to 30% (where the specified period was for 10 years). As TDL was for planning permission given for relatively short periods and has not been commonly encountered in practice, the authors do not propose to discuss this levy.

the TDL imposed under the Planning Act and collected by the URA as well as the DP which was collected by the Singapore Land Authority (SLA) as consideration payments for the varying of restrictive covenants in the State titles of any land. The DP formerly collected as a contractual payment for the varying of restrictive covenants in a State title, has been placed on a statutory footing and collected as a tax. It is to be noted that the determination of the "topping-up" premium payable for a site for an extension of the term of a State lease does not fall within the scope of the LBC Act and continues to be determined by way of individual valuations. Some of the changes brought about by the LBC Act are as follows:

(a) The replacement of DC and DP with the LBC which is collected by a single government agency i.e. SLA, which did away with any confusion arising from the earlier dual system where DC was collected by URA and DP by SLA;

(b) A standardized basis for the calculation of the LBC which provides a downward adjustment by way of a leasehold factor, in the case of properties with a residual tenure of 99 years or less. This adjustment for leasehold land was earlier available only for DP but not for DC[97];

(c) A consequential change is that there is no stamp duty chargeable in all instances of the imposition of the LBC as it is a tax, whereas this was only the case with regard to the DC and TDL which were also taxes. Stamp duty was earlier imposed in relation to the collection of DP which was a consideration payment on a contract for the sale and purchase of an interest in immovable property[98];

(d) The relatively obscure practice of charging DP on the basis of 100% of the enhancement in land value arising from the intensification

---

[97] As noted by the Second Minister for Law, Mr Edwin Tong at the second reading of the LBC Bill on 10 May 2021, the leasehold factor adjustment would make for a more accurate reflection of value, and that there was no adjustment for by a leasehold factor in the case of DC. However pursuant to a joint circular by URA and SLA on 1 September 2011, in the case of State leases that did not specify the nature of use and/ or maximum allowable intensity and with a residual tenure of 99 years or less, lessees who would otherwise had to pay DC, had been administratively allowed to apply to SLA to pay DP instead, with the benefit of the leasehold factor adjustment.

[98] The contract or agreement fell to be charged under Article 3(a) of the First Schedule to the Stamp Duties Act.

or change of land use in the cases of (i) directly allotted State titles, (ii) State titles with the "additional land premium" condition and (iii) the varying of restrictive covenants pertaining to non-subdivision and "controlled activity", has been put on a statutory footing and the circumstances for such levy have become apparent. A "controlled activity" is defined in section 2(1) of the LBC Act and "extends to cover a binding obligation expressed in a State title for land that requires the land owner to refrain from changing the composition of individuals who are members of or otherwise constitute the owner, or who may be licensed or otherwise allowed by the owner to enter and use the land, such as club membership if the land owner is a club"[99].

Despite the change in the labels (from DC, TDL and DP to LBC), the mechanics in the computation of the LBC are largely similar to those of the DC, TDL and DP. As the LBC is relatively new and there may be transitional cases where DC and DP are still being charged, the authors have also discussed the DC and DP in the way that they have operated before the coming into operation of the LBC Act, in this chapter. The discussion will help in the better understanding of the LBC.

The purpose of the LBC Act is set out in section 5 of the Act. The express statements on the purpose of the Act in section 5, will facilitate any purposive interpretation of the provisions of the Act under section 9A of the Interpretation Act. Basically, the purpose of the Act in the imposition of the LBC is to (a) recapture some of the economic benefits flowing from the grant of the "chargeable consent"; (b) provide certainty and transparency in the calculation of the LBC without the need for valuation; (c) promote land development activity which is consistent with the land planning and urban development system and the productivity enhancement measures for the construction industry and (d) promote and encourage environmentally sustainable development or use of land. It is refreshing to note that there is an elaboration of the purpose of the Act in the Explanatory Statement to the LBC Bill as set out below, which is instructive:

---

[99] See Explanatory Statement to the LBC Bill (No. 7 of 2021).

The Bill provides a transparent and certain process for determining the land betterment charge by making the amounts payable where consent is given for development or other use of the land in a large number of cases determinable by reference to a straightforward, simple (no valuations required) table of rates.

This should provide certainty and predictability for the property development industry because the land betterment charge can be determined upfront. Predictability allows for certainty in planning which should also reduce overall project risk. Finally, although there is public expenditure required to develop the table of rates and its periodic review, it is further anticipated that there will be savings in tax administration costs for cases which the Government does not need to refer for valuation.

Almost all development has some impact on the need for infrastructure, services and amenities. This may include new or safer road schemes, flood defences, schools, hospitals and other health and social care facilities, park improvements, green spaces and leisure centres. The land betterment charge is a way to raise funds from developers undertaking new building projects, and that money can be used to fund a wide range of infrastructure that is needed as a result of development.

Finally, almost all developments benefit from existing amenities and infrastructure, so it is also fair that those who benefit financially when planning permission, etc., is given should share some of that gain with the community to help fund the infrastructure services and amenities that are needed to make the development acceptable and sustainable.

3.1. Chargeable consent

With the coming into operation of the LBC Act, both DP and DC have been replaced by the LBC which is charged under section 6 of the Act in respect of each "chargeable consent" given in relation to a development or subdivision of, or a "controlled activity" of any land.

The term "chargeable consent" is defined in section 3(1) of the Act. In respect of cases governed by the Planning Act and which *do not involve the varying of any restrictive covenant in a State title*, the term "chargeable consent" refers to (i) the grant of planning permission; (ii) the grant of conservation permission or (iii) the acceptance of a lodgment of any plans for a development of the land deemed authorized without express WP under section 21(6) of the Planning Act.

In respect of cases which also *concern the varying of restrictive covenants in State titles*, the term "chargeable consent" refers to the varying of the restrictive titles in the State titles by SLA, as well. While all planning authorizations for the development of land would be regarded as "chargeable consents", the "chargeable consent" in respect of subdivision of land (even if accompanied by development), is the varying of a restrictive covenant. "The mere grant of a subdivision permission under the Planning Act or the mere lodgment of a subdivision plan for land pursuant to authorizations under section 21(6) of the Planning Act, does not attract tax liability under the [Act] if the State title to the land does not contain a restrictive covenant restraining subdivision"[100]. In this regard, it is also to be noted the definition of the word "subdivision" in section 2(1) of the LBC Act[101], differs from that of the word "subdivide" in section 4(1) of the Planning Act[102].

Statutory provisions in the LBC Act set out the applicable "chargeable consent" for the purpose of determining the LBC, in cases where multiple events may give rise to more than one "chargeable event" for the same development. Some of these instances may occur where both the requirements of the Planning Act and the contractual terms of the State title (where applicable) must be satisfied in order for a development, subdivision or controlled activity (as the case may be) to be lawfully carried out. In this regard, sections 3(3) and (4) of the LBC Act are "to ensure that taxable persons do not take advantage of the differential tax rates for different chargeable consents"[103].

---

[100] See Explanatory Statement to the LBC Bill (No 7 of 2021) on clause 3.

[101] In the LBC Act, the word 'subdivision' for any land, means 'the division of the land into 2 or more parts which can be conveyed, assigned, transferred, subleased or otherwise disposed of, and includes a strata subdivision of any building after completion of the building comprised in a development of land'.

[102] In the Planning Act, 'a person shall … be said to subdivide land if, by any deed or instrument, he conveys, assigns, demises or otherwise disposes of any part of the land in such a manner that the part so disposed of becomes capable of being registered under the Registration of Deeds Act or, in the case of registered land, being included in a separate folio of the land-register under the Land Titles Act'. Under the Planning (Leases and Disposal of Land)(Consolidation) Order made under s 4(3) of the Planning Act, (Cap 232, OR 1), the grant of any qualifying lease for a term not exceeding an aggregate of 21 years, shall not be regarded as a disposal of land.

[103] See Explanatory Statement to the LBC Bill (No 7 of 2021) on clause 3.

Essentially sections 3(3) and (4) are to provide that where multiple events may be regarded as the giving of "chargeable consents", the earliest event is to be regarded as the giving of "chargeable event", in the case where the various events give rise to the same rate of LBC of 70% of the increase of the land likely to accrue from the giving of the "chargeable consent". However, where the various events are such that some will provide for the 100% rate of LBC and others provide for the lower 70% rate of LBC, the event that provides for the higher rate of LBC, is to be regarded as the giving of "chargeable consent". In other words, the statutory provisions operate in the collection of the LBC in such a way that (a) the higher rate of LBC applies where more than one rate may be applicable; and (b) the LBC is collected at the earliest "chargeable event" where there may be more than one applicable "chargeable event".

3.2. Rates of land betterment charge

Generally, the LBC is payable at 70% of the increase in the value of the land likely to accrue from the giving of the chargeable consent[104], which is the same rate generally used for the calculation of the earlier DC and DP. The rate of 70% is factored into the Table of Rates[105] prescribed under section 65 of the Act (as was in the case of the earlier DC Table), such that the quantum of the LBC may be arrived at directly, by deducting the "pre-chargeable valuation of the land" from the "post-chargeable valuation of the land" as provided in section 11(1) of the Act[106], without having to multiply the net result by 70% in order to arrive at the quantum of the LBC. The LBC Act contemplates that it is possible that no LBC may be payable, where the "post-chargeable valuation" does not exceed the "pre-chargeable valuation", as may be seen from section 11(2) of the LBC Act.

In determining the "pre-chargeable valuation" of the land, the last "paid-up" authorized development of the land, usually measured in terms

---

[104] The rate is prescribed under s 7(2) of the LBC Act.

[105] The Table of Rates replaces the DC Table prescribed under the Planning (Development Charges) Rules.

[106] The terms 'post-chargeable valuation of the land' and 'pre-chargeable valuation of the land' largely correspond to the terms 'development ceiling' and 'development baseline' formerly used in the calculation of the development charge under the Planning Act.

of plot ratio or gross floor area, has to be taken into account, as provided in section 11(3)(a) of the Act. However, in the case of land which is the subject of a State title where a restrictive covenant provides a "comparably higher" value as compared with that of the last "paid up" authorized development, the restrictive covenant will be recognized for the purpose of determining the "pre-chargeable valuation" for the land as provided in section 11(3)(b) of the Act. This is provided a comparison may be made between the value of the last authorized development of the land and that pertaining to the restrictive covenant. "For example, if the State land only contains a use restriction but no gross floor area, there is no comparability, so the last authorized development of the land paid for will be recognized instead"[107]. Any exemption, remission, relief or non-liability granted in connection with the last authorized development has also to be taken into account in determining the "pre-chargeable valuation" as provided in paragraphs (c), (d) and (e) of section 11(3) of the Act.

The "post-chargeable valuation" of the land must take into account the entitlement arising from the "chargeable consent" which is given. The entitlement may pertain to the development of the land or "controlled activity" in relation to the land, as provided in section 11(5) of the Act.

While generally the LBC is levied at 70% of the increase in the value of the land that accrues from the giving of "chargeable consent", there are however situations where the LBC is levied at 100% of the increase in the value of the land[108] and is to be calculated by the valuation method and not by reference to the Table of Rates prescribed under section 65 of the Act[109]. These cases fall into the following three broad categories[110]:

(a) Cases where the land was earlier sold by the State directly to the lessee without the process of an open tender and State title contains a restrictive covenant on change of land use. The policy of the SLA has

---

[107] See Explanatory Statement to the LBC Bill on clause 11.

[108] S 8(2) of the LBC Act.

[109] S (9)(2) of the LBC Act.

[110] See the speech of the Second Minister for Law, Mr Edwin Tong at the second reading of the LBC Bill on 10 May 2021, available on the Ministry of Law website.

been to collect DP at 100% of the enhancement of land value in such cases, where there were to be a material change of use. While most land would have been sold by competitive tender, there are cases where land has been sold directly to a lessee such as that in *Chiu Teng @ Kallang Pte Ltd v Singapore Land Authority*[111]. In that case, it was also mentioned in the grounds of judgment that DP was charged at 100% of the enhancement of land arising from the change from car park use to office building use, in the case of the former site of the Market Street multi-storey car park building which was redeveloped into an office building, known as CapitaGreen. The earlier direct sale of the Market Street site to a government agency to erect a multi-storey car park building may have been necessary in the 1960s, to provide car parking in the Central Business District where some buildings did not provide the minimum car parking lots required and the developers of those buildings had to pay "car park deficiency charges" to the Government. The subsequent intensification and change of use of such directly allotted land would attract LBC at 100% of the enhancement of land value arising from such intensification and change of use.

The higher rate of LBC for this category of cases comprising directly allotted land is provided in section 8(2)(a) of the LBC Act where a "special condition" in a directly allotted State title, may have to be varied to allow a development or a subdivision of the land. The term "special condition" is in turn defined in section 2(1) of the Act as "a reservation, restriction or covenant expressed in a directly allotted State title, requiring the initial owner of the land that is the subject of the State title to refrain from abandoning or changing the use of the land in a particular way, failing which the lessor is entitled to demand the surrender of the land". The "special condition" will ostensibly include the condition in the "land return" clause in the State title in the *Chiu Teng* case. The statutory prescription of a LBC amounting to 100% of the increase in land value in such cases (unlike the earlier practices which were not legislated or published) will now be apparent to all and

---

[111] [2014] 1 SLR 1407.

will be in line with the purpose of the LBC Act, which is to provide certainty and transparency in the calculation of most LBCs, as stated in section 5(b) of the Act. As may be seen in the *Chiu Teng* case, the developer in that case seemed unaware that the DP was to be calculated at 100% of the increase in land value, on the basis of valuation, and not on the basis of the table of development charge rates prescribed under the Planning Act.

(b) Cases where the State title contains an "additional land premium" condition, requiring the lessee "to refrain from developing beyond a particular intensity or otherwise using the land in a particular way, failing which the lessor is entitled to demand an additional premium for the land"[112]. This condition is "typically inserted in a State title granted for a land parcel where the Master Plan does not stipulate a maximum gross plot ratio for the land parcel, where the land is alienated at a gross plot ratio that is lower than the Master Plan, or where more valuable uses for the land are envisaged but not reflected in the State title"[113].

Such a condition may be included in a State title to allow for the collection of the entire value enhancement arising from an intensification or change of use of that land, prior to a certain cut-off date, such as before the Temporary Occupation Permit of a development is obtained, or until certain conditions are met. The condition is to discourage landowners from changing their plans shortly after the purchase of the piece of land from the State. If such change in the land use (made not long after the purchase of the land) would instead only attract a LBC of 70% of the enhancement in value arising from the intensification or change of use, the land for the changed use would effectively have been acquired from the State at less than the full market rate for the land.

The higher rate of LBC for such cases is provided in section 8(2)(b)(i) of the LBC Act, where a restrictive covenant in a "concessional State title" has to be varied in the case of a chargeable consent given in relation to a development or subdivision of land. The term "concessional State title" is in turn defined in section 2(1) of the Act.

---

[112] See Explanatory Statement to the LBC Bill.
[113] See Explanatory Statement to the LBC Bill.

(c) Cases where the varying of the State title restrictions against subdivision, or against controlled activities which are unconnected to the development of land (such as club membership rules in the case where the land is developed with a club building). The higher rate of LBC for such cases, is provided in paragraphs (ii) and (iii) of section 8(2)(b) of the LBC Act, where a chargeable consent is given where there is a varying of a "controlled activity restrictive covenant" or a "subdivision control restrictive covenant" to allow a development or a subdivision of the land. The terms "controlled activity", "controlled activity restrictive covenant" and "subdivision control restrictive covenant" are in turn defined in section 2(1) of the Act.

Where a taxable person considers that the LBC calculated by reference to the Table of Rates under section 11 is excessive, he may pursuant to section 9(3)(a) of the LBC Act, elect to have the LBC determined by way of the Valuation method, before a liability order for the charge is given to him. An election under section 9(3)(a) is however irrevocable[114]. In the event that the Valuation method provides a LBC which is higher than that earlier provided by the Table of Rates, the taxable person is not at liberty to revert to the lower LBC earlier provided by use of the Table of Rates. The policy behind the irrevocable election is obviously to encourage the use of the fixed rates in the Table of Rates without the need for valuation[115]. Of course, the taxable person may choose to abort his planning application and re-start his planning application afresh. In that situation, his fresh application will have to meet the conditions of the prevailing planning policies at the time of re-application and the LBC is also to be calculated by reference to the then prevailing Table of Rates.

Where the Valuation method is adopted to ascertain the amount of the LBC, the valuation may be done by the Chief Valuer or another valuer appointed by the SLA according to section 10(2) of the Act. As the Table

---

[114] The Valuation method is also used where the Table of Rates is inapplicable as provided in s 9(3)(b) of the Act. This is uncommon but may occur where the use group as prescribed for the Table of Rates, may not be suitable or comparable to the uses of the development site.

[115] See s 5(b) of the LBC Act, on the purpose of the Act. As expressed in the Explanatory Statement to the Bill, 'it is further anticipated that there will be savings in tax administration costs for cases which the Government does not need to refer for valuation'.

of Rates is prepared by the Chief Valuer, there may be a perception that where the Chief Valuer performs a valuation under section 10 of the LBC Act, he may tend towards upholding the rates in the Table of Rates which he has earlier prepared. In the view of the authors, the appointment of another valuer who has not been involved in the preparation of the Table of Rates, for the purpose of the section 10 valuation, would provide a signal of independence. After all, private sector valuers have been routinely appointed by the SLA for the purpose of ascertaining the compensation to be awarded for properties acquired under the Land Acquisition Act.

In the interests of transparency and the saving of tax administration costs, it is further submitted that the Valuation method prescribed in section 9(2) of the Act in respect of the ascertainment of the LBC for certain cases where the LBC is levied at 100% of the enhancement of the land value arising from the varying of restrictive covenants, should be dispensed with altogether. Instead, the Table of Rates may readily be utilized for the purpose, by multiplying the relevant rate in the Table of Rates by a factor of 100/70 to ascertain the LBC in such cases. The use of the Table of Rates in this manner will promote the purpose of the LBC Act, i.e. to provide a transparent and certain process where the LBC is determinable upfront by reference to a straightforward and simple Table of Rates, which will provide certainty and predictability for the property development industry and reduce overall project risk[116].

4. Development Charge

The new LBC insofar as it is levied for the intensification and change of use of land beyond the parameters of the last "paid-up" authorized development, without the need to vary any restrictive covenant in a State title, operates very much like the development charge (DC) which it replaced. In this section, the authors will discuss the DC which had a longer history of operation and which will provide an understanding of the workings of the new LBC.

Planning permission which allows a landowner to develop his land obviously is of value to the owner. Where the planning permission confers a right to develop beyond the owner's legal entitlement in respect of the land,

---

[116] See Explanatory Statement to the LBC Bill (No 7 of 2021) on clause 5.

there is a "planning gain", "giving" or betterment conferred on the owner. Part of this betterment is to be captured and returned to the community[117]. Indeed, section 5(a) of the LBC Act states that one of the purpose of the imposition of the LBC is for "the return to the community of an appropriate proportion of economic benefits from the grant of rights to develop or otherwise use land".

Of course, whether there is in fact betterment in a particular case, is a question of fact. There may be situations where a landowner proposes a land use which may be of less monetary value than that based on the use permissible pursuant to the Development Baseline. For example, a landowner for his own reasons, may propose the use of valuable land zoned "Residential" which may otherwise accommodate high-rise apartment blocks, for the erection of an institutional building. Where such a development proposal is approved, the proposed land use may not give rise to an enhancement in the land value and hence no DC was chargeable. In the LBC Act, it is also envisaged that there may be situations where no LBC is to be levied in such situations[118].

DC was levied in respect of development land where planning permission was granted for a development in excess of the Development Baseline and which did not require any varying of restrictive covenants in State titles[119]. Quite obviously, where a significant amount of DC had to be paid for the development land, it would affect the price that the land would fetch in the market as any purchaser of such land would have to factor in the amount of DC payable in the development of the land[120].

---

[117] See John Good, 'Singapore's integrated transit-oriented planning and land value capture', in Stephen Hamnett and Belinda Yuen (eds.), *Planning Singapore: The Experimental City* (Routledge, 2019); Phang Sock Yong, 'Economic development and the distribution of land rents in Singapore,' *American Journal of Economics and Sociology* 55 (1996), 489–501, Edwin Loo, 'Land value capture: The impossible tax, Lessons from Singapore,' *IPPR Progressive Review*, 26(1) (2019) 61–68 and Susan Fainstein, 'Land value capture and justice,' in Gregory Ingram and Yu-Hung Hong (eds.), *Value Capture and Land Policies* (Lincoln Institute of Land Policy, 2012), pp. 21–40.

[118] Sections 10(3) and 11(2) of the LBC Act.

[119] For land which was sold by the State and where the State lease specified the permissible nature and intensity of the use of the land, the varying of the restrictive covenants on the use and intensity, required the payment of differential premium, which is discussed later in this chapter. Both the development charge and differential premium have since been replaced by the LBC with the coming into operation of the LBC Act.

[120] See *Kok Yin Chong and Others v Lim Hun Joo and Others*, [2019] 2 SLR 46, which discussed the influence of the development charge on the bid price of the site of Goodluck Garden, in an *en bloc* sale.

DC was essentially a betterment tax levied under the Planning Act and which took into account that the WP may confer an enhancement in the land value of the development site. Various countries have attempted to capture the land value enhancement in various ways[121]. In Singapore, the then Minister for National Development, Mr Mah Bow Tan at the second reading of the Planning (Amendment) Bill 2003, explained the development charge as follows[122]:

> The Development Charge is really a tax. It is levied where the value of land is enhanced as a result of some actions of the State, whether this is in the building up of infrastructure that would allow land to be used more intensively, or whether this is some change in planning parameters, or some change of policy regarding land use. All these are actions of the State which have created value in the land. The principle, is at first mooted when Development Charge was implemented in 1964, that where there are enhancements in land value, the State should share with the landowner in that enhancement.

As may be seen, DC was then levied in respect of the enhancement in land value, where the planning authorities approved a higher value use, beyond which the landowner was entitled to, pursuant to the planning legislation. In this regard, VK Rajah JA in delivering the judgment of the Court of Appeal in *Chua Choon Cheng and others v Allgreen Properties Ltd,* said[123]:

> Development charges are charges levied on the enhancement in land value resulting from the State approving a higher value development proposal: see *A Quick Guide on Development Charge* (Source: <http://www.ura.gov.sg/ dc/brochure-devtcharge.pdf> (accessed on 14 May 2009). Generally, a

---

[121] See Hiroaki Suzuki *et al.*, '*Financing Transit-Oriented Development with Land Values: Adapting Land Value Capture in Development Countries* (International Bank for Reconstruction and Development/The World Bank, 2015),' on the theory of land value capture and on how publicly-created land value increments are captured for public purposes, using various instruments, and Eddie Hui *et al.*, 'Land value capture mechanisms in Hong Kong and Singapore,' *Journal of Property Investment & Finance* 76 (2004) 22 and Chen Jianlin and Cui Jiongzhe, 'More market-oriented than the United States and more socialist than China: A comparative public property story of Singapore,' (2014) *Pacific Rim Law & Policy* 1.

[122] *Singapore Parliamentary Debates, Official Report,*11 November 2003, at col 3500.

[123] [2009] 3 SLR(R) 724 at [4].

development charge is payable where the "development ceiling" exceeds the existing "development baseline" (the formula is: Development Charge payable = Development Ceiling — Development Baseline — Development Charge Exemption). Therefore, the higher the existing development baseline of a project is, the lower the development charge will be. A lower development charge would, in turn, ordinarily translate into a higher realisable sale price for the land.

The development charge was computed by taking the difference between the Development Ceiling and the Development Baseline[124], as was prescribed in section 35(2) of the Planning Act which read:

> Subject to section 39, any development charge payable in respect of any development of land shall be the difference between the Development Baseline and the Development Ceiling for that land.

In addition, any applicable DC Exemption had to be deducted to arrive at the final amount of DC payable. In formulaic expression,

$$\text{Development Charge} = \text{Development Ceiling} - \text{Development Baseline} - \text{DC Exemption}$$

We will discuss the concepts of the Development Ceiling, Development Baseline and DC Exemption in turn. The numbers for Development Ceiling and Development Baseline were to be calculated in accordance with prescribed methods and rates as set out in the Planning (Development Charges) Rules[125].

4.1. Development ceiling

The Development Ceiling basically corresponded to the land value of the development site based on the parameters of the WP which was granted for

---

[124] The corresponding terms for 'Development Ceiling' and 'Development Baseline' in the LBC Act are 'post-chargeable valuation' and 'pre-chargeable valuation' respectively, referred to in s 11 of the LBC Act. In the Explanatory Statement to the LBC Bill, it was stated that 'clause 11 deals with the 'post-chargeable valuation' of the land and is similar to the Development Ceiling in the Planning Act'.

[125] Cap. 232, R5.

the proposed development of the site. The computation of the Development Ceiling was provided in section 35(7) of the Planning Act which read:

> The Development Ceiling for any land shall be the total of the following when calculated in accordance with the prescribed method and rates[126]:
>
> (a) the value of the authorised development of the land to be retained; and
> (b) the value of the development of the land to be authorised by the written permission.

For most developments where the existing authorized development on the development site was not to be retained or the development site was vacant land where there was no authorized development to be retained, the Development Ceiling was computed with reference to the parameters of the development allowed under the WP, as envisaged under section 35(7)(b) of the Planning Act. As explained by the then Minister for National Development, Mr Lim Hng Kiang at the second reading of the Planning Bill on 14 January 1998:

> When a developer submits a proposal for development of a site, there will be a value associated with it depending on factors like the usage and intensity. There is a need to introduce a new term "Development Ceiling" to reflect this value for development charge purposes. The development charge payable will be the difference between Development Ceiling and Development Baseline for a site.

4.2. Development baseline

The Development Baseline was defined in section 36(1) of the Planning Act as follows:

> Subject to this section, the Development Baseline for any land shall be the value of any authorized development of that land which satisfies any one or more of the following criteria:

---

[126] The prescribed method and rates are provided in the Planning (Development Charges) Rules discussed below.

(a) development charge, where payable in respect of the authorised development, has been paid;

(b) no development charge is payable in respect of the authorised development by reason of any exemption or remission under this Act or the repealed Act; or

(c) development charge is not payable in respect of the authorised development under the written law in force when the development was authorized.

As may be seen from the definition, the Development Baseline of a site was a historical number to be calculated on the basis of the authorized development for the site or may be broadly referred to as corresponding to the "paid up development rights"[127]. The Development Baseline was not to be computed on the basis of the development allowable under the provisions of the prevailing Master Plan.

The provisions of the Master Plan do not confer development rights and are not taken as the basis for determining the liability for the determination of the new LBC (and previously the DC)[128]. The Master Plan is presently a forward-looking plan as its contents and provisions are applied to guide development for the next 10–15 years[129]. As the provisions of the Master Plan are not shackled to the basis for the levy of LBC (or the DC that LBC replaces), the competent authority has been free to express its planning intentions in the Master Plan, taking into account the prevailing and foreseeable circumstances.

Had the provisions of the prevailing Master Plan been used as the basis to confer development rights, the competent authority will be wary of expressing its planning intentions in the Master Plan for fear that those

---

[127] This term was used by the then Minister of National Development, Mr Lim Hng Kiang on 14 January 1998 at the second reading of the Planning Bill 1998 which introduced the terms, 'Development Baseline' and 'Development Ceiling'.

[128] See Preface to the Written Statement of the 2019 Master Plan.

[129] The transition from a Master Plan which recorded approved developments, to a Master Plan as a forward-looking document expressing planning intentions which guide future developments, was achieved through the publication of a series of 55 non-statutory Development Guide Plans (DGPs) over time, culminating in the adoption of the DGPs as the statutory Master Plan in 1998: see Leung Yew Kwong and See Wei Hwa, *Property Tax in Singapore*, Third Edition (LexisNexis, 2015), pp. 341–342. On 11 April 2007, Professor S Jayakumar then Deputy Prime Minister and Minister of Law, in the context of a Parliamentary debate on the Land Acquisition (Amendment) Bill 2007, said, 'In Singapore ... we have adopted a forward-looking Masterplan regime where the Masterplan reflects the long-term planning intention for the land,' *Singapore Parliamentary Debates, Official Report*, vol. 83, col. 500.

intentions will confer a windfall gain on the owners of the land. Hence, there was the need to separate the system for the computation of DC from the provisions of the prevailing Master Plan. Such separation was effected with the coming into operation of the Planning (Amendment No. 2) Act 1989. At the second reading of the Planning (Amendment No. 2) Bill 1989 in Parliament, the then Minister for National Development, Mr S Dhanabalan explained[130]:

> The second aspect is the separation of the development charge system from the planning system. Sir, under the present section 26 of the Act, the zones and development intensities shown in the Master Plan form the basis for computing the development charge. The Master Plan is basically a 1958 document. Our present and future requirements as we see them today are quite different from what they would have appeared to planners in 1958. We may, for example, want to change an area that is zoned for industrial use in the Master Plan to residential use to reflect current needs and current standards. If the Master Plan is changed, the basis for computing development charge may be affected.
>
> As a result of this connection between the Master Plan and the development charge, the planning authority is reluctant to make changes to the Master Plan even though such changes may be necessary to show the long term planning intentions for an area. For example, if an area is zoned as green belt today and we want to change it to residential and the planners made the change, then the owner of a plot in the green belt would expect to be automatically allowed to develop housing in that area. For this reason, the planners are reluctant to make changes.
>
> To overcome this inflexibility, the Bill stipulates that the Master Plan to be used for the purpose of development charge will be the Master Plan approved in 1958, including of course all subsequent alterations and additions that have been made to it and for which development charge has already been paid. That will be the basis for calculating development charge. On the other hand, for purposes of guiding and approving development, the Master Plan could be a series of development guide plans, street plans and other documents which will incorporate the latest thinking of the planners.

---

[130] *Singapore Parliamentary Debates, Official Report*, 4 August 1989, vol. 54, cols. 439 and 440.

With this stipulation, the basis for computing development charge is fixed and the planning authority is free to make changes to the Master Plan without being concerned about how they will affect the development charge. This will give the planning authority the flexibility to update the current Master Plan, for example, by drawing up new development guide plans for various areas in Singapore and to make known the long term planning intentions of an area to the public.

Before the delinking of the system of the computation of the DC from the provisions of the prevailing Master Plan, the competent authority would only update the Master Plan when a development had been approved and DC paid, and would resort to "bottom drawer" plans which were not generally available to the public, to guide its development control work in the processing of applications for development[131]. As explained in *The Rule of Law and Urban Development*[132]:

> In the urban arena, it is noteworthy that Singapore's statutory Master Plan is publicly available on the URA's website. Anyone intending to purchase property or develop land can thus find out the zoning and plot ratio of not just his or her own plot, but of neighbouring plots as well.
>
> This was not the case before the 1990s. Even though there had been a statutory Master Plan passed in 1958 under the colonial government, it was widely considered inadequate for the needs of a growing city. But instead of updating this plan, the government prepared separate plans for the various sectors and regions of Singapore, but did not disclose them to the public. This lack of transparency not only inconvenienced the public and businesses (for example, a developer or landowner now needed to make a new development or redevelopment application to find out if what he had in mind was in fact aligned with the government's internal plan), it also created additional work for the government. Said former Minister for National Development Lim Hng Kiang: "Every development application submitted by the private sector required an individual decision ... there were piles and piles of development applications overwhelming the

---

[131] See Ole Johan Dale, 'The Singapore concept plan historical context/current assessment,' *PLANEWS* 14 (April 1993), 41–46, where the author explained that there were 'dual plans' as the then statutory Master Plan 'retained an artificial importance because of the development charge system'.

[132] Centre of Liveable Cities (2019), p. 51.

Permanent Secretary and all the officials ... Every decision had to go up and be decided by the Minister ... so we had to see how we could streamline the process."

The basis for the calculation of DC was measured against the Development Baseline (which was a historical measure). The term "Development Baseline" was first introduced by the Planning Act 1998[133], in relation to the computation of DC, in order to avoid any confusion with references to the prevailing Master Plan. As the then Minister for National Development, Mr Lim Hng Kiang explained at the second reading of the Planning Bill on 14 January 1998[134]:

> Sir, the term "Master Plan" in the existing Act has two different definitions. Each definition has a different usage. This has caused confusion.
>
> The first definition, retained in clause 6 of the Bill, means the original Master Plan approved in 1959 and all subsequent approved amendments to the Plan. This "Master Plan" refers to the approved development or planning intention for a site and is used to evaluate whether a proposed development could be allowed.
>
> The second definition, in section 32(4) of the existing Act, refers to the paid-up development rights of a site for the purpose of determining development charge.
>
> To distinguish the two clearly, we now propose to replace the second definition of the term "Master Plan" with a new term "Development Baseline" in clause 36 of the Bill to describe the base value more accurately. This is only a change in nomenclature which does not result in any change in substance or in practice.

The definition of "Development Baseline" was amended later to curtail the high historical baselines as prescribed in the 1958 and 1980 Master Plans, which were enjoyed by around 1,000 sites, most of which are situated in the city area. The legislative amendment for this purpose was made in the Planning (Amendment) Act 2003[135], although the amended definition

---

[133] Act No. 3 of 1998.

[134] *Singapore Parliamentary Debates, Official Report*, 14 January 1998, col. 50–51.

[135] Act No. 30 of 2003.

only came into operation on 1 January 2008, some four years later[136]. This deferred implementation of the amended definition of "Development Baseline", was explained by the then Minister for National Development, Mr Mah Bow Tan[137]:

> Sir, the deletion of references to MP 58 and MP 80 from the definition of Development Baseline, though a necessary and desirable move, will affect those landowners who have sites with MP 58 and MP 80 baselines that are higher than their approved Development Baseline. These landowners would be subject to a higher Development Charge upon rezoning and redevelopment of their sites.
>
> To mitigate the impact on these landowners, and to give ample time for landowners to adjust to the revised baseline definition, my Ministry intends to effect the revised baseline definition only in 4 years' time, i.e, on 1st January 2008. During this period, landowners who intend to redevelop their lands can submit development proposals and they can still make use of their historical baselines up to the MP 03 intensity for the purpose of computing Development Charge.

Essentially, the 4-year deferment of the implementation of the new definition of "Development Baseline" which deprived the landowners of the affected sites of the benefit of the high historical baselines in the 1958 and 1980 Master Plans, was to provide a window period up to 31 December 2007, for those landowners to take advantage of the high historical baselines which could shelter the incidence of DC. On or after 1 January 2008, the high historical baselines would be curtailed.

Those high historical baselines if not curtailed, would have resulted in an anomaly where DC may not be levied, if the sites were to be redeveloped after 2007. The amendment of the definition of "Development Baseline" for the purpose, was explained by the then Minister for National Development, Mr Mah Bow Tan at the second reading of the Planning (Amendment) Bill 2003 on 11 November 2003[138]:

---

[136] The definition was amended by the Planning (Amendment) Act 2003 (Act 30 of 2003), although it came into operation only on 1 January 2008: see Planning (Amendment) Act (Commencement) Notification 2007, S 755/2007.

[137] *Singapore Parliamentary Debates: Official Report*, 11 November 2003, at col. 3480.

[138] *Singapore Parliamentary Debates: Official Report*, 11 November 2003, at col. 3477.

Under the current Planning Act, the base value of a piece of land, i.e. the Development Baseline, is determined by comparing the values of the following three items:

(a) the 1958 Master Plan baseline;
(b) the 1980 Master Plan baseline;
(c) the approved development baseline.

The highest of the three values derived will be the Development Baseline. The Master Plan 58 and Master Plan 80 baselines have been included in the baseline definition due to historical reasons. The proposed amendment in clause 12 is to delete the first two items in the definition, i.e., the 1958 and the 1980 Master Plans.

With this amendment, the Development Baseline is the value of the approved development for the site for which Development Charge was paid, exempted, or not required to be paid. Any enhancement in value arising from redevelopment would be that above this base, and not that above a historically prescribed base that has no direct link with the actual development history of the site.

In reply to questions by Members of Parliament on the same day, the Minister explained that the anomaly created by the high historical baselines in the 1958 and 1980 Master Plans, was such that DC was not levied for the affected sites upon redevelopment[139]:

In this particular case, we have situations where pieces of land with high baselines, historically derived in 1958 and 1980, would actually result in no sharing of enhancement between the State and the landowner, if such lands were to be redeveloped in future whenever the Master Plan allows. Where such an anomaly exists, we should correct it. It does not matter whether there are many pieces of, land or not. The point is that this is an anomaly that has to be corrected because, if it is not corrected, we are not able to apply this principle [of Development Charge]. Having said that, of course, I can inform the Member that there are quite a few of these sites in the central area. URA has combed through the various sites and they have estimated that there are over 1,000 such sites, mainly in the central area, where there are such high baselines and which, if this Act is not amended, would result in the State not having the ability to share in any

---

[139] *Singapore Parliamentary Debates: Official Report*, 11 November 2003, at cols. 3500–3502.

enhancement in land values in the future. So that is the reason behind this change. It is not an administrative issue. It is not an issue where we are doing this just because we happen to go through and we see this anomaly and, therefore, we want to change it. I think there is a fundamental principle involved.

The other major point that she raised is whether, in this particular amendment, we are actually destroying value. Is it akin to, say, compulsory acquisition of land, where we are actually taking land and compensating based on a certain formula in the Act? Are we destroying value in this? Let me say that when we talk about destroying value, the Member is assuming that the high baselines in the 1958 and 1980 Master Plans are actually legal entitlements to the value of the land. In other words, you were given a high baseline, you are entitled to this value for eternity. The answer is no. It is not a legal entitlement. What is it? It is an expectation that you can develop these lands up to that particular value subject to what is stipulated in the current Master Plan. So even if the Master Plan 1958 or 1980 stipulates a very high baseline exceeding the current Master Plan — in this case, we are talking about Master Plan 2003 — it does not follow that that high baseline is what they are legally entitled to. They can only develop up to the Master Plan 2003. This is the main point that I would like to make. Historical baselines are not legal entitlements to land value. They are expectations of enhancements of development potential in the future. They are actually parameters in the Development Charge tax formula. We can change this parameter from time to time. I do not agree that there is a destruction in the value of the land in this particular case. As I have said, the proposal is to refine the tax formula to make it more in line with the principle of collecting Development Charge as and when lands are redeveloped and value is enhanced.

Why are we doing this? We are doing this simply because when value is enhanced as a result of State actions, particularly through the building of infrastructure, it is only fair that some of the benefits accruing from this enhancement in land value be channeled back to the State for public infrastructure works, for building of roads, building of MRTs, sewer lines, etc. The proposed revision in the baseline merely reestablishes this principle of sharing of enhancement gains from those sites which may have fallen through the system.

With the amended definition of "Development Baseline", section 36(1) of Planning Act made no reference to the baselines in the 1958 and 1980

Master Plan. Nevertheless, parts of the legacy of the baselines of the 1958 and 1980 Master Plans, lived on in the Planning (Development Charge — Exemption in relation to Historical Base Values) Rules 2008[140], which accorded DC exemption for the "safeguarded historical baselines". We will discuss the DC Exemption in the following section.

4.3. Development charge exemption

DC exemption was not commonly encountered in practice. Where DC exemption was applicable, the amount of DC exemption had to be deducted in determining the amount of DC payable. The DC exemption generally pertained to the value of the "safeguarded historical baseline" as provided in the Planning (Development Charge — Exemption in relation to Historical Base Values) Rules 2008[141] (2008 Rules), prescribed under section 40 of the Planning Act, for about 1,000 sites, in the city area[142].

Essentially when the high historical baselines in the 1958 and 1980 Master Plans for those sites were expunged by the 2003 legislative amendment for the purposes of the computation of DC, lower baselines up to those prescribed in the Master Plan 2003 (which was the prevailing Master Plan at that time), were nevertheless safeguarded for the affected sites. In other words, the high historical baselines in the 1958 and 1980 Master Plans may be said to be safeguarded but capped at the nature and intensity of development allowed under the Master Plan 2003.

With such safeguarding, no DC needed to be paid where the Development Ceiling of the affected sites in any future redevelopments, matched up to the Master Plan 2003 development baseline. In that sense, there was DC Exemption in those cases. This was explained by the then Minister for National Development, Mr Mah Bow Tan at the second reading of the Planning (Amendment) Bill 2003, on 11 November 2003[143]:

---

[140] S 112/2008.

[141] S 112/2008.

[142] Other DC exemptions include exemptions in respect of: (1) land sold or leased by the State or a statutory board where the nature and intensity of development are in accordance with those specified in the terms of sale or lease; (2) land leased by the State to statutory boards (for gross plot ratio of 2.5 for industrial land, 2.8 for public housing land, etc.) and (3) single dwelling houses on land, to the extent allowed under rules 5, 7 and 10, respectively, of the Planning (Development Charge — Exemption) Rules, Cap. 232, R6.

[143] *Singapore Parliamentary Debates: Official Report*, 11 November 2003, col. 3480.

For landowners who have no intention or are unable to redevelop their lands within this advance notice period [up to 31 December 2007], my Ministry will take a further step to safeguard and lock-in the historical baselines in MP 58 and MP 80 that is applicable to their site under the current legal provisions. This is capped at the maximum use and intensity allowed under MP 03 if the MP 58 or MP 80 baseline value is higher than the MP 03. In other words, the URA will preserve the value of historical baseline up to the development potential of the Master Plan 2003. Landowners will thus not the worse off than they are presently. The historical value locked-in will continue to be applicable after 1st January 2008. Any development proposal on these lands after 1st January 2008 will be exempted from Development Charge payment up to the difference between the locked-in value and the new Development Baseline, if the locked-in value is higher.

Although the Master Plan 2003 development baseline for the affected sites was safeguarded such that any DC applicable for the redevelopment of the affected sites up to the Master Plan 2003 development baseline was exempt, DC would have been payable had the Development Ceiling of the affected sites been raised beyond the safeguarded historical baselines, in any future redevelopment. This was explained by Mr Mah as follows[144]:

However, the revision [of the high historical baselines provided in the 1985 and 1980 Master Plans] will allow enhancement gains to be shared in future when the Development Ceiling is raised beyond the MP 2003 value. .... When the Development Ceiling is raised in future Master Plan Reviews, redevelopment can take place beyond the MP 2003. The enhancement in value beyond the MP 2003 will be liable to Development Charge. What this means is that it will bring these sites in line with other sites after 2008. Development Charge will now be payable for all sites which have their Development Ceiling raised beyond the MP 2003 value. ...

With the deferred implementation and safeguarding of the historical value up to the allowable uses under the prevailing Master Plan [2003], the impact of the redefinition of baseline will be minimal. However, it will allow a more equitable sharing of the value enhancement for redevelopment

[144] *Singapore Parliamentary Debates: Official Report*, 11 November 2003, col. 3482.

and Master Plan alteration in future Master Plan review. After 2008, the Development Charge system will be fairer and more effective.

Accordingly, in respect of sites with safeguarded historical baselines, the 2008 Rules still provided for DC Exemption, which would have helped to reduce the amount of DC payable upon redevelopment of the affected sites[145].

4.4. Development charge table[146]

The DC Table prescribed by the Planning (Development Charge) Rules is now replaced by the Table of Rates under the LBC Act. Before DC was replaced by the LBC, DC was generally computed at 70%[147] of the enhancement in land value arising from the grant of planning permission. In explaining the DC in Parliament, the then Minister for National Development. Mr Mah Bow Tan said[148]:

> Currently, ... DC rate is pegged at 70% of the enhancement in land value. The ... DC collected allows the State to provide the necessary infrastructure and services (e.g. roads, drainage and sewerage) without which the

---

[145] See URA Circular of 5 December 2007, *Implementation of Revised Definition of Development Baseline*.

[146] The DC Table first came into operation on 1 September 1989 to address the uncertainties with regard to the computation of the amounts of DC before then, where the amount of DC for every case was determined on a case-by-case valuation by the Chief Valuer: see comments of Mr Lim Hng Hiang (then Deputy Secretary at the Ministry of National Development) in dealing with the situation before the advent of the DC Table in 1989, in *Urban Redevelopment: From Urban Squalor to Global City* (Centre of Liveable Cities, 2016), p. 79 and R. Amirtahmasebi, M. Orloff, S. Wahba and A. Altman, *Regenerating Urban Land: A Practitioner's Guide to Leveraging Private Investment* (International Bank for Reconstruction and Development/The World Bank, 2016), p. 365.

[147] See rule 10(b) of the Planning (Development Charges) Rules, Cap. 232, R5, where the rate of 70% was specified. However, DC was charged at 100% of the enhancement of land value in relation to development of 'business zone commercial use' under rule 10(a). When the computation of DC by way of 'spot valuation' was first introduced on 1 February 1980, the DC was calibrated at 70% of the enhancement in land value arising from planning permission. The rate was reduced to 50% on 1 June 1985 at the time when the property market took a downturn. When the DC Table first came into operation on 1 September 1989, the rates in the table were computed at 50% of land values. The rate had been recalibrated to 70% since 18 July 2007 *via* the Planning (Development Charges) Rules 2007 (S 385/2007) when the property market showed signs of recovering and there was a feverish increase in *en bloc* sales. In 2007, the DC Table was therefore updated three times, i.e. on 1 March 2007, 18 July 2007 and 1 September 2007. Since 18 July 2007, the numbers in the DC Table reflect 70% of the land value of the relevant geographical sector and corresponding use.

[148] *Singapore Parliamentary Debates, Official Report*,19 July 2010, vol. 87, col. 815.

developer cannot materialise the higher development intensity in the area. The balance of the gain from the land value enhancement is retained by the land-owner and provides an incentive for him to undertake the development work.

In calibrating the DC rate, there is a need to balance between providing an equitable share of the land value enhancement for the State to fund the necessary infrastructure and services and, at the same time, providing a reasonable incentive for land-owners and developers to undertake development works. We believe that the current 70% DC rate is reasonable in the current market conditions.

While an applicant may have asked for DC to be determined by way of a "spot valuation" of his particular development site under section 39 of the Planning Act, this was only where he was dissatisfied with the DC determined in accordance with the rates in the DC Table contained in the Planning (Development Charges) Rules, *gazetted* under section 40 of the Planning Act[149].

The amount of DC was first to be determined by reference to the DC Table which was prescribed in Part II of the First Schedule to the Planning (Development Charge) Rules, and a new DC Table came into operation on 1 March and 1 September each year[150]. The date of the provisional permission of a development would determine the appropriate DC Table to be used for the determination of the DC. For example, where the date of the provisional permission (which is valid for 6 months) was 1 May 2020, the March 2020 DC Table (which was the DC Table then in force) was to be used for computing the DC[151]. With the provisional permission, the developer was expected to finalize his development proposals, pay the DC, obtain the WP and proceed with the development.

---

[149] In the vast majority of cases where DC has to be determined, the applicant has accepted the amount of DC computed in accordance with the DC Table and has not asked for a section 39 'spot valuation'. This phenomenon indicated that the rates in the DC Table are generally accepted as reasonable in relation to land values.

[150] After the DC Table first came into operation on 1 September 1989, the Table was updated annually with the updated DC Table coming into operation on each anniversary, i.e. on 1 September of the subsequent years. The frequency of updating the DC Table was changed to once every 6 months with effect from 1 March 2000, to take into account the greater volatility of land values. Before the DC Table was replaced by the Table of Rates for the LBC under the LBC Act, the DC Table was updated to come into operation on 1 March and 1 September each year.

[151] Rule 17(1)(a) of the Planning (Development Charges) Rules, Cap. 232, R5.

However, the developer may need more than 6 months for the finalization of his development proposals, and he may apply for an extension of the provisional permission. In this example, the validity of the provisional permission was extended for the first time on 1 November 2020 (6 months after the original provisional permission of 1 May 2020), in which case the March 2020 DC Table remained as the DC Table used for determining the DC (although the September 2020 has already come into force by then). This was because it may not be unreasonable to require more than 6 months to finalize their plans, before the developer is in the position to apply for the WP.

However, where the provisional permission goes into its second extension, it would have been at least 12 months since the original provisional permission is granted. The official position was that in such situations, the DC should reflect the market value of the development land, as at the date of the extension. Rule 17(2) of the Planning (Development Charges) Rules[152] thus provided that where the provisional permission went into its second or subsequent extensions, the appropriate DC table to be used would be those DC Tables in force as at the date of those extensions[153]. During a period of rising values, the delay in finalizing the development plans, would result in a higher development charges with each extension of the provisional permission. This procedure which had been in place since 1 January 1997, was to encourage developers to finalize their plans early and proceed to apply for the WP[154]. This policy is now provided for in paragraphs (d) and (e) of section 8(3) of the LBC Act, in respect of the LBC.

The DC table comprised a matrix of 118 geographical sectors and nine use groups, and the one in operation for the 6-month period from 1 September 2021 to 28 February 2022 is shown in Table 1[155].

---

[152] Cap. 232, R 5.

[153] Rule 17(2) of the Planning (Development Charges) Rules, Cap. 232, R5.

[154] *Skyline,* September/October 1996, published by the Urban Redevelopment Authority.

[155] This DC Table which came into operation with the Planning (Development Charges)(Amendment No. 2) Rules 2021, S 661/2021 on 1 September 2021. The earlier Planning (Development Charges) (Amendment No. 2) Rules, S 725/2020, which came into operation a year earlier on 1 September 2020, reflected a more severe adverse impact of the COVID-19 outbreak in Singapore: see 'Hotel, commercial use groups see biggest chops in DC rates,' *The Business Times,* 1 September 2020, and 'Development charges cut for commercial and hotel use,' *The Straits Times,* 1 September 2020.

Table 1:   DC Table.

Geographical Sectors	A	B1	B2	C	D	E	F	G	H
1	$12,950	$4,130	$12,250	$13,860	$840	$910	$10	—	$1
2	$12,950	$4,130	$12,250	$13,860	$840	$910	$10	—	$1
3	$12,950	$4,130	$12,250	$15,470	$840	$910	$10	—	$1
4	$12,950	$4,130	$12,250	$14,490	$840	$910	$10	—	$1
5	$12,950	$4,130	$12,250	$15,470	$840	$910	$10	—	$1
6	$12,950	$4,130	$12,250	$15,470	$840	$910	$10	—	$1
7	$11,340	$4,130	$12,250	$13,860	$840	$910	$10	—	$1
8	$10,850	$4,130	$12,250	$13,230	$840	$910	$10	—	$1
9	$11,550	$4,130	$12,250	$13,230	$840	$910	$10	—	$1
10	$10,850	$4,130	$12,250	$13,230	$840	$910	$10	—	$1
11	$13,300	$4,130	$12,250	$15,470	$840	$910	$10	—	$1
12	$13,300	$4,130	$12,250	$16,100	$840	$910	$10	—	$1
13	$9,450	$4,130	$12,550	$12,600	$840	$910	$10	—	$1
14	$9,450	$4,130	$12,250	$12,600	$840	$910	$10	—	$1
15	$11,900	$4,130	$11,550	$12,600	$840	$910	$10	—	$1
16	$11,900	$4,130	$11,690	$13,860	$840	$910	$10	—	$1
17	$10,850	$4,130	$11,550	$12,600	$840	$910	$10	—	$1
18	$10,850	$4,130	$11,550	$12,600	$840	$910	$10	—	$1
19	$10,850	$4,130	$12,040	$13,860	$959	$910	$10	—	$1
20	$10,850	$4,130	$10,500	$13,860	$959	$910	$10	—	$1
21	$11,900	$4,130	$10,500	$13,860	$959	$910	$10	—	$1
22	$7,420	$4,130	$10,500	$12,600	$840	$910	$10	—	$1
23	$10,850	$4,130	$12,040	$13,860	$840	$910	$10	—	$1
24	$9,450	$4,130	$8,540	$12,600	$840	$910	$10	—	$1
25	$9,100	$3,640	$8,540	$12,600	$840	$910	$10	—	$1
26	$9,450	$3,640	$8,540	$12,600	$840	$910	$10	—	$1
27	$9,450	$3,640	$8,540	$12,600	$840	$910	$10	—	$1
28	$9,100	$3,640	$7,840	$12,600	$840	$910	$10	—	$1
29	$9,100	$3,640	$7,840	$12,600	$840	$910	$10	—	$1
30	$9,100	$3,640	$7,840	$12,600	$840	$910	$10	—	$1
31	$9,800	$3,640	$7,840	$12,600	$840	$910	$10	—	$1

(*Continued*)

Table 1:   (*Continued*)

Geographical Sectors	A	B1	B2	C	D	E	F	G	H
32	$9,800	$3,640	$7,840	$12,600	$840	$910	$10	—	$1
33	$7,700	$3,640	$8,540	$12,600	$840	$910	$10	—	$1
34	$7,420	$5,250	$9,450	$12,600	$840	$910	$10	—	$1
35	$7,420	$5,250	$10,500	$12,600	$840	$910	$10	—	$1
36	$6,720	$5,250	$11,900	$12,600	$840	$910	$10	—	$1
37	$9,450	$5,250	$12,600	$12,600	$840	$910	$10	—	$1
38	$7,700	$9,100	$12,600	$12,600	$840	$910	$10	—	$1
39	$7,700	$12,600	$16,450	$14,490	$840	$910	$10	—	$1
40	$9,800	$9,100	$15,050	$14,490	$840	$910	$10	—	$1
41	$12,950	$5,950	$15,050	$16,100	$840	$910	$10	—	$1
42	$13,650	$9,100	$16,450	$16,100	$840	$910	$10	—	$1
43	$10,850	$9,100	$17,850	$15,470	$840	$910	$10	—	$1
44	$7,700	$12,600	$16,450	$13,860	$840	$910	$10	—	$1
45	$7,700	$9,100	$16,450	$13,860	$840	$910	$10	—	$1
46	$7,700	$7,350	$12,740	$11,970	$840	$910	$10	—	$1
47	$7,700	$7,700	$12,740	$11,970	$840	$910	$10	—	$1
48	$7,420	$7,350	$12,600	$11,970	$959	$910	$10	—	$1
49	$7,420	$3,640	$8,540	$9,310	$959	$910	$10	—	$1
50	$7,420	$3,640	$9,940	$9,310	$840	$910	$10	—	$1
51	$9,450	$3,850	$9,590	$10,430	$1,407	$910	$10	—	$1
52	$6,720	$3,780	$9,450	$8,680	$1,407	$910	$10	—	$1
53	$9,450	$3,850	$8,190	$11,340	$1,407	$910	$10	—	$1
54	$6,230	$3,780	$6,440	$6,650	$1,680	$910	$10	—	$1
55	$6,230	$3,780	$6,440	$6,650	$1,407	$910	$10	—	$1
56	$6,230	$3,780	$6,440	$6,650	$1,680	$910	$10	—	$1
57	$6,230	$3,850	$7,980	$6,650	$1,407	$910	$10	—	$1
58	$9,450	$5,040	$8,400	$10,430	$1,407	$910	$10	—	$1
59	$8,750	$5,040	$8,190	$11,970	$1,407	$910	$10	—	$1
60	$11,200	$4,760	$10,500	$12,600	$840	$910	$10	—	$1
61	$9,800	$6,610	$10,500	$12,600	$840	$910	$10	—	$1
62	$9,800	$9,100	$12,040	$12,600	$840	$910	$10	—	$1
63	$7,420	$7,700	$10,500	$10,010	$840	$910	$10	—	$1

Table 1: (*Continued*)

Geographical Sectors	A	B1	B2	C	D	E	F	G	H
64	$5,460	$7,700	$7,840	$8,680	$840	$910	$10	—	$1
65	$6,720	$9,100	$9,590	$9,310	$840	$910	$10	—	$1
66	$6,720	$12,600	$12,600	$12,600	$805	$910	$10	—	$1
67	$9,800	$14,000	$16,450	$13,860	$840	$910	$10	—	$1
68	$6,720	$11,760	$11,900	$10,010	$805	$910	$10	—	$1
69	$6,720	$11,760	$11,900	$10,010	$805	$910	$10	—	$1
70	$7,700	$12,600	$13,090	$12,600	$959	$910	$10	—	$1
71	$7,420	$6,300	$10,500	$12,600	$959	$910	$10	—	$1
72	$6,720	$4,550	$8,400	$7,980	$1,855	$910	$10	—	$1
73	$6,720	$3,850	$7,980	$7,980	$1,988	$910	$10	—	$1
74	$6,720	$3,850	$8,190	$8,680	$1,988	$910	$10	—	$1
75	$6,720	$3,850	$7,980	$7,980	$1,988	$910	$10	—	$1
76	$7,420	$3,990	$9,940	$7,980	$1,267	$910	$10	—	$1
77	$6,720	$3,990	$6,300	$7,980	$1,988	$910	$10	—	$1
78	$6,720	$3,990	$8,190	$7,980	$1,988	$910	$10	—	$1
79	$6,720	$3,850	$7,980	$7,980	$1,988	$910	$10	—	$1
80	$9,800	$3,990	$8,190	$7,980	$1,988	$910	$10	—	$1
81	$6,720	$3,850	$7,980	$7,980	$1,988	$910	$10	—	$1
82	$6,720	$3,990	$8,190	$7,980	$1,988	$910	$10	—	$1
83	$6,720	$3,990	$8,190	$7,980	$1,988	$910	$10	—	$1
84	$6,720	$3,850	$7,980	$7,980	$1,988	$910	$10	—	$1
85	$6,720	$3,990	$8,190	$7,980	$1,988	$910	$10	—	$1
86	$6,720	$3,990	$7,980	$7,980	$1,988	$910	$10	—	$1
87	$6,720	$3,850	$7,980	$7,980	$1,988	$910	$10	—	$1
88	$11,200	$5,250	$11,690	$12,600	$1,988	$910	$10	—	$1
89	$6,720	$3,640	$7,560	$7,980	$875	$910	$10	—	$1
90	$6,720	$3,640	$7,560	$7,980	$875	$910	$10	—	$1
91	$6,475	$7,700	$9,450	$6,020	$875	$910	$10	—	$1
92	$6,720	$6,160	$8,190	$9,310	$875	$735	$10	—	$1
93	$9,100	$6,160	$7,350	$10,010	$875	$735	$10	—	$1
94	$9,800	$6,160	$9,450	$10,010	$875	$735	$10	—	$1
95	$6,720	$6,160	$8,190	$6,020	$875	$735	$10	—	$1

(*Continued*)

Table 1: (*Continued*)

Geographical Sectors	A	B1	B2	C	D	E	F	G	H
96	$6,720	$5,950	$8,050	$6,020	$875	$735	$10	$34	$1
97	$6,475	$5,950	$6,650	$6,020	$805	$735	$10	$34	$1
98	$9,800	$5,040	$6,650	$6,020	$1,407	$735	$10	$34	$1
99	$6,230	$4,270	$5,600	$6,020	$1,022	$735	$10	$34	$1
100	$9,800	$4,270	$6,160	$4,970	$644	$735	$10	$34	$1
101	$9,800	$5,250	$8,050	$6,020	$2,093	$735	$10	$34	$1
102	$6,720	$3,850	$5,740	$9,310	$2,093	$735	$10	$34	$1
103	$9,800	$5,950	$8,190	$6,020	$2,093	$735	$10	$34	$1
104	$9,800	$5,950	$8,050	$5,320	$1,855	$735	$10	$34	$1
105	$9,800	$5,040	$6,160	$5,320	$1,715	$735	$10	$34	$1
106	$8,400	$3,640	$5,600	$4,970	$721	$735	$10	$34	$1
107	$7,420	$5,390	$7,910	$5,320	$1,512	$735	$10	$34	$1
108	$8,400	$11,550	$11,900	$7,980	$1,407	$735	$10	$34	$1
109	$7,420	$9,100	$9,590	$7,980	$959	$735	$10	$34	$1
110	$10,500	$7,350	$9,590	$7,980	$959	$735	$10	$34	$1
111	$9,450	$5,250	$8,400	$8,330	$2,261	$735	$10	$34	$1
112	$9,800	$5,250	$6,860	$7,980	$1,099	$735	$10	$34	$1
113	$9,450	$5,250	$6,650	$5,320	$889	$735	$10	$34	$1
114	$9,450	$3,640	$5,600	$4,970	$609	$735	$10	$34	$1
115	$9,450	$3,640	$5,600	$4,970	$812	$735	$10	$34	$1
116	$980	$910	$980	$910	$427	$385	$10	$34	$1
117	$8,400	$10,500	$12,040	$14,770	$371	$385	$10	$34	$1
118	$980	$910	$980	$910	$371	$385	$10	$34	$1

Essentially, land lots situated within the same geographical sector and having uses in the same use group, would have the same number in the DC Table.

The DC Table attempted to address the two main variables of "geographical location" and "nature of use" which impacted land values. The "time" or temporal variable which also impacted land values was addressed at least partially, through the periodic publication of the DC Table with updated values half-yearly on 1 March and 1 September each year. Of course, the value of a site may also be impacted by other factors, such as its configuration, physical contour, etc. These factors could not be addressed in the DC Table. Where those other factors were particularly adverse for a site such that the DC computed in accordance with the DC Table may be excessive, the landowner could request for a spot valuation under section 39 of the Planning Act, for the purpose of determining the DC.

For the purpose of the DC Table, Singapore was divided into 118 geographical sectors, with each sector having lands of similar value, in terms of dollars per square meter[156]. The geographical sectors varied tremendously in size and were depicted in the maps in the Second Schedule to the Planning (DC) Rules[157]. The geographical sectors in the city area, tended to be smaller in size, as compared to those in the outlying areas farther away from the city. This was because in the higher-value areas in the city, the variation in land values tended to be significant even where locations were close to each other. For example, the land values in Raffles Place would have been much higher than those in Telok Ayer Street, even though the two locations may not be very far apart. With such a phenomenon of land value differentiation, smaller geographical sectors were necessary in the city area in order to reflect the requirement that the land values within each of the geographical sectors are sufficiently proximate.

Obviously, as each piece of land was unique and varied in value from those of its neighboring lots, there needed to be a balancing exercise in the choice of the number of geographical sectors for the DC Table. If the DC Table was to reflect more accurately the value of each individual plot of land within each geographical sector, there would have to be many more geographical sectors than 118.

However, the number of geographical sectors must also not be too large, as otherwise it may have been unwieldy to prepare and use a large DC Table. Nevertheless, the number of geographical sectors had been expanded and sector boundaries had been changed, through the years. When the DC Table first came into operation on 1 September 1989, there were 47 sectors. Later, the number of geographical sectors was increased to 108 with effect from 1 September 1997, to 116 sectors with effect from 1 March 2000 and to 118

---

[156] As reflected over the gross floor area in the case of use groups A to E, and as reflected over the land area in the case of use groups F, G and H.

[157] Cap. 232, R5.

sectors with effect from 1 September 2000, until it was replaced by the Table of Rates under the LBC Act.

The nine use groups as prescribed in Part I of the First Schedule to the Planning (Development Charge) Rules[158] are as shown in Table 2 below:

Table 2: Use groups in DC Table.

Use Group	Purposes for Which Development is Permitted or to be Authorized
A	Shop, office, association office, cinema, place of entertainment, clinic, medical suite, restaurant, petrol station, auto-service center, commercial garage, market, sports and recreation building
B1	Residential (landed dwelling-house)
B2	Residential (non-landed residential building)
C	Hospital, hotel room and hotel-related uses
D	Industrial, warehousing, science park, business park, transport depot, airport, dock, port uses, utility installation, telecommunication infrastructure, Mass Rapid Transit Station, Light Rail Transit Station
E	Place of worship, community building, community sports and fitness building, educational and institutional uses, government building
F	Open space, nature reserve
G	Agriculture
H	Drain, road, railway, cemetery, Mass Rapid Transit Route, Light Rail Transit Route

The nine use groups in the Table only served the purposes of computing DC and they did not refer to the Master Plan zones[159]. Uses which were considered to provide similar values were grouped into the same use group. Obviously in deciding on the number of use groups, as in deciding on the number of geographical sectors, there needed to be a balance between simplicity (which dictated a lesser number of use groups) and having a sufficient number of use groups which gave similar land values for the uses within the groups. Where the conditions demanded or required the creation of a new use group to better reflect land values, this had been done. For example, with effect from 1 March 2000, there had been two use groups for residential use, i.e. Use Group B1 for landed dwelling-house and Use

---

[158] Cap. 232, R5.

[159] For example, B1 and B2 use groups (which came about from the splitting of the single use group B for residential developments into two sub-groups), referred to landed low-rise residential developments and high-rise residential developments respectively for the purposes of the DC Table. They did not refer to the Master Plan zones of B1 and B2 for industrial/warehouse developments.

Group B2 for non-landed residential building. Before then, there was only a single user group B for residential uses, regardless of whether the residential use was in respect of low-rise or high-rise developments[160]. The splitting of the single residential use group into the two from 1 March 2000, was obviously to reflect the phenomenon that land values/m^2 for low-rise and high-rise residential developments had deviated to the extent that required the creation of two use groups to accommodate the different rates of land value (in terms of \$/m^2) pertaining to the two use groups.

Each of the numbers stated in the DC Table (which comprised a matrix of 118 × 9) relating to use groups A to E, was essentially 70% of the rate of land value reflected over the gross floor area, corresponding to a particular geographical sector and a particular use group. For example, the rate which corresponded to Geographical Sector No. 1 (the Raffles Place area), and use group A (commercial use) in the DC Table was \$12,950/m^2 of gross floor area in Table 1 above. As the rate shown in the DC Table was computed at 70% of the land value, the indicative land value for commercial use in the Raffles Place area was \$18,500 (i.e. \$12,950/0.7)/m^2 of gross floor area. If for example, there is planning permission for the extension of a commercial building in Geographical Sector No. 1, which gave an additional gross floor area of 1,000m^2 above the Development Baseline, the DC payable according to the DC Table would have been \$12.95 million (i.e. \$12,950 × 1,000).

To provide another example, we may have a site zoned "Residential" in Geographical Sector No. 71, with an approved gross floor area of 4,800m^2 ("Development Baseline"), for which DC had earlier been paid. The proposed gross floor area as stated in the provisional permission for the site was 12,000m^2 (for a high-rise residential development). The rate for Geographical Sector No. 71 and B2 use group (non-landed residential use) read off the above DC Table above, was \$10,500. In that case,

DC payable = Development Ceiling (12,000 × \$10,500)
— Development Baseline (4,800 × \$10,500)
= \$75,600,000

[160] Compare Planning (Development Charges) (Amendment) Rules 1999 (S 373/1999) with Planning (Development Charges) (Amendment) Rules 2000 (S 82/2000).

In looking up the appropriate rate in computing DC, one has to be careful in selecting the correct use group. For example, an ancillary[161] showroom use within an industrial building (i.e. where the showroom is used in connection with an industrial use), the appropriate rate would be for use group D (i.e. for industrial use), as the showroom is not a separate and independent use. However, where the showroom was a separate and independent use, e.g. a retail showroom on its own and was not used as ancillary to or in connection with an industrial space in the building, the applicable rate was that for use group A (for commercial use). The difference in the rates in the use groups may have made a big difference in the DC payable[162].

In relation to use groups F (Open Space and Nature Reserve), G (Agriculture) and H (Drain, Road, Railway, Cemetery, Mass Rapid Transit Route, Light Rail Transit Route), the rates indicated the DC Table were essentially 70% of the rate of land value reflected over *the land area* of the development site[163]. In relation to such uses where any floor area was comparatively minimal, the rates were more meaningfully expressed as a rate over the land area. As may be observed from the DC Table, only 23 geographical sectors (i.e. Sectors 96–118) which were principally in the outlying areas in the north and north-east of Singapore, had rates of land value for the use group G (Agriculture). It is not meaningful to have rates of land value for use group G (Agriculture) in the rest of the geographical sectors, as such rates would not have been applicable for those sectors which are largely in urbanized parts of Singapore.

The rates in the DC Table generally reflected the land values of sites of a freehold or long leasehold[164] tenure. Therefore, where the development site concerned was of a relatively shorter leasehold tenure, the developer would be disadvantaged as compared with another developer with a similar

---

[161] The planning permission by the competent authority will indicate if the use is ancillary. See *Gallagher v Church of Jesus Christ of Latter-Day Saints*, [2008] 1 WLR 852, where the UK Supreme Court construed the words 'used in connection with the use of place of public worship' as implying a use ancillary to the use of public worship, and not a separate and independent use.

[162] See *RBC Properties Pte Ltd v Defu Furniture Pte Ltd*, [2015] 1 SLR 997.

[163] See rule 8 of the Planning (Development Charges) Rules, Cap. 232, R5.

[164] In Singapore, there are State leases which were granted in the 19th century and the earlier part of the 20th century, with leasehold tenures substantially in excess of 99 years. The market essentially treats land with such leases as freehold land.

development site but with a freehold tenure. This was because, both developers would be paying the same amount of DC, despite the difference in the tenure of their respective development sites. The differential premium system[165] was fairer, in that the amount of differential premium was adjusted lower from the rates given in the DC Table, in cases where the development sites were of leasehold tenure. The difference between DC and DP has since been addressed in the LBC Act, where the LBC (which replaces DC and DP), is adjusted downwards to reflect the leasehold tenure of 99 years or less of any development site.

Generally, the rates in the DC Table lagged behind the prevailing land values at any point in time. This is because the DC Table was published only twice a year, at six-month intervals, whereas property market conditions are dynamic. The DC rates stated in the DC Table at the coming into operation on 1 March each year, would have determined by placing greater weight on the more recent sale evidence in the 6-month period since the coming into operation of the last DC Table on 1 September. Similarly, the DC Table coming into operation on 1 September would have reflected the sales in the 6 months immediately before 1 September. If the land values had been rising since the coming into operation of the prevailing DC Table, one would have expected an increase in the rates in the next DC Table. Conversely, if the land values had been falling, one would have expected the rates in the next DC Table to trend lower. Therefore, one may have seen the phenomenon where developers may have wanted to accelerate the obtaining of planning permission, during a period of rapidly rising land values, so as to avoid being caught by the higher rates in the next half-yearly DC Table. Similarly, where land values were trending lower, one may have seen the phenomenon where developers may have delayed their applications of planning permission, so that the next DC Table with lower DC rates would have applied to their development site.

It may also be observed that almost every box in the DC Table matrix corresponding to each geographical group and each use group, was filled with a rate. However in the half-yearly preparation of the matrix, there may not have been sales of properties in every geographical sector and for every use group in the last 6 months, that would support the rate in each box

---

[165] See discussion on the differential premium system below, in this chapter.

of the matrix. Quite obviously, the rates in many of the boxes in the DC Table, were inserted to reflect the geographical relationship with each other as well as the historical relationship with the earlier DC Table, on the basis of judgments of the relativity of the rates to each other.

The workings of the DC Table were the subject of judicial comment in *Chiu Teng @ Kallang Pte Ltd v Singapore Land Authority*, where Tay Yong Kwang J (as then was) said[166]:

> The DC Table is split across different categories of land use and different geographical sector areas in Singapore. There is a specific rate for each category of land use in each particular sector area. The rates are revised half-yearly in March and September. The rates are not spot valuations but are based on past transactional prices of a preceding six-month period and on the average of such prices in a particular sector area. As the DC Table is a snapshot of rates determined in advance, the DC Table does not necessarily reflect the actual prevailing value of land. In a rising market, the DC Table's rates would be lower than spot valuations. In contrast, a spot valuation assesses the actual value of a piece of land at the time of assessment. A plot of land located in a more desirable location may have a much higher value than another plot of land in the same sector. The Chief Valuer takes into account various factors, including transactions involving similar developments (corrected for differences in time), the natural attributes of the land, its shape, and its accessibility.

While the DC Table was useful in providing a developer with an indication of the quantum of DC that may have been payable on account of his specific development proposal, it may sometimes have produced an excessive DC[167] for a particular development site for various reasons, some of which are as follows:

(a) The rates in the DC Table on a 118 × 9 matrix, by their nature, could only reflect the approximate land value for the entire geographical sector. As a particular development site may have had its own peculiarities such as disamenities, adverse contour and configurations, *etc*, the uniform

---

[166] [2014] 1 SLR 1047 at [10].

[167] Where the application of the DC Table does not give rise to an excessive DC, the developer will accept the quantum of DC.

rate applicable for an entire geographical sector may not have been representative of the value of the particular use for that particular site.

(b) The coming into being of exogenous factors may have rendered the rates in the DC Table no longer relevant. For example, the announcement of the increase of the rates of ABSD which came into effect on 6 July 2018 may have had an immediate dampening effect on residential land values. Such an exogenous factor could not have been reflected in the then prevailing DC Table in operation for the period from 1 March 2018 to 31 August 2018. Any adverse effect of the announcement could only be reflected with the coming into operation of the future DC Table, i.e. the ones coming into operation on or after 1 September 2018.

(c) As the quantum of DC was measured by the difference of the land value rates for two use groups as reflected in the DC Table, the difference may have had given rise to an excessive DC in certain situations due to a substantial increase of the land value rate for a particular use group and geographical sector on account of local factors, without the commensurate increase in the DC rate for another use group. For example, in the DC Table which came into operation on 1 March 2019, the land value rates pertaining to the use group for hotel (i.e. Use Group C) were given an increase of some 25% compared to those in the DC Table which came into operation 6 months earlier on 1 September 2018 due to record prices paid for some hotel sites in the earlier part of 2019[168]. The corresponding increases in respect of land value rates for commercial offices (i.e. Use Group A) in the DC Table which came into operation on 1 March 2019, were more modest on account of the absence or dearth of sales of commercial sites during the same period, to support a more substantial increase in the DC rates for Use Group A. This difference in the rates of increase of the DC rates for Use Groups A and C, resulted in the DC rate for Use Group C (for hotel) overtaking that for Use Group A (for commercial offices) by a substantial margin for the first time in many years for some geographical sectors. This would have resulted in a substantial DC in the case of the development

---

[168] See 'Club St hotel site sets record price for 99-year land at GLS tender,' *The Business Times*, 16 January 2019. The top bid of $562 million for the Club Street hotel site reflected a land value rate of $2,148 per square foot per plot ratio, which was more than 12% above the second highest bid.

of a hotel (which provided for the Development Ceiling) on a site zoned "Commercial" in the Master Plan (which provided for the Development Baseline)[169]. This phenomenon may not have been due to the land values for commercial office sites not rising in line with those of hotel sites. It may be just because there was little evidence from sales transactions to support a higher increase for the land value rates for commercial office sites, at the time of the preparation of the DC Table. This "jerky" increase of land value rates for particular Use Groups in the DC Table in response to particular sales of development sites or those of completed projects during particular periods, may have left some owners with the imposition of amounts of DC that they had not earlier planned for.

4.5. Section 39 valuation

Section 39 of the Planning Act provided for the owner/developer to apply for an alternative basis for computing the DC, i.e. by way of specific valuation of the development site (and not by reference to the DC Table), where he considered the amount of DC provided by the DC Table was excessive[170]. Section 39(3) provided that DC "shall be a prescribed percentage of *any* appreciation in the value of the land arising from the grant of the relevant permission to develop the land". Under section 39(4), the Chief Valuer or such other person as the Minister may appoint shall determine the appreciation in the value of the land. As may be seen the Minister may appoint a valuer other than the Chief Valuer, to conduct the case-by-case valuation under section 39. There is merit in the Minister so appointing another valuer as there may have been a perception that where the Chief Valuer conducted the section 39 valuation, he may be inclined to come up with valuations that were close to those reflected by the DC Table that he has earlier prepared. In other words, he may have been perceived as defending the numbers in the DC Table. In fact, a section 39 valuation need not necessarily have accorded with the valuations in the DC Table as the numbers in the DC Table were generalized approximate ones for

---

[169] See 'High hotel DC rates threaten to throw a spanner in the works for CBD Incentive Scheme,' *The Business Times*, 13 December 2019.

[170] Under the LBC Act, the election for a 'spot valuation' is provided in s 9(3)(a).

an entire geographical sector corresponding to particular use groups. In those uncommon cases where section 39 valuations were requested by the landowners, there may be features pertaining to the development sites concerned which were not or could not possibly have been reflected in the generalized approximate numbers in the DC Table.

The determination of DC under section 39 would usually have involved two valuations of the development site, as at the date of the grant of provisional permission for the proposed development. One valuation was done on the basis of the "Development Baseline" while the other was on the basis of the "Development Ceiling". With this "before and after" approach, where the "Development Ceiling" valuation exceeded the "Development Baseline" valuation, this indicated that there was an appreciation in land value arising from the grant of the planning permission. DC was then levied at 70% of the appreciation. On the other hand, where the "Development baseline" valuation exceeded the "Development Ceiling" valuation, this indicated that there was no appreciation in land value, and hence there was no DC to be levied. The word "any" in section 39(3) envisaged that there may be situations where there was no appreciation in the land value arising from the planning permission. As the then Minister for National Development Mr S Dhanabalan explained in Parliament at the second reading of the Planning (Amendment No. 2) Bill 1989:

> The development charge is a tax levied on a developer when he is allowed to use his land for a purpose that is more valuable than what is prescribed in the Master Plan.

While it may be generally the case that a landowner will propose a development with parameters which may confer a higher land value which gives an appreciation in the land value, there will be situations where the landowner will adopt a development with parameters that does not give such an appreciation in the land value. For example, the landowner may have his special or business reasons for adopting a "Development Ceiling" use of the land which is less valuable than its "Development Baseline" use. For example, a church organization may propose a church building on a valuable piece of land which may be zoned "Residential" in a particular location or a hotel chain may propose a hotel development on a valuable piece of land which may be zoned "Commercial" as it needed to maintain its market share in the location.

Hence, there could be no pre-ordained presumption that the "Development Ceiling" valuation would have always exceeded the "Development Baseline" valuation, and it is wrong to have assumed that the "Development Ceiling" use was the "higher and better" use as compared with the "Development Baseline" use such that a DC was to be levied in all cases. The two valuations of the "Development Ceiling" and "Development Baseline" based on the use and intensity, had to be conducted without any prior assumptions that one of the valuations had always to be greater than the other. For the purpose of illustration, we will use an example of a development site in the Hillview area.

4.5.1. Hillview example

It is of general knowledge that the competent authority's vision of or plan for the Hillview area off Upper Bukit Timah Road is for it to be a wholly residential area[171]. Nevertheless, the Hillview area was formerly a predominantly industrial area. Given its legacy, it is not surprising that there are still a few industrial buildings remaining in the area, although much of the earlier industrial land has been redeveloped into residential developments. The Development Baseline for the industrial properties would be based on its industrial use. However, it is expected that the competent authority would only allow a residential use in line with the Master Plan intentions, if the existing industrial properties were to be redeveloped.

If a DC valuation under section 39 of the Planning Act was required for the redevelopment of an industrial building in the Hillview area to a condominium housing development, the Development Baseline valuation had to be determined for an industrial use. In other words, the remit for the Development Baseline valuation was to value the subject land if it were to be used for an industrial development.

The remit was not to question the possibility of an industrial development on the site. It may well be that the competent authority will only allow a

---

[171] See the 2019 Master Plan, available at the website of the URA.

residential development on the site and that the possibility of any industrial redevelopment in the Hillview area is nil. Yet the valuation hypothesis was that the Development Baseline valuation was to be on the basis of the industrial use under section 39 of the Planning Act. The assumption of the Development Baseline use was required for the statutory valuation under the Planning Act, if there was to be a Development Baseline valuation at all. It would not have been correct to give a depressed or nil valuation for the Development Baseline just because there is no possibility of any industrial redevelopment given the competent authority's planning intentions for the area.

In the above Hillview example, an industrial property if it were to be transacted in the open market, would be on the basis of its potential for residential redevelopment. This is because the market recognizes such potential for residential redevelopment, and may accord the property with a higher value, than that on the basis of a pure industrial use corresponding to the Development Baseline. But the remit under the Planning Act would be to provide the Development Baseline valuation for an industrial use, and the valuer should neither depress nor increase the valuation by taking into account the nature of any other potential use being approved. If the valuer were to take into account the potential redevelopment into residential use in the aforesaid example, this would have provided a higher Development Baseline valuation. Such a valuation will in turn erode or diminish the differential between the Development Ceiling and Development Baseline valuations, and hence would have diminished the quantum of DC.

As may be seen from the above discussion, the *basis of valuation* under section 39 of the Planning Act was that of an assumption of a presence of a hypothetical development as *per* the Development Baseline. No assumption was to be made that any purchaser would in fact pay a higher price for the site in view of the potential for the redevelopment for a condominium housing development, as such an assumption would have the effect of diminishing the quantum of DC. At the same time, no assumption was to be made on any constraints or uncertainties with regard to the Development Baseline, which would depress the Development Baseline valuation and enhance the quantum of DC.

The Hillview site in the above example, cannot be sold in the open market on the basis that it can be redeveloped into an industrial building as such redevelopment would not be permitted by the competent authority, given the planning intentions expressed in the Master Plan for the area. Notwithstanding that fact, the Development Baseline valuation under the Planning Act, had still to be on the hypothetical basis of an industrial redevelopment on the site.

The principle illustrated by the above Hillview example, is that the valuation of the Development Baseline use under the Planning Act, was to be on the hypothetical basis of the Development Baseline use, notwithstanding that that use may even have been precluded by the competent authority.

The above principle cuts both ways. In the above example, the industrial land value (for Development Baseline) is usually lower than the residential land value (for Development Ceiling). We nevertheless have to adhere to the hypothetical basis for the valuation of the industrial land for the Development Baseline. In other instances, the valuation of the Development Baseline use may be higher than the Development Ceiling use. For example, the Development Baseline use may be that of a service station, and the developer chose to build commercial shops on the site which represent the Development Ceiling use. In such case and if based on sales evidence, the Development Baseline exceeded the Development Ceiling, there should be no DC payable. It would be unprincipled to make an argument that since the developer chose to develop commercial shops, the Development Ceiling valuation must be higher than the Development Baseline valuation.

4.6. History of development charge

While the workings of the DC system have been discussed above, it is proposed to briefly discuss the history of DC in Singapore, to provide a greater appreciation of the DC as has been implemented in Singapore since 1964, and also of the new LBC.

When the land use planning legislation in the form of the Planning Ordinance was first introduced in Singapore, there was no levy of DC or betterment charges as a result of an enhancement in land value as a result of land use prescribed under the Master Plan. At the same time, there was to be no compensation for any worsenment of the land value as a result of any adverse prescriptions in the Master Plan. At the second reading of the Planning Bill on 10 September 1958, the then Minister for Local Government, Lands and Housing, Dato Abdul Hamid bin Haji Jumat explained[172]:

> It has now been found impracticable, Sir, to recover betterment charges which have therefore had to be dropped. After very careful consideration, the Government has decided that as there was equally no practicable way of collecting charges for betterment in Singapore, it cannot accept the principle of compensation[173].

This early difficulty in imposing a DC was at least due in part to the fact that there was no existing statutory land use baseline[174], to measure any enhancement in land value for the purpose of computing the DC, as statutory land use zones were only introduced with the coming into operation of the 1958 Master Plan. DC was first introduced some 7 years later on 12 March 1965, with the coming into operation of the Planning (Amendment) Ordinance 1965. At the second reading of the Planning (Amendment) Bill 1964, the then Minister for National Development, Mr Lim Kim San gave the following rationale for the introduction of DC[175]:

> With a view to securing to the state the increases in value of land brought about by community development and not through the efforts of the

---

[172] *Singapore Legislative Assembly Debates, Official Report*, 10 September 1958, col. 751–752.

[173] While the collection of betterment charges are contemplated where the provisions of the Master Plan confer a gain for the owner, reciprocal compensation may have to be contemplated where there is 'down zoning' (e.g. where the zone of the land is changed from a higher-value one to a lower-value one, or where the intensity of development is curtailed) of the land by the Master Plan: see Edward Ti, *An Overlooked Overriding Interest in Singapore's Torrens System?* (2018) 82 Conv 280. The twin issues of compensation and betterment were the subject matter of consideration by the Uthwatt Committee in conjunction with the enactment of the Town and Country Planning Act 1947 in the UK: see Leung Yew Kwong, *Development Land and Development Charge in Singapore* (Butterworths, 1987), p. 133 and Leung Hok Lin, *Redistribution of Land Values* (University of Cambridge, Department of Land Economy, 1979), Occasional Paper No. 11.

[174] This is because until the coming into operation of the Master Plan in 1958, there was no comprehensive document which prescribes the permissible use and the intensity of use.

[175] *Singapore Legislative Assembly Debates, Official Report*, 3 November 1964, vol. 23, col. 146. In TTB Koh and William Lim, *Planning Law and Processes in Singapore*, [1969] 11 Mal LR 315 at 355, the authors nevertheless commented that it was more logical to introduce DC along with the adoption of the Master Plan in 1958.

landowner, the government has considered various measures including the acquisition of development rights in land, the acquisition of the freehold in land, and the freezing of land prices, but after very careful consideration, the government has decided that, as a practicable and immediate measure, a development charge should be made on all written permissions for the development of land beyond the existing permitted use. The broad principle is that any written permission granted which allows development over what is normally permitted in the present Master Plan will attract a development charge. In other words, landowners or other interested persons who will benefit from the grant of permission must pay to the state a part of this benefit in the form of a development charge.

The early DC system was based on prescribed rates. For example, the DC varied between $1,500 and $3,500 for each dwelling house permitted in excess of the allowable intensity under the prevailing Master Plan, depending on the location of the development site[176].

With escalating land values, it was decided to compute DC on the basis of the valuation of the enhancement in land value, arising from the planning permission for each individual development site. This was explained by the then Minister for National Development, Mr Teh Cheang Wan at the second reading of the Planning (Amendment) Bill 1979 as follows[177]:

> The present system of levying development charge for rezoning and for increases in plot ratio and density is based on flat rates. These rates were prescribed in 1965 and are now grossly unrealistic. In addition, the fixed-rate system does not accurately reflect the change in land value arising from rezoning since it does not take into account the original zoning and other factors such as location and accessibility which affect land value. Under the system, development charge is payable on rezoning even though there may be no increase in land value.

---

[176] See Planning (Development Charge) Rules 1965, Sp S 44/1965. In TTB Koh and William Lim, *Planning Law and Processes in Singapore*, [1969] 11 Mal LR 315 at 332, it was mentioned that a high official of the Ministry of National Development verbally stated that the DC was designed to capture between 25% and 50% of the incremental value for the State although it was not apparent how he arrived at the figures.

[177] *Singapore Parliamentary Debates, Official Report*, 11 December 1979, vol. 30, col. 525.

The Bill seeks to give effect to a new and equitable system of levying development charge. Under the new system, development charge will be at a prescribed percentage of the appreciation in land value or at revised fixed rates, whichever is higher. The percentage to be prescribed, under subsidiary legislation, will be 70%. This valuation method will reflect more accurately the increase in land value. The revised fixed rates are intended to serve as a guide to land-owners who wish to submit proposals which require rezoning.

With the coming into operation of the Planning (Amendment) Act 1979[178] and the Planning (Development Charge) Rules 1980[179] on 1 February 1980, DC was essentially levied at 70% of the enhancement in the land value arising from the planning permission, as determined by the Chief Valuer. The valuation of the DC for each development site was done on a case-by-case basis and there was as yet no DC Table until 1 September 1989, some 9½ years later.

The property market took a downward trend from 1982 and there were increasing pressures to reduce the rate of DC. The then Minister for National Development, Mr Lee Yock Suan had to explain the then measures available to developers to reduce their DC in a falling market, in Parliament on 18 March 1982[180]:

Development charge is intended to cream off part of the windfall gains from increases in land values arising from approvals to develop land not in conformity with the Master Plan. It is based on 70% of the increase in land value as determined on a case-by-case basis by the Chief Valuer. This system is fair to all, since land value varies widely from locality to locality and at different points in time. Development charges are as high or as low as property prices at the time of approval of the development project. In the event that developers dispute the quantum of development charge, there is an avenue of appeal to the Minister.

---

[178] No. 31 of 1979.

[179] S 129/1980.

[180] *Singapore Parliamentary Debates, Official Report*, 18 March 1982, vol. 4, col 1136 and 1137.

The present procedure for the determination of development charge ensures that development is not discouraged. Development charge is determined at the date of the grant of in-principle approval and remains valid for a period of 12 months or until written permission is issued, whichever is earlier. This protects the developer in both a rising as well as a falling property market. In a rising market, with development charge determined on the date of in-principle approval, the developer is protected for up to one year from having to pay higher development charges from rising land values. In a property downturn, the developer can get a new determination of development charge after the expiry of 12 months to benefit from falling land values. Alternatively, he can abort his original planning application before the 12-month period and resubmit for a new in-principle approval upon which development charge will be determined.

When the property market deteriorated, the rate of DC was reduced on 1 June 1985 from 70% to 50% of the enhancement in land value arising from any planning permission[181]. The DC Table was only introduced from 1 September 1989. At the second reading of the Planning (Amendment No. 2) Bill in Parliament, the then Minister of National Development explained the rationale for the introduction of the DC Table[182]:

... this new system is a simpler way of computing the development charge. The present development charge system requires the Chief Valuer to determine the enhancement of land value arising from each and every development approval when it is granted. Not only is this time-consuming but it also makes it difficult for the developer to know how much development charge is payable at the outset when he has to assess the viability of his development. For example, somebody may want to buy a piece of land where the plot ratio is, say, 1.2. But he is thinking in terms of developing something with a plot ratio of 2, or he might buy a piece of land where the density is 125 persons per hectare, and he might want to buy the piece of land to build something of 250 persons per hectare. Before he buys the piece of land he must know what development charge

---

[181] See Planning (Development Charges) (Amendment) Rules 1985, S 162/1985.
[182] *Singapore Parliamentary Debates, Official Report*, 4 August 1989, vol. 54, col 440.

he would have to pay in order to calculate the viability of the project. At present he would not know the development charge until he actually submits an application for developer and the valuer has valued that piece of land. Based on difference in valuation for the changed use, a certain development charge would be levied. So he would not know the development charge before he buys the piece of land.

Clause 9 of the Bill will introduce a simpler system which will enable the development charge to be computed in accordance with a set of prescribed rates determined by the Chief Valuer and with a definite method of calculation.

The DC Table which had been in operation for more than 30 years, was updated half yearly, with a new DC Table coming into operation on 1 March and 1 September each year. The corresponding Table of Rates for the LBC is now published pursuant to section 65 of the LBC Act.

5. Differential Premium

As may be seen from the above discussion, DC was levied in cases where the development land was not the subject of a State lease which required a varying of the restrictive covenants, for the purpose of an intensification or change of the use of the land. Where the land was the subject of such State leases, the betterment arising from the grant of planning permission, was levied by way of a differential premium (DP)[183]. Unlike DC which was charged as a tax under the provisions of the Planning Act, DP was collected by the State in its capacity as the lessor of the land, in exercise of its contractual rights where the lessee sought an amendment of the terms of the lease. Both DC and DP have been replaced by the LBC which is a tax levied under the LBC Act.

Where the State land was earlier sold, the price charged for the State land correlated with the nature and intensity of use of the land as specified

---

[183] For cases where the background facts concerned DP, see *RBC Properties Pte Ltd v Defu Furniture Pte Ltd*, [2015] 1 SLR 997 (which concerned the change of use of part of an industrial building for use as a furniture showroom) and *Parkway Properties Pte Ltd and another v United Artists Singapore Theatres Pte Ltd and Another*, [2003] 2 SLR(R) 103 (which concerned Parkway Parade Shopping Centre where the lessee proposed the addition of a cineplex to the shopping center).

in the State lease[184]. Hence where subsequent to the sale of the State land, the lessee obtains planning approval from the competent authority for a proposed development which is a higher-value use, the lessee is getting a higher-value commodity as compared what he has paid for earlier, to the lessor (i.e. the State). To be able to benefit from the planning approval, the lessee would first have to get the lessor (i.e. the State), to amend the terms of the lease, to accord with the terms of the planning approval. If the State (in its capacity as the lessor) were to vary the title restrictions in the State title to accord with the parameters in terms of nature and intensity of use of the land, given by the planning approval, it would have in exercise of its contractual rights, demanded a DP, the amount of which reflected the enhancement in the land value.

The charging of a premium by the State for the varying of title restrictions in a lease in Hong Kong was the subject matter of the Privy Council case of *Hang Wah Chong Investment Co Ltd v Attorney-General of Hong Kong*[185]. In that case, the appellant was the lessee of Crown land in Hong Kong which it held as successors-in-title to a company which had earlier purchased the right to a 75-year lease at a public auction in 1931. The conditions of sale restricted the development on the land to that of detached and semi-detached houses. In 1973, the appellant made plans to redevelop the land for four blocks of flats and applied to the Director of Public Works for a modification of the conditions of sale. In that case, the Director of Public Works besides his responsibilities under the Building Ordinance, was also acting as the Crown's land agent. It was held in that case, that the Director acting in his capacity as the Crown's land agent, could demand the payment of the premium, for the modification of the conditions of sale. Lord Edmund-Davies in delivering the judgment of the Privy Council said at page 1146:

---

[184] It would seem that in respect of State leases granted before 1991, while the nature of the use may be specified under the terms of the leases, the plot ratio may not have been stated: see 'Most CBD sites won't benefit from lower DP', *The Business Times*, 2 August 2000. In such cases, where there was to be a change in the plot ratio but no change in the nature of the use, there would have been no necessity to change the terms of the State lease. Consequently, DP could not have been charged. Instead, DC was charged as a tax under the Planning Act, where the Development Ceiling exceeded the Development Baseline.

[185] [1981] 1 WLR 1141.

It is sufficient, for present purposes, to say that, the applicant's seeking a concession from the landlords in relation to the development of land leased, the landlords were entitled to make the granting of that concession conditional upon the payment of a premium.

In Singapore, in respect of State leases which have title restrictions on the nature and intensity of use of the land, there may also be a clause in the leases which specifically provides for the payment of DP. Such a DP clause will typically read as follows[186]:

> The demised land shall not be used for other than the abovementioned development except with the prior permission of the Lessor. The lessee shall be required to pay a differential premium, as appropriate, in respect of any increase in floor area or change of use from a lower use category to higher use category from the existing use which will result in an enhanced value.

Where there are such title restrictions under the terms of the State lease, the lessee will have to apply to the lessor (as represented by SLA), to have the restrictions amended or lifted, upon the issue of the provisional permission (PP) by the Chief Planner[187]. Before 31 July 2000, SLA used to charge a DP which was computed on the *full* enhancement in value. There were pressures to align the amount of DP with that of DC which was levied at 70% of the enhancement in value, arising from the planning permission. There were also public comments that while the computation of DC by means of the DC Table was transparent, the case-by-case valuation of the DP was not so. Technically, there was no legal requirement to align the DP which was collected by the State in exercise of its contractual rights, with the DC which was collected as a tax pursuant to the provisions of the Planning Act. Nevertheless, on 31 July 2000 the Government decided to align the amount

---

[186] See *Chiu Teng @ Kallang Pte Ltd v Singapore Land Authority* [2014] 1 SLR 1047 at [4]. The terms 'lower use category' and 'higher use category' in the DP clause, refer to 'land uses which give lower value' and 'land uses which give higher value', respectively.

[187] See the Circular issued jointly by the Singapore Land Authority and the URA on 1 July 2013, in respect of *Revised Procedure for Development Applications Involving Lifting of Title Restrictions and Payment of Differential Premium*.

of the DP with that of the DC and the SLA circular issued in relation to the DP system stated as follows:

1 With effect from 31 Jul 2000, the Singapore Land Authority has implemented a transparent system of determination of differential premium (DP) for the lifting of State title restrictions involving change of use and/or increase in intensity. This is to encourage optimisation of land use and to facilitate the overall pace of redevelopment in Singapore. It will also provide greater certainty to landowners who will now be able to compute the DP payable themselves.

2 The determination of DP will be based on the published Table of Development Charge (DC) rates. The material date of determination of DP will be pegged to the date of Provisional Planning Permission (PP) or the start date of the validity of the second and subsequent PP extensions, similar to DC. The prevailing Table of DC rates at the date of grant of PP will be used.

3 In addition, where tenure of the land is leasehold, the DC rates will be adjusted to reflect the residual tenure of the land. In this regard, a Leasehold Table, which expresses the value of the residual tenure as a percentage of freehold value, will be applied to the DC rates to determine the DP payable. A copy of the Leasehold Table is at Appendix 1.

4 Where the use as spelt out in a particular title restriction does not fit into any of the Use Groups in the Table of DC Rates, the DP payable will be determined by the Chief Valuer on a case-by-case basis.

Although the computation of the DP was to be aligned with the computation of the DC, as may be seen from the Circular, the DP system had a feature which the DC system did not have. In respect of DP, where the tenure of the development site was leasehold, the rates in the DC Table were adjusted lower to reflect the actual leasehold tenure of the development site concerned. The computation of DC using the DC Table on the other hand, did not have this feature of downward adjustment for the leasehold tenure of the development site concerned. This disparity between the computations of DC and DP, may not have caused substantial grievances in practice, as most of the development sites (with State leases) of leasehold tenures of less than 99 years would have gone under the DP system, which accorded the adjustments for leasehold tenures. On the other hand, development land with freehold or long leasehold tenures in excess of 99 years (where their land titles would generally not restrict the nature and intensity the use of the land), would have gone under the DC system, and such land of with long-term tenures did not require the adjustments for leasehold tenures. Nevertheless with DC and DP being replaced by the LBC which may be adjusted lower for leasehold tenures of 99 years or less, this difference between DC and DP is a matter of history.

The leasehold value table[188] in Appendix 1 of the SLA Circular is reproduced in Table 3. It shows leasehold values as a percentage of freehold value. For example, according to the table, the value of a piece of land with a remaining term of 30 years is 60% of its freehold value, and the value of a piece of land with a remaining term of 60 years is 80% of its freehold value.

The payment of DP in relation to land which was subject to State leases with title restrictions, however did not result in double payment (i.e. first the payment of DP to SLA (as agent of the State) and another payment of DC to URA which was collected as a tax). Where DP was paid to SLA in respect of a particular proposed development, no DC needed to be paid to URA in respect of the same proposed development. This exemption from DC was provided in rule 8 of the Planning (Development Charge — Exemption) Rules which read as follows[189]:

> A person shall be exempted from liability to pay any development charge under section 35 of the Act for any development of land authorised on or after 1st March 2001 if the land is the subject of a lease from the State and

---

[188] The SLA leasehold table available on the SLA website, was used by the valuers giving expert evidence in *Su Ah Tee and others v Allister Lim and Thrumurgan (sued as a firm) and another (William Cheng and others, third parties)*, [2014] SGHC 159. See the article, 'Determining the value of leasehold land: A closer look at 'Bala's Table',' *CLC Insights*, Issue No. 20 (November 2016), on the background and explanation of the SLA leasehold table, formerly referred to as Bala's Table', being named after the Land Office valuer who first drew up the table for the computation of land values for leases of various terms. The Land Office later became part of the SLA. *CLC Insights* is a publication of the Centre of Liveable Cities.

[189] Cap. 232, R6. This exemption rule is obviously to avoid a double charge (i.e. both DP and DC being levied) in respect of the same development proposal.

Table 3: Leasehold values as a percentage of freehold value.

Term of Years	Percentage (%) of Freehold Value	Term of Years	Percentage (%) of Freehold Value	Term of Years	Percentage (%) of Freehold Value
1	3.8	32	61.9	63	81.8
2	7.5	33	62.8	64	82.4
3	10.9	34	63.7	65	83.0
4	14.1	35	64.6	66	83.6
5	17.1	36	65.4	67	84.2
6	19.9	37	66.2	68	84.5
7	22.7	38	67.0	69	85.4
8	25.2	39	67.7	70	86.0
9	27.7	40	68.5	71	86.5
10	30.0	41	69.2	72	87.0
11	32.2	42	69.8	73	87.5
12	34.3	43	70.5	74	88.0
13	36.3	44	71.2	75	88.5
14	38.2	45	71.8	76	89.0
15	40.0	46	72.4	77	89.5
16	41.8	47	73.0	78	90.0
17	43.4	48	73.6	79	90.5
18	45.0	49	74.1	80	91.0
19	46.6	50	74.7	81	91.4
20	48.0	51	75.2	82	91.8
21	49.5	52	75.7	83	92.2
22	50.8	53	76.2	84	92.6
23	52.1	54	76.7	85	92.9
24	53.4	55	77.3	86	93.3
25	54.6	56	77.9	87	93.6
26	55.8	57	78.5	88	94.0
27	56.9	58	79.0	89	94.3
28	58.0	59	79.5	90	94.6
29	59.0	60	80.0	91	94.8
30	60.0	61	80.6	92	95.0
31	61.0	62	81.2	93	95.2

Table 3: (*Continued*)

Term of Years	Percentage (%) of Freehold Value	Term of Years	Percentage (%) of Freehold Value	Term of Years	Percentage (%) of Freehold Value
94	95.4	98	95.9		
95	95.6	99	96.0		
96	95.7				
97	95.8				

land premium has been paid or is payable or required to be paid to the President —

    (a) by virtue of the development being not in accordance with the use of the land, or in excess of the maximum allowable intensity or plot ratio, specified in the lease; or

    (b) for the purpose of first specifying in the lease —

        (i) any restriction as to the use of the land; or

        (ii) the maximum allowable intensity or plot ratio for the development of the land.

However, there were cases where the State lands were earlier alienated directly to the lessee, without the requirement for competitive tender. In such cases, SLA may charge the DP by way of "spot valuation" by the Chief Valuer at 100% of the enhancement of the land value, and not by reference to the DC Table. This is now provided for in section 8(2) of the LBC Act. Such leases typically have a "land return" clause which reads as follows[190]:

The Lessee shall notify the Lessor in writing of such portions of the demised land which are not used for the purposes specified. If directed by the Lessor, the Lessee shall surrender to the Lessor such land not used for the purposes specified at rates equivalent to the compensation payable for

---

[190] See *Chiu Teng @ Kallang Pte Ltd v Singapore Land Authority*, [2014] 1 SLR 1047 at [4] and [62]. Besides the Kallang Avenue site (on which the development known as CT Hub has been built) which was the subject matter of the *Chiu Teng* case where DP was charged at 100% of the enhancement in land value, the other site mentioned in the case where DP was also charged at 100% of the enhancement in land value, was the Market Street car park site which has since been developed into the office development known as CapitaGreen situated at No. 138 Market Street.

such land if it had been acquired under the Land Acquisition Act on the date of the direction.

Provided that if the Lessor does not issue a direction for the surrender of such land within 1 year from the said notification by the Lessee under this clause or within such other period as may otherwise be mutually agreed between the Lessor and the Lessee, the Lessor shall, at the request of the Lessee, lift the restrictions in the Lease under [the DP Clause] in relation only to such land; subject to the Lessee obtaining the necessary approvals from the relevant authorities regarding the proposed use of such lands and the payment of a differential premium under [the DP Clause].

The rationale of the SLA for charging the DP at 100% of the enhancement in land value was stated in *Chiu Teng @ Kallang Pte Ltd v Singapore Land Authority* as follows[191]:

The SLA averred that it was not unreasonable for the DP to be assessed by a spot valuation at 100% value. It was in the interests of the public for the State to realise the full value of any land that it disposes of. Where directly alienated land is concerned, the State is in fact forfeiting its legal right to take back the land (pursuant to the Land Return Clause) and the chance to re-sell the land at a higher price in a competitive tender. The State must ensure that it obtains a DP that fully and accurately reflects the enhancement in value that the state is foregoing. Indeed, the SLA was merely discharging its statutory duties and functions. Section 6(1)(*a*) of the Singapore Land Authority Act (Cap. 301, 2002 Rev Ed) ("the SLA Act") states that it shall be the function and duty of the SLA "to optimise land resources". This necessarily entails a duty on SLA's part to obtain the full enhancement on land value where directly-alienated state lands are concerned.

In the opinion of the authors, even where the LBC (which replaced the DP) is to be charged at the *full* enhancement in value, useful reference may

---

[191] [2014] 1 SLR 1047 at [62]. In the *Chiu Teng* case, the High Court was receptive to the application of the doctrine of substantive legitimate expectations in Singapore. However, the state of the law on the reception of this doctrine in Singapore has yet to be settled: see *SGB Starkstrom Pte Ltd v Commissioner of Labour* [2016] 3 SLR 598, *Kardachi Jason Aleksander v Attorney-General* [2020] 2 SLR 1190, *Tan Hon Leong Eddie v Attorney-General* [2021] SGHC 196, Swati Jhaveri, 'The doctrine of substantive legitimate expectations: the significance of *Chiu Teng@Kallang Pte Ltd v Singapore Land Authority*, [2016] *Public Law* 1 and Eugene Tan, 'Commercial Judicial Review in Singapore: Strategic or Spontaneous', [2020] *Singapore Journal of Legal Studies* 448.

still be made to the Table of Rates prescribed under the LBC Act (formerly the DC Table) for the purpose. This is because although the rates in the Table of Rates are computed on the basis of 70% of the enhancement in value, one needs only to gross up the rates by the factor of 100/70, to derive the rate which reflects the full enhancement in value. Indeed, this had been done in respect of DC affecting "business zone commercial uses" where DC is charged at 100% of the enhancement in value[192]. Using the published Table of Rates to compute the LBC where the charge is to be computed on the basis of 100% of the enhancement in value pursuant to section 8(2) of the LBC Act, will provide certainty and transparency to the landowner.

5.1. "Topping up" premium

The LBC (formerly the DP) is levied where the proposed use of the land in terms of its nature and intensity does not accord with the terms of original State title and a varying of the restrictive covenants is required. The developer of the development site, in addition to proposing a use which does not accord with the terms of the original State title, may also want to extend the remaining term of the lease which may be less than 99 years, such that he has a full 99-year lease for the purpose of development[193]. Such an extension or topping up of the lease term is especially crucial in the case of the development of residential units for sale, as new residential units with leasehold tenures of substantially less than 99 years are not very marketable.

Where the SLA approves of such an extension of the term of the State lease, a "topping up" premium is payable to the SLA. The valuation of the "topping up" premium for a development, is done by the Chief Valuer, on a case by case[194]. As any valuation is to an extent subjective, the amount of "topping up" premium imposed, may be a matter of contention. There is no independent tribunal, to which a developer may make an appeal against the

---

[192] See Planning (Development Charges) Rules, Cap. 232, R5.

[193] Technically, the extension of the lease takes the form of the surrender of the existing lease and the re-grant of a fresh 99-year lease.

[194] See para 8 of the SLA Circular on *The Differential Premium System*, updated on 25 November 2010, available on the SLA website.

amount of "topping up" premium that is imposed. Strictly, the matter of the "topping up" premium does not fall within the scope of the LBC Act.

In the view of the authors, just as the computation of the LBC with the use of the Table of Rates under the LBC Act, has become a transparent exercise, it is possible to compute the "topping up" premium through the combined use of the Table of Rates and the SLA leasehold table, in a transparent exercise. Presently this valuation of the "topping up" premium is an opaque exercise within an otherwise largely transparent process for the computation of the LBC. This anomaly may be addressed, through the use of the Table of Rates and the SLA leasehold table, both of which are already readily available to the public. Through the use of the two tables, the 99-year leasehold value as well as the leasehold value corresponding to the actual remaining term of the State lease concerned, may be computed. The difference between those two leasehold values, will provide the amount of the "topping-up" premium.

6. Extension charges under the Residential Property Act

The matter of extension charges[195] levied under section 31(5A) of the Residential Property Act, is discussed here as those charges may have a significant impact on the finances of the developer, although they are not in essence a levy imposed in respect of the use of the development land.

The Residential Property Act has its genesis in the early 1970s when there was an escalation of property prices[196]. The Government in a press statement on 10 September 1973, announced that the restriction of the purchase of residential properties to Singapore citizens was to take effect the following day. Nevertheless, foreign developers[197] are allowed to buy residential land for development, as they add competition to the market and will be contributing to the supply of properties on to the housing market,

---

[195] Often referred to as QC charges, as the extension charges are paid where the terms of the conditions of the Qualifying Certificate issued to the developer under the Residential Property Act, have been breached.

[196] See 'The Residential Property Act: Citizenship and its entitlements,' *CLC Insights,* Issue No. 58, July 2020, Centre of Liveable Cities.

[197] Generally refer to any development company where any of its directors or shareholders are non-Singapore citizens.

which in turn will help to moderate the escalation of residential property prices.

The foreign developers are however required to apply for qualifying certificates (QCs) for such purchases under section 31 of the Residential Property Act[198]. From 6 February 2020 however, housing developers which are listed on the Singapore Exchange and which have a substantial connection to Singapore, may be exempted from the QC regime. Any application for the QC exemption by the listed housing developers is to be assessed according to the following criteria: (a) incorporation in Singapore; (b) primary listing is on the Singapore Exchange and principal place of business is Singapore; (c) the chairperson and the majority of the company's board are Singapore citizens; (d) a significant Singaporean substantial shareholding interest in the company; and (e) track record of developments in Singapore[199]. Where the substantial shareholding interest in the listed company is in the hands of non-Singapore citizens, the company will not be exempted from the application of a QC in the acquisition of residential properties.

For foreign developers not otherwise exempt, the conditions for the issue of QCs require compliance with a project completion period (PCP) where the developers are given 5 years from the date of the issue of the QC or the date of the collective sale order (whichever is applicable) to complete the project and another 2 years to sell all the units after the completion of the project. The purpose of the PCP is to prevent the hoarding or speculation in residential land[200]. A developer is usually able to comply with the 5-year period given for the completion of the development. He may however not be able to sell all the units developed, by the prescribed deadline. In that case,

---

[198] Before 20 July 2005, 43 foreign companies (principally developers which were listed on the Singapore Exchange), were exempted from having to apply for QCs in the purchase of residential land for development. With the revocation which took effect from 20 July 2005, those foreign companies had to apply for QCs in such purchases like all other foreign companies: see SLA website.

[199] See *Publicly Listed Housing Developers with Substantial Connection to Singapore to be Exempted from Qualifying Certificate Regime*, Press Release on 6 February 2020 by the Ministry of Law and the SLA. The restrictions of the Residential Property Act have been relaxed for the developers: see for example, Residential Property (Amara Holdings — Exemption) Notification 2020, S 710/2020, and Residential Property (Yanlord Land Group Limited — Exemption) Notification 2021, S 145/2021.

[200] See the speech of the Minister of Law, Mr K Shanmugam at the second reading of the Residential Property (Amendment) Bill 2010 on 22 November 2010. With the COVID-19 outbreak in 2020, there have been calls to review the PCP deadlines: see 'Time to review Project Completion Period deadlines,' *The Business Times*, 26 March 2020.

the developer may apply for an extension of the PCP. For such extension, the Controller of Residential Property imposes an extension charge under section 31(5A)[201] of the Residential Property Act, at 8% of the price at which the developer earlier bought the development land, for the first year of extension. The amount of extension charges may be pro-rated downwards to take into account the percentage of units which have already been sold by the prescribed deadline.

Part of the extension charge may be refunded, if the developer eventually does not need the full extension year to sell all the units. Where the developer thinks that he could sell all the units within the next half year, he may first pay half the annual extension charge and apply for further extension where necessary. Where the PCP goes into an extension for the second and third years, the rates of the extension charge increase to 16% and 24%, respectively[202]. The QC charges paid under the Residential Property Act are in addition to any clawback of the ABSD remission, which the developer has to bear under the Stamp Duties Act for the breach of the stricter ABSD rules of completing and selling all residential units within a 5-year period.

With the COVID-19 outbreak when circuit breaker measures were put in place from 7 April 2020, the PCP under the QCs was extended by 6 months, in respect of cases which satisfied both of the following conditions: (a) the QC is issued on or before 1 June 2020; and (b) the original timeline for the completion and sale of the residential units expired on or after 1 February 2020[203]. The 6-month extension of the PCP was given as there were suspensions of construction works, operations at housing developers' sales galleries and home viewings.

It is to be noted that in respect of sites with leases which are extended to a term of 99 years by the SLA, the SLA also imposes a PCP (whether or not

---

[201] Inserted by the Residential Property (Amendment) Act 2010, (Act 35 of 2010), which came into operation on 17 January 2011.

[202] The rates of 8%, 16% and 24% for the extension charges are indicated on the website of the SLA. The rates of extension charges and the requirement for the developer to provide a banker's guarantee of at least 10% of the purchase price of the land for its obligations under the qualifying certificate, were also mentioned in *Yoo Design Services Limited v Iliv Realty Pte Limited* [2021] EWCA Civ 560. In that English case, the interior designer based in England sued the Singapore developer for fees which were contingent upon the sale of the apartments built by the developer.

[203] *Temporary Relief Measures for Property Sector due to Coronavirus Disease (COVID-19) Pandemic*, Joint Press Release by the Ministries of National Development, Finance, Law and Trade & Industry on 6 May 2020.

the developer requires a QC) as a condition for the extension of the leases. Where an extension of the PCP is applied for and given, extension charges will also be applicable for such cases. The extension charges are however computed on the "topping up" premium paid for the extension of the lease, and not on the value of the entire development site.

For development sites sold under the GLS program since 1 May 2000, developers have to comply with a PCP for the completion of the project under the contractual terms of the sales which provide for the extension charges[204]. Before that date, the mechanism for enforcing the PCP for land sold under the GLS program, was to require the developer to pay liquidated damages at a rate of 2% of the land premium for each month of delay in the completion of the project. The switch from liquidated damages to extension charges was prompted by two considerations: (a) liquidated damages where interpreted as a penalty, is potentially unenforceable legally; and (b) the requirement to pay the extension charges prior to the PCP deadline as compared to the situation where liquidated damages are only triggered after the stipulated completion date, is considered more effective in encouraging developers to detect and resolve problems leading to any delay in the completion[205].

---

[204] The contractual PCP applies to commercial and industrial sites sold under the GLS program as well.

[205] See *Working with Markets: Harnessing Market Forces and Private Sector for Development*, Urban Systems Studies Series (Centre for Liveable Cities, 2017), p. 66 and 67.

CHAPTER 4

Real Estate Developers: A Much Regulated Sector

1. Introduction

In the Singapore context, the term "developer" is usually associated with a company that develops properties in the private sector for the purposes of sale[1]. As the product of a housing developer (i.e. the homes that it builds) interfaces with the public at large and the price to be paid by the man-in-the-street for the product represents a significant investment on his part, the operations of the developer in the private sector are regulated by the provisions of the Housing Developers (Control and Licensing) Act. The real estate market is also influenced by the supply of development land by the Government through the Government Land Sales program which is the main source of the land supply for new developments. The sale of land under the program is by way of open tender. The development land is normally awarded to the tenderer with the highest bid[2], subject to the bid

---

[1] In *Mount Elizabeth (Pte) Ltd v Comptroller of Income Tax*, [1985–1986] SLR(R) 950 at [28], Chan Sek Keong JC (as he then was) made the observation that 'a company which describes its business as a property development or itself as property developer is *prima facie* carrying on the business of property development for sale'. The largest developer of all is the Housing and Development Board which develops public housing which accommodates the vast majority of households in Singapore.

[2] Some land usually that for non-residential projects or where the non-residential component is a major part of the project, in prime locations may be sold through a Concept and Price Revenue approach, where tenderers are required to submit their concept proposals and their tender bids in two separate envelopes. Only tenders with concepts which substantially satisfy the evaluation criteria, will proceed to the next stage where their second envelope on their tender bids will be opened at which point, the site will be awarded to the highest bidder.

being not less than 85% of the estimated market value (which forms the reserve price) as determined by the Chief Valuer appointed under section 3(1) of the State Lands Act[3] whose function is to carry out valuations of State land for disposal as provided under section 4(1)(a) of the Act. The Chief Valuer submits his valuation at the close of the tender and does not have prior knowledge of the bids made by the various tenderers. The reserve price however is not disclosed so as not to influence the bids and to discourage cartel bidding.[4]

The developer company of residential properties is also subject to the provisions of the Residential Property Act[5] where any of its directors and shareholders are not Singapore citizens and is required to apply for a qualifying certificate when it acquires residential land for development.[6] The various taxes in Singapore also impact the developer, with some of the tax statutes having specific provisions pertaining to developers. We will start the discussion with stamp duty which in recent years has assumed particular importance, especially since the introduction of additional buyer's stamp duty (ABSD) in December 2011.

---

[3] Cap 314.

[4] *The Government Land Sales Programme: Turning Plans into Reality,* Urban Systems Studies series (Centre of Liveable Cities, 2021), p 52. Nevertheless in the case of sites on URA's Reserve List, an applicant may test the reserve price. Where an applicant submits a minimum tender price which is accepted by the Government, the Reserve List site is then put by for competitive tender. The applicant who submitted the minimum tender price to trigger the tender process, is obliged to make a bid at the competitive tender stage at no less than the minimum tender price earlier indicated. Equally, there is some sense of obligation on the part of the Government to award the site even if it turns out that there is only a single bid at the competitive tender stage, since the Government has earlier indicated that the minimum tender price was acceptable. With respect to the residential and hotel use site at Marina View, the Government awarded the site to the IOI Property Group on 29 September 2021, which made the sole bid which was $101 above the minimum tender price it has earlier indicated to trigger the tender process.

[5] Cap 274.

[6] With effect from 6 February 2020, a publicly listed housing developer may apply for exemption from the Qualifying Certificate regime where it has a 'substantial connection to Singapore'. Amongst other things, there must be a significant Singaporean substantial shareholding in the company. In this regard, a housing developer will be considered to have such shareholding, if Singaporean shareholders from the same family collectively hold at least 30% in the total voting rights and issued shares in the company. However, the largest single foreign substantial shareholder must hold not more than 30% of the voting rights and issued shares in the company.

2. Stamp Duty

2.1. Additional Buyer's Stamp Duty

A housing developer acquiring a residential development site, has to pay a buyer's stamp duty (BSD) of nearly 4% of the consideration[7]. In addition, he has to pay a non-remittable ABSD of 5% of the consideration. Effectively, he has to pay close to 9% of stamp duty up-front at the time of acquisition of the development site. In addition, there is a sum of ABSD amounting to 35% of the consideration, which may potentially be payable if the developer does not complete and sell all the housing units of the development within 5 years[8] of the acquisition of the development site. If at the end of the 5-year period, the developer does not manage to complete[9] and sell all the housing units, the 35% ABSD with interest at 5% per annum[10] has to be paid to the Commissioner of Stamp Duties. As may be seen, stamp duty may amount to almost 44% of the consideration for the development site[11], where the developer has to pay the full extent of the ABSD. In the case where a developer purchases a

---

[7] The duty on the first tranche of $180,000 of the consideration is levied at 1%, the duty on the second tranche of $180,000 is at 2%, the duty on the third tranche of $640,000 is at 3%, and the duty of any amount of the consideration in excess of $1 million is at 4%, as provided in Article 3(a)(iii)(A) of the First Schedule to the Stamp Duties Act.

[8] For developments of 4 housing units or less, the prescribed period is 3 years. In some large sites (comprising residential components) sold under the Government Land Sales program, the developer may be given up to 7 years to complete the project, but the requirement to sell all the housing flats within 5 years of the award of the site if ABSD is not to be paid, remains, as in the case of the residential and hotel site at Marina View awarded to the IOI Properties Group on 29 September 2021.

[9] There is usually no difficulty in complying with the milestones for the development of the site, except during the period of the COVID-19 pandemic in 2020. The difficulty usually encountered in compliance with the conditions for ABSD remission, concerns the sale of all the housing units within the prescribed period.

[10] The Commissioner charges an interest, as the ABSD is technically chargeable as at the time of acquisition of the site and is remitted on the condition that all the housing units are to be completed and sold within 5 years of the date of acquisition of the site. The interest for the entire 5-year period, is 25% on the ABSD payable. If say at the end of the 4th year, the developer thinks that he is unable to meet the 5-year deadline in any case, he may choose to pay up the ABSD earlier and an interest of 20% on the ABSD, for the 4-year period that the ABSD is not paid. For the years 2019 and 2020, about 85% of developments by licensed housing developers met the 5-year deadline: Minister of Finance Mr Lawrence Wong's Parliamentary reply on 1 November 2021.

[11] The increased amount of ABSD came into operation on 6 July 2018, after a sharp increase of 9.1% in residential property prices in the past year compared with a gradual decline for close to 4 years before then, and after developers started bidding aggressively for development land: see Joint Press Release by the Ministry of Finance, Ministry of National Development and the Monetary Authority of Singapore on 5 July 2018. The latest enhancement of ABSD rates came into operation on 16 December 2021.

development site *via* an *en bloc* sale, the Commissioner of Stamp Duties is prepared to consider the commencement of the 5-year prescribed period for the completion and sale of all the residential units, to be from the date of the Collective Sale Order issued by the Strata Titles Board under the Land Titles (Strata) Act. Where there is an appeal to the High Court or the Court of Appeal, the Commissioner is prepared to consider the commencement of the 5-year prescribed period to be the date of approval by the High Court or the Court of Appeal, as the case may be.[12]

If at the end of the 5-year period, the developer has only a few housing units left unsold, he may choose to sell the remaining units at reduced prices where necessary, so as not to incur the 35% ABSD on the original land price. Alternatively, if he considers that there may be a chance that the prices will recover in the future, he may choose to sell the units to a related company, which has to bear the stamp duty on the acquisition of the housing units. The BSD on the consideration of the housing units for the intra-group transfer may however be remitted under section 15 of the Stamp Duties Act if the relevant conditions are satisfied. The ABSD of 35% on the consideration of the housing units for the intra-group transfer, has to be paid by the transferee company and may not be remitted. Quite obviously, if the number of units left unsold at the end of the prescribed period is large, it may not be worthwhile to effect the intra-group transfer and incur the 35% ABSD computed on the consideration for the housing units, in order to avoid the clawback of the 35% ABSD on the original land price together with the interest at 5% per annum for 5 years.

The time table for the completion and sale of the housing units may be onerous considering that there are also the following measures that curb the demand by potential purchasers:

(a) Purchasers have to pay the 4% BSD on the consideration for the housing units. In addition, a Singapore-citizen purchaser has to pay an ABSD of 17% on his second residential property and 25% on his third and subsequent residential property, whereas permanent resident purchasers have to pay ABSD of 5% on his first residental property, 25%

---

[12] See the relevant page of the IRAS website on this matter.

on his second residential property and 30% on his third and subsequent residential properties. Foreigners buying any residential property have to pay an ABSD of 30%, whereas entities buying any residential property pays an ABSD of 35%.

(b) Loan-to-Value (LTV) limits on the first, second and third housing loans of 75%, 45% and 35%, respectively for individual borrowers. Where the loan tenure exceeds 30 years or extends past the age of 65 for the borrowers, the LTV limits drop to 55%, 25% and 15% for the first, second and third housing loans, respectively. For non-individual borrowers, the LTV limit is 15%.

(c) the Total Debt Servicing Ratio (TDSR) will impose limits on what a person may be able to borrow on the housing loan.

Housing developers building more than 4 housing units, are licensed and regulated under the Housing Developers (Control and Licensing) Act[13]. In granting a licence under section 4(5) of that Act, the Controller of Housing may impose conditions. The Controller may grant a "sale" licence to a licensed housing developer, which may allow the housing developer to sell the housing units even before the units are completed. Such a licence will assist the housing developer in complying with the 5-year "complete and sell" time frame under the ABSD conditions, and will provide him with incoming cash flows as the construction progresses.

The Controller of Housing may however grant a "no sale" licence to a housing developer, where the housing developer may only be allowed to sell the housing units upon the issue of the Temporary Occupation Permit (TOP) of the development. The Controller is known to have issued "no sale" licences, where there have been complaints of shoddy workmanship in the other residential projects of a housing developer and its related companies. However, the Controller of Housing may allow the sale of the housing units before the issue of TOP, where the developer undertakes to complete a Quality Mark assessment of all the units before applying for TOP[14]. The "no sale" licence or the undertaking to conduct a Quality Mark assessment will delay the launch of the sale of the housing units, which may

---

[13] Cap. 130.

[14] See 'Normanton Park gets green light to sell, but with conditions,' *The Straits Times*, 31 December 2020.

in turn affect the ability of the housing developer in complying with the ABSD time frame for completion and sale of the units.

The COVID-19 outbreak in 2020 saw the disruption of construction activities. In respect of the affected residential projects, the Government has extended the prescribed periods for developers, in respect of the clawback of ABSD.[15]

2.2. En bloc purchase

A developer may acquire a development site by way of an *en bloc* purchase of all the units in a development. In such a situation, the *ad valorem* stamp duty is computed on the entire purchase price. For example, if there are 20 residential units in a development and the *en bloc* purchase price is $60 million, the BSD is computed as follows:

1% of $180,000	=	$1,800
2% of $180,000	=	$3,600
3% of $640,000	=	$19,200
4% of ($60 million − $1 million)	=	$2,360,000
Stamp duty payable		$2,384,600

As may be seen from the tied-rate structure of the *ad valorem* stamp duty, the BSD on the tranches of the price below $1 million is computed at rates lower than the maximum 4% rate. Essentially, one may perform a quick computation of the BSD where the total price is $60 million, by multiplying the total consideration of $60 million by the rate of 4%, and deduct a sum of $15,400 (i.e. $5,400 + $3,600 + $6,400) which accounts of the tranches of the price computed at less than the rate of 4%. In other words, the BSD may be computed as follows:

$$4\% \text{ of } \$60 \text{ million} - \$15,400 = \$2,400,000 - \$15,400$$
$$= \$2,384,600$$

---

[15] The latest round of extension at the time of writing of this chapter is provided in the Stamp Duties (Housing Developers)(Remission of ABSD)(Amendment) Rules 2021, S 415/2021 and the Stamp Duties (Non-licensed Housing Developers)(Remission of ABSD)(Amendment) Rules 2021, S 416/2021.

The computation also shows up that had the *ad valorem* stamp duty been computed alternatively on the basis of the 20 individual purchases of the units at $3 million each, such that there are to be 20 computations of the BSD on an average price of $3 million, there would be a stamp duty savings of $292,600 ($15,400 × 19). However, in the case of an *en bloc* purchase, where the developer essentially tendered a global price for the entire development, the Commissioner of Stamp Duties would invoke the general anti-avoidance provisions in section 33A of the Stamp Duties Act, to thwart any such attempt at stamp duty savings by entering into separate sale and purchase agreements with each of the vendors of the units.

In *UOL Development (Novena) Pte Ltd v Commissioner of Stamp Duties*[16], the Commissioner of Stamp Duties was successful in invoking the general anti-avoidance provisions in section 33A of the Stamp Duties Act, to impose *ad volarem* stamp duty computed on the total consideration of $61 million paid by a developer in an *en bloc* purchase of 53 properties. In that case, there was a collective invitation to tender by the 53 vendors. When the tender bid was received from the developer, each of the 53 vendors then executed separate letters of acceptance. The price in each of the 53 letters of accepetance was essentially an apportionment of the total consideration of $61 million, based on the distribution formula agreed by the vendors before the launch of the *en bloc* sale. The facts were such that the vendors had to sell collectively to achieve a higher price and the developer had intended to purchase a collective interest for the purpose of redevelopment.

In that case, the Commissioner had the awkward situation of stamping one of the letters of acceptance on the basis of the total consideration of $61 million and the rest of the 52 letters of acceptance at the nominal rate of $10. This is an instance where the general anti-avoidance provisions in section 33A do not operate elegantly in respect of stamp duty, which is still very much a tax on documents[17].

---

[16] [2008] 1 SLR(R) 126.

[17] In the draft legislative amendments on s 33A which were made available for public consultation by the Ministry of Finance in 2020, there was a proposal to insert a sub-section to s 33A which read, 'An adjustment may be made under subsection (2) *whether or not there is an instrument.*' However in the Stamp Duties (Amendment) Bill 2020 (Bill No. 38 of 2020) introduced in Parliament on 5 October 2020, the said proposed subsection was not included in the Bill, probably on account of feedback received on the proposal. This episode perhaps indicates that stamp duty is still very much a duty on instruments. If there is no chargeable instrument to be stamped in the first place, there cannot be a situation of avoidance of stamp duty.

In the subsequent case of *Lai Ling Wan (alias Lai Lily) v Commissioner of Stamp Duties*,[18] where the taxpayer purchased 83 apartments from a developer and there were 83 separate agreements, the Commissioner also decided that the stamp duty was to be computed on the total consideration for all 83 apartments. There were however *bona fide* commercial reasons for the 83 separate agreements. The High Court held that each of the 83 agreements was to be stamped separately, based on the consideration stated in each agreement. In that case, Choo Han Teck J in deciding in favour of the taxpayer, said at [15]:

It was not the Commissioner's case that the Parties' contracts were structured for the purpose of reducing or avoiding tax liabilities such that s 33A(1) of the Act has to be invoked. There was also no evidence to show that that was one of the parties' purpose or intention. Although the Parties' bargain had the effect of reducing tax liabilities, the Appellant had offered persuasive and *bona fide* commercial reasons for structuring the bargain in that manner. The Appellant affirmed in her affidavit that she would not have accepted a single sale and purchase agreement to purchase all the units as a collective interest. A single agreement would have constrained her ability to obtain financing from more than one financial institution. She would also face difficulties in the event of the sub-sale of one or more of the units because the Developer would have to cancel the sale and purchase agreement and re-issue her with fresh sale and purchase agreements. These reasons bring the Appellant's case within the ambit of s 33A(3)(*b*) of the Act which states that the section shall not apply to "any arrangement carried out for bona fide commercial reasons and had not as one of its main purpose the avoidance or reduction of duty".

Some of the indications which the Commissioner may look at in determining whether there is a collective sale and purchase of the multiple properties, that would attract the higher *ad valorem* stamp duty computed on the total consideration of the properties, are as follows[19]:

---

[18] [2011] 4 SLR 845.

[19] IRAS e-Tax Guide, *Stamp Duty Treatment for the Acquisition of Multiple Properties*, Second Edition, 22 February 2012.

(a) Whether the letter of acceptance to purchase the multiple properties, corresponds with the letter of offer to sell the multiple properties.

(b) Whether all the purchase contracts for the multiple properties are dependent and conditional upon one another, such that the purchaser is not obliged to complete the entire transaction if any of the vendors does not sell his property.

(c) Whether there is an indemnity clause in the option or sale and purchase agreement stating to the effect that in the event of any default and/or failure by any vendor to complete the sale following the execution of the sale and purchase agreement, the defaulting vendor is liable to the other vendors of the properties and the purchaser and is to indemnify them against all costs.

2.3. Conveyance directions

A housing developer may use a company to bid for a site. On being awarded the site by the vendor, a contract is formed. Stamp duty is chargeable on the contract document for the sale and purchase of the land, and the duty has to be paid within 14 days of the execution of the sale and purchase agreement. In some cases, the housing developer for its own commercial reasons, may after being awarded the site with the consequential stamp duty liability, decide to direct the vendor to convey the site to another of its companies. Such "conveyance directions" may be made for various genuine business reasons. For example, a holding company may have tendered for the site and upon successful in the tender, it decides that a special purpose vehicle be incorporated for the purpose of undertaking the development. In such a case, the holding company may direct the vendor of the site, to convey the site to the special purpose vehicle. In another example, a company which is successful in the tender for a development site, may decide to invite other developers to participate in the joint development of the site and a special purpose vehicle may then be incorporated with all various participants having a shareholding in the special purpose vehicle. The successful tenderer then directs that the vendor convey the site to the special purpose vehicle.

Such conveyance direction attracts another set of stamp duties by virtue of the operation of secion 22(4) of the Stamp Duties Act.[20] As may be seen, this may end up with the developer having to pay two sets of stamp duties for what is essentially a single acquisition of a development site, i.e. one set being payable on the original agreement with the vendor of the property and another set on the conveyance direction.

In such situations, the developer may seek remission of the BSD on the conveyance direction under the Stamp Duties (Conveyance Duties) (Remission) Rules 2015[21] and the remission of any ABSD under the Stamp Duties (Housing Developers)(Remission of ABSD) Rules 2013[22] (2013 Rules).

Under rule 4(1) of the 2013 Rules, remission of the ABSD on the conveyance direction is available where the housing development company (referred to as "the first-mentioned company") has executed a contract or agreement for the acquisition of the property, with the intention that the property is to be transferred to another company (referred as "the subsidiary") for the purpose of a housing development. It is important that the first-mentioned company has documentary evidence of such intention, as the Commissioner may require the production of such evidence in any application for the remission of the ABSD on the conveyance direction. The following conditions for the remission are set out in rule 4(2) of the 2013 Rules:

(a) the conveyance direction for the conveyance or transfer of the property to the subsidiary is made not more than 2 months starting from the date of the execution of the contract or agreement;

---

[20] Section 22(4) which treats the conveyance direction as chargeable with stamp duty, was inserted by the Stamp Duties (Amendment) Act 1996 (No. 26 of 1996) to come into operation on 15 May 1996 as part of the property cooling measures. The duty on the conveyance direction was intended to curb the speculation and quick resales, as stamp duty would be imposed on the sale and purchase agreement for the first sale and another set of stamp duty would be imposed on the conveyance direction where the purchaser directs the vendor to convey the property to the sub-purchaser.

[21] S 778/2015.

[22] S 362/2013. In the case of non-licensed housing developers (building four housing units or less), the applicable subsidiary legislation is the Stamp Duties (Non-Licensed Housing Developers) (Remission of ABSD) Rules 2015, S 764/2015.

(b) no consideration passes between the first-mentioned company company and the subsidiary for the conveyance or transfer. As between companies, the subsidiary would have to reimburse the first-mentioned company, for any part of the consideration that the first-mentioned company has paid to the vendor before the completion of the sale. This reimbursement cannot be considered as "consideration" for the purpose of rule 4(2)(b), as otherwise the remission of conveyance direction would be an impossibility, since even between related companies, a reimbursement is required;

(c) at all times between the date of the execution of the contract or agreement and the date of issue of the Temporary Occupation Permit or Certificate of Statutory Completion for all units of housing accommodation that are the subject of the housing development (both dates inclusive), the first-mentioned company[23] —

  (i) has beneficial interest in more than 50% of the shares in the subsidiary; and

  (ii) holds more than 50% of the votes attached to the voting shares in the subsidiary.

The condition in rule 4(2)(c) will mean that the first-mentioned company has to maintain a majority interest in the subsidiary during the entire period of the development. Should the first-mentioned company's interest fall below the majority during that period, the ABSD remitted will then be payable to the Commissioner. This may occur when the first-mentioned company faces financial difficulties and its interests in the subsidiary may have to be transferred to another party.

Hence as far as possible, the use of the conveyance direction should be avoided, as there may still be a risk there may be a breach of the condition in rule 4(2)(c) in the future, triggering the clawback of the ABSD remitted earlier on the conveyance direction. The second set of ABSD on what is after all a single transaction to acquire the development site, then becomes payable.

---

[23] Rule 4(2)(c). In the case where a successful developer invites other developers to participate in the joint development of the site, the other incoming developers must together have less than 50% beneficial interest in the subsidiary and hold less than 50% of the votes attached to the voting shares in the subsidiary, for the remission of the ABSD.

The use of the conveyance direction may be avoided, with some pre-planning before the submission of the tender bid to buy a property. The special purpose company which is going to undertake the development (whether with the participation of partners or otherwise) should be incorporated in advance of the tender bid for the development site. With the special purpose company making the tender bid of the development site and subsequently undertaking the development of the site after being successful in its tender bid, there is then no need for any conveyance direction.

While the remission of the ABSD on the conveyance direction comes under the 2013 Rules, the remission of BSD on the conveyance direction comes under a separate set of subsidiary legislation, i.e. the Stamp Duties (Conveyance Directions) (Remission) Rules 2015[24] (2015 Rules). Conditions similar to those for the remission of ABSD on the conveyance, are also provided for the remission of the BSD on the conveyance direction in the 2015 Rules.

With respect to the reason for the existence of the two pieces of subsidiary legislation (i.e. one dealing with BSD remission and another dealing with ABSD remission) for the remission of stamp duty on the conveyance direction, we have to go back into history. The subsidiary legislation dealing with BSD remission came first, with the Stamp Duties (Conveyance Directions) (Remission) Rules 2005[25] (2005 Rules). Those Remission Rules were of general application and they dealt both residential as well as non-residential properties where the conveyance direction is used. They provided for the remission of the "second set of duty" on the conveyance direction.

ABSD made its debut on 8 December 2011 and the Stamp Duties (Housing Developers)(Remission of ABSD) Rules 2013[26] was subsequently enacted to provide housing developers with ABSD remission where they meet the conditions of the development and sale of the completed units within the prescribed period. While the remission of the ABSD on the conveyance direction is dealt with in the 2013 Rules, the BSD remission

---

[24] S 778/2015.

[25] S 446/2005 since revoked with the coming into operation of the Stamp Duties (Conveyance Directions) (Remission) Rules 2015, S 778/2015.

[26] S 362/2013.

rules on the conveyance direction remains with the 2005 Rules which were later superseded by the 2015 Rules. Hence, there are two pieces of subsidiary legislation that deal with remission of the duty on the conveyance direction, i.e. one for the BSD remission and another for the ABSD remission.

2.4. Additional conveyance duty

The subject of additional conveyance duty (ACD), which concerns the stamp duty payable on the acquisiton of "equity interest" of a "property holding entity", is dealt with in detail in Chapter 7. A developer which acquires a site for development purposes, will not usually encounter ACD, except perhaps in the situation set out in the next paragraph.

A developer may mitigate its development and business risks by having joint venture "partners" in a development company incorporated for the purpose of development of residential properties. Those "partners" would become shareholders of the development company. However, should any of the "joint venture partners" get into financial difficulties and wishes to sell its shares, the remaining "joint venture partners" may find themselves in the situation where they are only able to acquire the shares of the outgoing "joint venture partner", by paying the ACD. ACD is chargeable where (1) the acquirer of the shares is already a "significant owner" of 50% or more of the shares of the development company, and it acquires more shares in the company; or (2) the acquisition of the shares would result in the acquirer having 50% or more of the entire shareholding of the company.

2.5. Mixed-use developments

In the case of sites which may accommodate large scale mixed-use developments, it is not uncommon for the developer to use multiple entities to jointly acquire the entire site, such that the entities will own the site as tenants-in-common. The dedicated mission of those entities may be to develop and own specific components of the development on the site. For example, one entity may develop and own the office component on the site and bear all the land and development costs pertaining to the office component, while another entity may be dedicated to the development and ownership of the serviced apartment component and bear all the land and development costs pertaining to the serviced apartment component.

Nevertheless with the joint ownership of the land, the entities end up jointly owning the entire developed project as well. Given the respective missions of the entities, they will commonly enter into a joint development deed (JDD) for the development of the site. The JDD will provide for each entity to hold in trust, the component that is beneficially owned by the other entity. For example, the entity developing and bearing the costs of the land and construction for the office component, will hold in trust the serviced apartment component for the entity that develops and bears the costs of the land and construction of the serviced apartment component, and *vice versa*. This is so that upon completion of the entire development, the interests of the office component and serviced apartment component, may be partitioned and cross-transferred to their respective beneficial owners, such that "office" entity solely owns the office component and the "serviced apartment" entity solely owns the serviced apartment component. The partition and cross transfers to the respective beneficial owners do not attract further stamp duty, as the entities essentially got the respective components for which they have borne the land and development costs and of which, they are the beneficial owners. This is provided that no beneficial interest of any component passes from one entity to the other.

3. Income Tax[27]

Like a manufacturer who pays income tax on the gains from the manufacture and sale of his manufactured goods, property developers pay income tax on the profits emerging from the development and sale of their properties. In this section, we will focus on some of the peculiarities that pertain to the taxation of the profits of housing developers, which are also generally applicable to property developers at large.

In Singapore, a housing developer who undertakes the development of more than 4 units of housing accommodation is regulated by the Housing Developers (Control and Licensing) Act.[28] Licensed housing developers

---

[27] See IRAS e-Tax Guide, *Income Tax: Taxation of Property Developers*, Second Edition, 20 April 2022.
[28] Cap. 130.

have to use the standard sale and purchase agreements prescribed in the Housing Developers Rules[29].

The developer must also keep proper accounts and he must have a separate account called the "Project Account"[30] for the instalments paid in by purchasers. The monies in the project account render some protection to the purchasers, in the event that the developer run into financial difficulties[31]. The fact that the housing developer may not have access to the monies in the project account, until certain conditions are fulfilled, has an impact on the recognition of income for the developer for income tax purposes.

Many of the income tax issues that concern developers revolve around the time of recognition of income and the deduction of expenses. We will first discuss the issues pertaining to the recognition of the income of housing developers.

3.1. Time of recognition of income

In relation to the recognition of income for taxation purposes, section 10(1)(a) of the Income Tax Act provides as follows:

> Income tax shall, subject to the provisions of this Act, be payable at the rate or rates specified hereinafter for each year of assessment upon the income of any person accruing in or derived from Singapore or received in Singapore from outside Singapore in respect of —
>
> (a) gains or profits from any trade, business, profession or vocation, for whatever period of time such trade, business, profession or vocation may have been carried on or exercised.

The words "income accruing" in section 10(1) have been construed to refer to the point of legal entitlement of income. Hence, an amount is recognized as income when the recipient has become unconditionally entitled to the right to payment, even though that the amount may not yet be payable[32]. As to the

---

[29] Cap. 130, R1.

[30] Regulated under the Housing Developers (Project Account) Rules, Cap. 130, R2.

[31] See 'UOB reaffirms offer to buyers of two condo projects under receivership,' *The Business Times*, 17 June 2019.

[32] *Lategan v Commissioner of Inland Revenue*, (1926) 2 SATC 16.

meaning of the word "accrue", Yong Pung How CJ in *Pinetree Resort Pte Ltd v Comptroller of Income Tax* said[33]:

> Now, according to the cases of *Lategan v CIR* (1926) 2 SATC 16 and *CIR v People's Stores (Walvis Bay) (Pty) Ltd* (1990) 52 SATC 9 (Supreme Court of South Africa), the word "accrue" has been interpreted to mean "to which any person has become entitled". Although some other cases have ascribed the meaning of "due and payable" to the term "accrue", we were of the view that entitlement was a more suitable meaning in the context of transactions in this day and age. In any event, the parties did not seriously contest the meaning of the term.

Hence, for income to be accrued or "recognized" for income tax purposes, the taxpayer has to be entitled to the income. However, where a payment received is subject to contingencies, the contingent payment is not earned until the contingencies have been satisfied.[34] In the case of housing developers, income from the residential units which are sold, is recognized upon the issue of the TOP of the development. This is despite the fact that the purchase prices for the residential units may have been paid by the purchasers in instalments as the construction of the development progresses and the developer has used the "percentage of completion" method for the accounting of profits. The purchasers pay into the housing developer's project account and the withdrawal of monies from the project account by the developer is subject to the satisfaction of various conditions. As Kan Ting Chiu J said in *Comptroller of Income Tax v KE*[35]:

> The management of the finances of the development are governed by the [Housing Developers (Control and Licensing)] Act and the Housing Developers (Project Account) Rules (Cap. 130, R 2, 1997 Rev Ed) ("the Project Account Rules"). The Act requires housing developers to set up a project account for each development. Proceeds from the sale of the development have to be paid into the project account, and withdrawals from the project account can only be made for the purposes approved by

---

[33] [2000] 3 SLR(R) 136 at [23].
[34] *Edwards v Roberts*, (1935) 19 TC 618.
[35] [2006] 4 SLR(R) 197 at [4].

the Project Account Rules. Rule 7 however provides that after the grant of the TOP, the developer may withdraw any surplus money in the project account after making several mandatory deductions.

In view of the fact that the monies received by the housing developer are subject to various contingencies, the Income Tax Board of Review in *MPD Pte Ltd v Comptroller of Income Tax*[36] held that the developer's income from the sale of housing units is recognized only upon the issue of the TOP and stated as follows:

[34] ... we note that the Sales and Purchase Agreement provides for payment of the purchase price in instalments. However, the Sales and Purchase Agreement also stipulates various obligations that the Appellants had to do and because of these outstanding obligations, the Appellants could not be said to have the monies over all encumbrances and contingencies. In such a case the monies could not have been said to have "come home".

[35] This concept of "come home" monies was enunciated in the leading Australian case of *Arthur Murray (NSW) Pty. Ltd. v. FCT* 14 ATD 98. The issue there was whether fees received in advance for a course of dancing lessons were assessable income in the year of receipt. It was held that (at p. 101) *"the conclusion is not open that a receipt of fees for a specified number of dancing lessons to be given over a period subsequent to the receipt is a derivation of assessable income"*. In describing the characteristics of the gain or profits which constitute income, the Australian High Court referred to *Carden's case* (1938) 5 ATD 98 and stated (at p. 99):

"... It refers to amounts which have not only been received but have 'come home' to the taxpayer; and that must surely involve, if the word 'income' is to convey the notion it expresses in the practical affairs of business life, not only that the amounts received are unaffected by

[36] [1998] MSTC 5249, and mentioned in *ABD Pte Ltd v Comptroller of Income Tax*, [2010] 3 SLR 609 at [19–20]. Also reported as *HS v Comptroller of Income Tax*, [1998] SGITBR 2. See commentary on this case in Tan How Teck, *When is income under long-term contracts derived?* (2002) 12 Revenue LJ 93. The recognition of income upon the issue of the TOP is not affected by the coming into operation of the Financial Reporting Standard 115 (which deals with recognition of income) and s 34I of the Income Tax Act: see para 4.4 of the IRAS e-Tax Guide, *Tax Treatment Arising From FRS 115 or SFRS(I) 115 — Revenue from Contracts with Customers*, Second Edition, 16 November 2018.

legal restrictions, as by reason of a trust or charge in favour of the payer — not only that they have been received beneficially — but that the situation has been reached in which they may properly be counted as gains completely made, so that there is neither legal or business unsoundness in regarding them without qualification as income derived."

A receipt which is subject to contingencies is not income which has been realized and is therefore not subject to tax (*J.P. Hall & Co. Ltd* v. *IRC* [1921] 3 KB 152). Lord *Sterndale M.R.* held (at p. 156):

"... It would be wrong to carry into the accounts, as profits of one year, the estimated profits which would accrue in subsequent years and which might perhaps never be made at all."

[36] The contingencies that the Appellants could face are many such as:

(a) Refund part of the purchase price in certain circumstances;
(b) Reduction in the purchase price in the event of defects;
(c) Abatement of the purchase price in the event of a shortfall;
(d) The cost of construction which may increase due to the uncertainties in the economic and regulatory regime affecting its operation; and
(e) External risks over which the Appellants would have no control such as the insolvency of the main building contractor leading to engaging new contractor at unfavourable terms.

[37] Over and above these, it was common ground that these monies were deposited in the Special Project Account and cannot be commingled with any other monies. This fund cannot even be used to pay income tax or dividends or any other expenditure which is not related to the construction of the Melville Park project. Even when legal completion is reached or at TOP stage, the Appellants are not at liberty to utilise all the monies in the Special Project Account but has to set up a certain sum required to complete the building project and the sales under the Sales and Purchase Agreement together with a further 20% thereof for contention and inflation.

[38] From these contingencies and severe limitations imposed on the funds in the Special Project Account, it was abundantly clear that the

Appellants could not be deemed to have earned any income in respect of the development at Melville Park as of 30 June 1994. They have no control over the funds. The monies are, therefore, devoid of the vital element applicable in characterising them as income. There is a total absence of the money having "come home" as they are subject to legal contingencies and qualifications in their use and are also subject to various contingencies while the Appellants have substantial outstanding obligations to purchasers.

[39] Secondly, the relevant Act and Regulations allow the Appellants to adopt one or two accounting methods. The choice of a particular account method would not preclude the Appellants from arguing that the profits are not taxable (*Willingdale v. International Bank* [1978] AC 834; *FCT v. Thorogood* (1925) 40 CLR 454). It was always a question of fact and law whether a certain sum of money can be classified as income which is taxable.

[40] Thirdly, we hold the view that the Special Project Account should be viewed from the view point of a big picture. The whole purpose of the incorporation of the Appellants was to develop a particular project. In our view, the correct approach with regard to taxing of profits should be to take the project as a whole and look at monies received with regard to the total cost before any sum is considered taxable. We agree that there should be a difference between accounting profits and taxable profits in that the former is merely for accounting purposes (to reflect economic activity) and any profit deemed as accounting profits should not be liable to tax. To tax such accounting profits would otherwise create an unfair situation in which the profits of the first year might be wiped out by losses arising from various circumstances in subsequent years. In our view, this unfair situation can be avoided if we hold the big picture in view and take it into consideration.

[41] In our view, we think that a good time to have a big picture would be at the time TOP was granted. At this time it would then be possible to have all income and expenses known. Expenses still outstanding would not be of a substantive nature.

Besides the income from the sale of housing units, a developer may also receive other forms of income. However, the following categories of income (unlike the sale proceeds of units which are recognized upon the issue of TOP) are taxed as they accrue to the developer[37]:

(a) Compensation/liquidated damages from vendors for late completion of the purchase of the development site[38];

(b) Compensation/liquidated damages from contractors for late completion of construction;

(c) Interest/penalty from purchasers for late payment of their purchase prices;

(d) Forfeiture of booking fees of the purchasers for abortive sales;

(e) Rental income (net of revenue expenses wholly and exclusively incurred to earn rental income) derived from the lands/ properties acquired pending development for sale; and

(f) Interest income from temporary placement of excess funds in the developer's Project Account in short-term deposits.

3.1.1 Stakeholding money

In the MPD case, it was held that a receipt which is subject to contingencies is not income which has been realized and is therefore not subject to tax as yet. The sum is subject to tax only when the contingencies are satisfied. Therefore, purchase moneys paid into the housing developer's Project Account, are only to be taxed upon the issue of the TOP of the housing development.

The same reasoning should apply for the recognition of stakeholding money held by the Singapore Academy of Law in respect of moneys paid for the purchases of residential properties. The payment of stakeholding money to the Singapore Academy of Law, is provided for in the prescribed sale and purchase agreement in the Housing Developers Rules[39] read with

---

[37] See para 6.1 of the IRAS e-Tax Guide, *Income Tax: Taxation of Property Developers*, Second Edition, 20 April 2022.

[38] In *ZT v. Comptroller of Income Tax*, [2009] SGITBR 1, the Income Tax Board of Review held that the compensation moneys paid by the seller of the development land to the developer who bought the land, for the late completion of the sale of the development land was to be taxed as the compensation moneys accrued. The compensation moneys were not to be offset against the purchase price paid by the developer for the development land, to reflect a reduced purchase price paid for the development land, in the assessment of the profits of the developer from the subsequent sales of the completed units.

[39] Cap. 130, R1.

the Singapore Academy of Law (Stakeholding) Rules[40]. The purpose of the stakeholding money is to help the purchaser to pay for the costs of rectifying any defects in the properties purchased, which may only emerge during the defects liability period, after the issue of the TOP of the housing development.

The prescribed sale and purchase agreements are in Form 4 for non-strata titled properties and Form 5 for strata titled properties, set out in the First Schedule to the Housing Developers Rules. Clause 17.4 in the prescribed sale and purchase agreements provides as follows in relation to the defects liability period:

> If the Vendor, after having been duly notified under clause 17.2, fails to carry out the rectification works to make good the defect within the specified time, the Purchaser has the right to cause the rectification works to be carried out and to recover from the Vendor the cost of those rectification works. The Purchaser may deduct the cost of those rectification works from the sum held by the Singapore Academy of Law as stakeholder for the Vendor for this purpose.

The purchaser wanting to claim a deduction from the stakeholding money, in respect of rectification works, will then have to serve a notice of deductions on the developer pursuant to clause 5.4 of the prescribed sale and purchase agreement. Clause 5.4 reads as follows:

> If the Purchaser desires to make deductions from the 5% of the Purchase Price held or to be held by the stakeholder under items 4 and 5 of the Payment Schedule, the Purchaser may serve on the stakeholder and Vendor in writing a notice of deductions from the Purchase Price.

Where money is held by the Singapore Academy of Law as stakeholding money, the developer will not have use of the money. The developer may not eventually get the whole of the stakeholding money, as it may be subject of claims by the purchaser as provided for in the sale and purchase agreement prescribed under the Housing Developers Rules. As in the *MPD* case, the

---

[40] Cap. 294A, R2.

stakeholding money is subject to contingencies and limitations imposed on the funds which are held by the stakeholder.

Where the money is held by the Singapore Academy of Law, the money may still be subject to deductions for works rectifying defects, undertaken by purchasers. The developer has no access to the money while it is held as stakeholding money by the Singapore Academy of Law[41]. On the authority of the *Pinetree* case, the stakeholding money where it was held by the Singapore Academy of Law, had yet to accrue to the developer, as the developer was yet to be entitled to the stakeholding money. Accordingly, the stakeholding money while held by the Singapore Academy of Law, is not to be recognized as income for the purposes of section 10(1) of the Income Tax Act, until the contingencies are satisfied.

Authority for the above proposition may be found in *Building Contractors v Commissioner of Taxes (South Rhodesia)*[42]. In that case, under the terms of the building contract, 10% of the contract price was retained as "retention moneys" until a final certificate is issued by the engineer after a period of six months from the date of completion of the building. The building was completed on 28 January and the engineer's final certificate was issued and the builder received the retention moneys on 31 August. It was held that the date of accrual was the date of the engineer's final certificate, i.e. 31 August, as prior to that date the builder was not entitled to the retention moneys. In coming to his judgment, Hudson J in that case said at page 187:

> ... during the three months' maintenance period the engineer could not only call upon the appellants to remedy defects but could also rectify any mistakes that might have been made in measuring up the work actually done. The latter consideration is of importance with Clauses 26 and 27 [of the contract]. If any omissions or additions should be made then the amounts to be deducted or added to the contract price could not be taken as finally settled until the expiration of the maintenance period. There would in such case be no final ascertainment of the amount of the final payment until the engineer has given his final quittance.

---

[41] See *UOL Development (Jurong West) Pte Ltd v Chan Chong Neng and Another*, [2003] SGMC 38 on the dispute between the developer of Westwood Park and the purchaser on the deduction of costs of rectification works for defects in the purchased property, from the stakeholding money.

[42] (1941) 12 SATC 182.

The practice of the Comptroller of Income Tax may however be to subject the stakeholding money to tax at the same time as the rest of the sale price, on the basis that the developer has done all that is necessary for the completion of the properties and to earn the income. The correctness of this practice is yet to be determined by the Board of Review or the courts in Singapore.

3.2. Deduction of costs

The practice pertaining to the income taxation of housing developers is to capitalize all the costs directly attributable to the property development activities into a Development Cost Account. This accounting practice was pointed out by the Court of Appeal in *TH Ltd v Comptroller of Income Tax*[43], where Wee Chong Jin CJ in delivering the judgment of the court, said:

> The company treated each development project separately and individual cost records are kept for each project. Development expenses are "capitalised" in the balance sheet and are accumulated and carried forward from year to year until the project is completed. Upon completion, all expenses attributable to a particular project are deducted from proceeds of sale and the net profits, if any, are assessed to tax.

For each Year of Assessment after the development project has been completed, depending on the units sold, the proportionate costs attributable to the development of those units (such as the costs of the land acquisition, development costs, financing cost, development charge and property tax[44]) are apportioned and deducted against the sale proceeds of those units[45]. Obviously, where all the units have been sold in the basis period

---

[43] [1981–1982] SLR(R) 366 at [3].

[44] See *Thomson Hill Ltd v Comptroller of Income Tax*, [1983–1984] SLR(R) 297 where the property tax was held to be correctly attributable to the costs and expenses of the development project and they were only to be brought into account upon completion of the project. The property tax was not to be deducted as and when it was incurred in the years prior to the year of completion. See also Shue Tily, *The Resolution of Tax Disputes over the Taxpayer's Choice of Accounting Method*, (1982) 24 Mal LR 48, for a commentary on the *Thomson Hill* case, and Liu Hern Kuan, *Recognition of Income — The Choice between the Earnings or Cash Basis*, (1992) 4 SAcLJ 249.

[45] See para 5 of the IRAS e-Tax Guide, *Income Tax: Taxation of Property Developers*, Second Edition, 20 April 2022. The practice of capitalizing the development costs such as the site acquisition costs, costs of construction

pertaining to the date of issue of the TOP of the development or earlier, there is no need to apportion the costs of development. In that case, the entire costs of development are deducted against the sale proceeds that are recognized as income.

Various other costs may be deducted in the taxation of the income of the developers. Quite obviously, the interest expenses incurred in the development of the properties for sale are deductible. In *Comptroller of Income Tax v IA*[46], a housing developer acquired a development site and developed condominium housing units thereon, which were sold. In that case, the Comptroller did not dispute the deductibility of the interest expenses which were incurred in respect of the loan which was taken to acquire and develop the site. The Comptroller however disputed the deductibility of the following expenses on the basis that they were capital in nature and denied deduction under section 15(1)(c) of the Income Tax Act[47], but the deduction was however allowed by the courts:

(a) "Borrowing Expenses" which comprised payments of underwriting fee to the arranger of the syndicated loan, agency fees to the agent of the lending syndicate, facility fees, solicitor's fees and valuer's fees;

(b) "Prepayment Penalty" which was incurred on account of the early repayment of the syndicated loan, and the Comptroller argued that the condominium units could have been developed without incurring the Prepayment Penalty and that the Prepayment Penalty was not incurred "wholly and exclusively incurred in the production of income" within the meaning of section 14(1) of the Income Tax Act so as to be deductible; and

(c) "Guarantee Expenses" which arose as the developer used moneys in the project account to repay the syndicated loan. To do so, the developer was required to obtain a bank guarantee equal to the amount withdrawn

---

and interest expenses, in the Development Cost Account, for deduction against the sale proceeds of the units after the completion of the project was upheld in *Commissioner of Inland Revenue v. Secan Ltd & another*, [2000] 3 HKLRD 627. Marketing and promotional expenses are however not capitalized into the Development Cost Account, but are deductible in the year in which they are incurred: see para 7.2 of the IRAS e-Tax Guide, *Income Tax: Taxation of Property Developers*, Second Edition, 20 April 2022.

[46] [2006] 4 SLR(R) 161.

[47] S 15(1)(c) prohibits the deduction of 'any capital withdrawn or any sum employed or intended to be employed as capital except as provided under section 14(1)(h)', in ascertaining the income of any person.

from its project account. The guarantee expenses were expenses the developer incurred to obtain two bank guarantees, namely bank commissions, agency fees and solicitor's charges[48].

The Court of Appeal in allowing the deduction of the expenses, applied the "wider nexus test" in *Pinetree Resort Pte Ltd v Comptroller of Income Tax*[49], which provides that in determining whether a nexus is present between the incurrence of the expense and the production of income for the expense to be deductible under section 14(1) of the Income Tax Act, "the business has to be looked at as a whole set of operations directed toward producing income in which case an expenditure which is not capital expenditure is usually considered as having been incurred in gaining or producing income".

We turn next to the deduction of interest expenses which is a particularly vexed issue in certain circumstances. The simplest route towards the deduction of interest expenses is for the developer company to borrow directly from the financial institutions. In that case, the interest expenses incurred for the development of the properties for sale, are deductible against the sale proceeds from the developed properties.

In commercial life, it is frequently cheaper for the borrowing of funds to be made by the parent company. The parent company may then on-lend the borrowed funds to the development company and charge an interest with a slight mark-up. In this way, the parent company will be able to deduct its interest expense against its interest income from the development company. The development company may in turn deduct its interest expense against the development profits.

Issues may arise where the amount borrowed by the parent company from the financial insitutions, may not exactly match to the amount on-lent to the development company. There may also be a time lag between the borrowing by the parent company and its on-lending to the development company.

---

[48] The allowance of the deduction of the guarantee fees incurred by the housing developer in this case, puts into doubt the correctness of the earlier Income Tax Board of Review decision in *UDPL v. Comptroller*, [2005] MSTC 5331 that the guarantee fees incurred by the housing developer where a purchaser defaulted on his loan payments to the financier, were capital in nature.

[49] [2000] 3 SLR(R) 136 at [47].

Where the borrowed funds of the parent company become commingled with its interest-free funds, issues may arise with regard to the full deduction by the parent company of its interest expense on the borrowed funds. With the commingling, the Comptroller may argue that the parent company is lending from a mixed pool of funds comprising interest-bearing borrowed funds and interest-free internal funds. In that situation, the Comptroller may seek to restrict the full deduction of the interest expense incurred by the parent company for the purpose of on-lending to the development company. The Comptroller may require the parent company to trace the use of the borrowed funds to purposes which generate taxable income, where the company seeks a full deduction of the interest expense. As money is fungible, it may be quite impossible for the taxpayer to so trace the use of the borrowed funds unless the taxpayer sets up a dedicated bank account for the purpose which may not be practicable. It is to be noted that in the Australian case of *Federal Commissioner of Taxation v Smith and Roberts*[50], Hill J noted that "a rigid tracing of funds will not always be necessary or appropriate" in such cases of borrowing and on-lending of funds. The case of *Smith and Roberts* was cited with approval by the Singapore Court of Appeal in *Andermatt Investments Ltd v. Comptroller of Income Tax*[51].

Nevertheless, the taxpayer company may find it difficult to show that the entire borrowed funds were used to generate taxable income, given the fungibility of money. In such circumstances, taxpayers may find it problematic to persuade the Comptroller to allow the full deduction of the interest expenses. The restriction of the full deduction of interest expense is a particularly vexed issue of contention, given the commercial environment in which the taxpayer is operating. In the area of deduction of expenses, practical and commercial considerations have to be regarded. As Lord Brightman said in the Privy Council case of *Commissioner of Inland Revenue v Lo & Lo*[52]:

> In the opinion of their Lordships, commercial considerations are not wholly to be disregarded in the course of this process [of determining whether an expense is deductible or not]. They are relevant for the

---

[50] (1992) 23 ATR 495.
[51] [1995] 2 SLR(R) 866.
[52] [1984] 1 WLR 986 at 991.

purpose of deciding what can properly be treated as "outgoings and expenses ... incurred during the basis period ... in the production of profits in respect of which ..." the taxpayer is chargeable to tax.

Similarly, in the Australian case of *Hallstroms Proprietary Ltd v Federal Commissioner of Taxation*[53], Dixon J in considering the deductibility of an expense, said:

> What is an outgoing of capital and what is an outgoing of revenue depends on what the expenditure is calculated to effect from a practical and business point of view, rather than upon the juristic classification of legal rights, if any, secured, employed or exhausted in the process.

Towards such practical and commercial considerations, the Comptroller should provide guidelines for the eligibility of the full deduction of interest expanses where a taxpayer may borrow and on-lend within its group of companies, without the rigid tracing of the use of borrowed funds. Such guidelines may include:

(a) the time difference from the date of borrowing and the date of on-lending by the taxpayer company; and
(b) the allowable difference between the amount of funds borrowed and the amount of funds on-lent.

Meanwhile in the absence of such guidelines, the taxpayer should be prudent in establishing mechanisms including dedicated bank accounts for the tracing of the funds which are borrowed and on-lent within its group of companies, such that the full deduction of interest expenses incurred is not prejudiced.

3.3. Diminution in value

A housing developer may make a specific provision for the diminution in value of unsold property units of completed projects in its accounts, where the

---

[53] (1946) 72 CLR 634 at 648.

market value of those units have dropped below their costs. In such cases, the Comptroller in practice, allows for a deduction of the amount of the write-down to the market value where the write-down is supported by an independent valuation[54]. Once such a provision is claimed, a valuation has to be done for every unsold property unit every year. If the market value falls further in a particular year as compared to the written-down value of the earlier year, a further write-down may be deductible in that year. Where the market value has increased, the provision written back is taxable in the year of write-back[55].

The deduction of the write-down or the taxation of the write-back of any particular unit will eventually be reckoned with, when the property unit is finally sold. In the year of sale, the value of the property unit (net of any previous write-down and write-back) is deducted against the sale price of the property unit. Any profit or loss realized in the year of sale, will be taxed or allowed a deduction accordingly. As may be seen, the provision for the diminution in value of the unsold completed property units, is merely an interim measure of the loss. Whether the sale of a property unit is at a profit or at a loss, will only be known when the property unit is eventually sold. Nevertheless, a housing developer may still make such specific provisions in their accounting records, and any loss on account of the diminution may be used for group relief against the profits of any qualifying company within a group of companies[56]. From the perspective of the group, there is an advantage of such group relief, as it helps to defer the payment of tax for the profitable companies within the group in the interim.

While the deduction of the diminution in value of the completed property units is not specifically provided in section 14(1) of the Income Tax Act, the Comptroller's practice is in accordance with the English income tax law and practice. While the UK income tax legislation does not specifically refer to the valuation of trading stock for the measurement of the profits or loss, it requires income tax be levied on the "balance of profits and gains"

---

[54] In the case of banks and qualifying finance companies where money is generally treated as their trading stock, there is a specific provision in s 14I of the Income Tax Act which allows for the deduction of the provision for diminution in the value of their investments.

[55] See para 10.1 of the IRAS e-Tax Guide, *Income Tax: Taxation of Property Developers*, Second Edition, 20 April 2022.

[56] S 37B of the Income Tax Act.

of the period[57], and the value of the trading stock is taken into account at the beginning and at the end of the accounting period for this purpose, in the accounts. In this regard, the Lord President Clyde in *Whimster & Co v Commissioners of Inland Revenue* said[58]:

> ... the profits of any particular year or accounting period must be taken to consist of the difference between the receipts from the trade or business during such year ... and the expenditure laid out to earn those receipts the account ... must be framed consistently with the ordinary principles of commercial accounting, so far as applicable, and in conformity with the rules of the Income Tax Act .... For example, the ordinary principles of commercial accounting require that in the profit and loss account of a merchant's or manufacturer's business the values of the stock-in-trade at the beginning and at the end of the period covered by the account should be entered at cost or market price, whichever is the lower; although there is nothing about this in the taxing statute.

The *Whimster* case was cited with approval by the Court of Appeal in *TH Ltd v Comptroller of Income Tax*[59], where Wee Chong Jin CJ in delivering the judgment of the Court of Appeal said:

> That profit must be ascertained in accordance with the ordinary principles of commercial accounting, including the principle that stock-in-trade must be brought into account at the beginning and end of the year at its cost or market value whichever is the lower: see *Whimster and Co v the Commissioners of Inland Revenue* (1925) 12 TC 813 at 823.

---

[57] Similarly, in s 10(1)(a) of the Singapore Income Tax Act, it is provided that income tax is payable on the 'gains or profits' from any trade or business. S 14 which provides for the general deduction formula is not strictly needed for the deduction of the costs of the housing units. Lord Millet NPJ in *Commissioner of Inland Revenue v Secan Ltd & Another* [2000] 3 HKLRD 627 at 634, in commenting on the general deduction provisions in s 16 of the Hong Kong Inland Revenue Ordinance in a case concerning a developer, said: 'But the profits of a business cannot be ascertained without deducting the expenses and outgoings incurred in making them, and the [deduction] section is not needed to authorise them to be deducted. Sections 16 and 17 (which disallows certain deductions) are enacted for the protection of the revenue, not the taxpayer, and in my opinion s 16 is to be read in a negative sense. It permits outgoings to be deducted *only* to the extent to which they are incurred in the relevant year.'

[58] (1925) 12 TC 813 at 823.

[59] [1981–1982] SLR(R) 366 at [9], where the taxpayer was a developer.

More recently, in the Hong Kong Court of Final Appeal case of *Commissioner of Inland Revenue v Secan Ltd & Another*[60], Lord Millett NPJ said:

> The first step is to ascertain the trading profits or losses for the year. This is done by debiting the opening stock (which is a purchase from the previous year of account) and purchases during the year and crediting the closing stock (which is a sale to the next year of account) and sales made during the year. The balance represents the trading profit or loss for the year. ...
>
> The need to enter the opening and closing stock is well established by the authorities: see *Whimster & Co. v. I.R.C.* (1925) 12 TC 813; *I.R.C. v. Cock Russell & Co. Ltd* (1949) 29 TC 387; *Patrick v. Broadstone Mills Ltd* (1953) 35 TC 44; *Duple Motor Bodies v. Ostime* (1961) 39 TC 537; *B.S.C. Footwear Ltd v. Ridgway* (1971) 47 TC 495; *Gallagher v. Jones* [1994] Ch 107. In *Duple Motor Bodies v. Ostime* at p. 569 Lord Reid explained:
>
>> "It appears that at one time it was common to take no account of the stock-in-trade or work in progress for Income Tax purposes; but long ago it became customary to take account of stock-in-trade, and for a simple reason. If the amount of stock-in-trade has increased materially during the year, then in effect sums which would have gone to swell the year's profits are represented at the end of the year by tangible assets, the extra stock-in-trade which they have been spent to buy; and similar reasoning will apply if the amount of stock-in-trade has decreased. So to omit the stock-in-trade would give a false result. It then follows that some account must be taken of work in progress ..."

However, the Comptroller does not allow a deduction in the case where a provision for diminution in value is made for the land which is yet to be developed by the housing developer. The reason provided by the Comptroller for this practice is that "the cost of the land is capitalized in the Development Cost Account and deduction in the Year of Assessment [pertaining to the issue of the TOP], when the profits from the development project on the land are recognized and taxed"[61]. This practice seems to have

---

[60] [2000] 3 HKLRD 627 at 637–638.

[61] See para 8.1 of the IRAS e-Tax Guide, *Income Tax: Taxation of Property Developers*, Second Edition, 20 April 2022.

stemmed from or supported by the *dicta* in *Thomson Hill Ltd v Comptroller of Income Tax*, where Lord Templeman stated[62]:

> In the present case the recognized and accepted completed contract method leaves the calculation of profit until the year of completion and obviates the necessity for valuation of work in progress or land which is in effect stock in trade.

Lord Templeman's comments were made in the context where development has commenced on the land in that case, and the comments did not extend to the situation where development on the land has yet to commence. It is submitted that in the case where development on the land has yet to commence, the provision for the diminution in value of the vacant land is to be deducted just as the provision for the diminution in value of the completed property unit is allowed deduction by the Comptroller, as the land as much as the completed property unit, constitutes the trading stock of the developer. In this regard, Wee Chong Jin J (as he then was) in *Comptroller of Income Tax v QRS*, stated[63]:

> Gains or profits from a trade or business must, I think, be arrived at on ordinary commercial principles, subject to such provisions of the Income Tax Ordinance as require a departure from such ordinary principles. In so far as the business activity connected with the building and selling of houses and the development of land is concerned, land is trading stock and therefore has to be treated for tax purposes in the same way as trading stock of any other kind. It follows that land as trading stock, in accordance with ordinary commercial principles, has to be valued at its cost or market value whichever is the lower, there being no provisions in the Ordinance otherwise.

More recently, in *IA v Comptroller of Income Tax*[64] which is a case involving the deduction of the interest expense of a housing developer, the

---

[62] [1983–1984] SLR(R) 297 at [19].

[63] (1961) 27 MLJ 276.

[64] [2006] 1 SLR(R) 821.

learned judge also stated that land is just as much a part of trading stock as the completed apartments in that case. In that case, Woo Bih Li J stated at [88]:

> Furthermore, if the Board was correct that the loan must be to acquire trading stock *in specie*, that would mean that borrowing expenses for a loan to buy completed apartments for resale would be deductible but not borrowing expenses for a loan to acquire land for development and sale. I do not see why there should be a difference between the two as the land is just as much a part of trading stock as the completed apartments.

3.4. Timing of deduction

A qualifying expense may be deducted in the relevant basis period as long as it has been "incurred" within the meaning of section 14(1) of the Income Tax Act. In the case *New Zealand Flax Investments Ltd v Federal Commissioner of Taxation*[65], Dixon J in examining the meaning of the word "incurred" in the deduction provisions of the Australian income tax legislation, said at page 207:

> To come within that provision there must be a loss or outgoing actually incurred. "Incurred" does not mean only defrayed, discharged, or borne, but rather it includes encountered, run into, or fallen upon.

On the timing of the deduction, Van Dijkhorst J, the President of the Transvaal Income Tax Special Court in the South African case of *Income Tax Case No. 1587*[66], also said:

> It is clear that expenditure may be deducted only in the year in which it is incurred. *Sub-Nigel Ltd v Commissioner for Inland Revenue* 1984 (4) SA 580 (A) at 589–591; *Caltex Oil SA Ltd v Secretary for Inland Revenue (supra)* 674. It is not necessary for the expenditure to be regarded as "incurred" that it must be due and payable at the end of the year of assessment. As long as there is an unconditional legal liability to pay at the end of the year,

---

[65] (1938) 61 CLR 179.

[66] (1994) 57 SATC 97 at 104.

the expenditure is deductible even though actual payments may fall due only in a later year. *Nasionale Pers Bpk v Kommissaries van Binnelandse Inkomste (supra)* 563–4, *Silke on South African Income Tax* 11 ed Vol. 1 para 7.5 at pp. 7–13.

In *Comptroller of Income Tax v KE*[67], the taxpayer developer sold all the properties that it had developed on a particular site. Upon the issue of the TOP for the development, 85% of the sale proceeds were brought tax, as the remaining 15% of the sale proceeds only accrued upon the delivering of title to the purchasers. Under such circumstances, the taxpayer developer wanted to claim a deduction of only 85% of the costs of development which had been incurred, leaving 15% of the development costs to be deducted only when the title is delivered to the purchasers. In that case, Kan Ting Chiu J, in rejecting the taxpayer's contention, held that all the costs incurred have to be deducted and stated:

> In a situation where the sale proceeds received or receivable in YA 1999 represents 100% of the purchase price, all the costs accrued up to the same period should be deducted. Likewise if the sale proceeds recognised in YA 1999 amount to 85% of the purchase price, all the costs accrued up to YA 1999, should be deducted. The underlying principle is the same, i.e., all costs incurred up to the year of assessment are deducted from all the sale proceeds received or receivable up to that year of assessment. There is no reason or justification for deferring 15% of the accrued costs to a subsequent year of assessment, and then to treat the deferred costs and any further costs incurred in the subsequent year of assessment as one. Such a division and deferral is inconsistent with s 14(1) of the Income Tax Act, as I have explained in [23] hereof.

As may be seen from the *KE* case, the full costs may be deducted when they were incurred, although 85% of the purchase price was recognized as income. There need not be symmetry in the timing of the deduction of costs and timing of the recognition of income. In the *KE* case, part of the income only accrues in a future year when the full cost has already been incurred

---

[67] [2006] 4 SLR(R) 197 at [43].

earlier. There will be converse situations where the recognition of the entire income is in an earlier year, and the cost is only incurred in later year. That does not preclude the deduction of the costs in the later year.

In *Pinetree Resort Pte Ltd v Comptroller of Income Tax*[68], the initiation deposits which were considered as part of the consideration for the sale of memberships were held to have accrued to the taxpayer which operated a proprietary club. The initiation deposits were however refundable to the members after 30 years if qualifying conditions are met. Where the refunds are made years after the income (i.e. the initiation deposits) accrued to the taxpayer, the refunds are nevertheless deductible when they are incurred later. In this regard, Yong Pung How CJ in delivering the judgment of the Court of Appeal stated:

[49] The appellants' reliance on *Port Elizabeth Tramway Co Ltd v CIR* ([46] *supra*) to show that the refunds would not be deductible as they amount to expenditure payable out of income after it has been earned, such as a tax on profits, was misplaced. The term "payable out of income" was intended as a reference to expenditure such as tax on profits. The refund of the initiation deposits would not be in the same category as tax on profits. As stated above, they could be characterized as contractual buy-backs of the memberships, in which case, they would amount to expenditure incurred for the purpose of producing the income generated from selling club memberships.

[50] In view of this, there was little merit in the appellants' contentions that it was legally impossible for the respondent to deduct refunds of initiation deposits against the appellants' income tax for the year in which the refunds are made. As pointed out by the respondent, it is settled law in many jurisdictions that it is not necessary, in order to render an expense deductible, that the expense in question should produce assessable income in the same year in which the expenditure is incurred. Moreover, the respondent had implicitly acknowledged that the refunds would be deductible in the event that the appellants have to pay this out in the future. The appellants' concern that s 93(2) of the Income Tax Act would prevent them from claiming the deduction was also unfounded. Section 93 deals with the payment of excess income tax by a person and claims

---

[68] [2000] 3 SLR(R) 136.

related to it. This was not the case here. The appellants would only be claiming a deduction off their tax bill in the event that they had to refund the initiation deposits, not a refund of overpaid income tax.

3.5. The single project concession

In Singapore, it is common for housing developers to use a special purpose vehicle ("SPV") to acquire the development land and develop the land into residential units for sale. Upon the sale of all the units that are developed, the developer would normally wind up the SPV, after the expiry of the defects liability period pertaining to the units sold.

After most of its income has been recognized and taxed, the SPV may still have to incur costs on rectification works etc. These costs are deductible in the year in which they are incurred, although the income from the project has earlier been earned, as may be seen in the *Pinetree Resort* case discussed above.

Where such a "single project" SPV has post-TOP development costs, business expenses and trade losses after the Year of Assessment pertaining to the TOP (TOP Year of Assessment), it may not have sufficient income after the TOP Year of Assessment to absorb those expenses and losses. Since the SPV is generally incorporated for a single project, it would also not have future projects to produce income to absorb the unabsorbed losses, in future Years of Assessment. On such a scenario, the unabsorbed losses would have no utilization value for the developer.

In such situations, the Comptroller as an administrative concession and in fairness, has allowed for such post-TOP costs, allowances and losses to be carried back and set off against the assessable income of earlier Years of Assessments where there are profits which were taxed, up to the TOP Year of Assessment[69]. The concession is available up to 4 years after the TOP Year of Assessment.

3.6. Developer may hold investment properties

Developers like any other company, may intend to keep some of the units in their projects for long-term investment purposes, while intending to sell

---

[69] See 'Single-project concession for property development companies' at para 18 of IRAS e-Tax Guide, *Income Tax: Taxation of Property Developers*, Second Edition, 20 April 2022.

the rest of the units for profits. The gains from the units held to be long-term investment properties will not be taxed, when they are eventually sold. Where there is such intention of long-term investment, it is prudent that the developer indicate such intention *ab initio*, by providing the Comptroller with a schedule showing the specific units intended for the long term investment and their floor areas, together with the tax return for the year of assessment pertaining to the date of issue of the TOP of the project[70].

Normally, developers retaining units for long-term investment may pre-select those that are in a particular block in the development, or perhaps units at particular floors. Such selection may be based on the developer's own commercial reasons and the pre-selected units are not offered for sale with the rest of the other units, at the time of the launch of the sale. Where the "investment" units concerned are also offered for sale and subsequently retained for investment where those units are not sold, the Comptroller is less receptive to any suggestion that there has been any change of intention from trading stock to investment properites, with regard to those units. The gains from those "remnant units" may be taxed, when they are eventually sold. This may be seen in the case of *Mount Elizabeth (Pte) Ltd v Comptroller of Income Tax*[71], where the developer sold 51 out of 59 apartments in the development project between 1971 and 1973. In 1974, the developer's solicitors informed the Comptroller of Income Tax that the remaining 8 apartments were to be held for investment. In 1980, 6 of those apartments were sold. The Comptroller brought the gains from the sale of the 6 apartments to tax. The Comptroller's decision was upheld on the surrounding circumstances of that case.

Nevertheless there may be situations where a developer has investment properties which he may later want to redevelop for the purposes of sale. For example, a property owner may want to redevelop his hotel property which has been used in the operation of a hotel business for some time, into residential units for sale. The investment property may have been kept by the owner for a long period of time and the historic cost of the development may be low. When he converts the investment property into trading stock, he may "re-base" his cost, as at the time of change of intention from holding

---

[70] See para 17.3 of IRAS e-Tax Guide, *Income Tax: Taxation of Property Developers*, Second Edition, 20 April 2022.

[71] [1985–1986] SLR(R) 950.

the property as investment property to holding it as trading stock. This "re-basing" allows for the profits from the sale of the residential units, to be calculated by deducting the market value of the property as at the date it becomes trading stock (together with the other costs of development), instead of deducting the historic cost of the property which may be very low.

This procedure is provided in section 32A which was introduced by the Income Tax (Amendment) Act 2021[72], the essence of which is captured in the Explanatory Statement to the Income Tax (Amendment) Bill 2021[73] as follows:

> Clause 27 inserts a new section 32A to provide that in ascertaining the gains or profits of a person arising from the sale or disposal of any trading stock that was previously not trading stock, the market value of the property as at the date it became trading stock is treated as the cost of the trading stock.

An indicium of the date of change of intention from that of investment to trading stock, is the date of the written permission of the proposed development of the property issued by the competent authoriy under section 14(4) of the the Planning Act, especially where a land betterment charge may have been paid. Where there is such a change of intention, the taxpayer will then have to give notice of the occurrence of the property having become trading stock in the income tax return for the year of assessment relating to the basis period in which the property becomes trading stock as required under section 32A(4) of the Income Tax Act.

3.7 Change of intention from trading stock to investment

Conversely, a property developer or owner may also change his intention with regard to his trading stock, and decide to hold the properties as investment property going forward. Where the Comptroller of Income Tax were to accept that there is indeed such a change of intention, what is then the tax treatment?[74] With such a change of intention, there is no disposal of

---

[72] In Hong Kong, this procedure for the re-basing of the cost of the property upon a change of intention from holding as investment property to holding as trading stock, is provided in section 15BA of the Inland Revenue Ordinance, which came into operation for a year of assessment commencing on or after 1 April 2018.

[73] Bill No 27/2021.

[74] The Comptroller may however not accept that there is any change of intention at all, as may be seen in *Mount Elizabeth (Pte) Ltd v Comptroller of Income Tax* [1985–1986] SLR(R) 950, in which case, the

the property concerned. The issue then is whether the notional gain (which is the difference between the historic cost of the property value and the market value of the Property as at the date of change of intention), will be subject to income tax.

Section 10P introduced by the Income Tax (Amendment) Act 2021 essentially deals with the situation where a person appropriates his trading stock for a purpose other than for sale or disposal in the ordinary course of his trade or business. The most common situation encountered is one where the person appropriates the trading stock for investment purposes. With such appropriation, any increase in value of the trading stock up to the time of appropriation, has yet to be realised. Neverthless, section 10P essentially deems the open market value of the trading stock as at the date of appropriation as income for tax purposes, and the increase in value from the historic cost of acquisiton of the trading stock, as a taxable gain.

Where there is such a change of intenton, the person must give notice of the appropriation of the trading stock for non-trading purposes, in his income tax return for the year of assessment relating to the basis period in which the trading stock is appropriated. The essence of section 10P is captured in the Explanatory Statement of the Income Tax (Amendment) Bill 2021[75] as follows:

> Clause 3 inserts a new section 10P to provide the tax treatment where any trading stock of a person's trade or business is appropriated for a purpose other than for sale or disposal in the ordinary course of any trade or business of the person. For section 10P to apply, it must be reasonably inferred from the circumstances that the appropriation is permanent. If so, an amount equivalent to the open market value of the trading stock as at the date of appropriation is treated as income of that trade or business. However, where the appropriation is by way of a donation that qualifies for enhanced deduction under section 37(3)(b), (e) or (f) for any year of assessment, the cost of acquiring, making or constructing the trading stock is treated as income of that trade or business instead.
>
> Where the new section 10P applies, the following also apply:
>
> (a) the person must at the time of lodgment of the person's return of income for the year of assessment relating to the basis period in

---

Comptroller may attempt to tax any gains when the properties are eventually disposed.

[75] Bill No. 27/2021.

which the trading stock is appropriated, give notice of the appropriation to the Comptroller;

(b) in a case where the person has not been assessed for the resulting income, that income is treated as the person's income for the year of assessment in which the Comptroller discovers sufficient facts on the basis of which the Comptroller may reasonably conclude that there has been such appropriation.

Section 10P(1) of the Income Tax Act since renumbered as section 10J(1), reads as follows:

This section applies where, at any time on or after the date of commencement of section 3 of the Income Tax (Amendment) Act 2021, a person carrying on a trade or business appropriates any trading stock of that trade or business for a purpose other than for sale or disposal in the ordinary course of any of the person's trades or businesses in circumstances that give rise to a reasonable inference that the appropriation is permanent.

As may be seen, the provisions of section 10J have prospective operation. Before the introduction of section 10J, the Comptroller may have in certain instances taxed the notional gains that may have arisen from an appropriation of trading stock to investment property, following the English case of *Sharkey v Wernher*[76]. Section 61 of the Income Tax (Amendment) Act 2021 validates any such assessment which may have been made before the coming into force of section 10J.

3.7.1 *Analysis of Sharkey v Wernher*

It will be useful to examine *Sharkey* in some detail. In that case, the taxpayer, Lady Zia Wernher carried on business as a breeder of race horses for sale. She also owned and raced horses as a hobby. She thus owned racehorses in

---

[76] (1955) 36 TC 275. See Roger Kerridge, 'The Rule in *Sharkey v Wernher* — Time for a Reappraisal?', [2005] *British Tax Review* 287. The Comptroller's practice of taxing the notional gains is untested: see Tang Siau Yan, 'Capital and Revenue Divide' at [5.78] in Darren Koh, Poh Eng Hin and Tang Siau Yan, *The Law and Practice of Singapore Income Tax* (LexisNexis, Third Edition, 2020). At the second reading of the Income Tax (Amendment) Bill 2021 on 5 October 2021, Minister of Finance Mr. Lawrence Wong in referring to the insertion of s10P said: 'Without this amendment, there would be revenue loss from deductions claimed by the taxpayer when the asset was held as trading stock, whereas any gain on the subsequent disposal of the asset will be treated as capital in nature and not subject to tax in Singapore. We do not have capital gains tax.'

two capacities: some were owned in her private capacity as a hobby, and the rest were owned as the trading stock of her business. In 1948, Lady Zia transferred 5 horses from her business to her personal account. There was of course, no reason for her to pay herself for the horses and she did not do so.

From the Revenue's point of view, the transfer of the 5 horses was problematic because in previous years, Lady Zia had claimed (and had been permitted) to deduct expenditure incurred in connection with her business. Some of this expenditure had in fact been incurred in connection with the 5 horses which she had subsequently transferred to her personal stable. At the time she claimed to deduct this expenditure, the horses had been part of her stock in trade. The deduction of the expenditure had therefore been clearly appropriate on ordinary principles. But since Lady Zia had enjoyed the benefit of the deductions, the Revenue reasoned that she should not be permitted, simply to withdraw the horses from the business without making some appropriate adjustment to her accounts. The Revenue argued that the appropriate adjustment was that Lady Zia should be treated for tax purposes as if she had sold the 5 horses at market value.

Lady Zia was carrying on two separate and distinct activities with separate and distinct sets of accounts: one, that of a stud farm, and that other that of racing stables. It is to be noted that the relevant tax statutes required a dichotomy of those functions because it was only in relation to her "farming" activity that Lady Zia was chargeable to under Case I of Schedule D of the UK tax statutes. Throughout the case, it was conceded on behalf of Lady Zia that in the stud farm accounts a sum must be credited to represent the horses transferred to the racing stables.

The Revenue's approach in *Sharkey* was to concentrate on the figure which needed to be inserted in Lady Zia's stud farm accounts. She had inserted a figure. She had, therefore, so the Revenue claimed, conceded that a figure needed to be inserted. The problem, said the Revenue, was that she has inserted the wrong figure. She had inserted cost when she should have inserted market value.

When the case went up to the House of Lords, there was a majority decision with four judges in favour of the Revenue and one judge against. Of the five judges who sat in the House of Lords, three of them gave detailed reasons for their decisions (i.e. Viscount Simonds and Lord Radcliffe who were in favour of the Revenue and Lord Oaksey who was in favour of the taxpayer). The majority preferred the Revenue's solution: that for tax purposes, Lady Zia was to be treated as if she had sold at market value the 5 horses she had in fact simply transferred from her business to her personal use. The majority view established what has since been known as the principle in *Sharkey v Wernher.*

It is clear from the judgments in the House of Lords that, but for the concession by Lady Zia, the decision might well have been different. As Viscount Simonds said in that case:

> I do not understand why it is admitted that she [the taxpayer] should be credited as a receipt with the cost of production. In fact as a trader she received no more the cost of production than the market value: I do not understand, therefore, why the argument did not proceed that, as she received nothing, her trading account should be credited with nothing; that she suffered, so far as her trade was concerned, a dead loss in respect of these animals, and that the accounts of the stud farm should be made up so as to show this like any other dead loss. I do not understand how the adjustment could take the form of the fictitious entry of a receipt which had not been received.

The following observation was also made in the article *The Sharkey v Wernher Principle in Hong Kong*[77]:

> The decision of the court in *Sharkey v Wernher* was on a very narrow point: namely, whether the sum to be credited in the stud farm account in respect of the transferred animals should be at cost or at market value. The question as to whether it should have been credited at all was simply not one open to the court, the concession having been made *ab initio* on behalf of the taxpayer that the stud farm account had to be credited with a sum.

Lord Oaksey dissented in the *Sharkey* case and agreed with the Court of Appeal below. His Lordship would have permitted Lady Zia to add back in the deductions she had claimed in respect of the five horses and pay tax on that basis. Lord Oaksey said:

---

[77] (1976) 6 *Hong Kong Law Journal* 107 at 112.

Traders must show in their trading accounts the value of their assets. If they sell those assets they must credit the price obtained. If they do not sell them but get rid of them, either by using them themselves or in any other way, they must credit the figure at which the assets stand in their accounts or the profits of the account will be improperly diminished by the amount entered in the account as the value of the asset. Taxation under Schedule D [of the Income Tax Act 1918, under which Lady Wernher had been assessed to tax] is imposed on the balance of profits and gains. Profits and gains are actual commercial profits and gains, and similarly the deductions allowed by the Act which produce the balance are deductions which are considered to be properly attributable to the profits as being commercial expenses incurred in order to earn the profits. It follows, in my opinion that such expenses as have been incurred to produce an asset which is withdrawn from the trade cannot be deducted and must therefore be withdrawn from the account, which can only be done in accordance with accounting practice by crediting the amount of the expenses.

In England, the rule in *Sharkey* has since been codified in sections 172A–172F Income Tax (Trading and Other Income) Act 2005 (for income tax) and sections 156–161 Corporation Tax Act 2009 (for corporation tax)[78].

3.7.2 *Position in Hong Kong*

As Hong Kong's income tax legislation is similar to Singapore's, it is instructive to consider Hong Kong cases with respect to the principle in *Sharkey*[79]. The Hong Kong Inland Revenue Board of Review doubted the applicability of *Sharkey* to the Hong Kong's tax regime in the cases of *D41/91*[80] and *D47/91*[81].

---

[78] The doubts over the validity of the rule in *Sharkey* may be inferred from a technical note produced by the UK Government in December 2004 on Corporation Tax reform, where the Government stated at D.51, with regard to *Sharkey*, that 'the giving of statutory expression to the case law principles makes the law on issue more certain and transparent'.

[79] In Hong Kong, section 15BA (similar to section 10J) has been inserted into the Inland Revenue Ordinance to put the principle in *Sharkey v Wernher* on a statutory footing. Section 15BA operates in relation to a year of assessment commencing on or after 1 April 2018.

[80] (1991) 6 IRBRD 211.

[81] (1991) 6 IRBRD 256.

The chairman of the Board, Litton QC said respectively at [41] and [31] of the two decisions:

> The charge on 'profit' in section 14 of the Inland Revenue Ordinance is a charge on real profit, not on notional profit which a taxpayer never made... When it comes then to assess the Taxpayer, what principles of law, or of commercial accountancy, require the Taxpayer to be assess on the basis of a sale at a notional figure and not the actual figure? We are aware of none.

Lord Oaksey's dissenting view in *Sharkey* was also preferred in the Hong Kong case of *Commissioner of Inland Revenue v Quitsubdue Ltd*[82]. In that case, the Hong Kong Court of First Instance had refused to follow the principle in *Sharkey*. According to the Commissioner in that case, the taxpayer's intention from the time of acquisition of the properties was to trade in the properties but the taxpayer subsequently changed its intention to holding them as fixed assets. The Commissioner then sought to tax the notional profits on the basis that after the date of acquisition there was a change of intention when the taxpayer started holding the buildings as fixed assets.

The Commissioner then argued that the principle in *Sharkey* applied and based his tax assessment on the notional profit calculated from the difference between the cost and the market value of the properties as at the date of change of intention. At the Court of First Instance, Yuen J held that no tax could be imposed because there was no change of intention. In *obiter*, Yuen J stated her reasons for refusing to apply the principle in *Sharkey v Wernher*, at page 492:

> I start off with first principles. The undisputed principle is that a person cannot trade with himself (*Dublin Corp v M'Adam (Surveyor of Taxes)* 2 TC 387 at 397; *Sharkey v Wernher* [1956] AC 58, 36 TC 275 at pp 296, 298). If he cannot trade with himself, it must follow that he cannot make a profit out of trading with himself. The charge on profit is s. 14 of the Inland Revenue Ordinance (Cap. 112) is a charge on real profit. So, it follows that

---

[82] [1999] 2 HKLRD 481.

a person cannot be charged with profits tax on "self-trade" as it does not exist.

In the later case of *Nice Cheer Investment Limited v Commissioner of Inland Revenue*[83], the taxpayer carried on an investment trading business. With respect of securities held for trading purposes, the taxpayer followed standard accounting rules and revalued the securities at fair value at the end of the accounting period, which resulted in unrealised profits. The Commissioner of Inland Revenue sought to tax the unrealised profits. In that case, To J stated:

> [51] In my view, *Sharkey and Wernher* did not overrule the principle that a man cannot trade with himself as a principle of construction of income tax statutes. Viscount Simonds only held that the principle was qualified by the relevant statutory provisions in that case. In *Sharkey and Wernher*, what were subject to tax were profits from various taxable activities. Stud farm and racing stables were two different taxable activities. Under that tax regime, it was possible for the court to accept the construction that some figures from one activity of the taxpayer be treated as receipts in his other activity. The decision was explained on the basis of notional receipt. It is far from establishing any principle of general application that a man can trade with himself.

> [52] Furthermore, by way of contrast, under our simple tax regime, which Hong Kong is always so proud of, what are chargeable to profits tax are profits from such trade, business or profession. The word 'trade' could not have any other meaning than that ascribed to it by Lord Reid and Lord Wilberforce in *Ransom v Higgs*, i.e. buying and selling or exchange of commodities for profit between two parties to a commercial transaction. The meaning is confirmed by numerous authorities, including Lord Oaksey in *Sharkey v Wernher* and Palles CB in *Dublin Corporation v M'Adam*. The idea that a person can trade with himself is inconsistent with the meaning of the word 'trade'.

From the above discussion, it may be seen that the Hong Kong courts have rejected the principle in *Sharkey* on the basis that *Sharkey* appears to run contrary to two fundamental tax principles which have been accepted

---

[83] [2011] 6 HKC 169.

in Hong Kong, namely, that (1) a person cannot trade with himself; and (2) income tax is a charge on real profit, not on notional profit which a taxpayer never made.

3.7.3 *Position in Singapore*

In Singapore, the principle that a person cannot trade with himself (which is also referred to as the principle of mutuality) has been accepted by the courts. In *BLP v Comptroller of Income Tax*, Choo Han Teck J stated as follows, with respect to the treatment of monies collected by management corporations established under the Land Titles (Strata) Act[84]:

> The money is generally either put into a "sinking fund" or a "management fund". On the face of it, it would seem absurd that if there is money leftover in either fund after all expenditures are accounted for, that amount should be considered the management corporation's profit and hence liable to income tax. This is because that argument contravenes the basic principle of mutuality, which states that a man cannot make a profit by paying himself or trading with himself.

Further, at [19], the learned judge went on to state:

> In dealing with this contention, it is important to remind ourselves of the principle of mutuality. A man cannot make profit trading with himself.

From the above discussion, given the Singapore court's position that a man cannot make profit trading with himself, this would suggest that the principle in *Sharkey* does not apply in Singapore as a taxpayer cannot trade with himself. A person cannot make a profit from himself.

With respect to the second principle that a notional gain should not be taxed, Singapore like Hong Kong, also accepts the general fundamental position of income tax that tax is only chargeable on realized profits and gains. As stated by Andrew Phang JA in *ABD Pte Ltd v Comptroller of Income Tax*[85]:

---

[84] [2014] SGHC 127 at [8].

[85] [2010] 3 SLR 609 at [16].

It is a well-established principle of tax law that neither profit nor loss may be anticipated. Income accrues when a taxpayer becomes entitled to it.

In the House of Lords case of *Willingale v International Commercial Bank Ltd*[86], the taxpayer bank discounted and purchased bills issued by borrowers. The bank in that case usually, although not invariably, held the bills to maturity. The bank's profit and loss account included a time based proportion of the profit which the bank expected to receive in respect of each bill if it held it to maturity. Assessments were raised on this basis also, but the bank contended that the assessments infringed the principle that a profit is not to be taxed until it has been realised. This argument was upheld by the House of Lords. No profit in respect of the bank's holding of any such bill was regarded as realised until it matured or was sold. Lord Salmon in that case said:

> It is well settled by the authorities ... that a profit may not be taxed until it is realized. This does not mean until it has been received in cash but it does mean until it has been ascertained and earned. It follows in my view that ... tax cannot be levied in respect of the bank's transactions until the fiscal year in which the bank sells the bill, or if the bank holds it until maturity, until the fiscal year in which it matures.

The concept of "realisation" in income tax has to be understood and appreciated on the above basis as supported by case law. From an accounting perspective, "profits" may arise from the revaluation of a property. Such profits may in turn be distributed as dividends to shareholders under company law, if there is sufficient cash in the company. However, whether profits have arisen for accounting purposes or distributed as dividends to shareholders for company law purposes, does not determine whether profits are "realised" for income tax purposes.

Notional gain may be taxed if the tax legislation specifically provides so

However, notwithstanding the rule that tax should only be imposed on a realized profits, a notional gain may be subject to income tax if Parliament

---

[86] [1978] AC 834 at 841.

explicitly provides for the taxing of such a gain in the legislation. One example concerns the alignment of accounting profits with taxable profits with respect to financial instruments where sections 34A and 34AA of the Singapore Income Tax Act provides for the taxation of profits which may not be realized. Section 34A reads as follows:

> Notwithstanding the provisions of this Act, the amount of any profit or loss (as the case may be) or expense to be brought into account for the basis period for any year of assessment in respect of any financial instrument for the purposes of sections 10, 14, 14I and 37 is that which, in accordance with FRS 39 or SFRS for Small Entities (as the case may be) is recognized in determining any profit or expense in respect of that financial instrument for that year of assessment.

While there are specific provisions that bring unrealized profits in respect of financial instruments to tax, there were no such provisions which would bring the gains from revaluations of immovable property to tax in Singapore until the introduction of section 10J of the Income Tax Act.

Section 32 of the Income Tax Act

We will next consider whether section 32 of the Income Tax Act has provided for the statutory application of the principle in *Sharkey*. This flows from the Singapore High Court case of *HC & Anor v Comptroller of Income Tax* ("*HC*")[87], where Winslow J said that when the House of Lords arrived at its decision in *Sharkey*, it had the English equivalent of section 32 in mind. Section 32 reads as follows:

> (1) In computing for any purpose of this Act the gains or profits of a trade or business which has been discontinued or transferred, any trading stock belonging to the trade or business at the discontinuance or transfer thereof shall be valued as follows:
> (a) in the case of any such trading stock —

---

[87] [1968–1970] SLR(R) 742 at [42] to [43].

(i) which is sold or transferred for valuable consideration to a person who carries on or intends to carry on a trade or business in Singapore; and

(ii) the cost whereof may be deducted by the purchaser as an expense in computing for any such purpose the gains or profits of that trade or business,

the value thereof shall be taken to be the amount realised on the sale or the value of the consideration given for the transfer; and

(b) in the case of any other such trading stock, the value thereof shall be taken to be the amount which it would have realised if it had been sold in the open market at the discontinuance or transfer of the trade or business.

(2) In computing for any purpose of this Act the gains or profits of the purchaser of the trading stock of any trade or business which has been discontinued or transferred, such trading stock shall be valued as provided in subsection (1).

(3) Any question arising under subsection (1) regarding the value attributable to the trading stock belonging to any trade or business which has been discontinued or transferred shall be determined by the Comptroller.

(4) In this section, "trading stock", in relation to any trade or business, means property of any description, whether movable or immovable, being either —

(a) property such as is sold in the ordinary course of trade or business or would be so sold if it were mature or if its manufacture, preparation or construction were complete; or

(b) materials such as are used in the manufacture, preparation or construction of any such property as is referred to in paragraph (a).

As can be seen, section 32(1) provides for the basis of valuation for the following two scenarios:

(a) section 32(1)(a) scenario: Where the trading stock[88] is sold or transferred for valuable consideration to a person who carries on or intends to carry on a trade or business in Singapore. In this case, the amount realized

---

[88] Which includes any property whether movable or immovable: see section 32(4) of the ITA.

in such sale or transfer, is to be taken as the value of the trading stock for the purposes of computation of the gains or profits of the taxpayer. This scenario concerns the taxpayer who sells or transfers his trading stock for valuable consideration.

(b) section 32(1)(b) scenario: In the case of any other trading stock, the value is to be taken as the amount which the trading stock would have realized if it had been sold in the open market at the discontinuance or transfer of the trade or business. This scenario will require some discussion.

Section 32(1)(b) was construed in HC. In that case, the taxpayer company which was a developer, owned some land at Dunearn Road on which were houses under construction. The shares of the taxpayer company were acquired by another company, T&C Properties Ltd ("T&C"). The taxpayer company went into voluntary liquidation and the land was distributed *in specie* to T&C, being the shareholder of the taxpayer company. As the land was not sold or transferred for valuable consideration to T&C, section 32(1)(a) had no application. Nevertheless, the land was transferred to T&C upon the voluntary liquidation of the taxpayer company. In that case, the High Court held that section 32(1)(b) would apply, such that the land would be valued at its open market value and the gains are to be computed accordingly and taxed.

In *HC*, it has to be noted that the land was transferred to a separate entity. In the situation where there is a change in intention (e.g. a company decided to retain a property as investment asset as opposed to holding the property as trading stock for sale), the change of intention does not in itself result in any actual transfer or disposal of the property.

As may be seen, section 32(1) which merely provides the valuation formula for the purposes of computation of gains or profits, does not go so far as to deem the computation under that provision as "income chargeable with tax under this Act". In our view, section 32 does not provide for the application of the principle in *Sharkey v Wernher*. If it does, there would have been no necessity to introduce section 10J into the Income Tax Act and "it is a basic premise of statutory interpretation that Parliament does nothing in vain"[89].

---

[89] *per* Chao Hick Tin JA in *Li Weiming and other matters v Public Prosecutor* [2013] 2 SLR 1227 at [18].

4. Goods and Services Tax

Goods and Services Tax (GST) treatment of supplies made by developers depends on whether the developer makes taxable supplies or exempt supplies or a mixture of both taxable and exempt supplies[90]. Exempt supplies made by a developer are those that pertain to the development and sale of residential properties[91], whereas taxable supplies pertain to the development and sale of non-residential properties.

Where a developer makes only exempt or taxable supplies, the GST treatment is relatively straightforward. Where he makes only exempt supplies, the developer may not even register for GST purposes. Where he is registered (as he may also be making taxable supplies), he does not charge GST on the value of the exempt supplies and he is unable to claim the GST incurred on associated inward supplies (e.g. the GST paid to the contractor in respect of the development costs) as input tax. The unclaimable GST which has been incurred on the inward supplies, basically increases the costs of the development. However, where the developer makes only taxable supplies, he charges GST on the value of the taxable supplies and he is able to claim the GST incurred on the associated inward supplies as his input tax.

Some complication in the GST treatment arises, where a developer makes both taxable and exempt supplies, such as where he develops and sells or rents both residential and non-residential properties. The complications arise in relation to the GST treatment upon the acquisition of the land and in the construction of the mixed development.

We begin with discussion on the GST treatment upon the acquisition of land. Had the developer acquired a site which is zoned or approved for a residential development, the vendor (whether he is a private sector vendor or the State under the Government Land Sales program) does not charge GST on the value of the residential land. However, where the developer acquires land for a mixed-used development e.g. land zoned "Commercial and Residential" in the Master Plan, the vendor of the site will charge the

---

[90] See IRAS e-Tax Guide, *GST: Guide for Property Developer*, Fourth Edition, 18 September 2019.

[91] Para 2 of Part I of the Fourth Schedule to the Goods and Services Tax Act and Goods and Services Tax (Buildings, Flats and Tenements for Residential Purposes) Order 2010, S 825/2010.

developer, GST on the *entire* sale price, as the vendor makes a taxable supply[92].

For such acquisition by the developer, obviously the consideration paid will be partly for the land value pertaining to the non-residential component and partly for the land value pertaining to the residential component. In respect of the part of the consideration pertaining to the value of the site for non-residential development, the developer will be able to claim the GST incurred as input tax, just as the developer will be claim the input tax on the construction costs for the non-residential development paid to the contractor[93].

However under strict GST theory, the developer will not be able to claim the GST incurred on the value of the site pertaining to the residential development. This is because the GST is incurred in making exempt supplies (i.e. the sale or rental of the residential units). However such a denial of a claim of GST incurred by the developer, would put the developer who acquires a site where a mixed-use development (comprising a residential component) is allowed, at a disadvantage compared to the situation where the developer acquires a site which allows a wholly residential development where the vendor would not charge any GST at all. To address that comparative disadvantage, regulation 41(1) of the GST (General) Regulations, allows a claim of the GST incurred in respect of the "residential component"[94].

In other words, the developer would be able to claim the entire GST incurred on the acquisition price of the "mixed use" site. In respect of the GST incurred on the value of the non-residential component, the developer is entitled to claim the GST incurred as his input tax. In respect of the GST incurred on the value of the residential component, the developer is able to

---

[92] Only the supply of land zoned 'Residential' in the Master Plan or approved exclusively for residential or condominium development, constitutes an exempt supply: see para 2 of Part I of the Fourth Schedule to the Goods and Services Tax Act.

[93] See para 3.5 of the IRAS e-Tax Guide, *GST Guide on Purchase of Land for Residential Development*, Second Edition, 1 January 2018.

[94] See paras 3.1 to 3.4 of the IRAS e-Tax Guide, *GST Guide on Purchase of Land for Residential Development*, Second Edition, 1 January 2018. However where there are buildings supplied with the land and the buildings are not to be demolished and are to be used for making exempt supplies, the relief is not given for the GST incurred on the buildings as provided under reg 41(2) of the Goods and Services (General) Regulations: see paras 3.6 and 3.7 of the IRAS e-Tax Guide, *GST Guide on Purchase of Land for Residential Development*, Second Edition, 1 January 2018.

claim the GST incurred as a matter of exceptional relief under regulation 41(1) of the GST (General) Regulations[95].

In respect of the construction costs incurred for a mixed-use development, the input tax in respect of the making of taxable supplies will be claimable from the Comptroller, whereas the GST incurred for the making of exempt supplies will not be claimable. Insofar as the GST incurred may be separately identifiable for the making of taxable supplies, the input tax may be claimed. However, certain costs may be incurred for both the making of taxable and exempt supplies (e.g. the common area serving both the residential as well as the non-residential components of the developmet), in which case the GST incurred for those common areas[96] may have to be apportioned and attributed to that for the making of taxable supplies for the purposes of claiming the input tax.

5. Property Tax[97]

Property tax is payable on the basis of the "annual value" ascribed to the property by the Chief Assessor pursuant to the Property Tax Act. Generally for development land, the "annual value" is assessed at 5% of the land value pursuant to section 2(6)(b) of the Property Tax Act. The land value is to be determined on a freehold basis even though the development land is actually a leasehold property, on account of the operation of section 2(10)(b) of the Property Tax Act[98].

A straightforward case will be one where a developer successfully tendered for a piece of land under the Government Land Sales program. Upon the developer taking possession of the land, he will have to pay the property tax for the land. During the period of construction, the "annual value" of the property continues to be assessed at 5% of the freehold land value. The costs of construction are not included in the assessment of the annual value. After the issue of the TOP for the development, the land

---

[95] Cap. 117A, Rg 1.

[96] The GST incurred for the making of both taxable and exempt supplies, is generally known as the 'residual input tax'.

[97] For a more detailed understanding of property tax, see Leung Yew Kwong and See Wei Hwa, *Property Tax in Singapore*, Third Edition (LexisNexis, 2015).

[98] *Shell Eastern Petroleum Pte Ltd v Chief Assessor*, [1998] 3 SLR(R) 874.

assessment will be deleted from the date that the TOP takes effect. In place of the land assessment, the individual completed units will be assessed at "annual values" which are equivalent to the amounts of the expected annual rents of each of those units.

In the uncommon situation pertaining to large development sites, where the TOPs of the phased development may be staggered over a period of time, the land assessment may be reduced corresponding to the completion of each phase of the development. However, in the case of the completion of a substantial phase of the development where the footprint of the development covers almost the entire development site, the land assessment may be entirely deleted from the completion of that substantial phase.

As most developments are completed within three years of the acquisition of the land, the "annual value" based on 5% of the land value may remain the same for the period of development, where the land values may be relatively stable during the short period of construction. However, the period of construction may coincide with a period of volatile land values. In that situation, the "annual value" of the land may be revised upwards or downwards depending on the movement of land values during the period of construction.

A case in point is that of *Chief Assessor v Glengary Pte Ltd*[99] which concerned the development site of the residential development known as "The Sail at Marina Bay" in the Marina Bay Financial District. In that case, the development site was acquired by the developer in 2002 under the Government Land Sales program, when the residential property market was in the doldrums. By 2005 when the development was still under construction, the residential units have been pre-sold. Residential land and property prices began to rise thereafter. In 2007, the Chief Assessor increased the annual value of the land, based on the higher prevailing residential values then.

The developer in the Glengary case having pre-sold most of the units, was however unable to benefit from the higher residential property prices. Nevertheless, the Court of Appeal held that the Chief Assessor was empowered to amend the annual value of the development site in 2017,

---

[99] [2013] 3 SLR 339.

based on prevailing land values. It is to be noted that this decision cuts both ways. Where the property tax cycle takes a downturn after the units under development have been pre-sold, the annual value of the development site may still be reduced in accordance with prevailing market conditions, even though the developer has pre-sold the units under development earlier, at higher property prices.

A developer therefore has to be vigilant, and has to evaluate the annual value of his development site at least once a year, to see if the annual value ought to be reduced on account of the downward trend in the market. If so, he may then have to lodge an objection against the annual value pursuant to section 20A of the Property Tax Act, where he has not received a valuation notice under section 20(1) of the Property Tax Act from the Chief Assessor reducing the annual value of the development site. During the COVID-19 pandemic in 2020, the Chief Assessor has in pursuance of his duties under the Property Tax Act, reduced the annual values of many development sites.

Besides acquiring vacant land for development, developers may also acquire development land by way of *en bloc* purchases of all the residential units within an existing development, for the purposes of development. In such cases, the Chief Assessor may also assess the development site at 5% of the vacant land value pursuant to section 2(6) of the Property Tax Act, notwithstanding that the residential units may still be occupied and have yet to be demolished[100]. The annual value based on 5% of the vacant land value of the development site, is generally much greater than the sum of the annual values of the residential units situated on the site, based on the annual rental value of the units. In respect of such assessment where the property is to be redeveloped, the Comptroller of Property Tax may also "backdate" the assessment of annual value to a period before the year in which the Chief Assessor issues a notice under section 20(1) of the Property Tax Act proposing the assessment of annual value. This "backdating" under section 21(10) of the Property Tax Act may be made for example to the date of the grant of written permission for the development of the land under section 14(4) of the Planning Act.

However, where the developer intends to retain the existing development for letting meanwhile, the assessment based on 5% of the vacant land value

---

[100] *CDL Properties Ltd v Chief Assessor and Another*, [2012] 2 SLR 30.

may be deferred for a year initially and reviewed annually and the deferment will remain where the following conditions are satisfied[101]:

(a) At least 25% of the units in the original development are let on tenancies of at least 1 year, on arm's length basis and to parties not related to the developer. There must also not be any termination clause in these tenancy agreements to evict the tenants within the tenancy period; and

(b) The original development must be let and used for purposes approved by the authorities.

---

[101] IRAS e-Tax Guide, *Property Tax Treatment of En-Bloc Sales Sites*, 2 September 2014.

CHAPTER 5

Property Investment: Deriving Long-Term Recurrent Income

1. Introduction

After the acquisition or completion of the development of a property, the property may be let to produce rental income. The duration of leases in respect of units in office buildings, shopping centers, factories or warehouses is typically for 2–3 years and the leases may be renewed. In respect of longer leases, there is usually a rent review clause in the lease agreement, which enables the contractual rent to be re-set generally to market levels during the course of the lease[1].

From time to time, the use of parts of the property may also be changed in view of the operation of market dynamics. It is to be noted that material changes of use of a property are regulated under the Planning Act and they

---

[1] The basis of determining the prevailing market rental value at the time of rent review, is not usually a subject of contention. In *Ngee Ann Development Pte Ltd v Takashimaya Singapore Ltd*, [2017] 2 SLR 627, the prevailing market rental value would vary, depending on whether the rented area of 56,105 m² in Ngee Ann City were to be determined on the basis of the existing configuration of the area, or on the basis of 'highest and best use' on a hypothetical configuration (which would give a higher market rental value). The Court of Appeal held that given the specific relationship between the landlord and tenant in that case, the text and context of the lease agreement contemplated that the valuation was to be on the basis of the existing configuration of the rented area. In *Lucky Realty Co Pte Ltd v HSBC Trustee (Singapore) Ltd* [2016] 1 SLR 1069 which concerned the land at Simpang Bedok near the corner of Bedok Road and Upper Changi Road, the terms of the rent review clause were somewhat clearer in that the market rent to be determined at five-year intervals was to be 'based on the existing development and not some imaginary highest and best use consideration'. However, the dispute in that case was on the interpretation of the words 'existing development', i.e. whether the words meant only the two-storey market building or the entire development which comprised the three blocks of two-storey shophouses as well. The two cases show that landlords and tenants have to set out the terms of their agreement clearly insofar as is possible.

require planning permission[2]. Guidance on what amounts to a "material change of use" is provided by the Planning (Use Classes) Rules[3] which prescribed 18 use classes. The general rule is that if there is a change of use from one prescribed use class to another, or from one prescribed use class to a use which is not prescribed in the Rules or *vice versa*, there is a material change of use that requires planning permission. The 18 use classes prescribed in the Rules are as follows[4]:

<u>Use Classes</u>

Class I	Use as a shop
Class II	Use as an office
Class III	Use as a restaurant
Class IV	Use as a health center or an amusement center
Class V	Use as a motor vehicle showroom
Class VI	Use as a theatre
Class VII	Use as a light industrial building
Class VIII	Use as a general industrial building
Class IX	Use as a special industrial building
Class X	Use as a warehouse
Class XI	Use as a convalescent home
Class XII	Use as a childcare center
Class XIII	Use as a community building
Class XIV	Use as a sports and recreation building
Class XV	Use as a night club
Class XVI	Use as a pet shop
Class XVII	Use as a community spots and fitness building
Class XVIII	Use as a commercial shop

---

[2] S 3(1) of the Planning Act defines the word 'development' to mean 'the carrying out of any building, engineering, mining, earthworks or other operations in, on over or under land, or the making of any material change in the use of any building or land'. S 12(1) of the Planning Act provides that 'a person must not, without planning permission, carry out … any development of any land …'

[3] Cap. 232, R2. The Planning (Use Classes) Rules were also used in the Property Tax (Non-Residential Properties) (Remission) Order 2020, S 155/2020 as amended by S 305/2020, to define various categories of buildings which were eligible for the 100% and 30% remissions of the property tax payable during the COVID-19 outbreak in 2020.

[4] For a more detailed discussion of the Rules, see Leung Yew Kwong and See Wei Hwa, *Property Tax in Singapore*, Third Edition (LexisNexis, 2015).

Nevertheless, certain changes of use within certain buildings and locations have been "pre-qualified" and are considered to cause no or minimal disamenities to their immediate neighborhood. Hence, the owners and occupiers intending to have such changes of use, do not need to seek the prior approval of the competent authority, and have only to lodge the proposal documents required under the Planning (Changes of Use — Lodgment Authorization) Notification[5]. This lodgment authorization process is to help reduce both administrative and business costs and provide greater certainty to businesses.

With this preamble, we will discuss various tax issues as they affect properties held for investment.

2. Income Tax

2.1. Basis of taxation of rental income

2.1.1. *Section 10(1)(a) or section 10(1)(f)?*

Property rental income may be taxed under the head of charge namely "rents, royalties, premiums and any other profits arising from property" in section 10(1)(f) of the Income Tax Act, as "passive income"[6]. Although the word "rents" is specifically mentioned in section 10(1)(f), rents may still, depending on the relevant circumstances, qualify to be taxed as "trade or business income" under section 10(1)(a), which is sometimes referred to as "active income". Generally, the size of the portfolio of investment properties may provide an indication as to whether the letting of the investment properties would provide an "active" or "passive" income. The terms "active income" and "business income" generally connote that the income is derived, using a system of operations which will require the necessary extent of personnel and resources, whether the operations are outsourced or performed in-house. In *Comptroller of Income Tax v VJ*[7], Andrew Ang J made the following observations with regard to the word "business" in the Income Tax Act:

---

[5] Cap. 232, N5. See URA Circular, *Planning Authorisation for Chang of Use within Commercial, HDB shops and Industrial Premises*, 20 July 2009.

[6] The terms 'passive income' and 'active income' or 'passive source' and 'active source' are not used in the Income Tax Act itself, but they are commonly used in tax parlance.

[7] [2009] 2 SLR(R) 91.

[13] It is first of all a "business". In the well-known Singapore Court of Appeal case of *DEF v The Comptroller of Income Tax* [1961] MLJ 55, Buttrose J (at 58) held that "business" implies or connotes "a series or ... repetition of acts" in carrying on, or carrying out, a scheme for profit making. He also said at 59:

> [T]he word 'business' in section 10(1)(a) of the Ordinance is used in association with 'trade', 'profession' or 'vocation', all of which connote habitual and systematic operations, a continuity or repetition of acts or similar operations.

[14] In that same case, Ambrose J said at 61:

> [T]he fundamental idea underlying the three words 'trade, ... profession or vocation' in section 10(1)(a) of the Singapore Income Tax Ordinance is the continuous exercise of an activity. Considering the context, it seems to me that the same fundamental idea underlies the word 'business' which appears between the word 'trade' and the words 'profession or vocation'; and that the word 'business' must, therefore, be given its ordinary meaning, namely, an occupation habitually engaged in, especially for livelihood or gain.

[15] Thus, the carrying on of a business is to be distinguished from passive derivation of income ....

Further at [17] of the VJ case, Andrew Ang J made the following distinction with regard to section 10(1)(f):

> Secondly, if a company that owns properties merely lets them out but carries out minimal or no other activities, it will not be treated as carrying on a business either. Such a company will be assessed on its rental income under s 10(1)(f), which applies to income derived passively from "rents, royalties, premiums and any other profits arising from property..."

In *Management Corporation Strata Title XYZ v Comptroller of Income Tax*[8], the rent from the letting of minor spaces in the common property within

---

[8] (1993) 2 MSTC 5155.

the confines of a condominium housing development was treated as non-business income chargeable to tax under section 10(1)(f) of the Income Tax Act. In that case, there was no dispute that there was passive receipt of rental income from those spaces.

Depending on the facts, rental income may fall under section 10(1)(a) of the Income Tax Act. In the Privy Council case of *American Leaf Blending Co Sdn Bhd v Director-General of Inland Revenue*[9], the rental income was held to be business income. In that case, the taxpayer had earlier purchased land and built a factory for its tobacco business. Subsequently, the taxpayer found that it was not profitable to carry on its tobacco business and ceased to do so. The land and buildings were then let and the rental income was held to be business income. In delivering the judgment of the Privy Council in that case, Lord Diplock said at page 3:

> In the case of a private individual, it may well be that the mere receipt of rents from property that he owns raises no presumption that he is carrying on a business. In contrast, in their Lordships' view, in the case of a company incorporated for the purpose of making profits for its shareholders any gainful use to which it puts any of its assets prima facie amounts to carrying on of a business. Where the gainful use to which a company's property is put is letting it out for rent, their Lordships do not find it easy to envisage circumstances that are likely to arise in practice which would displace the prima facie inference in doing so it was carrying of a business.

Where the rental income is taxed as an "active income" under section 10(1)(a), the taxpayer will be entitled to claim capital allowances in respect of capital expenditure incurred in the provision of plant or machinery for the purposes of that business, under sections 19 and 19A of the Income Tax Act. On the other hand, where the rental income is taxed as a "passive income" under section 10(1)(f), no such claim may be made. Where rental income is taxed under section 10(1)(f), the Comptroller will generally allow the deduction of expenses incurred directly in producing the income, e.g. interest expense incurred to acquire the rental income, insurance premiums, expenses of repair and maintenance and property tax. "Indirect expenses"

---

[9]   [1979] 1 MLJ 1, on appeal from Malaysia.

such as directors' fees, office rent, telephone and utility charges, transport charges and staff salaries, which may be allowed deduction against "active income", are generally not allowed deduction against the "passive income"[10].

Another advantage in the tax treatment of "active income" under section 10(1)(a) vis-à-vis that of "passive income" as non-section 10(1)(a) sourced income, is that the expenses of the business are aggregated and set off against the entire business income. That is no necessity to match expenses against each source, as would be the case with non-section 10(1)(a) sourced income[11], as explained by Yong Pung How CJ in *JD Ltd v Comptroller of Income Tax*[12]:

> The distinction is significant because certain tax restrictions are not visited on s10(1)(a)-sourced income. For instance, only s 10(1)(a) losses can be set off against statutory income for the same year of assessment (see s 37(3)(a)), and unabsorbed s 10(1)(a) losses can be carried forward for set-off against statutory income of future years of assessment upon satisfying certain criteria in s 37(5). For non-s10(1)(a) sources, s14(1) requires a source-by-source concept to be applied, whereby the expenses incurred in the production of each source of income must be scrupulously matched against the source, i.e, expenses are not deductible on an aggregated basis against the total of all sources of income nor can they be set off against statutory income. The treatment of s10(1)(a) income therefore differs somewhat from that of non-s10(1)(a) income.

Prior to the enactment of section 10D[13] of the Income Tax Act which provides for a specific tax regime for a taxpayer who is in "any business of the making of investments" (which includes the business of letting immovable properties"), the taxpayer with an active source of property rental income could also carry forward unabsorbed losses and capital allowances to be deducted against future rental income. The provisions of section 10D(1)

---

[10]   In practice, the Comptroller limits the deduction of indirect expenses at not more than 5% of a passive investment holding company's gross investment income (e.g. rental income).

[11]   However, the Comptroller's practice known generally as 'block basis concession' is to treat the income producing properties as a single block, such that the net rental loss from one property is set out against the net rental income from other properties in any year. But the net loss for the year is still not allowed to be carried forward for set-off against the income for future years, for such s 10(1)(f) income.

[12]   [2006] 1 SLR(R) 484 at [45].

[13]   The operation of s 10D will be discussed later in Section 2.1.3.

have since denied such carrying forward from the Year of Assessment 1996, when those provisions first came into operation.

2.1.2. *Indicia of carrying on of business*

What then are the indicia of "income from the carrying on of a business" or "business income"? In *Mitsui-Soko International Pte Ltd v Comptroller of Income Tax*[14], Warren Khoo J in considering whether the taxpayer company was carrying on a business, gave the following guidelines on the scale of operations *etc*:

> I think it would be more appropriate to look at the company's activities themselves and, in the light of the facts and circumstances of the case as a whole, to consider whether those activities can reasonably and fairly be said to constitute carrying on business according to what the ordinary man (or ordinary businessman if you like) understands by that term. In *Calkin v Commissioner of Inland Revenue* (1984) 7 TRNZ 100 at 106, Richardson J in the New Zealand Court of Appeal said:
>
>> The decision whether or not a taxpayer is in business involves a two-fold inquiry as to the nature of the business carried on — including the period over which they are engaged in, the scale of operations and the volume of transactions, the commitment of time and effort, the pattern of activity and the financial results — as to the intention of the taxpayer in engaging in those activities.

The *Calkin* case was also cited with approval in *Brennan (Inspector of Taxes) v Deanby Investment Co Ltd*[15] where Carswell LCJ said:

> In construing a New Zealand taxing statute the court said that underlying ["business"] was the fundamental notion of the exercise of an activity in an organized and coherent way which is directed to an end result: *Calkin v Inland Revenue Commissioner.*

Hence, the scale of operations in an organized and coherent way is one indicium of the carrying on of a business. In *Mitsui-Soko*, the appellant

---

[14] (1998) MSTC 7349 at 7354.

[15] [2001] STC 536.

taxpayer Mitsui-Soko International Pte Ltd (MSI) leased its warehouse to its subsidiary Mitsui-Soko Singapore Pte Ltd (MSS) where MSS was to be responsible for maintenance and repairs for the warehouse while MSI was to pay the property tax. MSS in turn entered into a storage service agreement with Sony Logistics, a subsidiary of the Sony Group where the warehouse was used as a central distribution facility in Singapore for Sony products manufactured in South East Asia. On the facts, the rental income of MSI was assessed under section 10(1)(f) while the income of MSS was assessed under section 10(1)(a). In that case, Warren Khoo J said[16]:

> If anyone was in the business of lettings, it would be the subsidiary MSS. I understand that for the year of assessment 1990 (when the income from the warehouse fell to be assessed), the income received by MSS from Sony Logistics was assessed under para (a) on the footing that MSS was carrying on business, but the rental received by the appellant from MSS was assessed to tax under para (f) of s 10. The matter is not directly before me, but I am sure this treatment is correct.

2.1.3. *Section 10D of the Income Tax Act*

The rental income from the business of investment holding which may be taxed under section 10(1)(a), could be subject to the restrictions of section 10D of the Income Tax Act[17]. Section 10D basically introduces the concept of "business of the making of investments"[18]. It denies the carrying forward of unabsorbed losses[19] and capital allowances[20] for the purposes of deduction in future years of assessment, and the deduction of outgoings and expenses which do not produce any income, with respect to companies and trustees of property trusts falling within its scope[21].

---

[16]   (1998) MSTC 7349 at 7355.

[17]   S 10E (since renumbered to S 10D) inserted by the Income Tax (Amendment) Act 1995 (No. 32/1995) came into operation from Year of Assessment 1996. Its provisions are intended to apply to companies in the business of making investments: see *Comptroller of Income Tax v VJ*, [2009] 2 SLR(R) 91 at [19].

[18]   See the opening words of s 10D(1) and the words 'business of making of investments' are defined in s 10D(2) to include 'the business of letting immovable properties'.

[19]   S 10D(1)(b) of the Income Tax Act.

[20]   S 10D(1)(c) of the Income Tax Act.

[21]   S 10D(1)(a) of the Income Tax Act.

The denying of the carrying forward of the unabsorbed losses and capital allowances[22] under paragraphs (a) and (b) of section 10D(1) which came into operation from Year of Assessment 1996, was to prevent a situation where the taxpayer does not pay any tax or pays little tax during the period of investment as a result of such carrying forward[23], and also does not pay any tax on the disposal of the capital investment. Effectively then without section 10D, little tax will be exigible from such property investments. With the operation of section 10D, at least some tax will be forthcoming once the property investment becomes profit-making from its rental income (without the carrying forward of unabsorbed losses), even where capital gains upon disposal are not taxed.

The Comptroller of Income Tax does not consider the taxation of the profits from hotel business to be within the scope of the provisions of section 10D of the Income Tax Act[24], as hotel operations are not seen as letting of immovable properties *simpliciter*. In *Comptroller of Income Tax v VJ*[25], Andrew Ang J provided the following reasons for such tax treatment of hotels, and distinguished the treatment for the business of the operation of serviced apartments which the taxpayer was in:

[56] In my view, the analogy is strained. The business of a hotel is not normally that of *letting* immovable properties. A hotel guest is a mere licensee (without exclusive possession). Moreover, the hotel derives income not only from room rates paid by in-house guests but also from (i) its food and beverage outlets open to the public; and (ii) its banquet halls and function rooms for conventions, meetings and exhibitions. In contrast, the Respondent's income is from tenants.

---

[22] With the denying of the carrying forward of unabsorbed capital allowances, the taxpayer has to be judicious in claiming capital allowances. The taxpayer should commence claiming capital allowances on items of plant and machinery only to sufficiently offset the net profits after the deduction of expenses, such that he has to pay little or no tax of the year. The claiming of excess capital allowances on items of plant and machinery, will only result in those unabsorbed capital allowances being disregarded under s 10D(1)(c).

[23] Property investments are notoriously known for loss-making in its initial years when occupancy rates are picking up and there are many expenses especially interest expenses to defray. Such losses would be carried forward to deduction against future rental income before the introduction of s 10D.

[24] See *IE v Comptroller of Income Tax*, [2005] SGITBR 1 at [45] and *Comptroller of Income Tax v VJ*, [2009] 2 SLR(R) 91 at [55–56].

[25] [2009] 2 SLR(R) 91 at [56] and [57].

[57] The Respondent's suggestion that its holding of the Property is merely incidental to the carrying on of the business of providing services is perhaps aptly described as akin to the suggestion that the tail wags the dog.

In *IE v Comptroller of Income Tax*[26], the Income Tax Board of Review also held that the taxpayer which used its convention center in the business of organizing exhibitions and conventions was not "in the business of making investments" such that the strictures of section 10D did not apply, and it stated at [45]:

> Substantial portion of that came from activities that do not depend on the Appellant's proprietary interest in the Centre although that proprietary interest is a significant component of these activities. But the same activities could be and are often staged in premises rented for the occasion and in hotels by event organisers or the hotel management staff. Hotels are not assessed under section 10E [renumbered to section 10D] but under section 10(1)(a).

In contrast, the business of letting of shopping center units and service apartments would be "the business of the making of investments" within the meaning of section 10D[27]. However, the Comptroller does not apply the provisions of section 10D on non-owners of immovable property which include lessees of properties who sub-let their properties and main tenants of food courts who license their stalls to food operators[28]. The reason is that such taxpayers are not within the contemplation of section 10D which is to provide that owners of properties who may later claim the gains from the disposal of properties as non-taxable would have to pay some tax during the holding period. Such "non-owners" are not in the position to dispose of their rented properties for capital gains. The practice has since been put on a statutory footing with the insertion of section 10D(1B) by the Income

---

[26] [2005] SGITBR 1. The *IE* case is also discussed in *Comptroller of Income Tax v VJ*, [2009] 2 SLR(R) 91 at [35] – [37].

[27] See *Comptroller of Income Tax v VJ*, [2009] 2 SLR(R) 91.

[28] See paras 1.1 to 1.3 of Annex A of the IRAS e-Tax Guide, *Ascertainment of Income from Business of Making Investments*, Third Edition, 25 January 2021. Other such non-owners may be the operators of co-working and co-living spaces where they rent the spaces from property owners to conduct their businesses.

Tax (Amendment) Act 2020[29]. The new provision makes it clear that section 10D applies in the situation where the investment is an immovable property and the company or trustee of the property trust which is taxed on the rental income, is the legal owner of the investment or otherwise has a proprietary interest in the investment (including a lease or an easement) and would receive consideration if the proprietary interest is disposed of or transferred.

2.1.4. *"Same investment"*

The opening words "business of the making of investments" in section 10D(1) are defined in section 10D(2) to include "the business of letting immovable properties", and the word "investments" is also defined in section 10D(2) to mean "securities, immovable properties and immovable property-related assets".

Section 10D(1) then denies the deduction of any outgoings and expenses in respect of *investments* of the business which do not produce any income. Hence, where only part of the same or single investment does not produce income, the revenue expenses for that entire single investment are still allowable for deduction. In other words, where an investment as a whole is producing income, one does not seek to deny part of the expenses incurred in the production of income on account that part of the same investment is not producing income.

Such an issue was considered in the case of *AYH v Comptroller of Income Tax*[30], where the taxpayer initially built a shopping mall. Some 2 years after the completion of the original mall, the Housing and Development Board put up the neighboring land lot for tender. The taxpayer successfully tendered for the lot and started building an extension to the original mall. Upon completion of the extension mall, the two parts of the mall became an integrated mall which was managed and run as a single unit with no delineation between the original mall and the extension mall. During the period of construction of the extension mall, there was obviously no income from the extension works. Nevertheless, there were interest expenses pertaining to the erection of the extension mall which the taxpayer wanted to deduct against the rental

---

[29]   Act 41 of 2020.
[30]   [2011] SGITBR 4.

income of the original mall. The taxpayer's case was that the extension works were part of the same investment as the original mall. The Board held that the following facts, amongst others, pointed to the extension mall as a separate investment[31]: (a) the acquisition of the plots for the extension building occurred 4 years after the acquisition of the plot for the original mall and 2 years after the completion of the original mall; (b) the subsequent amalgamation of the original plots and the new plots of land such the leasehold tenures of the original and new plots were coterminous "only highlighted the obvious point that the two investments were separate in the first place and the second investment had to be trimmed to fit in with the first investment in order to create the new Integrated Mall sitting on the amalgamated plots".

The Board of Review in affirming the interest expense incurred in the construction of the extension mall was not to be deducted against the rental income of the original mall in that case, stated as follows:

[53] The meaning of "investments" in s 10E [since renumbered as 10D] is a question of law that should be determined, not according to the self-serving declared intention of the Company, but by objective reference to the principles of statutory interpretation and established case authorities. On a proper application of these results, the interest expenses incurred in respect of the construction on the New Plots are not deductible against the income of the existing Mall on Plot 1 during the period of construction when no income was produced by or on the New Plots. We would add that the Comptroller had allowed, and we believe rightly so, the deduction of interest expenses incurred in respect of the construction of the New Plots against any income from the Integrated Mall once TOP was issued for the New Plots.

[54] Acceding to the Company's argument would in fact be tantamount to rendering otiose the distinction that s 10E draws between income producing investments and non-income producing investments. The construction of s 10E is founded on the intent and plain reading of s 10E, read with s 14, that for the purpose of obtaining a deduction of an expense under s 10E, income must be produced by the investment before the expense can be deducted. An investment can produce no income if, being immovable property, it is in the process of construction, has not derived

---

[31] *AYH v Comptroller of Income Tax* [2011] SGITBR 4 at [52].

rental income and is not ready to receive tenants and customers. As shopping malls often strive to commence as soon as possible after TOP, either the TOP date or the commencement date of business may, depending on circumstances, be suitable markers in determining the point in time from which expenses may be deducted under s 10E.

[55] In the event that the Board has erred in its interpretation of s 10E(1)(a) in the context of the facts of this case, and all or part of the Interest Expense deductions sought for the period prior to the issuance of TOP could, in fact and in law, be regarded as having a causal effect in the generation of income in the existing Mall by reason of the fact that part of the construction works occurred within the existing Mall and its facade area for purpose of the physical integration with the new building structures on the New Plots, which was still generating rental income independent of such construction works, then any deductions should rightfully to be limited to such portion of the Interest Expense attributable to such portion of the construction loan for this very limited scope of construction works which occurred within the existing Mall and at the facade area. However, the Board would still dismiss the appeal on the following bases.

[56] Firstly, no evidence has been adduced by the Company as to what portion of the construction cost related to construction works in the existing Mall itself, for purposes of making it part of the new Integrated Mall. The construction works within the Original Mall and its façade, as highlighted by the Company were very minimal in comparison which the construction works required for the new buildings on Plot 2 and the Cul-de-sac Land. Absent such evidence, it would be impossible for the Board to determine what portion of the construction cost and hence, the corresponding portion of the Interest Expense, related to the existing Mall and any production of income in the existing Mall. Alternatively, it was likely to be *de-minimis*.

2.2. Deductions of outgoings and expenses

In ascertaining the income for any period for the purpose of imposition of income tax, section 14(1) of the Income Tax Act provides for the deduction of "all outgoings and expenses wholly and exclusively incurred during that period by that person in the production of the income". Many issues have arisen with respect to the deductibility of outgoings and expenses, and we shall deal with some of them.

As it is "gains or profits" from a trade or business that is chargeable to tax under section 10(1)(a) of the Income Tax Act, it is implicit that the net sum of the excess of revenues over expenses, is to be taxed. In this regard, Linden JA in *Tonn v The Queen* said[32]:

> Section 9 [of the Canadian Income Tax Act] sets out the basic rules for computing income or loss from a business or property. Subsection 9(1) is specifically relevant, and reads:
>
> > 9 (1) Subject to this Part, a taxpayer's income for a taxation year from a business or property is the taxpayer's profit from that business or property for the year.
>
> This subsection is the starting point in any analysis of the deductibility of business expenses and is important for two reasons. First, it stipulates that reference to business "income", such as those contained in sections 18 and 30, are references to "profit", which is a net concept. Second, by defining business income as a profit, subsection 9(1) implicitly authorizes the deduction of legitimate expenses. In other words, profit, as a net concept, refers to the excess of revenues over expenses. Thus profits are achieved only after expenses are deducted.
>
> Subsection 9(1) has therefore been regarded as the provision of "first recourse" in a deductibility analysis, and by its reference to "profit" has been interpreted to incorporate a business test for deductibility.

Similarly, in the House of Lords case of *Gresham Life Assurance Society v Styles*[33], Lord Herschell in regard to the profits and gains of a trader, said:

> When we speak of the profits and gains of a trader we mean that which he has made by his trading. Whether there be such a thing as profit or gain can only be ascertained by setting against the receipts the expenditure or obligations to which they have given rise ... The scheme of the Act obviously is to tax, not receipts, but profits properly so called ... I have

---

[32]   [1996] 2 FC 73 at 84.

[33]   (1892) 3 TC 185 at 194–195.

pointed out that in the charging provision it is the profits and gains properly so called, not the gross receipts, which are brought to charge.

It may be argued that section 14(1) is not needed for the deduction of expenses and is only to be read in the negative sense, in that expenses are generally deductible but section 14(1) permits outgoings to be deducted only to the extent to which they are incurred in the relevant year. In this regard, Lord Millett NPJ in construing the general deduction formula in section 16 of the Hong Kong Inland Revenue Ordinance (which is *in pari materia* with that in section 14(1) of the Singapore Income Tax Act) in *Commissioner of Inland Revenue v Secan Ltd* said[34]:

> Thus section 16 of the Ordinance lies at the heart of this case. It provides that in ascertaining the assessable profits for any year of assessment:
>
> > "there *shall* be deducted *all outgoings and expenses* to the extent to which they are incurred during the basis period for that year of assessment ... including —
> > (a) ... interest ..." (my emphasis).
>
> Both parties agree that the section is mandatory, that is to say, that it positively compels the taxpayer to deduct outgoings, including interest, in ascertaining its assessable profits. But the profits of a business cannot be ascertained without deducting the expenses and outgoings incurred in making them, and the section is not needed to authorise them to be deducted. Sections 16 and 17 (which disallows certain deductions) are enacted for the protection of the revenue, not the taxpayer, and in my opinion section 16 is to be read in a negative sense. It permits outgoings to be deducted *only* to the extent to which they are incurred in the relevant year.

2.2.1. *Commencement of business*

The threshold condition for the deduction of expenses of a business is that the business must have commenced. In other words, pre-commencement expenses are generally not deductible. The time at which a business

---

[34] [2000] 3 HKLRD 627 at [17].

commences is a question of fact and degree and may vary according to the nature of the business involved[35]. As Andrew Ang J said in *T Ltd v Comptroller of Income Tax*[36]:

> When then did the appellant's business commence? The answer to this question is of course dependent on the determination as to what the business of the appellant was.

In the case of a property investment business where a building is erected to be let, it has been held that the date of the grant of the Temporary Occupation Permit (TOP) of the rental property would be the date of commencement of letting business. In coming to his judgment in *T Ltd v Comptroller of Income* Tax, Andrew Ang J said[37]:

> In the present case, the degree of connection between the development of the property and the letting thereof is weaker. Certainly it cannot be said that the development of the property was "essential" to the letting. In theory, at least, a completed property could be bought or leased for the purpose of the letting. Besides, whereas the quarrying of limestone would be an ongoing activity throughout the life of the cement manufacturer's business, the property development in this case is a one-off affair.

As may be seen, the reason for deciding that the date of grant of the TOP as the date of commencement of the letting business, was that the property development was not an ongoing activity during the life of the letting business. In other businesses, we will have to examine the nature of the businesses and the type of activities that are ongoing throughout the life of the business to determine the date of commencement of the business. For example, in the case of company conducting a pharmaceutical business, the development of drugs is an ongoing activity throughout the life of the business. The business may be said to have commenced, as soon as the

---

[35] See IRAS e-Tax Guide, *Determination of the Date of Commencement of Business*, Second Edition, 23 March 2022.

[36] [2005] 4 SLR(R) 285 at [22].

[37] [2005] 4 SLR(R) 285 at [39].

company embarks on the development of a drug although the company has yet to earn any income at that stage.

The Court of Appeal in *T Ltd v Comptroller of Income Tax*[38] affirmed the judgment of the High Court and the treatment that a property rental business would commence from the date of the grant of the TOP and it stated:

> As found by the judge, the letting out of the shopping mall was the *only regular activity* and the primary source of the taxpayer's income. The business of the taxpayer was therefore the letting out of the shopping mall. Since this was the business of the taxpayer, it followed that its business could not have commenced before the TOP was granted for the shopping mall as it would not have been able to embark on its income-generating activity, which was the taking in of tenants. It was only upon the grant of the TOP that the shopping mall was capable of producing income and the taxpayer company was ready to begin its ordinary business operations. The purchase of the land and the construction works were preparatory steps taken towards the ultimate object of owning, managing and operating the business of letting out. (Emphasis added)

2.2.2. *Purpose test*

Where the business has commenced, the deductibility of outgoings and expenses is governed by the general deduction formula in section 14(1). The "purpose test" is applied in determining whether an expense is incurred in the production of income of the taxpayer. The application of the "purpose test" in construing the general deduction formula is endorsed by the Court of Appeal in *Comptroller of Income Tax v IA* where it stated[39]:

> It is our view that the "purpose test" is of the first importance inasmuch as given the significant difficulties in distinguishing revenue from capital transactions as stated at the outset of this judgment, this particular test provides an eminently appropriate starting-point for any inquiry of this

---

[38] [2006] 2 SLR(R) 618 at [13].

[39] [2006] 4 SLR(R) 161 at [62].

nature. In other words, the purpose of the taxpayer in entering into the transaction (here, loan) concerned must surely be of vital importance.

The "purpose" of an expenditure is to be distinguished from its "immediate reason". In the case of *KD v Comptroller of Income Tax*[40], the Singapore Income Tax Board of Review in endorsing the application of the "purpose" test, cited the Australian case of *The Herald and Weekly Times Ltd v Federal Commissioner of Taxation*[41] and it stated at [19]:

> The majority also expressed the view that the question whether money is expended in and for the production of income cannot be determined by considering only the immediate reason for making a payment and ignoring the purpose with which the liability was incurred.

For example, an employer may incur medical expenses in respect of an employee who has fallen ill. The immediate reason for the expenditure is to cure the employee. But the employer does not incur the medical expenses for an altruistic "purpose". The "purpose" of the expenditure is to render the employee fit for the production of income for the employer. Hence, medical expenses of employees incurred by the employer are deductible in ascertaining the taxable income of an employer.

Returning to the *KD* case, the taxpayer company there carried on the business of developing, manufacture and sale of *in-vitro* diagnostic tests for the detection of human infectious diseases. It was sued in Singapore by a French foundation for an infringement of its patent in respect of HIV diagnostic test kits manufactured by the taxpayer company. The matter was settled out of court and the taxpayer paid a settlement sum of $5,220,900 to the French foundation and its legal expenses amounted to $1,547,257. The Board of Review allowed the deduction of the settlement sum and the legal fees, and it stated at [25]:

> In our view, in determining whether an expenditure was incurred in the production of income, it is necessary to look at the business as a whole set

---

[40] [2006] SGITBR 3.

[41] (1932–1933) 2 ATD 169.

of operations directed towards producing income. It is an outgoing, not an incoming. Its character can be determined only in relation to the object which the person making the expenditure has in view. If the actual object is the conduct of the business on a profitable basis, then the expenditure is an expenditure incurred in producing the income.

As may be seen from the *KD* case, the immediate reason for the payment of the settlement sum and the legal fees was to bring to a conclusion the suit by the French foundation. That did not produce any income *per se*. But we do not look at the immediate reason in determining the deductibility of an expense under the general deduction formula. We look at the object or purpose of that expenditure. In expending the sums, the object and purpose of the taxpayer company in that case was for the conduct of its business on a profitable basis. On the purpose test, the expenses were held to have been incurred in the production of income and were tax-deductible, where the expenses are not capital in nature.

The Court of Appeal in *Comptroller of Income Tax v IA*[42] was of a similar view that the whole set of business operations directed towards producing income has to be looked at in considering any deduction of expenses, and it endorsed the earlier Court of Appeal case of *Pinetree Resort* and stated:

> The requisite nexus between the "expenses incurred" and "the production of income" under s 14(1) of the ITA was elucidated by the Singapore Court of Appeal in *Pinetree Resort Pte Ltd v Comptroller of Income Tax* [2000] 3 SLR(R) 136 ("*Pinetree's* case"). Chief Justice Yong Pung How held (at [47]) that:
>
> > Section 14(1) of the Income Tax Act provides that in ascertaining the income of a taxpayer for any period, there shall be deducted all outgoings and expenses wholly and exclusively incurred during that period by the taxpayer in the production of income as long as these are not expressly prohibited by other sections in the Income Tax Act. The important feature of when deductions may be made for the purposes of this case is the fact that s 14 requires a nexus between the incurrence of the expense and the production of income.

---

[42] [2006] 4 SLR(R) 161 at [98].

In determining whether this nexus is present, the business has to be
looked at as a whole set of operations directed toward producing
income, in which case an expenditure which is not capital expenditure
is usually considered as having been incurred in gaining or producing
income: *W Nevill & Co v FCT* (1937) 56 CLR 290.

In ascertaining the "purpose" of the taxpayer, the "wider nexus
test" is also used. In this regard, the Income Tax Board of Review in the
KD case, cited Australian income tax case of *The Herald and Weekly Times
Ltd v Federal Commissioner of Taxation* in support and stated at [19], [25]
and [26]:

[19] The wider approach can be seen in the decision of the majority in the
case of *The Herald and Weekly Times Ltd v Federal Commissioner of Taxation*
[1932–33] 2 ATD 169. In this case, the taxpayer which was the proprietor
and publisher of a newspaper sought to deduct compensation paid for
damages in respect of defamatory matters published in the newspaper, and
also for legal costs incurred to contest the claims against it and in obtaining
advice. The majority of the court allowed the deduction on the ground that
the claims arose from acts done for the earning of income, acts which
formed the essence of the business. The majority also expressed the view
that the question whether money is expended in and for the production of
income cannot be determined by considering only the immediate reason
for making a payment and ignoring the purpose with which the liability
was incurred. The narrower approach can be seen in the decision of the
minority in *The Herald and Weekly Times Ltd v Federal Commissioner of
Taxation* case. The minority would have disallowed the claim because the
expenditure was not productive of any income, it was incurred to pay
compensation for civil wrongs that have been committed. ...

[25] In our view, in determining whether an expenditure was incurred
in the production of income, it is necessary to look at the business as a
whole set of operations directed towards producing income. No
expenditure, strictly speaking, in itself actually gains or produces
income. It is an outgoing, not an incoming. Its character can be
determined only in relation to the object which the person making
the expenditure has in view. If the actual object is the conduct of the

business on a profitable basis, then the expenditure is an expenditure incurred in producing the income. In our view, for an expenditure to be incurred in the production of income, it is both sufficient and necessary that the occasion of the expense should be found in whatever is productive of the income.

[26] We agree with the Appellant's view that the settlement sum was incurred to deal with the liability arising out of the Appellant's business activities, namely the manufacture and sale of the HIV test kits without a licence for the relevant period. Such activities were carried out with the objective of producing income. We are also of the view that the legal expenses were incurred for the purposes of the Appellant's business activities, namely the manufacture and sale of the HIV test kits which were carried out with the objective of producing income.

The "wider nexus test" has also received endorsement by the Court of Appeal in the *IA* case, where it stated at [99] and [100]:

[99] In the Australian High Court decision of *W Nevill and Company Limited v The Federal Commissioner of Taxation* (1937) 56 CLR 290 (which was also cited in *Pinetree's* case, as noted in the preceding paragraph), Latham CJ stated (at 301):

The mere reduction of expenditure, though it decreases the expenditure side of an account, does not increase the receipts side of the same account. In my opinion the answer to this contention is to be found in a recognition of the fact that it is necessary, for income tax purposes, to look at a business as a whole set of operations directed towards producing income. No expenditure, strictly and narrowly considered, in itself actually gains or produces income. It is an outgoing, not an incoming. Its character can be determined only in relation to the object which the person making the expenditure has in view. If the actual object is the conduct of the business on a profitable basis with that due regard to economy which is essential in any well conducted business, then the expenditure (if not a capital expenditure) is an expenditure incurred in gaining or producing the assessable income. If it is not a capital expenditure it should be deducted in ascertaining the taxable income of the taxpayer.

Indeed, a holistic view that eschews artificiality and technicality ought to prevail (see also *per* Rich, Dixon and McTiernan JJ at 304, 307 and 309, respectively).

[100] Applying the wider nexus test as laid down by the Court of Appeal in *Pinetree's* case, the Prepayment Penalty and Guarantee Expenses permitted the respondent to obtain substantial interest savings thereby increasing the respondent's overall profitability. As such, these Expenses can be regarded as having been incurred "in the production of income" under s 14(1) of the [Income Tax Act].

In the *IA* case, the taxpayer which was a developer had to pay a prepayment penalty to the bank for prematurely terminating the borrowing on account of the ready sale of the apartments under development. The developer also had to incur guarantee expenses for the withdrawal of moneys from the project account maintained with the Controller of Housing, to pay the bank and for other expenses. Both the prepayment penalty and the guarantee expenses were not incurred for the erection and sale of the apartments. However, with the early repayment of the loan moneys to the bank, there were substantial interest savings which increased its overall profitability of the developer. The prepayment penalty and the guarantee expenses which were expenses incurred to reduce further expenses, were nevertheless held to have been incurred "in the production of income".

In considering a deduction of an expense, one has to apply the law on the facts as one finds them. As Innes CJ said in the South African case of *Commissioner of Inland Revenue v George Forest Timber Co Ltd*[43]:

> It is dangerous in income tax cases to depart from the actual facts; the true course is to take the facts as they stand and apply the provisions of the statute.

For example, an individual may incur interest expenses in respect of two apartments which he has acquired. One of the apartments is let while the other apartment is owner-occupied. The individual may use the rental income from the apartment which is let, to pay down the loan amount for the

---

[43] (1924) 1 SATC 20 at 23.

owner-occupied apartment. The deductibility of the interest expense against the rental income from the apartment which is let, is not to be challenged on the basis that the individual should have used the rental income to pay down the loan amount for the apartment which is let instead. The deductibility of the expense is to be considered on the facts, and not on an alternative hypothetical basis that the individual should have acted otherwise.

In applying the law to the facts as we find them, in determining the deductibility of the expenses, there can also be no question as to the necessity of the expenditure. As Romer LJ said in *Bentleys, Stokes and Lowless v Beeson (Inspector of Taxes)*[44]:

> Expenditure is permitted as a deduction under r. 3(a) if it is:
>
> > "wholly and exclusively laid out or expended for the purposes of the trade, profession ..." etc.
>
> and this language makes no reference to the necessity of the expenditure. If any particular expenditure is necessary for the purposes of a profession it presumably satisfies the test laid down by the rule, but there is no warrant for saying that the absence of necessity automatically prevents it from doing so. It is not for the commissioners to prescribe what expenditure is or is not necessary for the conduct of a profession or business, and they should not, in our judgment, have applied their minds to that question in the present case. The first reason, accordingly, on which the commissioners based their decision was wanting in the requisite element of relevance. (Emphasis added)

2.2.3. *In the production of income*

The words "in the production of income" which appear in the general deduction formula in section 14(1), impose no requirement that income must be produced in the same period in order for the relevant outgoings and expenses to be deductible.

The South African income tax case of *Sub-Nigel Ltd v Commissioner of Inland Revenue*[45], authoritatively establishes that the words "incurred in

---

[44] [1952] 2 All ER 82 at 86.

[45] [1948] (4) SA 580.

the production of income" do not mean that before a particular item of expenditure may be deducted, it must be shown that it produced any part of the income for the particular year of assessment. The important question is: "Was the expenditure incurred for the purpose of earning income?" In the *Sub-Nigel* case, it was held that the expense of premiums on insurance policies against loss of profits occasioned by fire, were incurred in the production of income, although the fire did not occur in the same year of assessment so as to trigger a payment from the insurance company. Whether or not the expense produced any income is not relevant, so long as the expense was incurred for the purpose of producing income. In this regard, Centlivres CJ in delivering the judgment of the Appellate Division in the *Sub-Nigel* case, said[46]:

> It seems to me clear on the authorities that the court is not concerned whether a particular item of expenditure produced any part of the income: what it is concerned with is whether that item of expenditure was incurred for the purposes of earning income ....
>
> The whole *raison d'etre* of the company is to earn profits, and in taking out these policies it was endeavouring to maintain its profits by making provision against loss in the event of a fire. Now, was the act entailing the expenditure of the amounts paid by way of premium performed for the purpose of earning income? In my opinion the answer to this question is in the affirmative. *The mere fact that no income [has] actually resulted is, in my view, irrelevant*: the purpose was to obtain income on the happening of a fire which would prevent the carrying on of income-producing operations. There can, to my mind, be no doubt that if a fire had occurred, the proceeds paid by the company's insurer in respect of the policies insuring net profits would have been a non-capital nature and would therefore have had to be include in the company "gross income".

In the Malaysian income tax case of *KHK Advertising Sdn Bhd v Ketua Pengarah Hasil Dalam Negeri*, KC Vohrah J similarly said[47]:

---

[46]   [1948] (4) SA 580 at 592–593.

[47]   [2001] 5 MLJ 177 at 184.

It is generally accepted that the phrase 'in the production of gross income' means that the *expenditure incurred need not produce income in the same year. In fact, an expenditure incurred may not produce income but may lead to a loss.* In *Vallambrosa Rubber Co Ltd v Farmer* STC 529, this principle that expenditure need not produce income in the same basis period is explained as follows:

> We find from your own admission that at present in this year, only a seventh of your rubber trees are in full bearing, and therefore, they say, we shall hold that only one-seventh of these expenses can be expenses of the ordinary business and as such deductible, and that the other six-sevenths are not deductible. Now, that somewhat startling result was before your Lordships argued on two grounds. The junior counsel for the Crown, encouraged by certain expressions which he found used by various learned judges who had given judgments in Tax Cases, wished your Lordships to accept this proposition, that nothing ever could be deducted as an expense unless that expense was purely and solely referable to a profit which was reaped within the year. I think that proposition has only to be stated to be defeated by its own absurdity.

An expense which is incurred after the production of income, may also be deductible, as was pointed out by Yong Pung How CJ in *Pinetree Resort Pte Ltd v Comptroller of Income Tax*[48]:

> As pointed out by the respondent [the Comptroller], it is settled law in many jurisdictions that it is not necessary, in order to render an expense deductible, that the expense in question should produce assessable income in the same year in which the expenditure is incurred. Moreover, the respondent [the Comptroller] had implicitly acknowledged that the refunds would be deductible in the event that the appellants have to pay this out in the future.

Some examples of the incurring of expenses after the production of income are as follows:

---

[48] [2000] 3 SLR(R) 136 at [50].

(a) A company owning a factory or shop used for its business may receive a notice from the Comptroller of Property Tax under section 22 of the Property Tax Act increasing the property tax or imposing the property tax for new buildings, such that the increase is retrospective to the previous years. The property tax expense would be incurred at the time that the notice is received and would be deductible, even though the factory or shop may have been used earlier to produce the income for the company.

(b) A company selling a product, may provide for a warranty of the product. In a subsequent year, the company may be asked to rectify the product without the ability to charge for the rectification. The cost of rectifying the product incurred in the subsequent year would be deductible in that year, although the assessable income has been earned in an earlier year.

(c) A company in its annual general meeting may decide on the director's fees for the services rendered by the directors in the previous years. The fees although incurred in a year subsequent to the year in which the director renders his services and produced the income for the company, may still be deductible in the subsequent year[49].

(d) The incurrence of the damages for torts committed or may have been committed by the taxpayer or its staff, where income may be been earned earlier, such as damages for defamation, accidents, breach of intellectual property rights, etc. In the Income Tax Board of Review case of *KD v Comptroller of Income Tax*[50], the Board held that the compensation payment made by the taxpayer to settle an infringement claim and the legal costs incurred in defending the claim were incurred in the production of the income and therefore deductible. In that case, the compensation was paid by the taxpayer on or about 8 September 2001 and amounted to $5,220,900 (or US$3 million),

---

[49] In practice, the Comptroller will typically allow deduction of director's fees approved in arrears for the year in which they are properly ascertained and accrued as expenses in the company's financial accounts in accordance with generally accepted accounting principles. This is provided that the payments are expected to occur shortly after they are accrued in the financial accounts. In the case of director's fees approved in arrears, the fees should be tabled and put to vote at the annual general meeting in which the financial accounts for the accounting year concerned are voted and approved. See IRAS e-Tax Guide, *Tax Treatment of Director's Fees and Bonuses from Employment*, Second Edition, 12 September 2014.

[50] [2006] SGITBR 3.

which was calculated using a rate of US$2.20 for every HIV test sold by the taxpayer for the period from 6 October 1992 to 3 February 2000 (the period of the infringement). The settlement sum was held to be deductible notwithstanding that the infringements occurred and the income earned, years before the incurrence of the compensation payment. In that case, the Board stated:

> In our view, in determining whether an expenditure was incurred in the production of income, it is necessary to look at the business as a whole set of operations directed towards producing income. It is an outgoing, not an incoming. Its character can be determined only in relation to the object which the person making the expenditure has in view. If the actual object is the conduct of the business on a profitable basis, then the expenditure is an expenditure incurred in producing the income.

(e) Similarly in *Port Elizabeth Electric Tramway Co Ltd v Commissioner of Inland Revenue*[51], a driver of the taxpayer which was a transport company met with a fatal accident while driving one of the trams belonging to the company. The company had to pay compensation to the estate of the deceased, which was held to be deductible. The result would be the same whether the liability to pay is in the same year of the death of the employee or in a subsequent year. Had the company paid a non-employee killed or injured by its negligent employee, such payment arising not from contract but from tort, will also be so deductible where they are incurred some years after the accident.

(f) A developer may have to do rectification works for the condominium that it may have sold. This may occur (a) during the warranty period where the purchasers may sue under contract, (b) outside the warranty period where the purchasers may sue under tort for negligence, or (c) where the developer may as a responsible developer decide to do the rectification works without any admission of liability under contract or tort in order that customers continue to buy their products. In all these cases, the expenses incurred years after the income is earned, have been deductible.

---

[51]   (1930) 8 SATC 13.

(g) A company upon the expiry of a tenancy, has to do some repair works for the rented premises. This may occur after the end of the financial year, after some long-drawn dispute with the landlord as to whether it is wear and tear or damage caused by the tenant. In such a situation, the expense would have been incurred after the income has been earned using the rented premises in the earlier year and would have been deductible.

2.2.4. Duality of purpose

The general deduction formula provides for the deduction of expenses which are "wholly and exclusively" incurred in the production of income. The word "exclusively" points to "exclusive in purpose".

The purpose or object of the taxpayer in incurring the expense must be distinguished from the effect of the expense. In the English income tax case of *Vodafone Cellular Ltd v Shaw (Inspector of Taxes)*[52], the taxpayer Vodafone made a substantial payment to rid the group of companies (of which Vodafone was the parent) of a trading liability, which also benefitted two subsidiaries within the group. The English Court of Appeal held that the trading liability in question was a liability of the taxpayer alone and the intentions of the directors of Vodafone in making the payment, whether articulated or not, was exclusively to serve the purposes of the taxpayer's trade. The fact that the payment might benefit the subsidiary companies was merely a consequential and incidental effect of the elimination of the liability. It was not the purpose of the taxpayer. In that case, Millett LJ (as he then was) in allowing the deduction of the payment, said at page 742:

> The object of the taxpayer in making the payment must be distinguished from the effect of the payment. A payment may be made exclusively for the purposes of the trade even though it also secures a private benefit. This will be the case if the securing of the private benefit was not the object of the payment but merely a consequential and incidental effect of the payment.

---

[52] [1997] STC 734.

Similarly in *Bentleys, Stokes & Lawless v Beeson*[53], the English Court of Appeal allowed the deduction of the expenditure as the purpose of the expenditure was for the promotion of the trade of the taxpayer, although a consequential effect is the element of hospitality. In that case, Romer LJ in delivering the judgment of the Court of Appeal said at page 84:

> The sole question is whether the expenditure in question was 'exclusively' laid out for business purposes, that is: What was the motive or object in the mind of the two individuals responsible for the activities in question? ... Entertaining involves inevitably the characteristic of hospitality. Giving to charity or subscribing to a staff pension fund involves inevitably the object of benefaction. An undertaking to guarantee to a limited amount a national exhibition involves inevitably supporting that exhibition and the purposes for which it has been organised. But the question in all such cases is: Was the entertaining, the charitable subscription, the guarantee, undertaken solely for the purpose of business, that is, solely with the object of promoting the business or its profit-earning capacity?
>
> It is, as we have said, a question of fact. And it is quite clear that the purpose must be the sole purpose. The paragraph says so in clear terms. If the activity be undertaken with the object both of promoting business and also with some other purpose, for example, with the object of indulging an independent wish of entertaining a friend or a stranger or of supporting a charitable or benevolent object, then the paragraph is not satisfied though in the mind of the actor the business motive may predominate. For the statute so prescribes. *Per contra*, if in truth the sole object is business promotion, the expenditure is not disqualified because the nature of the activity necessarily involves some other result, or the attainment or furtherance of some other objective, since the latter result or object is necessarily inherent in the act.

2.2.5. *Practical and business point of view*

Another guiding principle in the interpretation of the general deduction formula in section 14(1) of Income Tax Act is that practical and commercial considerations have to be taken into account in determining the deduction

---

[53] [1952] 2 All ER 82.

of expenses. In this regard, in the Australian income tax case of *Hallstroms Proprietary Ltd v Federal Commissioner of Taxation*[54], Dixon J in considering whether an expenditure is on revenue or capital account, said at page 648[55]:

> What is an outgoing of capital and what is an outgoing of revenue depends on what the expenditure is calculated to effect from a practical and business point of view, rather than upon the juristic classification of legal rights, if any, secured, employed or exhausted in the process.

In the Privy Council case of *Commissioner of Inland Revenue v Lo & Lo,* Lord Brightman also said[56]:

> In the opinion of their Lordships, commercial considerations are not wholly to be disregarded in the course of this process [of determining whether an expense is deductible or not]. They are relevant for the purpose of deciding what can properly be treated as "outgoings and expenses ... incurred during the basis period ... in the production of profits in respect of which ..." the taxpayer is chargeable to tax.

2.2.6. *Capital expenditure vs revenue expenditure*

"Generally, since income tax is levied in respect of only revenue receipts and not capital receipts, as a corollary, deductions are also allowed only in respect of revenue expenditure and not capital expenditure. The revenue-capital distinction is fundamental to the law of income taxation"[57]. Business expenses may therefore be denied deduction where they are capital in nature[58].

An "adequate working formulation" of the distinction between revenue and capital expenditures, as stated by the Court of Appeal in *BFC v Comptroller of Income Tax* is as follows[59]:

---

[54] (1946) 72 CLR 634.

[55] See *ABD Pte Ltd v Comptroller of Income Tax*, [2010] 3 SLR 609 at [59].

[56] [1984] 1 WLR 986 at 991, on appeal from Hong Kong.

[57] *per* Tay Yong Kwang JA in *BML v Comptroller of Income Tax*, [2018] 2 SLR 1009 at [30].

[58] S 15(1)(c) of the Income Tax Act.

[59] [2014] 4 SLR 33 at [12].

The distinction between capital expenditure and revenue expenditure is that between "the cost of creating, acquiring or enlarging the permanent (which does not mean perpetual) structure of which the income is to be the produce or fruit" on the one hand, and "the cost of earning that income itself or performing the income-earning operations" on the other.

The two major tests frequently used in determining if an expense is revenue or capital in nature are the "enduring benefit" test and the "identifiable asset" test. Where there is no "enduring benefit" or no "new asset" created, the expenses concerned are considered revenue in nature. On the other hand, where a new asset is created or there is enduring benefit, as a consequence of the incurring of the expense, the expense is capital in nature.

2.2.6.1. Enduring benefit test

In *ABD Pte Ltd v Comptroller of Income Tax*, Andrew Phang JA stated that the main test in discerning whether an expense is capital or revenue in nature is the "enduring benefit of the trade" test[60]:

> In the circumstances, it would appear that the "enduring benefit of the trade" test (enunciated by Viscount Cave LC in *Atherton* (see above at [45]) is, despite its weaknesses (see above at [48]), probably still — in substance at least — the main test.

The *dicta* of Viscount Cave LC referred to above, was earlier cited by Andrew Phang JA at [45] of the *ABD Ltd* case as follows:

> The *second* — and, arguably, most well-known as well as well-cited — test is to be found in the judgment of Viscount Cave LC in *Atherton*. In that decision, the learned law lord observed thus (at 213–214):
>
> > But when an expenditure is made, *not only once and for all*, but *with a view to bringing into existence and asset or an advantage for the enduring benefit of a trade*, I think that there is very good reason (in the absence

---

[60]   [2010] 3 SLR 609 at [69].

of special circumstances leading to an opposite conclusion) for treating such an expenditure as properly attributable not to revenue but to *capital*. [emphasis added in italics and bold italics in grounds of judgment]

The meaning of the words "enduring benefit" was earlier enunciated by Rowlatt J in *Anglo Persian Oil Co Ltd v Dale (HM Inspector of Taxes)*[61] (cited with approval in the Singapore Court of Appeal case of *Comptroller of Income Tax v IA*[62]):

> ... It means a thing which endures in a way that fixed capital endures. It is not always an actual asset, but it endures in the way that getting rid of a lease or getting rid of onerous capital assets or something of that sort as we have had in the cases, endures. I think that the Commissioners, with great respect, have been misled by the way in which they have been "enduring" to mean merely something that extends over a number of years.

As may be seen, the term "enduring benefit" does not therefore mean that the benefit endures for a number of years. The term is used in the sense of being in the nature of "fixed capital". The above *dicta* of Rowlatt J in the *Anglo Persian Oil* case was cited with approval by the Court of Appeal in *Comptroller of Income Tax v IA*, where the Court after citing the above passage from *Anglo Persian Oil*, stated[63]:

> What this means is that a payment may be made and be deductible as revenue expenditure even though it provides a long term advantage to the trade. This can be so even though the payment does not relate to anything which can be described as a capital asset. Even where it does, a deduction may be possible. Thus in the House of Lords decision of *Commissioners of Inland Revenue v Carron Company* (1968) 45 TC 18, Lord Reid said (at 68):
>
> > [M]oney spent on income account, for example on durable repairs, may often yield an enduring advantage. In a case of this kind what matters is the nature of the advantage for which the money was spent.

---

[61] (1931) 16 TC 253 at 262.

[62] [2006] 4 SLR(R) 161 at [106].

[63] [2006] 4 SLR(R) 161 at [106].

2.2.6.2. Identifiable asset test

Another test that has been used in determining whether an asset is capital in nature, is the "identifiable asset test". In this regard, Andrew Phang JA in the High Court case of *ABD Pte Ltd v Comptroller of Income Tax*[64], after evaluating various tests, proceeded to provide a composite and integrated approach in evaluating where an expense is capital or revenue in nature. In setting out the "First Principle (General)", Andrew Phang JA said at [71]:

> First, the court must, as a matter of general principle, look closely at the purpose of the expenditure and ascertain whether or not such expenditure either created a new asset or opened new fields of trading not hitherto available to the taxpayer ... in which case the expenditure concerned would be capital (and not revenue) in nature.

Having set out the guiding principles above, we will discuss the deduction of some of the expenses frequently encountered in property investment.

2.2.7. *Deduction of interest expense*

One significant expense incurred for the purpose of producing rental income is interest which may be incurred in the acquisition or development of the rental property. The "current position"[65] is that the interest expense may qualify for deduction under section 14(1)(a)(i) as "any sum payable by way of interest upon any money borrowed by that person where the Comptroller is satisfied that such sum is payable on capital employed in acquiring the

---

[64] [2010] 3 SLR 609.

[65] The words 'current position' were used by Tay Yong Kwang JA in delivering the judgment of the Court of Appeal in *BML v Comptroller of Income Tax*, [2018] 2 SLR 1009 at [37] following from the earlier Court of Appeal judgment in *BFC v Comptroller of Income Tax*, [2014] 4 SLR 33 where the Court held that interest expense incurred even during the period when a property is producing income is capital expenditure which qualifies for deduction under s 14(1)(a) which is an exception to s 15(1)(c) which otherwise denies deduction of capital expenditure. The position in *BFC* is a departure from the Court's earlier position in *T Ltd v Comptroller of Income Tax*, [2005] 4 SLR) 618 (where Tay Yong Kwang J (as he then was) delivered the judgment of the Court of Appeal) that interest expenses becomes a revenue expenditure as soon as the property started producing income. On that basis, the interest expense where it is revenue expenditure would have been deductible under the general deduction formula in s 14(1) or alternatively under s 14(1)(a).

income". Such a deduction is allowable even though the interest expense may be a capital expenditure, as section 14(1)(a) is an exception to section 15(1)(c) which prohibits the deduction of capital expenditure.

The interplay between the specific deduction provisions in section 14(1)(a)(i) with those in section 15(1)(c) which prohibits the deduction of an expense which is capital in nature, has been of some controversy[66]. Nevertheless from the practical standpoint, interest expense incurred directly in the acquisition of a rental property would be deductible upon the property producing income.

A number of cases on the construction of section 14(1)(a) of the Income Tax Act have been dealt with by the Singapore courts. In *Andermatt Investments Pte Ltd v Comptroller of Income Tax*[67], the rental property was acquired in an indirect manner, i.e. first by acquisition of the shares of the company that owned the rental property followed by the liquidation of the company such that the rental property was then distributed *in specie* to the shareholder who was the taxpayer in that case[68].

In *Andermatt*, the Court of Appeal in construing the words "capital employed in acquiring the income" in section 14(1)(a), has held that a direct link is required between the money borrowed and the income produced, in order that the interest expense is to be deducted. The direct link test has since been held as a universal test for section 14(1)(a) in *BML v Comptroller of Income Tax*[69], where the Court of Appeal reasoned that the direct link test is grounded in the statutory language of section 14(1)(a) at [48]:

[66] See Justin Jerzy Tan, 'A Big, Frustrating Conundrum: Reflections on Singapore's Deduction Regime for Interest and Other Borrowing Costs Following BFC v CIT, (2015) 27 SAcLJ 506. In *BML v Comptroller of Income Tax*, [2018] 2 SLR 1009, Tay Yong Kwang JA in delivering the grounds of judgment of the Court of Appeal noted at [37]: 'The interaction between ss 14(1), 14(1)(a) and 15(1)(c) is an important but perplexing issue. ... We appreciate that there has been some concern with the approach taken in BFC.'

[67] [1995] 2 SLR(R) 866.

[68] At that time, there was no *ad valorem* stamp duty for the distribution *in specie* of the immovable property to the shareholders upon liquidation of the company. Hence there were stamp duty savings with the indirect acquisition of the immovable property where the shares of the company holding the immovable property were first acquired which was followed by the liquidation of the company, as the stamp duty on the acquisition of the shares of the company were much lower than that on the acquisition of the immovable property. However since 2002, such distribution *in specie* attracts the stamp duty as a conveyance on sale of the immovable property with the coming into operation of the Stamp Duties (Amendment) Act 2002 (Act 38 of 2002).

[69] [2018] 2 SLR 1009 at [44].

In our view, the direct link test is grounded in the statutory language of s 14(1)(*a*) and in particular, the words "capital employed in acquiring the income". The language of the provision states that deductions are allowed in respect of interest paid on "any money borrowed" amounting to "capital" that to the satisfaction of the CIT is "employed in acquiring the income". This imports necessarily the requirement of a nexus — which we agree can be articulated conveniently as a "direct link" — between the loan and the acquisition of the income. In practical terms, to establish the deductibility of an interest expense, the taxpayer should ordinarily be able to particularise how it had employed the borrowed funds in the acquisition of the income against which a deduction is sought. Therefore, we do not think that the general applicability of the direct link test can be contested seriously.

In *BML*, the Court of Appeal in discussing *Andermatt*, stated as follows[70]:

[39] Traditionally, this phrase ["capital employed in acquiring the income"] is taken to imply a direct link requirement. The genesis of this direct link test is the Court of Appeal's decision in *Andermatt Investments Pte Ltd v Comptroller of Income Tax* [1995] 2 SLR(R) 866 ("*Andermatt*") where the court held that the phrase "capital employed in acquiring the income" in s 14(1)(*a*) required a direct link between the money borrowed and the income produced. In that case, the taxpayer company desired to purchase a property owned by another company. In order to take advantage of a tax concession in the applicable Stamp Duties Act (Cap. 312, 1985 Rev Ed), the taxpayer decided to acquire the property indirectly by purchasing the latter company's shares and thereafter initiating its voluntary winding up, rather than purchasing the property directly. The shares of the target company were accordingly acquired by the taxpayer on 8 December 1987. Two months later, on 8 February 1988, the taxpayer obtained an overdraft facility to finance the remaining consideration for the prior acquisition of the company. On 31 March 1988, the property was transferred to the taxpayer pursuant to the voluntary liquidation of the target company. The issue was whether the taxpayer was entitled to deduct the interest paid on the overdraft facility against the rental income derived from the transferred property.

---

[70] [2018] 2 SLR 1009.

[40] The Court of Appeal affirmed the direct link test in the context of s 14(1)(*a*) and held, on the facts, that the test was not satisfied as the overdraft had been taken out for the purpose of acquiring the shares of the target company rather than the property itself which generated the rental income (at [26] and [27]):

> [26] Reverting to the problem in hand, it seems to us that at the end of the day it is the few key words in the section which are going to decide the matter: 'capital employed in acquiring the income'. It is only when the answer to this question, whether the overdraft was employed in acquiring the rental income, is in the affirmative that the interest incurred would be deductible from the rental income. We do not think one should disregard the manner in which the appellant has gone about arranging the transaction. Whatever may be said to be the motive behind the arrangement, there is no denying that the overdraft was used to pay a debt, or the purchase price of the shares from the vendors. ... The overdraft has nothing to do with the acquisition of the ...property, except in the remote sense.

> [27] We endorse the view that under s 14(1)(*a*) there must be a direct link between the money borrowed and the income produced. ...

On the facts in *Andermatt*, the Court of Appeal had earlier denied the deduction of the interest expense on the ground that there was no direct link between the money borrowed and the rental income produced.

2.2.7.1. Interest expense in acquiring rental income — Capital expense?

The current position is that interest expense would be nevertheless deductible under section 14(1)(a) being an exception to the prohibition against deduction of capital expenditure under section 15(1)(c) of the Income Tax Act[71].

---

[71] *BFC v Comptroller of Income Tax*, [2014] 4 SLR 33. Although in deciding that s 14(1)(a) is an exception to s 15(1)(c) which prohibits the deduction of capital expenditure, the Court provided a practical solution to the deduction of interest expense incurred in producing income, it is not satisfactory as it runs counter with the express words in the opening words of s 15(1) which provide that 'notwithstanding the provisions of this Act, ... no deduction shall be allowed in respect of'. It is noted that within s 15(1)(c) itself, an express exception is provided for s 14(1)(h) but not s 14(1)(a).

However earlier in the Court of Appeal case of *T Ltd v Comptroller of Income Tax*[72], which concerned the development of a shopping mall which produced rental income for the taxpayer, the position was different. It was held in that case that once the shopping mall produces rental income, the interest expense becomes revenue in nature and therefore deductible under section 14(1)(a). Section 15(1)(c) which prohibits the deduction of capital expenditure simply does not apply in relation to interest expense incurred after the property is producing income. It is then not necessary to decide that section 14(1)(a) is an exception to section 15(1)(c) to enable the deduction of the interest expense against the rental income.

T Ltd in essence followed the Privy Council case of *Wharf Properties Ltd v Commissioner of Inland Revenue*[73] which concerned the development of Times Square at Causeway Bay in Hong Kong. There, the taxpayer claimed the deduction of the interest expense incurred during the period of development and before the shopping center produced income. In *Wharf Properties*, Lord Hoffman in denying the deduction, said:

> First, [counsel for the taxpayer] said that interest was by definition a revenue payment and could not be anything else. Their Lordships think that this confuses the position of payer and recipient. It is true that in the hands of the recipient, interest will be either the earnings of capital advanced or, in some cases, additional income derived from trading in money. In either case, it will have the character of income. From the point of view of the payer, however, a payment of interest may be a capital or revenue expense, depending upon the purpose for which it was paid. The fact that it is income in the hands of the recipient and a recurring and periodic payment does not necessarily mean that it must be a revenue expense. *Wages and rent are income in the hands of their recipients; periodic payments, in return for services or the use of land or chattels respectively. But whether such payments are of a capital or revenue nature depends on their purpose.* The wages of an electrician employed in the construction of a building by an owner who intends to retain the building as a capital investment are part of its capital cost. The wages of the same electrician

---

[72] [2006] 2 SLR(R) 618 at [24].
[73] [1997] AC 505, on appeal from Hong Kong.

employed by a construction company, or by the building owner in maintaining the building when it is completed and let, are a revenue expense.

For this purpose, their Lordships consider that there is no material distinction between interest and other periodic payments. As Lord Upjohn said in *Chancery Lane Safe Deposit and Offices Co. Ltd. v. Inland Revenue Commissioners* [1966] AC 85, 124 (in a passage quoted by the Commissioner in his correct and succinct reasons for disallowing the deduction): "the cost of hiring money to rebuild a house is just as much a capital cost as the cost of hiring labour to do the rebuilding". ....

Each payment of interest must be considered in relation to the purpose of the loan during the period for which the interest was paid. Once the asset has been acquired or created and is producing income, the interest is part of the cost of generating that income and therefore a revenue expense. (Emphasis added)

It is to be noted that we have to look at the use of the money during the period in respect of which "each payment of interest" is made. This ties back to the words of section 14(1)(a) which provide that deduction is to be made of "any sum payable by way of interest upon money borrowed on capital employed in acquiring the income".

The *dicta* in *Wharf Properties* was commented on favorably in an article, and the example of rent used Lord Hoffman in that case was elaborated on, as follows[74]:

The Privy Council's reference to rent is apt in the present context. Rent is the amount payable by a person for the use of another person's property. Interest is the amount payable by a person for the use of another person's money. Interest is really only rent of a very specific nature, and there is no policy reason for it to be treated differently. Like rent, interest can sometimes be a capital expenditure and sometimes a revenue expenditure, depending on the factual circumstances during the period for the interest is payable.

If a person pays rent to acquire the use of a building as office space for its employees or to house its manufacturing equipment, the rent is clearly

---

[74] See Michael Templeton in *The Earth is Not Flat — Gifford v The Queen* 2001 DTC 168, [2001] 2 CTC 2162, (2001) 49 *Canadian Tax Journal* 720 at 723.

a revenue expense. The rent is a recurring, ongoing expense that does not create an enduring asset. The payment of rent obtains the use of an asset for a limited time. The fact that the asset may be an item of capital does not change this analysis and make the rental payment a capital expenditure. Similarly, under a loan, the payment of interest obtains for a borrower of capital the use of a sum of money for a limited time. The fact that the borrowed money may be used to acquire a capital asset should not make the interest payment a capital expenditure.

If, however, rent is paid to acquire the use of a tool that is first used to construct a building and then to maintain it, the characterization of the rent will change as the use of the tool changes. During the period in which the tool is used to construct the building, it is being used for a capital purpose, to create an asset of enduring value; therefore, the payment of rent for this period would be a capital expenditure in the same way that payments for labour and other inputs into the creation of an asset would be capitalized. However, during the period in which the tool is used to maintain the building, it is no longer being used to create an asset of enduring value, and the rental payments for this period would be considered to be on revenue account.

However in *BFC v Comptroller of Income Tax*[75], the Court of Appeal held that interest expense payable on a loan remains capital in nature even after the capital asset acquired with the loan, has started producing income. Such a decision would render the interest expense non-deductible on account of section 15(1)(c) which prohibits the deduction of capital expenditure. The Court then decided that section 14(1)(a) was an exception to section 15(1)(c) paving the way for its deduction. In coming to its judgment, the Court reasoned as follows:

[30] We endorse the proposition of law enunciated in *T Ltd* and *IA*, which accords with first principles. A loan that is capital in nature is one that is taken for the purpose of acquiring or enlarging the permanent structure of a business. The paradigm example of a loan that is capital in nature would be one that is taken for the purpose of purchasing a capital asset, e.g, a piece of land or machinery. When interest is payable on such a loan, we

---

[75]   [2014] 4 SLR 33.

think the interest should be considered to be part of the overall cost of purchasing the capital asset. Let us say a taxpayer purchases some machinery for $100,000, and in taking a loan of this amount for that purpose, has to pay interest amounting to $10,000. It appears to us that the overall cost of the machinery is $110,000, being the purchase price of $100,000 plus the interest of $10,000. The capital asset being a component of the permanent structure of the taxpayer's business, the interest of $10,000 is part of the overall cost of acquiring or enlarging that permanent structure and is, for that reason, capital expenditure.

[31] What has just been stated is not confined to loans taken for the purpose of purchasing a capital asset. It also applies to any loan that is taken for the purpose of acquiring or enlarging the permanent structure of a business. In other words, it applies to any loan that is capital in nature, for the interest payable on such a loan would be part of the overall cost of acquiring or enlarging the permanent structure of a business and would, for that reason, be capital expenditure. In fact, we can generalise further, for interest is not the only type of borrowing cost that may be incurred on a loan. Let us say agency fees are incurred in taking a loan for the purpose of purchasing a capital asset. Such fees are, like any interest payable on the loan, part of the overall cost of purchasing the capital asset, and are therefore capital expenditure. This logic extends to all types of borrowing costs relating to all loans of a capital nature: any borrowing cost incurred on any loan that is capital in nature would be capital expenditure.

The authors prefer the position held in *T Ltd*, as it places emphasis on the entire phrase in section 14(1)(a), i.e. "any sum payable by way of interest upon any money borrowed by that person where ... the interest was payable on capital employed in acquiring the income", rather than the shorter phrase "capital employed in acquiring the income". With this emphasis, weight should be placed on each payment of interest. Normally, interest expense is payable over the period of loan and is a recurrent expense. With this reading, the following fall in place:

(a) There is no need to create an exception to section 15(1)(c) for section 14(1)(a) where the express language in section 15(1)(c) does not do so;

(b) There is no necessity for the administrative concession given by the Comptroller of Income Tax in respect of refinancing of loans.

In the authors' view, the words "any sum payable by way of interest upon any money borrowed" in section 14(1)(a) have to be read in the context of "each payment of interest" by the taxpayer. We will discuss this view, in relation to the case of *Andermatt*. An appreciation of the facts in *Andermatt* is crucial in understanding that decision. In that case, the taxpayer company purchased all the issued shares of a company called Wan Holdings Pte Ltd for a consideration of $20,000,030 on 8 December 1987 and became the holding company of Wan Holdings which in turn owned a property at No. 1 Jalan Remaja (the "Hillview property"). The purchase consideration was satisfied by the payment of $1 million and the remaining sum of $19,000,030 stood as a debt owing by the taxpayer to the vendors of the shares. The taxpayers subsequently on 8 February 1988 obtained an overdraft facility of $6 million and drew down $5.8 million to satisfy part of the purchase consideration.

On 31 March 1988, upon the winding up of Wan Holdings, the Hillview property was distributed to the taxpayer as a return of capital *in specie*. In the financial period from 28 November 1987 to 31 December 1988, the taxpayer derived dividend income amounting to $4,620,007 from its holding of the Wan Holdings shares. The dividends were received by the taxpayer on 5 January 1988. In the *same financial period*, the taxpayer also derived rental income amounting to about $600,000 from the direct holding of the Hillview property. An interest expense of about $200,000 was incurred in the *same financial period* from the drawdown of the overdraft.

The taxpayer claimed the deduction of the interest expenses against the rental income from the Hillview property but the claim was disallowed by the Comptroller of Income Tax. The disallowance was upheld by the Court of Appeal and Chao Hick Tin J (as he then was) in delivering the judgment of the court said[76]:

> The purchase of the shares did not in itself vest the Hillview property or the rental income in the appellant. They were brought about by an act of the shareholders of Wan Holdings in voluntarily winding-up the company. *The original assets which were the shares, and the original income, the dividends, which is a different source of income,* had all ceased to exist

---

[76] *Andermatt Investments Pte Ltd v Comptroller of Income Tax* [1995] 2 SLR(R) 866 at [29]

following the liquidation of Wan Holdings. The overdraft could not be attributable to the acquisition of the rental income. *We noted that counsel for the appellant has argued that s 14(1)(a) is concerned with how the capital was employed during the period in which the interest was incurred, not how the capital was employed when first raised or during some other periods. We are here concerned with the question how the capital (the overdraft) was employed when first raised; no question concerning subsequent years or periods arises.*

One may readily see that the main features of *Andermatt* are as follows:

(a) In that case, where the learned judge pointed to the two different sources of income (i.e. the dividends and rental income), he was referring to two different sources of income in the same financial period (i.e. 28 November 1987 to 31 December 1988). His Honour specifically stated that he was not addressing the issue for subsequent years where there was only one source of income (i.e. rental income) as there were no appeals against the assessments for the later years before the court.

(b) The facts were such that the year in which the capital was first raised (i.e. 1988) was also the same year in which the interest expenses (which was the subject of consideration for deduction) were incurred. In the *Andermatt* case, the court then decided that in 1988 when the capital was first raised to pay off the debts for the purchase of the Wan Holdings shares, it was not employed in acquiring the rental income received in the same year, 1988. The court did not deal with the nature of the interest expenses in the years subsequent to 1988, as that issue was not before the court. After the *Andermatt* case in 1995, we have the later cases of *Wharf Properties* in 1997 and *T Ltd* in 2006 cited above. In each of those later cases, it is stated that "each payment of interest must be considered in relation to the purpose of the loan *during the period for which the interest is paid*".

At this juncture, it will be useful to discuss the New Zealand Court of Appeal case of *Pacific Rendezvous Ltd v Commissioner of Inland Revenue*[77].

---

[77] [1996] 2 NZLR 567. This case was referred to by the Court of Appeal in *BML v Comptroller of Income Tax*, [2018] 2 SLR 1009, on a different aspect.

In that case, the provisions of section 106(1)(h)(i) of the New Zealand Income Tax Act which were construed, read as follows:

> Notwithstanding anything in section 104 of this Act, in calculating the assessable income derived by any person from any source, no deduction shall except as expressly provided in this Act, be made in respect of any of the following sums or matters:
>
> (h) *Interest* (not being interest of any of the kinds referred to in paragraph (g) of this subsection), except so far as the Commissioner is satisfied that:
> (i) *It is payable on capital employed in the production of the assessable income.*

One may see that the provisions of section 106(1)(h)(i) of the New Zealand Act although expressed as an exclusion subject to an exception, is similar to the provisions of section 14(1)(a) of the Singapore Income Tax Act. In construing section 106(1)(h)(i), Richardson J in delivering the judgment of the New Zealand Court of Appeal stated as follows:

> In concentrating on the employment of the borrowed capital rather than on the interest expended it proceeds on the premise that interest is paid for the use of the principal and is referable to the production of assessable income through the investment of principal moneys on which it is paid. *The paragraph speaks in the present. Its concern is with how the capital was employed during the period in which the interest in question was incurred, not how the capital was employed when first raised or during some other period.* It is both necessary and sufficient that the capital was employed in the production of assessable income. "Employed" bears its plain ordinary meaning and is synonymous with "used".

So, besides the authorities in *Wharf Properties* and *T Ltd*, we also have the authority in the New Zealand Court of Appeal case of *Pacific Rendezvous*, which support the proposition that in construing the deduction provisions in section 14(1) and section 14(1)(a), we have to look at how the capital was "employed" or "used" during the period in which the interest expense in question was incurred, and not look at how the capital was employed or the "purpose" of the loan when it was first raised. It has to be noted that the focus in section 14(1)(a), as was pointed out in relation to section 106(1)(h)(i) of the New Zealand Income Tax Act in *Pacific Rendezvous*, is on the "use" rather than on the initial "purpose" of the taxpayer in borrowing the funds.

An example will illustrate this principle better. If one were to borrow moneys to purchase a house for owner-occupation, the interest expenses are clearly not deductible as the expenses were not incurred to produce any income and the loan was obtained for a capital purpose. If after a period of owner-occupation, one is to let out the house to produce a rental income, the interest expenses incurred on the loan first raised to purchase the house for owner-occupation, would be deductible against the rental income. There can be no suggestion that the original loan has to be repaid and a new loan is to be obtained, in order for the interest expense to be deductible against the rental income. This example shows that we have to consider the purpose of the incurrence of the interest expenses during each period for which the interest is paid. The question is not: "What is the purpose of the loan when it was first raised?"[78]

2.2.7.2. Boosting interest expense

A property owner with a substantial rental income and relatively smaller sums of interest expense, will find that a large part of its rental income even after the deduction of interest expenses, would be subject to income tax. Some owners may not pay down the capital loan, such that the interest expense remains substantial and is available for deduction against the rental income. There may be situations where the rental income has grown substantially over time, such that even where the original capital loans are not paid down, the amount of interest expense that may be deducted against the amount of the rental income is relatively small.

A case concerning the deduction of interest expense may be seen in *BML v Comptroller of Income Tax*[79]. In that case, the taxpayer company owned a

---

[78]   The facts in this example are similar to those in *Case Q35*, (1993) 15 NZTC 5171, where the New Zealand Taxation Review Authority, allowed the deduction of interest expense against the rental income of properties.

[79]   [2018] 2 SLR 1009.

shopping mall which has been producing rental income, with a relatively minor interest expense[80]. The taxpayer company then embarked on a capital restructuring exercise which converted much of the shareholders' equity in the company into a debt investment. This was achieved by first capitalizing the retained earnings and the asset revaluation reserve and capital redemption reserves, and then reducing the share capital with a debt due to the shareholders. The taxpayer company then issued shareholder bonds to the shareholders for the same amount of the debt due to them, thus replacing the shareholders' equity in the company with debt in the shareholders' bonds.

On the substantial amount of the shareholders' bonds, the taxpayer company claimed a deduction of the boosted interest expense[81] against its rental income[82]. The facts regarding the taxability of the substantial interest income in the hands of the shareholders are not stated in the *BML* case, as they are not relevant to the issue of the deductibility of the interest expense for the taxpayer company.

If the substantial interest income is taxable in the hands of the shareholders, the amount of tax payable would merely have shifted from the taxpayer company to its shareholders. That would have been pointless. In order for the transaction to make commercial sense, the shareholders should receive a stream of interest income that would be tax-free or at least taxed at lower than the corporate tax rate, or otherwise have tax losses that may absorb the interest income. Although it is not stated in the case, presumably the bonds issued by the special purpose vehicle WM Limited which the shareholders subscribed to, would have been qualifying debt securities (QDS) such that the interest income in the hands of bond-holders was taxed at the concessionary rate of 10% pursuant to section 43H of the

---

[80] Amounting to a sum of $1,101,181 for the Year of Assessment 2005.

[81] Amounting to equal sums of $23,643,000 for the four Years of Assessment 2004 to 2009.

[82] At the Income Tax Board of Review, the taxpayer claimed the deduction of the interest expense against the rental income. On appeal at the High Court and the Court of Appeal, the taxpayer expanded the claim as against the rental income as well as against the interest income from the advances made to shareholders: see *BML v Comptroller of Income Tax*, [2018] 2 SLR 1009 at [89].

Income Tax Act[83]. The interest income would be tax-free in the hands of non-residents[84].

In the result, the Court of Appeal disallowed the deduction of the interest expense which arose from the conversion of the shareholders' equity into debt, as it was not directly linked to the taxpayer's acquisition of the rental income from the shopping mall.

2.2.7.3 Interest expense on refinanced loans

The taxpayer may decide to refinance the amount of loans taken up initially to finance his investment, in the sense that the amount of the outstanding loan is replaced by another loan of the same amount. For the interest expense incurred on the refinanced loan or debt refinancing to be deductible under section 14(1)(a) of the Income Tax Act as "any sum payable by way of interest upon any money borrowed by that person … where … such sum is payable on capital employed in acquiring the income", there has to be a "direct link" between the production of the investment income and the incurrence of the interest expense. In *Andermatt Investments Pte Ltd v Comptroller of Income Tax*[85], the Court of Appeal endorsed the view that there is a "direct link" in the case of refinanced loans or debt refinancing, and it stated:

> [22] In *Federal Commissioner of Taxation v J D Roberts & Smith* ([21] *supra*), a law partnership took out an overdraft to enable it to repay partners the capital they had put into the firm over the years to enable the firm to carry on its business. The object behind this repayment to the partners was to make it cheaper for new partners to buy into the partnership. The full Federal Court of Australia held that the interest paid on the overdraft was deductible as the interest was incurred on a loan used to repay working

---

[83] From the facts of the case, the shareholders had earlier on 20 October 2004 borrowed from the taxpayer to subscribe to the WM bonds, and there was a later loan in the other direction from the shareholders to the taxpayer, when the shareholders subscribed for the shareholders' bonds issued by the taxpayer, such that both the taxpayer and shareholders have interest income receivable from each other and interest expenses payable to each other.

[84] Interest income from QDS is exempt under s 13(1)(a) of the Income Tax Act. See also Income Tax (Qualifying Debt Securities) Regulations (Cap. 134, Rg 35).

[85] [1995] 2 SLR(R) 866.

capital originally advanced from partners. The court rejected the argument that the funds were used for a private purpose, namely, to pay the partners. It is important to note what Hill J said (at 4388):

> The funds to be withdrawn in such a case were employed in the partnership business; the borrowing replaces those funds and the interest incurred on the borrowing will meet the statutory description of interest incurred in the gaining or production by the partnership of the assessable income.
>
> In principle, such a case is no different from the borrowing from one bank to repay working capital originally borrowed from another; the character of the refinancing takes on the same character as the original borrowing and gives to the interest incurred the character of a working expense.

[23] In *Roberts & Smith* the money borrowed replaced the original funds employed in the same business ....

[27] We endorse the view that under s 14(1)(*a*) there must be a direct link between the money borrowed and the income produced. In both *Roberts & Smith* and *Yeung* the direct link was there. ...

The Australian case of *Roberts & Smith* was also cited by the Court of Appeal in *Comptroller of Income Tax v IA*[86]. The Court of Appeal in endorsing that the view that the interest expense incurred on the refinanced loan is revenue in nature where the expense on the original loan is itself revenue in nature, stated at [108]:

> The judge was of the view that the bank guarantees amounted to a refinancing which enabled the release of funds to pay the Syndicated Loan. Indeed, it is well established by cases such as *Federal Commissioner of Taxation v JD Roberts; Federal Commissioner of Taxation v Smith* (1992) 92 ATC 4,380 and *Federal Commissioner of Taxation v Jones* (2002) ATC 4,135 that expenses incurred in connection with the refinancing of a revenue loan are also revenue in nature. Further, there appears to be no reason why the respondent's claims for a deduction of the Guarantee Expenses should be denied when interest expenses incurred on loans taken up to refinance

---

[86] [2006] 4 SLR(R) 161.

earlier loans or borrowings are possibly deductible under the IRAS Interpretation and Practice Note 19, "Administrative Concession for Interest Incurred by Taxpayers on Loans to Refinance Earlier Loans on Borrowings" *IRAS Compass* (17 April 1995, 3(2)) at 4, if the refinancing is effected for genuine commercial reasons.

Following the *dicta* of the Court of Appeal in the cases of *Andermatt* and *IA*, the Comptroller has accepted that the interest expense incurred on refinanced loans or substituted financing (in the sense of debt refinancing rather than debt-to-equity restructuring), where the capital is employing in acquiring the investment income, would be deductible. This can be seen in the case of *GBK v Comptroller of Income Tax*[87], where had the facts of that case been one of substituted financing (i.e. debt refinancing), the interest expense would have been allowed by the Comptroller. In this regard, the Income Tax Board of Review in dealing with the facts of that case where the debt financing replaced equity capital, stated:

The present case is not a substituted financing

[35] The Appellant submitted that the matter before the Board was a "substituted financing" since the Shareholder Bonds replaced the equity capital that was reduced. "Substituted financing" is a case where a loan refinances a prior loan and assumes the character of the prior loan. If interest on the prior loan is deductible under section 14(1)(a), interest on the new loan is also deductible. Returning to the facts of the matter before the Board, there is no "substituted financing". The debt represented by the Shareholder Bonds was not a "substitute" for any type of financing. For all intent and purposes, this case was a restructuring of the Appellant's capital profile from equity to debt (rather than substituting of one form of debt or financing with another). The Shareholder Bonds did not replace an original loan (except for the *temporary* debt arising from capital reduction), but were issued as the second phase of the Appellant's capital restructuring from equity to debt.

[36] The reasoning in the Australian case of *Yeung v Federal Commissioner of Taxation* (1988) 88 ATC 4193 ("*Yeung*") cited by the Appellant as an

---

[87] [2006] SGITBR 3.

example of "substituted financing" is inapplicable here because the fact situation was quite different. The findings of fact in *Yeung's* case indicated that Dr Yeung had lent funds to the partnership for the purchase of properties, and this was replaced by the loan from Ozanu Pte Ltd. A clear link could be discerned between the loans and the properties purchased. Moreover, the partnership in *Yeung* was not a separate entity from its partners (unlike a company in the case of the Appellant). The 'capital contribution' of the shareholders and partners in *Yeung* (ultimately being advances / loans) is not equivalent to the share capital of a company. In *Yeung*, the loan / advances by the partners were replaced by a new loan. Hence, the *Yeung* case does not assist the Appellant on the issue of "substituted financing". Even if this Board is misdirected on this point of "substituted financing", we are satisfied that the Appellant still fails the "direct link" test under section 14(1)(a), which is the only question that truly matters in this case before us.

The case then went on appeal to the High Court, where the learned judge traced the IRAS's earlier stand from the time that the deduction of interest on refinancing was granted on the basis of an administrative concession, to *IA* where the Court of Appeal accepted that the interest expense incurred on a refinanced loan would be revenue in nature, where the interest expense on the original loan was itself revenue in nature. In this regard, Choo Han Teck J said[88]:

> ... For example, re-financing a loan that was previously borrowed to buy machinery or other assets used in income-producing activities is entitled to a deduction. The Inland Revenue Authority of Singapore ("IRAS") accepts that this is not allowed by the statute, because the money borrowed from re-financing would have been used to repay another loan rather than to purchase new assets. But IRAS allows a deduction by way of an "administrative concession" if the re-financing was carried out for genuine commercial reasons. The strict reading of the statute may thus not reflect the full commercial reality as IRAS sees it. In *Comptroller of Income Tax v IA* [2006] 4 SLR(R) 161, it was also there accepted (at [108]) that

---

[88] *BML v Comptroller of Income Tax* [2018] 4 SLR 1121 at [24]. Although the case was reported as *GBK v Comptroller of Income Tax* at the Board of Review level, it was reported as *BML v Comptroller of Income Tax* at both the High Court and the Court of Appeal.

expenses incurred in connection with the refinancing of a revenue loan are also revenue in nature, *ie*, the new loan takes on the same character as the previous loan....

The learned judge went on to deal with the term "substituted financing" and he said at [26]:

"Substituted financing" is not a term of art and does not in itself entitle the taxpayer to a deduction. There are various ways a company may change its sources of finance. The ultimate question will still be whether there can be said to be a direct link between the substituted finance and the income produced. I accept that there may be instances where it can reasonably be said that when loan capital replaces equity capital, there can still be a direct link between the money borrowed and the income, *eg*, in *Yeung*, where the partners were essentially paid back the same amount that they had invested into the business. Cases like *Yeung* would closely resemble the situation where a new loan replaces a previous loan. In the case of *FCT v Roberts* (1992) 23 ATR 494 decided by the Federal Court of Australia, Hill J interpreted *Yeung* as a case "involving a borrowing to fund the repayment of moneys originally advanced by a partner and used as partnership capital, particularly given that the original funds were used to purchase the rental property". He was clear that where the new borrowing did not operate as a "refund of a pre-existing capital contribution", deduction of the interest expenses on the new borrowing would not be allowed. Thus, interest on loans to replace partnership capital represented by internally generated goodwill would not be deductible.

The *BML* case finally reached the Court of Appeal, where the Court seemed to have pointed out that had the case been one of debt refinancing, the Income Tax Board of Review would have allowed the deduction of the interest expense. In this regard, the Court of Appeal stated[89]:

Third, the Shareholder Bonds were not substituted financing. The ITBR construed "substituted financing" narrowly to refer only to debt refinancing and not equity-to-debt restructuring. Since the Shareholder Bonds did not

---

[89] *BML v Comptroller of Income Tax* [2018] 2 SLR 1009 at [21(c)].

replace any loan, the cases on "substituted financing" did not assist the Taxpayer. See ITBR Judgment at [35]–[36].

As may be seen from the above discussion, there would be a "direct link" between the interest expense incurred in a case of debt refinancing or refinanced loans and the income acquired on the capital employed, and such the interest expense would be deductible under section 14(1)(a) of the Income Tax Act.

2.2.8. *Deduction of borrowing costs*

In addition to the deduction of interest expense provided specifically under section 14(1)(a)(i) of the Income Tax Act, the Income Tax (Deductible Borrowing Costs) Regulations 2008[90] made under section 14(1)(a)(ii)[91] also provide for the deduction of other borrowing costs, i.e. guarantee fees, bank option fees, discount and premium on debt securities payable on the maturity or early redemption of those securities, prepayment fees or early redemption fees, extension fees, increased costs (i.e. upward interest rate adjustments payable when certain event occurs as specified in the loan agreement), interest rate cap payments, interest rate swap payments, conversion fees or amendment fees, cancellation fees, and front-end and back-end fees.

The provisions of section 14(1)(a)(ii) and the Income Tax (Deductible Borrowing Costs) Regulations recognise that section 14(1)(a)(i) which provide for the deduction of interest expense incurred on capital employed in acquiring income, is not wide enough to cover borrowing costs which may be the economic equivalent of interest. This is because a "fundamental feature" of interest is that it accrues with time in that the total amount of interest payable "depends on the duration of the period for which the loaned money is in the borrower's hands"[92]. Such a feature generally does not exist

---

[90] S 115/2008. See IRAS e-Tax Guide, *Tax Deduction for Borrowing Costs other than Interest Expenses*, 15 January 2019.

[91] S 14(1)(a)(ii) provides for the deduction of 'any sum payable in lieu of interest or for the reduction thereof, as may be prescribed by regulations'.

[92] *BFC v Comptroller of Income Tax*, [2014] 4 SLR 33 at [49]. In *BFC*, the discount and redemption premium of a bond issue were held not to be 'interest' qualifying for deduction under the then s 14(1)(a). Such

with other borrowing costs, which may involve a one-time incurrence without explicit relationship to the period of borrowing.

2.2.9. Deduction of repair expenses

Repair expenditure has to be incurred periodically in the holding of properties for investment income. The expenses of "repair" besides qualifying for deduction under the general deduction formula in section 14(1) of the Income Tax Act, may also qualify for deduction specifically under section 14(1)(c) as "any expenses of repair of premises, plant, machinery or fixtures employed in acquiring the income or for the renewal, repair or alteration of nay implement, utensil or article so employed".

What then is the meaning of the word "repair"? "Repair" frequently will include replacement of parts of the entirety. For example, one may repair a television set (the "entirety") by replacing a defective chip (a subsidiary part of the entirety) in the television set with a new one. In this regard, in the English Court of Appeal case of *Lurcott v Wakely & Wheeler*[93], Fletcher Moulton LJ said:

> For my own part, when the word "repair" is applied to a complex matter like a house, I have no doubt that the repairs include the replacement of parts. Many, and in fact most, repairs imply that some portion of the total fabric is renewed, that new is put in place of old. Therefore you have from time to time as things need repair to put new for old.

In the same case, Buckley LJ said at page 924:

> Repair is restoration by renewal or replacement of subsidiary parts of the whole. Renewal, as distinguished from repair, is reconstruction of the entirety, meaning by the entirely not necessarily the whole but substantially the whole subject-matter under discussion. It follows that the question of repair is in every case one of degree, and the test is whether the act to be

---

borrowing costs have since been deductible, with the coming into operation of the Income Tax (Deductible Borrowing Costs) Regulations.

[93]   [1911] 1 KB 905 at 919.

done is one which in substance is the renewal or replacement of defective parts of the renewal or replacement of substantially the whole.

2.2.9.1. Identifying the entirety

It is therefore important to identify the "entirety", the replacement of parts of which, will still constitute "repair". Indeed, Rowlatt J in *O'Grady v Bullcroft Main Colleries Ltd*[94], in approving *Lurcott v Wakely & Wheeler,* said:

> But the critical matter is — as was pointed out in the passage read from Lord Justice Buckley's judgment, in the case which has been referred to — what is the entirety? The slate is not the entirety in the roof. You are repairing the roof by putting in new slates. What is the entirety? If you replace in entirety, it is having a new one and it is not repairing an old one.

In the UK First-tier Tribunal case of *Hopegar Properties Limited v The Commissioners for Her Majesty's Revenue and Customs*[95], which concerned the issue of deduction of "repair" expenses and where the two cases of *O'Grady v Bullcroft Main Collieries Ltd* and *Philips v Whieldon Sanitary Potteries*[96], were cited, the Tribunal summarized the issue succinctly at [55]:

> HMRC [Her Majesty's Revenue and Customs] have accepted in their guidance the concept of "entirety" to distinguish revenue, repairs and capital expenditure. They accept that the replacement of an entire asset is capital but if less than the entire asset is replaced then it is likely to be revenue expenditure. Expenditure on repairs and maintenance of an asset would involve restoring the asset or part of it to its original state so it performs its original function in a manner similar to that which was intended; it is this question of degree which must be examined.

The Tribunal accepted that the starting point in deciding whether works constitute "repairs" is to identify the "entirety", and discussed the two cases of *Bullcroft* and *Whieldon Sanitary Potteries* as follows:

---

[94] [1932] 17 TC 93 at 100.

[95] [2013] UKFTT 331.

[96] (1952) 33 TC 213.

[56] The starting point is to look to identify the relevant asset. A case which looks at the entirety is *O'Grady v. Bullcroft Main Collieries Limited* 17 TC 93 (*"Bullcroft"*). In this case, a colliery chimney became unsafe and needed to be replaced. It was a separate structure from the other buildings of the colliery but connected to the furnace by pipes. It was claimed that the cost of building a replacement chimney was revenue but the Commissioners decided it was capital. The chimney was held to be a separate entity and the expenditure on its replacement was therefore capital.

[57] The judge in the case, Rowlatt J, said:

> "Of course, every repair is a replacement. You repair a roof by putting on new slates instead of old ones, which you throw away. There is no doubt about that. But the critical matter is … what is the entirety? The slate is not the entirety of the roof. You are repairing the roof by putting new slates. What is the entirety? If you replace in entirety, it is having a new one and it is not repairing an old one. I think that is very largely a question of degree, but it seems to me the Commissioners have taken the only possible view here."

[58] The Court seems to have been influenced by the fact that a new chimney was functionally a significant improvement on the existing chimney. It was taller with greater dimensions and constructed of engineering brick as opposed to the original built in common brick. It was in effect a new structure.

[59] The concept of the new structure was explored in another case. In *Phillips v Whieldon Sanitary Potteries Ltd* [1952] 33 TC 213 the Court looked at the question of entirety. The company's factory was adjacent to a canal and had been protected by an embankment. There was subsidence in the embankment and water seeped into the factory. Consequently the factory suffered subsidence. The old brick and earth embankment was removed and an iron and concrete barrier constructed. The Judge decided that the work was of a capital nature. Donovan J said:

> "I am of the opinion that this is a clear case of capital expenditure. I reach this conclusion taking into account the extent of the work, the permanent nature of the new barrier, the enduring advantage it confers upon preserving part of the fixed capital of the business, and the contention of the Company that it was essential to enable the

trade to be carried on. It is irrelevant, in my view, in the present case to consider whether the new barrier, in point of size or effectiveness, is or is not an improvement on the old, and there is no finding upon that point. There can be cases where the work done may result in no improvement, but merely reinstatement, and yet be work involving capital expenditure on account of its size and importance."

[60] The case highlights the question of the "size and importance" of the work and concludes that because of those factors it cannot be an improvement but must be a reinstatement. In his view, the barrier itself was the entirety and since it was replaced with a new one, the work was not repair.

In *Whieldon Sanitary Potteries Ltd*, the "size and importance" of the barrier made it an "entirety" itself. Hence, the replacement of the new barrier with a new one, was held not to be "repair". There are also the two famous "chimney" cases, i.e. *O'Grady v Bullcroft Main Collieries* and *Samuel Jones & Co (Devonvale) Limited v Commissioners of Inland Revenue*[97].

In *Samuel Junes*, the replacement of the chimney was a repair of the factory, where the chimney was "physically, commercially and functionally an inseparable part of the factory". The Lord President (Cooper) in delivering his ground of judgment in the *Samuel Jones* case in a unanimous decision of the three-judge court, distinguished the case of *O'Grady v Bullcroft Main Collieries*, and said at page 518:

It is no part of our duty to review the decision of Rowlatt J as applied to the facts of the *O'Grady* case, but so far as this case is concerned the facts seem to me to demonstrate beyond a doubt that the chimney with which we are concerned is physically, commercially and functionally an inseparable part of an "entirety", which is the factory. It is quite impossible to describe this chimney as being in the words of Rowlatt J, the "entirety" with which we are concerned. It is doubtless an indispensable part of the factory, doubtless an integral part; but none the less a subsidiary part, and one of the many subsidiary parts, of a single industrial profit-earning undertaking.

---

97   (1951) 32 TC 513.

Lord Carmont in that case also said at page 519:

> In the present case I am clearly of the opinion that the unit to be considered is the factory and the chimney cannot be taken in isolation. There was no improvement in the factory, on the findings of the case, by the erection of the new chimney in place of the old.

It is also to be noted that even where new and different materials are used in the repair works, the expenses may nevertheless be those of "repair". In this regard, the First-tier Tribunal in the *Hopegar Properties* case, stated at [75]:

> In the case of *Conn (HM Inspector of Taxes) v Robins Brothers Ltd* 43 TC 266 ("Conn"), the repairs were treated as revenue even though different materials were used. The slate roof was replaced with one of corrugated asbestos, the floorings were replaced with concrete in the main shop, certain timbers were replaced with steel joist encased in oak and overall, modern materials had been used. The result was, in substance, to repair what was there before and the expenditure was treated as revenue. The case takes a common sense and practical approach to the issue of revenue expenditure. It cannot be expected that a contractor having modern and improved components would elect to use outdated and inferior materials to repair an asset especially where there is a legal obligation to observe current standard of safety and repair.

In *Cairnsmill Caravan Park v The Commissioners for Her Majesty's Revenue & Commissioners,* strips of grass were resurfaced with a hard-core surface. In that case, the First-tier Tribunal in deciding the costs of the resurfacing were revenue in nature, stated[98]:

> The most obvious advantage to the Appellants of re-surfacing in this matter was that it avoided a serious disruption of their lettings for touring caravans over an extended period. A "like for like" re-surfacing with grass would not have stabilised and been suitable for use for up to two years.

---

[98]   [2013] UKFTT 164 at [25].

2.3. Capital allowances

Capital expenditure may be incurred on the provision of plant and machinery used by the taxpayer in its business. Typical plant and machinery found in an investment property include lifts, escalators and air-conditioning plant. In relation to an office building held for investment, the Income Tax Board of Review in *IH v Comptroller of Income Tax*[99], also held that electrical switchgear, electrical transformers and electrical door opening systems constituted "plant", and in that case the Comptroller of Income Tax conceded that the wiring for building automation systems also constituted "plant".

However for the purposes of income tax, capital expenditure is not deductible against the income of the business, whereas revenue expenditure is so deductible[100]. In recognition that plant and machinery suffer from wear and tear and may eventually need to be replaced, the Income Tax Act provides for wear and tear allowances or capital allowances in respect of expenditure incurred in the provision of machinery and plant, to be set off against the taxable income. As Yong Pung How CJ said in *Comptroller of Income Tax v GE Pacific Pte Ltd*[101]:

> [6] Expenditure incurred in the production of the income is deductible under s 14 of the Act. However, it is only revenue expenditure that is so deductible and no deduction is made for expenditure of a capital nature. The Act does not provide for relief for capital losses nor for taxes on capital gains. This means that capital losses like the depreciation of fixed assets may not be deducted. However, the Act does provide for the depreciation of fixed assets to be written off against taxable income through the provision of various allowances. ...

> [27] ... As already stated, the cost of fixed assets like plant and machinery cannot be considered expenditure and so deducted from taxable income. However, since such assets depreciate, the Act recognises this inherent and periodic "loss" suffered by those who use machinery or plant in the course of their business and grants allowances to reflect this additional cost of producing the income. The rationale for capital allowances is the

---

[99] [2005] SGITBR 2.
[100] Sections 14(1) and 15(1)(c) of the Income Tax Act.
[101] [1994] 2 SLR(R) 948.

depreciation of fixed assets. Obviously, it is the taxpayer who owns and uses the plant or machinery that suffers this "loss" of depreciation and it is to him that the Act grants the allowance.

Similarly, in *Barclays Mercantile Business Finance Ltd v Mawson (Inspector of Taxes)*, Lord Nicholls of Birkenhead said[102]:

A trader computing his profits or losses will ordinarily make some deduction for depreciation in the value of the machinery or plant which he uses. Otherwise the computation will take no account of the need for the eventual replacement of wasting assets and the true profits will be overstated. ... Parliament therefore makes separate provision for depreciation by means of capital allowances against what would otherwise be taxable income.

A claim for capital allowances is available for the provision of "machinery or plant for the purposes of [a] trade" under sections 19(1) and 19A(1) of the Income Tax Act which read as follow:

19. —(1) Where a person carrying on a trade, profession or business incurs capital expenditure on the provision of machinery or plant for the purposes of that trade, profession or business, there shall be made to him, on due claim for the year of assessment in the basis period for which the expenditure is incurred an allowance, to be known as an "initial allowance", equal to one-fifth of that expenditure or such other allowance as may be prescribed either generally or for any person or class of persons in respect of any machinery or plant or class of machinery or plant.

19A. —(1) Notwithstanding section 19, where a person carrying on a trade, profession or business incurs capital expenditure on the provision of machinery or plant for the purpose of that trade, profession or business, there shall be made to him, on due claim for any year of assessment and in lieu of the allowances provided by section 19, an annual allowance of 33 $\frac{1}{3}$% in respect of the capital expenditure incurred.

As may be seen from the provisions of sections 19(1) and 19A(1), capital allowances are available for an asset which is either "machinery" or "plant"

---

[102] [2005] 1 AC 684 at [3].

used for the purposes of the trade of the taxpayer. On the meaning of the word "machinery", Andrew Ang J in the property tax case of *Pan-United Marine Ltd v Chief Assessor* said[103]:

> The word ["machinery"] is defined in *Collins English Dictionary & Thesaurus* (HarperCollins Publishers, 4th Ed, 2006) principally as:
>
>> 1 machines, machine parts, or machine systems collectively. 2 a particular machine system or set of machines. 3 a system similar to a machine.
>
> "Machine" is in turn defined, *inter alia*, to mean:
>
>> 1 an assembly of interconnected components arranged to transmit or modify force in order to perform useful work. 2 a device for altering the magnitude or direction of a force, such as a lever or screw. 3 a mechanically operated device or means of transport, such as a car or aircraft. 4 any mechanical or electrical device that automatically performs tasks or assists in performing tasks.

Where an object qualifies as "machinery" used for the purposes of the trade of the taxpayer, capital allowances are available on the capital expenditure incurred for the provision of the machinery. It is then not necessary to consider whether the object also qualifies as "plant".

Where it is necessary to consider whether an object may be characterised as "plant", one has to consider the function of the object in the context of the business or trade that is being actually carried on by the taxpayer. Whether an object is "plant" depends on the nature of the trade of the taxpayer and how the object is being used to promote his trade. A particular object may be "plant" for one trade but may not be "plant" for another. For example, in *Bridge House (Reigate Hill) Ltd v Hinder (HM Inspector of Taxes)*[104], sewage pipes laid to carry away effluent from a restaurant was held not to be "plant". Nevertheless, the sewage pipes may be "plant" for the sewerage authority which uses the pipes for the purposes for the conveying of the effluent. In that case, Lord Denning MR said at page 192:

---

[103] [2008] 3 SLR(R) 569 at [122].
[104] (1971) 47 TC 182.

Vis-a-vis the sewerage authority the [sewage] pipes may be part of their "plant", but vis-à-vis the restaurant proprietor they are not.

Or as Vinelott J said in *Cole Brothers Ltd v Phillips (HM Inspector of Taxes)*[105]:

> The word "plant" is a chameleon-like word which takes its colour from its context.

2.3.1. *Functional test*

One has therefore to examine closely the *function* of a particular object in the context of the trade or business being carried on by the taxpayer in considering whether the object constitutes "plant". As Andrew Ang J said in *ZF v Comptroller of Income Tax*[106]:

> The "functional" test entails an examination of the function of the apparatus in question in the context of the business of the taxpayer. This can be seen from the House of Lords case of *Scottish & Newcastle Breweries* ([7] *supra*). In that case, Lord Wilberforce said (at 299):
>
> > In the end each case must be resolved, in my opinion, by *considering carefully the nature of the particular trade being carried on, and the relation of the expenditure to the promotion of the trade.* ... [emphasis added]

The words of Lord Wilberforce echoed those of Lord Cameron in the same case in the court below at the Court of Session. Lord Cameron's *dicta* (as were conveniently cited by Lord Lowry in the House of Lords) were as follows (at 302):

> ... the question of what is properly to be regarded as 'plant' can only be answered in the context of the particular industry concerned and, possibly, in light also of the particular circumstances of the individual taxpayers' own trade. ... I think that much difficulty is caused by seeking to place *limitative interpretations* on the simple word 'plant': I do not think that the classic definition propounded in *Yarmouth v France* suggests that it is a word which is other than of comprehensive meaning-'whatever apparatus

---

[105] (1982) 55 TC 188 at 202.
[106] [2010] 2 SLR 350 at [13].

is used by a businessman for carrying on his business"-whatever the business may be. ... [emphasis added]

In other words, whether an asset functions as plant for a taxpayer has to be determined by consideration of that particular taxpayer's trade and examining the function of the asset in that particular taxpayer's trade. What is "plant" for one trade, may not be "plant" for another trade.

In considering whether an object constitutes "plant", there is no requirement to show that the object installed is effective for the purpose of its installation, just as advertising expenses incurred in the production of income of a business may be deducted under section 14(1) without the requirement to show the advertisements are effective in attracting customers. In this regard, Lord Wilberforce in *Inland Revenue Commissioners v Scottish and Newcastle Breweries Ltd*, in deciding that various decorative objects installed in hotel premises to create the ambience for the purposes of the trade, constituted "plant", said[107]:

It seems to me, on the commissioner's findings, which are clear and emphatic, that the taxpayer company's trade includes, and is intended to be furthered by, the provision of what may be called 'atmosphere' or 'ambience', *which (rightly or wrongly) they think may attract customers.* Such intangibles may in a very real and concrete sense be part of what the trader sets out, and spends money, to achieve.

As may be seen, an object does not have to be a requisite or essential for the business, for it to be considered as "plant". The relevant test as may be seen in *Scottish and Newcastle Breweries*, is whether the object installed, is considered by the taxpayer (whether rightly or wrongly) to promote its trade or business.

In *Leeds Permanent Building Society v Proctor (HM Inspector of Taxes)*[108], the taxpayer installed decorative screens bearing its name and logo, at the windows of the shopfronts of its branch offices. The purpose of the screens was to attract the attention of passers-by in the hope that they might notice the society's display cards, giving particulars of investments and other

---

[107] (1982) 55 TC 252.
[108] (1982) 56 TC 293.

facilities offered by the building society. The display cards were placed in front of or beside the decorative screens. The English High Court in that case held that the screens were plant, as they were "part of the apparatus employed in the commercial activities of the society's business" and "were part of the means by which the relevant trade was carried out". There was no legal requirement for the decorative screens in that case, to have to be a requisite or essential for the business, for the screens to qualify as "plant". The facts of that case were such that "the Society considers that there is no specific evidence as to the effect of the screens as they form part of the general advertising policy. They are, however, a very important part of the Society's visual presentation of its branches, together with the high level of fascia signs and projecting signs".

Objects used in the creation of atmosphere and ambience for the promotion of trade, have been held to be plant in respect of hotels and licensed public houses (in the *Scottish and Newcastle Breweries* case), restaurants (in *Wimpy International Ltd v Warland*[109]) and branch offices of a building society (in the *Leeds Permanent Building Society* case). However, that does not mean that such objects may only qualify as "plant" where they are installed in such buildings. Ultimately, one has to look at the principles established in case law and apply those principles to the facts of each case, in the characterisation process. In this regard, Lord Wilberforce in the *Scottish and Newcastle Breweries* case said:

> In the end each case must be resolved, in my opinion, by considering carefully the nature of the particular trade being carried on, and the relation of the expenditure to the promotion of the trade.

2.3.2. *Business use, premises and completeness tests*

Although the functional test is the primary one in determining if an object constitutes "plant" used in the business of the taxpayer, the "business use", "premises" and "completeness" tests have also been used to consider whether an object is "plant". As the Income Tax Board of Review in *IH v Comptroller of Income Tax* stated[110]:

---

[109] (1989) 61 TC 51.
[110] [2005] SGITBR 2 at [20].

We feel that the 'business use', 'premises', 'completeness" test are tools to assist one to form the view, whether on the facts of a particular case, the items in dispute are plant or machinery provided by the taxpayer for the purpose of its business.

However, the business use, premises and completeness tests, are not necessarily conclusive. For an object to qualify as "plant", it must be used for the business purposes of the taxpayer and satisfy the "business use" test. The object must also satisfy the "premises" test in that the object should not be part of the premises. Where the object visually retains its separate identity and is distinct from the superstructure of the premises, the object is not likely to be part of the premises and would pass the "premises" test. However, the converse does not necessarily apply. The "completeness" test was enunciated in the case of *Cole Brothers* case and cited by the Income Tax Board of Review in the *IH* case. Under the "completeness" test, an asset is not likely to be "plant" where the premises are incomplete without the asset. However, where an asset embellishes a complete building, the indication is that the asset functions as plant.

2.3.3. *Plant may be fixed in location*

The following *dicta* of Lindley LJ in the English Court of Appeal decision of *Yarmouth v France*[111] has often been cited in relation to cases concerning "plant":

> There is no definition of plant in the Act: but, in its ordinary sense, it includes whatever apparatus is used by a business man for carrying on his business, not his stock-in-trade which he buys or makes for sale; but all the goods and chattels, fixed or moveable, live or dead, which he keeps for permanent employment in his business.

As may be seen from the above-mentioned *dicta*, the fact that an object is "fixed" does not preclude its characterisation as "plant". Plant by its very nature would also have some durability for it to be in "permanent"

---

[111] (1887) 19 QBD 647 at 658 and cited with approval by the Court of Appeal in the ZF case [2011] 1 SLR 1044 at [22].

employment in the business. It may therefore be seen that "permanence" is not necessarily to be equated with "premises" or "building". Indeed, silos which are permanent structures erected on land, have been held to be plant in *Schofield v R&H Hall Ltd*[112]. In that case, the silos were concrete structures into which were built concrete bins, and machinery which included gantries, conveyor belts and mobile chutes.

The House of Lords case of *Inland Revenue Commissioners v Barclay, Curle & Co Ltd*[113] which concerned the capital expenditure on excavation and concrete work in the construction of a dry dock, also shows that a construction may be plant although it is deeply and firmly fixed to the land. In that case, Lord Reid said at pages 238–239:

> ... buildings or structures and machinery and plant are *not mutually exclusive*, and that was recognised in *Jarrold v John Good & Sons Ltd* 40 TC 681. Undoubtedly this concrete dry dock is a structure, but is it also plant? The only reason why a structure should also be plant which has been suggested or which has occurred to me is that it fulfils the function of plant in the trader's operations. And, if that is so, no test has been suggested to distinguish one structure which fulfils such a function from another. I do not say that every structure which fulfils the function of plant must be regarded as plant, but I think that one would have to find some good reasons for excluding such a structure.

Therefore, the fact that an object is fixed or connected to something that is fixed does not necessarily preclude it from being characterised as plant. Much depends on its function in the promotion of the trade carried on by the taxpayer.

2.3.4. *Lighting as plant*

A taxpayer company may have a shopping centre as an investment property and may install decorative lights at the premises. Let us examine if such lightings may be considered to be plant, on which capital allowances may be claimed.

---

[112] [1975] STC 353. See also the recent case of *JRO Griffiths Limited v The Commissioners for Her Majesty's Revenue and Customs* [2021] UKFTT 257.

[113] (1969) 45 TC 221.

It has to be noted that the modern shopping centres are not just convenient places for shopping. Ambience and facilities that provide recreation, are also important factors in attracting shoppers. As stated in the article, *"Managing the Shopping Center Ambience Attributes by Using Importance-Performance Analysis: The Case from Serbia"*[114]:

> ... shopping centers are not only places for shopping but also for other activities such as entertainment, recreation, etc. Shopping center companies have to compete with Internet based e-shopping and small format stores, so they need to attract customers by creating a pleasant shopping experience in order to keep the customers in the shopping center longer, get them to spend more money and come again.... Scientists emphasize that many customers make their decisions about the shopping place based on their relation towards the mix of stores, prices of merchandize and the ambience of the retail facility.

The above statements in the article are equally applicable to shopping malls in Singapore. In the article *"ION Orchard: atmosphere and consumption in Singapore"*, the following is also stated[115]:

> All malls deploy whatever sensory stimulation is available to encourage consumption; all must continually recreate spectacles and atmospheres to maintain the modes of re-enchantment necessary to attract customers.

Lightings and other decorative objects may be used as apparatus to create spectacles and atmospheres in shopping centres, to attract customers. In considering whether such lighting may qualify as plant, let us first look at Item 10 of Annex C of the IRAS e-Tax Guide: *"Machinery and Plant: Section 19/19A of the Income Tax Act"* (updated 20 April 2011), for some guidance on the role of lightings in trades or business, in the context of the claim for capital allowances. The following is stated at Item 10 of Annex C of the Guide, where the exceptions stated in Item 10 may be considered as plant:

---

[114] Markovic JJ, *et al.*, *Central European Business Review*, (June 2014, Vol 3 No 2), pp 18–27.
[115] Chris Hudson, *Visual Communication*, 2015, Vol 14(3), pp 289–308.

General lightings and electrical works to provide general illumination or general supply of electricity, *except those meant to provide for the specific requirements of the trade. For example, floodlight to illuminate sports pitches may qualify* but not the general lighting in changing rooms and areas available to the general public.

Lightings which are to provide for the specific requirements of the taxpayer's trade, qualify as plant. The example provided in the IRAS e-Tax Guide is that of floodlights which are used to illuminate sports pitches. On that score, lightings installed for night-time golfing will similarly qualify as plant. Yet another example would be lighting in a hotel as may be seen in *Inland Revenue Commissioners v Scottish & Newcastle Breweries Ltd,* where Lord Wilberforce[116]:

The type, design, and layout of the lighting arrangements, particularly in the common living areas, are selected with the aims of producing the atmosphere appropriate to attract the type of customers sought.

The provision of lighting to create an atmosphere or ambience in order to attract customers is not confined to the hotel industry. In a nightclub or discotheque, lightings also function in the promotion of trade. Some other examples are stated in the book *"Practical Capital Allowances"* by Peter Newbold and Martin Wilson[117]:

Building specifications will often refer to 'special light fittings' or some such term. In order to be successfully claimed, such fittings really must perform a special function, for example:

(1)   providing ambience in a trade dealing with members of the public;

(2)   providing daylight lamps for examining fabrics etc;

(3)   display lighting in shops.

Floodlighting

In general terms, there can only be two reasons for the installation of floodlighting:

---

116   [1982] STC 296 at 298.

117   Butterworths, (1995) at page 251.

(1)   to draw attention to a property at night, to advertise its pleasant aspect and its occupiers' trades; and

(2)   for security purposes.

In either case, it is likely that the lighting performs a function in the trade of the building's owners or tenants.

As may be seen from the above excerpt from the book, floodlights which function as plant are not limited to those at sports pitches or stadia. Basically, a floodlight would be one where an extraordinary intensity of light is brought to bear in the circumstances for the function of the trade.

In *Wimpy International Ltd v Warland (HM Inspector of Taxes)*[118], light fittings in a restaurant were held to be plant on the basis that they were installed to meet the particular commercial requirements of the taxpayer company. In that case, Hoffman J (as he then was) said at page 88:

Light Fittings. This is the only item on which I think the Commissioners were wrong. ... They found that Wimpy considered the volume of light important for the purposes of their business and that it had been progressively increased for business reasons: "The object is to create an atmosphere of brightness and efficiency, suitable to the service and consumption of fast food meals and attractive to potential customers looking in from outside", This is in my view a finding that the provision of lighting was specific to the trade. ... If the provision of such lighting is a necessary feature of the setting for the trading of preparing and serving meals, the light fittings must be apparatus used in that trade.

In *JD Wetherspoon plc v The Commissioners for Her Majesty's Revenue and Customs*[119] concerning public houses or "pubs" as they are commonly referred to in the United Kingdom, the First Tier Tribunal held that the "front of the house" lightings, the toilet lightings and the kitchen fittings were "plant". The Tribunal held that in distinguishing between "trade-specific" and "general" lighting, there were two aspects to consider. The first was to look at the light fittings themselves to see if there is anything that

[118]   (1988) 61 TC 51.
[119]   [2009] UKFTT 374.

sets them apart from being ordinary light fittings such as might be found in any residential or other premises to provide illumination and something that makes them suitable for the particular trade in question. For example, in the context of the film industry, bright lights in any film studio would be trade specific. The second aspect is whether the light fittings performed an appreciable function in carrying on the business.

The above-mentioned approach was accepted by both the taxpayer and the Revenue in the *Wetherspoon* case. Thus, the "front of house" lighting was accepted as being trade-specific. The Tribunal also accepted that toilet lighting fell within the accepted meaning of trade-specific assets as there was a degree of ambience within these areas. Kitchen lighting was accepted by the Tribunal as trade-specific, specifically because of the high hygiene standards required for a pub kitchen.

On the above-mentioned authorities and principles, lightings (other than those for general illumination) which are used as apparatus in the promotion of the business of investment holding of shopping centres, should qualify as plant for which capital allowances may be claimed.

2.3.5. *Other decorative objects and equipment as plant*

Lightings in the context of the shopping centre investment is but an example of the objects which are used as apparatus with which the taxpayer carries on its business. In the *Wimpy International* case where the taxpayer carried on a business of operating pubs, the following decorative objects were held to be plant:

a) decorative brickwork, where the court stated at page 74 of the case: "As we understand it, the premises were complete without the brickwork, which was added as a purely decorative feature in selected areas to achieve a particular effect in the ambience of the restaurant";

b) decorative designs glued to the wall for ornamental effect, where the court stated at page 78 of the case: "We find that both types of mural constitute plant. Each is added to the wall by way of ornamentation and contributes to the ambience offered to [Associated Restaurants'] customers".

In the context of the shopping centre, capital expenditure may also be incurred in playground equipment, sculptures and various objects such as miniature tree houses and mushroom houses, to create an ambience of excitement to attract children and shoppers. Caregivers of young children who are a key client sector for the shopping centre, would be attracted to shopping centres with such facilities for children. There the children may be let to run off some energy at such facilities while the caregivers shop. In such instances, the objects installed should qualify as plant, for which capital allowances may be claimed.

3. Goods and Services Tax[120]

A property owner may have residential properties and/or non-residential properties to let for rental income. The letting of non-residential properties amounts to the making of a taxable supply whereas the letting of "properties used or to be used principally for residential purposes"[121] amounts to the making of an exempt supply. Within that broad classification, there are nuances. The letting of a building or part of a building for use as: (a) homes for the aged; (b) serviced apartments; (c) students' hostels; (d) workers' dormitories; and (e) welfare homes for the destitute, or families or individuals in crisis, amounts to the making of an exempt supply[122]. On the other hand, the letting of a building or part of a building for use as: (a) boarding houses or guest houses; (b) chalets; (c) convalescent homes, nursing homes or hospices; (d) hospitals; (e) hotels; (f) sports and recreational clubs with accommodation facilities; and (g) welfare homes for purposes of rehabilitation, amounts to the making of taxable supplies[123].

Where the property owner is GST-registered and makes a taxable supply in letting a non-residential property, he will have to charge GST on the rent.

---

[120] As there are detailed explanations set out with respect to the GST impact on property investment in the IRAS e-Tax Guide, *GST: Guide for Property Owners and Property Holding Companies*, Sixth Edition, 8 January 2021, the discussion of GST in this chapter is intended to be brief.

[121] Para 2(c) of Part I of the Fourth Schedule to the GST Act.

[122] Para 2 of the Goods and Services Tax (Buildings, Flats and Tenements for Residential Purposes) Order 2010, S 825/2010.

[123] Para 3 of the Goods and Services Tax (Buildings, Flats and Tenements for Residential Purposes) Order 2010, S 825/2010.

To that extent, the GST-registered person is acting as a tax collector, and pays over to the Comptroller of GST, the excess of his output tax (i.e. GST that he charges on the value of its taxable supplies) over his input tax (i.e. GST incurred on his inward supplies used in making the taxable supplies).

On the other hand, where the GST-registered property owner makes an exempt supply in letting a residential property, he will not have to charge GST on the rent from the residential property[124]. Correspondingly, the GST-registered property owner will not be able to claim any input tax on supplies, used in making the exempt supplies.

4. Property Tax

Property tax is an expense in the business of letting properties. It amounts to about 10% of the rental income for non-residential properties and up to 20% of the rental income for residential properties[125]. Property tax is payable each year on the basis of the "annual value" as assessed by the Chief Assessor under the Property Tax Act. The term "annual value" is defined in section 2(1) of the Property Tax Act as the gross rental value of a property on the basis that the landlord pays for the expenses of repairs, maintenance, insurance and property tax.

As rents may fluctuate from time to time, the Chief Assessor may re-assess the annual value from year to year. Where he does so, he will send a notice under section 20(1) of the Property Tax Act informing the owner of the proposed annual value. The proposed annual value may take effect from any time in the year in which the notice is sent, as long as the proposed annual value is supported by the rental evidence of the period. The owner

---

[124] A property owner making annual taxable supplies of less than $1 million, is not required to register for GST supplies. He may choose to be so registered, if he so wishes. A GST-registered person may in fact in the course of his business, be making both taxable supplies and exempt supplies. For example, the owner which operates serviced apartments, makes exempt supplies insofar as the accommodation at the serviced apartments are concerned. But he is also making taxable supplies, in relation to the provision of furniture, furnishings and services.

[125] For a more detailed discussion on the topic of property tax, see Leung Yew Kwong and See Wei Hwa, *Property Tax in Singapore,* Third Edition (LexisNexis, 2015). Residential properties are subject to greater progressivity in terms of the applicable tax rate. In the Budget 2022 announcement made on 18 February 2022, the appliable tax rate for non-owner occupied residential properties in respect of annual values above $60,000 is set to increase to 27% with effect from 1 January 2023 and 36% with effect from 1 January 2024.

may object to the proposed annual value within 30 days of the date of the section 20(1) notice, if he considers the annual value to be excessive. This process is generally known as an objection to the valuation notice. The owner has to use a prescribed form that is available at the IRAS website, for the purpose of the objection.

It is however to be noted that the proposed annual value may not equal to the annual rent that the owner is getting for his property for various reasons. Firstly, the annual value is the estimated annual rent of the property based on the evidence of the current rents of similar properties and is not based on the actual rent of a property alone[126]. Hence, the annual value may not coincide exactly with the annual rent of a particular property. Secondly, the contracted rent of a particular property is usually fixed for a period of 2 or 3 years, whereas the annual value is based on the current prevailing market rent and is not constrained by the contractual arrangements of the landlord and tenant. Hence during a period when rents are on the uptrend, an owner may find that the annual value goes up each year while he is only able to increase the rent upon the expiry of the tenancy period or upon "rental review" during the term of the tenancy where such review is provided in the tenancy agreement. Correspondingly, when rents are on the downtrend, annual values may be reduced although an owner may still be enjoying a higher rent which has been fixed earlier during a good rental market. Needless to say, an owner has to be vigilant in monitoring the annual value of his property.

At any time where an owner considers the annual value of his property to be excessive, it is incumbent upon him to lodge an objection against the annual value of the property, using the prescribed form that is available on the IRAS website, even where he does not receive a section 20(1) valuation notice amending the annual value. Technically, this process of objecting to the annual value where a section 20(1) valuation notice has not been received by the owner, is known as an objection to the Valuation List. The owner may object against the annual value prescribed in the prevailing Valuation List at any time in the year. But he has to do so, before the end of the calendar year.

---

[126] In respect of a retail unit in a shopping center, there is a greater tendency that the actual rent is adopted by the Chief Assessor in assessing the annual value of the unit as it is much harder to derive the annual value based on some average or median, as rents of retail units vary tremendously depending on their location and size, even where they are situated within the same shopping center.

There is no mechanism in the Property Tax Act that provides for an owner to object to the annual value of his property, in respect of the Valuation Lists of past years.

4.1. Annual value

For the purpose of charging the property tax, the Chief Assessor assesses the annual value of a property. The term "annual value" is defined in section 2(1) of the Property Tax Act generally to mean the gross amount at which a property may be let from year to year, with the landlord paying the expenses of repair, maintenance, insurance and property tax. The annual property tax payable is then computed by multiplying the tax rate[127] with the annual value.

For most properties which are let, the "annual value" bears a close relationship with the actual rents received for the properties, as the "annual value" is assessed using the rental evidence of properties which are let. In respect of strata-titled properties, where the tenant pays a rent which includes a conservancy charge is levied by the management corporation, whether or not such charge is expressly stated in the tenancy agreement with the landlord, the annual value generally does not include the amount of the conservancy charge. This is because the definition of "annual value" does not include the amount paid by the tenant for services, such as those relating to provision of security, cleaning, refuse disposal and pest control services. However, where the tenant pays a specific amount towards to the sinking fund (levied by the management corporation on the landlord who is a subsidiary proprietor), the contribution to the sinking fund is not excluded in the determination of the annual value[128].

The property investor may encounter various practices concerning property tax assessments, some of which are discussed below:

(a) Since 2014, when the property tax refund for vacant buildings was abolished, there has been a greater tendency for individual units within

---

[127] For non-residential properties, the applicable tax rate is 10% per annum.

[128] *Tan Hee Liang v Chief Assessor and Another*, [2009] 1 SLR(R) 335 and IRAS e-Tax Guide, *Property Tax: Treatment of Contributions to Management Fund and Sinking Fund,* 2 September 2014.

a building which have been let, to be assessed with their separate annual values. Before 2014, such buildings where they were under a single ownership, may have been assessed with a single annual value for an entire building. In such "global" assessments, a "global discount" was usually given from the total sum of the individual rental values of the component units, in order to arrive at the global annual value of the entire building. The "global discount" was given in view of the size of the entire building and took into account that where the entire building is let in a single tenancy, the rent for the building would be lesser than the sum of the total rental values of the individual component units and that there may be vacancies in the entire building from time to time[129]. To continue with the assessments of entire buildings with the "global discount" after the abolition of property tax refund for vacant buildings, may seem to be providing for a "vacancy refund" in an indirect way. Hence, there has a greater tendency for the separate assessments of the component units in a building, with each unit having with its individual annual values even though the entire building may be under a single ownership.

However, with the individual assessments of the component units, the focus in the assessments is then on the annual rental values of the individual component units, sometimes with scant regard on the overall fairness of the assessments when considered together. A case in point is *HSBC Institutional Services (Singapore) Limited (as Trustee of Capitaland Mall Trust) v Chief Assessor*[130] which concerned the assessment of the car park at the IMM Building (which also comprised retail and warehouse units) situated in Jurong East. In order to attract patronage at the IMM Building, the owner of the building had a policy of providing free parking during lunch time. The free parking policy had the effect of depressing the business receipts of the car park. The Valuation Review Board in that case held that the profits method of assessment based on the actual receipts was not to be used, as the receipts were depressed on account of the free parking policy. Instead, the annual value of the

---

[129] See *DBS Bank Ltd v Chief Assessor* [2005] SGVRB 3, where the former DBS Building (since refurbished and is part of OUE Downtown) at Shenton Way was assessed with a global annual value and a 'global discount' of 20% was given.

[130] [2007] SGVRB 1.

car park was to be determined by comparison with the assessments of other car parks. While from the perspective of the narrow jurisdiction of the Board, that conclusion may be correct, one has to be mindful of the objective of the property owner in providing the free parking, from the broader perspective of fairness in tax administration. The objective of the property owner was to increase the overall rental income from the other parts of the building that it also owned. Those other units in the building had been assessed with annual values which reflected the rents which were obtained for those units, which in turn would have reflected the free parking policy during lunch time. It may be argued that had there been no free parking during lunch time, the patronage at the building may be lower and consequently the rents and the assessed annual values of the other parts of the building, would have been lower. After all, why would a property owner give up part of its car park revenue without a commercial purpose. It will be difficult to prove the relationship between free parking and the rents of other parts of the building in a scientific manner but that relationship is a matter of common sense. Indeed, valuation itself is very much based on common sense, and is not a science.

The contradictory positions borne out of individual assessments of various parts of a building which is under a single ownership, may be seen from the example of the car park at IMM Building. In assessing the annual value of the car park, the free parking policy was to be disregarded. But in assessing the annual values of the other parts of the building, the free car parking policy was implicitly taken into account, through the use of the actual rents in the assessments. In the days of global assessments, such individual "maximization" of the annual values of parts of a building may be moderated through taking the overall perspective of the entire building which was under a single ownership. A lower assessment of the car park through taking into account the actual receipts, would not have stood out when the car park was assessed with the rest of the building with a global annual value, and may be justified on the basis that the otherwise higher annual values for the rest of the building compensated for the lower annual value for the car park.

The above phenomenon which may affect the assessment of a car park in a building under a single ownership goes beyond just the case of the car park. In a shopping centre under a single ownership, the owner may "sub-optimise" the revenue of a space so as to optimize the overall revenue of the entire building. For example, a retail unit may be let for a bookshop or a traditional Chinese medicine shop, in order to portray the shopping centre as a place that caters to the needs of the entire family so as to attract patronage to the shopping centre. Typically, the use of the unit as a bookshop will provide a lower rent (expressed in terms of the rent per square foot) as compared with the rent the unit will fetch if it were to be used as a boutique for fashion clothes. On the basis of the principle of hypothetical tenancy underlying property tax assessments, the actual use of the unit is disregarded, and a higher annual value of the unit occupied by the bookshop may be assessed on the basis of the rent that the unit would fetch if it were vacant. Again, one has to bear in mind that the property owner did not rent the unit out for use as a bookshop for altruistic reasons. His commercial objective is in optimizing the rental income of the entire building, not just that of an individual unit. It would have been easier to accommodate the issues discussed above in a global assessment of the entire building. Otherwise, a pragmatic approach of assessing the annual values of component units or parts of the building, by taking into account the actual circumstances, would ensure that there is no "over-assessment" on an overall perspective.

(b) Another issue encountered in property tax assessments is that concerning rent-free periods. In *BFC Development LLP v Comptroller of Property Tax*, Chao Hick Tin JA in delivering the judgment of the Court of Appeal, observed[131]:

> It is a well-established in the property rental market in Singapore that tenants which require a big space for their business often ask for a rent-free fitting-out period to do the necessary pre-occupation works in order to ensure that the premises would be in a state to mee the physical needs of their business.

---

[131] [2014] 2 SLR 462 at [50].

The use of rent-free periods has enabled landlords to maintain a higher "signing" or "headline" rent and achieve a market rent or "effective" rent over the term of the lease. The effective rent is computed by dividing the total sum of the rents receivable for the term of the lease by the number of months in the term, and would be lower than the "signing" rent. The extent of the rent-free period given to each tenant, may vary and will depend on the individual circumstances of each tenancy. The landlord in the negotiations with each tenant, will be able to tailor the extent of rent-free period to be given for each tenancy. This is no different from the situation where the landlord agrees in negotiations to a particular rent with each tenant and the amount of rent in each case may vary somewhat. Nevertheless, the "effective rents" should be used as market evidence for the purpose of property tax assessment[132]. After all, the landlord would not want to give away any rent-free period to the tenant, if the market demand for rental space is such that no rent-free period is necessary to attract the tenant. The rent-free period is a marketing device for the rental package as in the case of discounts given by a developer to purchasers in the sale of residential apartments. The discounts may vary with individual purchasers (e.g. a bigger "early bird" discount may be given to the first purchasers), but the market values of the residential apartments are to be analysed on the basis of the agreed prices, net of the discount.

Nevertheless, the effective rent for a particular tenancy is a piece of market evidence amongst other market evidence. It does not necessarily follow the effective rent for a particular unit, *ipso facto* provides the annual value of that unit. In determining the annual value of a unit, all relevant market evidence has to be considered although greater weight may have to be given to the market evidence of the actual unit. In *DBS Bank Ltd v Chief Assessor*[133], the Valuation Review Board decided that "rent rebates" (which were effectively the amount of notional rent for the rent-free period) should not be taken into account, on the evidence in

---

[132] Where no rent-free period is given for a particular tenancy, the effective rent will be the signing rent. See *Sinofit (HK) Ltd v Full Gain Investment Ltd* [2000] CPR 1 where the Hong Kong Lands Tribunal accepted that in the analysis of market rents, the rent-free periods if any, were to be factored in to provide adjusted effective rents which may be used for rent comparison.

[133] [2005] SGVRB 3.

that case. One of the factors that the Board may have taken into account was that "rental rebates are not assured rebates but contingent upon the tenant adhering to the entire tenancy term. They are contracted on the basis that they provide an incentive for the tenant to remain throughout the contracted tenancy". The same may be said of the agreed rent itself. The amount of rent was agreed on the basis that the tenant was to remain for the full term and not for a shorter term by prematurely terminate the lease. With respect, it is submitted that the fact that the "rent rebates" were so contingent and varied with different tenancies, is no reason for disregarding them. Instead, the effective rents should be calculated for each tenancy, so that a standardized basis may be used for comparison of the market rents in the assessment of the annual values.

4.1.1. *Installation of fixtures*

Where the tenant installs fixtures in the property, the annual value of the property may be increased such that the landlord as owner of the property has to pay the increased property tax. This is because property tax is essentially a tax on immovable property which includes the fixtures. The impact of such increased property tax is especially substantial for properties such as cinemas and food courts, where the tenants typically install tenant's fixtures of substantial costs. In such cases, the landlord may have to provide in the tenancy agreements entered into with the tenants, that increases in property tax on account of the installation of tenant's fixtures have to be borne by the tenants. In this regard, in *HSBC Institutional Trust Services (Singapore) Ltd (trustee of Capitaland Mall Trust) v Chief Assessor*, Andrew Phang JA in delivering the judgment of the Court of Appeal in that case where the property was let to a cinema operator which installed various fixtures such as cinema seats, said[134]:

> The appellant's argument hinges at least in part on the fact that the Works were installed by its tenant, GV, rather than itself. The identity of the

---

[134] [2020] 1 SLR 621 at [6]. In *FC Retail Trustee Pte Ltd (in its capacity as Trustee-Manager as Sapphire Star Trust) v Chief Assessor and Another* [2021] SGVRB 2, the Valuation Review Board similarly upheld the increase in annual value where the fixtures were installed in a food court by the tenant which was a food court operator.

person who installed the fixtures may be relevant to the court's determination as to whether the Works are fixtures or chattels, and, in fact, the appellant had raised this issue before the Judge below. However, once the Works are found to be fixtures, the statutory tax regime does not differentiate between landlord's fixtures and tenant's fixtures. Property tax attaches to the property and not the person, although we note that there can be a separate arrangement between landlord and tenant where the tenant agrees to pay the landlord any increase in property tax over and above the property tax payable based on the rent under the existing tenancy agreement (which is, in fact, the case here).

A form of fixtures which are excluded from property tax assessment, is machinery affixed to the premises, which falls within the scope of section 2(3) of the Property Tax Act. Section 2(3) [renumbered from section 2(2), since 31 December 2021] reads as follows:

In assessing the annual value of any premises in or upon which there is any machinery used for any of the following purposes:

(a) the making of any article or part thereof;
(b) the altering, repairing, ornamenting or finishing of any article; or
(c) the adapting for sale of any article,

the enhanced value given to the premises by the presence of such machinery shall not be taken into consideration, and for this purpose 'machinery' includes the steam engines, boilers and other motive power belonging to that machinery.

The meaning of the word "article" in section 2(3) is wide and may include substances which are in solid, liquid or gaseous form. In this regard, Andrew Phang JA in *Skyventure VWT Pte Ltd v Chief Assessor and Another person* said[135]:

The word "article", at its broadest, may refer to commodities or substances in general, in either solid, liquid or gaseous form. Under this broad definition, water, steam and coal gas may all be articles (see the English

---

[135] [2021] 2 SLR 116. Section 2(2) referred to in the grounds of judgment, has been renumbered as section 2(3) in the 2020 Revised Edition of The Property Tax Act 1960. For a commentary on this case, see 'Is property tax ready for the future economy?' KPMG Tax Alert, September 2021 and *The Business Times*, 30 November 2021.

Court of Appeal decision in *Cox v S. Cutler & Sons, Ltd. and Hampton Court Gas Co.* [1948] 2 All ER 665 at 667). Indeed, natural elements may be considered articles in themselves (see the House of Lords decision in *Longhurst v Guildford, Godalming and District Water Board* [1963] 1 AC 265 ("*Longhurst*") at 277 – 278). We would further observe that it was undisputed in *First DCS (CA)* that chilled water was an article for the purposes of s 2(2) of the Act (at [8]). It follows that things occurring in nature, such as water, air and so on, may be "articles" for the purposes of s 2(2) of the Act. Manufactured items may also be articles, as is clear from s 2(2)(*a*) of the Act. Taken together, the term "article" in s 2(2) of the Act, in our view, is *ordinarily* capable of referring, at its broadest, to any matter or *thing* whether occurring in nature or otherwise.

The application of section 2(3) is also not limited to manufacturing machinery. As Andrew Phang JA said in *Skyventure* at [21]:

> … in order for s 2(2) of the Act to apply to a particular piece of machinery, it must be shown that the machinery in question must be used *for the purposes* of making, altering, repairing, ornamenting, finishing, or adapting for sale any *article*, a term which the Act does not define. As long as the machinery in question satisfies these criteria, the type of machinery and the premises in or upon which it is situated are irrelevant considerations, since the terms "any premises" and "any machinery", as used in the provision, ordinarily refer to "any and all" premises and machinery without any limitation (see also the decision of this court in *Li Shengwu v Attorney-General* [2019] 1 SLR 1081 at [170]).

Earlier in *Chief Assessor and Another v First DCS Pte Ltd*[136]. the Court of Appeal has held that chiller machinery which were fixtures and was used in the provision of district cooling services in that case, fell within the scope of the then section 2(2) and was to be excluded from property tax assessment. In *Skyventure*, the Court of Appeal observed that in *First DCS*, the cooling or chilling effect of the water was sold[137].

Following the Court of Appeal decision in *First DCS* in 2008, machinery installed in data centres for the purpose of controlling, maintaining or

---

[136] [2008] 2 SLR(R) 724.

[137] [2021] 2 SLR 116 40 at [54]–[58].

modifying the temperature and the humidity of the data centre properties, was not included in property tax assessment, on the basis that the machinery which are fixtures fall within the scope of the then section 2(2). If the fixtures were to be included in the property tax assessment, the annual values of the data centre properties would be increased substantially, in view of the cost of data centre machinery and the data centre redundancy requirements.

In 2017, there was a proposal by the Ministry of Finance to introduce legislation to amend the then section 2(2), and the draft legislation was published by the Ministry for public consultation. In the draft Property Tax (Amendment) Bill, there were specific proposals to include some machinery for property tax assessment, which would otherwise fall within the scope of the then section 2(2). The proposed section 2(2AA)(a)(v) which was to amend the then section 2(2), reads as follows:

Subsection (2) does not apply to —

(a) any machinery which is the setting or environment for the carrying out of necessary work and business on the premises, and the purpose of which is —

   (i) for the provision of heating, cooling, ventilation or lighting in the premises;

   (ii) for the draining or supplying of water in or from the premises;

   (iii) for the transmission, distribution or supply of electricity and the provision of back-up power to or within the premises (such as a solar panel, stand-by generator, transformer, or switch gear);

   (iv) for telecommunications;

   (v) for the controlling, maintaining or modifying of the temperature, atmospheric pressure, humidity or air quality in the premises.

   (vi) to protect the premises from any trespasser, danger, theft, fire, over-heating, or other hazards (such as security and fire protection systems); or

(b) machinery that is used or intended to be used for the storage of articles.

The proposed statutory provisions if enacted, would have the effect of including the machinery in the data centre properties and similar machinery in other properties, in property tax assessment. However, following the public consultation[138], the Ministry decided not to proceed with the proposed legislative amendments with respect to the then section 2(2). In a Ministry statement published on its website on 5 September 2017, it was stated as follows: "We will study further the proposed amendment relating to the exemption of machinery from property tax, and not include this in the Bill."

There was therefore a reprieve for owners of data centre properties and other properties with similar machinery. Nevertheless, it is to be observed that the existing provisions of section 2(3) are rather archaic and hark back to the industrial age of the 19th century and are generally not in tune with the modern economy. Under section 2(3), machinery which has become fixtures and are used for the manufacturing of shoes, beverages, electricity *etc*, are not assessed for property tax. It would seem that some of the machinery used for the new economy and in furtherance of Singapore's position as a regional hub, are treated as not falling within the scope of section 2(3) and are treated as taxable for property tax purposes by the authorities. Some of the machinery are as follows:

(a) Machinery for the provision of cold chain logistical facilities to store vaccines and other perishables, which can significantly reduce loss and wastage;

(b) Machinery for the provision of contamination-free or sterile environment for the life sciences industry (including the medical technology, biotechnology, pharmaceuticals and medical devices industries), where vaccines and drugs may be manufactured and filled into vials and syringes in fill-and-finish processes;

(c) Machinery comprising photovoltaic systems and inverters for the provision of solar power in specialized factories;

(d) Machinery for the automatic storage and retrieval systems (ASRS) to store goods, designed to meet the objectives of faster deliveries, shorter

---

[138] Information on the efforts of the data centre industry in providing feedback to the Ministry was published on the SGTech website. See also 'Can property tax promote Industry 4.0', *The Business Times,* 24 October 2017.

storage time, higher efficiency and lower costs. Buildings with ASRS generally need less land for their operations;

(e) Machinery with state-of-the-art sorting technologies used by the logistics industry designed to meet the requirements of e-commerce;

(f) Machinery such as robotics, Internet of Things (IoT) enabled carts and automated guide vehicles used for the lifting and conveying of goods;

(g) Wind tunnel machinery for the testing of the aerodynamics of objects in the aerospace industry;

(h) Urban farming machinery which provides multiple levels of hydroponic vegetable growing space with precisely-controlled lighting and other conditions essential to such farming; and

(i) Machinery for high-technology aquaculture with advanced water treatment processes, for farming of fish, shrimps and shellfish.

In comparison, the statutory provisions for the annual value system in England, have been updated to cater to modern industries, where plant and machinery which are essentially "tools of the trade" of businesses are excluded from assessment. In England, following the publication of the Wood Report on "Rating of Plant and Machinery" in March 1993, the Valuation for Rating (Plant and Machinery) (England) Regulations 2000 were enacted. The 2000 Regulations list plant and machinery under four classes, in its Schedule. In Class 2 in the Schedule to the 2000 Regulations, plant and machinery used for manufacturing operations or trade processes, are excluded from rating. Class 2 provides as follows:

Plant and machinery specified in Table 2 below ... which is used or intended to be used in connection with services to the hereditament or part of it, other than any such plant or machinery which is in or on the hereditament and is used or intended to be used in connection with services mainly or exclusively as part of manufacturing operations or trade processes.

The exclusion from assessment, of plant and machinery used or intended to be used mainly or exclusively as part of trade processes, may potentially exclude much of the "tools of the trade" or machinery of modern industries mentioned above, from property tax assessment. It is interesting to note that in *Iceland Foods Ltd v Berry (Valuation Officer)*[139], the United Kingdom Supreme Court has held that the air handling systems used for the freezing or refrigeration of goods to preserve them in a retail store, are to be excluded from assessment on the basis of the Valuation for Rating (Plant and Machinery)(England) Regulations 2000.

Hong Kong has followed the English position and machinery used for "trade processes" is similarly excluded from assessment, under section 8(b) of the Hong Kong Rating Ordinance which reads as follows:

> For the purpose of ascertaining the rateable value of a tenement ... no account shall be taken of the value of any machinery in or on the tenement for the purpose of manufacturing operations or trade processes.

It may be seen that Singapore is lagging behind in updating its property tax legislation in this respect. Ultimately, it is matter of fiscal policy as to whether Singapore is to follow the English and Hong Kong positions. It would seem that there is a good policy case for Singapore to do so, if it were to encourage investments in modern technologies needed by the emerging sectors of the economy.

It is a legacy from colonial legislation that we have used the English legal doctrine of fixtures for the purposes of the levy of property tax. Under that doctrine, an article which was originally a movable chattel may by virtue of its physical annexation to the land or the purpose of such annexation, become part of the land, even where the chattel may be affixed by the tenant. The doctrine of fixtures itself drew inspiration from the ancient Roman doctrine of *accessio* where an accessory property was acceded to the principal property, the owner of the principal property became the owner of the accessory property as well. The policy behind the Roman doctrine was the preservation of value as the physical removal of the accessory property may cause damage and loss of value[140]. That policy is not necessarily aligned with that for property tax. The colonial government in cognizance that the operation of the common law of fixtures may have the dragnet effect of

---

[139] [2018] 1 WLR 1277.
[140] See Lars Van Vliet 'Accession of Movables to Land' in Elizabeth Cooke (ed), *Modern Studies of Property Law* Vol 1 (Hart Publishing, 2000) and *Elitestone Ltd v Morris* [1997] 1 WLR 687.

taxing productive machinery, carved out the exceptions in the provisions of section 2(3). The policy for property tax seems to be to encourage the investment in such machinery which is affixed to the property more for use in the productive processes, than for the enjoyment of the property. However as the provisions in section 2(3) of the Property Tax Act which were first enacted in the 19th century, now stand, they would encourage investments in machinery for the more traditional manufacturing and processing industries, but not those for the new economy.

4.2. Property tax rebates

As property tax in Singapore is treated as a tax on ownership of a property and as a form of wealth tax, relief from tax is generally not given. There is no refund of tax given in the case of an unoccupied building[141]. However in the unprecedented circumstances of the COVID-19 pandemic outbreak in 2020, property tax rebates were given to the owners of non-residential properties for the year 2020 under the Property Tax (Non-Residential Properties) (Remission) Order 2020[142]. The rebate was 100%[143] of the property tax for properties such as hotels, serviced apartments, MICE[144] venues, cinemas, theatres, amusement centers, foreign worker dormitories, shops and tourist attractions, which were more severely impacted by the outbreak, such that no property tax was charged for the year 2020. In respect of office buildings, factories and warehouses, the rebate was for 30% of the property tax. The integrated resorts of Marina Bay Sands and Resorts World Sentosa (each with components comprising hotels, retail shops and casino, and in the case of Resorts World Sentosa, also a theme park) were given rebates of 60%. Although the hotels, retail shops and theme park would have been given a

---

[141] Property tax refund for vacant buildings was abolished from 1 January 2014 with the coming into operation of the Property Tax (Amendment) Act 2014 (Act 18 of 2013).

[142] S 155/2020 as amended by the Property Tax (Commercial Properties) (Remission) Order 2020, S 305/2020. See IRAS e-Tax Guide, *Property Tax Rebate for Non-Residential Properties in 2020*, Second Edition, 22 April 2020. This is the first time that property owners are required by law, to pass on the benefit of the property tax rebates to tenants. In earlier rebates, property owners were only exhorted to pass on the benefits.

[143] With the 100% rebate, no property tax was payable for the year 2020.

[144] Meetings, Incentive Travel, Conventions and Exhibitions venues, namely Suntec Singapore Convention and Exhibition Center, Singapore EXPO and Changi Exhibition Center.

100% remission of their property tax, had they been standalone properties with their individual annual values, the intermediate rate of rebate of 60% for the entire integrated resorts, perhaps reflected the perception that there may be less public receptiveness for according total remission of the property tax payable on the casino component of those properties.

Where a property is let or licensed, the owner who is given the property tax rebate has to pass the benefit of the reduction in property tax to his lessees or licensees, with the coming into operation of Part 6 of the COVID-19 (Temporary Measures) Act 2020[145]. As property tax for a non-residential property is payable at 10% of the annual value which is roughly equivalent to the annual rental value of the property, the benefit to be passed on with respect to properties accorded 100% and 30% rebates amounts to about a month's rent and one-third of a month's rent respectively.

The benefit was generally to be passed on in two parts, by 31 July and 31 December 2020[146]. Such a procedure would also cater to a situation where there may be a change of tenants or licensees during the year, such that the benefit may be apportioned between the tenants or licensees concerned. Some owners have for commercial reasons, chosen to go beyond what is required and have provided a rental rebate greater than the amount of property tax rebates received or have passed on the benefit of the entire reduction in property tax in a single lump sum before 31 July 2020.

Where a property is assessed with a single annual value and has multiple tenants or where a tenant only occupies a part of the property, the basis of the apportionment of the property tax rebates for the transfer of the benefit of the property tax reduction, is set out in Part 3 of the COVID-19 (Temporary Measures) (Transfer of Benefit of Property Tax Remission) Regulations 2020[147]. Any dispute in this regard may be heard and determined by a Valuation Review Panel[148].

---

[145] Act No. 14 of 2020. Part 6 of the Act dealing with the passing of the benefit of in property tax reduction came into operation on 22 April 2020: see COVID-19 (Temporary Measures) Act 2020 (Commencement) (No. 3) Notification, S 310/2020.

[146] See paras 9.28 and 9.29 of the IRAS e-Tax Guide, *Property Tax Rebate for Non-Residential Properties in 2020*, Fifth Edition, 29 December 2020.

[147] S 375/2020.

[148] S 30(2) of the COVID-19 (Temporary Measures) Act 2020.

5. Stamp Duty

A landlord of a property may enter into a tenancy agreement with a tenant, in respect of the letting of his property. The tenancy agreement is chargeable with *ad valorem* stamp duty pursuant to section 4(1) and Article 8 of the First Schedule, of the Stamp Duties Act. The duty is payable by the tenant, unless there is an agreement to the contrary by the parties[149]. In some cases, the parties may first enter into an agreement which sets out the essential points of agreement for the tenancy to facilitate the tenant moving into the premises, where it is anticipated that the tenancy agreement may take some time to prepare. In that case, the agreement for lease is chargeable with stamp duty instead[150]. An agreement for lease has the same effect as a formal lease[151].

5.1. Lease vs licence

While a lease of an immovable property is subject to stamp duty, a licence for the use of an immovable property is not. In Singapore, licence arrangements are commonly encountered with respect to student accommodation in a hostel, stalls in a food court and accommodation in workers' dormitories and service apartments. An essential and distinguishing feature of a lease is the "exclusive possession" of the property by the tenant. In *Tan Sook Yee's Principles of Singapore Land Law*, the following is stated on the feature of exclusive possession[152]:

> The problem lies in determining whether exclusive possession has been given. Gray and Gray contend that the two distinctive features of exclusive

---

[149] Section 34(a) and Article 4 of the Third Schedule, of the Stamp Duties Act.

[150] Prior to the coming into operation of the Stamp Duties (Amendment) Act 2011 (No 23 of 2011), the lease was liable to a nominal $2 stamp duty where the *ad valorem* duty was earlier paid on the agreement to lease. Article 8(d) which provided for the nominal duty in the case of a 'lease executed in pursuance of a duly stamped agreement for the production on production of the agreement to the Commissioner, was deleted by the legislative amendment.

[151] *Walsh v Lonsdale* (1882) 21 Ch D 9 cited in *Golden Village Multiplex Pte Ltd v Marina Centre Holdings Pte Ltd* [2002] 1 SLR(R) 169 and Tan Sook Yee, *Equitable Leases, Subdivision and Section 4 Planning Act*, (2002) 14 SAcLJ 133.

[152] Tan Sook Yee, Tang Hang Wu and Kelvin FK Low, *Tan Sook Yee's Principles of Singapore Land Law* (LexisNexis, 2009), para 17.38.

possession are (i) the exclusionary power of the occupier, and (ii) the occupier's immunity from supervisory control. With regard to exclusory power, this must mean a right of territorial control the tenant may vindicate by action in trespass even against his own landlord. Exclusive possession also means that the occupier is immune from supervisory control by the freehold owner. Where the occupier is subject to control by the freehold owner, this indicates that the occupier has not been granted exclusive possession.

Exclusive possession which is an attribute of a lease or tenancy is to be distinguished from exclusive occupation which merely gives the occupant a right of sole occupation. Exclusive occupation, whilst giving the occupant the exclusive physical occupation of the premises, does not give him the overall control over the use of, and access to, the premises. Thus, students in hostels, lodgers in boarding houses and patients in nursing homes, may all enjoy exclusive occupation, but they do not have exclusive possession of the premises. In this regard, in the House of Lords case of *Street v Mountford*, Lord Templeman said[153]:

> In the case of residential accommodation there is no difficulty in deciding whether the grant confers exclusive possession. An occupier of residential accommodation at a rent for a term is either a lodger or a tenant. The occupier is a lodger if the landlord provides attendance or services which require the landlord or his services to exercise unrestricted access to and use of the premises. A lodger is entitled to live in the premises but cannot call the place his own. In *Allan v Liverpool Overseers* (1874) LR 9 QB 180, 191–192, Blackburn J said:
>
>> A lodger in a house, although he has the exclusive use of rooms in the house, in the sense that nobody else is to be there, and though his goods are stowed there, yet he is not in exclusive occupation in that sense, because the landlord is there for the purpose of being able, as landlords commonly do in the case of lodgings, to have his own servants to look after the house and the furniture, and has retained to himself the occupation, though he has agreed to give the exclusive enjoyment of the occupation to the lodger.

---

[153] [1985] AC 809 at 818.

If on the other hand residential accommodation is granted for a term at a rent with exclusive possession, the landlord providing neither attendance nor services, the grant is a tenancy ....

Hence, the occupant is a lodger if the landlord provides attendance or services which require the landlord or his servants to exercise unrestricted access to the premises. It is the occupant's inability to resist intrusion by the owner who requires access to supply the service or attendance which affects any finding of exclusive possession or a lease[154]. In this regard, Lord Donaldson MR in *Aslan v Murphy* said[155]:

> ... if the true bargain is that the owner will provide genuine services which can only be provided by having keys, such as frequent cleaning, dialing bed-making, the provision of clean linen at regular intervals and the like, there are materials from which it is possible to infer that the occupier is a lodger rather than a tenant. But the inference arises not from the provisions as to keys, but from the reasons why those provisions formed part of the bargain. ...

5.2. Lease duty

The lease duty in respect of leases not exceeding 4 years is computed at 0.4% of the "total" rent and other consideration payable for the period of the lease. For leases exceeding 4 years, the lease duty is computed at 0.4% of 4 times the "average" rent and other consideration calculated for a whole year (or "average annual rent", AAR) during the period of the lease. The "other consideration" used in the computation of the lease duty will include consideration payments payable by the tenant for the provision of furniture, chattels, fittings or equipment, services and facilities in connection with the lease[156].

Where there is also a premium payable for a lease, the additional lease duty is computed at 1% of the first tranche of $180,000 of the premium,

---

[154] See also *Antioniades v Villiers* [1990] 1 AC 417 at 459 and 467.
[155] [1990] 1 WLR 766 at 773.
[156] See Article 8 of the First Schedule to the Stamp Duties Act.

2% of the second tranche of $180,000 and 3% of the tranche in excess of $360,000[157].

The calculation of the total rent or AAR payable under the lease for the purpose of computing the *ad valorem* stamp duty, is relatively straight-forward for shorter terms where there is no provision of rent reviews during the period of the lease, and the rent and other consideration are specified in absolute amounts in the agreement. For longer leases however, there may be provisions for stepped-up rents and rent reviews at periodic intervals. Where the stepped-up rents (whether in absolute amounts or as may be ascertained by a fixed formula) are ascertainable from the lease, the total rent or AAR may also be easily calculated for stamp duty purposes. However, there may be a rent review clause in the lease agreement where the rent at each review is to be based on the prevailing rental value, which may be subject to some minimum and/or maximum increase.

Since the future rents are to be based on the prevailing market rent at the point of rent review, they are unascertainable at the time of the stamping of the lease. In such circumstances, the Stamp Office uses the contingency principle developed by the courts in the UK with respect to stamp duty law[158], for the purpose of the calculation of the "average rent" for the entire period of the lease, as specified in Article 8(aa) of the First Schedule to the Stamp Duties Act, to determine the stamp duty. With respect to the contingency principle, Brightman J in *Coventry City Council v Inland Revenue Commissioners* said[159]:

> It was submitted that the authorities establish the proposition that where ad valorem duty is payable on an instrument by reference to a sum payable thereunder, the duty is charged not only by reference to any sum which is unconditionally payable but also by reference to a sum specified in the

---

[157] It would seem that the higher rates of stamp duty would apply in the case of premiums paid for leases of residential property, in accordance with the rates in Article 3(a)(iii)(A) of the First Schedule to the Stamp Duties Act. This issue remains academic, as the payment of a premium for leases of residential properties, is unheard of in Singapore.

[158] The contingency principle was developed as the liability of an instrument to stamp duty is determined on the circumstances at the time of executive of the instrument and is not affected by subsequent events. In this regard, Lord Reid in *William Cory & Son Ltd v Inland Revenue Commissioners* [1965] 2 WLR 924 at 933, said: 'the liability of an instrument to stamp duty depends on the circumstances which exist when the instrument is executed'.

[159] [1978] 2 WLR 857 at 860.

instrument which is payable contingently or conditionally, that is to say, on a sum which may become payable. That, it was said, is a principle of general application under the Stamp Act. If, per contra, the form of the instrument is such that a sum is payable but the instrument does not name what that sum is, or what it may be, so that the sum could, in theory, be any figure, subject to due quantification by reference to some formula, then there is nothing by reference to which ad valorem duty can be calculated. If a minimum sum is expressed as that which may be payable, ad valorem duty is to be assessed on that minimum sum. If a maximum sum is expressed, ad valorem duty is to be assessed on that maximum sum as a sum which may be payable. *If both a maximum and a minimum sum are expressed*, ad valorem duty is perhaps, in theory, assessable on both, but the greater charge to duty will, of course, absorb the smaller charge in order to avoid a double charge.

The contingency principle subject to the provisions of section 25 of the Stamp Duties Act[160], operates as follows in determining the amount of stamp duty payable on the lease where an initial rent[161] is stated:

(a) where the maximum rate of increase of the rent is stated in the lease agreement but no minimum rate of increase is stated, the rents at each rent review is calculated on the basis of the maximum rate of increase, in order to arrive at the AAR for the entire period of lease. The AAR is arrived at by dividing the total rent for the period of the lease by the number of years in the lease[162];

(b) where the maximum and minimum rates of increase of rent are stated in the lease agreement, the maximum rate is used to calculate the rents at each rent review, in order to arrive at the AAR for the entire period of lease[163];

---

[160] S 25 was amended by the Stamp Duties (Amendment) Act 1999 (Act 33 of 1999) and the purpose of the legislative enactment was stated in the Explanatory Statement to the Stamp Duties (Amendment) Bill 1999 (No 28 of 1999) as follows: 'Clause 12 amends section 25 by empowering the Commissioner to assess a lease with regard to its open market rent where the rent is indeterminable or the rent is below open market rent.'

[161] In the situations set out in paragraphs (a) to (d) in this section, where the Commissioner considers the initial rent to be below open market rent, he may substitute the initial rent with the 'open market rent' for the purposes of calculation of the lease duty.

[162] *Coventry City Council v Inland Revenue Commissioners* [1978] 2 WLR 857.

[163] *Coventry City Council v Inland Revenue Commissioners* [1978] 2 WLR 857.

(c) where the minimum rate of increase is stated in the lease agreement but no maximum rate of increase is stated, the minimum rate is used to calculate the rents at each rent review, in order to arrive AAR for the entire period of lease[164];

(d) where there is no maximum or minimum rate of increase stated in the lease agreement, and the rate of increase at each rent review is to be based on the prevailing market rent at the time of review, the rate of increase is hence *unascertainable*. In such a situation, the initial rent at the commencement of the lease, is used as the AAR for the entire period of lease as explained below[165]; and

(e) where the amount of rent as specified in the lease agreement cannot be ascertained e.g. where the rent may be based solely on the gross sales turnover of the tenant after the commencement of the lease, section 25(2) of the Stamp Duties Act empowers the Commissioner to use the "open market rent" to calculate the stamp duty chargeable on the lease agreement. Section 25(2) reads as follows:

> If the rent or any other consideration payable by the lessee under a lease cannot be ascertained or estimated at the time that the lease is presented for stamping (whether because the consideration depends on some future contingency or for any other reason), the Commissioner may assess the duty payable based on the open market rent for the leased property as if the open market rent were the rate or average rate of rent per annum under the lease and there were no other consideration payable under the lease.

As may be seen, section 25(2) deals with the situation where the rent "*cannot* be ascertained" (i.e. unascertainable) from the tenancy agreement, as the rent may depend on a future contingency (e.g. the amount of sales turnover). But for section 25(2), there is no *ad valorem* stamp duty chargeable on a lease where the rent "cannot be ascertained" on account of the contingency principle[166]. As stated by Scrutton J in *Underground*

---

[164] *Underground Electric Railways Co of London Ltd v Inland Revenue Commissioners* [1906] AC 21.

[165] *Independent Television Authority v Inland Revenue Commissioners* [1961] AC 427.

[166] *Harbour Centre Development Limited v Collector of Stamp Revenue* (1968) 1 HKTC 822.

Electric Railway and Glyn, Mills, Currie & Co v The Commissioners of Inland Revenue[167]:

> ... if you cannot ascertain from the instrument a fixed sum which may become payable, though on contingencies, you cannot stamp ad valorem.

With respect to the situations stated in paragraphs (a) to (d) above, section 25(3) of the Stamp Duties Act may come into operation, where the initial rent at the commencement of the lease is considered by the Commissioner to be below open market rent. Under that circumstance, the Commissioner may substitute the "open market rent" over the initial rent as stipulated in the lease agreement pursuant to the powers under section 25(3), but otherwise the operation of the contingency principle remains as stated in paragraphs (a) to (d) above. Section 25(3) reads as follows:

> If the consideration payable by the lessee under a lease can be ascertained or estimated at the time that the lease is presented for stamping but the duty that may be charged on the instrument (whether as a lease or a conveyance on sale or both) apart from this section is less than the duty that would be payable based on the open market rent for the property, the Commissioner may assess the duty payable based on the open market rent as if the open market rent were the rate or average rate of rent per annum under the lease and there were no other consideration payable under the lease.

As may be seen, section 25(3) deals the situation where the rent "can be ascertained or estimated at the time that the lease is presented for stamping", as opposed to the situation in section 25(2) where the rent "cannot be ascertained or estimated". Under section 25(3), where the Commissioner considers the rent which "can be ascertained" (i.e. ascertainable), to be below the "open market rent", he may assess the stamp duty based on the "open market rent".

The term "open market rent" in section 25(3) is defined in section 25(5), as "the consideration ... that a lessee might reasonably be expected

---

[167] [1914] 3 KB 210 at 220.

to pay ... if it were unoccupied and offered for renting, expressed as a *rate of rent per annum*". The "open market value" is determined by the Chief Valuer. Quite obviously, the Chief Valuer is not clairvoyant and he can only determine the "open market value" as at the commencement of the lease. He is in no position to determine any market rent in respect of any future periods. It is to be noted that the "open market rent" in section 25(5) is expressed as a "rate of rent per annum".

For the operation of section 25(3), the "open market rent" is then to be treated "*as if* the open market rent were the *rate* or *average rate* of rent per annum under the lease". The application of the "open market rent" as if it is (1) the "rate per annum" *or* (2) the "average rate per annum", in section 25(3) is meant to cater to the following two different situations:

(a) *"Open market rent" treated as if it is the "rate of rent per annum"*

The "open market rent" is treated as if it is the "rate of rent per annum" where the stipulated rent under the lease is below the "open market rent". Where the stipulated rent remains the same for the entire period of the lease, the "open market rent" instead of the stipulated rent, is then used to compute the *ad valorem* lease duty. Where the stipulated initial rent under the lease is subject to rent review and the rate of rent increase at each rent review is *stipulated* (whether in terms of a maximum, minimum or fixed rate) in the rent review clause in the lease agreement, the contingency principle (as discussed above) operates such that the applicable rate of increase is used to calculate the rents at each rent review. The AAR (which contemplates varying rents during the term of the lease, which are then averaged) is then obtained by an averaging process (i.e. dividing the total rents to be collected during the entire period of lease by the number of years in the entire period of lease). Therefore in such a case, the "open market rent" at the commencement of the lease provides "the rate of rent per annum", and the AAR is derived by using the applicable rate of rent increase; and

(b) *"Open market rent" treated as if it is the "average rate of rent per annum"*

The "open market rent" is treated as if it is the "average rate of rent per annum" or the AAR under the lease, where there is no further "averaging process" needed. This occurs where the rate of rent increase at each rent review is *not stipulated* in the rent review clause (i.e. the rent at each rent review is to be determined at the prevailing open market rent at that time). As the rent at the time of rent review is unknown, then there can be no step-up or step-down of the rent for the purposes of the calculation of the AAR for stamp duty purposes, In that situation, the "open market rent" which is the open market rent at the commencement of the lease, is treated as if it is the "average rate of rent per annum" itself, for the purposes of the calculation of the lease duty under Article 8(aa) of the First Schedule to the Stamp Duties Act.

In other words, section 25(3) only serves to empower the Commissioner to substitute the "open market rent" over the stipulated initial rent which "can be ascertained" at the commencement of the lease. Section 25(3) does not disturb the operation of the contingency principle in arriving at the AAR.

Where the lease has a stipulated rate of increase of the rent at each rent review, the applicable rate of increase is then used to calculate the rents at each rent review so as to derive the AAR over the entire period of the lease. On the other hand, if the revised rent at each rent review is to be based on the prevailing market rent (and there is no stipulated maximum, minimum or fixed increase in the rent for the purpose of the rent review) as in situation (d) above, the initial rent (as substituted with the "open market rent" by the Commissioner under section 25(3) where he considers the stipulated initial rent to be below the open market rent) at the commencement of the lease, is itself the "average rent" under Article 8(aa) of the First Schedule to the Stamp Duties Act for the purpose of the calculation of the lease duty.

5.3. Revision of rent during the term of the lease

During the term of the lease, the rent may be revised pursuant to the rent review clause in the lease agreement. A memorandum may be prepared which records the revised rent. This memorandum is not chargeable with duty as it is not a lease falling under the head of charge in Article 8 of the

First Schedule to the Stamp Duties Act. It is to be noted that the original lease has already been duly stamped, with the application of the contingency principle as may be necessary.

The rent that is reserved under the original lease includes the rents that are payable throughout the term of the lease, the non-payment of which may give rise to a determination of the lease by the landlord, as the liability to pay rent remains so long as the lease exists. The memorandum of the revised rent at each rent review does not by itself create the obligation to pay the revised rent. The revised rent arises by virtue of the terms of the original lease itself and not by reason of the memorandum outside the lease. In this regard, in *Landlord and Tenant Series — Rent Review*, the author stated[168]:

> Varying rent does not normally result in the payment of stamp duty under the Stamp Act 1891. If the lease provides for the rent to be reviewed and a memorandum is entered into to record the new rent, there will be no liability to duty under s 77(5) of the 1891 Act. Accordingly, stamp duty is chargeable at rent review only if the document effecting the review actually varies the rent, and this will occur rarely (for example, where the lease did not contain rent review provisions but the parties have agreed to a review).

Similarly, the leading stamp duty lawyer, Reginald S Nock in *Stamp Duty for Property Transactions* stated[169]:

> Section 77(5) of the Stamp Act 1891 provides that any instrument whereby the rent reserved under a lease is increased is to be charged with stamp duty as though the instrument were itself a lease. Duty will thus be charged by reference to the amount of the increase (not the total rent as increased) as a percentage appropriate to the period during which the rent will be increased (not necessarily the whole of the remainder of the term of the lease). This does not apply to a memorandum recording an increase in rent under a rent review provision. Section 77(5) has no application to instruments recording the result of normal rent review since the increase

---

[168] Jill Alexander, *Landlord and Tenant Series — Rent Review,* (Blackstone Press, 2001), para 5.8 at p 132.
[169] Reginald S Nock, *Stamp Duty for Property Transactions* (Key Haven Publications, Second Edition, 1996), p 382.

arises by virtue of the terms of the lease itself and not by reason of a separate instrument outside the lease.

Section 77(5) of the English Stamp Act 1891 is *in pari materia* with section 26(3) of the Stamp Duties Act which reads as follows:

> An instrument *whereby* the rent reserved by any other instrument chargeable with duty and duly stamped as a lease is increased shall not be charged with duty otherwise than as a lease in consideration of the additional rent thereby made payable.

It is to be noted that the memorandum which records an increased rent, where there is a rent review clause in the original lease agreement, is not an instrument "whereby" the rent is increased, as the increased rent arises by virtue of the terms of the lease itself. Hence, section 26(3) can have no application in the case of a memorandum of which records an increased rent. Section 26(3) is in any case, not a charging provision and cannot impose a duty on the memorandum which is not a lease. An instrument which increases the rent without actually granting a new lease does not attract lease duty, as such an instrument does not fall under any of the heads of charge in the First Schedule.

For an understanding of the operation of the provisions of section 26(3) which are adopted from section 77(5) of the English Stamp Act 1891, it is instructive to consider *Gable Construction Ltd v Inland Revenue Commissioners*[170] which concerned the operation of section 77(5). In that case, the lease did not provide for a rent review clause and the parties entered into a deed of variation during the term of the lease. In that case, Goff J (as he then was) accepted that lease duty only applied to leases and therefore an instrument that increased rent without actually granting a new lease was not subject to stamp duty altogether. The outstanding question then concerned the possibility of stamping the instrument under the head of charge on "bond, covenant" where an instrument which provided for the payment of periodical sums, was subject to duty. The bond covenant duty at that time provided for

---

[170] [1968] 1 WLR 1426. The *Gable Construction* case was approved by the English Court of Appeal in *Jenkin R Lewis & Son Ltd v Kerman* [1971] 1 Ch 477 at 497 insofar as it decided that the rent increasing document did not operate to create a new lease.

a greater amount of duty as compared with the lease duty in England and section 77(5) was considered a relieving provision. In other words, as the deed of variation was not a lease, it attracted the higher bond covenant duty and section 77(5) operated to apply the lower lease duty[171]. Section 77(5) was not a charging provision. In that case, Goff J said at pages 1434 and 1435:

> … it follows in my judgment that the deed of variation is not a lease or tack, it follows equally that it is prima facie chargeable under the heading, "bond, covenant," etc. … Then, section 77(5) fits into place as a relieving provision limiting the higher duty which would be payable as a bond or covenant to the lesser amount attributable to a lease or tack for the amount of the increase in rent.

In Singapore as in England, the head of charge for "bond, covenant" in the First Schedule has been amended substantially. The existing "bond, covenant" head of charge in Article 1 of the First Schedule to the Singapore Stamp Duties Act amended in 1998, reads as follows[172]:

> Bond, Covenant or Instrument for securing the payment of securing the payment for the hire of furniture, chattels, fittings or equipment in connection with the lease of immovable property and for the provision for services or facilities or to other matters or things in connection with such lease.

The deed of variation does not fall under the terms of bond covenant duty in Article 1 of the First Schedule. Since the deed of variation is also not a lease, the deed does not attract any stamp duty at all, as it does not fall under any of the heads of charge in the First Schedule. In this regard, it has to be noted section 26(3) does not operate as a charging provision to impose stamp duty on the deed of variation. Section 26(3) which has its origins in section 77(5) of the English Stamp Act 1891, is a relieving provision which has been rendered defunct by the 1998 legislative amendment of the head of charge concerning bond and covenant in Article 1 of the First Schedule to the Stamp Duties Act.

---

[171] See *Sergeant and Sims on Stamp Duties and Stamp Duty Reserve Tax,* (Butterworths, 10th edition, 1992) at p 170 for an annotation of s 77(5) of the Stamp Act 1891.

[172] The head of charge for 'bond, covenant' was amended by the Stamp Duties Act (Substitution of Schedules) Notification 1998 (S 284/1998) and came into operation on 28 February 1998.

In the above discussion on section 26(3), one has to bear in mind that the original lease agreement has been duly stamped and the actual period of the lease has been taken into account in the calculation of the stamp duty paid on the original lease agreement. It is just that, section 26(3) does not serve to impose any additional duty on (a) the memorandum of increased rent where there is a rent review clause in the lease agreement or (b) the deed of variation which is usually executed where there is no rent review clause, where such memorandum or deed may be executed during the term of the original lease.

CHAPTER 6

Acquisition and Disposal of Real Estate: Asset Sale Transactions

1. Introduction

Singapore has a buoyant real estate market which has time and again outperformed those in other jurisdictions. For year 2020, the country is ranked number 1 for real estate investment prospects in terms of increase in value[1]. The real estate market in Singapore is not only underpinned by strong local demand[2], but also by the huge amount of foreign investments which flow into the country every year. Political instability in other jurisdictions is also known to drive up the demand for Singapore real estate, as evident by the surge in investment from Hong Kong when the jurisdiction was rocked by a series of protests in 2019[3].

In year 2019, property investment sales in Singapore hit $29.5 billion and was forecasted to increase by another 6% to $31.3 billion in 2020[4]. Of the transactions recorded in 2019, commercial properties, residential properties,

---

[1] 'S'pore tops region for property investment prospects,' *The Straits Times*, 13 November 2019.

[2] Singapore has a home ownership rate of more than 90%, one of the highest in the world. See Population Trends 2019, Department of Statistics, MTI, Republic of Singapore.

[3] 'Singapore top choice for Hong Kong real estate investors in first half of 2019: Report,' *The Straits Times*, 27 August 2019.

[4] 'Colliers forecasts Singapore property investment sales to cross S$31b in 2020,' *The Business Times*, 29 January 2020. Colliers' definition of investment sales transactions includes all private property sales which transacted for S$10 million and above, and all awarded state land tenders. The forecast however did not materialize due to the onset of the COVID-19 pandemic in early 2020.

hospitality properties and industrial properties accounted for 40%, 23%, 19% and 14% respectively, with mixed-use developments and shophouses making up the remaining 4%[5]. Notably, the hospitality sector experienced its best year in 2019, with investment sales quadrupling to an all-time high of $5.7 billion, driven by increasing tourist arrivals as well as major meetings, conferences and exhibitions held in Singapore[6]. As for commercial property investment sales, the largest office transaction of year 2019 was that of Allianz Real Estate and Gaw Capital Partners acquiring Duo Tower and Galleria from M+S, a joint venture between Singapore's Temasek Holdings and Malaysia's Khazanah, for $1.58 billion or $2,570 per square foot.

The real estate market in Singapore is also powered by the strong demand from real estate investment trusts listed on the Singapore Exchange (S-REITs)[7]. In year 2019, the largest real estate transactions include Lendlease's injection of 313@Somerset, a shopping mall located in the prime shopping district of Orchard Road, into Lendlease Global Commercial REIT for $1 billion[8], and Mapletree Investments' injection of Mapletree Business City II, a business park located at the Pasir Panjang area, into Mapletree Commercial Trust for $1.55 billion[9].

In this chapter, we will examine the tax and non-tax issues associated with the acquisition and disposal of real estate in Singapore.

2. Acquisition of Real Estate in Singapore

The acquisition of immovable property in Singapore is subject to stamp duty[10], which can be up to a rate of 44% in instances where additional buyer's stamp duty (ABSD) is triggered. In addition, various rules have been

---

[5] 'Bright prospects into 2020,' *Colliers Quarterly*, 29 January 2020.

[6] With the spread of the coronavirus, COVID-19 in Singapore in early 2020, the investment demand for Singapore's hospitality assets was subdued due to the drop in visitor arrivals and cancellation of meetings, incentives, conferences and exhibitions (MICE) events.

[7] 'Singapore property investment sales more than double to $16.7b on quarter: Report,' *The Straits Times*, 14 October 2019.

[8] 'Lendlease preparing for S-REIT listing that will include Orchard mall,' *The Business Times*, 17 August 2019.

[9] 'Mapletree trust to buy $1.55b business park in Pasir Panjang,' *The Straits Times*, 28 September 2019.

[10] Strictly speaking, the stamp duty is a document tax imposed on instruments relating to the sale or transfer of immovable property in Singapore.

imposed to regulate the amount of loans which a person may undertake to acquire immovable property in Singapore. The commonly encountered tax and non-tax issues arising from the acquisition of immovable property in Singapore are discussed in turn.

2.1. Buyer's stamp duty

2.1.1. *Imposition of buyer's stamp duty*

Stamp duty is a tax imposed on executed instruments (i.e. documents). Stamp duty of up to 4% is imposed on executed instruments for the sale or transfer of any interest in immovable property situated in Singapore. Such stamp duty is to be borne by the buyer[11] and is hence commonly referred to as Buyer's Stamp Duty (BSD).

Instruments which are chargeable to BSD include executed contracts such as the exercised option to purchase (OTP) and the sale and purchase agreement (SPA). Instruments effecting the transfer of interest in Singapore immovable property are also chargeable to BSD, albeit that a remission is available in instances where BSD has already been paid in respect of the contract[12]. The effect of the remission is such that stamp duty is only paid once for the same transaction, notwithstanding the fact that more than one instrument may be executed in respect of the same transaction (e.g. the execution of the SPA followed by the subsequent execution of the transfer instrument in respect of the same immovable property).

The BSD payable is based on the higher of (i) the purchase price or consideration payable in respect of the immovable property and (ii) market value of the immovable property. The applicable BSD rates with effect from 20 February 2018 are set out in Table 1.

Prior to the change on 20 February 2018, the maximum BSD rate applicable for both residential and non-residential immovable properties was 3%. In announcing the increase in the top marginal BSD rate from 3% to 4% for residential immovable property worth more than $1 million, Finance Minister Heng Swee Keat explained during the annual budget statement on 19 February

---

[11] Unless otherwise contractually agreed with the seller.

[12] S 22(3) of the Stamp Duties Act.

Table 1:   BSD rates.

Higher of Purchase Price or Market Value of the Property	BSD Rates[a]	
	Residential Property	Non-Residential Property
First $180,000	1%	1%
Next $180,000	2%	2%
Next $640,000	3%	3%
Above $1,000,000	4%	

Note:
[a]Article 3(a) of the First Schedule to the Stamp Duties Act.

2018 that the change was to make the tax system more progressive[13]. In this regard, it is noted that most purchasers of Housing and Development Board (HDB) flats will not be affected by the change given that the value of HDB flats typically does not cross $1 million, with the exception of a small handful of HDB transactions in prime locations which may exceed the million dollar threshold.

BSD is payable within 14 days of the execution of the instrument (if executed in Singapore) or 30 days of receiving the executed instrument in Singapore (if executed outside Singapore).

2.1.2. Relief from stamp duty

Where stamp duty is payable in respect of executed instruments for the sale or transfer of Singapore immovable property[14], relief (i.e. exemption) from stamp duty may be available under certain prescribed situations[15]. These include situations involving (i) a transfer of undertaking under a scheme of reconstruction or amalgamation of companies[16] or (ii) a transfer of assets between associated permitted entities[17].

---

[13] 'Singapore Budget 2018: Top marginal buyer's stamp duty to go up from 3% to 4% for residential properties worth over $1 million,' The Straits Times, 19 February 2018.

[14] See Section 3.5 of Chapter 7 for a discussion on the relief of stamp duty arising from instruments executed to transfer Singapore shares.

[15] S 15 of the Stamp Duties Act. For a detailed discussion on the stamp duty relief provisions under the Stamp Duties Act, see Tan Kay Kheng and Leung Yew Kwong, LexisNexis Annotated Statutes of Singapore: Stamp Duties Act 2015 (LexisNexis, 2015). The 2022 edition of the book is available in electronic version from the publisher.

[16] Stamp Duties (Relief from Stamp Duty upon Reconstruction or Amalgamation of Companies) Rules (R 3).

[17] Stamp Duties (Relief from Stamp Duty upon Transfer of Assets between Associated Permitted Entities) Rules 2014 (S 28/2014).

2.1.2.1. Transfer of undertaking pursuant to a scheme of reconstruction or amalgamation of companies

Where Singapore immovable property is transferred as part of the transfer of a business undertaking, the stamp duty which is otherwise payable may qualify for relief under section 15(1)(a) of the Stamp Duties Act, provided that the transfer is undertaken pursuant to a scheme of reconstruction or amalgamation. Such relief is commonly referred to as "Reconstruction relief" or "Amalgamation relief", as the case may be.

(a) Reconstruction

Broadly speaking, the effect of a reconstruction is such that following the transfer of the business undertaking, the transferee company has substantially the same shareholders as the transferor company[18], and is carrying on substantially the same business as that earlier carried on by the transferor company. In other words substantially the same persons should be carrying on that business, either directly or indirectly, following the reconstruction[19]. Such a reconstruction includes the transfer of a business undertaking or part of a business undertaking of an existing company (i.e. the transferor company) to another company (i.e. the transferee company, which is often, but not always, newly incorporated), with substantially the same persons as owners of the transferred business undertaking, either directly or indirectly, before and after the reconstruction[20].

In general, in such a scheme of reconstruction, the existing business undertaking and the ultimate owners of the existing business undertaking are substantially the same before and after the reconstruction, but the company through which the business undertaking is carried on is changed. The concept of reconstruction is illustrated in Figures 1 and 2.

For the purposes of the Reconstruction relief, a high threshold of 90% substantiality in the same shareholding or ownership before and after the

---

[18] The 'transferor company' is referred to as the 'existing company' which transfers the undertaking in rule 3(1)(a) of the Stamp Duties (Relief from Stamp Duty upon Reconstruction or Amalgamation of Companies) Rules (R 3).

[19] Re South African Supply and Cold Storage Company Ltd, [1904] 2 Ch 268.

[20] Brooklands Selangor Holdings Ltd v IRC, [1970] 1 WLR 429.

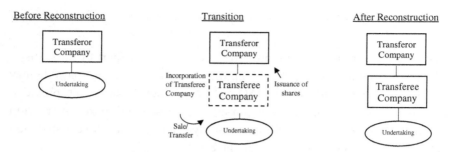

Figure 1: Reconstruction involving the transfer of undertaking by Transferor Company to newly incorporated Transferee company, in return for the issuance of shares by Transferee Company to Transferor Company.

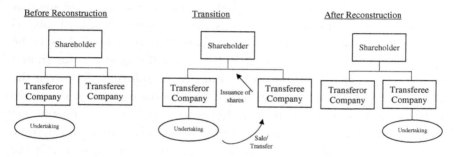

Figure 2: Reconstruction involving the transfer of undertaking by Transferor Company to Transferee Company, in return for the issuance of shares by Transferee Company to the shareholder of the Transferor Company.

Note: Transferee Company may issue shares to either the Transferor Company or the shareholder(s) of the Transferor Company.

reconstruction, is generally required[21]. In other words, a capital-ownership retention of at least 90% by the transferor(s) or the shareholder(s) of the transferor(s), will be required. The introduction of new capital from a third party or a change in shareholding beyond a 10% tolerance will generally result in the stamp duty relief being denied.

(b) Amalgamation

Broadly speaking, an amalgamation involves the merger or fusion into common ownership of what was previously held in separate ownership.

---

[21] *Clifford Development Pte Ltd v Commissioner of Stamp Duties*, [2009] 3 SLR(R) 363.

The term is used to describe a merger of the business undertakings of two or more companies into a single undertaking. Such a merger can be achieved in various ways and the resultant undertaking may become that of one of the companies concerned or of a new company altogether[22].

In general, in a scheme of amalgamation, two separate corporate businesses are brought together, with the shareholders ceasing to be discrete groups interested in their respective businesses only. Instead, they become fellow owners of a merged corporate business.

It is to be noted that the term "amalgamation" refers not only to the statutory amalgamation of companies effected pursuant to sections 215A to 215K of the Companies Act[23], but also the common law concept of amalgamation[24]. In the case of a statutory amalgamation, the amalgamating companies may be merged into the amalgamated company (i.e. the merged company), such that the amalgamating companies may automatically cease to exist as separate companies post-amalgamation. In contrast, in the case of a common law amalgamation, the companies involved in the amalgamation may continue to exist as separate legal entities.

The common law concept of amalgamation (which in recent times has been overshadowed by the more widely known statutory amalgamation) is depicted in Figures 3 and 4.

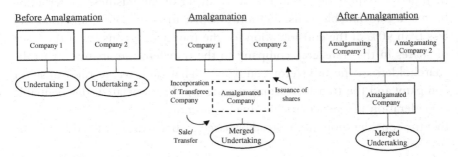

Figure 3: Amalgamation of two separate undertakings as a single undertaking held by a newly incorporated company.

Note: Company 1 and Company 2 may or may not be related prior to the amalgamation.

---

[22] *Crane Fruehauf Ltd v Inland Revenue Commissioners*, [1975] 1 All ER 429.

[23] Cap. 50.

[24] It is worthwhile noting that the term 'amalgamation' has been in s15(1)(a) of the Stamp Duties Act even before the statutory amalgamation procedure was introduced into the Companies Act in 2005.

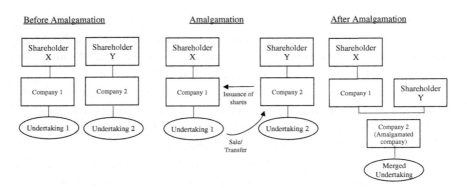

Figure 4: Amalgamation of two separate undertakings as a single undertaking held by an existing company.

Note: Company 1 and Company 2 may or may not be related prior to the amalgamation. Company 2 may issue shares to either Company 1 or the shareholder(s) of Company 1.

(c) Other Key Conditions

There are a number of other prescriptive conditions attached to the Reconstruction/Amalgamation relief in respect of the transfer of Singapore immovable property (as part of the transfer of a business undertaking). These include the requirement that the sale/transfer of the business undertaking be made for valuable consideration at open market value[25] and that not less than 90% of the consideration for the transaction consists of the issue of shares in the transferee company to the transferor company[26] or to the shareholders of the transferor company[27]. That said, where the transferor company and the transferee company are wholly associated, the "valuable consideration at open market value" condition may be substituted, such that the consideration may instead be based on book value[28]. In addition, the

---

[25] Rule 3(1)(a) of the Stamp Duties (Relief from Stamp Duty upon Reconstruction or Amalgamation of Companies) Rules (Reconstruction/Amalgamation rules).

[26] The 'transferor company' is referred to as the 'existing company' which transfers the undertaking in rule 3(1)(a) of the Reconstruction/Amalgamation rules.

[27] Rule 3(1)(b)(i) of the Reconstruction/Amalgamation rules.

[28] Rule 3(3)(a) of the Reconstruction/Amalgamation rules.

"issue of shares" condition may be substituted, such that the consideration may instead be in cash[29].

Other key conditions that need to be observed to avoid triggering a clawback of the stamp duty relief include observing the following 2-year moratoria: (i) the transferor company or the shareholder of the transferor company (as the case may be) must not cease to be the beneficial owner of the shares in the transferee company issued in connection with the scheme[30] and (ii) the transferee company must not cease to be the beneficial owner of the undertaking which it had acquired in connection with the scheme[31]. The purpose of the moratoria is to ensure that the transferred business undertaking continues to be retained by the existing owner(s), whether directly or indirectly, or even jointly with another person.

An exception may however be made for failing to observe the 2-year moratoria where the breach is due to qualifying reasons such as a further reconstruction, amalgamation or liquidation[32].

2.1.2.2. Transfer of assets between associated permitted entities

The transfer of Singapore immovable property also qualifies for stamp duty relief where such transfer is undertaken between associated permitted entities. Such relief is provided under section 15(1)(b) of the Stamp Duties Act and is commonly referred to as "Transfer of Assets relief"[33]. Unlike the "Reconstruction/ Amalgamation relief", the transfer of immovable property qualifying for "Transfer of Assets relief" does not have to be made as part of a transfer of business undertaking.

To qualify for the "Transfer of Assets relief", the transferor and transferee must be permitted entities — defined to be companies, limited liability partnerships and statutory bodies[34]. The transferor and transferee must also be "associated" (i.e. related) by virtue of at least 75% voting capital and

---

[29] Rule 3(3)(b) of the Reconstruction/Amalgamation rules.

[30] Rule 7(1)(a) of the Reconstruction/Amalgamation rules.

[31] Rule 7(1)(b) of the Reconstruction/Amalgamation rules.

[32] Rule 7(1)(a) and (b) of the Reconstruction/Amalgamation rules.

[33] Stamp Duties (Relief from Stamp Duty upon Transfer of Assets between Associated Permitted Entities) Rules 2014 (S 28/2014) (Transfer of Assets rules).

[34] Rule 4(b) read with rule 2 of the Transfer of Assets rules.

more than 50% voting power. Such association may be via direct or indirect holdings, or via a common holding entity[35]. As a general rule, the transferor entity and the transferee entity should have already been associated for at least 12 months unless the transferee entity is newly incorporated[36].

Other Key Conditions

There are a number of other prescriptive conditions attached to the Transfer of Assets relief. These include the requirement that the transferor entity and the transferee entity are part of a group which comprises only permitted entities[37].

The sale/transfer of the asset is also be undertaken for valuable consideration at open market value[38] and the consideration for the transaction is to be paid in cash or shares[39] issued by the transferee entity to the transferor entity by the time of the completion of the transfer[40]. That said, where the transferor entity and the transferee entity are wholly associated, the "valuable consideration at open market value" condition may be substituted, such that the consideration may instead be based on the transferor entity's book value of the asset[41]. In addition, the settlement of the consideration may be deferred i.e. the consideration payable may be left outstanding as an indebtedness owed by the transferee to the transferor, such as in the form of an outstanding debt or note payable[42].

Other key conditions that need to be observed to avoid triggering a clawback of the stamp duty relief include observing the following 2-year moratoria: (i) the transferor entity and the transferee entity must not cease to be associated[43] and (ii) the transferee entity must not dispose of the asset

---

[35] Rule 4(d)(ii) read with rule 3 of the Transfer of Assets rules.

[36] Rule 4(d)(ii) read with the Second Schedule of the Transfer of Assets rules. It is to be noted that there are additional prescriptive conditions for the scenario where the transferee entity is newly incorporated.

[37] Rule 4(b) of the Transfer of Assets rules.

[38] Rule 4(e) read with the Third Schedule of the Transfer of Assets rules.

[39] Or voting capital, in the case where the transferee is a limited liability partnership.

[40] Rule 4(e) read with the Third Schedule of the Transfer of Assets rules.

[41] Rule 4(e) read with the Third Schedule of the Transfer of Assets rules.

[42] Rule 4(e) read with the Third Schedule of the Transfer of Assets rules. In this regard, it is noted that the Third Schedule to the Transfer of Assets rules specifically provides that the consideration may be provided 'after the time of execution of the instrument for the transfer'.

[43] Rule 7(1)(a) of the Transfer of Assets rules. Based on a strict reading of rule 7(1)(a)(i), stamp duty relief is not to be disallowed under rule 7(1)(a) merely because there is a change in the transferee's ownership

acquired[44]. The purpose of the moratoria is to ensure that the transferred asset continues to be retained by the associated entities as a corporate group.

An exception may however be made for failing to observe the 2-year moratoria where the breach is due to qualifying reasons[45] such as a reconstruction, amalgamation or a qualifying liquidation[46].

2.2. Additional buyer's stamp duty

2.2.1. *Imposition of additional buyer's stamp duty*

In addition to normal BSD which applies to the acquisition of immovable property in Singapore, an additional stamp duty known as ABSD is payable on the acquisition of residential immovable property in Singapore[47]. ABSD is payable within 14 days of the execution of the relevant transaction instrument (if executed in Singapore) or 30 days of receiving the executed instrument in Singapore (if executed outside Singapore), as in the case for the payment of BSD.

ABSD was first introduced on 8 December 2011 as a property cooling measure to ensure a stable and sustainable residential property market in Singapore. In the joint press release issued by the Ministry of Finance (MOF) and Ministry of National Development (MND) on the eve of the imposition of ABSD (i.e. 7 December 2011), the following rationale was provided for the introduction of ABSD[48]:

> The Government's objective is to promote a sustainable residential property market where prices move in line with economic fundamentals. Prices of private residential properties have continued to rise, albeit more slowly in the last two quarters. Prices are now 13% above the peak in 2Q1996 and 16% above the more recent peak in 2Q2008.

---

of the voting capital/voting power in the transferor. This is in view that under such a scenario, the target asset is still retained within the original corporate group ownership.

[44] Rule 7(1)(b) of the Transfer of Assets rules.

[45] Rule 7(1)(a) and (b) of the Transfer of Assets rules.

[46] Fourth Schedule to the Transfer of Assets rules.

[47] Strictly speaking, the ABSD is imposed on executed instruments instead of the transactions in question.

[48] Press release, *Additional Buyer's Stamp Duty for a Stable and Sustainable Property Market*, issued by MOF and MND, 7 December 2011.

Even with the current economic uncertainties, the demand for private residential property remains firm. Given the uncertainty in stock markets and with interest rates remaining low, private property in Singapore continues to attract investors, local and foreign. Excessive investment demand will however make the property cycle more volatile, and thus increase the risks to our economy and banking system.

The Government has therefore decided to impose the ABSD to moderate investment demand for private residential property and promote a more stable and sustainable market. A higher ABSD rate for foreign buyers in particular is necessary, in view of the large pool of external liquidity and strong buying interest from abroad, and the relatively small size of the Singapore market. Foreign purchases account for 19% of all private residential property purchases in 2H2011, up from 7% in 1H2009.

Despite the introduction of ABSD, the prices of residential real estate in Singapore continued to rise. This in turn forced the Government to increase the ABSD rates on 12 January 2013, just 13 months after ABSD was first introduced. In announcing the ABSD hike, the joint press release issued by MOF, MND, Monetary Authority of Singapore (MAS) and Ministry of Trade and Industry (MTI) explained that[49]:

The Government has implemented several rounds of measures to cool demand and expand supply, so as to moderate the increase in housing prices. While these measures have dampened speculative buying, the demand for residential property remains firm and prices have continued to rise.

The continued buoyancy of the property market reflects the very low interest rate environment and continued income growth in Singapore. These factors supported a record level of housing transactions last year, particularly from investment demand. Housing prices have also shown signs of reaccelerating in recent months, in both the private residential and HDB resale flat markets. Price increases, if not checked, will run further ahead of economic fundamentals and raise the risk of a major, destabilising correction later on.

The Government has therefore decided to implement a further set of measures to cool the private and public housing markets. These measures

---

[49] Press release, *Additional Measures to Ensure a Stable and Sustainable Property Market*, issued by MOF, MND, MAS and MTI, 11 January 2013.

are calibrated to be tighter on property ownership for investment, as well as on foreign buyers. To discourage over-borrowing, financing conditions for housing have also been tightened. In addition, structural measures have been implemented to strengthen the policy intent of public housing and executive condominiums.

Following the first increase of ABSD rates on 12 January 2013, the private residential property market declined gradually for close to 4 years. Private residential prices however began rising in the third quarter of 2017 and increased sharply by 9.1% over the subsequent 12-month period. Demand for private residential property also saw a strong recovery, as transaction volumes continued to rise[50]. It was also reported that private home prices had risen to the highest point in four years in the April to June quarter of 2018, as transactions increased and liquidity from *en bloc* sales flowed into the market, with analysts predicting that prices could soon recover to 2013 peak levels[51].

In light of the situation, the Government announced on 5 July 2018 that ABSD rates[52] on residential property purchases would be increased from the next day to cool the property market and keep price increases in line with economic fundamentals. The announcement came shortly after official data showed that private residential prices had risen to a 4-year peak in the second quarter of 2018, and analysts were predicting that prices could soon recover to the peak levels in 2013.

In announcing the change, the then Minister for National Development, Mr Lawrence Wong, explained that "The government has been monitoring the property market closely. We are very concerned that prices are running ahead of economic fundamental". Minister Wong added that "There is a large supply of units coming on stream and interest rates are going up. We want to avoid a severe correction later, which can have more destabilising consequences. Hence we are acting now to maintain a stable and sustainable property market".

After a brief period of stabilisation in the residential property market, the upward trajectory of property prices was again observed. Private housing prices rose by 9% and HDB resale flat prices rose by 15% during the 2-year period

---

[50] Press release, *Raising Additional Buyer's Stamp Duty Rates And Tightening Loan-To-Value Limits To Promote A Stable And Sustainable Property Market*, issued by the MOF, MND and MAS, 5 July 2018.

[51] See 'Private home prices inch towards new peak after 3.4% jump in Q2,' <https://www.channelnewsasia.com/news/singapore/private-home-property-prices-q2-ura-singapore-10490090> (accessed 2 July 2018).

[52] It was announced at the same time that loan-to-value (LTV) limits would be tightened.

from 2020 to 2021, despite the ongoing COVID-19 pandemic. The Government responded by announcing on 15 December 2021 a new round of property cooling measures, including a hike in ABSD rates which took effect the next day.

Following the recent change, the top ABSD rate applicable from 16 December 2021 is 40%. The total maximum BSD and ABSD payable is therefore up to 44% (i.e. 4% BSD plus 40% ABSD)[53]. The top ABSD rate of 40% comprises a 35% ABSD payable by all entities (i.e. non-individuals) and a 5% non-remissible ABSD payable by housing developers.

The applicable ABSD rate broadly depends on various factors including the profile of the buyer (e.g. whether the buyer is a Singapore citizen, permanent resident, foreigner or non-individual) and the number of residential properties owned by the individual buyer in Singapore, immediately prior to the acquisition of the property in question.

Table 2 shows the relevant ABSD rates applicable for the periods from 8 December 2011 to 15 December 2021, as well as the prevailing rates which took effect from 16 December 2021.

Less than 5 months after the hike in ABSD rates in December 2021, the Government introduced further refinement to the ABSD rules such that with effect from 9 May 2022, the 35% ABSD will similarly apply to residential properties which are sold or transferred to a "living trust", albeit that a remission may be available in certain situations (such as where there

---

[53] Remission of ABSD is available under certain prescribed circumstances, such as the joint purchase of a second residential property by a married couple (at least one of whom must be a Singapore citizen), where their first residential property is disposed of within 6 months of acquiring the second residential property. For this purpose, the 6-month period commences from the date of purchase of the completed property. In the case where the acquired property was uncompleted at the time of purchase, the 6-month period commences from the issue date of the Temporary Occupation Permit (TOP) or Certificate of Statutory Completion (CSC), whichever is earlier. In effect, the stringent ABSD rules require the married couple to make an upfront payment of the hefty ABSD in respect of the acquisition of their second residential property and thereafter seek a refund after the disposal of their existing residential property within the prescribed 6 month period. This posed significant challenges, especially to those who genuinely intended to upgrade from a HDB flat to a private apartment, given that it could be a number of years before the construction works in respect of the uncompleted private apartment is completed. It would be almost impossible for the married couple to accelerate the ABSD refund process by disposing of their existing HDB flat at an earlier date, as they often have no alternative but to continue staying in their existing HDB flat until the construction of the uncompleted private apartment is completed. In response, private housing developers had resorted to re-issuing OTPs to the same buyers, such that the buyers would not face the cashflow pressure of having to pay up the ABSD within 14 days of exercising the OTP. Such practices have since been subject to clampdown by the Government in September 2020. See 'REDAS calls for ABSD deferment for first-time HDB upgraders to private property,' *The Business Times*, 30 September 2020. Notably, the buyers of new executive condominium units do not face similar issue with the upfront payment of ABSD, as a remission of the ABSD is granted automatically upon approval of the acquisition by HDB, and there is no need for the buyers to go through the ABSD refund process.

Table 2: ABSD rates.

Profile of Buyer	ABSD Rates			
	8 December 2011 to 11 January 2013	12 January 2013 to 5 July 2018	6 July 2018 to 15 December 2021	From 16 December 2021
Singapore citizens buying 1st residential property	Not Applicable	Not Applicable	Not Applicable	Not Applicable
Singapore citizens buying 2nd residential property	Not Applicable	7%	12%	17%
Singapore citizens buying 3rd residential property	3%	10%	15%	25%
Singapore permanent residents buying 1st residential property	Not Applicable	5%	5%	5%
Singapore permanent residents buying 2nd residential property	3%	10%	15%	20%
Singapore permanent residents buying 3rd and subsequent residential property	3%	10%	15%	30%
Foreigners buying any residential property	10%	15%	20%	30%
Entities buying any residential property	10%	15%	25% Plus additional 5% (non-remissible) ABSD payable by Housing Developers	35% Plus additional 5% (non-remissible) ABSD payable by Housing Developers

is an identifiable individual beneficiary qualifying for reduced ABSD). The change is targeted at closing a then existing loophole where ABSD was not imposed in the situation where a "living trust" was structured with no identifiable beneficial owner at the time when the residential property was transferred into the trust.

2.2.2. *Remission for housing developers*

A remission of the 35% ABSD is available to housing developers, subject to certain conditions including commencing the housing development within 2 years from the date of execution of the instrument (i.e. acquisition date) as well as completing the housing development and selling all units of housing accommodation in the development within 5 years[54] from the acquisition date. A shorter period of 3 years from the acquisition date applies for the

---

[54] Stamp Duties (Housing Developers) (Remission of ABSD) Rules 2013 (S 362/2013).

sale of all units in housing development which comprises 4 or less units. Where the housing developer fails to meet its obligations, the ABSD which was earlier granted remission, will be payable with a 5% interest per annum.

In light of the global outbreak of the COVID-19 pandemic in year 2020, the Government made an unprecedented but not unexpected announcement on 6 May 2020, that housing developers affected by disruptions to construction timelines and sale of housing units due to the imposition of "circuit breaker" measures[55], would be provided with an additional 6 months to fulfil their obligations to commence, complete and sell their residential development projects, in order to qualify for the remission of ABSD[56].

The 6-month extension took into account the fact that the economy came to a virtual standstill during the "circuit breaker" period, when all non-essential businesses were required to stop operations at their workplaces. In particular, the circuit breaker measures implemented from 7 April 2020 saw the suspension of work at construction sites, operations at housing developers' sales galleries, as well as home viewings. The delay in the progress of construction projects as well as the sale of housing units in turn impeded the ability of housing developers to meet the original timeline imposed for the remission of ABSD.

Subsequently, on 8 October 2020, a further 6-month extension for the commencement and completion of residential development projects was announced[57], in light of the continued disruption faced by the construction industry due to the COVID-19 pandemic. The construction sector, which relied heavily on foreign workers, many of whom lived in purpose-built dormitories, was especially hard hit by the pandemic, with many of the workers subject to strict quarantine rules[58]. In contrast, there was no further extension of the remission condition timeline for the sale of all housing units in the residential development project.

---

[55] The 'circuit breaker' measures were imposed by the Government from 7 April 2020 to 1 June 2020 to halt the spread of COVID-19 coronavirus within the community.

[56] Press release, *Temporary Relief Measures for Property Sector Due to Coronavirus Disease 2019 (COVID-19) Pandemic*, issued by MND, MOF, Ministry of Law (MinLaw) and MTI, 6 May 2020.

[57] Press release, *Additional Temporary Relief Measures for Property Sector Due to Coronavirus Disease 2019 (COVID-19) Pandemic*, issued by MND, MOF, MinLaw and MTI, 8 October 2020. See also 'Government relief measures for developers hit by construction disruptions,' *The Business Times*, 9 October 2020.

[58] 'Nearly half of migrant workers in dormitories have had Covid-19,' *The Straits Times*, 15 December 2020.

It was subsequently further announced on 28 June 2021 that an additional 6-month extension of the commencement and completion timelines of residential development would be granted.

2.3. Goods and services tax

Apart from BSD and ABSD, another tax cost which may be borne by the buyer who acquires immovable property in Singapore is goods and services tax (GST). The prevailing rate of GST is 7%, but is slated to increase to 8% on 1 Janaury 2023 and 9% on 1 January 2024.

GST is chargeable only in respect of transactions involving the acquisition of non-residential property in Singapore. The acquisition of residential property is exempt for GST purposes[59].

Whether GST is chargeable also depends on the GST registration status of the seller[60] of the non-residential property. Where GST is charged by the seller to the buyer, the buyer may nevertheless be able to claim input tax credits in respect of the GST paid provided that the buyer is a GST registered person. In addition, the input tax must be attributable to supplies made in the furtherance of the business of the buyer, and the relevant conditions prescribed for the claim of input GST must be fulfilled[61].

2.4. Qualifying certificate and clearance certificate issued under the Residential Property Act

Apart from the taxes payable on the acquisition of immovable property, there are various other non-tax considerations relevant to the acquisition of immovable property in Singapore. These regulatory requirements include those imposed under the Residential Property Act[62].

The Residential Property Act was enacted in the 1970s with the aim of restricting the purchase or transfer of residential properties (including vacant land) to Singapore citizens and approved purchasers[63]. It serves the purpose of preventing foreign housing developers from hoarding and

---

[59] Para 2 of the First Part of the Fourth Schedule to the GST Act.

[60] See section 3.3 for a discussion on the charging of GST by the seller of non-residential properties.

[61] See s 19 and 20 of the GST Act.

[62] Cap. 274.

[63] See preamble of the Residential Property Act.

speculating in residential land. As explained by the then Minister for Law and the Environment, Mr E. W. Barker, at the second reading of the Residential Property Bill on 19 August 1975[64]:

> On 10th September, 1973, a Government press statement made it known that as from the day following the announcement only citizens of Singapore would be permitted to purchase residential property without any restriction. This decision was arrived at after considerable thought. For many months before that, the cost of real estate had been sharply on the increase and had almost doubled over the previous year. Government was concerned about the rise and decided that it should confine its efforts at keeping down the cost of residential property, leaving the market value of commercial and industrial properties to find their levels by the interaction of factors governing supply and demand.

Under the Residential Property Act[65], a Singapore company[66] may seek, and the Controller of Residential Property may issue, a certificate (commonly referred to as the "clearance certificate") which allows the Singapore company to acquire and retain residential properties in Singapore.

On the other hand, all foreign persons are required to seek the prior approval for the acquisition and retention of restricted[67] residential properties in Singapore[68]. While foreign individuals may be allowed to acquire a restricted residential property for owner occupation (with conditions attached), such approval is seldom provided to foreign companies. As an exception[69], "foreign" housing developers may apply to the Controller of

---

[64] Available on the website of the Parliament of Singapore.

[65] Pursuant to s 10 of the Residential Property Act.

[66] Singapore companies are those incorporated in Singapore with all shareholders and directors being Singapore citizens or Singapore companies.

[67] The following residential properties are non-restricted under s 4(1): any unit of flat, any unit of condominium and any unit of executive condominium. It is however to be noted that under s 4(2), the following residential properties will not be regarded as non-restricted: all the flats in every building in a development, all the units in a condominium development and all the units in an executive condominium development. Hence, a foreign person is not allowed to purchase the entire development without approval. In practice, such persons have resorted to using two entities to purchase the entire development.

[68] S 25(2) of the Residential Property Act.

[69] S 31(1) and (2) of the Residential Property Act.

Residential Property for approval for the acquisition of any estate or interest in any private[70] residential property for development[71].

For this purpose, "foreign" housing developers broadly refer to any person who is not a Singapore citizen or a Singapore company, who or which constructs or intends to construct flats or dwelling houses for sale[72]. The term "Singapore company" is in turn defined to be a company which is incorporated in Singapore, and its directors and shareholders are all Singapore citizens or Singapore companies[73]. Based on the definition, a Singapore incorporated company even with a single shareholder or director who is not a Singapore citizen, will be regarded as a foreign (i.e. non-Singapore) company for the purpose of the Residential Property Act.

Upon obtaining the Controller's approval, which is provided in the form of a Qualifying Certificate (QC), foreign housing developers are required to adhere to the stringent QC rules. These rules include completing the construction of the residential development and obtaining the Temporary Occupation Permit (TOP) or Certificate of Statutory Completion (CSC) within 5 years from the date of issue of the QC or the collective sale order, as well as disposing of all the residential units in the residential development within 2 years from the date of issue of the TOP or CSC, whichever is earlier (i.e. a maximum total of seven years from the acquisition of the land). Housing developers which fail to satisfy the conditions of the QC risk forfeiting a banker's guarantee to the extent of 10% of the land purchase price[74].

---

[70] S 33(e) of the Residential Property Act provides that the prohibition does not extend to the acquisition by a foreign person of any estate or interest in any residential property from URA or any person or body that is duly appointed as an agent of the Government. For residential lands sold by the Government, all housing developers (including Singapore companies with a clearance certificate) are required to comply with the applicable conditions of tender sale imposed by the Government, including the conditions pertaining to the project completion period.

[71] An exception applies to residential developments on Sentosa Cove. See Residential Property (Exemption — Sentosa Cove) Notification 2004 and 2006 (S 483/2004 and S543/2006).

[72] See s 31(18) of the Residential Property Act for the full definition of 'housing developer'.

[73] See s 2(1) of the Residential Property Act for the full definition of 'Singapore company'.

[74] See s 31(3)(c) of the Residential Property Act. The current practice of the Controller of Residential Property is to require a banker's guarantee for a sum at 10% of the purchase price of the land. The 'foreign' housing developer is also not allowed to sell the land in its vacant or undeveloped state, unless otherwise approved. See: *Chi Liung Holdings Sdn Bhd v Attorney-General* [1994] 2 SLR(R) 314 where the Court of Appeal held that the Controller of Residential Property was wrong in forfeiting the developer company's money for an alleged breach of undertaking where the company granted options to purchase its land, to a purchaser, conditional upon the purchaser obtaining a qualifying certificate from the Controller.

Housing developers which are Singapore companies with clearance certificates are not required to apply for a QC to acquire private residential property for development.

The underlying rationale of the QC rules is to allow foreign housing developers to build and sell, thus contributing to the housing supply and hopefully a reduction in prices. In the absence of the QC rules, the foreign developers might simply hold onto their unsold units and wait for prices to go up, or for existing property cooling measures to be dismantled[75].

A foreign housing developer which requires more time to meet the deadlines imposed under the QC may seek approval from the Singapore Land Authority and pay the requisite charges to extend the deadlines. The extension charges are currently set at 8% of the land purchase price for the first year of extension, 16% for the second year and 24% from the third year. The charges for extension of the 2-year sale deadline is to be prorated based on the number of unsold units[76]. In contrast, there is no prorating of the charges for the extension of the 5-year completion deadline. In practice, housing developers do not usually have difficulties meeting the 5-year completion deadline, in the overall time framework of 5 years to complete and an additional 2 years to sell, under the QC rules.

In light of the global pandemic caused by COVID-19 in early 2020, the Government made an unprecedented but not unexpected announcement on 6 May 2020 that foreign housing developers affected by disruptions to construction timelines and sale of residential units, would be provided with an extension of the project completion period and/ or disposal period, for up to a total of 6 months, for the purposes of the QC rules[77].

The 6-month extension took into account the implementation of the "circuit breaker" measures imposed by the Government from 7 April to 1 June 2020 to curtail the spread of the coronavirus within the community. The circuit breaker measures effectively placed the country in a partial lock-down, where all non-essential businesses were required to temporarily cease

---

[75] 'Developers face hefty extension charges over unsold units,' *The Business Times*, 20 May 2015.

[76] See website of the Singapore Land Authority.

[77] Press release, *Temporary Relief Measures for Property Sector Due to Coronavirus Disease 2019 (COVID-19) Pandemic*, issued by MND, MOF, MinLaw and MTI, 6 May 2020. This extension is in line with the similar extension for meeting the deadline for ABSD.

operations at their worksite for almost 2 months. The delay in the progress of construction projects as well as the sale of residential units in turn impeded the ability of property developers to meet the original deadlines imposed under the QC rules.

Subsequently, on 8 October 2020, a further 6-month extension of the project completion period was announced for residential projects under the QC regime for foreign housing developers[78]. This was in light of the continued challenges faced by the construction industry which saw many of the workers subject to strict quarantine rules due to the COVID-19 pandemic. In contrast, there was no further waiver of extension charges for the extension of the existing deadline to dispose of all housing units in the residential development project.

It was subsequently further announced on 28 June 2021 that an additional 6-month extension of the project completion period would be granted for residential projects under the QC regime.

2.4.1. *Reaction to the QC rules and extension charges*

Since the extension charges framework was introduced in January 2011[79], it was reported in an article in early 2020 that housing developers have paid a total of about $200 million in extension charges[80]. In order to avoid the stringent QC rules and the hefty extension charges imposed on unsold residential units, a number of housing developers were reported to have chosen to delist their shares from the Singapore Exchange (if they were listed) or sell the residential units to a privately held Singapore company[81].

Notably, under the existing definition of "Singapore company", it is practically impossible for Singapore incorporated housing developers

---

[78] Press release, *Additional Temporary Relief Measures for Property Sector Due to Coronavirus Disease 2019 (COVID-19) Pandemic*, issued by MND, MOF, MinLaw and MTI, 8 October 2020. See also 'Government relief measures for developers hit by construction disruptions,' *The Business Times*, 9 October 2020.

[79] See s 31(5A) of the Residential Property Act which comes into operation on 17 January 2011.

[80] 'New rules on qualifying cert offer reprieve to Singapore developers,' *The Business Times*, 7 February 2020.

[81] The sale of residential property is however subject to BSD and ABSD, which are currently imposed at up to 44%. Developers will therefore have to weigh the cost and benefits arising from their decision (i.e. savings on the QC charges vs additional costs arising from the stamp duty payable by the privately-held Singapore company).

which are publicly listed to qualify as a "Singapore company", given that these companies invariably have foreign shareholders. In this regard, it was reported that the Soilbuild Group delisted in 2010 and subsequently applied successfully to have its QCs cancelled, presumably on the basis that it had become a "Singapore company" with only Singapore shareholders and directors after its delisting and privatisation[82]. Other examples of publicly listed housing developers which delisted on account of the QC regime include SC Global[83] and Popular Holdings, both of which were previously listed on the Singapore Exchange.

As for examples of companies which sold units in their residential development to their related companies, these include Hiap Hoe which is listed on the Singapore Exchange. In the case of Hiap Hoe, it sold its entire high-end condominium development near Orchard Road to its privately held parent company in December 2014. Prior to that, Hiap Hoe also sold some residential units in another project to a subsidiary in view of the QC extension charges payable on its unsold units[84].

2.4.2. *Change in rules for publicly listed housing developers with substantial connection to Singapore*

In light of the various arrangements put in place by listed companies to overcome the QC rules, it was eventually announced on 6 February 2020, and subsequently refined on 29 June 2021, that publicly listed housing developers with substantial connection to Singapore will be treated as a Singapore company within the meaning of the Residential Property Act when they acquire residential land for development. The policy rationale

---

[82] The group subsequently re-listed on the Singapore Exchange in 2013. See: 'Qualifying certificate scheme: Time for review,' *The Straits Times*, 6 March 2015.

[83] Market watchers were initially of the view that the QCs which SC Global had earlier obtained for its residential developments would still be applicable notwithstanding the delisting of the company from the Singapore Exchange. However, SC Global successfully applied to the Singapore Land Authority to cancel the QCs on all its residential developments. The application was on the basis that SC Global is a 'Singapore company' for the purposes of the Residential Property Act after its delisting, and hence not required to be bound by the QC rules. With the cancellation of the QCs, SC Global was allowed to hold on to its unsold residential units and not have to pay the extension charges which amounted to millions of dollars. See 'Qualifying certificate scheme: Time for review,' *The Straits Times*, 6 March 2015.

[84] 'Qualifying certificate scheme: Time for review,' *The Straits Times*, 6 March 2015. See also 'Spike in extension fees paid by developers,' *The Straits Times*, 7 November 2016.

behind the change is to better align the QC rules and the objectives of the Residential Property Act[85].

Following the change, housing developers listed on the Singapore Exchange may now apply for exemption from the QC rules for both their existing and new projects, on the basis that they have a substantial connection to Singapore. Such applications are to be assessed by reference to a set of criteria, including having a significantly Singaporean substantial shareholding interest in the company. This requires one of the following two conditions to be met: (i) substantial shareholders who are Singapore citizens, Singapore companies or Singapore Government entities holding at least 50% interest in the voting rights and issued shares in the company; or (ii) the largest single substantial shareholder[86] is a Singapore citizen, Singapore company or a Singapore Government entity and holding at least 25% interest in the total voting rights and issued shares in the company, and the largest single foreign substantial shareholder holds not more than 25% of the voting rights and issued shares in the company.

The rules were subsequently refined on 29 June 2021, such that a housing developer will be considered to have a significantly Singaporean substantial shareholding interest if Singaporean shareholders from the same family collectively form the largest substantial shareholder and hold at least 30% interest in the total voting rights and issued shares in the company. At least one of the shareholders in the family has to be a substantial shareholder and identified as the primary shareholder. Further, the largest single foreign substantial shareholder must hold not more than 30% of the voting rights and issued shares in the company.

In addition, the housing developer must be incorporated in Singapore, has its principal place of business in Singapore, has a track record in Singapore and has its primary listing on the Singapore Exchange. Further, the company's chairperson and majority of its board must be Singapore citizens.

Prior to the change, substantially Singapore-owned listed housing developers were regarded as foreign companies for the purposes of the Residential Property Act. Following the change, the treatment of these

---

[85] 'New rules on qualifying cert offer reprieve to Singapore developers,' *The Business Times*, 7 February 2020.

[86] Defined as those with at least 5% shareholding.

substantially Singapore-owned listed companies will now be aligned with that of private housing developers. Such a move will help alleviate the burden of substantially Singapore-owned listed housing developers, given that they are no longer subject to the hefty extension charges.

As at 6 January 2020, immediately prior to the announcement of the change, there were 122 QC holders (entities/companies) which were developing 136 projects that come under the QC rules. Of the 122 QC holders, 37 were wholly-owned by companies listed on the Singapore[87]. Many of these developers, which have "substantial connection to Singapore", are expected to benefit from the relaxation of the QC regime.

It is however to be noted that all housing developers are still subject to the ABSD rules, which are comparatively more stringent. The ABSD rules require housing developers to undertake to develop the acquired residential site and sell all units in the development within five years as a condition for upfront remission of ABSD on the acquisition of the land. The remissible ABSD for residential developers will be clawbacked if all the residential units in the development are not developed and sold within five years. Unlike the QC extension charges, there is no pro-rating of the ABSD to be clawed back, even if the housing developer managed to sell some of the residential units within the development.

2.5. Rules for new housing loans

The acquisition of real estate (in particular, residential properties) are also subject to various restrictions imposed by the MAS in relation to the loans undertaken to finance the transaction. These restrictions are discussed in turn below.

2.5.1. *Overview*

For most individuals, real estate loans constitute a substantial portion of their long-term liabilities. The Government is therefore concerned with ensuring that individuals borrow responsibly and not overexpose themselves to leverage.

---

[87] 'Listed property developers with 'substantial connection to Singapore' can be exempted from qualifying certificate scheme,' *The Straits Times*, 6 February 2020.

Various housing loan rules have been introduced by the MAS over the years to encourage financial prudence among borrowers, ensure long-term household economic health, strengthen credit underwriting standards at financial institutions as well as ensure long-term stability in the real estate market[88]. The rules imposed on new housing loans include maximum limit on loan tenure, loan-to-value ratio, mortgage servicing ratio and total debt servicing ratio. These rules are discussed in the following sections[89].

2.5.2. Loan tenure

The maximum housing loan which borrowers can undertake depends on various factors including, the age of the borrowers[90], the duration of the loan, the type of the property as well as whether the borrowers have other existing housing loans[91]. The maximum loan tenure for housing loans is capped at 30 years for HDB flats and 35 years for non-HDB properties.

The imposition of a maximum limit on loan tenures helps ensure that borrowers do not overstretch themselves when purchasing property, particularly in the years after their retirement when their income earning capacity is reduced.

2.5.3. Loan-to-value

The loan-to-value (LTV) ratio expresses the permissible loan amount as a percentage of the property's value, and has the effect of limiting the amount of housing loan which a person can borrow. It takes into account the tenure of the loan, the age of the borrower, whether the borrower has other existing loans and whether the borrower is an individual or a company[92]. The LTV limit helps ensure that borrowers do not overstretch themselves financially

---

[88] See MAS website <https://www.mas.gov.sg/regulation/explainers/new-housing-loans> (accessed 8 August 2020).

[89] See MAS Notice 825, Residential Property Loans, 27 August 2013 (last revised on 5 July 2018) for further details.

[90] Joint borrowers are assessed based on their income-weighted average age.

[91] See MAS website <https://www.mas.gov.sg/regulation/explainers/new-housing-loans/loan-tenure-and-loan-to-value-limits> (accessed 8 August 2020).

[92] See MAS website <https://www.mas.gov.sg/regulation/explainers/new-housing-loans/loan-tenure-and-loan-to-value-limits> (accessed 8 August 2020). The LTV for HDB granted loans was 85% with effect from 16 December 2021. Immediately prior to 16 December 2021, the LTV was 90% for HDB granted loans.

Table 3: LTV limit and minimum cash downpayment.

Number of Outstanding Housing Loan	LTV Limit	Minimum Cash Downpayment[a]
1st Housing Loan	75% or 55%, if the loan tenure is more than 30 years* or extends past age 65	5% or 10%, if the loan tenure is more than 30 years* or extends past age 65
2nd Housing Loan	45% or 25%, if the loan tenure is more than 30 years* or extends past age 65	25%
From 3rd Housing Loan	35% or 15%, if the loan tenure is more than 30 years* or extends past age 65	25%

* 25 years, where the property purchased is a HDB flat.

Note:

[a] Prior to 30 August 2010, property buyers were required to make cash payment of at least 5% of the valuation limit. With effect from 30 August 2010, the cash payment was increased from 5% to 10% of the valuation limit. The measure was applied only to buyers of residential properties who intended to take housing loans from financial institutions and who already had one or more outstanding housing loans at the time of applying for a housing loan for the new property purchase. With effect from 12 January 2013, the minimum cash down payment required for such individuals was raised to 25%.

(e.g. in the acquisition of multiple properties for speculative purposes, through debt financing).

On 5 July 2018, it was announced that the LTV limit will be further tightened as part of a package of measures to cool the property market and keep price increases in line with economic fundamentals. The LTV limits and minimum cash downpayment, as set out in Table 3, currently apply to loans undertaken by individuals from financial institutions in respect of residential properties where the option to purchase is granted on or after 6 July 2018.

In essence, a lower LTV limit would apply if the loan tenure exceeds 30 years (or 25 years for HDB flats), or the loan period extends beyond the borrower's age of 65 years[93].

---

[93] It was announced on 19 February 2010 that LTV limit would be lowered from 90% to 80% for all housing loans provided by financial institutions. Loans granted by HDB for HDB flats (including DBSS flats) would retain a LTV cap of 90%. This is because HDB flats are already subject to other criteria to prevent speculation and encourage financial prudence e.g. minimum owner occupation period and restriction on ownership to one flat per household. HDB loans are offered to only eligible first-time flat buyers or second-timers who are upgrading. They are required to utilize all of their CPF Ordinary Account balance before HDB loans will be granted. This is in line with HDB's home ownership policy of helping eligible buyers, especially first-time

In instances where the borrower is a shell company or not an individual, a 15% LTV limit will apply[94].

The LTV limit for HDB housing loans was reduced from 90% to 85% from 16 December 2021. However, the LTV limit for loans granted by financial institutions for public housing remains unchanged (as per Table 3)

2.5.4. *Mortgage servicing ratio*

The mortgage servicing ratio (MSR) is a restriction imposed to limit the proportion of a borrower's gross monthly income that may be utilized for the repayment of all property loans, including the loan which the borrower is applying for[95].

MSR is capped at 30% of a borrower's gross monthly income for housing loans granted by financial institutions[96]. In other words, no more than 30% of a borrower's gross monthly income should go towards the repayment of his/her property loans to financial institutions. The MSR applies only to housing loans for the purchase of a HDB flat or an executive condominium, where the minimum occupation period of the executive condominium has not expired. In essence, the MSR limits the amount of such loans which a borrower may borrow[97].

The following formula applies to the calculation of the MSR:

$$\frac{\text{Monthly repayment instalment for all property loans}}{\text{Gross monthly income}} \times 100\%$$

---

buyers, purchase public housing in a financially prudent manner. The LTV limit for housing loans provided by financial institutions was subsequently lowered on 14 January 2011 from 70% to 60% for property purchasers who are individuals with one or more outstanding housing loans at the time of the new housing purchase. Prior to 12 January 2013, the LTV limits for individuals who had one or more outstanding housing loans and were obtaining second or subsequent housing loans were 60%, or 40% if the loan tenure exceeded 30 years or the loan period extended beyond the borrower's retirement age of 65. This was subsequently reduced with effect from 12 January 2013 to 50% (or 30% if the loan tenure exceeded 30 years or the loan period extends beyond the borrower's retirement age of 65) for individuals obtaining a second housing loan, and 40% (or 20% if the loan tenure exceeded 30 years or the loan period extends beyond the borrower's retirement age of 65) for individuals obtaining third or subsequent housing loans.

[94] With effect from 14 January 2011, a LTV limit on housing loans granted by financial institutions property buyers who are not individuals was set at 50%. It was subsequently further lowered to 40% before being further reduced to 20% from 12 January 2013.

[95] See MAS website <https://www.mas.gov.sg/regulation/explainers/new-housing-loans/msr-and-tdsr-rules> (accessed 8 August 2020).

[96] With effect from 12 January 2013.

[97] Prior to 12 January 2013, HDB offered housing loans with MSR of up to 40% of a borrower's gross monthly income. From 12 January 2013, HDB would only offer housing loans with MSR of up to 35% of the gross monthly income.

2.5.5. *Total debt servicing ratio*

The Total Debt Servicing Ratio (TDSR) was introduced on 29 June 2013 to limit the proportion of a borrower's gross monthly income that may be utilized for the repayment of his/her total monthly debt obligations[98]. The underlying policy objective is to encourage home buyers to borrow within their means.

The TDSR ratio is currently capped at 55%. In other words, no more than 55% of a borrower's gross monthly income should go towards repaying all his/her debt obligations (including those for credit card, personal loans, car loans, renovation loans, mortgage loans)[99]. This serves to limit the amount of loan which an individual may borrow to finance the acquisition of real estate.

The TDSR rules apply to any individual applying for a loan to purchase a property or a loan secured by a property, as well as the refinancing of the aforementioned loans. It is to be noted that the TDSR rules apply to loans for both residential and non-residential properties (e.g. industrial and commercial properties), and cover properties in and outside Singapore. The TDSR rules however do not apply to bridging loans where the outstanding balance will be repaid within 6 months[100].

The TDSR rules also do not apply to loans for companies, as companies are subject to a different set of credit assessment criteria. That said, if the borrower is a sole proprietor or an individual setting up a company solely to purchase property, the TDSR rules will be applied to the individual.

The following formula applies to the calculation of the TDSR:

$$\frac{\text{Borrower's total monthly debt obligations}}{\text{Borrower's gross monthly income}} \times 100\%$$

Monthly debt is defined to include all outstanding debt obligations of the borrower, including property-related loans (including the loan being

---

[98] See Guidelines on the application of TDSR for property loans under MAS Notices 645, 1115, 831 and 128, MAS, June 2013 [Last revised on 15 December 2021 (with effect from 16 December 2021)].

[99] Nevertheless, it may be possible for financial institutions to grant property loans to borrowers whose TDSR exceeds the threshold on an exceptional basis, subject to enhanced credit evaluation.

[100] See MAS website <https://www.mas.gov.sg/regulation/explainers/tdsr-for-property-loans/who-tdsr-applies-to> (accessed 8 August 2020).

applied for), car loans, student loans, renovation loans, credit card loans as well as any other secured or unsecured loans (e.g. revolving loans)[101].

When simulating the monthly interest payable, financial institutions are required to apply the medium-term interest rate to the property purchase loan or loan secured by property under application (i.e. the medium-term interest rate should not be applied to existing property loans). Table 4 below sets out the prescribed interest rates in respect of the different types of property loan[102].

Table 4: Prescribed interest rates.

Type of Loan	Interest Rate
Residential property or secured residential property	Not less than 3.5% or the prevailing market interest rate, whichever is higher
Non-residential property or secured by non-residential property	Not less than 4.5% or the prevailing market interest rate, whichever is higher

Medium-term interest rates are applied in view of the long-term nature of property loans. The use of medium-term interest rates helps ensure that borrowers are not over-extended in their property purchases and are able to continue servicing their monthly repayments even where interest rates increase in the medium to long term. The medium-term interest rates used for different types of properties (as shown in Table 4) reflect the differing risk premium associated with the types of properties.

As regards the denominator of the TDSR formula, the term "gross monthly income" refers to the borrower's monthly income before tax, and excludes any CPF contribution made by the employer.

In computing the "gross monthly income", a minimum haircut of 30% is imposed in respect of variable income (e.g. commission, bonus and allowance) as well as rental income, in view of the potential fluctuation of such income. In addition, certain eligible financial assets may also be included, subject to haircuts and an amortization schedule over 48 months.

If a borrower has an existing residential property loan and is taking a second loan to buy a property, his monthly loan obligations for the existing property may be excluded from the TDSR calculation under certain

---

[101] See MAS website <https://www.mas.gov.sg/regulation/explainers/tdsr-for-property-loans/calculating-tdsr> (accessed 8 August 2020).

[102] See MAS website <https://www.mas.gov.sg/regulation/explainers/tdsr-for-property-loans/calculating-tdsr> (accessed 8 August 2020).

circumstances. For such exclusions to apply, the borrower is required to meet the following conditions, set out in Table 5[103]:

Table 5: Exclusion rules for borrowers with existing residential property loan(s).

Existing Property	Borrower Needs to Provide
• A HDB flat • An executive condominium (EC) where the minimum occupation of the EC has not expired	Both these documents: • A copy of a signed undertaking to the HDB committing to complete the sale of their current property within the period stipulated in the undertaking • A written declaration that they will take steps, in accordance with the signed undertaking, to sell their current property
• An EC where the minimum occupation of the EC has expired • A private property	Both these documents: • A sale and purchase agreement signed by both the borrower (as seller) and the buyer of the existing property • A certificate from the IRAS showing that stamp duty has been paid on the signed agreement
• A HDB flat that is being sold	A letter from the HDB approving the sale of the flat

In approving any loans, financial institutions are also required to ensure that borrowers are the mortgagors of the property. Furthermore, guarantors of the loan are to be brought in as co-borrowers if they are standing guarantee for borrowers who have not met the TDSR threshold requirements.

Exemptions from the TDSR rules are available in relation to the refinancing of existing property loans. More specifically, an existing borrower looking to refinance his loan to purchase a property is exempted from the TDSR rules if he/she is an owner–occupier. This is a concession provided to borrowers who have purchased properties for their own stay, and are seeking refinancing for existing loans in respect of their owner-occupied homes[104].

As for those with an existing investment property loan, they are allowed to refinance their investment property loans above the TDSR ratio, provided certain conditions are satisfied, as shown in Table 6[105].

---

[103] See MAS website <https://www.mas.gov.sg/regulation/explainers/tdsr-for-property-loans/calculating-tdsr> (accessed 8 August 2020).

[104] Previously, owner-occupier home loans were exempted only if the property had been bought before 29 June 2013.

[105] Previously, investment property loans were allowed to be refinanced above the TDSR ratio of 60% only if the borrower applied by 30 June 2017.

Table 6: Refinancing above the TDSR ratio.

Type of Property Loan	Does the TDSR Limit/MSR Limit Apply at the Time of Refinancing
Owner-occupied housing loan	No
Investment property loan	No, provided that the borrower meets both of these conditions: • Commits, at the point of refinancing, to a debt reduction plan with the financial institution, comprising a repayment of at least 3% of the outstanding balance over a period of not more than 3 year • Fulfil the financial institution credit assessment

The above rules were introduced on 1 September 2016 after the MAS received feedback that some borrowers who wanted to refinance their home loans to take advantage of the prevailing lower interest rates were unable to do so because of the TDSR threshold[106].

Despite the purportedly onerous requirements imposed under the TDSR rules, the objectives of the TDSR framework have gradually been met. According to an update from the MAS in early 2016, less than 10% of existing borrowers have a TDSR of above 60% and this group of borrowers is expected to decline over time[107].

2.5.6. *Borrower–Mortgagor requirement*

A borrower named on a residential property loan is required to also be the mortgagor of the property in respect of which the loan is granted. This requirement applies to any loan for the purchase of residential property where the option to purchase is granted on or after 29 June 2013, or any re-financing of such a property-secured loan. The requirement does not apply if the housing loan is not secured on the property being financed.

2.5.7. *Guarantor–Borrower requirement*

If a borrower is unable to meet the TDSR threshold on his own, another individual may be brought in to assist him in servicing the loan. This person

---

[106] 'Changes to TDSR rules: 6 things you need to know,' *The Straits Times*, 2 September 2016.

[107] 'TDSR objectives gradually being met: MAS,' *The Business Times*, 1 February 2016.

will be considered a co-borrower rather than a guarantor, and lower LTV limits will apply to the person's subsequent housing loan applications.

The guarantor-borrower requirement applies to (i) any loan for the purchase of residential property where the option to purchase is granted on after 29 June 2013, or any refinancing of such a property-secured loan in certain situations and (ii) any loan otherwise secured by residential property, if the application date is on or after 29 June 2013, or any refinancing of such a property-secured loan in certain situations.

3. Disposal of Real Estate in Singapore

The disposal of residential and industrial immovable property in Singapore is subject to stamp duty imposed on the seller, if the disposal takes place within the minimum holding period[108]. Such duties which are commonly referred to as Seller's Stamp Duty (SSD) can be up to a rate of 12% for disposal of residential immovable property and up to a rate of 15% for disposal of industrial property. The rules relating to SSD which arises on the disposal of residential and industrial immovable property are discussed below.

3.1. Seller's stamp duty

3.1.1. *Residential properties*

On 19 February 2010, the Government announced that it would be re-introducing SSD[109] on sellers who acquired residential property on or after 20 February 2010 and disposed of them within the specified holding period. In the press release issued by the MOF and MAS on 19 February 2010, the rationale behind the (re)introduction of SSD was explained as follows[110]:

> In September last year, the Government introduced a set of measures to temper the exuberance in the private residential market. The Government

---

[108] Strictly speaking, the stamp duty is imposed on instruments relating to the sale or transfer on sale of immovable property in Singapore.

[109] First introduced in 1996 under the repealed s 22A.

[110] Press release, *Measures to Ensure a Stable and Sustainable Property Market,* issued by MND, MOF and MAS, 19 February 2010.

has continued to monitor the property market closely. While the September 2009 measures helped to cool the property market, there are recent signs that it is starting to heat up again.

Demand for private housing units has spiked sharply in January this year. The number of units sold by developers in January was triple that in December 2009 and was the highest monthly total since September 2009. Prices have also increased sharply in the second half of 2009, at a faster rate compared to previous rebounds from the troughs of property cycles, and the price increase has continued in January. Mortgage lending has also increased steadily by around 12% year-on-year through 2009.

While the current level of speculative activity in the market is still lower than what it was at the height of the property market boom, and overall price levels are below the previous peak, there is a risk that the market could overheat in the next few months, fueled by low global interest rates and positive sentiments associated with the economic recovery.

Any excessive exuberance will make the property market vulnerable to the continuing risks in the global economy. Should growth turn out weaker than expected, property buyers and speculators could face capital losses as the market corrects. Conversely, if the recovery stays on course, interest rates will eventually rise and drive up financing costs with severe implications for those who have overextended themselves.

Therefore, the Government has decided to introduce calibrated measures now to temper sentiments and pre-empt a property bubble from forming. We will tighten the supply of credit to the housing market to encourage greater financial prudence among property purchasers. The Government prefers to take small steps early, rather than be forced to impose more drastic measures after a bubble has formed.

The Government will continue to monitor the property market closely and will introduce additional measures if required later, to promote a stable and sustainable property market.

The announcement of the (re)introduction of SSD was soon followed by the amendment of the Stamp Duties Act[111]. At the second reading of the Stamp Duty (Amendment) Bill 2010 in relation to the imposition of SSD on instruments relating to the sale or transfer on sale of residential

---

[111] Cap. 312.

property, the then Minister for Finance, Mr Tharman Shanmugaratnam, said the following[112]:

> Sir, the Government had previously amended the Stamp Duties Act to introduce a seller's stamp duty in 1996 to cool down the over-heating property market then. The seller's stamp duty was suspended in Nov 1997, and the relevant provisions in the Stamp Duties Act were subsequently repealed in 2005. To pre-empt the emergence of a bubble in the property market, we reintroduced the seller's stamp duty from 20 February this year. The Stamp Duties (Amendment) Bill 2010 will give legislative effect to this reintroduction of the seller's stamp duty.
>
> A seller's stamp duty is part of the range of policy instruments that the Government may use from time to time to pre-empt or mitigate property market bubbles. However, the process of introducing and repealing provisions in the Stamp Duties Act each time we have to introduce, vary or remove a seller's stamp duty is not efficient, especially when we have to respond in a timely and calibrated fashion to changes in the property market cycle.
>
> The Amendment Bill will therefore introduce general provisions on a seller's stamp duty and allow the Government to introduce, vary or remove the seller's stamp duty via a Ministerial Order.
>
> The objective of this new tax measure is to discourage short-term speculative activity that could distort underlying prices. It is not targeted at the purchase of properties for owner-occupation or longer term investment.

Despite the (re)introduction of SSD, residential real estate prices continued to increase significantly by 11% in the first half of 2010, and price levels even exceeded the historical peak in the second quarter of 1996. This in turn led to another round of property cooling measures being introduced with effect from 30 August 2010, which included an increase in the SSD rates[113].

---

[112] Available on the website of the Parliament of Singapore.

[113] Press release, *Joint Press Release on Measures to Maintain a Stable and Sustainable Property Market*, issued by MND, MOF and MAS, 30 August 2010.

Since then, the SSD regime was revised another two times — on 14 January 2011 and 11 March 2017.

The SSD rates applicable to instruments relating to the sale or transfer of residential property since 20 February 2010, are set out in Table 7.

Table 7:   SSD rates — Residential properties.

Date of Purchase or Date of Change of Zoning/Use	Holding Period	SSD Rate (On the Higher of Purchase Price or Market Value)
Between 20 February 2010 and 29 August 2010 (inclusive)	Up to 1 year	1% on the first $180,000 2% on the next $180,000 3% on the remainder
	More than 1 year	No SSD payable
Between 30 August 2010 and 13 January 2011 (inclusive)	Up to 1 year	1% on the first $180,000 2% on the next $180,000 3% on the remainder
	More than 1 year and up to 2 years	0.67% on the first $180,000 1.33% on the next $180,000 2% on the remainder
	More than 2 years and up to 3 years	0.33% on the first $180,000 0.67% on the next $180,000 1% on the remainder
	More than 3 years	No SSD payable
Between 14 January 2011 and 10 March 2017 (inclusive)	Up to 1 year	16%
	More than 1 year and up to 2 years	12%
	More than 2 years and up to 3 years	8%
	More than 3 years and up to 4 years	4%
	More than 4 years	No SSD payable
On or after 11 March 2017	Up to 1 year	12%
	More than 1 year and up to 2 years	8%
	More than 2 years and up to 3 years	4%
	More than 3 years	No SSD payable

As can be seen from Table 7, the SSD rates have increased sharply since 20 February 2010. At one point in time, the highest SSD rate was 16% for residential real estate acquired between 14 January 2011 and 10 March 2017 and disposed of within 1 year of acquisition.

The highest SSD rate was subsequently lowered to 12% for residential property acquired on or after 11 March 2017 and disposed of within 1 year of acquisition. At the same time, it was announced that SSD would no longer apply to residential property sold after the third year of acquisition, on account that the number of property sales within 4 years of acquisition has fallen significantly over the years[114]. This marked the first time the SSD regime was relaxed since its (re)introduction in February 2010[115].

The impact of the SSD is especially significant as it is payable regardless of whether the property is sold at a gain or loss. SSD on residential property is payable within 14 days of the execution of the document (if executed in Singapore) or 30 days of receiving the executed documents in Singapore (if executed overseas).

3.1.2. *Industrial properties*

While SSD was initially imposed only in respect of residential property, the scope of taxation was subsequently expanded to include industrial property from 12 January 2013. The rationale for the imposition of SSD on instruments relating to industrial property was set out in the joint press release issued by the MOF, MND, MAS and MTI, which stated[116]:

> Prices of industrial properties have doubled over the last three years, outpacing the increase in rentals. In addition, there has been increasing speculation in industrial properties: in 2011 and the first eleven months of 2012, about 15% and 18% respectively of all transactions of multiple-user factory space were resale transactions carried out within three years of purchase. This is significantly higher than the average of about 10% from 2006 to 2010.
>
> The Government is introducing Seller's Stamp Duty (SSD) on industrial property to discourage short-term speculative activity which could distort the underlying prices of industrial properties and raise costs for businesses.

---

[114] Press release, *Joint Press Release on Measures Relating to Residential Property, issued by MND*, MOF and MAS, 10 March 2017.

[115] 'Singapore property market finally sees slight easing — and a new stamp duty,' *The Business Times*, 11 March 2017.

[116] Press release, *Additional Measures To Ensure A Stable And Sustainable Property Market,*' issued by MOF, MND, MAS and MTI, 11 January 2013.

SSD is imposed in respect of instruments relating to the sale or transfer on sale of industrial property acquired on or after 12 January 2013 and disposed of within three years of the date of acquisition. The applicable SSD rates are shown in Table 8:

Table 8:   SSD rates — Industrial properties.

Holding Period	SSD Rate (On the Higher of Purchase Price or Market Value)
Up to 1 year	15%
More than 1 year and up to 2 years	10%
More than 2 years and up to 3 years	5%
More than 3 years	No SSD payable

Similar to the SSD on residential property, the SSD imposed in relation industrial property is payable within 14 days of the execution of the instrument (if executed in Singapore) or 30 days of receiving the executed instrument in Singapore (if executed outside Singapore).

3.1.3. *Relief from seller's stamp duty*

Relief from SSD is available subject to meeting the relevant prescribed conditions. The relief framework is the same as that for the relief of BSD (i.e. Reconstruction relief, Amalgamation relief or Transfer of Assets relief) as set out in Section 2.1.2.

3.1.4. *Exemption/Remission of seller's stamp duty*

Instruments executed by a licensed housing developer or an industrial property developer for the sale of residential property or industrial property (as the case may be), are exempt from SSD[117]. As regards the instruments executed by a non-licensed housing developer for the sale of any housing accommodation constructed in the course of its business of housing development, remission of SSD will be granted for such companies and businesses[118].

---

[117] Stamp Duties (Exempt Instruments under Section 22A) Rules 2010, S 208/2010.
[118] Stamp Duties (Non-Licensed Housing Developers) (Remission) Rules 2011, S 590/2011.

Clearly, there are good policy reasons for not charging SSD in these situations as the sale of the residential/industrial properties by the housing developer and industrial property developer (as the case may be), help increase the available supply of properties. This in turn has the effect of keeping in check any price hikes arising from a shortage of supply.

3.2. Income tax

Apart from SSD, a person who disposed of Singapore real estate will have to be mindful of the potential income tax and GST obligations. These obligations are discussed in turn.

From an income tax perspective, the gains arising from the disposal of real estate in Singapore may or may not be taxable, depending on the specific nature of the disposal gains (i.e. revenue or capital in nature). Revenue gains arising from the disposal of real estate situated in Singapore are subject to income tax at the prevailing tax rate. On the other hand, capital gains arising from the disposal of real estate in Singapore are not taxable in view that there is no capital gains tax in Singapore.

3.2.1. *Badges of trade test*

The tax legislation however does not specifically define what constitute capital gains. As such, whenever a gain is realized on the disposal of an asset (e.g. real estate or shares of a real estate holding company), the practice is to rely upon a set of commonly-applied rules (commonly referred to as the "badges of trade") to characterize the gain as capital or revenue in nature.

The badges of trade test includes an examination of the following factors: (i) subject matter (i.e. what is the nature of the asset in question), (ii) frequency of similar transactions entered into by the taxpayer, (iii) length of period of ownership of the disposed asset, (iv) circumstances leading to the disposal of the asset, (v) motive of the taxpayer, and (vi) whether supplementary work was carried out prior to disposing the asset. The "badges of trade" are not necessarily conclusive on their own, and depending on the circumstances, there may be other relevant factors that may be taken in account in characterizing the nature of the gain. In addition, whilst certain badges would normally carry more weight than others, the badges are generally looked upon holistically in their totality (together with all other relevant circumstantial evidence) in order to determine the character of the gain.

There are a number of cases dealing with the characterization of gains arising from the disposal of assets. Some of these are discussed below, with specific reference to the framework set out by the badges of trade.

3.2.1.1. Motive and intention

Whether the gain from the disposal of an asset is taxable or not, depends on the intention for its acquisition at the time of the acquisition. In the House of Lords case of *Simmons v Inland Revenue Commissioners*[119], Lord Wilberforce said the following:

> Trading requires an intention to trade: normally the question to be asked is whether this intention existed at the time of the acquisition of the asset. Was it acquired with the intention of disposing of it at a profit, or was it acquired as a permanent investment?

The *Simmons* case was cited with approval in the Singapore Income Tax Board of Review case of *TN v Comptroller of Income Tax*[120] and by the Singapore High Court in *NP and Another v Comptroller of Income Tax*[121].

(a) Intention *ab initio*

As the taxability of any gain arising from the disposal of assets depends on the intention at the time of its acquisition, it will be critical to examine the intention of the taxpayer closely. The actual intent may be proved by way of direct evidence or may be inferred from the surrounding circumstances, as Pennycuick VC said in *Lloyds Bank Ltd v Marcan*[122] (and cited with approval

---

[119] [1980] 1 WLR 1196 at 1199.
[120] [2007] SGITBR 2 at [33].
[121] [2007] 4 SLR(R) 599 at [32].
[122] [1973] 2 All ER 359 at 367.

by the Singapore Court of Appeal in *Ng Bok Eng Holdings Pte Ltd and Another v Wong Ser Wan*[123]):

> A man's intention is a question of fact. Actual intent may unquestionably be proved by direct evidence or may be inferred from surrounding circumstances.

In this regard, the indicia that may point to an investment intention in respect of the acquisition of the asset include the principal activities of the company which acquired and disposed of the asset, as reflected in the company's constitution, business profile and financial statements. In addition, the resolutions passed at the time of acquiring the asset in question would also provide useful information with regard to the intention behind the acquisition of the asset.

(b) Accounting classification

The accounting classification of the asset in the financial statements of the company which acquired and disposed of the asset, may also shed some light on the intention at the time of acquisition of the asset. In this regard, when the Income Tax Board of Review in the case of *TN v Comptroller of Income Tax*[124] held that the disposal of 17 apartments were held in capital, it was stated at [53] that one of the reasons for the Board's decision was "the consistent classification of the activities of the appellant and the property in its accounts as 'property investment' and 'fixed assets', respectively".

(c) Feasibility study

While the existence of a feasibility study may provide evidence of the intention with regard to the acquisition of the asset, the absence of such a feasibility study should not in itself be regarded as a red flag. For instance, in practice, it is not uncommon for the investor to do a simple mental or "back-of the envelope" analysis or calculation when acquiring a single property unit (as compared to the acquisition of a large commercial property that

---

[123] [2005] 4 SLR(R) 561 at [31].
[124] [2007] SGITBR 2.

requires tens of millions of dollars of investment, which may then require some sophisticated or formal feasibility studies).

In the case of *HZ and Another v Comptroller of Income Tax*, where no feasibility study was prepared, the Income Tax Board of Review nevertheless held that the gains were capital in nature. In that case, the taxpayer bought the shop premises from HDB under the Sale of Tenants Shops Scheme in October 1993 and sold them shortly thereafter in February 1994, on account of an attractive offer by a purchaser. In deciding that the gains were capital in nature, the Board stated[125]:

> ... there was every reason for Appellants to purchase the shop from HDB. This was a very good offer from HDB under a national scheme given with a generous discount and there was no assurance it will be repeated on the same terms. It also would protect them from future rental hikes. The fact that no feasibility study was taken out was not of significant weight in this case as the simple analysis showed that the Appellant were able to finance the regular outgoings relating to the purchase of the shop.

(d) Intention to be determined based on holistic assessment of all evidence

While direct documentary evidence is useful for the purposes of corroborating the intention of the person who acquired and disposed of the asset, the absence or dearth of documentary evidence does not mean that an explanation or narration of the facts that transpired is to be rejected out of hand. As observed by Tan Ah Tah J in the Singapore High Court case of *STU v Comptroller of Income Tax*[126]:

> In this case certain explanations given by the Appellant to the officers of the Income Tax Department were rejected on the ground that there was no documentary evidence to support them. No doubt documentary evidence can in many cases be very cogent and convincing. The lack of it, however, should not invariably be a reason for rejecting an explanation. Not every transaction is accompanied or supported by documentary evidence. Much

---

[125] [2004] SGITBR 8 at [61].
[126] [1962] MLJ 220 at 221.

depends on the facts and circumstances of the case, but if the person who is giving the explanation appears to be worthy of credit, but does not reveal any inconsistency and there is nothing improbable in the explanation, it can, in my view, be accepted.

Direct evidence may therefore be given by the persons in effective control of a company as to what was the intention or purpose in relation to any matter at any given time. As Botha JA in the South African income tax case of *Secretary for Inland Revenue v The Trust Bank of Africa Ltd*[127], said:

> ... I can see no reason in principle why the persons who are in effective control of a company cannot give evidence as to what was the intention or purpose of the company in relation to any matter at any given time.

In the Singapore context, the Income Tax Board of Review has similarly taken into account the documentary evidence and the testimony of the persons involved in the case of *HZ and Another v Comptroller of Income Tax*, where it stated[128]:

> Having observed their demeanour and having weighed their respective testimonies with the evidence in its entirety including the documentary evidence, the Board found no reason not to accept the evidence of the First Appellant and Second Appellant. The Board found their testimonies to be truthful, cogent and consistent with the objective documentary evidence presented before the Board.

Notably, the intention has not only to be ascertained from the expression of intention by the taxpayer itself (e.g. through board resolutions and other contemporaneous documentation), but has to be tested against other facts and inferred from the surrounding circumstances, to determine if the actual intention at the time of acquisition of the asset is for the purpose of trading or for investment. As Mortimer J said in the Hong Kong case of *All Best Wishes Limited v Commissioner of Inland Revenue*[129] (and cited with approval

---

[127] [1975] 37 SATC 87 at page 106.
[128] [2004] SGITBR 8 at [54].
[129] [1992] 3 HKTC 750 at 771.

by Judith Prakash J in the Singapore High Court case of *NP v Comptroller of Income Tax*[130]):

> The intention of the taxpayer, at the time of acquisition, and at the time when he is holding the asset is undoubtedly of very great weight. And if the intention is on the evidence, genuinely held, realistic and realisable, and if all the circumstances show that at the time of the acquisition of the asset, the taxpayer was investing in it, then I agree. But as it is a question of fact, no single test can produce the answer. In particular, the stated intention of the taxpayer cannot be decisive and the actual intention can only be determined upon the whole of the evidence.

3.2.1.2. Subject matter of realization

Some categories of assets such as manufactured articles will usually be the subject matter of trading rather than for investment. Other categories of assets such as real estate or shares which produce recurrent income, may however be the subject matter of investment as well as that of trading.

Where the subject matter of realization is real estate which generates recurring rental income or shares in a real estate holding company which generates recurring dividend income, such assets are generally more likely to be viewed as investments and not as trading stock.

3.2.1.3. Frequency of similar transactions

Where a person has no history of trading or dealing, and the disposal of the asset is the only such transaction undertaken by the person, there should be strong grounds to contend that the person is not a trader merely because of the disposal of a single asset. On the other hand, a series of transactions over a relatively short period of time is more likely to connote trading than an isolated transaction would. As Harman J said in *J Bolson & Son Ltd v Farrelly*[131]:

> A deal done once is probably not an activity in the nature of a trade, though it may be. Done three or four times it usually is. Each case must depend on its own facts.

---

[130] [2007] 4 SLR(R) 599 at [32].
[131] [1952] 34 TC 161 at 167.

Notwithstanding the above, where an investment is made in the expectation that someday it may be realised, that does not mean that the original intention is to acquire the asset as trading stock or make the gains from realisation, income. As Lord Buckmaster said in *Jones v Leeming*[132]:

> [A]n accretion to capital does not become income merely because the original capital was invested in the hope and expectation that it would rise in value; if it does so rise, its realisation does not make it income.

Frequently, one may even hear an investor saying that he may sell his property at the appropriate time, should there be a favorable opportunity like an en-bloc sale. But that does not turn his investment asset into trading stock when it is sold. In this regard, in the English income tax case of *Dodd and Tanfield v Haddock (HM Inspector of Taxes)*[133], Buckley J said:

> If the project was continuously of one character from the date when Mr Tanfield bought, the question must be whether he then intended to buy with a view to reselling as a trading transaction, or whether he then bought the property as an investment or capital asset, albeit with the idea that he might resell in the future, even in the near future, if a favourable opportunity arose.

3.2.1.4. Length of period of ownership of the disposed asset

As a general rule, the longer the period of ownership of the asset disposed of, the stronger is the inference that the asset was held as a long term investment (i.e. capital asset). On the other hand, where an asset is disposed of shortly after acquisition, it may be difficult to demonstrate that the asset was held as an investment to enjoy either income return or capital appreciation. However, there is no magic figure with regard to the number of years of holding, which would safely classify the gains from the disposal of asset as non-taxable gains.

---

[132] [1930] AC 415 at 420.
[133] [1964] 42 TC 229 at 245.

As highlighted by the Singapore Income Tax Board of Review in the case of *NO v Comptroller of Income Tax*[134], whether the gain on disposal derived by a taxpayer is capital or revenue in nature, depends largely on the facts. As can be seen from the *NO* case which concerned a family company which purchased commercial premises from the Housing and Development Board, a relatively short holding period is not determinative of the issue. In the *NO* case, the Board stated as follows in its grounds of decision:

38. "The Length of Period of Ownership
Generally speaking, property meant to be dealt with is realised within a short period of time after acquisition. But there are many exceptions from this as a universal rule".

39. The Respondent [i.e. the Comptroller of Income Tax] highlighted the fact that the Property was sold to M on a back-to-back basis on the same day that completion of the sale to *NO* was to take place. *NO*, it was submitted, did not even get to the position of acquiring the property and this, it was submitted, goes to show that *NO* intended to trade.

40. Whilst it is true that *NO* did not get to the stage of acquiring the Property, *NO* nevertheless had an option to buy the property and, with the consent of HDB, had assigned the benefit of that option to M. *NO* therefore can be said to have "held" the Property from the date (02/09/1994) when HDB agreed to sell the Property to it to the date (21/11/1994) when it granted an option to M: a period of about 2½ months. Considering the nature of the property, this is, undoubtedly, a short period of ownership.

41. Short though the period of holding was, we see merit in Appellant's [i.e. *NO*'s] submission that the price offered by M was so exceptionally high that it made sense for *NO* to dispose of the asset and take the profit, the more so since the anticipated usages of the second floor were not materialising. The short period of ownership did not, it was submitted, negative the fact that NO, in buying the Property from HDB, was buying it for its own long-term use.

Notably, in the *NO* case, the holding period was merely 2½ months but the Board was not deterred from deciding that the gain is capital in nature.

---

[134] [2006] SGITBR 5.

3.2.1.5. Circumstances leading to the disposal

The circumstances leading to the disposal of the immovable property is another important factor to be considered.

(a) Unsolicited offer

Where the seller disposed of the asset pursuant to an unsolicited offer, there are strong grounds to contend that the disposal gain is capital in nature and hence not taxable.

In the Singapore Income Tax Board of Review case of *TN v Comptroller of Income Tax*[135] (where the taxpayer company sold 17 out of 18 units in a residential development), the Board of Review pointed to the unsolicited offer in coming to the conclusion that the gain was capital in nature. In coming to its conclusion in that case, the Board of Review stated as follows in its grounds of decision:

> 26. The Appellant also submits that the sale of the Property was unsolicited as the Appellants and D did not set out to look for a buyer but was approached by Jones Lang Wootton Properties Consultant Pte Ltd (as it was then known), who informed them that a party was interested in the purchase of the Property en-bloc.
>
> 27. The Appellant cited the decision of the Special Commissioners in *HCM v Director-General of Inland Revenue* (1993) 2 MSTC 539:
>
> ... if special exertion is made to find or attract purchasers such as the opening of an office or advertising extensively, such facts will indicate the presence of a profit-making undertaking... From the evidence of the appellant and the witness we find no evidence to show that the appellant had done anything to attract purchasers to the lands least of all opening up an office, or even advertising extensively for the sale of the said lands. Therefore according to this criterion the appellant cannot be said to be engaged in stock-in-trade.

In the *TN* case, the Board of Review in concluding that the gain of the collective disposal of 17 apartments was capital in nature, relied on the

---

[135] [2007] SGITBR 2.

ground amongst others, that the properties were "sold collectively in one lot to an unrelated buyer pursuant to an unsolicited offer made by the buyer": see paragraph 53(ii) of the grounds of decision in the *TN* case.

Similarly, in the Malaysian income tax case of *ALF Properties Sdn Bhd v Ketua Pengarah Jabatan Hasil Dalam Negeri*[136], Mokhtar Sidin JCA in deciding the gains of disposal of properties in that case were capital in nature at the Court of Appeal, pointed to the unsolicited offer in support and stated:

> In July 1990 the unused portion was sold when there was a good offer from Chanrai Investment Corporation. In respect of the sale of the unused portion, there was no evidence to show that the appellant made preparation for the sale such as advertising or that the appellant had opened an office just for the purpose of selling the unused portion or other activity pertaining to sale or development of the unused portion. The evidence shows that the sale of the unused portion was by chance in that there was a good offer by Chanrai Investment Corporation ....

(b) Exceptionally high price offered

The fact that the seller disposed of the asset pursuant to an exceptionally high offer price is yet another reason for contending that the seller had not earlier contemplated the disposal of the asset.

In the *NO* case, the testimony of the appellant that the disposal of the asset was pursuant to an exceptionally high offer price was also cited by the Board of Review, in making its finding that the gain was capital in nature. In that case, the appellant's testimony quoted in paragraph 29 of the Board's grounds of decision was as follows:

> He offered $15.5 million. I respected him. He had given me a very good price. Before that, I could not imagine I could sell the premises. So, on 21.11.1994, I agreed to sell.

In the Privy Council case of *Beautiland Co Ltd v Commissioner of Inland Revenue*[137] (on appeal from Hong Kong and where it was held that the gain

---

[136] [2005] 3 CLJ 936 at 979.
[137] [1991] STC 467 at 473.

was capital in nature), the circumstances under which capital assets were disposed of was a relevant factor considered by Lord Keith of Kinkel who said:

> The true view is that the appearance of a fortuitous offer at a very good price caused the taxpayer company to decide to sell part of its capital structure.

3.2.1.6. Supplementary work carried out prior to disposal

Generally speaking, the mere carrying out of supplementary work in relation to an asset prior to its disposal, is of itself neutral in determining if there is a trading of assets. For example, improvement or alteration works may be made to an investment property merely with a view to enhancing its rental yield. On the other hand, if work is carried out in order to put the investment into a more saleable condition, or if any special exertions are made to find or attract buyers for the investments, the carrying out of that work may point towards a trading intention.

As the Lord President said in the case of *Inland Revenue Commissioners v Livingston*[138], the work will indicate a trade if "the operations involved in it are of the same kind, and carried on in the same way, as those which are characteristic of ordinary trading in the line of business in which the venture was made". Therefore, if special exertions are made to find or attract purchasers, there is evidence of trading. Similarly, where there is an organized effort to obtain profit, this would point to trading, giving rise to taxable income.

Of course, at the point of disposal, some marketing efforts may have to be made to obtain a good price for an investment. But that by itself should not turn an investment into a trading stock. As Viscount Dilhorne said in *Simmons v Inland Revenue Commissioners*[139]:

> An investment does not turn into trading stock because it is sold. I entirely agree with my noble and learned friend, Lord Wilberforce, that no such concept can be accepted.

---

[138] (1926) 11 TC 538 at 542.
[139] [1980] 1 WLR 1196 at 1203.

3.2.1.7. Capacity to hold the real estate for the long term

Beyond the badges of trade, a relevant factor to be considered in determining whether an asset was held for investment or trading purpose, is the financial capacity of the person to hold the asset for the long term. This in turn depends on the income (e.g. rental income) derived from the holding of the asset and the interest expense arising in connection with the acquisition of the asset.

Where the income (e.g. rental income, dividend income, etc.) generated from the holding of an asset is significantly greater than the interest expenses incurred in financing the acquisition of the asset, it may be inferred that the person has the financial capacity to hold the asset as a long term investment. In the *TN* case (where the gain from the disposal of 17 apartments was held to be capital in nature), the Board of Review similarly relied on the ground amongst others, that "the Appellant [taxpayer] was in a position to hold the Property for the long-term and was actually in a tax-paying position for most of the years during which it held the Property": see paragraph 53(iii) of the grounds of decision.

3.2.1.8. Mode of financing the acquisition

Yet another relevant factor to be considered is the mode of financing the acquisition of the real estate. As a general guide, where a higher proportion of equity capital is invested by the person acquiring the asset, it may be inferred as pointing to a long term investment intention. That said, it is worthwhile noting that in the case of *NO*, the family company needed 100% financing for the purchase of the commercial premises from HDB and yet the Income Tax Board of Review held that the gain on disposal after the 2½-month holding period was capital in nature.

As regards the *TN* case, where the disposal gains were held to be capital in nature, the term loan facility undertaken by *TN* was $6,640,000, which was 62% of the purchase price of $10,767,000 and there was an interest free loan of $4,127,000 from the parent company.

On a related note, where the third-party loans undertaken to finance the acquisition of the asset come with a longer tenure (e.g. 20 years), it may also be inferred that the person had intention to hold the asset for the long term.

3.3. Goods and Services Tax

In the last section of this chapter, the focus will now turn to the GST implication arising in connection with the disposal of immovable property situated in Singapore.

The sale of non-residential properties in Singapore (including any movable furniture and fittings) by a taxable person is currently subject to GST at the prevailing standard rate of 7%. In contrast, the sale of residential properties situated in Singapore by a taxable person is an exempt supply which is not subject to GST[140]. It is however to be noted that GST remains chargeable on the supply of movable[141] furniture and fittings made in connection with the sale of furnished residential properties.

3.3.1. *Taxable person*

A taxable person for GST purposes is one who is or is required to be registered under the GST Act[142]. A person is required to register for GST if his taxable supplies[143] exceeds or is expected to exceed $1 million on an annual basis[144]. For this purpose, it is to be noted that proceeds from the sale of capital assets (e.g. sale of machinery/equipment, office building) should be excluded when determining the value of taxable supplies for GST registration purpose.

3.3.2. *Residential properties vs non-residential properties*

For GST purposes, residential properties include vacant residential land as well as residential flat and building. The sale of residential properties situated in Singapore is an exempt supply and no GST is chargeable, except

---

[140] Para 2 of Part 1 of the Fourth Schedule to the GST Act provides that the grant, assignment or surrender of any interest in or right over residential properties or of any licence to occupy such residential properties is an exempt supply. Where the property comprises both a residential and non-residential component, only the non-residential component is subject to GST.

[141] Fixtures such as built-in cabinets and wardrobes, kitchen and sanitary wares, wall-mounted air conditioners that are attached permanently to the residential property are exempt from GST together with the residential property.

[142] Cap. 117A.

[143] Taxable supplies include all supplies but exclude exempt supplies.

[144] First Schedule to the GST Act.

in respect of movable furniture and fittings made in connection with the sale of furnished residential properties.

Land is considered residential if it is vacant land zoned "Residential" in the Master Plan[145] and the use of the land is approved for residential or condominium development. Residential land also includes vacant land or land with existing building (to be demolished), which is supplied by the Government or public authority and approved exclusively for residential or condominium development.

On the other hand, a building is a residential building if it is approved for use or approved to be used for residential purposes. Examples of residential properties for GST purposes include dwelling houses, upper floor of shop-houses approved for dwelling only, as well as serviced apartments.

Properties that do not fall within the definition of residential properties (land or building) are regarded as non-residential properties. Examples of non-residential properties for GST purposes include chalets, holiday bungalows as well as lower floor of shop-houses approved for non-residential use[146].

---

[145] Under the Planning Act.

[146] See also: Goods and Services Tax (Buildings, Flats and Tenements for Residential purposes) Order 2010 (S825/2010).

Acquisition and Disposal of Real Estate Holding Entities: Equity Sale Transactions

1. Introduction

The acquisition and disposal of real estate may be effected directly via the outright transfer of the real estate (i.e. an asset deal) or indirectly via the transfer of equity interests in the entity[1] which holds the real estate (i.e. an equity or share deal). An equity deal involving the transfer of equity interests in the entity which holds[2] real estate is usually more complex than an asset deal. This is because inquiries have to be made into the various aspects of the entity, given that the acquisition of equity interests in the entity will mean that the buyer will also be inheriting the liabilities of the entity.

Some of the key tax issues that commonly arise in an equity deal (also referred to as a share deal, where the acquired entity is a company), are as follows[3]:

---

[1] Such an entity may be a company, a partnership, a trust, etc.

[2] The real estate may be held either directly by the entity or indirectly via one or more intermediate entities.

[3] As real estate holding entities are predominantly set up in the form of companies, the discussion in this chapter will be focused on transactions involving transfer of shares in real estate holding companies, unless otherwise specifically stated. Where applicable, the key differences in tax treatment in respect of the acquisition of real estate holding companies vis-a-vis acquisition of other types of real estate holding entities (e.g. limited partnerships or trusts) are set out either in the body of the main text or in the footnotes.

(a) There is no "uplifting" or "step-up" in the cost base of the underlying real estate held by the acquired company (also referred to as the target company). In other words, the historic cost of acquisition of the underlying real estate held by the real estate holding company may be much lower than the corresponding costs of acquisition of the shares paid by the buyer of the real estate holding company. The lower historic cost of the underlying real estate may be a significant concern to the buyer of the real estate holding company, where the gains arising from the subsequent disposal of the underlying real estate are subject to income tax.

(b) The interest expense incurred on the acquisition of the shares has no tax deduction value, where the income arising from the holding of the shares is not subject to income tax[4].

(c) There is risk of exposure to "legacy" tax and other legal issues relating to activities carried on by the target company prior to being acquired by the buyer, e.g. under-reporting of income and over-claiming of expenses, etc by the target company previously.

(d) The imposition of stamp duty and additional conveyance duty (ACD) on the acquisition of shares in the real estate holding company, including the issues involved in determining the quantum of duties payable in respect of any earn-outs.

The transaction costs involved in a share deal are also expected to be higher than that of an asset deal, given the additional due diligence and other work required to be undertaken in respect of the target company (on top of those required in respect of the underlying real estate).

2. ACD: An Added Complexity

We will first discuss the ACD[5] regime which was introduced in 2017 to neutralize the advantage of lower stamp duty rate applicable to equity

---

[4] The dividend income received from a Singapore tax resident company is tax exempt under s 13(1)(za) of the Income Tax Act. Consequently, the interest expenses incurred on the acquisition of the shares has no tax deduction value. In contrast, interest expenses incurred on the direct acquisition of real estate is tax deductible against the rental income generated from the letting out of the real estate.

[5] The ACD is imposed under ss 23, 23A to 23D of the Stamp Duties Act and the subsidiary legislation.

deals involving underlying residential property, as compared to the then significantly higher stamp duty rate applicable to asset deals involving residential property[6]. The advent of the ACD which is targeted at the acquisition and disposal of equity interests in entities known as property holding entity (PHE)[7], has added complexity to equity deals. As the term "prescribed immovable property" (which in turn characterizes whether an entity is a PHE) is defined widely in the Stamp Duties Act, an entity which seems to be holding non-residential properties may nevertheless be a PHE, such that the acquisition and disposal of the interests in the entity may have ACD consequences.

Given that the ACD, which carries a punitive rate of duty of up to 44%, is a potential deal-breaker for transactions involving the acquisition and disposal of equity interests in PHEs, it will be useful to have an in-depth discussion of the ACD regime.

2.1. Introduction of the ACD regime

On 10 March 2017, an urgent bill[8] was introduced and passed in a single sitting in the Singapore Parliament to legislate the imposition of a new stamp duty known as the ACD. The ACD took effect the very next day[9] with rates of up to 18%[10]. The pace[11] at which the legislation was passed caught many by surprise, as new bills are typically introduced and passed at different sittings of the Parliament, usually weeks or months apart.

The ACD is targeted at residential property transactions which involve the transfer of equity interest of the entities that hold residential property which prior to the introduction of ACD, was subject to significantly lower stamp duty compared to that for the direct acquisition or disposal of

---

[6] See: Ministry of Finance Fact Sheet for Stamp Duty (Amendment) Bill, 10 March 2017.

[7] See Section 2.4.2 for further details on 'PHE'.

[8] Stamp Duties (Amendment) Bill 2017, Bill 18 of 2017.

[9] The Stamp Duties (Amendment) Act 2017 (Act 13 of 2017) came into operation on 11 March 2017 by operation of the Stamp Duties (Section 23) Order 2017 (S 100/2017).

[10] 'Parliament: New stamp duty rule on residential property transactions via share sales,' *The Straits Times*, 10 March 2017. The top ACD rate has since been increased to 44% with effect from 16 December 2021.

[11] The relevant legislation was introduced and passed at a single sitting of the Parliament due to the market sensitive nature of the imposition of ACD.

residential property[12]. Basically, with the advent of the ACD, the stamp duty payable for the *indirect* acquisition of residential properties, through the acquisition of equity interests in an entity which in turn holds residential property, is increased to be on par with the stamp duty payable for the *direct* acquisition of the residential property.

Just three days before the ACD legislation was introduced and passed, the Second Minister for Finance, Mr Lawrence Wong, had hinted at changes to the then existing stamp duty regime. Many market watchers however did not expect the changes to be put in place so quickly, when Mr Lawrence Wong told the Parliament on 7 March 2017 that[13]:

> In principle, we should treat transactions in residential property on the same basis, regardless of whether a property is transferred directly or through a transfer of shares in a company whose primary business is in residential property in Singapore.

The objective for the introduction of ACD is set out in the joint press release issued by the Ministry of Finance (MOF), the Ministry of National Development (MND) and the Monetary Authority of Singapore (MAS) on 10 March 2017, announcing the implementation of the ACD[14]:

> The 2nd Minister for Finance will be introducing legislative changes in Parliament today aimed at treating transactions in residential properties on the same basis irrespective of whether the properties are transacted directly or through a transfer of equity interest in an entity holding residential properties. ... Significant owners of residential property-holding entities or PHEs will be subject to the usual stamp duties when they transfer equity

---

[12] Immediately prior to the introduction of ACD, a direct acquisition of residential property was subject to buyer's stamp duty of up to 3% and additional buyer's stamp duty of up to 15% of the market value of the residential property. In contrast, the acquisition of shares in a company which owned the residential property was subject to stamp duty of only 0.2% of the value of the company. With the introduction of ACD, significant owners of residential property-holding entities, or PHEs for short, are now subject to equivalent stamp duties when transacting in the shares, as though they were directly acquiring or disposing of the residential property.

[13] The Minister was responding to a suggestion from Member of Parliament, Yee Chia Hsing. See also 'Transfer of home-owning entities: Government plans to apply residential stamp duties,' *The Business Times*, 8 March 2017 and 'Government to plug loophole in residential property stamp duty,' *The Straits Times*, 9 March 2017.

[14] See para 7 of the press release, *Joint Press Release on Measures Relating to Residential Property*, issued by MOF, MND and MAS, 10 March 2017.

interest in such entities, similar to what would happen if they were to buy or sell the properties directly.

The rationale for the introduction of ACD is further set out in the Fact Sheet for the Stamp Duties (Amendment) Bill 2017 released by the MOF on 10 March 2017, which states the following at paragraphs 2 and 3 of the Fact Sheet:

> 2 Currently, the acquisition of shares in companies is subject to 0.2% stamp duty. In comparison, the purchase of residential properties in Singapore attracts Buyer's Stamp Duty (BSD) of 1% to 3%[15], and Additional Buyer's Stamp Duty (ABSD) of up to 15%[16]. The sale of residential properties in Singapore may also be subject to Seller's Stamp Duty (SSD). Hence, this results in a stamp duty rate differential between the direct buying/selling of residential properties, and indirect buying/selling of residential properties through PHEs.
>
> 3 The new stamp duty measure seeks to address the stamp duty rate differential by subjecting the acquisition and disposal of equity interest in entities whose primary tangible assets are in residential properties in Singapore to Additional Conveyance Duty (ACD). ...

The imposition of ACD came after several high-profile residential real estate transactions were effected via sale of shares in real estate holding companies, as opposed to an outright sale of the residential real estate. The most widely reported of such transactions occurred just two months earlier in January 2017, when 45 unsold units at upmarket condominium The Nassim were acquired for $411.6 million, via the acquisition of a 100% stake in the company, Nassim Hill Realty[17].

The decision to introduce ACD was somewhat surprising because the Inland Revenue Authority of Singapore (IRAS) had earlier in January 2013 stated (or rather, suggested) that the Commissioner of Stamp Duties may (already have powers to) disregard or vary arrangements to counteract any

---

[15] The highest marginal stamp duty rate in respect of the acquisition of residential property has since been raised to 4% with effect from 20 February 2018.

[16] The highest ABSD rate in respect of the acquisition of residential property has since been raised to 44% with effect from 16 December 2021.

[17] 'Banker Wee Cho Yaw buys all 45 unsold units at The Nassim for $411.6m,' *The Straits Times*, 17 January 2017.

reduction in or avoidance of duty payable by the person, in the scenario where residential property is indirectly acquired via the purchase of shares in special purpose companies which hold such residential property[18].

The enactment of the ACD provisions thus indicates the implausibility of imposing ABSD[19], or its equivalent, on the transfer instrument relating to shares of a "land rich" company, by invoking the general anti-avoidance provisions in section 33A of the Stamp Duties Act[20]. Consequently, new statutory provisions had to be enacted to impose the ACD on the agreement for the sale and purchase of "property holding entity", in order that additional stamp duty equivalent to the ABSD, may be effectively imposed on the instruments (i.e. documents) pertaining to equity transactions involving PHEs.

2.2. Overview of the ACD regime

The ACD[21] is targeted at residential property transactions which involve the transfer of equity interest of the entities that primarily hold residential property. Such entities, which could be a company, general partnership, limited partnership, limited liability partnership, trust, etc., are referred to as a PHE[22] in the ACD legislation.

The ACD is intended to mirror the BSD, SSD and ABSD, which apply to the direct acquisition and disposal of residential property. It plugs the then existing loophole by aligning the stamp duty rates for the indirect sale of residential property with those for direct sales. The ACD rules are however not targeted at the ordinary buying and selling of shares in listed companies by retail investors[23].

---

[18] 'Residential property buys via SPV may not escape ABSD,' *The Business Times Weekend*, 26/27 January 2013 and 'Residential property of firm subject to top ABSD rate of 15%,' *The Business Times Weekend*, 26/27 January 2013.

[19] ABSD is chargeable on the sale and purchase agreement relating to residential property.

[20] In *Comptroller of Income Tax v AQQ and another appeal* [2014] 2 SLR 847, the Court of Appeal in construing the general anti-avoidance provisions in s 33 of the Income Tax Act which are *in pari materia* with those in s 33A of the Stamp Duties Act, adopted the scheme and purpose approach.

[21] For an in-depth discussion of the ACD regime, see Vincent Ooi, *The New Additional Conveyance Duties Regime in the Stamp Duties Act*, [2018] 30 SAcLJ 119 and Justin Tan, 'Singapore Stamp Duty: Strengthening the additional conveyance duty rules,' *Asia-Pacific Tax Bulletin* 26(1) (2020).

[22] See Section 2.4.2 for further details on 'PHE'.

[23] See para 7 of the press release, *Joint Press Release on Measures Relating to Residential Property*, issued by MOF, MND and MAS, 10 March 2017.

The tax is imposed on executed instruments (e.g. the exercised Option to Purchase, Sale and Purchase Agreement, etc.) relating to the acquisition or disposal of equity interests in PHEs, regardless of whether any profit or loss arises from the transaction in question. Such a feature of the ACD regime makes it particularly punitive, compared to income tax which is only imposed if the seller derives a gain from the transaction. Where ACD is triggered, the tax is to be paid within 14 days of executing the instrument (if executed in Singapore) or 30 days of receiving the executed instrument in Singapore (if executed outside Singapore).

Although the ACD legislation is widely crafted, the ACD regime does not extend to all transactions involving PHEs. Instead, the ambit of the ACD regime is limited to execution of instruments relating to the purchase or sale involving "significant owners"[24] of PHEs.

2.3. ACDB and ACDS

With the introduction of ACD, the execution of instruments for the acquisition of equity interests in a PHE (e.g. the acquisition of shares of a Singapore-incorporated company[25] with assets comprising substantially residential properties), attracts ACD for the buyer (ACDB), if the buyer is a significant owner of the PHE immediately before the execution of the instrument, or becomes one upon the execution of the instrument. On the other hand, the execution of instruments for the disposal of equity interests in a PHE, attracts ACD for the seller (ACDS), if the seller is (or was) a significant owner of the PHE and disposed of equity interests within 3 years of acquiring the equity interests[26].

A simplified diagrammatic illustration of the ACDB and ACDS regimes are set out in Figures 1 and 2.

---

[24] See Section 2.4.4 for further details on 'significant owners'.

[25] The ACD regime also applies to acquisition and disposal of shares in foreign incorporated companies where the share register of such companies is kept in Singapore. See s 36(d) of the Stamp Duties Act which provides that exemption of stamp duty is not available for the transfer of shares in a foreign incorporated company which has its register kept in Singapore.

[26] ACDS would not apply to any conveyance that is executed in the period between the time the transferor (including the transferor's associates) ceases to own any equity interests in the PHE and the time the transferor becomes a significant owner of the PHE again. See s 23(4) of the Stamp Duties Act.

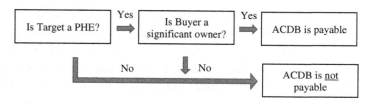

Figure 1: ACDB.

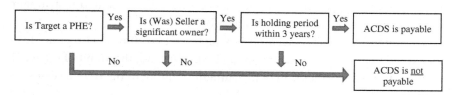

Figure 2: ACDS.

The ACD payable by buyers (i.e. ACDB) is currently imposed at a rate of up to 44% whereas the ACD payable by sellers (i.e. ACDS) is imposed at a flat rate of 12%.

2.4. Fundamental concepts of ACD

In respect of the imposition of ACD, quite obviously the legislation has to define:

(a) the types of immovable property holdings which may be caught under the ACD provisions;
(b) the profile of the entity which may be caught under the ACD provisions;
(c) the nature of the interests in the relevant entity that may be caught under the ACD provisions; and
(d) the minimum amount of interest in the entity which has to be acquired or disposed of, before ACD applies.

In this regard, the ACD provisions introduced the concepts of:

(a) "prescribed immovable properties", to set out the types of immovable property holdings which may be caught under the ACD provisions;

(b) "property holding entities", (i.e. PHEs) to address the issue on the profile of entity which may be caught under the ACD provisions;

(c) "equity interest", to address the issue on the nature of the interests in the relevant entity which may be caught under the ACD provisions; and

(d) "significant owner", to address the issue on the minimum amount of interests in the entity which has to be acquired or in ownership before ACD applies.

All four threshold conditions pertaining to "prescribed immovable properties", "PHE", "equity interests" and "significant owner" must be satisfied before ACD is triggered. All the other complexities of ACD in turn revolve around providing for various conceivable situations where there may be a PHE and where a person may effectively be or become a "significant owner". The key concepts of "prescribed immovable properties", "PHE", "equity interest" and "significant owner" are discussed in turn below.

2.4.1. *Prescribed immovable properties*

A "prescribed immovable property"[27] for the purposes of the ACD legislation is broadly defined to include any immovable property that is zoned or situated on land that is zoned under the Master Plan as "Residential", "Commercial and Residential", "Residential/Institution", "Residential with Commercial at 1st Storey" or "White"[28]. This definition in effect casts the ACD net very wide as properties which are clearly non-residential in nature (such as the two integrated resorts at Marina Bay and Sentosa, which sit on land zoned "White" in the Master Plan) technically fall within the definition of "prescribed immovable property" for ACD purposes. Other examples where the properties are deemed as prescribed immovable property despite the non-residential usage of the property, include office buildings such as One Raffles Quay, Asia Square Tower One and Asia Square Tower Two, all of which are situated on land zoned "White" in the Master Plan.

---

[27] As defined in para 5 of the Stamp Duties (Section 23) Order 2017 (S 100/2017), read with s 23(21) of the Stamp Duties Act.

[28] This definition mirrors that for residential property which are subject to ABSD upon their acquisition, as ACD is basically targeted at the indirect acquisition of residential property.

The definition of the term "prescribed immovable property" also extends to any immovable property permitted[29] to be used for solely residential purposes or for mixed purposes one of which is residential, as well as those used[30] for solely residential purposes or for mixed purposes one of which is residential.

As can be seen from the definition of "prescribed immovable property", the scope of ACD is far-reaching and extends beyond what is normally regarded as "residential" property. In practice, however, it is noted that a remission from ACD may be sought (in many situations), where the underlying property is not approved and used for residential purposes.

2.4.2. Property holding entity

A property holding entity (PHE) is an entity which has at least 50% of its total tangible assets comprising prescribed immovable properties in Singapore. For ACD purposes, a PHE is categorized as either a Type 1 PHE or a Type 2 PHE.

Generally speaking, a Type 1 PHE is one which has significant *direct* holdings in prescribed immovable properties whereas a Type 2 PHE is one which has significant *indirect* holdings in prescribed immovable properties.

In the article, "The New Additional Conveyance Duties Regimes in the Stamp Duties Act", the learned author, Vincent Ooi, made the following insightful comment on the concept of PHE which will help the reader navigate the complexities of ACD[31]:

> To understand the concept of a PHE, the phrase "property holding entities" can be broken down into its constituent terms: (a) property, (b) holding, and (c) entity.
>
> "Property", in this context, refers to prescribed immovable properties (PIPs), which correspond with the residential properties defined under the direct stamp duties regime. "Entities", subject to the ACD regime, are companies, partnerships and property trusts. "Holding" is a more complex

---

[29] By way of (1) a written permission given under s 14(4) of the Planning Act (not being one that is given for a period of 10 years or less) or (2) a notification under s 21(6) of the Planning Act.

[30] Where the property was so used on 1 February 1960 and has not been put to any other use since that date, and where such use is not the subject of a written permission or notification.

[31] [2018] 30 SAcLJ 119 at [12] and [13].

concept. An entity is not a PHE simply because it holds residential property; there are requirements on how much it must hold. At least 50% of the market value of an entity must be made up of PIPs before an entity may be classified as a PHE under the ACD regime. This will be referred to as the "property-heavy" condition hereinafter.

The concept of "prescribed immovable property" is discussed in Section 2.4.1. As for the concept of "entity", such an entity may be a company, partnership, limited partnership, limited liability partnership or a property trust[32]. With regard to the concept of "holding", the threshold is 50% of the market value of the total tangible assets of the entity.

An entity may own prescribed immovable properties *directly* and where the market value of 50% or more of its total tangible assets as at the end of the most recent completed accounting period comes from prescribed immovable properties, it is a Type 1 PHE[33]. A Type 2 PHE, on the other hand, is an entity which *indirectly* owns prescribed immovable properties through one or more Type 1 PHE[34], in which it has a "significant stake". The threshold of 50% similarly applies[35].

In determining whether an entity has a "significant stake" in one or more Type 1 PHE, a threshold of 50% equity interests applies. In other words, an underlying Type 1 PHE held directly or indirectly by an entity is to be disregarded, unless the entity holds a significant stake of at least 50% in the underlying Type 1 PHE (whether through multiple chains of entities or otherwise).

The concept of "significant stake" is set out under sections 23(13) to (16) of the Stamp Duties Act and takes into account the direct/indirect beneficial ownership which one entity has in another entity[36]. As an

---

[32] S 23(21) of the Stamp Duties Act.

[33] S 23(13)(a) of the Stamp Duties Act and para 4(3) of the Stamp Duties (Section 23) Order 2017, S 100/2017.

[34] A Type 2 PHE may also directly hold prescribed immovable properties.

[35] In the case of a Type 2 PHE, the calculation is to be computed by reference to (i) the sum of the market value of prescribed immovable properties held by the entity and proportionate market value of prescribed immovable property held through Type 1 PHE which the entity has a significant stake of at least 50%, divided by (ii) the sum of the entity's total tangible assets and proportionate total tangible assets of the Type 1 PHE which the entity has a significant stake of at least 50%. See s 23(13)(b) of the Stamp Duties Act and para 4(4) of the Stamp Duties (Section 23) Order 2017, S 100/2017.

[36] S 23(13) to (19) of the Stamp Duties Act.

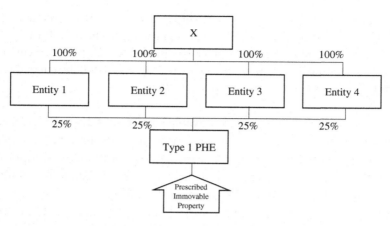

Figure 3:   Determination of "significant stake".

illustration (see Figure 3), an entity (X) may own a significant stake of 100% in 4 other entities, each of which owns a 25% stake in a Type 1 PHE. While each of the 4 other entities does not have a significant stake in the Type 1 PHE, the ACD legislation provides that all the equity interests, directly and indirectly held by the entity (X), are to be added together, for the purposes of determining whether it has a significant stake in the underlying Type 1 PHE[37]. Accordingly, in the example illustrated in Figure 3, the entity X has a significant stake in the Type 1 PHE.

In the above example, the prescribed immovable properties held indirectly through the various layers of intermediate entities are to be taken into account for the purpose of determining the 50% prescribed immovable property threshold for the entity in question (i.e. X).

2.4.3. *Equity interest*

An "equity interest" in relation to an entity is defined in section 23(21) of the Stamp Duties Act. "Equity interest" is defined to mean the issued share (but not a treasury share) where the entity is a company, and a "share" in the partnership in the case where the entity is a partnership, limited partnership or limited liability partnership, and a "unit" where the entity is a property trust.

---

[37] S 23(16) to (19) of the Stamp Duties Act.

For a company, the "equity interest" will include ordinary shares and preference shares. The debt instrument issued by a company will thus not fall under "equity interest". The word "share" in a partnership, limited partnership or limited liability partnership or a "unit" in a property trust, are also defined in section 23(21) of the Stamp Duties Act, and the definitions are as follows:

> "share", in relation to a partnership, limited partnership or limited liability partnership, means —
> - (a) the proportion of the partnership property that a partner is entitled to on the dissolution or winding up of the partnership, as specified in the partnership agreement; or
> - (b) if none is specified, the proportion of the profits of the partnership that a partner is entitled to;
>
> "unit", in relation to a property trust, means —
> - (a) a share in the beneficial ownership in the property subject to the trust; or
> - (b) a share in the profits, income or other payments or returns from the management of the property or operation of the business premised on the property.

It is to be noted that even where the "unit" of a property trust does not entitle the "unit holder" to a share in the beneficial ownership in the property subject to the trust, it is still treated as an "equity interest" for the purposes of ACD where the "unit" provides the "unit holder" with a share in the profits, income or other payments or returns from the management of the property or operation of the business which are accommodated at the property.

2.4.4. Significant owner

A significant owner of a PHE is a person who beneficially owns at least 50% of the equity interests in the entity[38]. The 50% threshold may also be

---

[38] S 23(11)(a) of the Stamp Duties Act and para 4(1) of the Stamp Duties (Section 23) Order 2017, S 100/2017.

separately determined with reference to the voting power held by the person in the PHE[39].

A person who is or becomes a significant owner of a PHE immediately after the execution of instrument for the acquisition of equity interests in the PHE will be subject to ACDB[40]. In addition, a person who is (or was) a significant owner of a PHE, will be subject to ACDS[41], if he or she executes an instrument for the sale of equity interest in a PHE within 3 years of acquisition.

As a person may nevertheless avoid the condition of "significant owner" by arranging for others (referred to as "associates") to acquire or dispose some of the equity interests, detailed rules have been prescribed to counter the "avoidance effect" of such arrangement. In determining whether a person,

(a) is a "significant owner", equity interests beneficially owned by the person's "associates" in the entity, are treated as beneficially owned by the person[42]; and

(b) becomes a "significant owner", equity interests beneficially owned by the person's "associates" (including those conveyed, transferred, assigned or agreed to the sold to the person's "associates"), at or around the same time as the time of execution of the conveyance to the person, are treated as beneficially owned by the person[43].

---

[39] S 23(11)(b) of the Stamp Duties Act and para 4(2) of the Stamp Duties (Section 23 Order) 2017, S 100/2017.

[40] In s 23 of the Stamp Duties Act, ACDB is referred to as duty A (where the grantee is or becomes a 'significant owner' of the target entity and does not have related interests in other entities) and duty C (where the grantee besides being or becoming a 'significant owner' of the target entity, also has related interest in other entities). In determining the incidence of duty C, the holdings of the grantee in the other entities are also taken into account, and duty C is chargeable where the target entity and the other entities would have been a PHE, had they been a single entity.

[41] In s 23 of the Stamp Duties Act, ACDS is referred to as duty B (where the grantor is a 'significant owner' of the target entity and does not have related interests in other entities) and duty D (where the grantor besides being a 'significant owner' of the target entity, also has related interests in other entities. In determining the incidence of duty D, the holdings of the grantor in the other entities are also taken into account, and duty D is chargeable where the target entity and the other entities would have been a PHE, had they been a single entity.

[42] S 23(12)(a) of the Stamp Duties Act.

[43] S 23(12)(b) of the Stamp Duties Act.

In other words, for the purposes of determining whether a person is a significant owner of an entity, the 50% equity interest threshold is to be determined by taking into account the equity interests in the PHE held by the person and all his associates. This will in turn have an impact on whether ACD is triggered as well as the quantum of ACD payable.

2.4.5. *Associates*

The term "associate" is defined very broadly[44]. A person is an associate of another person if the first-mentioned person is the spouse, parent, grandparent, child, grandchild or sibling of the second-mentioned person. Two persons who are partners in a partnership, limited partnership or limited liability partnership will also be regarded as associates of each other.

Apart from the abovementioned scenarios, a person (i.e. an entity or an individual) is associated with another entity if the first-mentioned person beneficially owns the voting capital and voting power in the second-mentioned entity to a significant extent (see Figure 4 for illustration). Two entities are also associated with one another if a third person (i.e. an entity or an individual) beneficially owns the voting capital and voting power in the two entities to a significant extent (see Figure 5 for illustration).

For the purposes of determining whether such an associate relationship exists, the term "significant extent" is defined to be at least 75% of the voting capital of an entity and more than 50% of the voting power of an entity[45].

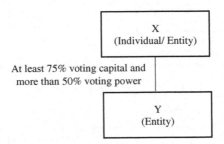

Figure 4: Determination of "associates".

---

[44] S 23(20) of the Stamp Duties Act.
[45] Para 6 of Stamp Duties (Section 23) Order 2017, S 100/2017.

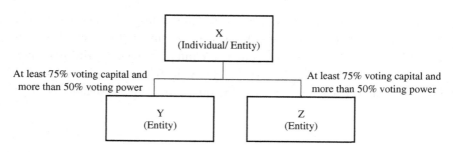

Figure 5: Determination of "associates".

Where there is one or more chain linking the two entities, each entity in the chain must directly own the entity immediately below it in the chain to a significant extent, in order for the two entities to be "associated".

As an exception to the general rule, the entity immediately above the lowest tiered entity, is not required to beneficially own the voting capital and voting power of the lowest tiered entity directly and to a significant extent. The exception rule is illustrated in Figure 6 where W and Z are

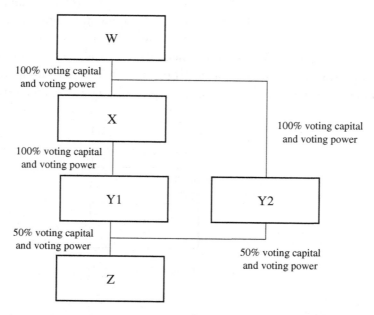

Figure 6: Determination of "associates" — exception rules.

associates even though the entities Y1 and Y2 (which are immediately above the lowest tiered entity, Z) does not beneficially own the voting capital and voting power of Z to a significant extent of 75% voting capital and more than 50% voting power in Z.

Apart from the above, the term "associate" also includes a person with whom another person has an agreement or arrangement, whether oral or in writing and whether express or implied, to act together with respect to the acquisition, holding or disposal of equity interests in, or with respect to the exercise of their votes in relation to, the entity in question. These "acting in concert" provisions in the ACD legislation[46] are widely crafted and may need some discussion.

Broadly speaking, the "acting in concert" provisions contemplate the following situations:

(a) Concert parties may act together to acquire more than 50% of the shares of a company and avoid the incidence of ACDB on the acquisition of the shares if there is no statutory provision to treat them as acting together. The percentages of shares owned by the concert parties after the acquisition, are therefore to be added together to determine if ACDB applies on the acquisition of shares; or

(b) Concert parties which together own more than 50% of the shares of a company, may dispose of their shares in a company, and avoid the incidence of ACDS on the disposal of shares within the specified 3-year holding period. The percentages of shares owned by the concert parties are therefore to be added together to determine if the ACDS applies on the disposal of shares.

In other words, the "acting in concert" provisions contemplate a situation where parties act together from the same side, i.e. either in acquiring or in disposing the shares. The "acting in concert" provisions do not contemplate a situation where a seller and a buyer may be said to be "acting in concert" in the same transaction with the seller selling and the buyer buying, as quite obviously if the parties are to enter into a transaction, they have to come to an agreement.

---

[46] S 23(20)(c) of the Stamp Duties Act.

2.5. ACD rates

ACD is imposed in addition to the existing 0.2% stamp duty imposed on the acquisition of shares. The applicable ACDB rate is intended to mirror the BSD and ABSD rates imposed on the acquisition of residential real estate whereas the ACDS rate is intended to mirror the SSD rate imposed on the disposal of residential real estate. When the ACD regime first came into operation on 11 March 2017, the ACDB payable by buyers was of up to 18% whereas the ACDS payable by sellers was 12%, in line with the then existing BSD, ABSD and SSD rates.

Over the years, ACDB first crept up to 19% (from 20 February 2018) before jumping to 34% (from 6 July 2018) and most recently to 44% (from 16 December 2021), as shown in Table 1. The ACDS rate has however remained at 12% since its introduction on 11 March 2017, as shown in Table 2.

The duty is levied on the prevailing market value of the underlying "residential" properties (more accurately referred to as "prescribed immovable properties"[47]) held by the PHE, and is to be pro-rated based on the percentage of equity interest acquired or disposed of. The value of the underlying

Table 1:   ACDB, BSD and ABSD rates over the years.

	From 11 March 2017	From 20 February 2018	From 6 July 2018	From 16 December 2021
ACDB rate	Up to 18%	Up to 19%	Up to 34%	Up to 44%
BSD rate	Up to 3%	Up to 4%	Up to 4%	Up to 4%
ABSD rate	15%	15%	30%	40%

Table 2:   ACDS and SSD rates over the years.

	From 11 March 2017	From 20 February 2018	From 6 July 2018	From 16 December 2021
ACDS rate	12%	12%	12%	12%
SSD rate	12%	12%	12%	12%

---

[47] See Section 2.4.1 for further details on 'prescribed immovable properties'.

residential property is in turn dependent on the component of the prescribed immovable property deemed attributable for residential purposes[48].

Where the prescribed immovable property directly/indirectly owned by the PHE is a vacant land or an entire building with land, the component deemed "residential" by the Commissioner of Stamp Duties is as indicated in Table 3[49]:

Table 3: "Residential" component.

Zoning of the Land	Component Deemed Residential
Residential	100% of the gross floor area
Residential/Institution	100% of the gross floor area
White	100% of the gross floor area
Commercial and Residential	60% of the gross floor area
Residential with Commercial at 1st storey	Total gross floor area less the minimum gross floor area which must be set aside for commercial uses under the Master Plan

On the other hand, where the prescribed immovable property directly/indirectly owned by the PHE is part of an entire building, the component of the property deemed residential by the Commissioner of Stamp Duties is the part of the property permitted for residential use.

2.6. Anti-avoidance provisions

The ACD regime contains various provisions which are aimed at counteracting the effects of arrangements put in place to avoid ACD. In particular, the anti-avoidance provisions are targeted at certain arrangements[50] which have the effect of increasing or reducing a person's equity interests in a PHE (whether in terms of absolute amount or percentage), where ACD would otherwise have been chargeable had the equity interests been conveyed to or by the person.

---

[48] See Article 3A to the First Schedule of the Stamp Duties Act, which provides that 'In this Article, the market value of the underlying property of a PHE is the amount of the value of the part of the property that is attributable to a residential purpose, as defined in paragraphs (2A), (2B) and (2C) of Article 3.'

[49] Article 3A to the First Schedule of the Stamp Duties Act read with paras (2A), (2B) and (2C) of Article 3.

[50] Such arrangements may or may not involve the execution of an instrument.

Such arrangements include (amongst others) (i) an acquisition by an entity of its equity interests, (ii) an issue by an entity of equity interests, (iii) a cancellation or redemption of equity interests in an entity, (iv) the conversion of equity interests into instruments that are not equity interests, (v) the conversion of instruments that are not equity interests into equity interests, (vi) the conversion of equity interests from one class to another class, (vii) the conversion of an entity to another type of entity, (viii) a change of partners of a partnership, limited partnership or limited liability partnership, (ix) an amalgamation of entities and (x) any other arrangement that, in the Commissioner's opinion, has as its purpose or one of its purposes the effect of increasing or reducing a person's equity interests in a PHE.

It is to be noted that a person who may be liable to pay ACDB or ACDS in respect of any of the abovementioned arrangements, will have to give a notice of the arrangement in the form prescribed by the Commissioner of Stamp Duties[51]. The matters as set out above are generally those that are within the knowledge of the persons concerned and they will be able to give the required notice. However, in respect of "any other arrangement that in the Commissioner's opinion, has as its purpose or one of its purposes the effect of increasing or reducing a person's equity interests in a PHE", quite obviously, a person will not be able to provide any notice of arrangement, as he is not in the position to determine the Commissioner's opinion.

In another provision which seems to be an over-kill or an attempt at catching the "unknown unknown", section 23C(9) also provides that an "equivalent arrangement" may be prescribed for the purposes of implementing the ACD regime under sections 23, 23A and 23B of the Stamp Duties Act. The "equivalent arrangement", which is yet to be prescribed, shall have effect even if it is carried out for *bona fide* commercial reason[52].

The abovementioned anti-avoidance provisions, which are set out in section 23C of the Stamp Duties Act, are cast widely like a driftnet and in the process they catch both targeted "arrangements" and non-targeted "arrangements". For example, technically where a sole shareholder of a PHE

---

[51] Para 7 of the Stamp Duties (Section 23) Order 2017, S 100/2017 and s 23C(3) of the Stamp Duties Act.

[52] The word 'arrangement' for the purposes of section 23C is defined in s 23C(11) to mean 'any scheme, trust, grant, covenant, agreement, disposition or transaction, whether or not it is or is part of a business or family dealing or is carried out for a bona fide commercial reason, and includes all steps by which it is carried into effect'.

injects equity capital into the PHE, and he gets additional shares in the PHE, ACDB is applicable based on a plain reading of the language of the legislation[53]. Similarly, where joint venture partners proportionately inject equity capital into a PHE of which they are joint shareholders, and they get proportionate shares of the PHE in return, ACDB is applicable based on a plain reading of the language of the legislation. This cannot be the legislative intent, as none of the shareholders concerned acquired any additional interests in the PHE.

In light of the extremely broad anti-avoidance provisions of the ACD regime, the Commissioner of Stamp Duties has since clarified that he is satisfied that an issuance of equity interest for capitalization purposes will not be subject to ACD, provided that there are no changes in the persons holding the equity interests and their respective proportions of holdings of equity interests, before and after the issuance. Accordingly, there is no longer any need to seek the Commissioner's opinion on the non-application of the ACD provisions for such a situation[54].

Notably, the term "arrangement" in the context of the anti-avoidance provisions under ACD rules, does not take into account whether the arrangement is carried out for a *bona fide* commercial reason[55]. This is in stark contrast with the general anti-avoidance provisions in section 33A of the Stamp Duties Act, where the existence of a *bona fide* commercial reason is a defense against the invocation of the anti-avoidance provision. Presumably, regardless of whether there exists any *bona fide* commercial reason behind the purported arrangement, the legislative intent is to confer the Commissioner of Stamp Duties with the discretionary powers to align the stamp duty rate differential pertaining to a direct sale of residential real estate *vis-à-vis* an indirect sale of residential real estate, which is purportedly the intention of introducing ACD.

It is also worthwhile noting that where an arrangement results in a change in composition of the tangible assets of an entity, such that the entity ceases to be a PHE, the Commissioner of Stamp Duties has the powers to

---

[53] S 23C(1) and (3) of the Stamp Duties Act.

[54] IRAS e-Tax Guide, *Stamp Duty: Additional Conveyance Duties on Property Holding Entities*, Third Edition, 5 July 2018.

[55] S 23C(11) of the Stamp Duties Act.

disregard such an arrangement which took place within one year of the execution of the instrument (which would otherwise not be chargeable with ACD if not for the anti-avoidance provision). An exception however applies if the Commissioner of Stamp Duties is of the opinion that the arrangement was not (whether solely or partly) carried out for the purpose of avoiding the liability to pay ACD. Presumably, the aforementioned exception rules would allow the anti-avoidance rules to be disapplied in situations where the change in composition of the tangible assets of the PHE was due to reasons such as the outright disposal of the underlying prescribed immovable properties.

3. Stamp Duty

We next turn to the 0.2% stamp duty (sometimes referred to as "conveyance duty" or share duty") imposed on executed instruments for the sale or transfer of shares in real estate holding entities. The duty rate of 0.2% is imposed on the higher of the consideration payable and the value of the shares, and is significantly lower than the rate payable in respect of instruments executed for the direct sale or transfer of immovable property[56].

The stamp duty is payable within 14 days of executing the instrument (if executed in Singapore) or 30 days of receiving the executed instrument in Singapore (if executed outside Singapore).

3.1. Advancement of the duty point from the transfer instrument to the sale and purchase agreement

In connection with the introduction of ACD on 11 March 2017, an amendment[57] was also made to section 22(1)(b) of the Stamp Duties Act, such that an executed contract (e.g. a sale and purchase agreement) for sale of shares would attract stamp duty. Prior to the amendment, the execution of a contract relating to the sale of shares would not trigger stamp duty, and

---

[56] The highest marginal stamp duty rate in respect of the transfer of residential property and non-residential property is currently 4% and 3%, respectively. The stamp duty rate differential between the direct transfer of residential property and the indirect transfer of residential property (via the transfer of shares in PHE), has since been equalized with the introduction of ACD on 11 March 2017.

[57] The words 'and stock or shares' were deleted from s 22(1)(b). See Stamp Duties (Amendment) Act 2017, Act 13 of 2017.

stamp duty would only be triggered by the execution of the share transfer instrument (also known as the share transfer form). In other words, with the amendment of the Stamp Duties Act, which came into operation with effect on 11 March 2017, the incidence of stamp duty for all share transactions (i.e. regardless of whether ACD would be triggered) would be advanced to the executed contract or agreement, instead of the executed transfer instrument.

The advancement of the stamp duty point to the execution of the contract, however, brought about much complications for share transactions which do not attract ACD, such as those which do not involve underlying residential property. This eventually led to the enactment of the Stamp Duties (Agreements for Sale of Equity Interests) (Remission) Rule 2018[58] which provides for the automatic remission of stamp duty payable in respect of sale and purchase agreement, in instances where ACD is not applicable.

Further details of the remission rules are set out in the next section.

3.2. Remission of stamp duty payable in respect of the sale and purchase agreement

A share deal between two unrelated parties typically involves a "completion period" during which the transferor and transferee are usually required to fulfil certain conditions precedent or pre-completion conditions (such as obtaining shareholders and/or directors' approval, or seeking the requisite approval from regulatory bodies). The transferee may also make use of the completion period to complete the necessary due diligence work. In the event that the conditions precedent are not satisfied, the transacting parties may abort or call off the share deal, and not proceed with the share transfer.

Prior to 11 March 2017, the execution of a sale and purchase agreement in respect of Singapore shares would generally not attract stamp duty. Instead, the instrument chargeable to stamp duty was the transfer instrument (i.e. the share transfer form which effects the share transfer).

However, with the advancement of the duty point to the sale and purchase agreement (see Section 3.1), stamp duty would have already been paid following the execution of the sale and purchase agreement. In the event that the transacting parties decided not to proceed with the share transfer,

---

[58] S 201/2018.

the transferee may then had to write to the Commissioner of Stamp Duties to seek a refund of the stamp duty paid, subject to meeting the relevant conditions[59]. This situation is now avoided with the remission of stamp duty on the executed agreement in respect of non-ACD cases, as discussed below.

The amendment of section 22(1)(b) in the Stamp Duties (Amendment) Act in March 2017, had at least one other inadvertent effect. By advancing the incidence of the duty to the sale and purchase agreement for share transactions, the acquisition and disposal of shares listed on the Singapore Exchange, also became subject to stamp duty, where a contract or agreement was entered into in respect of a transaction involving the sale and purchase of shares listed on the Singapore Exchange. This may be the situation in the case of a married deal involving the vendor and buyer of such listed shares, where the parties enter into a written agreement for the transaction.

Before the amendment of s 22(1)(b) on 11 March 2017, in respect of share transactions, the chargeable instrument was the transfer instrument, but not the sale and purchase agreement. There is generally no transfer instrument with respect to scripless shares listed on the Singapore Exchange, as the legal owner of the shares is the Central Depository (Pte) Ltd and the settlement of the transaction is by way of book entries. Hence, the execution of a transfer instrument[60] is not required and no stamp duty is therefore chargeable in respect of transactions of shares listed on the Singapore Exchange.

In light of the unintended consequences caused by the advancement of the stamp duty point to the execution of the contract, stamp duty remission had been granted with effect from 11 April 2018 (slightly more than a year after the 2017 amendment of section 22(1)(b)), in respect of executed contracts or agreements for:

(1) The sale of shares in non-ACD cases[61] — With the remission, the chargeable instrument for share transactions for non-ACD cases, effectively reverts to the transfer instrument (which was the case, pre 11 March 2017).

---

[59] See s 57 and s 75 of the Stamp Duties Act.

[60] In *The Enterprise III Fund Ltd and others v OUE Lippo Healthcare Limited*, [2019] 2 SLR 524, the Court of Appeal noted at [98] 'transfers of [scripless] shares are made by way of book-entry in the Depository Register and not by way of an instrument of transfer'.

[61] Under r 2 of the Stamp Duties (Agreements for Sale of Equity Interests) (Remission) Rules 2018, S 201/2018.

(2) The sale of listed shares where ACD would otherwise be applicable[62] — With the remission, stamp duty (including ACD) is no longer payable on the contract or agreement for the sale of any listed shares (referred to as book-entry securities, in the remission rules). Such remission reflects the policy that stamp duty and ACD are not to be charged on any contract or agreement pertaining to shares of companies listed on the Singapore Exchange, even where the companies are PHEs.

Given that the execution of a physical transfer instrument is also not required in respect of scripless shares listed on the Singapore Exchange, stamp duty and ACD are effectively not applicable to transactions involving shares listed on the Singapore Exchange from 11 April 2018 (which was the case pre-11 March 2017)[63].

3.3. Stamp duty on deferred consideration and earn-outs[64]

Another stamp duty issue commonly encountered in relation to the acquisition and disposal of real estate holding entities, is that relating to deferred consideration and earn-outs.

The consideration payable in respect of a share transaction is normally set out in the sale and purchase agreement and/or share transfer form. However, the total consideration in respect of the share transaction may not always be payable at the time of executing the share transfer instrument. This could be due to various *bona fide* commercial reasons, such as the deferment of the payment of the consideration for cashflow optimization reasons. The delayed payment of the full consideration could also be due to the fact that the final consideration would only be determined after the completion of the share transfer (e.g. at such time when the finalized version of the completion accounts prepared up to and including the completion date is ready and post-completion adjustments are made to the consideration, e.g. one month after the completion of the share transfer).

---

[62] Under r 2 and 3 of the Stamp Duties (Agreements for Sale of Equity Interests) (Remission) Rules 2018, S 201/2018.

[63] The electronic transfer of scripless shares listed on the Singapore Exchange is exempt under the Stamp Duties (Exempt Record) Rules 2018, S657/2018.

[64] See Tan Kay Kheng and Leung Yew Kwong, *LexisNexis Annotated Statutes of Singapore: Stamp Duties Act 2015* (LexisNexis, 2015), for further details. The 2022 edition of the book is available in electronic version from the publisher.

In other instances, total consideration may be unascertainable as earn-outs could be payable after the completion of the transaction, based on a future contingency or event (e.g. the earnings of the target company in a future year after the completion of the share transfer). It is to be noted that stamp duty is a tax assessed on the basis of the circumstances existing at the time that the chargeable instrument is executed[65], and the liability to duty cannot be altered or affected by subsequent events[66]. In this regard, stamp duty may not be levied on a chargeable instrument by reference to the amount of consideration which is unascertainable at the time when the instrument is executed[67].

That said, where the consideration payable is merely uncertain (as opposed to unascertainable), stamp duty is assessed on the sum which may become payable and which can be calculated in advance as at the time of execution. For example, in the situation where the quantum of consideration, payable based on the value of the target shares as at the date of transfer, may only be finalised and fixed after the completion of the share transfer (e.g. one month after the completion of the share transfer), stamp duty should nevertheless be payable within the stipulated deadline of 14 days[68]/30 days[69] based on the initial or estimated quantum of consideration agreed between the transacting parties (e.g. based on the completion accounts prepared up to 3 months before the completion date).

Subsequently, when the quantum of consideration is finalised and determined after the completion of the share transfer, upstamping (i.e. topping up the stamp duty shortfall) may be required where the actual amount of stamp duty payable is higher than that earlier paid. On the other hand, where the actual amount of stamp duty payable is lower than that earlier paid, a refund may be sought within 6 months of the execution of the share transfer, subject to meeting the relevant conditions[70]. In such instances, the recommended practice is for the share transfer form to make reference

---

[65] See *William Cory & Son Ltd v IRC*, [1965] AC 1088, at 1105 and 1109 *per* Lord Reid and Lord Donovan respectively.

[66] *Carlill v Carbolic Smokeball Co*, [1892] 2 QB 484.

[67] *Per* Carnwath J in *LM Tenancies 1 plc v IRC*, [1996] STC 880, at 884.

[68] 14 days of executing the instrument is in Singapore.

[69] 30 days of receiving the executed instrument in Singapore, where the instrument is executed outside Singapore.

[70] See s 57 and s 75 of the Stamp Duties Act.

to the consideration clause of the sale and purchase agreement (as opposed to indicating the quantum of the initial or estimated consideration), so as to avoid the need of subsequently amending the share transfer form when the final quantum of consideration is determined.

In the scenario where the instrument provides for the payment of an earn-out which is unascertainable as at the date of execution of the instrument (e.g. no specific quantum of earn-out is stated and the formula does not provide for a minimum or maximum amount — such as where the earn-out is based on X% of profit before tax one year after the completion of the share transfer), no stamp duty is chargeable in respect of the earn-out, under the contingency principle of stamp duty[71].

However, where it is possible to ascertain from the instrument a fixed sum of earn-out which may be payable, though subject to contingencies, stamp duty will be charged on that amount. This may be a minimum or a maximum amount, or a specified sum subject to increase or decrease.

More specifically, where there is a definite minimum earn-out payable, stamp duty is payable in respect of the minimum earn-out. On the other hand, where there is a maximum earn-out payable, stamp duty is payable in respect of the maximum earn-out, regardless of whether the maximum earn-out is likely to be payable or not[72]. In the scenario where there are both definite maximum and minimum earn-outs stipulated under the transaction document, stamp duty is payable on the maximum sum.

3.4. Stamp duty and partnership interests

The limited partnership is generally recognized as the preferred investment vehicle for private funds, in view of the limited liability accorded to investors as well as the contractual flexibility and tax transparent treatment of the limited partnership. With respect to the subscription, transfer and redemption of a limited partner's interest in a Singapore limited partnership where the underlying assets of the limited partnership comprise Singapore real estate and shares of Singapore-incorporated companies, it seems that

---

[71] See: *Independent Television Authority v IRC*, [1961] AC 427, at 443 and *IRC v Coventry City Council*, [1978] STC 151.

[72] *Underground Electric Railways v IRC*, [1906] AC 21.

the practice of the Commissioner of Stamp Duties is that no stamp duty is chargeable on the instruments for such subscription, transfer or redemption.

For an understanding of the basis of the practice, we have to first understand the nature of the Singapore limited partnership. The Singapore limited partnership does not have a separate legal personality and is governed by the Limited Partnerships Act[73]. Section 4(1) of the Limited Partnerships Act reads as follows:

> Subject to the provisions of this Act, the Partnership Act 1890 and the rules of equity and common law applicable to partnerships (except so far as they are inconsistent with the express provisions of the Partnership Act 1890) shall apply to limited partnerships.

In this regard case law pertaining the nature of a partner's interest in the partnership property of a general partnership, is instructive as to the nature of a limited partner's interest in the partnership property of a limited partnership. With respect to the nature of the partner's interest in the partnership property of a general partnership, Sundaresh Menon CJ in delivering the judgment of the Court of Appeal in *Chiam Heng Hsien (on his own behalf and as partner of Mitre Hotel Proprietors) v Chiam Heng Chow (executor of the estate of Chiam Toh Say, deceased) and others*[74], said:

> [116] It is apparent from these cases that there are two periods in the life of the partnership — first, while it is continuing, and, second, after a general dissolution; and there is both an internal and an external perspective of the nature of a partner's interest in partnership property. During the continuation of the partnership, and as against the outside world, the partners are *collectively* entitled to each and every asset of the partnership in which each of them has an undivided share. However, as between themselves, none of the partners are entitled *individually* to assert proprietary rights over any specific part of the partnership property to the exclusion of the other partners. This follows from their having subjected

---

[73] Cap 163B.
[74] [2015] 4 SLR 180.

their proprietary interests to the terms of the partnership agreement. Therefore, each partner's interest in the partnership property is in the nature of an interest in their use and application for the benefit of the partnership until the time of its determination. At such time, each partner's beneficial interest in the partnership property will, unless the partners have agreed otherwise, take effect by the division of any surplus (after the settlement of the debts and liabilities) amongst the partners in their proportionate share.

[117] The nature of the partner's interest in the partnership property in relation to the other partners is the result of the implied agreement between the partners that all partnership property (including land) will be sold upon the dissolution of the partnership and which equity deems to have been performed. Hence, in the absence of any agreement to the contrary, the default position is that a partner's share in the partnership property as against the other partners is a proportionate share in the net proceeds of sale of the partnership property after all the firm's debts and liabilities have been paid or provided for upon dissolution.

[118] Because of this, the traditional view in the common law has been to treat the partner's interest in the partnership property as an equitable chose in action (*ie*, a right enforceable by action or the right of action itself) .... What is pertinent, however, is that they do not support the conclusion that a partner (or his personal representatives) can demand as against the other partners that any particular partnership asset (or a share thereof) be transferred to him (or his personal representatives).

In the view of the authors therefore, the nature of the limited partner's interest in the partnership property of a limited partnership generally does not confer the limited partner with any equitable, beneficial or proprietary interest in specific underlying assets of the limited partnership. Such a characterization of the nature of the partner's interest, which is a chose in action, supports the stand of the Commissioner of Stamp Duties that the subscription, transfer and redemption of the limited partnership's interest in a limited partnership do not attract stamp duty, even where the underlying assets of the limited partnership comprise Singapore real estate or shares of Singapore-incorporated companies.

3.5. Relief from stamp duty

Where stamp duty is payable in respect of the transfer of Singapore shares[75] (other than in scenarios where ACD is imposed), relief from stamp duty may be available under certain prescribed scenarios[76]. These include scenarios involving (1) a transfer of undertaking under a scheme of reconstruction or amalgamation of companies[77] or (2) a transfer of assets between associated permitted entities[78]. The relief framework in respect of the transfer of Singapore shares is the same as that for the relief of BSD arising from the transfer of Singapore immovable property as set out in Section 2.1.2 of Chapter 6, and includes Reconstruction relief, Amalgamation relief and Transfer of Assets relief.

4. Income Tax

Apart from stamp duty and ACD, another tax which is applicable to the acquisition and disposal of real estate holding entities, is income tax.

4.1. Badges of trade test

Where a person derives any gain from the disposal of a real estate holding entity, the gain could be subject to income tax, to the extent that the gain is revenue in nature. On the other hand, where the gain is capital in nature, no tax is to be imposed. The tax legislation however does not specifically define what constitute revenue or capital gains. In this regard, whenever a gain is realized on the disposal of an asset (such as shares of a real estate holding company), the practice is to rely upon a set of commonly-applied

---

[75] See Section 2.1.2 of Chapter 6 for a discussion on the relief of stamp duty arising from instruments executed for the sale/transfer of Singapore real estate.

[76] S 15 of the Stamp Duties Act. For a detailed discussion on the stamp duty relief provisions under the Stamp Duties Act, see Tan Kay Kheng and Leung Yew Kwong, *LexisNexis Annotated Statutes of Singapore: Stamp Duties Act 2015* (LexisNexis, 2015). The 2022 edition of the book is available in electronic version from the publisher.

[77] Stamp Duties (Relief from Stamp Duty upon Reconstruction or Amalgamation of Companies) Rules (R 3).

[78] Stamp Duties (Relief from Stamp Duty upon Transfer of Assets between Associated Permitted Entities) Rules 2014 (S 28/2014).

rules (referred to as the "badges of trade") to characterize whether the gain is revenue or capital in nature.

The badges of trade test[79] includes an examination of the following factors: (i) subject matter (i.e. what is the nature of the asset in question), (ii) frequency of similar transactions entered into by the taxpayer, (iii) length of ownership of the disposed asset, (iv) circumstances leading to the disposal of the asset, (v) motive of the taxpayer, and (vi) whether supplementary work was carried out prior to disposing the asset. The "badges of trade" are not necessarily conclusive on their own, and depending on the circumstances, there may be other relevant factors that may be taken in account in characterizing the nature of the gain. In addition, whilst certain badges may carry more weight than others, the badges are generally looked upon holistically in their totality (together with all other relevant circumstantial evidence) in order to determine the character of the gain.

In view of the complexity involved in the application of the badges of trade test, and in order to provide a greater certainty to taxpayers on the tax treatment of gains derived on the disposal of their equity investments, a safe harbour rule has been in force with effect from 1 June 2012.

4.2. Safe harbour rule

Under the safe harbour rule in section 13W of the Income Tax Act, gains derived by a company from the disposal of ordinary shares in another company will be exempt from Singapore income tax if the divesting company directly and beneficially held at least 20% of the ordinary shares in the investee company (i.e. target company) at all times during a continuous period of 24 months immediately prior to the disposal of such shares. The safe harbour rule is applicable for disposal of ordinary shares during the period between 1 June 2012 and 31 December 2027 (both dates inclusive), regardless of the country of incorporation or tax residency of the investee company.

It is however to be noted that the disposal of shares in an unlisted investee company that is in the business of trading or holding Singapore immovable properties (other than the business of property development)

---

[79] For a more detailed discussion of the 'badges of trade' test, please see Section 3.2.1 of Chapter 6.

is specifically excluded from the safe harbour rule. In other words, while the disposal of shares of listed companies that trade or hold Singapore real estate could qualify for the safe harbour rule, the disposal of shares in an unlisted company which holds Singapore real estate for investment or trading purposes would not be accorded the benefit of the safe harbour rule. An exception is however available if the disposed shares are unlisted shares in a company which is in the business of property development.

In the recent Singapore annual Budget Statement released on 18 February 2020, it was announced that the safe harbour rule would be further tightened and would no longer be available to disposals of unlisted shares that is in the business of trading, holding or developing immovable properties in Singapore or abroad, with effect from 1 June 2022. The rationale provided for the change was "to ensure consistency in the tax treatment for property-related businesses". It is however puzzling as to why the exclusion should be extended to companies which invest or trade in overseas real estate, when the policy has always been to encourage Singapore companies to venture or invest abroad. This is especially so given that such trading, holding or development of overseas real estate does not in any way contradict the measures put in place to cool the local real estate market.

Under the Income Tax (Amendment) Act 2020, section 13W(8)(ba) has been inserted to exclude the following disposals from the safe harbour rule:

> the disposal of shares on or after 1 June 2022 not listed on a stock exchange in Singapore or elsewhere, being shares in a company that the Comptroller is satisfied —
>> (i) is in the business of trading immovable properties situated whether in Singapore or elsewhere;
>> (ii) principally carries on the activity of holding immovable properties situated whether in Singapore or elsewhere; or
>> (iii) has undertaken property development, except where —
>>> (A) the immovable property developed is used by the company to carry on its trade or business (including the business of letting immovable properties), not being a business mentioned in sub-paragraph (i); and

> (B) the company did not undertake any property development for a period of at least 60 consecutive months before the disposal of shares.

As may be seen, the gains from the disposal of shares in companies which are in business of trading immovable properties or property development, are excluded from the safe harbour rule. It is to be noted that companies which carry on the "activity of holding immovable properties" are also excluded from the safe harbour rule. However, the term "activity of holding immovable properties" in section 13W(8)(ba)(ii) is defined in section 13W(9) to exclude the "holding of immovable properties where such properties are used to carry on a trade or business, including the business of letting immovable properties". Hence, where for example, a company holds immovable property which is used by the company to operate a hotel or a data center or for the carrying on of a trade/ business involving the letting the immovable property (such as that of a company subject to tax under section 10(1)(a) of the Income Tax Act and subject to the provisions of section 10D), the disposal of the shares of such a company is not excluded from the safe harbour rule. It would therefore seem that the term "activity of holding immovable properties" is intended to cover the situation where the company merely holds the immovable property without making beneficial use of the property meanwhile, probably with the intention of selling the property.

As provided in section 13W(8)(ba)(iii), the disposal of shares of a company which has undertaken the "property development" is excluded from the safe harbour rule. The term "property development" is in turn defined in section 13W(9) to mean the:

> construction or causing the construction of any building or part of a building and acquisition of land or building for such construction, and for this purpose "construction" means —
>
> (a) any building operations, or demolition and rebuilding operations, in, on, over or under any land for the purpose of erecting a building or part of a building; and
> (b) any alteration or addition to, or partial demolition and rebuilding of, any building or part of a building,

that requires the approval of the Commissioner of Building Control under the Building Control Act 1989 or (if carried out in a country outside of Singapore) would have required such approval if it had been carried out in Singapore.

The definition of the term "property development" which envisages construction works, generally accords with what is generally envisaged in the process of "property development". The words "alteration or addition" in the definition, perhaps need some discussion. In the context of the other terms like "building operations", "demolition and rebuilding operations", "for the purpose of erecting a building or part of a building" and "partial demolition and rebuilding of any building of part of a building" in section 13W(9), the words "alteration or addition" contemplate substantial "alteration or addition" works which would require approval of the Commissioner of Building Control in the Singapore context. Minor renovation works which do not require such approvals, would not to be considered as "alteration or addition" within the meaning of section 13W(9).

Where the safe harbour rule is not available to the disposal of equity interests in a real estate holding entity, the tax treatment of such transactions will be based on the application of the badges of trade test which takes into account the facts and circumstances of the specific case.

4.3. Singapore-sourced or foreign-sourced?

Where (i) the disposal gain is assessed to be revenue in nature under the badges of trade test, and (ii) protection under the safe harbour rule is not available, it may nevertheless still be necessary to examine if the disposal gain may be regarded as having its source outside Singapore depending on the facts.

Singapore adopts a territorial basis of taxation whereby income tax is imposed in respect of Singapore-sourced income. Where the income is sourced outside Singapore, no income tax is payable, unless the foreign-sourced income is received or deemed received in Singapore[80].

Gains arising from the disposal of real estate holding entities are arguably sourced outside Singapore if the deliberation, negotiation and execution of

---

[80] The remittance basis of taxation only applies to corporates. Where an individual derives foreign-sourced income, such income is not taxable in Singapore.

the share transfer are wholly undertaken outside Singapore, such as in the case where both the buyer and the seller are non-Singapore persons situated outside Singapore. Foreign-sourced income derived by non-individuals are subject to tax on a remittance basis[81]. Where such foreign-sourced income is not received or deemed received in Singapore, no income tax is payable[82].

4.4. Other income tax related issues

Other income tax related issues commonly arising in connection with the acquisition and disposal of real estate holding companies are discussed below.

4.4.1. *No "uplifting" or "step-up" in the cost base of the underlying real estate*

In the case of the acquisition of a real estate holding company, there is no "uplifting" or "step-up" in the cost base of the underlying real estate held by the acquired company. In other words, the cost base of the underlying real estate remains unchanged in the books of the real estate holding company, for income tax purposes.

Consequently, the cost base[83] of the real estate held by the real estate holding company may be much lower than the corresponding costs of acquisition of the shares paid by the buyer of the real estate holding company. The lower historic cost of the underlying real estate may be a significant concern to the buyer of the real estate holding company, where the gains arising from the subsequent disposal of the underlying real estate is subject to income tax. In such instances, the buyer of the real estate holding company may have to negotiate for a reduction of the purchase price to take into account the potential income tax liability which may arise in the event of a future sale of the underlying real estate.

---

[81] Foreign-sourced income derived by individuals are exempt from tax unless such income is received by a tax-resident individual through a partnership. See s 13(7A) of the Income Tax Act.

[82] As an administrative concession, the IRAS is prepared not to tax foreign-sourced income received in Singapore, where such foreign-sourced income is received by foreign businesses which are not operating in or from Singapore. The concession is granted so as not to discourage foreign businesses from using Singapore's banking and fund management facilities.

[83] In general, the cost base will be the historic cost of acquisition of the real estate.

In the alternative, the buyer (who will become the new owner of the real estate holding company) may consider "kicking the can down the road", by similarly choosing to dispose of the shares of the real estate holding company to the next buyer, instead of directly disposing of the underlying real estate.

4.4.2. *Non-deductibility of interest expenses*

Another issue which commonly arises from the acquisition of a real estate holding company (as opposed to an outright acquisition of the real estate), is that the interest expense incurred on the acquisition of the shares has no tax deduction value, where the income arising from the holding of the shares is not subject to income tax. Such a scenario may arise where the future dividend income derived from the acquired shares of the real estate holding is exempt from income tax in Singapore — e.g. where the real estate holding company is tax resident in Singapore such that the dividend paid by the company is tax exempt[84]. In contrast, interest expenses incurred on the direct acquisition of real estate is generally tax deductible against the rental income generated from the letting out of the real estate.

5. Goods and Services Tax

From a goods and services tax (GST) perspective, the transfer of ownership of an equity security is an exempt supply[85]. It follows that the transfer of ownership of an equity security is exempt from GST, regardless of whether the equity security relates to the shares of a company which holds residential or non-residential real estate.

The transfer of interest in or rights to a share in the capital of a limited liability partnership (which is regarded in law as a body corporate) should similarly qualify as an exempt supply. This is on the basis that the term "equity security" has been specifically defined to mean any interest in or right to a share in the capital of a body corporate or any option to acquire

---

[84] Pursuant to s 13(1)(za) of the Income Tax Act.

[85] Para 1(f) Part 1 of the Fourth Schedule to the GST Act.

any such interest or right[86]. As for the transfer of ownership of a unit under any unit trust or business trust, such transactions should similarly be an exempt supply[87], regardless of whether the trust holds residential or non-residential real estate.

6. Property Tax

The acquisition of shares in a real estate holding company typically does not in itself have a direct impact on the property tax payable in respect of the underlying real estate. Nonetheless, it is worthwhile noting that the Chief Assessor may take into account the consideration paid or value passing on the sale of 75% or more of the issued ordinary shares of a land-owning company, in determining whether there is a need to amend the annual value of the underlying real estate[88]. In other words, the consideration paid or value passing on the sale of ordinary shares is one of the factors which the Chief Assessor may rely upon in determining whether or not to amend the annual value of the immovable property in the Valuation List. Any such amendment of the annual value will in turn have an impact on the quantum of property tax payable in respect of the underlying real estate owned by the real estate holding company. In practice, the Chief Assessor has generally not relied on the consideration passing on the sale of ordinary shares of a company for the purpose of amendment of the annual value of a property for the following reasons:

(a) There is usually sufficient sales evidence of other properties which may be used by the Chief Assessor as the basis for an amendment of the annual value of the property concerned;

(b) The sale price of the ordinary shares of a company may not be easily analysed to discern the value of the underlying real estate, as there may be various assets and liabilities of the company which affect the sale price.

---

[86] Para 1(f) of Part 1 of the Fourth Schedule to the GST Act, read together with the definition of 'equity security' in para 1 of Part III of the Fourth Schedule to the GST Act.

[87] Para 1(p) of Part 1 of the Fourth Schedule to the GST Act.

[88] S 20(2)(a)(iii) of the Property Tax Act.

7. Due Diligence Work

In the penultimate section of this chapter, we turn to the due diligence work typically carried out in connection with the acquisition of equity interests in a real estate holding company.

One of the major risks arising from the acquisition of real estate holding entities (as opposed to the outright acquisition of the real estate) is the exposure to "legacy" tax and other legal liabilities relating to activities carried on by the target company prior to being acquired by the buyer. Hence, the buyer will have to conduct due diligence work (i.e. investigative work) on the target entity. Such due diligence work may involve legal, accounting as well as tax aspects.

In respect tax due diligence work, the primary objective of such an exercise is to identify any possible tax exposure and protect the buyer of the real estate holding entity against any potential tax exposure, by any of the following actions:

(a) calling off the deal where the tax exposure is serious enough;
(b) reduction of the price of the share deal;
(c) taking up insurance for the tax exposure[89];
(d) retention of part of the price for example in an escrow account until the tax issue is resolved;
(e) seeking appropriate tax warranties, indemnities or price adjustment mechanism from the seller.

Apart from checking on the tax compliance status of the target entity, the tax due diligence process typically involves (i) identifying any under-provisioning of taxes, (ii) identifying any ongoing tax disputes, and (iii) identifying potential tax disputes or issues which may arise.

---

[89] See 'Warranty and Indemnity Insurance in Today's M&A Environment,' *The Singapore Law Gazette*, November 2010, pp. 29–32. In 'Private M&A trends: report on warranty and indemnity insurance,' *PLC Magazine*, July 2020, pp. 12–13, it is reported that W&I insurance is behind some fundamental developments in private M&A deal structure, with more 'nil' seller recourse structure and fewer escrows, and that W&I insurance challenges M&A practitioners to think in new ways about the purpose of due diligence, the function of warranties and the integrity of the disclosure process.

8. Tax Warranties and Indemnities

Following the tax due diligence, certain specific tax issues may be revealed, and the vendor and purchaser will have to come to an agreement on the allocation of the tax risks between themselves, if there is to be an agreement on the sale of the shares of the target company. This is because a purchaser who buys the shares of the target company and becomes its shareholder will effectively inherit the target company's liabilities, which include its tax liabilities which may surface after the completion of the sale. It is therefore customary for the purchaser to receive from the vendor some form of assurances (in the form of warranties and indemnities) with respect to the liabilities which affect the target company typically for the period before the completion of the sale of the shares of the target company.

8.1. Tax warranties

The warranties are normally listed in a schedule to the sale and purchase agreement. The warranties which shift the risk to the vendor and provide a means of redress to the purchaser, have a secondary purpose during the sale transaction, of serving as a checklist of those matters that the purchaser requires the vendor to check before signing the sale and purchase agreement. Some of the tax warranties that a vendor may give to the purchaser include the following:

(a) The target company has duly filed all its tax returns in compliance of the relevant tax statutes;

(b) All taxes due to be paid by the target company has been duly paid to the relevant tax authorities;

(c) There are no circumstances existing which would require or result in additional tax liability for the target company or which may require the amendment of returns filed with the relevant tax authorities;

(d) The target company has complied with the requirements of the Income Tax Act with respect to withholding tax requirements for all payments made to non-residents;

(e) There is no audit or investigation currently being undertaken by the relevant tax authorities into the tax matters of the target company; and

(f) The target company has not entered into or been engaged in or been a party to any transaction or arrangement of which the main purpose or one of the main purpose was the avoidance of tax.

A warranty is simply a term to the agreement under which the vendor warrants a particular statement of fact. In other words, it is a promise made in contract by one party to another that a state of affairs exists. If the factual situation is not as stated in the warranty, the warrantor is liable for any consequential damages. Had there been no warranty and in the absence of misrepresentation by the vendor, the purchaser would have no remedy against the vendor, in view of the doctrine of *caveat emptor.*

The warranty provides the purchaser with the means of redress based on contract, against the vendor should there be a breach of the warranty. The remedy for a breach of warranty is damages such that a purchaser must normally prove that he has suffered financial loss if he is to enforce a claim against the vendor/warrantor. The measure of the damages is the loss which could reasonably have been expected to arise at the date of the contract.

A case which concerned a breach of warranty is the Privy Council case of *Lion Nathan Ltd v CC Bottlers Ltd*[90]. In that case, there was an agreement that the defendants would sell the entire issued share capital of a soft drinks company to the claimants. The claimants brought proceedings for damages for breach of a warranty given by the defendants as to the accuracy of their forecast of the company's expected profits up to the date of completion. In that case, Lord Hoffman said at page 1441:

> This difference over construction has an important effect on the way in which damages are calculated. In the case of a warranty as to the quality of the goods, the purchaser is *prima facie* entitled to the difference between what the goods as warranted would have been worth and what they were actually worth. If the vendor had warranted that the earnings in the last two months would be $2,223,000, there would have been an

---

[90] [1996] 1 WLR 1438.

analogy with a warranty of quality and the damages would *prima facie* have been the difference between what the shares would have been worth if the earnings had been in accordance with the warranty and what they were actually worth. The Court of Appeal was saying that although the vendor had not warranted that the earnings would be $2,223,000, it had effectively warranted that the company could be valued on the assumption that they would be in the region of $2,223,000. As the region would be a range above and below the figure of $2,223,000, the reasonable buyer would value such a company, as the actual purchaser had done, on the assumption that the earnings would be the mean figure of $2,223,000. Accordingly, the measure of damages was the difference between the company valued on that basis and the actual value of the company, calculated by applying the same multiple to the actual earnings after tax.

On the other hand, if one construes paragraph 32 as a warranty that reasonable care has been taken in the preparation of the forecast, there is no analogy with a warranty of quality. The forecast, though prepared with reasonable care, may on account of unknown or unforeseeable factors turn out to be substantially inaccurate. It therefore does not warrant that the company has any particular quality. The prima facie rule for breach of a warranty of quality of goods cannot be applied. One must therefore return to the general principle of which that rule is only one example, namely that damages for breach of contract are intended to put the plaintiff in the position in which he would have been if the defendant had complied with the terms of the contract. In this case the vendor represented to the purchaser that $2,223,000 was a figure upon which he could rely in calculating the price. The figure was in fact used in the calculation of the price. If the vendor had made a forecast in accordance with the terms of the warranty, he would have produced a lower figure and the price would have been correspondingly lower. The damages are therefore the difference between the price agreed on the assumption of $2,223,000 earnings and what the price would have been, using the same method of calculation, if the forecast had been properly made.

As may be seen, the measure of damages is the difference between (i) the value of the shares purchased if the warranties had been true and (ii) the actual value of the shares in the light of the breach of warranties.

In this regard, in *Zayo Group International Limited v Michael Ainger and Others*[91], Simon Bryan QC sitting as Deputy Judge of the High Court said at [116]:

> It is well established, and not disputed by Zayo (see paragraph 77 of Zayo's Skeleton Argument), that the measure of loss for breach of warranty as to shares in a share sale and purchase agreement is the difference in value between (1) the value of shares purchased if the warranties had been true (usually, but not necessarily, the price paid), and (2) the actual value of the shares (i.e. in the light of the breach of warranty) — see, for example, *Ageas (UK) Ltd v Kwik-Fit (GB) Ltd* [2014] EWHC 2178 (QB) where Popplewell J stated as follows:
>
> The measure of loss for breach of warranty in a share sale agreement is the difference between the value of the shares as warranted and the true value of the shares: *Lion Nathan Ltd. v C-C Brothers Ltd* [1996] 1 WLR 1438, 1441F-H, *Eastgate Group Ltd v Lindsey Morden Group Inc* [2002] 1 WLR 446.

8.2. Disclosure letter

The vendor may also issue a disclosure letter to the purchaser and disclose specific information, which would, if not so disclosed, result in a breach of warranty. Hence, the disclosure letter serves to relieve the vendor of any liability in relation to matters specifically covered in the letter and shifts the specific known risk to the buyer. The purpose of such disclosure letters has been set out in some detail in the recent case of *Triumph Controls UK Ltd v Primus International Holding Company*[92], where O'Farrell J said:

> [330] The commercial purpose of such disclosure clauses is to afford a seller who wishes to avoid a breach of warranty the opportunity to give specific notice of a matter to the buyer: *Levison v Farin* [1978] 2 All ER 1149 (QBD) per Gibson J at 1157:
>
> "I do not say that facts made known by disclosure of the means of knowledge in the course of negotiation could never constitute

---

[91] [2017] EWHC 2542.
[92] [2019] EWHC 565.

disclosure for such a clause as this but I have no doubt that a clause in this form is primarily designed and intended to require a party who wishes by disclosure to avoid a breach of warranty to give specific notice for the purpose of the agreement, and a protection by disclosure will not normally be achieved by merely making known the means of knowledge which may or do enable the other party to work out certain facts and conclusions."

[331] In *Daniel Reeds Ltd v EM ESS Chemists Ltd* [1995] CLC 1405, the Court of Appeal held that an omission of a pharmaceuticals licence from a disclosure list was not sufficient to amount to fair disclosure of the fact that the licence had expired. As Beldam LJ stated:

"... fair disclosure requires some positive statement of the true position and not just a fortuitous omission from which the buyer may be expected to infer matters of significance."

[332] In *New Hearts Ltd v Cosmopolitan Investments Ltd* [1997] 2 BCLC 249 (Court of Session), Lord Penrose referred to Gibson J's comments in *Levison* and stated at pp. 258–259:

"The disclosure letter is distinguished, even in comparison with the agreement, by the obscurity of its language. It incorporates by reference a list of documents, including the last accounts and the management accounts and purports to disclose their content and terms...

This repetitive and omnibus approach of an invitation to the purchasers and their representatives to make what they will of the documents with reference to which warranties have been given by the vendors cannot by any stretch of the imagination be considered fair disclosure, with sufficient detail to identify the nature and scope of any matter purportedly disclosed...

Mere reference to a source of information, which is in itself a complex document, within which the diligent enquirer might find relevant information will not satisfy the requirements of a clause providing for fair disclosure with sufficient details to identify the nature and scope of the matter disclosed."

[333] The case of *Infiniteland Ltd v Artisan Contracting Ltd* [2005] EWCA Civ 758 concerned the construction of a share purchase agreement under

which the seller warranted that: *"the contents of the Disclosure Letter and of all accompanying documents … fully, clearly and accurately disclosed every matter to which they related"*. The Disclosure Letter stated that matters previously disclosed to the purchasers' accountants and in the accompanying disclosure bundle were deemed to be disclosed. In finding that this satisfied the contractual warranty, Chadwick LJ made the following observations at [70]:

> "It would have been open to the Purchaser to refuse to accept disclosure made in general terms by reference to what had been supplied to its reporting accountants; and to insist that it would only accept disclosure which was specific to each individual warranty. But the Purchaser did not choose to take that course. It was content to rely on its reporting accountants to identify from the documents supplied to them — and to report on — the matters about which it needed to be informed. That is the effect of the terms in which disclosure was made under the disclosure letter; and, for whatever reason, those were the terms upon which the purchaser was content to accept disclosure. In those circumstances, as it seems to me, the disclosure requirement was satisfied in relation to such matters as might fairly be expected to come to the knowledge of the reporting accountants from an examination (in the ordinary course of carrying out the due diligence exercise for which they were engaged) of the documents and written information supplied to them (including board meeting packs and the contents of the Disclosure Bundle)."

[334] The necessity of considering the material terms of the contract was emphasised in *Man Nutzfahrzeuge AG v Freightliner Ltd* [2005] EWHC 2347 (Comm). In that case, the relevant clause stated that *"any matter which is or should be revealed by inspection of the statutory registers and books…"* was disclosed. A submission that various VAT frauds were disclosed by reference to the financial records from which the fraud could be deduced was rejected by Moore-Bick LJ (giving judgment in a case heard in the commercial court) at [178]:

> "The natural meaning of the words the parties have chosen to use is that only matters that can be directly ascertained from an inspection of the relevant documents are to be treated as having been disclosed."

[335] The following principles can be derived from those cases:

(i) The commercial purpose of such disclosure clauses is to exonerate the seller from its breach of warranty by fairly disclosing the matters giving rise to the breach.

(ii) The disclosure requirements of the contract in question must be construed applying the usual rules of contractual interpretation, by reference to the express words used, the relevant factual matrix and the above commercial purpose.

(iii) The adequacy of disclosure must be considered by careful analysis of the contents of the disclosure letter, including any references in the disclosure letter to other sources of information, against the contractual requirements.

(iv) A disclosure letter which purports to disclose specific matters merely by referring to other documents as a source of information will generally not be adequate to fairly disclose with sufficient detail the nature and scope of those matters. For that reason, disclosure by omission will rarely be adequate.

(v) However, it is open to the parties to agree the form and extent of any disclosure that will be deemed to be adequate against the warranty. That could include an agreement that disclosure may be given by reference to documents other than the disclosure letter, such as by list or in a data room.

(vi) Where disclosure is by reference to documents other than the disclosure letter, only matters that can be ascertained directly from such documents will be treated as disclosed.

8.3. Tax indemnity[93]

The purchaser may also seek tax indemnities with respect to certain tax matters where the purchaser considers that there may be a serious tax exposure, or otherwise seek to reduce the consideration for the transaction. Such actions will be the subject matter of negotiations between the vendor and the purchaser.

---

[93] See 'Tax indemnities in mergers and acquisitions and other commercial transactions,' *Bulletin for International Taxation* (IBFD, August 2011), pp. 469–479, and Mehdi Tedjani, 'Indemnities in private share deals,' (2019) 40 *The Company Lawyer* 39.

Essentially, an indemnity is a contractual promise by one party (usually the vendor in this case) to ensure that the other is kept harmless against a certain loss[94]. An indemnity provides for the vendor to reimburse the claimant in respect of a specified loss suffered. Unlike the case for warranties, there is no obligation on the part of the claimant to prove that the loss has occurred as a result of any inaccuracy of the information provided by the vendor.

---

[94] *Firma C-Trade SA v Newcastle Protection and Indemnity Association (The Fanti)*, [1992] 2 AC 1.

CHAPTER 8

Singapore Real Estate Investment Trusts: 20 Years of Phenomenal Growth

1. Introduction

In less than two decades since the first successful listing of a real estate investment trust (REIT)[1] on the Singapore Exchange in 2002, the Singapore REIT (S-REIT) market has grown to become one of the largest globally, with a market capitalization of more than \$100 billion[2]. As at 1 January 2020, the S-REITs[3] listed on the Singapore Exchange accounted for more than 10% of the total market capitalization of the Singapore stock market[4].

---

[1] The inception of REIT may be traced to the United States where it was first introduced in the 1960s, with legislative amendments made to the Internal Revenue Code in order to facilitate real estate investment by small, unsophisticated investors and create a vehicle that provides limited personal liability while allowing income to flow directly to investors: See Michael Torkin, 'Real Estate Investment in the 1990s: An Analysis of REITS' (1997) 12 BFLR 199, and Marc Louargand, 'The Global REIT revolution,' *Real Estate Issues* (Spring 2007 issue).

[2] Singapore has the 5th largest REIT market globally, behind United States, Japan, Australia and United Kingdom. See REIT Association of Singapore (REITAS) website <https://www.reitas.sg/singapore-reits/overview-of-the-s-reit-industry/> (accessed 1 January 2022).

[3] Includes stapled trusts where S-REIT and business trust securities are stapled together and traded as one (also referred to as stapled securities).

[4] The daily average value of S-REITs traded on the Singapore Exchange accounted for close to 25% of the day-to-day turnover in the Singapore Exchange. See 'Risks in REITs are not what they once were,' *The Business Times*, 13 February 2020.

The rise of S-REITs, as an alternative asset class to the traditional stocks and shares listed on the Singapore Exchange, can also be observed from the market trend that the largest initial public offerings (IPOs) on the Singapore Exchange in recent years have all been dominated by S-REITs (and business trusts)[5]. For year 2019, S-REIT listings[6], remarkably accounted for a whopping 98% (or $3 billion out of $3.06 billion) of funds raised through IPOs[7]. Of the worldwide REIT IPOs in year 2019, 45% debuted on the Singapore Exchange[8].

In Asia, Singapore has the largest REIT market, excluding Japan[9]. The other Asian jurisdictions with a REIT market include Hong Kong, Malaysia, South Korea, Taiwan, and Thailand. The latest to jump onto the REIT bandwagon in Asia are India and the Philippines, which successfully launched their first REIT in March 2019[10] and August 2020[11], respectively. As at mid-2020, China, was reported to be working on its REIT regime for launch[12].

Since the first S-REIT IPO in 2002, the S-REIT sector in Singapore has grown faster than that in anywhere else in Asia[13], earning it the title of "REITs Growth Capital of Asia". The phenomenal growth of the S-REIT market can be attributed to the consultative regulatory regime as well as the favorable tax regime for S-REITs, which includes "tax transparency" treatment for income tax purpose, and tax exemption of foreign-sourced

---

[5] Examples include Cromwell European REIT, Keppel-KBS US REIT and Netlink NBN Trust in 2017, Sasseur REIT in 2018 and Prime US REIT, Lendlease Global Commercial REIT, Eagle Hospitality Trust and ARA US Hospitality Trust in 2019.

[6] Includes stapled trusts where S-REIT and business trust securities are stapled together and traded as one (also referred to as stapled securities).

[7] 'REIT IPOs reign in Singapore, but more diversity welcome,' *The Business Times*, 13 December 2019.

[8] 'SGX to launch two international REIT futures, in Asian first,' *The Business Times*, 4 August 2020.

[9] 'S-REITs placements, rights hit 8-year high of S$4.3b in 2018,' *The Business Times*, 14 February 2019.

[10] 'Blackstone plans 7 per cent yield for India's first REIT IPO,' *The Business Times*, 24 September 2018, and 'India's first REIT up 21% since March listing,' *The Business Times*, 19 June 2019.

[11] 'Ayala REIT's IPO to blaze trail for other Philippine issuers,' *The Business Times*, 4 September 2020.

[12] 'China takes first steps towards launching US$3 trillion REIT market,' *The Business Times*, 3 June 2020.

[13] 'Singapore REITs set for broader recovery after Q1 Covid-19 hit,' *The Business Times*, 23 September 2020.

income[14]. Most notably, an individual investing in S-REITs is exempt from tax on distributions made by S-REITs[15].

In this chapter, we will trace the development of the S-REIT market, outline the regulatory regime governing S-REITs and examine the various concessionary tax treatments accorded to S-REITs. In the next chapter, the discussion will turn to business trusts and property trusts listed on the Singapore Exchange. This is followed by a discussion on the private real estate fund market in the subsequent chapter.

2. S-REITs: An Overview of the Key Milestones

In the Singapore context, a "real estate investment trust" refers to one which is authorized under section 286 or recognized under section 287 of the Securities and Futures Act[16]. The term generally refers to a collective investment scheme that is constituted as a trust that invests primarily in real estate and real estate related assets and the units of which are listed on an approved exchange[17].

There were 41 S-REITs listed on the Singapore Exchange as at 1 January 2020 (see Table 1)[18]. These S-REITs invest in a portfolio of real estate ranging

---

[14] For an overview of the regulatory and tax regime pertaining to S-REITs, see Lee Suet Fern and Linda Esther Foo, *Real Estate Investment Trusts in Singapore, Recent Legal and Regulatory Developments and the Case for Corporatization* (2010) 22 SAcLJ 36, Allen Tan, James Choo and Justin Tan, 'An Investor's Guide to the Regulatory and Tax Framework for S-REITs,' *Derivatives and Financial Instruments*, May/June 2011, IBFD, p137 and Joseph Chun, *Are Reits Green? An Environmental Analysis of Real Estate Investment Trust Law in Singapore* (2007) 19 SAcLJ 47. See also Joseph A. Daniels, Securitizing Spectacle: Property, Real Estate Investment Trusts, and the Financialization of Retail Space in Singapore, University of British Columbia, 2015.

[15] S 13(1)(zh) of the Income Tax Act.

[16] S 286 deals with collective investment schemes constituted in Singapore whereas s 287 deals with collective investment schemes constituted outside Singapore. The usage of the term 'real estate investment trust' is restricted under s 283A of the Securities and Futures Act. See also Securities and Futures (Offers of Investments) (Use of term 'Real Estate Investment Trust') Order 2007, S 227/2007.

[17] See s 2(1) and s 137S(2) of the Securities and Futures Act for the definition of the term 'real estate investment trust'. The Income Tax Act contains a narrower definition where the term 'real estate investment trust' is limited to those authorized under s 286 of the Securities and Futures Act and listed on the Singapore Exchange. See s 43(10) of the Income Tax Act.

[18] Includes stapled trusts where S-REIT and business trust securities are stapled together and traded as one (also referred to as stapled securities). Other S-REITs which were previously listed include Saizen REIT(listed 9 November 2007 and delisted 6 October 2017) and Fortune REIT (listed 12 August 2003, delisted 11 October 2019). Fortune REIT was the first S-REIT whose portfolio wholly comprised overseas

Table 1: S-REITs listed[a] as at 1 January 2020.[b]

S/N	Name	Primary Property Portfolio	Listing Date	Stapled Trusts
1	CapitaLand Mall Trust[c]	Retail	17-07-02	
2	Ascendas REIT	Industrial	19-11-02	
3	CapitaLand Commercial Trust[d]	Office/Retail	06-02-04	
4	Suntec REIT	Office/Retail	09-12-04	
5	Mapletree Logistics Trust	Industrial	28-07-05	
6	Starhill Global REIT	Retail/Office	20-09-05	
7	Keppel REIT	Office	28-11-05	
8	Frasers Commercial Trust[e]	Office	30-03-06	
9	Ascott Residence Trust[f]	Hospitality	31-03-06	√
10	Frasers Centerpoint Trust	Retail	05-07-06	
11	CDL Hospitality Trusts	Hospitality	19-07-06	√
12	ESR-REIT[g]	Industrial	25-07-06	
13	CapitaLand Retail China Trust[h]	Retail	08-12-06	
14	First REIT	Healthcare	11-12-06	
15	AIMS APAC REIT[i]	Industrial	19-04-07	
16	Parkway Life REIT	Healthcare	23-08-07	
17	Lippo Malls Indonesia Retail Trust[j]	Retail	19-11-07	
18	ARA LOGOS Logistics Trust[k]	Industrial	12-04-10	
19	Mapletree Industrial Trust	Industrial	21-10-10	
20	Sabana Shariah Compliant Industrial REIT[l]	Industrial	26-11-10	
21	Mapletree Commercial Trust	Office/Retail	27-04-11	
22	Ascendas Hospitality Trust[m]	Hospitality	27-07-12	√
23	Far East Hospitality Trust	Hospitality	27-08-12	√
24	Mapletree North Asia Commercial Trust[n]	Office/Retail	07-03-13	
25	SPH REIT	Retail	24-07-13	
26	Soilbuild Business Space REIT	Industrial	16-08-13	
27	OUE Commercial REIT	Office/Hospitality/Retail	27-01-14	√
28	Frasers Hospitality Trust	Hospitality	14-07-14	√
29	IREIT Global	Office	13-08-14	
30	Keppel DC REIT	Industrial	12-12-14	
31	BHG Retail REIT	Retail	11-12-15	
32	Manulife US REIT	Office	20-05-16	
33	Frasers Logistics and Industrial Trust[o]	Industrial	21-06-16	

Table 1:   (Continued)

S/N	Name	Primary Property Portfolio	Listing Date	Stapled Trusts
34	EC World REIT	Industrial	28-07-16	
35	Keppel Pacific Oak US REIT[p]	Office	09-11-17	
36	Cromwell European REIT	Office/Retail/Industrial	30-11-17	
37	Sasseur REIT	Retail	28-03-18	
38	ARA US Hospitality Trust	Hospitality	09-05-19	√
39	Eagle Hospitality Trust	Hospitality	24-05-19	√
40	Prime US REIT	Office	19-07-19	
41	Lendlease Global Commercial REIT	Retail/Office	02-10-19	

Notes:

a   Includes stapled trusts where S-REIT and business trust securities are stapled together and traded as one (also referred to as stapled securities).

b   Two additional S-REITs, Elite Commercial REIT and United Hampshire US Real Estate Investment Trust have since listed on the Singapore Exchange on 6 February 2020 and 12 March 2020 respectively. Another two S-REITs, Daiwa House Logistics Trust and Digital Core REIT, listed on 26 November 2021 and 6 December 2021 respectively.

c   CapitaLand Mall Trust has since merged with CapitaLand Commercial Trust on 21 October 2020. The merged entity is named CapitaLand Integrated Commercial Trust.

d   Formerly known as CapitaCommercial Trust. CapitaLand Commercial Trust has since merged with CapitaLand Mall Trust on 21 October 2020. The merged entity is named CapitaLand Integrated Commercial Trust.

e   Formerly known as Allco REIT. Frasers Commercial Trust has since merged with Frasers Logistics & Industrial Trust on 15 April 2020. The merged entity is named Frasers Logistics & Commercial Trust.

f   Following the merger of Ascott Residence Trust and Ascendas Hospitality Trust, the combined vehicle known as Ascott Residence Trust commenced trading on 2 January 2020.

g   Formerly known as Cambridge Industrial Trust. ESR-REIT merged with Viva Industrial Trust in year 2018.

h   Formerly known as CapitaRetail China Trust. It has since been renamed CapitaLand China Trust from 26 January 2021.

i   Formerly known as MacarthurCook Industrial REIT. It was renamed AIMS AMP Capital Industrial REIT before changing to its current name in April 2019.

j   Formerly known as Lippo-Mapletree Indonesia Retail Trust.

k   Formerly known as Cache Logistics Trust.

l   Sabana Shariah Compliant Industrial REIT has since been renamed Sabana Industrial REIT from 21 October 2021.

m   Following the merger of Ascendas Hospitality Trust and Ascott Residence Trust, the combined vehicle known as Ascott Residence Trust commenced trading on 2 January 2020.

n   Formerly known as Mapletree Greater China Commercial Trust.

o   Frasers Logistics & Industrial Trust has since merged with Frasers Commercial Trust on 15 April 2020. The merged entity is named Frasers Logistics & Commercial Trust.

p   Formerly known as Keppel-KBS US REIT.

from commercial properties (e.g. shopping malls and offices) to healthcare-related properties (e.g. hospitals and nursing homes) to hospitality-related properties (e.g. serviced residences and hotels) and industrial properties (e.g. factories, warehouses, business park space, distribution centers, logistics facilities, data centers)[19].

2.1. The initial years

The first S-REIT to be successfully listed on the Singapore Exchange was CapitaLand Mall Trust[20], sponsored by CapitaLand. Prior to the successful listing of CapitaLand Mall Trust in July 2002, there was an earlier IPO attempt by CapitaLand to list SingMall Property Trust in November 2001. Unfortunately, the response of the market to SingMall Property Trust was lacklustre and the listing was eventually aborted.

The successful listing of CapitaLand Mall Trust in July 2002 was quickly followed by a series of listings of S-REITs over the period from 2002 to 2007, including those of Ascendas REIT[21], Suntec REIT, Mapletree Logistic

---

real estate. It was primary listed on the Hong Kong Stock Exchange and secondary listed on the Singapore Exchange following a conversion exercise of Fortune REIT's listing status on the Singapore Exchange from a primary listing to a secondary listing which became effective on 21 December 2015. On 19 June 2019, the manager of Fortune REIT announced that Fortune REIT would voluntarily delist from the Singapore Exchange and continue to maintain its primary listing on the Hong Kong Exchange. The reasons provided for the delisting in Singapore include (i) to eliminate the additional administrative overhead and costs of compliance associated with Singapore regulatory requirements, (ii) to better reflect the investor profile and geographical asset profile of Fortune REIT in line with its closer nexus with Hong Kong, (iii) the low trading liquidity of the units on the Singapore Exchange and (iv) the primary listing on Hong Kong Stock Exchange is sufficient to meet Fortune REIT's debt and equity fund raising requirements.

[19] In year 2020, Singapore has seen the listing of a S-REIT which has a portfolio of grocery-anchored malls in the US. Typically a grocery-anchored mall will have the main anchor grocery tenant accounting for 50% to 70% of the mall space, with other tenants such as hairdressers and drycleaners providing lifestyle services, accounting for less than 5% of mall space each: 'S-Reit universe may soon welcome a new asset class: grocery-anchored malls,' *The Business Times,* 30 August 2019. See also 'United Hampshire US REIT launches IPO at US$0.80 per unit,' *The Business Times,* 4 March 2020.

[20] Formerly known as CapitaMall Trust. CapitaLand Mall Trust has since merged with CapitaLand Commercial Trust on 21 October 2020. The merged entity is named CapitaLand Integrated Commercial Trust. See 'CMT to be renamed CapitaLand Integrated Commercial Trust on Nov 3,' *The Business Times,* 21 October 2020. See also Seek Ngee Huat, Sing Tien Foo and Yu Shi Ming, *Singapore's Real Estate, 50 Years of Transformation,* World Scientific series on Singapore's 50 years of Nation Building, 2016, for information on S-REITs.

[21] Formerly known as A-REIT. With the listing of CapitaLand Mall Trust and A-REIT, the Editorial in *The Business Times,* 23 July 2002, with the caption 'REITs: A respectable report card,' commented favorably on the development of the REIT market in Singapore.

Trust, Starhill Global REIT[22], Keppel REIT[23], Frasers Centrepoint Trust and Parkway Life REIT. The S-REIT listing fever was so hot during that period that of the 41 S-REITs listed on the Singapore Exchange as at 1 January 2020, 17 (or more than 40%) were listed during the period from 2002 to 2007 (see Table 1).

During the initial wave of S-REIT listings, CapitaLand was a first mover and pioneer at the forefront of the developments[24]. In the short span of 5 years from 2002 to 2006, it spearheaded the listing of 4 S-REITs — including, the first S-REIT (CapitaLand Mall Trust), the first commercial S-REIT (CapitaLand Commercial Trust), the first China retail S-REIT (CapitaLand Retail China Trust) and the first hospitality-related S-REIT (Ascott Residence Trust; through Ascott which is the serviced residence arm of CapitaLand).

Another significant milestone reached during the initial wave of S-REIT listings was in year 2006 when CDL Hospitality Trusts, the first stapled trusts (also referred to as stapled securities) comprising a S-REIT and a business trust[25], was listed on the Singapore Exchange. The structure of CDL Hospitality Trusts is such that the S-REIT holds the real estate to generate passive rental income, and where the need arises (e.g. when the S-REIT is unable to appoint a master lessee for any of the hotels), the business trust will serve as the master lessee of the hotel and undertake the hotel operations.

Notably, during the initial wave of S-REIT listings from 2002 to 2007, the initial portfolio of many of the S-REITs comprises entirely Singapore real estate (see Table 2). Many of these S-REITs have however since diversified their property portfolio to seek growth abroad, and now hold real estate both within and outside Singapore.

As investors' familiarity and confidence with S-REITs grew, the number of S-REIT listings in a single year hit an all-time high of seven listings in a

---

[22] Formerly known as Prime REIT.

[23] Formerly known as K-REIT Asia.

[24] At the successful launch of CapitaLand Mall Trust, the then President and CEO of CapitaLand Ltd Liew Mun Leong pointed out that the remaking of the Singapore real estate market has begun: See 'A new look for the real estate sector,' *The Business Times*, 9 August 2002.

[25] There are six stapled trusts listed on the Singapore Exchange as at 1 January 2020. See Chapter 9 for a discussion on business trusts.

Table 2: Initial property portfolio of selected S-REITs.

Name	Initial Property Portfolio	Year of Listing
CapitaLand Mall Trust	• Junction 8 • Tampines Mall • Funan the IT Mall	2002
Ascendas REIT	• The Alpha, The Aries, The Capricorn and The Gemini at Singapore Science Park II • Techplace I and Techplace II at Ang Mo Kio Industrial Park I and II • Techlink at Kakit Bukit • Honeywell Building at Changi Business Park	2002
CapitaLand Commercial Trust	• Capital Tower • 6 Battery Road • Starhub Center • Robinson Point • Bugis Village • Golden Shoe Car Park • Market Street Car Park	2004
Suntec REIT	• Suntec City Mall • Suntec City Office Towers	2004
Mapletree Logistics Trust	• 15 logistics properties located across Singapore	2005
Starhill Global REIT	• Wisma Atria • Ngee Ann City	2005
Keppel REIT	• Prudential Tower • Keppel Towers • GE Towers • Bugis Junction Towers	2005
Frasers Centrepoint Trust	• Causeway Point • Northpoint • Anchovale Point	2006
CDL Hospitality Trusts	• Grand Copthorne Waterfront Hotel • Copthorne King's Hotel • M Hotel • Orchard Hotel and Shopping Arcade	2006
ESR-REIT	• 27 industrial properties located across Singapore	2006
AIMS AMP Capital Industrial REIT	• 12 industrial properties located across Singapore	2007
Parkway Life REIT	• Mount Elizabeth Hospital • Gleneagles Hospital • Parkway East Hospital[a]	2007

Note:

[a] Formerly known as East Shore Hospital.

single year in 2006 (see Table 1)[26]. The year also marked a turning point in the S-REIT market, with the initial portfolio of more than 50% of the newly listed S-REITs (or four out of the seven listings in 2006) comprising substantially overseas real estate. These include Frasers Commercial Trust with almost 50% of its initial real estate investment in Australia, Ascott Residence Trust with about 67% of its initial real estate portfolio in China, Vietnam, Indonesia and the Philippines, CapitaLand Retail China Trust with 100% of its initial portfolio in China, and First REIT with 100% of its initial portfolio in Indonesia.

The first wave of S-REIT listing fever was unfortunately interrupted by the onset of the subprime mortgage crisis in 2007 which snowballed into the worst global financial crisis since the Great Depression of the 1930s. During the peak of the global financial crisis between 2008 and 2009, the number of S-REIT listing fizzled out as the S-REIT IPO market came virtually to a standstill. The overall value of REIT units plunged more than 50% in the second half of 2008 and credit and refinancing risks were cited as a major reason for the decline in the unit prices as the REITs themselves do not have much liquidity on account of the requirement to distribute 90% or more of its taxable income to enjoy tax transparency[27].

The global financial markets rebounded shortly thereafter, and the interest in S-REIT listings revived. The S-REIT sector bounced back with the completion of recapitalization exercises and major refinancing exercises[28].

2.2. Internationalization of S-REITs

A second wave of S-REIT listings started from around 2010, and hit a new peak in 2013 when Mapletree North Asia Commercial Trust[29] raised $1.6 billion to become the largest S-REIT IPO in Singapore[30]. Notably, the

---

[26] Excluding stapled trusts where a S-REIT and a business trusts are stapled together (also referred to as stapled securities).

[27] 'S-REITs face worst crisis,' *The Business Times*, 28 March 2009, where it was reported that the overall value of units plunged 60%.

[28] 'Refinancing fears recede but REITs still cautious on outlook,' *The Business Times*, 2–3 May 2009 and 'S-REIT sector bounces back from global crisis,' *The Business Times*, 21 April 2010.

[29] Formerly known as Mapletree Greater China Commercial Trust.

[30] Press release, *Mapletree Greater China Commercial Trust IPO Debuts Strongly on the Singapore Exchange*, issued by Mapletree Greater China Commercial Trust, 7 March 2013.

Mapletree group of companies was seen to be actively pushing the S-REIT agenda during this period, and sponsored the listing of 3 S-REITs during the 4-year period from 2010 to 2013: Mapletree Industrial Trust in 2010, Mapletree Commercial Trust in 2011 and Mapletree North Asia Commercial Trust[31] in 2013.

Over the years, Singapore's reputation and credentials as a global hub for REIT listing grew and a third wave of S-REIT listings may be observed from 2015. In a clear departure from the first two waves of S-REIT listings, there has been no S-REIT IPO with pure play Singapore real estate portfolio since 2014. It is further noted that all S-REITs newly listed on the Singapore Exchange from 2015 comprise wholly overseas real estate, with the sole exception of Lendlease Global Commercial REIT, which has a Singapore shopping mall in its initial portfolio[32]. Most of the S-REITs listed from 2015 were also sponsored by non-Singapore based sponsors such as BHG, Manulife, KBS and Lendlease[33]. The above trends are testament to the increasing global recognition garnered by S-REITs.

As of year 2020, the Singapore Exchange has more foreign REITs than anywhere else in the world[34]. Many of the "foreign" REITs listed in Singapore (instead of the home country of the sponsors or the country where the real estate is located) because of Singapore's rising reputation as an international REIT hub[35]. Unlike the situation in Singapore, the REIT markets in many other Asia Pacific jurisdictions are primarily focused on their domestic real estate.

Riding on its growing reputation as an international REIT hub, Singapore is fast becoming a preferred listing platform for United States property trusts. Since the first pure-play United States focused S-REIT (i.e. Manulife US REIT) listed on the Singapore Exchange in 2016, there has been five other listings of S-REITs with 100% of their real estate portfolio

---

[31] Formerly known as Mapletree Greater China Commercial Trust.

[32] In 2019, the IPO of Lendlease Global Commercial REIT, comprises a Singapore shopping mall (i.e. 313@ Somerset), and a property in Milan, Italy.

[33] 'S'pore still seen as major Asia REIT hub,' *The Business Times*, 20 April 2015.

[34] 'Singapore is REIT hub with most foreign IPOs,' *The Business Times*, 24 February 2020.

[35] 'SGX explains why Singapore is Asia's largest global REIT platform,' *The Edge Singapore*, 6 May 2019. See also, 'The way forward for S-REITs,' *The Edge Singapore*, 21 February 2022.

in the United States — Keppel Pacific Oak US REIT[36] which listed in 2017, ARA US Hospitality Trust, Eagle Hospitality Trust and Prime US REIT all of which listed in 2019[37], as well as United Hampshire US REIT which listed in 2020.

The internationalization of the S-REIT market can also be attributed to the diminished stock of attractive real estate available in Singapore for acquisition and listing[38], as well as increasing interest in overseas real estate for investment opportunities[39]. Other contributing factors include Singapore's position as the leading international wealth and financial hub with an increasingly sophisticated investor base, the strong corporate governance framework in Singapore, as well as the favorable regulatory and tax regimes[40]. REITs in general have benefitted the financial system as they added breadth and liquidity to the capital markets. They also reduce the property sector's dependence on bank loans by broadening the financing options[41].

Of the 41 S-REITs listed as at 1 January 2020, 14 (or 34%) have portfolios which wholly comprise overseas real estate situated across Asia Pacific, Europe and North America (see Table 3). It is further noted that as at 1 January 2020, only 4 S-REITs[42] did not diversify their investment portfolio beyond Singapore: ESR-REIT[43], Sabana Shariah Compliant Industrial REIT, Mapletree Commercial Trust and Far East Hospitality Trust.

---

[36] Formerly known as Keppel-KBS US REIT.

[37] 'US Reits in Singapore,' *The Business Times*, 14 September 2019.

[38] It was reported that more than 70% of Singapore Central Business District Grade A-office stock is already owned by S-REITs and developers. See 'S-REITs seek faster approval turnaround for related-party deals,' *The Business Times*, 5 July 2019.

[39] 'Issues with tenants 'unavoidable' but unlikely to concern REITs: DBS,' *The Business Times*, 18 April 2019.

[40] 'Singapore's strong corporate governance and tax support big draws for foreign REITs,' *The Business Times*, 5 July 2019 and 'Will local investors take to foreign REITs?' *The Edge Singapore*, 16 April 2018. See also 'Keeping Singapore's status as Asia-Pacific's global REIT hub,' *The Business Times*, 12 January 2022.

[41] *Financial Stability Review* (MAS Macroeconomic Surveillance Department, December 2006).

[42] Includes stapled trusts where S-REIT and business trust securities are stapled together and traded as one (also referred to as stapled securities).

[43] 'ESR-REIT focusing on S'pore after merger,' *The Straits Times*, 21 January 2019. ESR-REIT has since announced on 6 May 2021 that it would be acquiring a 10% interest in ESR Australia Logistics Partnership which holds 37 assets in Australia. See: 'ESR-REIT to raise S$150m as it acquires Singapore and Australia assets,' *The Business Times*, 7 May 2021.

Table 3: S-REITs with portfolio which wholly comprises overseas real estate.[a]

S/N	Name	Location of Real Estate Portfolio[b]	Year of Listing
1	CapitaLand Retail China Trust	China	2006
2	Lippo Malls Indonesia Retail Trust	Indonesia	2007
3	Mapletree North Asia Commercial Trust	China, Hong Kong, Japan	2013
4	IREIT Global	Germany	2014
5	BHG Retail REIT	China	2015
6	Manulife US REIT	United States	2016
7	Frasers Logistics and Industrial Trust	Australia, Germany, Netherlands	2016
8	EC World REIT	China	2016
9	Keppel Pacific Oak US REIT	United States	2017
10	Cromwell REIT	Europe	2017
11	Sasseur REIT	China	2018
12	ARA US Hospitality Trust	United States	2019
13	Eagle Hospitality Trust	United States	2019
14	Prime US REIT	United States	2019

Notes:

[a] Four additional S-REITs with portfolios which wholly comprises overseas real estate situated outside Singapore, Elite Commercial REIT, United Hampshire US Real Estate Investment Trust, Daiwa House Logistics Trust and Digital Core REIT, have since listed on the Singapore Exchange in 2020 and 2021. Elite Commercial REIT holds commercial real estate in the United Kingdom, United Hampshire US REIT holds retail real estate and self-storage facilities in the United States, Daiwa House Logistics Trust holds logistics properties in Japan and Digital Core REIT holds data centres in North America.

[b] As at 1 January 2020.

2.3. REIT exchange traded funds and futures: The next engine of growth

Since late 2016, a number of exchange traded funds[44] which track the performance of S-REITs have been launched. As at 1 January 2020, there

---

[44] An exchange traded fund is a basket of securities that is listed and traded on an exchange, just like a stock or S-REIT. An exchange traded fund may invest in different types of securities such as listed equities or REITs.

Table 4: REIT exchange traded funds listed as at 1 January 2020.

S/N	Name	Underlying REITs[a]	Year of Listing
1	Phillip SGX APAC Dividend Leaders REIT ETF[b]	Comprises 30 highest total dividend paying REITs in the Asia Pacific ex-Japan region (including Link REIT, Scentre Group and Stockland).	20 October 2016
2	NikkoAM-Straits Trading Asia Ex-Japan REIT ETF[c]	Comprises REITs which tracks the performance of the FTSE EPRA/NAREIT Asia ex-Japan Net Total Return REIT Index (including CapitaLand Mall Trust, Ascendas REIT and Link REIT)	29 March 2017
3	Lion-Phillip S-REIT ETF	Comprises 28 S-REITs (including CapitaLand Mall Trust, CapitaLand Commercial Trust and Mapletree Commercial Trust)	30 October 2017

Notes:

[a] As at 1 January 2020.

[b] Besides being the first REIT exchange traded fund to be listed in Singapore, Phillip SGX APAC Dividend Leaders REIT ETF is also the first REIT exchange traded fund to be dividend weighted, with its investment allocation based on dividends, rather than following the traditional market capitalization weighted approach.

[c] NikkoAM-Straits Trading Asia Ex-Japan REIT ETF is weighted based on market capitalization, similar to most other exchange traded funds. In contrast, Phillip SGX APAC Dividend Leaders REIT ETF is dividend weighted.

were 3 REIT exchange traded funds listed on the Singapore Exchange[45], with the latest, i.e. Lion-Phillip S-REIT ETF, focusing exclusively on S-REITs (see Table 4). These REIT exchange traded funds are widely seen to be the engines that drive the next phase of growth and liquidity of the S-REIT market[46].

From the perspective of the investors, one major advantage of investing in REIT exchange traded funds is that such funds offer diversification through a pool of REITs with lower transaction cost as compared to that for investing in each REIT individually. Exchange traded funds typically offer significantly lower management fees than those offered by actively managed mutual funds or unit trusts. In addition, investing in REIT exchange traded funds also help reduce the investors' effort in research given that such funds are professionally managed.

---

[45] *Chartbooks: SREITs & Property Trusts* (SGX Research, December 2019). Two additional REIT ETFs, CSOP iEdge S-REIT Leaders Index ETF and UOB APAC Green REIT ETF have since listed on 18 November 2021 and 23 November 2021 respectively. Singapore currently has the largest REIT exchange traded fund market in Asia (excluding Japan), with combined asset under management of close to $800 million. See 'Retail interest picks up in S-REIT ETFs,' *The Business Times*, 14 February 2022.

[46] 'S-REITs' next growth phase to be supported by REIT ETFs,' *The Edge Singapore*, 19 March 2018.

The increasing popularity of REIT exchange traded funds also helps create an additional source of demand for S-REITs, given that the exchange traded funds will have to acquire units in the underlying S-REITs which constitute the exchange traded funds. This in turn attracts additional liquidity from the region into the S-REIT market, especially for S-REITs which are constituents of the exchange traded funds.

For the above reasons, REIT exchange traded funds are perceived to be more attractive to foreign investors compared to investment in individual S-REITs given that such investors may be less familiar with the S-REIT market[47]. The first REIT exchange traded fund to be listed on the Singapore Exchange, Phillip SGX APAC Dividend Leaders REIT ETF, raised more than US$30 million mainly from local investors in its first closing. About two thirds of its investors are institutional investors and the remaining one third are retail investors[48].

More recently in August 2020, the Singapore Exchange launched Asia's first international REIT futures, the SGX FTSE EPRA Nareit Asia ex-Japan Index Futures and the SGX iEdge S-REIT Leaders Index Futures amid rising global investor demand for real estate-related investment products and trading solutions[49].

2.4. Ongoing mergers and consolidations

Another noteworthy recent development is the consolidation wave which has been sweeping through the S-REIT universe from early 2018 when ESR-REIT announced its merger with Viva Industrial Trust. Since then, at least seven other consolidation exercises have been announced: the mergers of (i) OUE Commercial REIT and OUE Hospitality Trust[50], (ii) Ascott Residence Trust

---

[47] 'The case for investing in an S-REIT ETF,' *The Business Times*, 18 October 2016. See also 'Singapore REIT ETFs holding up amid global REITs rout', *The Business Times*, 3 May 2022.

[48] 'SGX still in talks on potential tax waiver on REIT ETF,' *The Business Times*, 21 October 2016.

[49] The FTSE EPRA Nareit Global Real Estate Index series is a widely followed global benchmark, with about US$340 billion of assets actively benchmarked against or passively tracking the indices, whereas The iEdge S-REIT Leaders Index is the most liquid index-basket representation of the S-REIT market. See also 'SGX to launch two international REIT futures in Asian first,' *The Business Times*, 4 August 2020 and 'Singapore REITs set for broader recovery after Q1 Covid-19 hit,' *The Business Times*, 23 September 2020.

[50] Press release, *Proposed merger of OUE Commercial REIT and OUE Hospitality Trust by way of a Trust Scheme of Arrangement*, issued by OUE Commercial REIT, 8 April 2019. See also 'Plan to merge OUE C-REIT and OUE H-Trust,' *The Straits Times*, 9 April 2019 and 'REIT consolidation continues as OUE C-REIT

and Ascendas Hospitality Trust[51], (iii) Frasers Logistics & Industrial Trust and Frasers Commercial Trust[52], (iv) CapitaLand Mall Trust and CapitaLand Commercial Trust[53], (v) ESR-REIT and Sabana Shariah Compliant[54] Industrial REIT[55] (vi) ESR-REIT and ARA LOGOS Logistics Trust, as well as (vii) Mapletree Commercial Trust and Mapletree North Asia Commercial Trust. See Section 5.3 for further discussion on the ongoing consolidation trend.

The ongoing mergers of S-REITs is viewed as the third stage of the development of the S-REIT market — with the first stage being the initial growth phase when REIT IPOs were first introduced and became popularized, and the second stage being the diversification phase where REITs start diversifying into different asset classes or acquiring overseas real estate due to the saturation in the local market. The third stage is the consolidation phase when growth opportunities become limited and REITs are compelled to merge to be in a stronger position to effectively compete globally. The S-REIT market is in the midst of transiting from the diversification phase to the consolidation phase[56].

2.5. Increasing focus on environmental and sustainability factors

Yet another emerging trend is the increasing focus on environmental and sustainability factors, as Environment, Social and Governance (ESG) related initiatives come into greater focus. In recent years, a number of green REIT indices have been launched globally, including Dow Jones US Green REIT

---

proposes to acquire OUEHT for $1.49 billion; unitholders to suffer dilution again,' *The Edge Singapore*, 15 April 2019. This marks the first intra-sponsor S-REIT merger in Singapore as both OUE C-REIT and OUE H-Trust are under the same sponsor, OUE Ltd.

[51] 'CapitaLand to merge Ascott REIT, Ascendas unit to form Asia Pac's' largest hospitality trust,' *The Business Times*, 3 July 2019.

[52] 'Frasers' logistics and commercial REITs propose S$1.58b merger,' *The Business Times*, 3 December 2019.

[53] 'CCT, CMT unveil plan for REIT juggernaut in S$8.27b merger,' *The Business Times*, 23 January 2020.

[54] See: 'ESR-REIT, ARA LOGOS propose S$1.4b merger,' *The Business Times*, 15 October 2021 and 'Mapletree Commercial Trust, Mapletree North Asia Commercial Trust propose merger,' *The Straits Times*, 31 December 2021.

[55] 'ESR-REIT plans growth by merger with Sabana REIT,' *The Edge Singapore*, 20 July 2020. The proposed merger of ESR-REIT and Sabana Shariah Compliant Industrial REIT was however voted down by the latter's unitholders. See 'Sabana Reit's proposed merger with ESR-Reit voted down in rare win for activists,' *The Straits Times*, 4 December 2020.

[56] 'Singapore Exchange can offer diversity as other exchanges enter REIT game,' *The Business Times*, 9 September 2020.

Index[57] in 2019, and FTSE EPRA Nareit Green Indexes in 2018, which help investor identify REITs that meet ESG criteria. Closer to home, the trend accelerated in year 2020, with the launch of Nikkei ESG-REIT Index, a Japanese REIT index which takes into account ESG performance, and Solactive CarbonCare Asia Green REIT Index, which focuses on green REITs in the Asia-Pacific region[58].

Notably, in developed regions such as Europe and the United States, green buildings are already enjoying rent premiums because the policy of some multinational companies is such that they will only occupy buildings which are "green"[59]. Over time, increasing government intervention in the form of environmental and sustainability related legislation is likely to further strengthen the competitive advantage which "green" REITs have over "non-green" REITs. In this regard, S-REITs and their investors are also expected to gravitate towards responsible investing and takes into account ESG factors in the deployment of their funds, as the culture of ESG further strengthens.

3. Key Events Leading to the Listing of the First S-REIT

The introduction of the REIT to the Singapore market was first recommended by the Property Market Consultative Committee in 1986 in its report, *Action Plan for the Property Sector*[60], to help reinvigorate the real estate sector which was adversely affected by the 1985 recession. In its report, the Committee recommended that tax exemption should be granted to REITs on their net income for at least the first 10 years of their operations. In addition, the

---

[57] Part of the Green Real Estate Index Series of S&P Dow Jones Indices.

[58] The REITs were assessed based on their carbon emission targets and their proportion of green-certified building in their portfolio, subject to certain market capitalization and liquidity criteria. Of the REITs constituting the Solactive CarbonCare Asia Green REIT Index, 8 are S-REITs. These include CapitaLand Integrated Commercial Trust, Frasers Centrepoint Trust, Keppel REIT, Manulife US REIT, Mapletree Commercial Trust, Mapletree North Asia Commercial Trust, SPH REIT and Suntec REIT. Notably, the S-REITs in the index tend to be the larger S-REITs. This raises the question of whether size and maturity, either of the REIT or sponsor or both, help these S-REITs in their green efforts. Also, whether the green REITs perform better because they are the bigger REITs, rather than because they are green. See 'Rising ESG focus sees launch of another green REIT index,' *The Business Times*, 17 December 2020.

[59] 'Rising ESG focus sees launch of another green REIT index,' *The Business Times*, 17 December 2020.

[60] Ministry of Finance (MOF), *Action Plan for the Property Sector: Report of the Property Market Consultative Committee* (1986), pp. 73–76.

Committee urged the Government to take up a substantial equity, via an appropriate public sector organization such as Temasek Holdings Pte Ltd or a statutory board, in the first REIT to be set up, and hold the equity at least until public participation is invited.

There was however a general lack of momentum until after the 1997 Asian Financial Crisis when the Monetary Authority of Singapore (MAS) released guidelines in May 1999 in relation to the setting up of property funds in Singapore[61]. The MAS guidelines were in response to the release of the *Report of the SES Review Committee* in July 1998 which recommended the introduction of REITs in Singapore[62].

While the MAS acknowledged in its press release on 14 May 1999 that the introduction of property funds would widen the range of financial products available to investors and is consistent with the Government's efforts to make Singapore a global financial hub, it was announced at the same time that property funds (including S-REITs) would not be accorded concessionary tax treatments. In other words, property funds were to be taxed according to the same general tax principles as ordinary companies and trusts[63]. The market response then was that some form of tax transparency was required for REITs to take off[64].

It was another 2 years before the Inland Revenue Authority of Singapore (IRAS) finally agreed in July 2001[65] that, subject to conditions, S-REITs would be accorded "tax transparent" treatment whereby the income of S-REITs would not be taxed in the hands of the S-REITs or their trustees. Instead, the pre-taxed income of the S-REITs would be deemed to be derived by the investors and taxed according to the profile of the various investors. This in turn meant that the incomes of the S-REITs are potentially subject to

---

[61] MAS announcement, *Introduction of Property Funds will add to Breadth and Sophistication of Singapore's Financial Center*, 14 May 1999.

[62] See recommendation 39 of *Report of the SES Review Committee*, 29 July 1998.

[63] 'No tax breaks for property trusts in MAS guidelines,' *The Business Times*, 15 May 1999.

[64] 'Guidelines on REITs draw mixed response,' *The Straits Times*, 15 May 1999, 'REITs need tax breaks to take off,' *The Business Times*, 18 May 1999 and 'No rush on property trusts,' *Property Review*, 22 July 1999.

[65] 'REITs clear hurdle with IRAS,' *The Business Times*, 24 July 2001. The IRAS tax ruling on tax transparency treatment was also set out at page A-102 of the SingMall Property Trust prospectus dated 29 October 2001.

tax at a lower rate or not taxed at all (e.g. in the case where the investor is a Singapore tax resident individual).

Shortly after the IRAS announcement, CapitaLand launched the IPO of the first S-REIT, SingMall Property Trust, with three shopping malls (namely Junction 8, Tampines Mall and Funan the IT Mall) within its initial portfolio. Unfortunately, there was a lack of demand from investors for the 530 million units offered, and the IPO was aborted on 12 November 2001[66].

About 8 months later in July 2002, CapitaLand relaunched the REIT as CapitaMall Trust with the same three shopping mall properties, but with a smaller public tranche of 213 million units offered to the public and institutional investors. CapitaMall Trust units were more than four times oversubscribed and became the first S-REIT to be successfully listed[67] on the Singapore Exchange.

4. The S-REIT Advantage

4.1. Real estate companies

Traditionally, real estate companies in Singapore such as CapitaLand, City Developments, Far East, Frasers and Keppel Land, were known to develop and retain a significant proportion of real estate on their balance sheets either for owner occupation or as long-term investment. Such strategy however ties up much of their capital and generate relatively low recurring annual yield, compared to their higher risk, higher return property development business. Following the introduction of a regulatory and tax framework for S-REITs, many of the real estate companies in Singapore with an asset-heavy business model started exploring the feasibility of using the S-REIT as a vehicle to unlock the value of the real estate on their balance sheets.

In particular, it has been noted that the setting up and listing of S-REITs offer real estate companies the opportunity to convert their relatively illiquid real estate assets into the units in S-REITs which are publicly traded on an

---

[66] 'CapitaLand calls off SingMall float,' *The Business Times*, 13 November 2001 where it was reported demand fell short by about 20% of the 530 million units on offer.

[67] For a detailed case study of the launch of CapitaMall Trust, see Seek Ngee Huat, Sing Tien Foo & Yu Shi Ming, *Singapore's Real Estate, 50 Years of Transformation*, World Scientific series on Singapore's 50 Years of Nation-Building, 2016.

exchange. Real estate companies, especially those which act as the sponsor of S-REITs, also have the option of injecting or divesting their real estate assets to the S-REITs. This in turn allows real estate companies to operate on an asset light business model with reduced assets, debts and liabilities on their balance sheets. The additional capital freed-up from the disposal of assets may either be recycled back into the core business of the real estate companies or returned to shareholders.

In many instances, companies with significant real estate on their balance sheets will enter into sale-and-leaseback arrangements with S-REITs and continue to occupy the premises for a long period of time after the disposal of the real estate to the S-REITs, with no change to the day-to-day activities and operations carried on within the properties[68]. Under such a scenario, the companies disposing of the real estate secure an upfront cash flow advantage from the sale of the properties and derive additional benefits from the tax deduction of rental expenses paid to the S-REITs. The first of such arrangements involving S-REITs is the sale-and-leaseback arrangement between Ascendas REIT and OSIM International announced in May 2003 which involved Ascendas REIT buying OSIM's headquarters at Ubi Avenue 1 for $35 million and leasing it back to OSIM for a period of 12 years. The acquisition of OSIM's headquarters was the first addition to Ascendas REIT's real estate portfolio after its IPO in the previous year[69].

Notwithstanding the offloading of the real estate from their balance sheets, many of these real estate companies hold controlling stakes in the S-REITs, continue to enjoy regular, stable income stream from the properties held through the S-REITs, and at the same time derive a new stream of fee income through the provision of asset and property management services to the S-REITs.

The dedicated teams of professionals serving the S-REITs have also raised the bar of managing of the underlying portfolio of real estate. For example, shopping malls owned by S-REITs regularly refresh its tenant mix

---

[68] There are hazards where REITs are to acquire properties at inflated prices where the vendors agree to lease back at inflated rents which are not sustainable after the lease-back period expires: 'Temasek chief warns of hazards in REITs market,' *The Business Times*, 29 July 2005. 'Master leases: Income stability at a cost,' *The Edge Singapore*, 15 January 2018.

[69] *Tenacity: A Decade of Enabling Businesses — Ascendas REIT* (Straits Times Press, 2014).

to attract shoppers, as well as undergo renovation and refurbishment works to maintain their appeal to shoppers.

4.2. Investors

From the perspective of the investors, S-REIT as an asset class is also becoming increasingly popular as an alternative to the conventional direct investment or ownership in real estate. S-REIT essentially allows individual investors to pool their capital to invest in a portfolio of professionally managed real estate investment with lower capital commitment from each investor. Such investment in S-REITs may be made via a subscription for new units during an IPO, private placement or preferential offering exercise, or acquisition of existing units which are traded on the stock exchange.

Compared to conventional direct investment in real estate (which is a relatively illiquid asset), investment in S-REITs offers significant liquidity. Investors in S-REITs may easily acquire and dispose of their investments, given that the S-REIT units are publicly traded on an exchange. Investors are not also bogged down by day-to-day operational and management issues as these are professionally managed by the asset and property managers of the S-REITs.

Another benefit of investing in S-REITs is that they offer an attractive and stable distribution yield[70] arising from the rent or other cashflow generated from the S-REIT's portfolio of real estate The regular S-REIT distributions, which typically take place quarterly or half-yearly , are particularly attractive to individual investors because such distributions are specifically exempt from tax in the hands of individuals. Further, such distributions may be paid using the operating cashflow of the S-REITs, unlike the dividends of a company which must be paid out of profits.

In addition, S-REITs offer investors an exposure to the upward cycle of the property market, which is reflected in the appreciation in unit price of the S-REITs. In this regard, it is worthwhile noting that in the first quarter of

---

[70] During times when the distribution of certain S-REITs are adversely affected by exceptional events, it have been observed that the S-REIT may voluntarily choose to top up its distribution to unitholders. For example, in late 2019, when Festive Walk, one of the primary assets in the real asset portfolio of Mapletree North Asia Commercial Trust (MNACT) in Hong Kong, suffered damages inflicted by protesters, MNACT announced that it would top up its distribution to unitholders to mitigate the impact of the closure of Festival Walk on its distribution to unitholders. See 'Singapore REIT tops up payouts after HK mall closure,' *The Straits Times*, 21 January 2020.

year 2019 itself, the top five performing S-REITS achieved an average return of 19.6% whereas the top 20 performing S-REITs achieved an average return of 15.7%[71].

S-REIT units are in essence a hybrid of equity and fixed income securities. During periods of prolonged low interest rates, S-REITs are particularly attractive as an asset class to investors given the lower cost of capital on debt used to acquire property, the lower financing risk faced by S-REITs as well as the relatively higher yield generated from investments in S-REITs compared to those of other low yield investments (such as treasury bills and bonds). This in turn translates to higher prices for S-REITs during a low interest rate environment[72].

The recent moves by central banks of major economies to cut benchmark interest rates to historical lows in year 2020 to counteract the COVID-19 pandemic-induced recession, have once again brought renewed interests in the attractive yield of S-REITs[73]. This is especially so, given that that low interest rate environment is likely to persist in the foreseeable future.

S-REITs are also known for their defensiveness and resilience during times of uncertain economic outlook, particularly given that S-REITs generally have a diversified tenant base and many of the leases would have already been locked in for the short to medium term, with rental deposits of up to 6 months from the tenants which the S-REIT can draw on[74]. That said, as with all other investments, investing in S-REITs comes with the associated market risks[75].

5. S-REITs: Growing the Real Estate Portfolio

5.1. Acquisition of yield-accretive assets

S-REITs are known to grow their real estate portfolio via the acquisition of yield-accretive assets. A recent example is SPH REIT which undertook its

[71] 'Top five performing S-REITs averaged 20% returns in Q1,' *The Business Times*, 3 April 2019.
[72] 'S-REITs tipped for further gains as rate hike fears subside,' *The Business Times*, 8 April 2019.
[73] 'Singapore REITs set for broader recovery after Q1 Covid-19 hit,' *The Business Times*, 23 September 2020.
[74] 'REITs have cushion against tenants in trouble': DBS, *The Business Times*, 19 April 2019.
[75] 'Risks in REITs are not what they once were,' *The Business Times*, 13 February 2020.

first post-listing acquisition during year 2018 by acquiring The Rail Mall for a consideration of $63 million. In the press release issued to the public in April 2018, SPH REIT announced that it expects the acquisition of The Rail Mall to be yield accretive to its unitholders[76].

In another example, Keppel DC REIT announced in September 2019 that it was planning to raise about $473.8 million to partially fund the highly yield accretive acquisition of two data centers (Keppel DC Singapore 4 and 1-Net North Data Center). The proposed fundraising comprises a combination of equity via private placement and preferential offering, as well as debt[77].

Other well-known examples of S-REITs pursuing an aggressive growth strategy include CapitaLand Mall Trust which has increased its portfolio more than five-fold from the initial three properties as well as Ascendas REIT which similarly expanded its initial portfolio multiple fold and now holds real estate in Australia, the United Kingdom and the United States. Frasers Centerpoint Trust has also grown its real estate portfolio over the years, and recently announced that it would be acquiring from its sponsor, Frasers Property, the remaining 63.1% of AsianRetail Fund which owns five retail malls in Singapore — Tiong Bahru Plaza, White Sands, Hougang Mall, Century Square and Tampines 1. Upon completion of the transactions, Frasers Centerpoint Trust would have 11 retail properties in its portfolio, and its net lettable area would expand by about 64% to 2.3 million square feet. Its portfolio size would also increase to approximately from $3.96 billion to $6.65 billion[78].

The acquisition of additional real estate by S-REITs post listing is typically funded by a mix of bank loan, issuance of debt securities as well as equity funding (e.g. via private placement, preferential offering). On the latter, it is noted that Singapore has a strong secondary fund-raising market as evident from the strong secondary fund-raising market recorded for year

---

[76] Press release, *SPH REIT's Acquisition — The Rail Mall*, issued by SPH REIT, 30 April 2018.

[77] 'Keppel DC REIT to raise S$473.8m to help fund data centre acquisitions,' *The Business Times*, 17 September 2019.

[78] 'Frasers Centrepoint Trust to raise up to S$1.39b to buy rest of AsiaRetail Fund,' *The Business Times*, 4 September 2020.

2019[79], where S-REITs and property trusts raised $7.66 billion, of a total of $8.82 billion in secondary fundraisings[80].

5.2. Asset enhancement initiatives

Many S-REITs have also grown their portfolio organically via asset enhancement initiatives (AEI) which involve the complete redevelopment of existing properties, undertaking AEI in phases or creating higher yielding space by decanting lower-yielding ones. A notable example is Suntec REIT which undertook a $410 million AEI in four phases from June 2012 to June 2015[81]. The AEI involved the decanting of lower-yielding space, converting levels 1 and 2 of Suntec Singapore Convention and Exhibition Center to retail use with the aim of increasing its retail net lettable area by 14%. Another example of AEI is that by OUE Hospitality Trust before its merger with OUE Commercial REIT, where the Mandarin Gallery was created and the hotel lobby of the Mandarin Hotel was shifted from the ground floor to the 5th floor, to provide higher-value retail space with Orchard Road frontage[82]. While such initiatives provide S-REITs with attractive returns on investment, they have an adverse impact on the distribution per unit (DPU) of the S-REITs during the period of the AEI[83].

5.3. Mergers and consolidations

In more recent times, it has been observed that S-REITs are merging and consolidating among themselves with a view to growing their overall asset portfolio. In early 2018, ESR-REIT announced that its manager was in discussions with the manager of Viva Industrial Trust to acquire all units in the latter by way of a trust scheme of arrangement. The merger and

---

[79] 'Singapore, Thailand driving South-east Asia's IPO momentum,' *The Straits Times*, 27 November 2019.

[80] 'S-REITs key driver of market turnover in 2019: SGX,' *The Business Times*, 7 January 2020.

[81] Press releases, *Remaking of Suntec City* and '*Suntec City Completes S$410 million Remaking*, issued by Suntec REIT, 31 October 2011 and 22 October 2015.

[82] Harminder C Rajan, Gareth Tan Guang Ming and Tan Beng Kai Even, *Unlocking Hidden Potential: Strategic Transformation and Value Creation at Mandarin Orchard Singapore and Mandarin Gallery* (NUS Press and World Scientific, 2019).

[83] 'Asset enhancements seen boosting retail REIT income,' *The Business Times*, 11 December 2012.

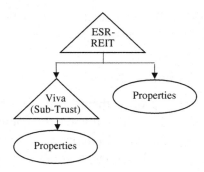

Figure 1: Simplified illustration of ESR-REIT post-merger with Viva Industrial Trust.

acquisition which was subsequently completed in October 2018 resulted in a combined entity with assets of about \$3 billion[84]. This marks the first ever merger and acquisition involving two S-REITs[85].

A simplified illustration of the trust structure of ESR-REIT after its merger with/acquisition of Viva Industrial Trust is set out in Figure 1[86]. In essence, Viva Industrial Trust became a sub-trust of ESR-REIT after the merger.

A trust scheme of arrangement, in compliance with the Singapore Code on Take-Overs and Mergers (Take-Over Code)[87], facilitates the transfer of the existing units in the target S-REIT to the acquirer. A typical trust scheme of arrangement involves obtaining certain approvals from the unitholders[88]

---

[84] 'Scheme for merger of ESR-REIT and Viva Industrial Trust takes effect,' *The Business Times*, 15 October 2018. In view of the ESR Cayman's cross ownership of the managers of ESR-REIT and Sabana Shariah Compliant Industrial REIT, there have been calls for the merger of the two REITs given that the investment mandates of the REITs overlap: See 'Activist fund calls for merger of Sabana REIT and ESR REIT,' *The Business Times*, 15 November 2019.

[85] 'First REIT M&A in 15 years as ESR-REIT primes portfolio,' *The Edge Singapore*, 12 February 2018. Prior to the merger between ESR-REIT and Viva Industrial Trust, the first merger and acquisition transaction involving a S-REIT took place in 2015 when the assets of Saizen REIT was acquired by US private equity firm Lone Star Funds for JPY 44.66 billion. See 'Saizen REIT to sell all Japan assets to Triangle TMK for 44.7b yen,' *The Business Times*, 1 November 2015.

[86] Based on information available on the website of ESR-REIT <https://www.esr-reit.com.sg/trust_structure.html> (accessed 1 January 2021).

[87] Issued by the MAS, on the advice of the Securities Industry Council, pursuant to s 139(2) of the Securities and Futures Act.

[88] The trust scheme is required to be approved by a majority in number representing at least 75% in value of unitholders or class of unitholders present and voting either in person or by proxy at a meeting

as well as the court[89]. The S-REIT which has been acquired will subsequently be delisted from the exchange[90].

ESR-REIT's rationale for the merger is that it would result in the creation of a sizeable industrial S-REIT with larger market capitalization, higher trading liquidity, a larger investor base and potential index inclusion. Index component S-REITs are known to trade with higher trading volume at a tighter yield, since they are tracked and followed by global institutional investors[91]. The tighter yield (or yield compression) in turn confers more opportunities for these enlarged S-REITs to undertake yield accretive acquisitions from a wider pool of assets.

Moreover, the enlarged ESR-REIT could potentially enjoy a positive re-rating of its unit price as well as more competitive costs of capital[92]. Larger S-REITs are more likely to be followed by institutional investors and analysts; and it would be easier for larger S-REITs to undertake private placements of their units to grow their portfolio of real estate. All these would ultimately benefit the unitholders.

With the successful merger of ESR-REIT and Viva Industrial Trust in 2018, a series of mergers was announced by various S-REITs in year 2019. In April 2019, OUE Commercial REIT announced its intention to acquire OUE Hospitality Trust through another trust scheme of arrangement to create one of the largest property trusts listed on the Singapore Exchange with

---

convened to approve the trust scheme, in order to be exempt from certain compliance requirements under the Take-Over Code.

[89] Under O 80 of the Rule of Court (R 5).

[90] Under s 288(7) of the Securities and Futures Act, the MAS may withdraw the authorization or recognition of a S-REIT, upon an application in writing made to it by the responsible person for the S-REIT. Under s 295(2) of the Securities and Futures Act, where the MAS revokes or withdraws the authorization of an S-REIT, the responsible person (and, where applicable, the trustee) shall take the necessary steps to wind up the S-REIT. That said, it is possible to seek an exemption under s 337(1) of the Securities and Futures Act from the requirement to wind up the S-REIT: See Securities and Futures (Exemption of Ascendas Hospitality Real Estate Investment Trust) Regulations 2020 (S 3/2020), which provides that Ascendas Hospitality Real Estate Investment Trust (Ascendas H-REIT) shall be exempt from the requirement under s 295(2) of the Securities and Futures Act to take the necessary steps to wind up Ascendas H-REIT following the withdrawal of the MAS' authorization of Ascendas H-REIT. With the merger, MAS also deregistered the Ascendas Hospitality Business Trust with effect from 3 January 2020: see *Gazette* notification No. 49/2020, 3 January 2020.

[91] 'Activist fund calls for merger of Ascendas Hospitality Trust, Ascott REIT,' *The Business Times*, 26 April 2019.

[92] Unitholders' Circular dated 7 August 2018 issued by ESR-REIT.

assets of $6.8 billion[93]. This was followed by an announcement on 3 July 2019 that Ascott Residence Trust and Ascendas Hospitality Trust would be merged to create the largest hospitality trust in the Asia Pacific region and the eighth largest globally[94].

The announcement to merge Ascott Residence Trust and Ascendas Hospitality Trust was made following the completion of CapitaLand's acquisition of Ascendas-Singbridge on 1 July 2019, which resulted in CapitaLand owning both Ascott Residence Trust and Ascendas Hospitality Trust which have overlapping mandates. One of the key justifications for the merger was that it would provide "access to a larger capital base and a higher debt headroom" which would in turn provide the combined trust with "greater financial flexibility to seek more accretive acquisitions and value enhancements"[95].

Before the year drew to a close, it was announced on 2 December 2019 that Frasers Logistics & Industrial Trust and Frasers Commercial Trust (both of which were sponsored by Frasers Property) would be merging[96]. The enlarged REIT would hold about $5.7 billion in assets across the Asia-Pacific, Europe and the UK, and is expected to be one of the top 10 S-REITs by market capitalization[97].

---

[93] Press release, *Proposed merger of OUE Commercial REIT and OUE Hospitality Trust by way of a trust scheme of Arrangement*, issued by OUE Commercial REIT, 8 April 2019. See also 'Plan to merge OUE C-REIT and OUE H-Trust,' *The Straits Times*, 9 April 2019 and 'REIT consolidation continues as OUE C-REIT proposes to acquire OUTHT for $1.49 billion; unitholders to suffer dilution again,' *The Edge Singapore*, 15 April 2019. This marks the first intra-sponsor S-REIT merger in Singapore as both OUE C-REIT and OUE H-Trust are under the same sponsor, OUE Ltd.

[94] Press release, *Ascott Residence Trust and Ascendas Hospitality Trust Enter Combination Deal to Become Asia Pacific's Largest Hospitality Trust with Asset Value of S$7.6 Billion*, issued by Ascott Residence Trust and Ascendas Hospitality Trust, 3 July 2019.

[95] 'CapitaLand to merge Ascott REIT, Ascendas unit,' *The Straits Times*, 4 July 2019.

[96] Press release, *Frasers Logistics & Industrial Trust and Frasers Commercial Trust Announce Proposed Merger by way of Trust Scheme*, issued by Frasers Logistics & Industrial Trust and Frasers Commercial Trust, 2 December 2019. See also 'Frasers' logistics and commercial REITs propose S$1.58b merger,' *The Business Times*, 3 December 2019 and 'Search for scale likely to keep S-REITs on M&A prowl,' *The Business Times*, 3 December 2019.

[97] One of the issues raised in connection with the proposed merger of Frasers Logistics & Industrial Trust (FLT) and Frasers Commercial Trust (FCOT) was whether the scheme consideration, which was priced based on historical trading prices (rather than net asset value) undervalued FCOT. In this regard, it was noted that S-REITs with different underlying asset classes would typically trade at different multiples to their net asset values. Industrial/logistics S-REITs tend to trade at significant premium to their net asset value per unit, at around 1.4 times on average. On the other hand, commercial S-REITs tend to trade at a discount to or around their net asset value per unit. The aforementioned trend was similarly observed in the market prices of FLT and FCOT prior to the announcement of the proposed merger. See 'Considering

The consolidation trend continued in the new decade when on 23 January 2020, CapitaLand Mall Trust and CapitaLand Commercial Trust announced their intention to merge to form Singapore's biggest S-REIT and the third largest in the Asia-Pacific after Hong Kong's Link REIT and Australia's Scentre Group. The merged entity, CapitaLand Integrated Commercial Trust, was expected to have a market capitalization of $16.8 billion and a combined property value of S$22.9 billion. The merged entity would also have greater funding capacity with a debt headroom of $2.9 billion, and the flexibility to undertake larger redevelopments[98].

More recently on 16 July 2020, the managers of ESR-REIT and Sabana Shariah Compliant Industrial REIT announced the proposed merger of the two REITs via a trust scheme of arrangement[99]. Post-merger, the enlarged REIT was expected to remain a 100% pure-play S-REIT in that its entire real estate portfolio comprises Singapore real estate. The combined REIT would have assets of about $4.1 billion, putting it in a stronger position for inclusion in key global indices such as FTSE EPRA Nareit[100]. The proposed merger was however voted down by the unitholders of Sabana Shariah Compliant Industrial REIT; the first time in the history of S-REITs that a proposed merger has been voted down[101].

It is expected that the S-REIT market will continue to see more consolidation in the coming years[102], particularly given the limited acquisition opportunities in Singapore and the increasingly competitive

the FLT-FCOT merger holistically,' *The Business Times*, 7–8 March 2020. See also 'The debate between DPU and NAV,' *The Business Times*, 7 October 2020.

[98] 'CCT, CMT unveil plan for REIT juggernaut in S$8.27b merger,' *The Business Times*, 23 January 2020.

[99] ESR-REIT and Sabana Shariah Compliant Industrial REIT were earlier discussing a potential merger of the two S-REITs, but the negotiations stalled in 2017. ESR-REIT then went on to merge with Vivia Industrial Trust in 2018. Both ESR-REIT and Sabana Shariah Compliant Industrial REIT currently have the same sponsor, ESR Cayman. This was not the case in 2017 when the two S-REITs were exploring a potential merger. See also 'Second time's the charm as ESR-REIT, Sabana REIT revive merger proposal,' *The Business Times*, 17 July 2020.

[100] The earlier merger of ESR-REIT and Viva Industrial Trust in 2018 also cited potential index inclusion as a reason for the proposed merger.

[101] 'Sabana REIT's proposed merger with ESR-REIT voted down in rare win for activists,' *The Straits Times*, 4 December 2020. One of the key reasons cited for the lack of support from unitholders was that the proposed merger undervalued Sabana Shariah Compliant Industrial REIT. See 'A closer look at the ESR-Sabana deal', *The Business Times*, 6 January 2022.

[102] See 'S-REITs set for wave of consolidation: CIT Chief,' *The Business Times*, 24 March 2016, 'More M&A could be in the offing for S-REITs,' *The Business Times*, 10 April 2019. In 'Who will be next to merge in the S-REIT universe?' *The Business Times*, 19 December 2019, the speculation was that the three mergers

regulatory and economic environment. Merger is generally seen to be the fastest way for S-REITs to scale up their expertise and resources and grow their asset portfolio. S-REITs which consolidate may also benefit from having access to a wider pool of investors, greater funding capacity, cost savings from synergies, greater trading volume, liquidity and visibility to global investors, and even inclusion in a leading benchmark index[103] which may in turn attract a valuation premium. Ideally, the merger and consolidation of two or more S-REITs into one should bring about an enlarged portfolio with diversification of geography and client base and at the same time expand the range of asset classes[104].

On the other hand, S-REITs which do not grow could be penalized with lower trading volume and liquidity due to the lack of attention from investors. The smaller S-REITs which are trading at steep discount and offering inflated yield to investors, will also find it difficult to grow via yield accretive acquisitions. This is due to the comparatively smaller pool of available assets which may offer a yield exceeding that provided by the S-REIT. Such REITs may eventually choose to go down the privatization and delisting route[105]. In the worst case scenarios, these smaller S-REITs may end up as potential acquisition targets, particularly where their units are trading below net asset value[106].

6. Typical Structure of S-REITs

A typical structure commonly adopted by S-REITs is set out in Figure 2, and comprises the S-REIT, the trustee, the S-REIT manager, the property manager and the unitholders (one of which is usually the sponsor of the S-REIT).

---

between (a) ESR REIT and Sabana REIT, (b) Cache Logistics Trust and Cromwell European REIT and (c) CapitaLand Mall Trust and CapitaLand Retail China Trust may be forthcoming.

[103] An example is the FTSE EPRA/NAREIT Global Real Estate Index Series (Global Developed Index), which is an international real estate investment index developed by FTSE Group in cooperation with the European Public Real Estate Association (EPRA) and the National Association of Real Estate Investment Trusts (NAREIT) to track the performance of listed real estate companies and REITs worldwide.

[104] 'Search for scale likely to keep S-REITs on M&A prowl,' The Business Times, 3 December 2019.

[105] See 'High yield a key factor in Soilbuild REIT's privatization exercise, but will investors accept the deal?' The Business Times, 17 December 2020 and 'Soilbuild Group chairman, Blackstone to take Soilbuild REIT private at 55 cents per unit,' The Straits Times, 14 December 2020.

[106] 'Issues with tenants 'unavoidable' but unlikely to concern REITs: DBS,' The Business Times, 18 April 2019.

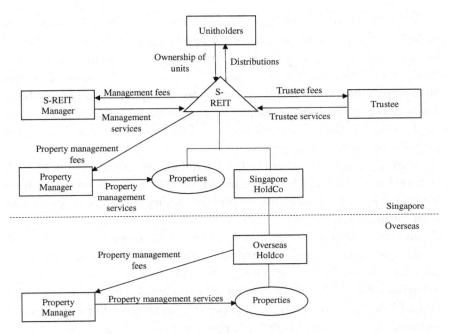

Figure 2: Typical S-REIT structure.

Source: Based on prospectus of Sasseur Real Estate Investment Trust available on the website of the Singapore Exchange.

6.1. S-REIT

A REIT is constituted by a trust deed, which sets out the trust and contractual rights and interest of the unitholders as well as the role and responsibilities of the trustee and manager of the S-REIT. The trust deed typically provides that the S-REIT is constituted as a trust to invest in real estate and real estate related assets. In the Singapore context, a S-REIT is often sponsored by a real estate company which will hold a significant interest in the units of the S-REIT post listing.

S-REITs which hold Singapore real estate typically hold such real estate directly, with the legal title and ownership of the real estate vested with the trustee of the S-REIT. Such direct holding of the Singapore real estate facilitates the flow-through of rental and other income from the S-REIT to the beneficiaries under the "tax transparency" treatment[107].

---

[107] See Section 8 for details on the tax transparency treatment accorded to S-REITs.

As an alternative to the direct holding of real estate, S-REITs are known to hold real estate through the use of another trust (commonly referred to as a "sub-trust"), as such a sub-trust may similarly qualify for "tax transparency" treatment. As an example[108], in the redevelopment of Golden Shoe carpark by CapitaLand Commercial Trust, CapitaLand and Mitsubishi Estate into a mixed-used development, two single-purpose sub-trusts were used — one for the commercial portion of the development and the other for the serviced residence portion.

With the introduction of the limited liability partnership in year 2005 as a new business vehicle, a number of S-REITs are now opting to hold their Singapore real estate through limited liability partnerships, given that such business vehicles are "tax transparent" for income tax purpose (i.e. the income is taxable in the hands of the partners instead of the limited liability partnership itself). For example, in January 2019, Keppel DC REIT converted Keppel DC Singapore 5 Pte. Ltd. (a Singapore incorporated company which holds a data center at 13 Sunview Way in Jurong) to a limited liability partnership (i.e. Keppel DC Singapore 5 LLP) pursuant to section 27 of the Limited Liability Partnerships Act[109]. Keppel DC REIT had earlier acquired 99% of the shareholding in the company from unrelated third parties. Following the acquisition of the 99% shareholding in Keppel DC Singapore 5 Pte. Ltd. and the conversion of the company into a limited liability partnership, Keppel DC REIT has been granted tax transparency treatment for its share of the taxable income of Keppel DC Singapore 5 LLP, similar to that which was granted for its other Singapore data centers[110].

As for overseas real estate, a common practice of S-REITs is to hold such real estate through one or more levels of holding companies or special purpose companies (incorporated in Singapore and/or outside Singapore). Alternatively, the overseas real estate may be held through a trust or registered branch office established in the overseas jurisdiction. The foreign dividend income, foreign branch profit, foreign interest income and foreign trust distribution received in Singapore may in turn qualify for tax exemption in

---

[108] 'S$1.82b redevelopment of Golden Shoe Carpark unveiled,' *The Business Times*, 14 July 2017.

[109] Cap. 163A.

[110] Press release, *Conversion of Keppel DC Singapore 5 Pte. Ltd., Which Holds Keppel DC Singapore 5, into a Limited Liability Partnership*, issued by Keppel DC REIT, 18 January 2019.

Singapore, subject to meeting prescribed conditions under section 13(8) or 13(12) of the Income Tax Act.

6.2. Sponsor

In the Singapore context, a S-REIT is often sponsored by a real estate holding or development company which provides the initial real estate portfolio of the S-REIT. The sponsor typically holds a significant stake of the S-REIT post listing (see further discussion on unitholders below)[111] and in many instances, has a pipeline of real estate available for injection into the S-REIT to grow its portfolio of real estate post listing. In many instances, the sponsor will also provide the S-REIT with a right of first refusal in respect of real estate to be divested by the sponsor[112]. In this regard, the industry experience of the sponsor in managing and growing the real estate portfolio of a S-REIT is usually a relevant factor taken into consideration by potential investors when deciding which S-REIT to invest.

The sponsor also often provides financial support to the S-REIT when the latter undertakes fund raising to expand its property portfolio. Such financial support is especially critical for S-REITs given that they have limited retained earnings available to fund acquisition of real estate, due to the requirement to distribute at least 90% of the income in order to enjoy "tax transparency" treatment for income tax purposes[113]. For the above reasons, investors generally prefer S-REITs with strong sponsors, such as CapitaLand Mall Trust, CapitaLand Commercial Trust and CapitaLand Retail China Trust which are sponsored by CapitaLand, as well as Mapletree Logistics Trust, Mapletree Industrial Trust, Mapletree Commercial Trust, Mapletree North Asia Commercial Trust which are sponsored by Mapletree.

One of the S-REITs, which was previously independent and not sponsored by a property developer, was Cambridge Industrial Trust, which was seen to be underperforming the market. It subsequently found

---

[111] The retention of a significant stake in the S-REIT also serves to signal the alignment of the sponsor's interests with that of the other investors.

[112] The injection or sale of a real estate by the sponsor to the S-REIT is an interested party transaction which requires the approval of unitholders. For such interested party transactions, the sponsor will have to abstain from voting.

[113] See discussion on 'tax transparency treatment' at Section 8.

a sponsor in e-Shang Redwood (ESR), a pan-Asian logistics property developer, owner and operator. ESR's co-founders and management team comprise executives of Prologis, one of the world's largest logistics property developer, owner and operator. Cambridge Industrial Trust was renamed as ESR-REIT and shortly thereafter went on an aggressive expansion drive by acquiring Viva Industrial Trust to become the fourth largest industrial S-REIT[114].

While the sponsor may be committed to supporting the growth of the sponsored S-REIT (e.g. by injecting real estate into the S-REITs or providing financial support), any such actions cannot be undertaken unilaterally. This is particularly so, given that the S-REITs are separately listed vehicles, with their own stakeholders. In this regard, any transaction involving the sponsor and the sponsored S-REIT would have to be undertaken on an arm's length basis and the respective board of directors would have to be satisfied with the commerciality of the proposed transaction.

6.3. Unitholders

The beneficiaries of a real estate investment trust are the unitholders of the S-REIT. Each unit held by the unitholders represents an interest in the S-REIT. The unitholders typically have no equitable or proprietary interest in the underlying assets of the S-REIT. In other words, a unitholder is not entitled to request for the transfer of the underlying real estate (or any interest or part thereof) to him in his capacity as a unitholder[115].

The primary rights of unitholders include the rights to receive income and other distributions attributable to the units held, receive audited accounts and the annual reports of the S-REIT and participate in the termination of the S-REIT by receiving a share of all net proceeds derived from the realization of the assets of the S-REIT less any liabilities, in accordance with their proportionate interests in the S-REIT.

---

[114] 'ESR-REIT and VIT plan merger as REITs race to grow bigger,' *The Edge Singapore*, 28 May 2018.

[115] See Aaron Seah, *Conceptualising the Singapore Real Estate Investment Trust*, (2010) 24(3) Tru. L.I., pp. 155–175, for a discussion on the rights of unitholders. An abridged version of the article is published in *Singapore Law Gazette*, February 2011.

In addition, unitholders have the right to require due administration of the S-REIT in accordance with the provisions of the trust deed, including, without limitation, by suit against the trustee or the manager.

6.4. Trustee

The main responsibilities of the trustee, as provided under a typical trust deed, are primarily custodial and administrative. Such responsibilities include holding the assets of the S-REIT (e.g. real estate or shares) in trust for the benefit of the unitholders, safeguarding the rights and interests of the unitholders, ensuring that the S-REIT manager invests according to mandate, and exercising powers as trustee of the S-REIT.

The trustee is typically entitled to a trustee fee determined as a percentage of the value of the underlying assets held in trust (e.g. 0.015% of the value of the deposited property held in trust), subject to a minimum absolute amount (see Table 5 for an overview of the fee structure of selected S-REITs).

The trust deed typically provides that the trustee may be removed by a resolution passed by at least 75% of the total number of votes represented by all the units in issue at a duly convened unitholders' meeting.

6.5. S-REIT manager

The manager of a S-REIT exercises general powers of management over the assets of the S-REIT. In the Singapore context, the external manager model is commonly adopted[116]. An externally managed S-REIT operates like a fund, with the manager being a third party that earns a fee for managing the S-REIT. In contrast, an S-REIT which is internally managed will employ the manager and support staff, instead of outsourcing the functions to a third party.

Under the external manager model in Singapore, the manager of a S-REIT in Singapore is typically a wholly owned subsidiary or related party of the sponsor of the S-REIT. The external manager model provides incentives for the sponsors, especially if they are property developers, to continue to inject

---

[116] 'A model that works,' *The Edge Singapore*, 30 December 2019.

real estate into the S-REIT and grow the vehicle post-IPO[117]. It has however been noted that calls for S-REIT managers to be internalized have grown stronger over time[118].

The main responsibilities of the S-REIT manager as provided under a typical trust deed include setting the strategic direction of the S-REIT, managing assets and liabilities of the trust for the benefit of unitholders, and giving recommendations to the trustee on the acquisition, divestment or enhancement of the assets of the S-REIT in accordance with the investment strategy of the S-REIT[119].

The trust deed typically provides that the manager may be removed by way of a resolution passed by a simple majority of unitholders present and voting at a general meeting. However, this may be difficult to achieve in many instances given that the S-REIT manager is typically wholly owned by the sponsor of the S-REIT which often holds significant interest in the units of the S-REIT.

With regard to the remuneration package of the S-REIT managers, such packages are typically structured in a manner which encourage the managers to focus on growing the S-REIT through yield-accretive acquisitions and increasing the distributable income to unitholders. More specifically, the S-REIT manager is often entitled to a management fee (comprising an annual base fee and a periodic performance fee which is subject to meeting certain conditions) for managing the affairs of the S-REIT, an acquisition fee for growing the portfolio and distributable income of the S-REIT through acquisition of real estate assets (which in turn result in an increase in the quantum of the base fee), a divestment fee for the disposal of real estate assets which no longer generate the desired yield, and a development management fee for managing development projects undertaken on behalf of the S-REIT (see Table 5 for an overview of the fee structure of selected S-REITs).

---

[117] 'A model that works,' *The Edge Singapore*, 30 December 2019.

[118] In the United States, the internally managed model is more predominant. It has been suggested that under the externally managed model, the REIT manager may not always act in the best interest of the unitholders, given that the external managers are working for fees based largely on the REIT's total property value or assets under management. See 'Do REIT managers have as much stake as unitholders?' *The Business Times*, 21 April 2020.

[119] 'ARA Asset Management's John Lim on what it takes to be a REIT manager,' *The Edge Singapore*, 25 June 2018.

In practice, it is observed that the abovementioned fees are commonly determined as follows[120]:

- **Annual base fee:** A percentage of the value of underlying assets held in trust (e.g. 0.5% of the value of the deposited property) and more recently, the distributable income of the S-REIT (e.g. 10% of distributable income). A common criticism of the external manager model is that the annual base fee is usually tied to the size of the S-REITs, which may unduly incentivize the S-REIT manager to acquire assets, even if such acquisitions are not yield-accretive to the unitholders[121]. In this regard, the alternative of computing the annual base fee based on the distributable income of the S-REIT better aligns the interests of the managers with that of the unitholders.
- **Performance fee:** A percentage of the net investment income (e.g. 5% of net property income or distributable income), the increase in distribution per unit compared to the preceding year (e.g. 25% of the increase in distribution) or the amount by which the total returns of the S-REIT outperforms a benchmark index[122].
- **Acquisition fee:** A percentage of the value of the real estate acquired by the S-REIT (e.g. up to 1% of the value of the acquisition).
- **Divestment fee:** A percentage of the value of the real estate divested by the S-REIT (e.g. up to 0.5% of the value of the divestment).
- **Development management fee:** A percentage of the total project cost incurred in development projects undertaken by the S-REIT manager on behalf of the S-REIT (e.g. 3% of the total development or project cost)[123].

---

[120] Based on the IPO prospectus of various S-REITs. See also, 'The lowdown on REIT fees,' *The Edge Singapore*, 20 September 2021.

[121] 'A model that works,' *The Edge Singapore*, 30 December 2019.

[122] 'MGCCT's fee model for future Mapletree REITs,' *The Business Times*, 20 May 2013. When the model where no performance fee is earned where there is no growth in the DPU featured in Mapletree Greater China Commercial Trust, it was well received by the market as being aligned to the interests of unitholders, whereas a performance fee based on a percentage of income motivates the REIT manager to grow the size of the REIT portfolio.

[123] In relation to the undertaking of development projects, Ascendas REIT is the widely known to be the first S-REIT to do so on its own balance sheet — its first two developments were the Courts Megastore and Giant Hypermart (both situated at Tampines), which commenced in 2006 and worth a total of $128 million. See *Tenacity: A Decade of Enabling Businesses — Ascendas REIT* (Straits Times Press, 2014).

Table 5: Typical fee structure of S-REITs (based on information available in the IPO prospectus of the S-REITs).

Type of Fee	Ascendas REIT (Listed in 2002)	Parkway Life REIT (Listed in 2007)	SPH REIT (Listed in 2013)	Frasers Logistics & Industrial Trust (Listed in 2016)
Trustee Fee	0.03% per annum of the deposited property, subject to a minimum of $10,000 per month	Up to 0.03% per annum of the value of the deposited property, subject to a minimum of $10,000 per month	Up to 0.02% per annum of the value of the deposited property, subject to a minimum of $15,000 per month	Up to 0.015% per annum of the value of the deposited property, subject to a minimum amount of $15,000 per month
Management Fee (payable to the REIT Manager)	**Base fee:** 0.5% per annum of the deposited property **Performance fee:** 0.1% per annum of the deposited property if annual growth in distributions per unit exceeds 2.5% 0.2% per annum of the deposited property if annual growth in distributions per unit exceeds 5.0%	**Base fee:** 0.3% per annum of the value of the deposited property **Performance fee:** 4.5% per annum of the net property income	**Base fee:** 0.25% per annum of the value of the deposited property **Performance fee:** 5.0% per annum of the net property income	**Base fee:** 0.4% per annum of the value of the deposited property **Performance fee:** 5.0% per annum of the distributable income
Acquisition Fee (payable to the REIT Manager)	Maximum of 1.0% of the acquisition price for any real estate purchased	1.0% of the enterprise value of any real estate or real estate related asset acquired Where the asset acquired is a real estate, "Enterprise Value" shall mean the value of the real estate Where the asset acquired are shares in special purpose vehicle whose primary purpose is to hold/own real estate (directly or indirectly), "Enterprise Value" shall mean the sum of the equity value and the total net debt attributable to the shares being acquired	0.75% for acquisitions from related parties and 1.0% for all other acquisitions, computed on the following: • Acquisition price of real estate purchased plus any other payment made in connection with the purchase • Underlying value of real estate taken into account when computing the acquisition price payable for the acquisition of the equity interest of entities which holds real estate plus any other payment made in connection with the purchase; or	0.5% for acquisitions from related parties and 1.0% for all other acquisitions, computed on the following: • Acquisition price of real estate purchased plus any other payment made in connection with the purchase; • Underlying value of real estate taken into account when computing the acquisition price payable for the acquisition of the equity interest of entities which holds real estate plus any other payment made in connection with the purchase; or

Divestment Fee (payable to the REIT Manager)	—	Maximum of 0.5% of the sale price of any real estate sold or divested	0.5% of the enterprise value of any real estate or real estate related asset sold or divested	Acquisition price of investment in debt securities of any property corporation or other special purpose vehicles ("SPVs") owning or acquiring real estate 0.5% of the following as is applicable: • Sale price of real estate sold or divested plus any other payment received made in connection with the sale or divestment • Underlying value of real estate taken into account when computing the sale price for the sale or divestment of the equity interest of entities which holds real estate plus any other payment made in connection with the sale or divestment; or • Sale price of investment in debt securities of any property corporation or other SPVs owning or acquiring real estate	• Acquisition price of investment in debt securities of any property corporation or other SPVs owning or acquiring real estate or any debt securities which are secured whether directly or indirectly by the real income from real estate 0.5% of the following as is applicable: • Sale price of real estate sold or divested plus any other payment received made in connection with the sale or divestment; • Underlying value of real estate taken into account when computing the sale price for the sale or divestment of the equity interest of entities which holds real estate plus any other payment made in connection with the sale or divestment; or • Sale price of investment in debt securities of any property corporation or other SPVs owning or acquiring real estate or any debt securities which are secured whether directly or indirectly by the real income from real estate
Development Management Fee (payable to the REIT Manager)	—	—	—	—	3.0% of the total project costs incurred in a development project undertaken by the manager

(Continued)

475

Table 5: *(Continued)*

Type of Fee	Ascendas REIT (Listed in 2002)	Parkway Life REIT (Listed in 2007)	SPH REIT (Listed in 2013)	Frasers Logistics & Industrial Trust (Listed in 2016)
Property Manager Fee[a]	• **Property management fee:** 2.0% per annum of the gross revenue of each property • **Lease management fee:** 1.0% per annum of the gross revenue of each property • **Property tax service fee:** Up to 7.5% of the property tax savings • **Marketing Services Commission:** ➤ Up to 2 months of gross rent inclusive of service charge for new lease and up to 1 month of gross rent inclusive of service charge for renewal of existing lease ➤ If a third party agent secures a lease, the manager will be entitled to up to 2.4 month of gross rent inclusive of service charge, and will be responsible for all marketing services commission payable to such third party agent • **Project management fees** (in relation to the development,	• **Property management fee:** 2.0% per annum of revenue for the managed property (excluding the Mount Elizabeth Hospital, Gleneagles Hospital, Parkway East Hospital for the duration of the master lease agreement) • **Lease management fee:** 1.0% per annum of the revenue of the managed property (excluding the Mount Elizabeth Hospital, Gleneagles Hospital, Parkway East Hospital for the duration of the master lease agreement) • **Marketing Services Commission:** ➤ Up to 2 months of gross rent inclusive of service charge for new lease and up to 1 month of gross rent inclusive of service charge for renewal of existing lease ➤ If a third party agent secures a lease, the manager will be entitled to up to 2.4 month of gross rent inclusive of	• **Property management fee:** ➤ 2.0% per annum of gross revenue for the relevant property; ➤ 2.0% per annum of the net property income for the relevant property; and ➤ 0.5% per annum of the net property income for the relevant property in lieu of leasing commissions otherwise payable to the property manager and/or third party agents. • **Project management fee** (in relation to the development and redevelopment, refurbishment, retrofitting and renovation works of property): ➤ Up to 5.0% of the construction costs	• **Property management fee:** Australia properties ➤ 1.2% per annum of the PMA Net Property Income (i.e. gross revenue less property expenses) of each property; where any property is not fully leased, A$1,000 per month per property in the event there is vacant lettable area in such property Non Australia properties ➤ Up to 2.0% per annum of the PMA Gross Revenue of each property • **Lease management fee:** Non Australia properties ➤ Up to 1.0% per annum of the PMA Gross Revenue of each property • **Marketing services commission:** Australia properties ➤ One-time commission of 13.0% of the Year 1 PMA Gross Revenue derived from new lease and one-time commission of

redevelopment, refurbishment, retrofitting and renovation of property): ➤ Up to 3.0% of the construction costs	service charge, and will be responsible for all marketing services commission payable to such third party agent • **Project management fee** (in relation to the development and redevelopment, refurbishment, retrofitting and renovation works of a property): ➤ Up to 5.0% of the capital expenditure	7.0% of the Year 1 PMA Gross Revenue derived from the renewal of existing lease Non Australia properties ➤ 0 to 2 months PMA Gross Revenue for new lease. The commission is reduced by 50% for renewal of existing lease. • **Project management fee** (in relation to the refurbishment, retrofitting, addition and alteration or renovation works of a property under management): ➤ Up to 3.0% of the construction costs

Note:

[a] In the case of Parkway Life REIT, the REIT manager is also responsible for performing some of the roles of typically performed by the property manager. In return for performing such services, the remuneration of the REIT manager includes property management fee, lease management fee and marketing services commission.

6.6. Property manager

The property manager is responsible for the day-to-day management or maintaining of the properties of the S-REIT. In the Singapore context, the property manager is typically a wholly owned subsidiary or related party of the sponsor or manager of the S-REIT. There are nevertheless instances where the routine property management and maintenance works are outsourced to third party property managers.

The main responsibilities of a property manager generally include managing, maintaining, marketing and leasing the properties of the S-REIT. The property manager is typically entitled to various streams of fees from the S-REITs for its efforts (see Table 5 for an overview of the fee structure of selected S-REITs, based on information available in the respective IPO prospectus). Such fees include a property management fee which is often determined as a percentage of the gross or net income of each property under management (e.g. 2% of the annual gross revenue of the managed property) as well as a lease management fee for managing the lease of the property (e.g. 1% of the annual gross revenue of the managed property). In addition, the property manager is typically entitled to a leasing commission when it secures a new tenant or a tenancy renewal. The commission is often determined based on the monthly rent and the duration of the lease (e.g. up to 2 months of gross rent).

It is further noted that the property manager typically receives a project management fee in relation to the development, refurbishment, retrofitting or renovation of its managed property (e.g. up to a rate of 5% of the capital expenditure of the project). A number of S-REITs also remunerate their property manager for its effort in managing the property tax payable on the annual value of the real estate of the S-REIT (e.g. up to a rate of 7.5% of the property tax savings).

7. Code on Collective Investment Scheme for Property Funds

A S-REIT constituted as unit trust is regulated as a collective investment scheme under the Securities and Futures Act[124]. Broadly speaking, S-REITs

---

[124] Cap. 289.

structured as unit trusts are regulated with a relatively light touch compared to unit trusts investing in securities or other financial instruments regulated under the collective investment scheme regime, or REITs in other jurisdictions[125].

The best practices on management, operation and marketing of collective investment schemes that managers and trustees are expected to observe are set out in the Code on Collective Investment Scheme (CIS Code) issued by the MAS pursuant to section 321 of the Securities and Futures Act. The Code was first issued on 23 May 2002 and has been revised over the years, as the S-REIT market developed and evolved. The most recent revision of the CIS Code was on 1 July 2021.

Appendix 6 of the CIS Code sets out the guidelines for property funds such as S-REITs which invest primarily in real estate and real estate-related assets. While the CIS Code is non-statutory in nature, a breach of the guidelines may be taken into account by the MAS in determining whether to revoke or suspend the status of the S-REIT or to refuse to authorize or recognize new collective investment schemes proposed to be offered by the same responsible person.

The CIS Code pertaining to property funds such as S-REITs takes into account the following key differences between a S-REIT (being a CIS which invests in real estate) and CIS which invests in securities or other financial instruments (Securities CIS)[126]:

- **Structural differences:** S-REITs are close-ended investment vehicles and investors have to exit their investments by selling them on the exchange. Market sentiment and confidence will play a part in determining the price at which investors can acquire or exit their investments, which may result in S-REITs not trading at or near their net asset value. In contrast, securities CIS are open-ended investment vehicles and its manager is required to sell or redeem units of the CIS at net asset value.

---

[125] For an overview of the regulatory regime pertaining to S-REITs, see Lee Suet Fern and Linda Esther Foo, *Real Estate Investment Trusts in Singapore, Recent Legal and Regulatory Developments and the Case for Corporatization* (2010) 22 SAcLJ 36 and Allen Tan, James Choo and Justin Tan, 'An investor's guide to the regulatory and tax framework for S-REITs,' *Derivatives and Financial Instruments*, May/June 2011, IBFD, p. 137.

[126] *Consultation Paper P006-2005: Review of the Regulatory Regime Governing REITs* (MAS, June 2005).

- **Liquidity of underlying assets:** The underlying real estate held by S-REITs are less liquid and the time required to dispose the real estate is generally longer compared to that for the underlying securities held by securities CIS.
- **Valuation of underlying assets:** The valuation of real estate held by REITs is more subjective in nature compared to securities held by securities CIS where market quotations of the underlying financial instruments are readily available.
- **Related party transactions:** S-REITs are usually sponsored by property holding or development companies and acquire their initial real estate portfolio from such related parties. In this regard, many S-REITs continue to transact with related parties after their formation and listing.

The guidelines pertaining to property funds set out under Appendix 6 to the CIS Code include (amongst others) the types of permissible investments which may be acquired, the limitation on the types of revenue streams to be derived, restriction on development activities, limitation on borrowings and leverage as well as guidance on valuation of the underlying real estate assets. These guidelines are in turn discussed in the following sections.

7.1. Permissible investments

The CIS Code provides that the investment portfolio of S-REITs should generally be limited to real estate, real estate related assets, debt securities and listed shares issued by non-property corporations, government securities and securities issued by a supranational agency or a Singapore statutory board, and cash and cash equivalent items.

The real estate may either be freehold or leasehold, situated within or outside Singapore. Such real estate may range from commercial properties (e.g. shopping malls and offices) to healthcare-related properties (e.g. hospitals and nursing homes) to hospitality-related properties (e.g. serviced residences and hotels) and industrial properties (e.g. factories, warehouses, business park space, distribution centers, logistics facilities, data centers). It may also extend to heritage shophouses and infrastructure real estate such as the Changi Airport terminals[127]. The investment in real estate may be made by the S-REIT via direct ownership or a shareholding in an unlisted SPV constituted to hold or own real estate. An investment in another property fund that is authorized under section 286(1) of the Securities and Futures Act and Appendix 6 of the CIS Code will also be regarded as an investment in real estate.

The term "real estate" does not include "real estate related assets" which refers to listed or unlisted debt securities and listed shares of or issued by property corporations, mortgage-backed securities, other property funds, and assets incidental to the ownership of real estate (e.g. furniture).

As a general guideline, at least 75% of the S-REIT's deposited property should be invested in income-producing real estate. Real estate would be considered income-producing if its yield (without any arrangement which could artificially enhance the yield of the property) is greater than the risk-free rate. The risk-free rate is taken as the highest yield of 5-year Singapore Government Securities for the 12 months preceding the date of the draft valuation report that is submitted to the MAS at the time of application for authorization.

In respect of the S-REIT's investment other than real estate and real estate related assets, not more than 5% of the S-REIT's deposited property should be invested in any single issuer's securities or any single manager's funds. An exception applies for deposits placed with eligible financial institutions and investments in high-quality money market instruments or debt securities.

7.2. Limitation on sources of other revenue

In addition to the above guidelines on the permissible investments which may be acquired by S-REITs, the CIS Code contains guidelines on the revenue streams to be derived by S-REITs. As a general rule, S-REITs should not derive more than 10% of its revenue from sources other than rental payments from

---

[127] 'Could a heritage shophouse REIT take off,' *The Business Times*, 25 April 2018, 'Airport REIT proposal sets analysts abuzz,' *The Business Times*, 7 March 2019, 'A Changi Airport spin-off may benefit investors more so than Singaporeans,' *The Business Times*, 12 March 2019 and 'Could a full-fledged Airport REIT work?' *The Business Times*, 26 March 2019.

the tenants of the real estate held by the S-REIT or interest, dividends, and other similar payments from SPVs and other permissible investments of the S-REIT. For this purpose, rental payments include income that is ancillary or incidental to the leasing of real estate. This includes income from use of signage space and advertising contributions by tenants.

7.3. Restriction on development activities

Under the CIS Code, and in line with Government policy that REITs are to be "stable, high pay-out and pass-through vehicles", S-REITs should also not undertake property development activities whether on its own, in a joint venture with others, or by investing in unlisted property development companies, unless the S-REIT intends to hold the developed property upon completion. In addition, S-REITs should not invest in vacant land and mortgages (except for mortgage-backed securities), albeit that S-REITs are not prohibited from investing in real estate to be built on vacant land that has been approved for development or other uncompleted property developments. However, where potential assets suitable for acquisition are lacking and the capital available for acquisition is expensive, REITs have embarked on development activities[128].

As a general guideline, the total contract value of property development activities undertaken and investments in uncompleted property developments should not exceed 10% of the S-REIT's deposited property. This serves to limit the extent of development activities undertaken by S-REIT and in turn reduce the overall risk borne by a S-REIT in undertaking any such activities which may adversely affect the cash flow and distribution of the S-REIT.

The total contract value of property development activities may be increased from 10% to 25% of the S-REIT's deposited property provided that (i) the additional allowance of up to 15% of the property fund's deposited property is utilized solely for the redevelopment of an existing property that has been held by the S-REIT for at least 3 years and which the S-REIT will continue to hold for at least another 3 years after the

---

[128] 'REITs may well have to go down development path,' *The Business Times*, 12 December 2017, where it was also reported that CapitaLand Commercial Trust did not buy CapitaLand's Temasek Tower and Chevron House which were sold to third parties, probably on account that the prices offered by the third parties were probably at a level which were not yield-accretive for the REIT.

completion of the redevelopment and (ii) the S-REIT obtains the specific approval of participants at a general meeting for the redevelopment of the property. Prior to the introduction of the new 25% limit, the total contract value of property development activities undertaken and investments in uncompleted property developments was capped at 10% of the S-REIT's deposited property.

The effect of the general restriction on development activities effectively means that S-REITs are more likely to acquire completed buildings instead of developing new buildings. Nevertheless, there are a number of S-REITs which are actively undertaking development activities. These include Ascendas REIT which would be developing Grab's new $181.2 million headquarters building in the one-north business park[129], and CapitaLand Commercial Trust which has redeveloped Golden Shoe Car Park into a 51-storey integrated development comprising office space, serviced residence, retail shops, a food center, and a multi-storey carpark[130]. In the case of CapitaLand Commercial Trust, it entered into a joint venture arrangement to comply with the 10% guideline stipulated under the CIS Code on development activities[131].

In the proposed redevelopment of 403-room Novotel Singapore Clarke Quay by CDL Hospitality Trust, it first sold the existing hotel to the CapitaLand and City Developments Limited (CDL) as part of the consortium's redevelopment of the Liang Court site, and would buy back a new hotel with 460–475 rooms to be built on the site under a forward purchase agreement with CDL at the lower of $475 million or 110% of the actual development costs[132].

7.4. Limitations on borrowings and leverage

Under the CIS Code, the aggregate leverage (which includes total borrowings and deferred payments, whether to be settled in cash or in units

---

[129] 'Ascendas REIT to develop, manage Grab's HQ,' *The Straits Times*, 31 January 2019.

[130] '$1.82b tower to replace Golden Shoe Car Park,' *The Straits Times*, 14 July 2017.

[131] '$1.82b redevelopment of Golden Shoe Carpark unveiled,' *The Business Times*, 14 July 2017.

[132] 'River Valley hotel plot offers CapitaLand-CDL integration potential with Liang Court,' *The Business Times*, 25 July 2019 and 'CDLHT hotel deals 'not prejudicial' to securityholders' interests: IFA,' *The Business Times*, 4–5 January 2020.

of the S-REIT) of a S-REIT should in general not exceed 45% of the value of the S-REIT's deposited property. Such a restriction prevents S-REITs from undertaking excessive debts, and in turn protects the interests of investors by mitigating the risk of a S-REIT having to liquidate a portfolio asset at the bottom of a property cycle, in order to service its debt during a liquidity or credit crunch[133]. This is an important safeguard put in place for investors given that the cost of debt financing is generally lower than that of equity financing, and *ceteris paribus* there is a general preference to fund the acquisition of real estate using borrowings.

As at 31 May 2019, the aggregate leverage of S-REITs stands at an average of 34%, more than 10 percentage points below the limit of 45%[134]. This is attributed to the fact that S-REITs typically try to maintain a sufficient buffer, in anticipation of any changes to market conditions such as declining property prices.

The 45% limit on aggregate leverage was announced in 2015 and supersedes the previous guidelines where (i) the aggregate leverage of a S-REIT was not to exceed 35% of the S-REIT's deposited property, and (ii) the 35% limit on aggregate leverage may be increased to 60% provided that a credit rating of the S-REIT from Fitch Inc., Moody's or Standard and Poor's is obtained and disclosed to the public. The adoption of a single-tier leverage limit of 45% in 2015 was on account of the fact that credit ratings may not sufficiently distinguish a good quality REIT from a poor one.

More recently, on 2 July 2019, the MAS issued a consultation paper proposing to amend the CIS Code to increase the leverage limit from the current 45%, subject to the S-REIT meeting a certain minimum interest coverage ratio (ICR)[135] or having demonstrated strong financial discipline

---

[133] During the Global Financial Crisis, it was reported that MAS reassured REIT managers that the increase in the leverage beyond the stipulated limit due to the fall in the property valuations, was not considered a breach of the regulatory limits, see 'No Panaceas for maladies of REITs,' *The Business Times*, 22 January 2009. While low interest rates will make increased borrowing attractive in boosting yields, high leverage levels may adversely affect unit prices, as may be seen especially during the global financial crisis: see 'Debt turns from foe to friend for many REITs,' *The Business Times*, 21 February 2011.

[134] 'MAS seeks views on raising 45% leverage limits for S-REITs,' *The Business Times*, 3 July 2019.

[135] ICR is a ratio that is calculated by dividing the trailing 12 months earnings before interest, tax, depreciation and amortization (excluding effects of any fair value changes of derivatives and investment properties, and foreign exchange translation), by the trailing 12 months interest expense and borrowing-related fees.

(such as having higher ICR threshold)[136]. The minimum ICR, which is a measure of an entity's debt servicing ability, is proposed at 2.5 times by the MAS[137]. The increase in leverage limit is expected to benefit the majority of the S-REITs given that the S-REIT sector currently have an average ICR of 5.8 times[138].

The rationale of such an increase in the leverage limit is (i) to provide S-REITs with more flexibility in managing their capital structure and (ii) to enable S-REITs to better compete against private equity funds, real estate companies and foreign REITs when making acquisitions to increase their real estate portfolio[139]. In proposing to recalibrate the leverage limits, the MAS took into account S-REITs' general preference to raise capital through debt financing, particularly given that debt tends to be a cheaper source of capital than equity and takes less time to raise. More importantly, the MAS acknowledges that, "This flexibility is particularly important when REITs acquire overseas assets from third parties, which has been the trend in recent years, driven partly by the search for assets with higher yield spreads. Unlike acquisitions from a REIT's sponsor, such acquisitions tend to involve a competitive bidding process and are highly time-sensitive". During such competitive bidding processes, competitors of S-REITs, which include private equity funds, real estate companies and foreign REITs which are not subject to such stringent leverage limits, have the additional flexibility of utilizing debt, which is a cheaper source of funding[140], to lower their overall cost of capital.

Another benefit which may arise from the proposed increase in leverage limit is the possibility of an increase in the distribution made by S-REITs to unitholders. This is in view that debt-funded property acquisitions are more likely to be accretive to distribution per unit (DPU) given that the

---

[136] *Consultation Paper on Proposed Amendments to the Requirements for REITs* (MAS, 2 July 2019). See also 'Leverage limit announcement for REITs won't come so soon: MAS,' *The Business Times*, 16 December 2019.

[137] Separately, the MAS has also proposed to streamline the fund-raising process for S-REITs by removing the requirement for them to submit a notification to MAS to obtain a 'Restricted Scheme' status when they make an offer of units to accredited and other investors. This will make the fund-raising process for S-REITs more efficient, and bring it in line with the fund-raising process for companies and business trusts.

[138] 'Higher gearing limits will improve REITs' DPU,' *The Business Times*, 4 July 2019.

[139] 'Good buys for REITs harder to come by with lower debt limits,' *The Business Times*, 23 March 2016.

[140] Interest rates have remained low since the days of the Global Financial Crisis more than a decade ago.

rental yields of the acquired assets will probably exceed the interest rate of borrowing. In addition, the higher leverage limits could also reduce the instances where S-REITs issue perpetual securities[141] to raise funds[142], in order to overcome the leverage limits. Perpetual securities are essentially bonds with no maturity date but may be structured and characterized as equity instead of debt for the purpose of determining the aggregate leverage of S-REITs[143]. Perpetual securities typically carry coupon rates[144] higher than the interest payable on bonds or loans[145], but are cheaper than equity.

A potential drawback of increasing the existing leverage limit is that it may entice S-REIT managers to engage in more aggressive acquisition activity to generate additional fees for the S-REIT managers, even in instances where the acquisition is not yield accretive and not in the overall interests of the unitholders. However, S-REITs which aggressively pursue leverage may not be well received by investors and may lead to lower valuation of their units[146].

Currently, Hong Kong REITs are subject to a leverage limit of 45% whereas Malaysian REITs are subject to a leverage limit of 50%. In Thailand, REITs are permitted to undertake leverage of up to 60%, provided the REITs have an investment-grade credit rating. European Union countries such as

---

[141] A perpetual security is a hybrid security. In order for a perpetual issued by a S-REIT to be treated as equity instead of debt, the perpetual security will have to fulfil certain conditions, including being deeply subordinated with non-cumulative distributions and no step-ups. These features, particularly no step-ups, differentiates perpetual securities issued by S-REITs from those typically issued by companies. See 'A model that works,' *The Edge Singapore*, 30 December 2019.

[142] In year 2019, S$7.1 billion was raised in Singapore via issuance of 20 perpetual securities. This dropped to S$1.4 billion in year 2020 when the financial market was rocked by the COVID-19 induced recession. See 'Share of perps in bond issues hits 6-year low as demand, yields dip,' *The Business Times*, 6 October 2020.

[143] 'A model that works,' *The Edge Singapore*, 30 December 2019. It is however to be noted that perpetual securities could potentially be regarded as debt instrument for Singapore income tax purposes. See Appendix 3 of IRAS e-Tax Guide, *Income Tax Treatment of Hybrid Instruments*, Second Edition, 21 October 2019.

[144] Perpetual securities have no legal maturity dates and are considered to be higher risk instruments than plain vanilla bonds. Issuers of perpetual securities in Singapore tend to be financial institutions looking to replenish capital to satisfy capital adequacy ratios, real estate investment trusts trying not to exceed their leverage limits, and Temasek-linked companies. On the other hand, investors of perpetual securities tend to be institutions such as insurance companies and fund managers, as well as private banking clients. See 'Share of perps in bond issues hits 6-year low as demand, yields dip,' *The Business Times*, 6 October 2020.

[145] 'Higher gearing limits will improve REITs' DPU,' *The Business Times*, 4 July 2019.

[146] 'Higher gearing limits will improve REITs' DPU,' *The Business Times*, 4 July 2019.

Belgium, Germany and Netherlands have leverage limits ranging from 60% to 66.25%. On the other hand, developed REIT markets such as the United States, Canada, Australia, France and Japan, do not impose any leverage limits, and neither does the United Kingdom, although it requires REITs to maintain a minimum ICR of 1.25 times[147].

In light of the onset of the COVID-19 global pandemic, it was announced on 16 April 2020 that the leverage limit for S-REITS would be temporarily raised from 45% to 50% with immediate effect, to provide S-REITs greater flexibility to manage their capital structure and to raise debt financing amid the challenging environment[148]. The MAS further announced that the new minimum ICR requirement of 2.5 times would not be implemented until 1 January 2022. In other words, from 1 January 2022, the leverage limit of 45% would apply, but may be increased to a maximum of 50% if the S-REIT has a minimum ICR of 2.5 times (after taking into account the interest payment obligations arising from the new borrowings).

The decision of the MAS took into account that the ICRs of S-REITs are expected to come under pressure in the short term as a result of the adverse impact of the COVID-19 pandemic on their earnings and cashflows. At the same time, the MAS announced that it would require S-REITs to disclose their leverage ratios and ICRs in annual reports and interim financial results, to provide investors with timely information about the financial position of S-REITs and the impact of higher leverage on their risk profiles.

As at 31 August 2020, the average leverage of the S-REIT sector stood at 36.4%, well below the 50% limit[149].

7.5. Valuation of the underlying real estate assets

The CIS Code also provides that a full valuation of each of the S-REIT's real estate assets should be conducted at least once a financial year, in

---

[147] 'MAS seeks views on raising 45% leverage limits for S-REITs,' *The Business Times*, 3 July 2019.

[148] Press release, *New Measures to Help REITs Navigate Operating Challenges Posed by COVID-19*, issued by MOF, IRAS and MAS, 16 April 2020.

[149] 'Singapore REITs set for broader recovery after Q1 Covid-19 hit,' *The Straits Times*, 23 September 2020.

accordance with any applicable code of practice for such valuations[150]. In addition, where the manager of the S-REIT proposes to issue new units for subscription or redeem existing units, and the property fund's real estate assets were valued more than 6 months ago, the manager should exercise discretion in deciding whether to conduct a desktop valuation of the real estate assets, especially when market conditions indicate that real estate values have changed materially. These measures increase transparency and help protect the interests of unitholders.

8. Income Taxation of S-REITs, Approved Sub-Trusts and Approved REIT Exchange Traded Funds[151]

Since the listing of the first S-REIT in year 2002, Singapore has introduced a wide array of tax concessions on income tax, goods and services tax (GST) and stamp duty, to promote the S-REIT sector. These concessionary tax rules which are aimed at enhancing the overall yield and attractiveness of S-REITs to investors, are widely seen as a major factor leading to the success of Singapore as an international hub for the listing of REITs.

In particular, the tax transparency treatment is widely regarded as the trigger which led to the taking off of the S-REIT market. Since then, the Singapore Government has introduced and extended various other concessionary tax treatments to enhance the attractiveness of S-REITs, often during the annual budget statement. This has in turn allowed a thriving S-REIT ecosystem, comprising S-REIT managers, trustees, bankers, lawyers,

---

[150] The regulatory arm of The Singapore Exchange SGX RegCo, in an initiative to raise investors' confidence in asset valuation reporting, has partnered the Singapore Institute of Surveyors and Valuers (SISV), in setting standards for property valuations. This follows an earlier incident where 3 separate property valuation firms had come up with the same valuation of $23 million for an industrial property which was also the price at the REIT sponsor proposed to sell to the REIT concerned: see 'SGX RegCo partners SISV to raise valuation standards,' *The Business Times,* 16 October 2019 and 'SGX RegCo seeks tougher standards for audits and property valuations,' *The Business Times,* 16 January 2020.

[151] For income tax purposes, the term 'real estate investment trust' generally refers to a trust that is constituted as a collective investment scheme authorized under s 286 of the Securities and Futures Act and listed on the Singapore Exchange, and that invests or proposes to invest in real estate and real estate related assets. See s 43(10) of the Income Tax Act for definition of S-REIT, approved sub-trust and approved REIT exchange traded fund for income tax purposes.

financial and tax advisers, valuers, investment analysts, etc, to emerge, offering a full suite of S-REIT related services.

In the 2004 annual budget statement[152], the then Deputy Prime Minister and Minister for Finance, Mr Lee Hsien Loong, announced that all Singapore-sourced investment income derived directly by individuals (i.e. not through a partnership) from financial instruments including S-REITs would be exempt from tax from 1 January 2004 (i.e. Year of Assessment 2005). In the subsequent annual budget statement in 2005[153], Mr Lee Hsien Loong who had then became the third Prime Minister of Singapore, announced various measures to strengthen Singapore's position as the preferred Asian hub for listing of REITs and attract foreign non-individual investors to participate in the S-REIT market. These include the waiver of stamp duty payable on sale or transfer of Singapore real estate into REITs to be listed or already listed on the Singapore Exchange for a 5-year period, the removal of most of the qualifying conditions for tax transparency and the reduction of withholding tax rate on REIT distribution from 20% to 10% for a 5-year period.

In the following year, additional measures were announced by Mr Lee Hsien Loong in the 2006 annual budget statement[154] to encourage S-REITs to venture overseas. These include the exemption of foreign-sourced interest and foreign trust distributions received by S-REIT as well as the recovery of GST incurred on the setting up of SPVs and the acquisition and holding of overseas non-residential properties by the SPVs. The market reacted positively to the announcements made, and the initial portfolio of 4 of the 7 newly listed S-REITs in 2006 (i.e. Frasers Commercial Trust, Ascott Residence Trust, CapitaLand Retail China Trust and First REIT) comprises substantially of overseas real estate. This marks a turning point in the history of the S-REIT market and the asset portfolio of subsequent S-REITs listed on the Singapore Exchange became increasingly international in nature.

The income tax and GST concessions for S-REITs were subsequently extended for another 5 years in the 2015 annual budget statement, to

---

[152] Minister for Finance's annual budget statement, 27 February 2004.
[153] Minister for Finance's annual budget statement, 18 February 2005.
[154] Minister for Finance's annual budget statement, 17 February 2006.

31 March 2020[155] by Mr Tharman Shanmugaratnam, the then Deputy Prime Minister and Minister for Finance. Enhancement was further made to the GST concession to facilitate fundraising by SPVs set up by S-REITs.

More recently, in the 2018 annual budget statement by Minister for Finance, Mr Heng Swee Keat[156], the S-REIT tax regime was enhanced when the income tax legislation was expanded to deal with exchange traded funds listed on the Singapore Exchange which invest or propose to invest in REITs as their underlying investment portfolio. With the extension of the tax transparency treatment to REIT exchange traded funds, the yield of REIT exchange traded funds are significantly enhanced, and investors who invest in a diversified portfolio of S-REITs through approved REIT exchange traded funds are now put at a level playing field *vis-à-vis* investors who directly invest in individual S-REITs. Prior to the change, investors in REIT exchange traded funds were at a tax disadvantage compared to those who invested directly in individual S-REITs. It took 2 years of lobbying before the tax transparency treatment accorded to S-REITs was extended to REIT exchange traded funds[157].

In the 2019 annual budget statement[158], Mr Heng Swee Keat further announced the removal of the sunset clause for tax exemption of distributions received by individuals from S-REITs and approved REIT exchange traded funds (which was due to expire on 31 March 2020), to make the exemption a permanent feature of the income tax regime. In addition, the other tax concessions earlier conferred on S-REITs, including (i) the tax transparency treatment for approved REIT exchange traded funds, (ii) the exemption of qualifying foreign-sourced income (such as interest income and trust distribution) derived by S-REITs and their wholly-owned Singapore resident subsidiary companies, and (iii) the remission of GST, were extended to 31 December 2025 in a bid to promote Singapore's position as a hub for the listing of S-REITs.

---

[155] Minister for Finance's annual budget statement, 23 February 2015.

[156] Minister for Finance's annual budget statement, 19 February 2018.

[157] 'SGX still in talks on potential tax waiver on REIT ETF,' *The Business Times*, 21 October 2016, 'SGX, MAS intensify lobbying against REIT ETF withholding tax,' *The Business Times*, 16 February 2018 and 'REIT ETFs to enjoy tax transparency,' *The Business Times*, 20 February 2018.

[158] Minister for Finance's annual budget statement, 18 February 2019.

In the subsequent sections, we will discuss in detail the various tax concessions conferred on S-REITs, approved sub-trusts of S-REITs and approved REIT exchange traded funds.

8.1. Income tax transparency treatment

A trust is a vehicle constituted by a trust deed and does not have separate legal personality. Under a trust arrangement, the trustee is the legal owner of the underlying trust assets and the income arising from the use of the assets held under trust. In this regard, for income tax purposes, the general rule is that the income of a trust constitutes the statutory income of the trustee[159] and is chargeable to tax in the hands of the trustee at the prevailing corporate income tax rate (currently 17%). Nevertheless, where the beneficiaries of a trust are entitled to a share of the income of the trust, a corresponding share of the income may be charged at a lower rate or not charged with any tax, as determined by the Comptroller[160].

In the case of a S-REIT (which is essentially a trust), the Comptroller of Income Tax may accord the abovementioned concessionary tax treatment to "specified income" distributed by the trustee of the S-REIT, such that it is the beneficiaries, instead of the trustee of the S-REIT, who are subject to tax on the "specified income" (hereafter referred to as "tax transparency treatment"). Where tax transparency treatment is accorded, the "specified income" distributed by the trustee of the S-REIT to the beneficiaries, is in many instances subject to a lower tax rate or not charged with any tax at all in the hands of the beneficiaries. As an example, such distributions made by the trustee of a S-REIT will be exempt from tax in the hands of an individual beneficiary unless such distributions are derived by the individual through a partnership in Singapore or is derived from the carrying on of a trade, business or profession[161].

The conditions attached to the grant of tax transparency treatment to S-REITs include the requirement for the trustee to distribute at least 90% of the taxable specified income of the S-REIT to the unitholders

---

[159] S 35(11) of the Income Tax Act.
[160] S 43(2) of the Income Tax Act.
[161] S 13(1)(zh) of the Income Tax Act.

in the same year in which the income is derived by the trustee of the S-REIT[162]. In this regard, most if not all S-REITs distribute their income to unitholders on a quarterly or half-yearly basis. Where the income of the last quarter of the S-REIT's financial year is distributed within the first 3 months of the subsequent financial year, the requirement to distribute the income in the same year in which the income is derived, would be considered satisfied[163].

The 90% minimum distribution requirement is widely understood to be the "sacred cow" or most important consideration for the grant of tax transparency treatment. This was reiterated by Ms Lim Hwee Hwa, then Senior Minister of State for Finance and Transport, in a speech made during the global financial crisis of 2008/2009 to address the question of whether the 90% minimum distribution requirement would be relaxed[164]:

> ... I would also like to take this opportunity to clarify our position on the REITs' dividend payout ratio. I understand that many are concerned whether the payout ratio for REITs to qualify for tax transparency treatment would be lowered to help REITs conserve cash. MOF and MAS have deliberated this issue and have decided that the minimum payout ratio would not be changed. The key characteristics of REITs as a stable, high-payout, pass-through vehicle are important considerations for investors, and hence, must be preserved.
>
> In addition, while we appreciate the re-financing difficulties faced by REITs, there are, at present, no strong grounds to justify a special tax treatment for REITs that is not made available to other entities. ...

It is to be noted that the requirement to distribute at least 90% of taxable income is to be measured on the basis of the S-REIT's accounting and taxable profits, instead of actual cashflow or rental collected. Where there is significant difference between the taxable income and actual cashflow

---

[162] The high payout ratio leaves REIT with limited retained earnings and makes them more dependent on the debt and equity markets: *Financial Stability Review,* MAS macroeconomic surveillance department, December 2006.

[163] IRAS e-Tax Guide, *Income Tax Treatment of Real Estate Investment Trusts and Approved Sub-Trusts,* Eighth Edition, 17 November 2021.

[164] Speech at the Asian Public Real Estate Association Singapore REIT Summit, *Navigating the Storm: Responding to the Challenges in Singapore's REIT Market,* 20 February 2009.

collected during a particular year (e.g. significant number of tenants delayed their rental payment during an economic crisis), the S-REIT may face difficulty in satisfying the distribution requirement.

In recognition of such challenges faced by S-REITs when the COVID-19 global pandemic broke out in early 2020, the MOF, IRAS and MAS allowed S-REITs up to 12 months after the end of financial year 2020 to make distribution of income derived during financial year 2020[165]. The objective was to provide S-REITs more flexibility to manage their cash flows during the global pandemic, in recognition of the fact that S-REITs generally have a low cash reserves due to the requirement to distribute at least 90% of their income. A key difference between the response of the authorities during the global financial crisis of 2008/2009 and the COVID-19 pandemic in 2020, is that at the height of the COVID-19 crisis, emergency legislation[166] was passed on 7 April 2020 to require landlords to suspend rent collections by up to 6 months for tenants who were unable to pay as a result of the pandemic. No such drastic measures were implemented during the global financial crisis of 2008/2009.

Besides adhering to the 90% minimum distribution requirement to qualify for tax transparency treatment, the trustee and manager of the S-REITs are also required to comply with certain compliance related requirements such as those relating to withholding tax, rollover income adjustment[167], provision of information to unitholders and submission of audited financial statements and tax computations, amongst other conditions. In addition, the trustee and manager of the S-REIT are required to submit a joint letter of undertaking to the Comptroller of Income Tax, so as to avail the S-REIT of the tax transparency treatment.

---

[165] Press release, *New Measures to Help REITs Navigate Operating Challenges Posed by COVID-19*, issued by MOF, IRAS and MAS, 16 April 2020. While the measure had an adverse impact on the distribution received by the unitholders during the COVID-19 pandemic, it was recognized that the alternative of mandating S-REITs continue with the distribution of at least 90% of their taxable income in the same year, would put significant strain on the financial position of the S-REITs.

[166] COVID-19 (Temporary Measures) Act, No. 14 of 2020.

[167] This refers to adjustments made to the specified income/exempt income for the next distribution as a result of rounding differences arising from the rounding off of distribution per unit to the nearest cent and differences in the taxable specified income as computed by the Comptroller of Income Tax from that determined by the trustee for distribution purpose.

With effect from 1 July 2018, the Income Tax Act has been amended to extend the abovementioned tax transparency treatment to REIT exchange traded funds listed on the Singapore Exchange and managed by a Singapore fund manager[168]. Prior to that, investors investing in REIT exchange traded funds were put at a disadvantage due to the higher effective tax rate of 17% on the distributions received by the REIT exchange traded funds from the underlying S-REITs, compared to the situation where the investors directly invest in the underlying S-REITs[169].

The grant of the aforementioned tax transparency treatment is subject to the satisfaction of certain conditions[170], including the requirement that the REIT exchange traded fund invests solely in REITs (whether solely in S-REITs or both in S-REITs and foreign REITs) and that the REIT exchange traded fund distribute 100% of the distributions received from S-REITs (net of expenses) in each relevant period (quarterly or half yearly as the case may be) to unitholders by the next distribution period. In addition, the trustee and manager of the REIT exchange traded fund are required to submit a joint letter of undertaking to the Comptroller of Income Tax so as to avail the REIT exchange traded fund of the tax transparency treatment.

8.1.1. *Specified income qualifying for tax transparency*

The tax transparency treatment accorded by the Comptroller of Income Tax is only available in respect of certain specified income[171] of S-REITs and their approved sub-trusts as set out below, and does not include gains from the disposal of immovable property which the Comptroller reserves his right to impose tax on such disposal gains of a revenue nature. Any income of the S-REIT which does not qualify for tax transparency treatment will be taxed in the hands of the trustee. Distributions made out of such income which

---

[168] IRAS e-Tax Guide, *Income Tax Treatment of Real Estate Investment Trust Exchange-Traded Funds*, Fifth Edition, 17 November 2021.

[169] When the investors invest directly into the S-REIT, the tax rate could be lower at 0% or 10%. See 'SGX, Mas intensify lobbying against REIT ETFs withholding tax,' *The Business Times*, 16 February 2018.

[170] *Tax Transparency Treatment for Exchange-Traded Funds Investing in Real Estate Investment Trusts*, FDD Cir 04/2018 (MAS, 12 April 2019).

[171] S 43(2A) of the Income Tax Act.

is taxed in the hands of the trustee will not be subject to further taxation in the hands of the beneficiaries.

In the case of an approved REIT exchange traded funds, only qualifying S-REIT distributions (i.e. distributions made by the trustee of a S-REIT out of the specified income of the S-REIT that has been accorded tax transparency treatment) will be accorded tax transparency treatment[172].

The various types of specified income which may qualify for tax transparency treatment are discussed below.

8.1.1.1. Rental income or income from the management or holding of immovable property

Rental income which constitutes the single largest component of the recurring income derived by S-REITs qualifies for tax transparency treatment. Service charges and car park fees which constitute a significant portion of the recurring income derived by S-REITs from the management or holding of immovable properties also qualify for tax transparency treatment. In addition, damages or compensation received by S-REITs from tenants (including payments made by tenants who "over-stay" or fail to deliver vacant possession at the expiry of the tenancy, to compensate the S-REIT for any shortfall in rental income) should qualify as "income from the management or holding of immovable property".

8.1.1.2. Income that is ancillary to the management or holding of immovable property

Apart from the income which S-REITs derive directly from the management or holding of immovable property, income which is ancillary to such activities also qualifies for tax transparency treatment. The word "ancillary" contemplates a more remote nexus with the management or holding of immovable property. Such income is subsidiary, subordinate or appurtenant to the management or holding of the immovable property. Examples of such income includes interest income derived by the trustee from placing cash surpluses in bank deposits or debt securities.

---

[172] S 43(2A)(ba) of the Income Tax Act.

8.1.1.3. Income that is payable out of rental income or income from the management or holding of immovable property in Singapore

Other income that is payable out of rental income or income from the management or holding of immovable property in Singapore will also qualify for tax transparency treatment. This serves as a catch-all for all other types of income that may be derived by the S-REITs from its core activities of managing and holding immovable property in Singapore.

8.1.1.4. Rental support payment

In recognition that the provision of rental support is a prevalent practice in the industry, rental support payments derived by S-REITs and approved sub-trusts from 29 December 2016 will also qualify for tax transparency treatment. This is provided that the rental support payments are paid to the trustee by the seller who sold the property or any interest in the owner of the property to the trustee, a person who wholly owns (directly or indirectly) the seller, or any other person approved by the Comptroller of Income Tax.

The rental support payment must be made under an agreement entered into at the time of the sale of the immovable property to the S-REIT or approved sub-trust (as the case may be). The agreement must provide for the payments to be made only for a fixed period of time, with a view to compensating a party to the agreement in the event that the amount of rental income from the property over a period of time is less than an amount agreed as the expected rental income for the same period, taking into account prevailing and forecasted market conditions at the time of that sale[173].

The rental support payment should be on an open market value basis. Any amount of rental support payment which is in excess of the shortfall in market rental income will not be granted tax transparency by the Comptroller of Income Tax, and will instead be taxed in the hands of the trustee.

In practice, it is observed that S-REIT sponsor or other parties which inject or sell immovable properties to S-REITs will in many instances provide rental or income support in respect of "non-mature" properties where the rental yield has yet to reach a stabilized state. The rental support

---

[173] S 43(10) of the Income Tax Act.

is essentially a guarantee provided to the S-REIT that it will be able to achieve a certain level of minimum rent during the initial period after the acquisition of the property. Where the actual rental income arising from the property is less than the amount guaranteed, the S-REIT will be entitled to receive rental support payments. The availability of such rental support is a critical consideration for the S-REITs prior to making any decision to acquire such "non-mature" properties given that the S-REIT will want to ensure that the acquisition is yield-accretive. Examples of S-REITs which have relied on rental support to maintain its distribution per unit include Keppel REIT and OUE Commercial REIT.

8.1.1.5. Distribution from an approved sub-trust

Distributions which the S-REIT receives from an approved sub-trust may also qualify for tax transparency treatment. For this purpose, the sub-trust must have an approved sub-trust status during the period which it derived income (out of which the distribution is made to the S-REIT) and at the point of distribution to the REIT. To qualify for tax transparency treatment, the distribution made by the approved sub-trust to the S-REIT must be in cash.

An "approved sub-trust", in relation to a S-REIT, refers a trust which is not listed on the Singapore Exchange or elsewhere, where the trustee of the S-REIT holds any right or interest in the property of the trust for the benefit of the beneficiaries of the S-REIT, and approved as such by the Comptroller of Income Tax[174]. The income derived by the trustee of an approved sub-trust will be accorded tax transparency treatment where that part of the approved sub-trust's specified income is distributed to the trustee of a S-REIT in the same year the income is derived. The types of specified income qualifying for tax transparency treatment in the hands of the trustee of an approved sub-trust are limited to rental or other income from the management or holding of immovable property, income that is ancillary to the management or holding of immovable property and rental support payment as discussed above. In approving any sub-trust of a S-REIT as an

---

[174] S 43(10) of the Income Tax Act.

"approved sub-trust", the Comptroller of Income Tax requires the following conditions to be fulfilled[175]:

(a) The sub-trust must be an unlisted special purpose vehicle that is constituted to hold/own real estate;
(b) The S-REIT has acquired interest in the sub-trust and is free to dispose of such interest;
(c) The joint venture agreement, memorandum and articles of association and/or other constitution documents of the sub-trust should provide for, inter alia:
  (i) a specified minimum percentage of distributable profits that will be distributed to the beneficiaries, of which the S-REIT should be entitled to receive its pro rata share;
  (ii) veto rights of the REIT over key operational issues, including:
      (a) amendment of the joint venture agreement, memorandum and articles of association or other constitutive documents;
      (b) cessation or change of the business;
      (c) winding up or dissolution;
      (d) changes to the equity capital structure;
      (e) changes to the distribution policy;
      (f) issue of securities;
      (g) incurring of borrowings;
      (h) creation of security over the assets;
      (i) transfer or disposal of the assets;
      (j) approval of asset enhancement and capital expenditure plans for the assets; and
      (k) entry into interested party transactions;
  (iii) a mode for the resolution of disputes between the property fund and joint venture partners; and
(d) The sub-trust has in place a mechanism to properly track and differentiate the distributions made to beneficiaries that are S-REITs vis-à-vis beneficiaries that are non S-REITs.

---

[175] See IRAS e-Tax Guide, *Income Tax Treatment of Real Estate Investment Trusts and Approved Sub-Trusts*, Seventh Edition, 24 June 2020.

8.1.2. *Distributions out of specified income in units (in lieu of cash)*

The distributions made by the trustees of the S-REITs and approved REIT exchange traded funds to unitholders may either be in cash or units in the S-REIT. Where the distributions are made in units in the S-REIT, the trustee has to provide written confirmation at the time of submitting the tax return, that the relevant conditions have been met[176].

In particular, the distribution must be made out of specified income and the distribution is made in the same year in which the income is derived by the trustee. Prior to making the distribution, the trustee of the S-REIT must have given all unitholders receiving the distribution an option to receive the distribution, either in cash or units in the S-REIT. In addition, the trustee must have sufficient cash available on the date of such distribution to make the distribution fully in cash. For this purpose, the credit facilities which the trustee of the S-REIT has obtained from its banks/financial institutions for the specific purpose of making the distribution may be taken into account.

8.1.3. *Application for tax transparency treatment*

In order for tax transparency treatment to apply, an application should be made to the Comptroller of Income Tax at least 3 months before the S-REIT/REIT exchange traded fund derives the income for which the tax transparency treatment is sought. Where an application for tax transparency treatment is approved, the tax transparency treatment will take effect from the listing of the S-REIT/REIT exchange traded fund on the Singapore Exchange.

9. Income Tax Treatment of Trustee

Where the tax transparency treatment applies, specified income which is distributed to the unitholders will not be taxed in the hands of the trustee of the S-REIT, approved sub-trust and approved REIT exchange traded fund (as the case may be). In other words, the trustee is only subject to tax on income which does not qualify for tax transparency treatment. Income which does not qualify for tax transparency treatment includes specified income

---

[176] Section 43(2B) of the Income Tax Act.

not distributed to the beneficiaries in the same year in which the income is derived as well as non-specified income (e.g. gains from the disposal of immovable properties and shares of a revenue nature)[177]. Any distribution made by S-REITs from such after-tax income is capital in nature and will not be subject to any further tax when received by the relevant unitholders and beneficiaries of the S-REIT, approved sub-trust and approved REIT exchange traded fund (as the case may be).

Where the tax transparency treatment does not apply, the trustee will be subject to tax on the income of the S-REIT, approved sub-trust and approved REIT exchange traded fund (as the case may be), at the prevailing corporate tax rate of 17%. Proceeds which are not in the nature of income (e.g. capital gains) will not be subject to tax.

The trustee of a S-REIT, approved sub-trust and approved REIT exchange traded funds is required to file a tax return (i.e. Form UT) annually. The form UT must be filed together with the audited accounts and tax computation by 15 April each year. Where an extension is required for the filing of the Form UT, the trustee will be required to furnish the estimated chargeable income under section 63 of the Income Tax Act.

10. Income Tax Treatment of Unitholders

The tax treatment of distributions made by S-REITs and approved REIT exchange traded funds, in the hands of the unitholders depends primarily on the type of distribution received by the unitholder and the profile of the unitholder.

10.1. Types of distribution

The types of S-REITs and approved REIT exchange traded funds distribution received by unitholders may be made out of (i) specified income accorded with tax transparency treatment, (ii) income subject to tax in the hands of the trustee or (iii) non-taxable amounts (e.g. capital gains or tax exempt income).

---

[177] Other examples of income not qualifying for tax transparency include specified income derived by an approved sub-trust but distributed to non-S-REIT beneficiaries.

10.2. Profile of unitholders

For income tax purposes, unitholders of S-REITs and approved REIT exchange-traded funds are categorized as either qualifying unitholders (who are accorded tax transparency treatment) or non-resident non-individual unitholders (for which certain distributions are subject to withholding tax).

The first category of unitholders — qualifying unitholders — who are accorded tax transparency treatment, is not subject to withholding tax on distributions received from S-REITs and approved REIT exchange traded funds. Qualifying unitholders include (i) any individuals[178], (ii) any company incorporated and resident in Singapore[179], (iii) any Singapore branch of a company incorporated outside Singapore[180], (iv) any body of persons incorporated or registered in Singapore[181], (v) any organization which is exempt from tax on distributions from S-REITs or approved REIT exchange traded funds by reason of an order made under the International Organizations (Immunities and Privileges) Act[182], and (vi) approved REIT exchange traded funds[183].

Unitholders who fall under the second category (i.e. non-resident non-individual unitholders) are subject to withholding tax on distributions received from S-REITs and approved REIT exchange traded funds. The withholding tax applies to distributions received by non-resident non-individual unitholders, where the distributions are made out of "tax transparent" specified income (i.e. taxable income which are not taxed at the hands of the S-REITs/approved REIT exchange traded fund, but taxed in the hands of the unitholders instead).

10.3. Distributions out of specified income accorded with tax transparency treatment

As a general rule, distributions out of specified income accorded with tax transparency treatment are subject to tax in the hands of the unitholders,

---

[178] S 45G(1)(b)(i) of the Income Tax Act.

[179] S 45G(1)(b)(ii) of the Income Tax Act.

[180] S 45G(1)(b)(iii) read together with S 45G(4A) of the Income Tax Act.

[181] S 45G(1)(b)(iv) of the Income Tax Act. This includes a charity registered under the Charities Act or established by any written law, a town council, a statutory board, a co-operative society registered under the Co-operative Societies Act and a trade union registered under the Trade Unions Act.

[182] S 45G(4B) of the Income Tax Act.

[183] S 45G(5) of the Income Tax Act.

unless otherwise exempt. The specific income tax treatment of such distribution in the hands of the unitholders depends on the profile of the unitholder in question. For this purpose, the unitholders may broadly be categorized as "qualifying unitholders" or "non-resident non-individual unitholders". The two broad categories may further be broken down into different sub-categories. The income tax treatment pertaining to each of these sub-categories is further described below.

10.3.1. *Qualifying unitholders*

Qualifying unitholders who are individuals are exempt from tax on the distribution, unless they have derived the distribution through a partnership in Singapore or from the carrying on of a trade, business or profession[184]. The availability of the exemption is not contingent on the citizenship, nationality or tax residency status of the individual. Qualifying unitholders which are international organizations[185] and REIT exchange traded funds which have been accorded tax transparency treatment, are similarly not subject to tax on the distribution received[186].

Distributions received by other qualifying unitholders (such as Singapore incorporated and tax resident companies, Singapore branches of foreign incorporated companies and bodies of persons incorporated or registered in Singapore) are subject to the normal tax rules as though the respective qualifying unitholders have received the income of the S-REIT and approved REIT exchange traded funds directly.

Unless otherwise exempt from tax, distributions received by a unitholder who holds the units in S-REITs/approved REIT exchange traded funds for trading purpose will be subject to tax under section 10(1)(a) of the Income Tax Act whereas distributions received by a unitholder who holds the units in S-REITs/approved REIT exchange traded funds for long-term investment purposes will be subject to tax as a "charge" under section 10(1)(e) of the Income Tax Act.

---

[184] S 13(1)(zh) of the Income Tax Act.

[185] This includes an international organization which is exempt from tax by reason of an order made under the International Organizations (Immunities and Privileges) Act.

[186] S 43(2) and (2AA) read together with S 43(2A)(ba) of the Income Tax Act.

10.3.2. *Non-resident non-individual unitholders*

As a general rule, the trustee of a S-REIT or an approved REIT exchange-traded fund is required to withhold tax from the gross distributions made to non-resident non-individual unitholders out of specified income accorded with tax transparency treatment[187]. A reduced 10% withholding tax rate applies where the distribution is made to a "qualifying non-resident non-individual unitholder"[188]. Otherwise, the prevailing corporate tax rate should apply.

The term "qualifying non-resident non-individual unitholder" refers to a non-resident non-individual unitholder who does not have any permanent establishment in Singapore or who carries on an operation in Singapore through a permanent establishment in Singapore, where the funds used by that person to acquire the units in S-REIT or approved REIT exchange-traded fund (as the case may be) are not obtained from that operation in Singapore[189].

Following the 2019 annual budget statement[190] made by the Minister for Finance, Mr Heng Swee Keat, qualifying non-resident funds under sections 13CA, 13X and 13Y, which were since re-numbered as sections 13D, 13U and 13V respectively, of the Income Tax Act will also be able to avail themselves of the 10% concessionary tax rate applicable to qualifying non-resident non-individuals when investing in S-REITs and approved REIT exchange traded funds. The change will apply to S-REIT and approved REIT exchange traded fund distributions made during the period from 1 July 2019 to 31 December 2025.

10.4. Distributions out of income subject to tax in the hands of trustee (i.e. where tax transparency does not apply)

Where the distributions are made out of income that has been subject to tax on the trustee, no additional taxes are payable by the unitholders. Similarly,

---

[187] S 43(1) read together with S45G(1) to (3) of the Income Tax Act.

[188] S 43(3B) and (3C) read together with S 45G of the Income Tax Act. The 10% rate applies to distributions made by the trustee of a S-REIT for the period from 18 February 2005 to 31 December 2025 (both dates inclusive) and distributions made by the trustee of an approved REIT exchange-traded fund for the period from 1 July 2018 to 31 December 2025 (both dates inclusive). An additional condition attached to the reduced 10% withholding tax rate for distribution from the trustee of an approved REIT exchange-traded fund is that the distribution must be made out of a distribution by a REIT that is in turn made out of income qualifying for tax transparency.

[189] S 43(3B) and (3C) of the Income Tax Act.

[190] Minister for Finance's annual budget statement, 18 February 2019.

the trustee of a S-REIT will not be taxed on any distribution from the trustee of an approved sub-trust of a REIT that is made out of income that has been subjected to tax at the sub-trust level. If the trustee of the REIT onward distributes such distribution to its unitholders, such distribution will also not be taxed in the hands of the unitholders.

10.5. Distributions out of non-taxable amounts (e.g. capital gains or tax exempt income)

Where the distributions are made out of non-taxable amounts (e.g. capital gains or tax exempt income) which are not subject to tax in the hands of the trustee, such distributions are similarly not taxable in the hands of the unitholders[191]. On the other hand, where the distribution is regarded as a "return of capital" to the unitholders (e.g. where the distribution is made out of unrealized revaluation gains on properties, etc.), the unitholders are required to reduce the cost of investment of the units by the amount of return of capital[192]. It follows that a unitholder who trades in units of S-REITs and REIT exchange traded funds (and who is taxable on trading gains arising from the units) are to use the reduced cost of investment to determine the quantum of taxable trading gains subject to income tax[193].

10.6. Summary table

Table 6 summarizes the tax treatment of the distribution in the hands of unitholders.

11. Income Tax Exemption of Foreign-Sourced Income

Apart from tax transparency treatment, S-REITs also enjoy concessionary income tax treatment in respect of certain foreign-sourced income received in Singapore. A S-REIT may directly or indirectly invest in foreign properties through various business vehicles including a company (or a branch), a

---

[191] S 35(15) of the Income Tax Act.
[192] S 35(15C) of the Income Tax Act.
[193] Where the amount of return of capital exceeds the cost of investment of the units, the excess is to be subject to tax as trading income of the unitholder.

Table 6: Tax treatment in the hands of unitholders.

Type of Distribution	Profile of Unitholder	Tax Treatment in the Hands of Unitholder
• Income subject to tax in the hands of the trustee (i.e. where tax transparency does not apply) • Non-taxable amounts (e.g. capital gains)	• All unitholders	• Tax exempt
• Distributions out of specified income accorded with tax transparency treatment	• Qualifying unitholders	
	➢ Individuals who derive the distribution through a partnership in Singapore or from the carrying on of a trade, business or profession	• Subject to tax at the individual's marginal tax rate which ranges from 0% to 22%[a]
	➢ Other Individuals	• Tax exempt[b]
	➢ Companies incorporated and resident in Singapore ➢ Singapore branches of companies incorporated outside Singapore ➢ Bodies of persons incorporated or registered in Singapore	• Subject to tax at the prevailing corporate income tax rate of 17%[c] (unless otherwise exempt from tax)
	➢ International organizations that are exempt from tax[d]	• Tax exempt
	➢ REIT exchange traded funds which have been accorded tax transparency treatment	• Not subject to tax in the hands of the trustee of the REIT exchange traded fund[e]
	• Non-Resident Non-Individual Unitholders	
	➢ Qualifying non-resident non-individual unitholders (including qualifying non-resident funds)	• 10% final withholding tax[f]
	➢ Others	• 17% withholding tax[g]

Notes:

[a] S 13(1)(zh), read together with s 42(1) and 43(1) of the Income Tax Act.

[b] S 13(1)(zh) of the Income Tax Act.

[c] S 43(1) of the Income Tax Act.

[d] Pursuant to an order made under the International Organizations (Immunities and Privileges) Act.

[e] S 43(2) and (2AA) read together with s 43(2A)(ba) of the Income Tax Act.

[f] S 45G(1)(a) and s 45G(2) read together with s 43(3B) to (3F) of the Income Tax Act. The 10% rate applies to distributions made by the trustee of a S-REIT for the period from 18 February 2005 to 31 March 2025 (both dates inclusive) and distributions made to a qualifying non-resident fund for the period from 1 July 2019 to 31 March 2025 (both dates inclusive).

[g] S 45G(1)(b) of the Income Tax Act. The tax deducted is not a final tax. In other words, the unitholder may submit a tax return to claim allowable expenses and tax credits.

trust or a limited liability partnership and in turn derive various streams of income including dividend income, trust distribution and interest income. Foreign-sourced income received in Singapore by a S-REIT could qualify for exemption under section 13(8) which is available to Singapore tax resident companies, or section 13(12) of the Income Tax Act where certain concessionary tax treatment is only available to S-REITs and not other companies.

11.1. Automatic tax exemption under section 13(8)

Under section 13(8) of the Income Tax Act, specified foreign-sourced income received in Singapore by the trustee of a S-REIT who is tax resident in Singapore, will qualify for automatic tax exemption subject to meeting certain conditions. Such specified foreign-sourced income includes dividend income derived from any territory outside Singapore and profits derived from the carrying on of a trade or business carried on by a foreign branch of a Singapore tax resident company. The "automatic" tax exemption under section 13(8) is subject to the satisfaction of 3 conditions[194], commonly referred to as the "subject to tax" condition, "headline tax rate" condition and "beneficial to taxpayer" condition.

To satisfy the "subject to tax" condition, the specified foreign-source income must have been subject to tax of a character similar to income tax in the foreign territory from which it is received. With regard to the "headline tax rate" condition, the headline tax rate, i.e. the highest rate of tax of a character similar to income tax, in the foreign territory from which the specified foreign-source income is received must be at least 15% in the year in which the specified foreign-sourced income is received in Singapore. The third condition, i.e. the "beneficial to taxpayer" condition, is regarded as met if the Comptroller of Income Tax is satisfied that the exemption of the specified foreign-sourced income will be beneficial to the taxpayer.

The "subject to tax" condition and "headline tax rate" condition serve the purpose of preventing abuse[195]. The "subject to tax" test condition is intended

---

[194] S 13(9) of the Income Tax Act.

[195] Parliament of Singapore, *Official Reports — Parliamentary Debates (Hansard): Second Reading of Income Tax (Amendment) Bill 2003*, available at <https://www.parliament.gov.sg/parliamentary-business/official-reports-(parl-debates)>.

to prevent the double non-taxation of income[196], whereas the "headline tax rate" condition limits the granting of an exemption to foreign-sourced income derived from territories which impose a comparable or significant level of tax vis-à-vis Singapore. On the other hand, the "beneficial to taxpayer" condition ensures that the taxpayer would be better off under the exemption scheme than continuing under the tax credit scheme that would otherwise be applicable[197]. A taxpayer can elect to opt out of the exemption if it is not beneficial for the company to be under the exemption regime for any reason.

11.2. Tax exemption under section 13(12)

Where the foreign-sourced income received in Singapore by a trustee of a S-REIT does not qualify for automatic exemption under section 13(8), an alternative avenue for tax exemption may nevertheless be available under section 13(12) of the Income Tax Act. This is provided that the foreign-sourced income originates from income/gains derived from ownership of foreign properties, property related activities or other activities permitted under the regulatory framework for S-REITs[198].

Notably, the scope of the exemption under section 13(12) is broader than that under section 13(8) and extends to foreign-sourced interest income, distributions from a non-resident trustee of a trust that holds foreign properties. Such exemption of foreign-sourced interest income and trust distributions is only available to S-REITs and is not conferred on other Singapore tax resident companies. The qualifying conditions for the purpose of the section 13(12) tax exemption are set out in Table 7.[199]

---

[196] As a concession, specified foreign income that has been exempt from tax in the foreign territory as a result of carrying out substantive business operations is regarded as having satisfied the 'subject to tax' test. IRAS e-Tax Guide, *Tax Exemption for Foreign Source Income*, Third Edition, 23 January 2019.

[197] Parliament of Singapore, *Official Reports — Parliamentary Debates (Hansard): Second Reading of Income Tax (Amendment) Bill 2003*, available at <https://www.parliament.gov.sg/parliamentary-business/official-reports-(parl-debates)>.

[198] See IRAS e-Tax Guide, *Income Tax: Tax Exemption under Section 13(12) for Specified Scenarios, Real Estate Investment Trusts, and Qualifying Offshore Infrastructure Project/Asset*, Eighth Edition, 17 May 2021, for further details. See also Income Tax (Elite Commercial Real Estate Investment Trust — Section 13(12) Exemption) Order 2020, S 7/2020 in respect of the s 13(12) exemption given for interest and dividend income received in Singapore for Elite Commercial REIT.

[199] See IRAS e-Tax Guide, *Income Tax: Tax Exemption under Section 13(12) for Specified Scenarios, Real Estate Investment Trusts, and Qualifying Offshore Infrastructure Project/Asset*, Eighth Edition, 17 May 2021.

Table 7: Qualifying conditions for section 13(12) tax exemption.

S/N	Foreign-Sourced Dividends/Trust Distributions by Foreign Trusts/Foreign Branch Profits	Foreign-Sourced Interest
1	The entity from which the income originates, owns overseas properties or engages in property-related activities, or other activities in line with the regulatory requirements imposed on S-REIT and the overseas properties are situated in a foreign tax jurisdiction with headline tax rate of at least 15%.	Same condition applies.
2	Dividend/trust distribution/branch profits must originate from: (i) Property rental income from underlying overseas property; or (ii) Capital gains from disposal of overseas property or special purpose vehicle that holds the overseas property, or (iii) Income derived from property-related activities, or other activities in line with the regulatory requirements imposed on S-REIT.	Same condition applies.
3	In respect of property rental income, tax has been paid in the foreign tax jurisdiction in which the property is situated.	Tax has been paid in the foreign tax jurisdiction on the interest income. Where there is no foreign tax paid on the interest income, the interest must be incurred on borrowings by the payer to acquire the underlying overseas properties and the income and/or capital gains from such properties are subject to tax in the foreign tax jurisdiction unless tax incentives apply to exempt the income and/or gains.
4	Funds channeled out of Singapore to finance the investment in the entity [specified in (1) above] must originate from the following sources: (i) Funds received by the trustee of a S-REIT from issue of its units; (ii) Permissible borrowings under the Property Trust Fund guidelines; (iii) Security deposits from tenants or properties owned by the trustee of a S-REIT; (iv) Undistributed income of the trustee of a S-REIT.	Funds channeled out of Singapore to finance the loan to the entity [specified in (1) above] must originate from the following sources: (i) Funds received by the trustee of a S-REIT from issue of its units; (ii) Permissible borrowings under the Property Trust Fund guidelines; (iii) Security deposits from tenants or properties owned by the trustee of a S-REIT; or (iv) Undistributed income of the trustee of a S-REIT.
5	There is no round tripping of locally-sourced income via the overseas investment and there is no setting up of artificial structure (e.g. incorporation of a shell company in Singapore) to avoid Singapore tax.	Same condition applies.

Table 7:   (*Continued*)

Foreign-Sourced Dividends/Trust Distributions by Foreign Trusts/Foreign Branch Profits	Foreign-Sourced Interest
Where the section 13(12) tax exemption is sought by a wholly-owned Singapore resident subsidiary company of a S-REIT, the full amount of the remitted income less incidental expenses associated with the remittance, statutory expenses and administrative expenses incurred by the subsidiary company, must be passed through to the S-REIT.	Same condition applies.
The CIT is satisfied that the above conditions are met.	Same condition applies.

Other Taxes

Goods and Services Tax (GST)

general rule, GST is imposed on the supply of goods and services by ple persons. It is however to be noted that the issuance or transfer vnership of a unit under any unit trust (including a S-REIT) or any ness trust is an exempt supply for GST purposes under the Fourth dule of the GST Act. In addition, there are a number of GST rules cable specifically to S-REITs and their SPVs to help ease their cash flow educe their business costs. The GST rules and concessionary treatment nent to S-REITs are discussed in turn.

.1. *Self-accounting for GST by S-REITs and their SPVs*

ecific rule applicable to GST-registered S-REIT or its GST-registered SPV at they are allowed to self-account the GST payable for the purchase on-residential properties (including movable assets therein such as ture, furnishings, fittings, appliances, equipment and machinery) from T-registered seller[200]. Such a concessionary treatment helps ease the flow of GST-registered S-REITs and their SPVs when acquiring non-

S e-Tax Guide, *GST: Self-Accounting of GST by Listed REITs and their SPVs for Property Purchases*, d Edition, 1 January 2018.

residential properties, as they are able to self-account for the GST payable and claim the corresponding input GST in the same GST return, without any need to pay GST upfront to the seller of the non-residential properties.

The concession for GST-registered S-REITs to self-account for the GST payable on the purchases of non-residential properties first came into effect from 1 July 2006. It was subsequently extended to GST-registered SPVs of GST-registered S-REITs with effect from 1 January 2009. More recently, GST-registered S-REITs and SPVs are allowed to self-account for the GST payable on the movable assets bought by the S-REITs or SPVs together with the non-residential properties, with effect from 1 January 2018.

The self-accounting of GST payable by S-REIT and their SPVs is provided for under section 38 of the GST Act, read together with Regulation 104A of the GST (General) Regulations which provides that a taxable supply of immovable property and movable assets therein made to a GST-registered S-REIT or a GST-registered SPV of a GST-registered S-REIT is a prescribed supply for the purpose of section 38 of the GST Act. Under the normal rules which would otherwise be applicable, where the seller is a taxable person for GST purposes, the seller will be required to charge and account for GST on the sale of the non-residential property made to the buyer. The buyer of the non-residential property, on the other hand, will incur GST upfront on the acquisition (and consequently suffer a cash flow disadvantage), but is allowed to subsequently claim the GST incurred through the filing of a monthly/quarterly GST return (which could be 3 months later), provided that the buyer is GST-registered[201].

12.1.2. Recovery of GST on expenses

Apart from the self-accounting of GST payable by S-REITs and their SPVs, another concessionary GST treatment available for S-REITs relates to the recovery of GST on expenses which was first introduced by Prime Minister Lee Hsien Loong in the 2006 annual budget statement[202]. Under the 2006 concession, S-REITs are allowed to recover GST on expenses incurred to set

---

[201] The claim of input GST is subject to the input tax claim conditions under sections 19 and 20 of the GST Act.

[202] Minister for Finance's annual budget statement, 17 February 2006.

up various tiers of SPVs to hold overseas non-residential properties, as well as GST on expenses incurred on the acquisition of overseas non-residential properties and the operating of the SPVs. The concession was however available only to GST registered S-REITs.

The GST concession was enhanced 2 years later in the 2008 annual budget statement[203] to allow all S-REITs and qualifying registered business trusts (S-RBTs) to claim GST incurred on business expenses[204], irrespective of whether the S-REIT or S-RBT is eligible for GST registration and whether they hold the underlying assets directly or indirectly through multi-tiered structures such as SPVs/sub-trusts. The enhanced concession effectively allows S-REITs and qualifying S-RBTs to treat all supplies made by the multi-tiered structure as if they are taxable or exempt supplies made by the parent S-REIT and qualifying S-RBT for the purpose of computing GST claims, regardless whether the S-REITs and qualifying S-RBTs make any taxable supplies.

A further enhancement on the GST concession was announced in the 2015 annual budget statement[205], such that with effect from 1 April 2015, S-REITs and qualifying S-RBTs are allowed to claim GST on expenses incurred to set up SPVs used solely to raise funds for the S-REITs or qualifying S-RBTs (Financing SPVs), even where the Financing SPVs do not directly or indirectly hold qualifying assets of the S-REITs or qualifying S-RBTs. In addition, S-REITs and qualifying S-RBTs are allowed to claim GST on the business expenses of such Financing SPVs (other than disallowed expenses). The enhanced concession will be granted on the basis that the funds raised by the Financing SPVs must be on-lent to the S-REITs or qualifying S-RBTs and be used to finance the business activities of the S-REITs or qualifying S-RBTs, as the case may be.

The abovementioned concessionary GST treatments[206] were extended in the 2019 annual budget statement[207] to 31 December 2025.

---

[203] Minister for Finance's annual budget statement, 15 February 2008.

[204] Excluding expenses which are specifically disallowed under Regulation 26 and 27 of the GST (General) Regulations (RG 1).

[205] Minister for Finance's annual budget statement, 23 February 2015.

[206] IRAS e-Tax Guide, GST: Concession for REITs and Qualifying Registered Business Trusts Listed in Singapore, Fifth Edition, 23 September 2019.

[207] Minister for Finance's annual budget statement, 18 February 2019.

12.2. Stamp duty

Stamp duty is a tax imposed on executed documents pertaining to transactions involving Singapore real estate and shares. In the final section of this chapter, the stamp duty issues relating to the acquisition of S-REIT units by investors as well as the acquisition and divestment of Singapore real estate and shares by S-REITs, are discussed.

12.2.1. *Acquisition of units in S-REITs*

The acquisition or transfer of scripless units in a S-REIT (which are essentially unit trusts which invest in real estate and related assets) by investors does not attract stamp duty. In this regard, it is worthwhile noting that 10 years before the listing of the first S-REIT, the then Minister for Finance, Dr Richard Hu, had announced during the 1992 annual budget statement that stamp duty would not be imposed on transfer of units in units trusts[208]:

> *Stamp Duty on Financial Derivatives*
> Singapore has been developing as a centre for trading in regional securities. To cater to the increased sophistication of regional investors and the growth in interest in financial derivatives, the Stock Exchange of Singapore will soon launch trading of stock options on securities traded on the exchange. To encourage such trading, I have decided not to levy stamp duty in respect of transactions in stock options. With effect from 1st April 1992, **stamp duty will also not be imposed on** contract notes and **instruments of transfers relating to** share warrants, rights in shares and **units in unit trusts.**

In any case, given that the transfer of S-REITs via the Singapore Exchange is effected without the execution of any physical instrument between the transferor and transferee, stamp duty is not chargeable in the absence of any such instrument. In addition, any entry made by the Central Depository (CDP) in its depository register by electronic means that effects a transfer

---

[208] Minister for Finance's annual budget statement, 28 February 1992.

of book-entry securities between depositors (i.e. beneficial owners) is an exempt record which does not attract stamp duty[209]

In practice, it is noted that the Stamp Office takes the view that the transfer of units in a unit trust does not attract stamp duty, where the units do not confer unitholders any legal and beneficial interest in the underlying real estate or shares held through the unit trust. It follows that the transfer of units in a S-REIT (where the unitholders typically have no equitable or proprietary interest in the underlying assets of the S-REIT) does not attract stamp duty[210].

12.2.2. *Acquisition of Singapore real estate or Singapore shares by S-REITs*

S-REITs are known to grow their real estate portfolio via the acquisition of yield-accretive real estate assets and disposal of real estate assets which no longer generate the desired yield. The acquisition or disposal of Singapore real estate or Singapore shares by S-REITs currently does not qualify for any special or concessionary stamp duty treatment. In other words, the normal stamp duty rules relating to buyer's stamp duty, additional buyer's stamp duty, seller's stamp duty, share duty and additional conveyance duty will apply to Singapore real estate and share transactions entered into by S-REITs, with no exception.

Prior to 1 April 2015, stamp duty remission was available in respect of agreements or instruments relating to the transfer on sale of any real estate or any interest thereof from any vendor to a S-REIT. Such transactions undertaken by an unlisted REIT would also enjoy the remission provided that it became listed within a prescribed period of time. The said remission which earlier took effect from 18 February 2005 was first announced in the annual budget statement of the same year[211], by the then Minister for Finance, Mr Lee Hsien Loong who said the following:

---

[209] Stamp Duties (Exempt Record) Rules 2018 (S 657/2018).

[210] See Section 6.3 for further discussion on the rights of the unitholders.

[211] Minister for Finance's annual budget statement, 18 February 2005.

To broaden our capital markets, we will continue to encourage the development of Real Estate Investment Trusts (REITs), Islamic financial products, and exchange-traded commodity derivative trading.

We will strengthen Singapore as the preferred location in Asia for listing REITs.

Promoting REITs will help enlarge our capital market, grow our local fund management business, and benefit other areas of the financial sector. While we have made good progress, Australia, Malaysia and Hong Kong are all actively developing their REITs markets. We therefore need to do more.

To attract more REITs listings, I will waive stamp duty on the instruments of transfer of Singapore properties into REITs to be listed, or already listed on the SGX, for a five-year period. Most of the qualifying conditions for tax transparency will also be removed.

The remission was effected via Stamp Duties (Real Estate Investment Trusts) (Remission) Rules 2005[212], 2007[213] and 2010[214], which have since lapsed.

The aforementioned stamp duty remission was enhanced with effect from 1 January 2006 pursuant to the 2007 remission rules. With the enhancement, stamp duty was remitted for instruments relating to the transfer on sale of 100% of the issued share capital of any company incorporated in Singapore, where such company directly or indirectly held immovable property situated outside Singapore, and was set up for the sole purpose of directly or indirectly holding such property. The stamp duty remission was initially due to lapse after 17 February 2010, but was subsequently enhanced and extended for another 5 years to 31 March 2015. Under the 2010 remission rules, in recognition that the listing of a S-REIT took time, the remission was enhanced such that it would be available as long as the REIT listed within a 6-month period.

The stamp duty remissions have since lapsed on 31 March 2015. In not renewing the stamp duty remission, the then Deputy Prime Minister and Minister for Finance, Mr Tharman Shanmugaratnam, explained in the

---

[212] S 734/2005.
[213] S 364/2007.
[214] S 515/2010.

2015 annual budget statement[215] that the stamp duty remission was earlier granted with the intention to enable the S-REIT industry to acquire a critical mass of local assets, as a base from which the S-REITs can expand abroad. As the objective has been achieved, the concession would not be extended.

Indeed, the S-REIT market went through a period of explosive growth during the 10-year period from 2005 to 2015 and many high yielding assets were snapped up by S-REITs during this period in part due to the stamp duty remission which significantly reduced the transaction costs borne by S-REITs in the acquisition of Singapore real estate. Following the lapse of the stamp duty remission, transaction cost for the acquisition of Singapore real estate is now higher, making such investments less attractive for S-REITs. Noticeably, the focus of S-REITs has since shifted to the acquisition of overseas real estate, and almost all S-REITs listed on the Singapore Exchange from year 2015 comprise wholly overseas real estate.

---

[215] Minister for Finance's annual budget statement, 23 February 2015.

CHAPTER 9

Business Trusts:
An Alternative to REITs?

1. Introduction

Shortly after the successful listing of the first real estate investment trust (REIT) on the Singapore Exchange in July 2002, the business trust was introduced as an alternative business vehicle in Singapore[1], with the intention to create a new asset class for investors, and add depth and vibrancy to Singapore's capital markets[2]. The first real estate focused business trust to be listed on the Singapore Exchange, was CDL Hospitality Business Trust (CDL HBT)[3], which became listed on 19 July 2006, about 4 years after the listing of the first Singapore REIT (S-REIT).

There were 15 business trusts listed on the Singapore Exchange as of 1 January 2020 (see Table 1)[4], of which nine are considered property

---

[1] Business trusts were commonly used for trading in the United States for more than 100 years until corporations gain popularity and became the pre-dominant form of business vehicle; see: Tang Hang Wu, 'The Resurgence of "Uncorporation": The Business Trusts in Singapore,' [2012] *Journal of Business Law* 683 and Jonathan Silberstein-Loeb, 'The Transatlantic Origins of the Business Trust,' (2015) 36 *The Journal of Legal History* 192. Apart from the United States, similar structures are also in used in other jurisdictions such as Australia and Canada. See: Ministerial speech at the second reading of the Business Trust Bill, 1 September 2004, available on the website of the Parliament of Singapore.

[2] Monetary Authority of Singapore (MAS) press release, *MAS Releases Consultation Paper on Regulation of Business Trusts*, 10 December 2003. The Business Trusts Act was enacted in October 2004. For an overview of the regulatory and taxation regimes applicable to Registered Business Trusts, see: Shantini Ramachandra, 'The Business Trust Regime,' *Asia-Pacific Tax Bulletin*, November/December 2013, p. 410.

[3] Listed together with CDL Hospitality Real Estate Investment Trust as the stapled trusts known as CDL Hospitality Trusts.

[4] Including stapled trusts where a S-REIT and a business trusts are stapled together (also referred to as stapled securities).

trusts[5]. The 15 business trusts invest in a wide portfolio of assets ranging from real estate (e.g. hotels, serviced apartments, offices, retail malls) to infrastructure-related projects (e.g. container ports, power plants, desalination plants, television, broadband and fiber networks) to ships and vessels. Apart from business trusts which are listed on the Singapore Exchange, there are also a number of unlisted business trusts[6].

Table 1: Business trusts listed as of 1 January 2020.[a]

S/N	Name	Primary Portfolio	Listing Date	Stapled Trust[b]	Property Trust[c]
1	CDL Hospitality Trusts[d]	Hospitality	19-07-06	√	√
2	Keppel Infrastructure Trust[e]	Desalination plant, NEWater plant, waste-to-energy plant, gas network, power plant, data center, etc.	12-02-07		
3	First Ship Lease Trust	Ship	27-03-07		
4	Ascendas India Trust	Office/Industrial	01-08-07		√
5	Hutchison Port Holdings Trust	Container port	18-03-11		
6	Ascendas Hospitality Trust[f]	Hospitality	27-07-12	√	√
7	Far East Hospitality Trust[g]	Hospitality	27-08-12	√	√
8	RHT Health Trust[h]	Healthcare	19-10-12		√
9	Asian Pay Television Trust	Television/Broadband network	29-05-13		
10	Frasers Hospitality Trust[i]	Hospitality	14-07-14	√	√
11	Accordia Golf Trust[j]	Golf course	01-08-14		
12	Dasin Retail Trust	Retail	13-01-17		√
13	NetLink NBN Trust	Fiber network infrastructure	19-07-17		
14	ARA US Hospitality Trust[k]	Hospitality	09-05-19	√	√

---

[5] Property trusts are business trusts which hold property assets. See: *Chartbooks: SREITs & Property Trusts* (SGX Research, December 2019).

[6] These include Greenship Gas Trust, Greenship Holdings Trust, TOP-NTL Shipping Trust which are registered with the MAS.

Table 1: *(Continued)*

S/N	Name	Primary Portfolio	Listing Date	Stapled Trust[b]	Property Trust[c]
15	Eagle Hospitality Trust[l]	Hospitality	24-05-19	√	√

Notes:

a   Including business trusts and stapled trusts.

b   Where S-REIT and business trust securities are stapled together and traded as one (also referred to as stapled securities).

c   Based on classification by Singapore Exchange. See: *Chartbooks: SREITs & Property Trusts*, published by SGX Research, December 2019.

d   Comprises CDL Hospitality Real Estate Investment Trust and CDL Hospitality Business Trust.

e   Formerly known as CitySpring Infrastructure Trust. CitySpring Infrastructure Trust merged with Keppel Infrastructure Trust on 18 May 2015. The enlarged trust was renamed from CitySpring Infrastructure Trust to Keppel Infrastructure Trust.

f   Comprises Ascendas Hospitality Real Estate Investment Trust and Ascendas Hospitality Business Trust. Following the merger of Ascendas Hospitality Trust and Ascott Residence Trust, the combined vehicle known as Ascott Residence Trust commenced trading on 2 January 2020. The decision to merge the two trusts was announced following the completion of CapitaLand's acquisition of Ascendas–Singbridge on 1 July 2019, which resulted in CapitaLand owning the two trusts which have overlapping mandates. One of the key justifications for the merger was that it would provide 'access to a larger capital base and a higher debt headroom' which would in turn provide the combined trust with 'greater financial flexibility to seek more accretive acquisitions and value enhancements'.

g   Comprises Far East Hospitality Real Estate Investment Trust and Far East Hospitality Business Trust.

h   Formerly known as Religare Health Trust. As of 1 January 2020, RHT Health Trust is a cash trust, as it had earlier disposed of its entire portfolio of healthcare assets to its controlling unit holder, Fortis Healthcare, in January 2019.

i   Comprises Frasers Hospitality Real Estate Investment Trust and Frasers Hospitality Business Trust.

j   Accordia Golf Trust has since sold the trust's interests in all its golf courses, and was wounded up and delisted shortly thereafter.

k   Comprises ARA US Hospitality Property Trust and ARA US Hospitality Management Trust.

l   Comprises Eagle Hospitality Real Estate Investment Trust and Eagle Hospitality Business Trust.

The business trust structure is generally regarded as being suited for businesses with high initial capital outlay but stable operating cashflow and growth, such as real estate, infrastructure businesses, as well as vehicle leasing and chartering businesses. It follows that all business trusts listed on the Singapore Exchange are in the real estate, infrastructure, and shipping sectors. Due to the nature of the underlying business and assets (which are mainly in industries where income flow is regular and stable), business trusts generally have better yield and at the same time are less price volatile, compared to general equities[7]. However, despite the first business trust being listed a mere 4 years after the first S-REIT, the number of business trusts listed on the Singapore Exchange is nowhere near that of S-REITs which has seen phenomenal growth[8] (15 business trusts vs 41 S-REITs, as of 1 January 2020). The performance of business trusts was also reported to be inferior to that of S-REITs[9].

From the perspective of the investors (particularly individual investors), one significant difference between registered business trusts and S-REITs is that the latter qualify for tax transparency treatment which effectively results in no tax payable by individual investors in respect of the income derived through S-REITs[10]. In contrast, there is no such beneficial tax treatment available for individual investors of registered business trusts. The difference in tax treatment in turn translates to a lower yield for investments in registered business trusts vis-à-vis S-REITs, *ceteris paribus*.

In this chapter, we will trace the development of the business trust as an alternative business vehicle in Singapore, outline the regulatory regime governing business trusts and examine the tax treatment of business trusts (*vis-à-vis* that of S-REITs).

2. Business Trusts: An Overview of the Key Milestones

The first business trust to be listed on the Singapore Exchange was Pacific Shipping Trust, which acquired vessels and leased them to charterers on either a time or bareboat charter basis. It was listed on 26 May 2006. It was, unfortunately, also the first Singapore-listed business trust to be delisted and privatized[11].

2.1. Listing of the first real estate focused business trust

The first real estate focused business trust to be listed on the Singapore Exchange was CDL HBT, which together with CDL Hospitality Real Estate

---

[7] 'Business trusts to give good yield,' *The Business Times*, 10 December 2007.

[8] There are 15 business trusts listed on the Singapore Exchange as of 1 January 2020 compared to 41 S-REITs.

[9] 'Business trusts' spotty showing spells caution,' *The Business Times*, 17 June 2013.

[10] S 13(1)(zh) read with s 43(2) of the Income Tax Act.

[11] Circular to unitholders in relation to the proposed voluntary delisting of Pacific Shipping Trust pursuant to Rules 1307 and 1309 of the SGX-ST Listing Manual dated 28 November 2011.

Investment Trust (CDL H-REIT), constitutes the stapled trusts known as CDL Hospitality Trusts[12]. CDL Hospitality Trusts was listed on 19 July 2006 with an initial real estate portfolio comprising four hotels and a shopping arcade in Singapore — Grand Copthorne Waterfront Hotel, Copthorne King's Hotel, M Hotel, Orchard Hotel, and Orchard Hotel Shopping Arcade.

CDL HBT, which primarily serves as "a master lessee of last resort", was initially dormant as of the date of listing. In this regard, it was stated in the prospectus of CDL Hospitality Trusts that CDL HBT would become active if CDL H-REIT is unable to appoint a master lessee for any of the hotels in its portfolio at the expiry of the relevant master lease agreement or for a newly acquired hotel. In addition, it was stated in the prospectus that CDL HBT may become active if it undertakes certain hospitality and hospitality-related development projects, acquisitions and investments which may not be suitable for CDL H-REIT. CDL HBT subsequently became active at the end of year 2013 when it became the master lessee of the Jumeirah Dhevanafushi resort in the Maldives[13].

Over the years, CDL Hospitality Trusts has grown to become one of Asia's leading hospitality trusts with assets valued at S$3.1 billion. It currently owns 18 properties with a total of 4,630 hotel rooms, comprising six hotels and a retail mall in Singapore, two hotels in Australia, one hotel in New Zealand, two hotels in Japan, two hotels in United Kingdom, one hotel in Germany, one hotel in Italy and two resorts in the Maldives[14].

Although CDL HBT was the first real estate focused business trust to be listed on the Singapore Exchange (as part of the stapled securities CDL Hospitality Trusts), it was initially dormant as of the date of listing. In this regard, the first standalone[15], non-dormant real estate focused business trust listed on the Singapore Exchange was CitySpring Infrastructure Trust (now known as Keppel Infrastructure Trust), which invests in and operates infrastructure assets. CitySpring Infrastructure Trust was listed on 12 February 2007, about 7 months after the listing of CDL Hospitality Trusts.

---

[12] See also: website and prospectus of CDL Hospitality Trusts.

[13] Annual report of CDL Hospitality Trusts for financial year ended 2013.

[14] Based on the website of CDL Hospitality Trust, http://www.cdlht.com/overview.html (accessed 1 January 2021).

[15] Without being listed together with a S-REIT as stapled trusts.

Its core business involves the production and sale of town gas[16] and water desalination[17]. Such infrastructure and utility businesses are very stable due to the constant day-to-day demand for energy and water usage[18].

2.2. Largest IPO of a business trust and first merger between business trusts

The most high-profile initial public offering (IPO) of units in a business trust in Singapore was that of Hutchison Port Holdings Trust in March 2011, which raised US$5.5 billion, making it one of the world's largest IPO of the year. The performance of Hutchison Port Holdings Trust in the stock market has however been lackluster.

Another major milestone for business trusts was reached in 2014 when CitySpring Infrastructure Trust and Keppel Infrastructure Trust announced that they would be the first two business trusts to merge[19]. The enlarged trust would become the largest Singapore infrastructure-focused business trust, with total assets of over S$4 billion. The merger of the two business trusts set a precedent for the subsequent wave of merger and consolidation, which took place from early 2018 following the merger of ESR-REIT (a S-REIT) and Viva Industrial Trust (a stapled S-REIT and business trust).

2.3. Proliferation of hospitality trusts

In more recent years, the number of hospitality trusts listed on the Singapore Exchange has proliferated. In the year 2019, the Singapore Exchange saw the listing of the first two United States pure play hospitality trusts — ARA US Hospitality Trust and Eagle Hospitality Trust[20], both of which invest

---

[16] Through the entity known as City Gas (now known as City Energy).

[17] Through the entity known as SingSpring.

[18] 'Business trusts to give good yield,' *The Business Times*, 10 December 2007.

[19] 'Singapore's CitySpring to merge with Keppel Infrastructure Trust,' *The Business Times*, 18 November 2014.

[20] Unfortunately, Eagle Hospitality Trust soon ran into problems, adding to the list of business trusts facing woes. See: 'Troubles mount for Eagle Hospitality Trust,' *The Straits Times*, 24 April 2020 and 'Eagle Hospitality Trust to use maiden distribution to pay for sponsor's liabilities,' *The Business Times*, 28 May 2020.

in and operate hotels situated in the United States[21]. This brings the total number of hospitality business trusts listed on the Singapore Exchange to a total of six out of a total of 15 (or 40%) as of 1 January 2020.

Notably, all hospitality trusts listed on the Singapore Exchange are "stapled trusts", which comprise S-REIT and business trust securities stapled and traded together (see Table 1). In a stapled trust structure, the S-REIT will hold the underlying hospitality real estate whereas the business trust, which is usually dormant, could be activated when the hospitality real estate needs to be actively managed. As stapled trusts, hospitality trusts are essentially hybrids of S-REITs and business trusts.

Similar to a standalone S-REIT, the S-REIT of a stapled trust is governed by the Code on Collective Investment Schemes (CIS Code), which requires, among others, the S-REIT to derive stable income from its underlying assets[22]. However, unlike commercial real estate such as office buildings and shopping malls which typically have longer leases and more stabilized income, hospitality real estate such as hotels typically have a much shorter average length of stay. Consequently, the revenue from hospitality real estate tends to fluctuate[23].

In order to overcome these inadequacies, it is common for hospitality trusts to enter into master lease agreements in respect of their underlying assets. The master lease arrangements are typically contracted with the sponsor(s) of the hospitality trusts, to provide a layer of stability to the cashflow of the trusts and downside protect the trusts. Where the S-REIT of a hospitality trust is unable to appoint a master lessee, such as in the case ARA US Hospitality Trusts where the sponsor did not guarantee a minimum rent or provide a master lease in respect of the hotels, the business trust will be activated to be the master lessee of last resort to actively manage the hotels[24].

Due to the sizeable component of variable rent which exposes investors to the vagaries of running a hospitality business (as opposed to the situation

---

[21] 'ARA plans first US hospitality trust on SGX,' *The Business Times*, 25 April 2019 and 'Another US hospitality trust looks to list on SGX,' *The Business Times*, 26 April 2019.
[22] Paragraph 7.2 of Appendix 6 of the CIS Code.
[23] 'A model that works,' *The Edge Singapore*, 30 December 2019.
[24] 'A model that works,' *The Edge Singapore*, 30 December 2019.

of mere rental collection), hospitality trusts are generally regarded as having more cyclical businesses compared to the other S-REITs and property trusts. For example, while more than 90% of net property income at CDL Hospitality Trusts in 2019 came from hotels with leases, about 50% of the rental revenue was fixed and the other 50% was variable[25], and hence subject to the vagaries of the business.

2.4. Other observations

In the Singapore context, it is noted that the trend of securitizing and listing non-traditional assets has been slow to catch on[26]. This is unlike other jurisdictions such as the United States where an increasing number of non-traditional assets (such as fiber optics networks, mobile towers, old aged homes and even prisons) are being securitized and listed on the exchange. As can be seen in Table 1, of the 15 business trusts listed on the Singapore Exchange as of 1 January 2020, only six business trusts hold non-traditional assets — Keppel Infrastructure Trust (infrastructure assets), First Ship Lease Trust (ships), Hutchison Port Holdings Trust (container ports), Asian Pay Television Trust (television/broadband networks), Accordia Golf Trust (golf courses) and NetLink NBN Trust (fiber network infrastructure). These constitute just 12% (or six out of 50) of the S-REITs and business trusts[27] listed on the Singapore exchange listed as of 1 January 2020.

It is also worthwhile noting that in less than 15 years since the listing of the first business trust, nine business trusts have been delisted due to various reasons (see Table 2). Notably, there were a number of business trusts whose units were acquired in a take-over or merger transaction[28].

---

[25] 'Risks in REITs are not what they once were,' *The Business Times*, 13 February 2020.

[26] 'Could a full-fledged Airport Reit work?', *The Business Times*, 26 March 2019.

[27] See: Table 1 of Chapter 8 for the other 44 S-REITs and property trusts which holds traditional real estate assets.

[28] The Singapore Code on Take-overs and Mergers (Take-Over Code) issued pursuant to section 139(2) of the Securities and Futures Act by the MAS, on the advice of the Securities Industry Council (SIC), sets out the rules pertaining to acquisition of units in a registered business trust as well as S-REIT. Registered business trusts are business trusts which are registered with the MAS. The Take-Over Code allows the SIC to exempt such a trust from certain compliance requirements if certain conditions are met. A trust scheme of arrangement, in compliance with the Take-Over Code, facilitates the transfer of the existing units in the target registered business trust to the acquirer. A typical trust scheme of arrangement involves obtaining certain approvals from the unitholders as well as the court pursuant to O 80 of the Rule of Court (Cap.

Table 2: Business trusts delisted as of 1 January 2020.[a]

S/N	Name	Primary Portfolio	Listing Date	Delisting Date	Remarks
1	Pacific Shipping Trust	Ship	26-05-06	08-03-2012	Acquired by Pacific International Lines
2	Perennial China Retail Trust	Retail	09-06-11	05-02-15	Acquired by Perennial Real Estate Holdings[b]
3	Forterra Trust[c]	Office/Retail	21-06-10	13-02-15	Acquired by Nan Fung[d]
4	K-Green Trust (renamed Keppel Infrastructure Trust, and thereafter renamed Crystal Trust)	Infrastructure	29-06-10	22-05-15	Merged with CitySpring Infrastructure Trust[e]
5	Rickmers Maritime Trust	Ship	04-05-07	30-08-17	Wounded up due to insolvency[f]
6	Viva Industrial Trust	Industrial	04-11-13	22-10-17	Merged with ESR-REIT[g]
7	Croesus Retail Trust	Retail	10-05-13	26-10-17	Acquired by Blackstone[h]
8	Indiabulls Properties Investment Trust	Office	11-06-08	11-12-17	Acquired by Indiabulls Real Estate[i]
9	OUE Hospitality Trust	Hospitality	25-07-13	17-09-19	Merged with OUE Commercial REIT[j]

Notes:

[a] Including business trusts and stapled trusts.

[b] 'Buyout of Singapore-listed Perennial China Retail Trust finalized,' *The Straits Times*, 24 December 2014.

[c] Formerly known as Treasury China Trust.

[d] 'Forterra Trust receives mandatory takeover offer from Nan Fung at S$1.85 per share (Amended)', *The Business Times*, 4 November 2014.

[e] 'Singapore's CitySpring to merge with Keppel Infrastructure Trust,' *The Business Times*, 18 November 2014.

[f] 'Shipping trust Rickmers Maritime bites bullet with winding up announcement,' *The Straits Times*, 12 April 2017.

[g] 'ESR-Reit, Viva Industrial Trust to merge, forming group with $3b in assets,' *The Straits Times*, 18 May 2018.

[h] 'Croesus Retail Trust unitholders approve Blackstone's $900.6m buyout offer,' *The Straits Times*, 13 September 2017.

[i] 'Indiabulls Properties Investment Trust gets takeover offer of 90 S cents apiece,' *The Business Times*, 12 October 2017.

[j] 'Plan to merge OUE C-REIT and OUE H-Trust,' *The Straits Times*, 9 April 2019.

These include Croesus Retail Trust, a retail business trust that invests primarily in retail real estate in Japan and the rest of the Asia Pacific region, which was acquired by affiliates of the Blackstone Group LP[29]. Considering that there are currently only 15 business trusts listed on the Singapore Exchange, the sheer number and proportion of business trusts which have delisted is clearly stark.

3. Business Trusts: Key Features

3.1. What is a business trust

A business trust is essentially a business set up with a trust structure instead of the traditional corporate structure[30]. It is constituted via a trust deed and does not have separate legal personality.

A business trust may be established in respect of any business or property. The purpose or effect of the trust is to enable the unitholders to participate in or receive returns arising from the management of the property or management or operation of the business. A business trust differs from traditional trusts (such as private trusts and unit trusts), in that the business trust is running and operating a business enterprise[31].

The setting up of a business trust may involve raising funds (for the purpose of acquiring the trust assets; e.g. via an IPO) from investors, who will become the unitholders of the trust. Unitholders of a business trust do not have day-to-day control over the management of the trust assets. Instead, the underlying properties or assets of the business trust are legally owned and held in trust by a trustee and managed by the trustee or another person on behalf of the trustee. In return for their investment in the business trust, unitholders receive regular distributions from the income generated from the underlying business and assets of the business trust.

322, R 5). In particular, the trust scheme is required to be approved by a majority in number representing three-fourths in value of unitholders or class of unitholders present and voting either in person or by proxy at a meeting convened to approve the trust scheme, in order to be exempt from certain compliance requirements under the Take-Over Code.

[29] 'Croesus Retail Trust unitholders approve Blackstone's $900.6m buyout offer'. *The Straits Times*, 13 September 2017.

[30] See: s 2 of the Business Trusts Act for the definition of 'business trust'. For an annotation of the Business Trusts Act by Vincent Ooi, see: *Woon's Corporations Law* (LexisNexis, 2019).

[31] See: Ministerial speech at second reading of the Business Trust Bill, 1 September 2004, available on the website of the Parliament of Singapore.

The business trust legislation further provides that (i) the units in the trust that are issued should be exclusively or primarily non-redeemable or (ii) the trust invests only in real estate and real estate-related assets specified by the Monetary Authority of Singapore (MAS) in the CIS Code referred to in section 284 of the Securities and Futures Act and is listed on an approved exchange[32].

Similar to a traditional company, a business trust is a business vehicle which may undertake active business activities with no restriction on the underlying asset or investment portfolio. A key feature of the business trust structure is the ability of the trust to make distributions to unitholders out of its operating cashflow or cash profits. This is in contrast to the traditional corporate structure, whereby a company can only pay dividends out of its profits (i.e. after deducting non-cash expenses such as depreciation)[33]. It follows that the business trust structure is particularly suitable for infrastructure, utilities and transportation related businesses and assets, which generally requires high initial capital expenditure (and hence high depreciation expenses) but offers stable operating cashflow over the long term[34]. In this regard, a key advantage conferred by the business trust structure is that it converts capital intensive and illiquid assets into liquid business trust units, which may be listed and publicly traded on an exchange.

Typically, the trust deed of a listed trust will expressly state that the unitholders do not have any equitable, proprietary or beneficial interests of the underlying trust assets. In this regard, Aedit Abdullah J in *Re Croesus Retail Asset Management Pte Ltd*, noted this feature of the business trust in that case[35]:

> Croesus differs from an orthodox and traditional trust since unit holders are expressly stated not have any equitable proprietary interest in the trust property but only a right to compel due performance by the trustee ....

Listed business trusts generally offer higher yields to the investors, and at the same time are less price-volatile, compared to listed equities. That

---

[32] See: Definition of 'business trust' at s 2 of the Business Trusts Act. Given that the units in business trusts are exclusively or primarily non-redeemable, business trusts should generally be considered as a 'closed-end fund' and hence falling outside the definition of a collective investment scheme under section 2 of the Securities and Futures Act.

[33] Compare s 33 of the Business Trusts Act and s 403 of the Companies Act.

[34] MAS consultation paper, *Regulation of Business Trusts*, 10 December 2003.

[35] [2017] 5 SLR 811 at [11].

said, the growth opportunities conferred by listed business trusts are lesser when compared to listed equities, which may experience more volatility in terms of income[36].

3.2. Registration under the Business Trusts Act

As a general requirement, a business trust must be a registered business trust or a recognized business trust, if its units or the derivative of its units are to be offered to the public or listed[37]. It is otherwise not mandatory for business trusts in Singapore to be registered with the MAS under the Business Trusts Act.

Nonetheless, a business trust may voluntarily register as one under the Business Trusts Act[38]. Business trusts which are not registered with the MAS under the Business Trusts Act will continue to be subject to the Trustees Act[39], which sets out the general obligations of trustees. In this regard, the following was said by the then Minister for Education, Mr Tharman Shanmugaratnam, at the second reading of the Business Trusts Bill on 1 September 2004[40]:

> The Business Trusts Bill sets out the requirements for the governance of business trusts registered under the Bill. The Securities and Futures (Amendment) Bill will make it mandatory for business trusts offered to the retail public to be registered under the Business Trusts Bill. Other business trusts, such as those offered to accredited and institutional investors will not require registration under the Bill. This is because such investors are generally better able to protect their own interests. Such business trusts may however be voluntarily registered under the Bill where, for instance, the offeror considers that the investors targeted prefer to have the assurance that the business trust is one which is registered under the Bill. Business trusts which are not registered under the Bill will continue to be subject to the Trustees Act, which sets out the general obligations of trustees.

---

[36] 'Business trusts to give good yield,' *The Business Times*, 10 December 2007.

[37] S 239C of the Securities and Futures Act.

[38] MAS consultation paper, *Regulation of Business Trusts*, 10 December 2013.

[39] Cap. 337.

[40] See: Ministerial speech at the second reading of the Business Trusts Bill, 1 September 2004, available on the website of the Parliament of Singapore.

In the subsequent paragraphs, the term "registered business trust" will be used to refer to business trusts which are registered under the Business Trusts Act, whereas the term "business trust" will be used to refer to business trusts in general, regardless whether such business trusts are registered under the Business Trusts Act.

3.3. Registered business trusts vs S-REITs vs companies

Generally, business trusts which undertake active business and/or development activities with respect to its asset portfolio, do not have a choice of adopting the S-REIT structure, which is reserved for real estate which receives "passive" rental income. For this reason, it is common for business trusts to be constituted to own, manage and operate infrastructure assets (e.g. Keppel Infrastructure Trust), hospitality assets (e.g. Far East Hospitality Trust), shipping assets (e.g. Rickmers Maritime Trust) and real estate portfolio where a significant proportion of the assets are non-rental yielding or undergoing development activities (e.g. Perennial China Retail Trust). Such business trusts may otherwise be constituted as companies, but the corporate structure does not offer the attractiveness of the flexibility of making distributions out of the company's operating cashflow or cash profits.

The income tax treatment of a registered business trust and a company is however less favorable compared to that of a S-REIT (as further discussed in section 5 below). The tax transparency treatment enjoyed by a S-REIT effectively means that individual investors are not subject to tax on the income derived through the S-REIT. In this regard, a S-REIT enjoys a significant tax advantage in that it is able to provide its individual investors with a higher rate of return compared to a registered business trust and a company.

While both the registered business trust and the S-REIT are essentially constituted as trusts and share various similarities, there are also a number of key differences between the two vehicles. It is further noted that while the registered business trust regime is more closely aligned with the regulatory regime for companies than that of S-REITs, there remain a number of key differences between the different regimes, as discussed below[41].

---

[41] See also: 'REIT or business trust,' *The Business Times Weekend*, 30 April/1 May 2011, and Jerry Koh and Liu Hailing, 'Diversifying and Deepening Singapore's Capital Markets: The Impact of Real Estate Investment Trusts and Business Trusts', (2011) 17 *Securities Law* 22.

3.3.1. Legislation/regulatory regime

Business trusts and S-REITs are constituted under trust deeds and do not have separate legal personalities. In contrast, companies have separate and distinct legal personalities from their shareholders. From a regulatory standpoint, a registered business trust is regulated under the Business Trusts Act, a S-REIT is regulated under CIS Code[42] whereas a company is incorporated pursuant to the Companies Act[43].

3.3.2. Investment/asset composition and other regulatory requirements

A primary distinction between a business trust and a S-REIT is that the business trust may actively undertake business activities (similar to companies), whereas the S-REIT is essentially required under the CIS Code to be a "passive" collective investment scheme which primarily engages in passive investments. Unlike the S-REIT which is largely restricted to investing in real estate and real estate related assets[44], there is no similar restriction on the business trust which can accommodate various classes of assets including infrastructure projects, hotels, ships and aircraft.

Other regulatory restrictions imposed on S-REITs under the CIS Code include a debt limit of 50%[45] of the value of the S-REIT's deposited property and a restriction of property development activities to 25% of the value of the S-REIT's deposited property. No such restrictions apply to business trusts and real estate companies which have flexibility to borrow funds to grow their business (particularly in today's low interest rate environment), and to undertake development activities in accordance with their own business strategies.

---

[42] See: Section 4.3 of Chapter 8 for an overview of the guidance set out under the CIS Code.

[43] Cap. 50.

[44] As provided under the CIS Code issued by the MAS pursuant to s 321 of the Securities and Futures Act.

[45] Press release, *New Measures to Help REITs Navigate Operating Challenges Posed by COVID-19*, issued by the Ministry of Finance (MOF), IRAS and MAS, 16 April 2020. The announcement to increase the leverage limit of S-REITs from 45% to 50% was made in the midst of the COVID-19 global pandemic, to provide S-REITs greater flexibility to manage their capital structure and to raise debt financing amid the challenging environment.

Given the absence of regulatory restrictions on borrowings, a business trust may take advantage of the prevailing low interest rate environment to acquire yield accretive assets, with the use of debt financing. It is up to the various business trusts to set their strategy, assess their risk appetite and self-impose any restrictions. In this regard, a business trust structure confers more flexibility and less restrictions compared to a S-REIT structure which is generally subject to more regulation under the CIS Code.

As an example[46], Perennial China Retail Trust, which was listed in June 2011 as Singapore's first listed pure-play China retail development business trust, was structured as a business trust instead of a REIT, in view of its investment objective of acquiring attractively priced, predominantly retail development projects that on completion would provide unitholders with both capital gain and regular distributions from stabilized assets. Given the significant property development activities to be undertaken by Perennial China Retail Trust, it was not feasible to constitute Perennial China Retail Trust as a S-REIT[47]. In this regard, Perennial China Retail Trust was structured as a business trust to offer not only yield but also growth opportunities to the investors.

3.3.3. Responsible entity

Unlike a S-REIT where the role of the trustee and the role of the manager are undertaken by two separate entities, in the case of a registered business trust, the roles are merged into a single responsible entity, known as a "trustee-manager"[48]. Having a single responsible entity not only makes it easier to manage the activities of the registered business trust but also helps eliminate the extra cost involved in appointing separate trustee and manager. It is in any case difficult for a separate independent trustee to be appointed to supervise the manager of the registered business trust, given the active nature of the business conducted by the trust.

---

[46] 'Perennial China play should take REIT route,' *The Business Times,* 14 March 2011 and 'Constituting PCRT as a REIT could stifle its growth,' *The Business Times,* 18 March 2011.

[47] Given that the CIS Code imposes a limit on the development activities which may be undertaken by S-REITs.

[48] See: Section 4.3 for a further discussion on the role of the trustee-manager.

In contrast, given the "passive" nature of the S-REIT, the appointed trustee is better placed to perform the independent role of monitoring the manager of the REIT, and ensuring that the real estate portfolio is managed in accordance with the terms of the trust deed constituting the S-REIT.

In the case of a company, its affairs are typically overseen by a board of directors as well as a management team.

3.3.4. *Distributions to unitholders/shareholders and taxation*

While a business trust is similar to a company in that both run and operate business enterprises and are taxed on their respective income, a business trust, unlike a company, may make distributions to its unitholders out of its operating cashflow (instead of its accounting profits which take into account non-cash expenses such as depreciation). In this regard, a business trust is similar to a S-REIT in that both the business trust and the S-REIT are not restricted or limited by their accounting profits when making distributions. There is however a notable exception in that the S-REIT is required to distribute at least 90% of its distributable income in the same year[49], in order to enjoy "tax transparency" treatment[50]. No such "tax transparency" treatment is available for registered business trusts.

While there is no requirement for business trusts to distribute at least 90% of their distributable income, it is nevertheless observed that certain registered business trusts (e.g. Accordia Golf Trust) adopted a deliberate policy of distributing at least 90% of their distributable income. Given that there is no requirement mandating business trusts to distribute a specified proportion of their income, the distribution yield offered by business trusts may not be as stable as that of S-REITs[51].

In the case of S-REITs, the 90% minimum distribution requirement is widely understood to be the hallmark of S-REITs. At the height of the Global Financial Crisis in early 2009, the authorities even rejected the

---

[49] Where the income of the last quarter of the S-REIT's financial year is distributed within the first 3 months of the subsequent financial year, the requirement to distribute the income in the same year in which the income is derived, would be considered satisfied. See: IRAS e-Tax Guide, *Income Tax Treatment of Real Estate Investment Trusts and Approved Sub-Trusts*, Eighth Edition, 17 November 2021.

[50] See: Section 8 of Chapter 8 for further details on the tax transparency treatment.

[51] 'Are REITs a better alternative to Hutchison Port Trust?', *The Business Times*, 31 March 2011.

requests made by S-REIT managers to lower the minimum distribution ratio of 90%, despite the severity of the ongoing economic crisis then[52]. A decade later, during the outbreak of the COVID-19 global pandemic and the ensuing economic crisis in early 2020, the authorities took a comparatively more liberal stance and allowed S-REITs up to 12 months after the end of financial year 2020 to make distributions of income derived during financial year 2020[53].

Although S-REITs and business trusts are able to make distributions based on their operating cashflow without regard to the non-cash depreciation expenses, investors who are holding on to units in S-REITs and business trusts should be cognizant of the relevance of depreciation given that the underlying assets of the S-REIT/business trust typically have limited useful life (e.g. in the case of an infrastructure project such a desalination plant), may become redundant or obsolete (e.g. in the case of a television or fiber network), and may require significant capital outlay to refurbish or upgrade (e.g. in the case of hotels, data centers or NEWater plant)[54]. A summary of the key similarities and differences pertaining to registered business trusts, S-REITs and companies is provided in Table 3.

3.4. Other unique features pertaining to business trusts

Under the Business Trusts Act, the trustee-manager of a registered business trust is prohibited from carrying on any business other than the management and operation of the registered business trust as its trustee-manager[55]. The rationale behind such a rule is that if a trustee-manager is

---

[52] Speech at the Asian Public Real Estate Association Singapore REIT Summit, *Navigating the Storm: Responding to the Challenges in Singapore's REIT Market*, 20 February 2009.

[53] Press release, *New Measures to Help REITs Navigate Operating Challenges Posed by COVID-19*, issued by MOF, IRAS and MAS, 16 April 2020. While the measure had an adverse impact on the distribution received by the unitholders during the COVID-19 pandemic, it was recognized that the alternative of mandating S-REITs continue with the distribution of at least 90% of their taxable income in the same year, would put significant strain on the financial position of the S-REITs. A key difference between the response of the authorities during the Global Financial Crisis of 2008/2009 and the COVID-19 pandemic in 2020, is that at the height of the COVID-19 crisis, emergency legislation (i.e. Covid-19 (Temporary Measures) Act) was enacted on 7 April 2020 to require landlords to suspend rent collections by up to 6 months for tenants who were unable to pay as a result of the pandemic. The suspension of rent collection had a substantial impact on the ability of S-REITs to distribute at least 90% of their distributable income in the same year.

[54] 'Mind the depreciation in REITs, business trusts,' *The Business Times*, 9 May 2006.

[55] S 6(3) of the Business Trusts Act.

Table 3: Registered business trusts vs S-REITs vs companies.

	Registered business Trusts	S-REITs	Companies
Legislation/ Regulatory regime	Business Trusts Act	Code on Collective Investment Schemes[a]	Companies Act
Legal personality	Not a separate legal entity	Not a separate legal entity	Separate legal personality
Investment/Asset composition	No restriction	Real estate and related assets	No restriction
Debt limit	None	Limited to 50%[b] of the value of the S-REIT's deposited property	None
Development Activities	No restriction	Limited to 25% of the value of the S-REIT's deposited property	No restriction
Responsible entity	Trustee-Manager is the single responsible entity with its role similar to the combined roles of the S-REIT's manager and trustee	S-REIT's trustee and manager are separate and distinct entities	Board of directors and management
Distributions to unitholders/ shareholders	Not limited by the accounting profits of the trust	Not limited by the accounting profits of the S-REIT; Required to distribute at least 90% of its distributable income in order to qualify for "tax transparency" treatment	Subject to the company's accounting profits which take into account non-cash expenses such as depreciation
Taxation	Subject to income tax in the hands of the registered business trust	Not subject to income tax; instead, the income of the S-REITs is deemed to be derived by the investors and taxed according to the profile of the respective investors, which is usually at a lower rate compared to that imposed on companies and registered business trusts	Subject to income tax in the hands of the company

Notes:
[a] Issued by the MAS pursuant to s 321 of the Securities and Futures Act.
[b] Press release, *New Measures to Help REITs Navigate Operating Challenges Posed by COVID-19*, issued by MOF, IRAS and MAS, 16 April 2020. The announcement to increase the leverage limit of S-REITs from 45% to 50% was made in the midst of the COVID-19 global pandemic, to provide S-REITs greater flexibility to manage their capital structure and to raise debt financing amid the challenging environment.

allowed to undertake other businesses or manage other registered business trusts, conflicts of interest may inevitably arise[56].

It is further to be noted that since a business trust does not have separate legal personality from its trustee-manager, creditors of a registered business trust may seek to wind-up the trustee-manager in the event that the registered business trust defaults on the repayment of its debts. With that in mind, if a trustee-manager is allowed to run more than one registered business trust, the creditors' winding up of a trustee-manager in respect of a specific registered business trust could have an adverse knock-on impact on the running of other registered business trusts operated by the same trustee-manager as well as on their unitholders[57].

It is also interesting to note that the creditors of a unitholder of a registered business trust is specifically prohibited from claiming on the trust property of the registered business trust[58]. This recognizes the fact that the unitholders are essentially the beneficial owner of the assets of the registered business trust[59], and creditors of the unitholders would, but for the statutory prohibition, be entitled to claim against the trust property of the registered business trust.

4. Typical Structure of Registered Business Trusts

A typical structure commonly adopted by registered business trusts in Singapore is set out in Figure 1, and comprises the business trust, the trustee-manager and the unitholders (one of which is usually the sponsor of the trust).

---

[56] MAS consultation paper, *Regulation of Business Trusts*, 10 December 2013.

[57] MAS consultation paper, *Regulation of Business Trusts*, 10 December 2013.

[58] See: s 34 of the Business Trusts Act which provides that 'No creditor of a unitholder of a registered business trust shall have any right to obtain possession of, or otherwise exercise any legal or equitable remedy with respect to, the trust property of the registered business trust'.

[59] See: s 2 of the Business Trusts Act, where the term 'unitholder' is defined as a person who holds units in a business trust. The term 'unit' in relation to a business trust, is in turn defined as a share in the beneficial ownership in the trust property of the business trust. Nevertheless, in *Re Croesus Retail Asset Management Pte Ltd* [2017] 5 SLR 811 at [11], it has been pointed out that the trust deed of the registered business trust in question had expressly provided that the unitholders do not have any equitable proprietary interests in the underlying assets of the registered business trust in that case.

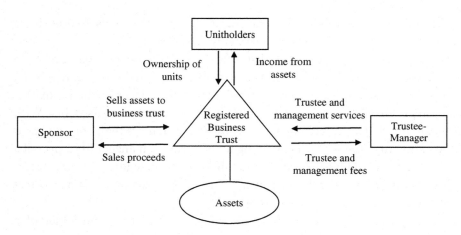

Figure 1: Typical registered business trust structure.

4.1. Registered business trust

A business trust is a business vehicle which has features of both a trust and a company. It is constituted by a trust deed which sets out the mechanism governing the trust, the purpose of the business trust and the classes of assets to be held in trust, the role and responsibilities of the trustee-manager as well as the rights and entitlement of the unitholders. A business trust which is registered with the MAS under the Business Trusts Act is referred to as a "registered business trust".

Under a registered business trust structure, the underlying trust properties or assets are legally owned and managed by a trustee-manager for the benefit of unitholders who are the beneficiaries of the trust. Business trusts may differ from an orthodox and traditional trust in that the trust deed may expressly state that the unitholders do not have any equitable proprietary interest in the trust property but only a right to compel due performance by the trustee[60].

---

[60] *Re Croesus Retail Asset Management Pte Ltd* [2017] 5 SLR 811 at [11]. See also: Hans Tjio, 'Merrill and Smith's Intermediate rights lying between contract and property: Are Singapore trusts and secured transactions drifting away from English law towards American law?', [2019] *Singapore Journal of Legal Studies* 235 and Hans Tjio, 'Restructuring business trusts as unregistered companies,' NUS Law Working Paper 2021/023, November 2021.

4.2. Sponsor

In the Singapore context, a registered business trust is often sponsored by a company which provides the initial asset portfolio of the trust. The sponsor typically holds a significant stake in the registered business trust post listing as unitholder[61], as well as control the trustee-manager[62] of the trust. In many instances, the sponsor has a pipeline of assets available for injection into the registered business trust to grow its portfolio post listing, and will also provide the business trust with a right of first refusal in respect of similar classes of assets to be divested by the sponsor to the trust.

The setting up of a registered business trust in Singapore generally involves the sponsor transferring its assets (e.g. infrastructure projects, hotels, etc.) to the trustee-manager for a sum of money which would be raised from the unitholders subscribing for units in the business trust. In return, the unitholders receive returns generated from the trust assets.

The reasons motivating a sponsor to set up a registered business trust are largely similar to those incentivizing a real estate company to set up a S-REIT. In particular, the injection of assets (e.g. infrastructure projects or a fleet of ships or aircraft) into a registered business trust provides the sponsor the opportunity to convert its relatively illiquid assets into units in the business trust which are offered to members of the public. This in turn allows the sponsor to operate on an asset-light business model with reduced assets, debts and liabilities on its balance sheets. The additional capital freed-up from the disposal of assets into the registered business trust provides the sponsor with liquidity and may either be recycled and used to fund new projects or returned to its shareholders.

Notwithstanding the disposal of the assets, the sponsor typically continues to hold significant stakes in the registered business trust and as such continue to enjoy stable income stream in the form of distributions from the units which it holds in the business trust. The retention of a significant stake in the registered business trust also serves to signal the alignment of the sponsor's interests with that of the other investors. At the

---

[61] See further discussion in Section 4.4. The retention of a significant stake in the registered business trust also serves to signal the alignment of the sponsor's interests with that of the other investors.

[62] See further discussion in Section 4.3.

same time, as the trustee-manager is commonly owned or controlled by the sponsor, the sponsor would enjoy the benefit of the recurring fee income derived by the trustee-manager from the provision of services relating to the trust.

4.3. Trustee-manager

The trustee-manager of a registered business trust must be a company incorporated in Singapore[63]. Given that the registered business trust is seen as an active investment scheme where the manager must run the day-to-day business, the conventional split between the roles of the trustee and the manager as in the case of a S-REIT is deemed impractical as it may hinder the day-to-day running of the business. This was explained by the then Minister for Education, Mr Tharman Shanmugaratnam during the second reading of the Business Trusts Bill on 1 September 2004[64]:

> The Bill requires that the business trust be run by a single responsible entity known as the trustee-manager. The trustee-manager must be incorporated in Singapore. The trustee-manager has the dual responsibility of safeguarding the interests of unitholders and managing the business of the business trust.
>
> This requirement ensures that fiduciary responsibility towards unitholders of a business trust is clearly placed on a single entity. The alternative would be a bifurcated structure, involving a manager of the business trust and a separate independent trustee. However, the running of a business trust involves management of an operating business and the making of business decisions on a day-to-day basis. It would be difficult for an independent trustee to oversee the manager's business decisions. It would also be impracticable for a separate trustee to set out an operating mandate for the manager, without fettering the manager's ability to run the business as an operating enterprise. More importantly, it would be difficult to apportion liability for breaches of trust between the trustee and the manager. Adopting the single responsible entity model avoids this

---

[63] S 6 of the Business Trusts Act. The trustee-manager must also not be an exempt private company under the Companies Act.

[64] Available on the website of the Parliament of Singapore.

problem. This was the approach taken in Australia, in response to a number of cases in which the Court found difficulty in apportioning liability between the trustee and the manager.

The shares in the trustee-manager company are typically owned by the sponsor of the registered business trust, which sponsored the business trust by injecting its assets into the trust. The board of directors of the trustee-manager has a fiduciary duty to manage the trustee-manager company in the best interests of the company and its shareholders, and at the same time, is required to safeguard the interests of the unitholders of the registered business trust.

The Business Trusts Act provides that the trustee-manager may be removed subject to a special resolution passed by not less than 75% of the voting rights exercised at a meeting by the unitholders voting in presence or by proxy[65]. The relatively high threshold of 75% is aimed at balancing the need to guard against the frivolous removal of a trustee-manager with the need to provide sufficient rights to unitholders to remove a trustee-manager who is considered to be under-performing or not acting in the interests of the unitholders[66]. In practice, however, unitholders are put at a severe disadvantage, as it may be difficult for the unitholders to remove an under-performing trustee-manager, if the sponsoring entity (which typically controls the trustee-manager at the outset), holds more than 25% of the units in the business trust.

The high threshold required to remove the trustee-manager inevitably favors the sponsors and trustee-manager unduly, at the expense of the other unitholders. The sponsors are basically able to (i) dispose of 74% of their effective interest in the assets to the registered business trust at full market value, (ii) retain only 26% effective interest in the assets as unitholders of the registered business trust, but yet at the same time retain 100% management and control of the assets through their ownership of the trustee-manager (which is disproportionate to their unitholding in the registered business trust). In contrast, in the case of a listed company, the sponsor would have

---

[65] S 20 of the Business Trusts Act.

[66] See: Ministerial speech at the second reading of the Business Trusts Bill, 1 September 2004, available on the website of the Parliament of Singapore.

lost control of the listed company, if the sponsor retains or holds a mere 26% shareholding[67].

On the other hand, in the case of the S-REITs, the CIS Code specifically provides that the trust deed of a property fund such as S-REITs should contain a provision to authorize removal of the manager by way of a resolution passed by a simple majority of participants present and voting at a general meeting. This effectively avoids the situation where the position of the S-REIT manager is unduly entrenched (which is the situation faced by registered business trusts, where the position of the trustee-managers may be entrenched as long as the owner of the trustee manager holds more than 25% of the units in the trust).

In view that the trustee-manager of a registered business trust may encounter situations where its interests (or those of the sponsor) conflict with those of the unitholders, the Business Trusts Act requires the directors of the trustee-manager of a registered business trust to give priority to the interests of all the unitholders of the registered business trust as a whole over the interests of the trustee-manager in the event of a conflict of interests[68].

As additional safeguards, the composition of the board of directors of the trustee-manager of a registered business trust is subject to stricter rules in relation to the independence of the directors. In particular, it is to be noted that (i) the majority of the directors is to be independent from management and business relationships with the trustee-manager, (ii) at least one-third of the directors is to be independent from management and business relationships with the trustee-manager and from every substantial shareholder of the trustee-manager, and (iii) the majority of the directors is be independent from any single substantial shareholder of the trustee-manager[69].

More recently, in November 2021, the MAS issued a consultation paper to seek the public's view on the proposed amendment of the Business Trusts Act to lower the threshold required to remove the trustee-manager, to a simple majority. The rationale provided by the MAS is that such a change will help to instil greater market discipline by allowing investors to hold

---

[67] 'Business trusts scrutinized,' *The Business Times Weekend*, 17–18 November 2012.

[68] S 11(1)(b) of the Business Trusts Act.

[69] R 12(1) of the Business Trusts Regulations (Rg 2), read with s 14(1) of the Business Trusts Act.

trustee-managers accountable for their performance. In the event that the proposed amendment is legislated, it would be possible to remove a trustee-manager of a registered business trust so long as a resolution to remove the trustee-manager is passed by unitholders who hold in total more than 50% of the voting rights of all the unitholders present and voting at a general meeting.

4.4. Unitholders

The units held by the unitholders represent their proportionate interest in the registered business trust. As beneficiaries of the business trust, unitholders are entitled to the distributions made by the trustee-managers out of the income generated from the trust assets.

The Business Trusts Act specifically provides that a unitholder's liability is limited to the amount which the unitholder expressly agreed to contribute to the registered business trust[70]. Such limitation of liability is to apply notwithstanding any provision to the contrary in the trust deed or the winding up of the registered business trust[71]. In other words, the liability of the unitholders is effectively limited by statute notwithstanding the fact that the registered business trust does not have separate legal personality. This provides certainty and protection to unitholders by limiting their liability and puts them in an equivalent position to shareholders of companies. In the absence of the specific statutory provision, under common law, unitholders may be exposed to unlimited liability for the obligations of the trust[72].

5. Taxation of Registered Business Trusts

5.1. Income tax

5.1.1. *No tax transparency treatment*

In the case of the S-REITs, the various concessionary tax treatments (and in particular the tax transparency treatment) which have the effect of

---

[70] S 32(1) of the Business Trusts Act.

[71] S 32(2) of the Business Trusts Act.

[72] See: Ministerial speech at the second reading of the Business Trusts Bill, 1 September 2004, available on the website of the Parliament of Singapore.

enhancing the overall yield and attractiveness of S-REITs to investors, are widely accredited as a major factor leading to the successful take off of the S-REIT market[73]. In particular, the major tax advantage conferred by treating the S-REIT as a tax transparent vehicle is that, the income of the S-REIT is potentially not subject to any taxation, where such income is distributed to the individual investors[74].

In the case of the registered business trusts, however, such trusts which are registered under the Business Trusts Act are to be treated as companies for Singapore income tax purposes[75], and no tax transparency treatment is available. The rationale given for the different tax treatments for business trusts and S-REIT is that the economic purpose, structure and operation of a registered business trust are similar to those of a company[76], which carries on an active business. In contrast, S-REITs are regarded as passive collective investment schemes which primarily engage in passive investments.

The different tax treatment invariably puts registered business trusts at a disadvantage *vis-à-vis* the S-REITs, which are able to provide their investors with a higher distribution and yield, *ceteris paribus*. Such tax difference could be as high as 17% (i.e. tax rate imposed on the registered business trust) in the case of the individual investors. Nevertheless, the policy decision in relation to the tax treatment of registered business trusts has been clearly articulated by the then Minister for Education, Mr Tharman Shanmugaratnam, in his response to comments from Nominated Member of Parliament, Mrs Fang Ai Lian, at the second reading of the Business Trusts Bill on 1 September 2004[77]:

> The tax position on REITs, if they choose to register under the Business Trusts Act, will be no different from what it is for other business trusts. In

---

[73] See: Chapter 8 for more details of the concessionary tax treatments accorded to S-REITs.

[74] The tax transparency treatment for S-REITs is provided under ss 43(2) and (2A) of the Income Tax Act. The exemption of S-REIT distributions in the hands of individual investors is provided under s 13(1) (zh) of the Income Tax Act.

[75] See: S 36B of the Income Tax Act. Where the business trust is not registered under the Business Trusts Act, the general taxation rules pertaining to trusts would apply instead.

[76] IRAS e-Tax Guide, *Income Tax Treatment of a Trust registered under the Business Trusts Act*, Third Edition, 10 March 2021.

[77] See: Ministerial speech at second reading of the Business Trusts Bill, 1 September 2004, available on the website of the Parliament of Singapore.

other words, the fact that they are REITs and they can alternatively be registered as a collective investment scheme will not change the tax treatment if they register as a business trust. So, REITs have a choice as to where they want to register. If they register under the Business Trusts Act, they will not be able to use the name "REITs" and they will be subject to the tax treatment that applies to all business trusts. In other words, they will be taxed at the corporate rate, at the trustee level, and distributions of the trust would be treated as exempt one-tier dividends in the hands of unitholders. I am sure the Minister for Finance heard Mrs Fang Ai Lian's arguments and will consider them. But the position at this point remains quite clear.

Given the more favorable tax treatment conferred on S-REITs, it is no surprise that most property trusts (i.e. trusts which hold real estate) are set up in the form of S-REITs as opposed to business trusts. Of the 44 property trusts listed on the Singapore Exchange as of 1 January 2020[78], there exists only three property trusts which are set up as pure business trusts (i.e. without being stapled to any S-REITs) — Ascendas India Trust, RHT Health Trust and Dasin Retail Trust. For these property trusts, presumably the limitations imposed under the CIS Code (such as those restricting borrowings and development activities[79]) which are applicable to S-REITs but not business trusts, are of greater concern from a commercial perspective, as compared to the tax disadvantage arising from the business trust structure.

5.1.2. *Taxation of income derived by registered business trusts*

The income of a registered business trust is subject to tax in the hands of the trustee at the prevailing corporate tax rate of 17% unless it enjoys specific tax incentive. The tax is a final tax and the unitholders of the registered business trust will not be subject to tax on their entitlement of the trust income[80]. It follows that no credit will be granted to the unitholders in respect of tax paid by the trustee of the registered business trust.

Additionally, the following key features of the Singapore corporate income tax regime will apply to registered business trusts, with relevant

---

[78] *Chartbooks: SREITs & Property Trusts*, published by SGX Research, December 2019.

[79] See: Section 7 of Chapter 8 for more details on such restrictions.

[80] S 13(1)(zg) of the Income Tax Act.

modifications to the qualifying conditions to take into account the differences between a company and a registered business trust: (i) group relief system pertaining to the transfer of unutilized capital allowances, trade losses and donation[81], (ii) application of "shareholding test" for the carrying forward of unutilized capital allowances, trade losses and donations[82], (iii) tax neutral transfer of plant and machinery between related parties at tax written down value[83], (iv) allowances conferred under the mergers and acquisitions scheme[84], and (v) the "safe harbour rule" in respect of gains arising from the disposal of ordinary shares[85].

For Singapore income tax purposes, a business trust that is not a registered business trust is subject to tax based on the general rules applicable to a normal trust.

5.1.3. Tax residence of registered business trusts

A registered business trust will be regarded as a Singapore tax resident for corporate income tax purposes to the extent that the trustee of the registered business trust in his capacity as such, carries on a trade or business in Singapore and the control and management of the business of the registered business trust is exercised in Singapore. As Singapore tax resident, the registered business trust is entitled to claim foreign tax credits in respect of foreign tax suffered overseas on its foreign-sourced income.

5.1.4. Exemption of foreign sourced income derived by registered business trusts

Given that registered business trusts are treated as companies for income tax purposes, the exemption of specified foreign-sourced income (such as foreign-sourced dividends) under section 13(8) of the Income Tax Act, which is available for Singapore tax resident companies, is similarly available to Singapore tax resident registered business trusts. In addition, exemption

---

[81] S 37B of the Income Tax Act.
[82] S 23(4) of the Income Tax Act.
[83] S 24 of the Income Tax Act.
[84] S 37O of the Income Tax Act.
[85] S 13W of the Income Tax Act.

is available under section 13(12) in respect of foreign-sourced dividend and interest income received in Singapore by listed resident entities (which include registered business trusts) or their wholly-owned Singapore resident subsidiary companies, from qualifying offshore infrastructure project/asset[86], subject to conditions[87]. This puts registered business trusts receiving foreign sourced income in a tax advantage compared to a traditional company which typically does not enjoy any tax exemption of foreign sourced interest income.

5.1.5. *Tax incentives for registered business trusts and their trustee-manager*

For Singapore income tax purposes, registered business trusts may qualify for tax incentives, just like any company. In addition, an approved trustee-manager of a qualifying registered business trust could potentially enjoy a concessionary tax rate of 10% on its income from providing service in respect of infrastructure assets or projects situated outside Singapore[88]. For this purpose, a "qualifying registered business trust" in relation to an approved trustee-manager refers to a registered business trust which (i) is listed or to be listed on the Singapore Exchange within one year from the date the approved trustee-manager is so approved and (ii) owns any offshore infrastructure assets or any assets used in an offshore infrastructure project, or debt securities or shares of any company that owns any offshore infrastructure asset or any asset used in an offshore infrastructure project. The 10% concessionary tax rate for trustee-managers of qualifying registered business trusts is however scheduled to lapse after 31 December 2022.

---

[86] A qualifying offshore infrastructure project/asset includes the following:
(a) electricity generation, distribution, transmission and/or alternative energy generation;
(b) gas distribution, transmission and/or generation;
(c) waste management including waste treatment and incineration plants;
(d) roads, rail infrastructure;
(e) ports (sea and air) and/or terminals;
(f) broadcasting and/or communication facilities and/or networks;
(g) telecom facilities and/or networks;
(h) water treatment (including desalination) and/or distribution;
(i) hospitals and/or clinics;
(j) schools including tertiary institutions; and
(k) such other areas as may be approved by the Minister or such person as he may appoint.

[87] IRAS e-Tax Guide, *Income Tax: Tax exemption under section 13(12) for specified scenarios, real estate investment trusts and qualifying offshore infrastructure project/asset*, Eighth Edition, 17 May 2021.

[88] S 43S of the Income Tax Act.

5.2. Goods and Services Tax

Goods and Services Tax (GST) concession is also available in respect of Singapore-listed registered business trusts carrying on qualifying infrastructure business, aircraft leasing and ship leasing. Under the GST concession (similar to those granted to S-REITs), qualifying registered business trust are allowed to claim GST[89] incurred in respect of allowable expenses incurred for their business and their special purpose vehicles (SPVs), regardless of whether they are eligible for GST registration. The concession allows a qualifying registered business trust to treat all supplies made by the multi-tiered structure as if they are taxable or exempt supplies made by the parent registered business trust for the purpose of computing GST claims. This is regardless of whether the qualifying registered business trust makes taxable supplies[90].

In order to qualify for the GST concession, the registered business trust must have veto rights[91] over key operational issues[92] of its SPVs holding the underlying assets.

The GST concession, which was first granted in 2006, was initially only granted to GST-registered S-REITs and available in respect of expenses incurred to set up various tiers of SPVs. Subsequently, in 2008, the concession was extended to S-REITs and qualifying registered business trusts, regardless of their GST registration status. The list of expenses for which input tax is claimable was also expanded to include all business expenses[93].

---

[89] Excluding disallowed expenses under Regulation 26 and 27 of the GST (General) Regulations (RG 1).

[90] See also: IRAS e-Tax Guide, *GST: Concession for REITs and Qualifying Registered Business Trusts Listed in Singapore*, Fifth Edition, 23 September 2019.

[91] The registered business trust can provide for veto rights over its SPVs in the joint venture agreement, memorandum, articles of association, trust deed or other constitutive document of the SPV. In the absence of any documentation or where veto rights are not clearly provided for, the veto rights condition will be satisfied only if the registered business trust holds more than 50% of the unit-holdings or shareholdings in the SPVs.

[92] Key operational issues include: (i) amendment of the joint venture agreement, memorandum and articles of association, trust deed, or other constitutive document of the SPV; (ii) cessation or change of the business of the SPV; (iii) winding up or dissolution of the SPV; (iv) changes to the equity capital structure of the SPV; (v) changes to the dividend distribution policy of the SPV; (vi) issue of securities by the SPV; (vii) borrowings by the SPV; (viii) creation of security over the assets of the SPV; (ix) transfer or disposal of the assets of the SPV; (x) approval of asset enhancement and capital expenditure plans for the assets of the SPV; and (xi) entry into interested party transactions.

[93] Excluding disallowed expenses under Regulation 26 and 27 of the GST (General) Regulations.

To facilitate fundraising by registered business trusts through SPVs, the GST concession was subsequently enhanced from 1 April 2015 to allow the claim of GST on business expenses incurred to set up SPVs that are used solely to raise funds (financing SPVs) for the qualifying registered business trusts, and which do not hold qualifying assets of the registered business trusts, directly or indirectly. Such registered business trusts are also allowed to claim GST on the business expenses of these financing SPVs. The enhanced concession is granted based on the additional condition that the funds raised by the SPVs must be on-lent to the qualifying registered business trusts and be used to finance the business activities of the qualifying registered business trusts.

The aforementioned GST concessions for qualifying registered business trusts have since been extended to 31 December 2025, as announced in the 2019 annual budget statement[94], with a view to continue facilitating the listing of registered business trusts in the infrastructure business, ship leasing and aircraft leasing sectors. However, to-date, notably no business trust has been constituted and registered in Singapore to carry on aircraft leasing activities.

5.3. Stamp duty

Where a business trust acquires or disposes of Singapore real estate or Singapore shares, the stamp duty treatment is broadly the same as those set out in Chapters 6 and 7.

Stamp duty relief for the transfer of chargeable assets (i.e. shares of Singapore-incorporated companies or Singapore real estate) between associated entities[95], is also available to registered business trusts where they make such transfers as the transferor and/or transferee, subject to meeting the relevant conditions[96]. However, the Stamp Duties (Relief from Stamp Duty Upon Transfer of Assets between Associated Permitted Entities)

---

[94] Available on the website of the Parliament of Singapore.

[95] Including companies and limited liability partnerships.

[96] S 15 of the Stamp Duties Act. In this regard, it is noted that the term 'entity' has been specifically defined to include a registered business trust under s 15(12) of the Stamp Duties Act. See: Section 2.1.2 of Chapter 6 and Section 3.5 of Chapter 7 for further discussions on the stamp duty relief regime.

Rules 2014[97], which specifically mentioned companies, limited liability partnerships and statutory bodies as permitted entities which may avail themselves of the stamp duty relief, do not make specific mention of business trusts. It may be that the registered business trust is omitted from the 2014 Rules, as the concepts of an "entity" holding "not less than 75% of the voting capital" and "more than half the voting power" in another "entity", are not readily accommodated in a registered business trust. Nevertheless, where a registered business trust is involved in a transaction which has a transfer of chargeable assets from another registered business trust or an "associated entity", it may still be eligible for a waiver of stamp duty under section 74 of the Stamp Duties Act, where such waiver is consistent with the spirit of the 2014 Rules.

Whether or not, the transfer of units of a business trust (which is not a legal entity) itself attracts stamp duty, will depend on a number of factors. Where the business trust is listed on the Singapore Exchange, such transfers do not attract stamp duty as in the case of scripless shares of companies. Where the trust deed of the non-listed business trust provides that the unitholders do not have any equitable, beneficial or proprietary interests of the underlying assets of the trust, transfers of the units will also not attract any stamp duty. Even where the unitholders have such interests and where the underlying assets comprise ships (which are movable assets) for example, such transfers do not fall within the provisions of Articles 3(a) or 3(c) of the First Schedule to the Stamp Duties Act and hence also do not attract stamp duty.

---

[97] S 28/2014.

CHAPTER 10

Private Real Estate Funds: A Platform to Enhance Value

1. Introduction

While the market capitalization of S-REITs, property trusts[1] and business trusts listed on the Singapore Exchange recorded two decades of phenomenal growth since their inception in the early 2000s, the private real estate market is also reported to be growing at a neck-breaking pace during the same period. In fact, global private market capital has grown at more than double the rate of public capital over the past two decades, causing private market valuations to surge and businesses to stay private longer[2].

Globally, the total real estate asset under management (AUM) is estimated at US$3.6 trillion as at 2019, with Blackstone being the market leader with total real estate AUM of US$278.7 billion[3]. Within the Asia Pacific region, total real estate AUM of US$588.8 billion was recorded as at 2018, of which non-listed[4] real estate made up 73.6% of AUM[5]. Examples of such non-listed

---

[1] Property trusts are business trusts which hold property assets. See *Chartbooks: SREITs & Property Trusts* (SGX Research, December 2019).

[2] Global Private Equity Report 2019, Bain & Company.

[3] Based on Fund Manager Survey 2020 published by Asian Association for Investors in Non-Listed Real Estate Vehicles (ANREV), European Association for Investors in Non-Listed Real Estate Vehicles (INREV) and National Council of Real Estate Investment Fiduciaries (NCREIF). The top three managers globally are Blackstone, Brookfield Asset Management and PGIM Real Estate. Others in the top 10 include Prologis, AXA Investments Management and CBRE Global Investors.

[4] Including funds, separate accounts, joint ventures, club deals, funds of funds and debt products. Non-listed funds make up more than half of non-listed real estate vehicles AUM at 57.2% in Asia Pacific.

[5] Based on ANREV, INREV, NCREIF Fund Manager Survey 2019. See also 'CapitaLand tops for Asia-Pacific real estate assets under management with US$55.9b,' *The Straits Times*, 22 May 2019.

real estate funds include the PGIM Real Estate AsiaRetail Fund[6], the largest non-listed retail mall fund in Singapore as at mid-2020[7], with five suburban malls within its Singapore portfolio — Tiong Bahru Plaza, White Sands, Hougang Mall, Century Square and Tampines 1.

In Singapore, CapitaLand, Global Logistics Properties, Mapletree, Ascendas-Singbridge and Alpha Investment Partners are reported to have the highest asset under management (AUM)[8]. In particular, it is noteworthy that CapitaLand has since vaulted into the top 10 real estate investment managers globally, with AUM of $123.4 billion following its acquisition of Ascendas-Singbridge in year 2019[9].

In this chapter, we will focus on non-listed real estate fund platforms, as well as outline the regulatory and tax regimes applicable to private real estate funds.

2. Fund Platforms of Singapore Real Estate Developers

In recent years, many real estate developers in Singapore which have diversified into fund management are actively building up fund platforms and integrating such fund management activities to complement their traditional real estate development business[10].

---

[6] PGIM Real Estate AsiaRetail Fund is managed by PGIM Real Estate, the real estate investment business of PGIM Inc, the global investment management business of Prudential Financial listed in New York. PGIM Real Estate AsiaRetail Fund is reported to be jointly owned by Frasers Property (63.1%) and Frasers Centrepoint Trust and (36.89%). See 'Analysts bullish on FCT as it ups stake in PGIM Real Estate AsiaRetail Fund,' *The Business Times*, 2 July 2020 and 'FCT to buy further 12% stake in PGIM's Asia Retail Fund,' *The Straits Times*, 2 July 2020.

[7] On 3 September 2020, Frasers Centrepoint Trust announced its plan to acquire the remaining 63.1% stake in AsiaRetail Fund for S$1.06 billion from its sponsor, Frasers Property. See 'Frasers Centrepoint Trust's proposed acquisition of AsiaRetail Fund comes as suburban malls show resilience,' *The Business Times*, 5–6 September 2020.

[8] Based on survey jointly conducted by ANREV, INREV and NCREIF. See also 'AUM up 12% for top 5 Singapore property funds targeting Asia-Pacific,' *The Business Times*, 23 May 2019.

[9] 'CapitaLand's acquisition of Ascendas-Singbridge gets overwhelming nod from shareholders,' *The Business Times*, 13 April 2019. CapitaLand further announced that it will use its newly-acquired exposure in industrial, logistics and business parks, arising from the acquisition of Ascendas-Singbridge, to cross-sell across various asset classes and countries. It will also step up on capital recycling, either through divesting to third parties or to its own REIT. See also 'CapitaLand to build on S$11b ASB deal in Singapore, China, India, Vietnam,' *The Business Times*, 10 April 2019.

[10] 'Fund platforms give developers flexibility,' *The Business Times*, 4 November 2016. In contrast, traditional real estate private equity firms typically pool money from investors to acquire third party real estates,

These fund management platforms confer real estate developers with the opportunity to move up the value chain beyond their conventional build-to-sell or build-to-lease business model, and generate new streams of fee-based revenue through the management of such real estate funds and assets. In addition, the fund platform allows real estate developers to unlock capital from divesting or injecting their own properties into the funds invested by third parties, and redeploy the capital raised from third parties into their other real estate development projects. Such recycling of capital through asset injection allows real estate companies to grow their asset base without being overly reliant on external debts and at the same time operate on an "asset light" model.

On the demand side, there is growing demand from institutional investors around the world, including pension plans, financial institutions, funds-of-funds, insurance companies, endowments, foundations, universities, family offices, sovereign wealth funds, as well as high net worth individuals who are seeking diversified global real estate exposure. Increasingly, many of these investors prefer to do so with experienced local players such as real estate developers rather than global funds[11].

As an example, CapitaLand Investment's real estate fund and asset management arm is responsible as manager for the group's five REITs and business trusts listed in Singapore and Malaysia[12] as well as real estate private funds' including discretionary funds[13]. CapitaLand Investment also manages 30 real estate private platforms many of which are invested into Chinese real estate[14]. These funds are the platforms which CapitaLand can inject its stabilized assets into (similar to the S-REITs which it sponsored in Singapore), in the absence of a robust REIT framework in China. Additionally, CapitaLand's private funds allow it to co-invest in third party assets with other capital partners. CapitaLand's subsidiary, The Ascott, for

---

enhances the assets over time through redevelopment or repositioning, sells the assets and distributes capital back to investors.

[11] 'Fund platforms give developers flexibility,' *The Business Times*, 4 November 2016.

[12] The five REITs and business trusts are CapitaLand Integrated Commercial Trust, Ascendas REIT, Ascott Residence Trust, CapitaLand China Trust, Ascendas India Trust and CapitaLand Malaysia Trust.

[13] See: CapitaLand Investment website <https://www.capitalandinvest.com/our-businesses.html> (accessed 9 January 2022).

[14] 'Fund platforms give developers flexibility,' *The Business Times*, 4 November 2016.

example, has set up a US$600 million serviced residence global fund, with Qatar Investment Authority to buy serviced residences and rental housing properties in Asia Pacific and Europe[15].

City Developments (CDL), another major real estate developer in Singapore, has similarly securitized its various real estate development projects and redeploy the capital into other development projects. The then chief executive officer of CDL, Grant Kelly, announced that since embarking on its funds management strategy in 2014, CDL was on track to achieve its target of S$5 billion in funds under management (FUM) within 5 years[16]. Notably, CDL's portfolio includes CDL Hospitality Trust, which is the first hotel REIT in Asia (excluding Japan) which has since grown to become one of Asia's leading hospitality trusts[17]. It is also reported that CDL is exploring the possibility of floating a REIT which invests in commercial properties in the United Kingdom[18].

Besides, CapitaLand and CDL, other Singapore headquartered companies such as the Keppel group and Mapletree group, are also known to be active in the fund management space.

Keppel group, through its asset management arm, Keppel Capital, manages three Singapore-listed REITs and one business trust, as well as various private funds[19]. The diversified portfolio of assets under management includes data centers as well as strategic infrastructure such as waste-to-energy plants, desalination plant and NEWater plant in Singapore.

---

[15] 'Fund platforms give developers flexibility,' *The Business Times*, 4 November 2016.

[16] 'CDL monetises Nouvel for $977.6 mil via profit participation securities,' *The Edge Singapore*, 21 October 2016.

[17] See CDL website <https://www.cdl.com.sg/index.php/diverse-portfolio/fund-management> (accessed 8 August 2020).

[18] 'CDL mulls Singapore Reit for UK commercial properties,' *The Business Times*, 27 February 2020 and 'Qatar Investment Authority in talks to inject HSBC HQ into CDL REIT,' *The Straits Times*, 20 May 2021.

[19] The three S-REITs are Keppel REIT (which invests in commercial properties across the Asia Pacific), Keppel DC REIT (which is the first pure play data center REIT) and Keppel Pacific Oak US REIT (which invests in commercial properties in the United States). The sole business trust managed by Keppel Capital is Keppel Infrastructure Trust, which is the largest diversified business trust listed in Singapore with a portfolio of strategic infrastructure businesses and assets, including various waste-to-energy plants, desalination plant, NEWater plant and town gas production plant. See Keppel website <https://www.kepcapital.com/en/> (accessed 8 August 2020).

Mapletree, on the other hand, manages four Singapore listed S-REITs[20] and seven private equity real estate funds[21]. Its private funds business is focused on various sectors including: (i) student accommodation, (ii) data centers, (iii) logistics facilities, (iv) corporate housing and (v) office sector. There is also intention for the assets of the private funds to eventually migrate over to the public platform at the right configuration and price[22].

In an interview with The Business Times published in June 2019, Mapletree Group CEO Hiew Yoon Khong shared the following[23]:

> One of the things that we focus on in terms of how we migrate our products is that we look at the possibility of initially forming a private platform. At the end of the platform's (lifespan), if the portfolio is suitable and the value is correct, one option is that we can divest the assets to return the capital and profits to investors, or maybe monetize them using a public platform — so that's an option that's available, but it's not something that we have decided.

With regard to the injection of the assets in Mapletree's existing private funds into S-REITs of similar mandates at the point of exit, Mr Hiew said:

> The flexibility that we have for private funds is that while the returns expectations are higher, a lot of the investors don't mind if the returns come from capital value appreciation rather than pure (recurring) yield.
>
> So, the maturity and profile of these assets are actually slightly different (from those of REITs). For REITs, the focus is very much on just the yield much more than the capital value (appreciation).

---

[20] The four S-REITs are Mapletree Logistics Trust, Mapletree Industrial Trust, Mapletree Commercial Trust and Mapletree North Asia Commercial Trust.

[21] The seven private real estate funds are Mapletree China Opportunity Fund II (MCOF II), Mapletree Global Student Accommodation Private Trust (MGSA), Mapletree US & EU Logistics Private Trust (MUSEL) and Mapletree Australia Commercial Private Trust (MASCOT) Mapletree Europe Income Trust (MERIT), Mapletree US Income Commercial Trust (MUSIC) and Mapletree US Logistics Private Trust (MUSLOG). See: Mapletree website <https://www.mapletree.com.sg/Our-Business/Capital-Management.aspx> (accessed 9 January 2022).

[22] 'Mapletree planning up to 2 REIT listing in next five years,' The Business Times, 10 June 2019.

[23] 'Mapletree planning up to 2 REIT listing in next five years,' The Business Times, 10 June 2019.

Mr Hiew further added that the private fund platform plays an instrumentation role in helping to gauge investors' demand for a product prior to listing; and as such, Mapletree doesn't bypass the private fund stage to go straight into stage of launching a REIT.

3. Fund Management Ecosystem in Singapore

In the last decade, an increasing number of fund managers are managing and domiciling their funds in Singapore, which has established a reputation of being a wealth and asset management hub in the Asia Pacific region. As at year 2019, 76% of the total AUM in Singapore originated from outside the country, and 69% of the AUM was invested into the Asia Pacific region[24].

Singapore has a thriving fund management ecosystem offering a full suite of fund management related services and is regarded by many fund management companies and investors, as an ideal location to manage and domicile their funds vis-à-vis traditional tax havens such as the British Virgin Islands and Cayman Islands. This is particularly so in light of the base erosion and profit shifting (BEPS) project led by the Organization of Economic Cooperation and Development (OECD) and Group of 20 (G20), which called for businesses to be based in jurisdictions where they have substantive operations (colloquially referred to as "business substance")[25]. An additional advantage which Singapore has over these traditional tax haven jurisdictions is that Singapore has an extensive network of tax agreements which offers protection from double taxation (e.g. via the elimination or reduction of withholding tax).

In recent years, the Monetary Authority of Singapore (MAS) has been working towards positioning Singapore as a full-service Asian hub for fund management and domiciliation[26], with a view to capturing a greater share of the fund management and fund domiciliation value chain, and creating new

---

[24] MAS, 2019 Singapore Asset Management Survey: Singapore — The Asset Management and Sustainability Center in Asia Pacific.

[25] Although the funds may be set up in certain traditional offshore tax haven jurisdictions, the day-to-day management of the funds may not be carried on in the same jurisdiction. The OECD initiated BEPS project is targeted at such arrangements which are perceived as lacking 'business substance'.

[26] See Industry Transformation Map for Financial Services available at the Ministry of Trade and Industry website <https://www.mti.gov.sg/-/media/MTI/ITM/Modern-Services/Financial-Services/Financial-Services-ITM-Infographic-2.pdf> (accessed 28 September 2020).

business collaboration and job opportunities within the fund ecosystem[27]. As at end-2019, Singapore was home to over 895 registered and licensed fund managers, spanning both the traditional[28] and alternative[29] investments space[30]. AUM in Singapore expanded at 11% compound annual growth rate over a 5 year period, reaching S$4.0 trillion at the end of 2019[31], This was an increase of almost S$600 billion from the AUM of S$3.4 trillion recorded in 2018, reflecting an annual growth of 15.7%[32].

For the previous year, 2018, the growth in total AUM was a modest 5.4%, riding on the back of a 15% surge in alternative assets. Private equity, venture capital and real estate saw strong inflows and continued valuation gains as investors increased their exposures to private assets, to enhance returns and diversify portfolios[33]. Notably, real estate AUM grew 44% from $101 billion in 2017 to $145 billion in 2018, and leapfrogged REIT AUM which clocked a 0.4% modest growth from $106 to $107 billion[34] (see Table 1). The alternative assets sector continued to see sustained growth of 12% in year 2019, with venture capital recording a growth of 86% (see Table 1). At the same time, the traditional asset sector also registered a strong 25% growth.

Overall, the fund management industry is a key component of Singapore's financial sector, and contributed 12.4% of the overall financial sector's nominal value-add in 2017[35]. The industry has immense growth

---

[27] Service providers such as lawyers, accountants, tax advisors, fund administrators and fund custodians are expected to benefit from the Singapore's reputation as a full-service Asian hub for fund management and domiciliation. These service providers work alongside fund managers in areas of expertise, including fund structuring and administration, fiduciary oversight, tax advisory, regulatory and compliance.

[28] Traditional funds include equities and fixed income.

[29] Alternative funds include private equity funds, real estate funds, venture capital funds, etc.

[30] 'Singapore-based asset managers' AUM jumps 15.7% last year: MAS survey,' *The Business Times*, 30 September 2020.

[31] In comparison, the AUM in Singapore was S$1.2 trillion 10 years ago in year 2009. See MAS' 2009 Singapore Asset Management Industry Survey.

[32] 'S'pore AUM up 5.4% to $3.4 trillion last year: MAS poll,' *The Straits Times*, 19 September 2019. See also 'Singapore's asset management industry clocks strong growth; AUM up 19% to S$3.3 trillion in 2017,' *The Business Times*, 25 October 2018.

[33] 'Singapore's asset management industry grew at slower 5.4% pace to S$3.4 trillion last year: MAS,' *The Business Times*, 18 September 2019.

[34] MAS, 2017 Singapore Asset Management Survey: Asian Hub for Fund Management and Domiciliation, and 2018 Singapore Asset Management Survey: The Gateway to Asset Management Opportunities in Asia.

[35] See second reading of the Variable Capital Companies Bill by Ms Indranee Rajah, Second Minister for Finance, 1 October 2018.

Table 1: Alternative Assets Under Management (2017, 2018 and 2019).[a]

	Year 2017		Year 2018		Year 2019	
	AUM (S$ billion)	Percentage Change	AUM (S$ billion)	Percentage Change	AUM (S$ billion)	Percentage Change
Private Equity	186	23%	213	14%	243	14%
Hedge Fund	162	18%	175	8%	199	14%
REIT	106	13%	107	0.4%	126	19%
Real Estate	101	13%	145	44%	142	(2.5%)
Venture Capital	4	(9%)	6	40%	11	86%

Note:
[a] MAS, 2017 Singapore Asset Management Survey: Asian Hub for Fund Management and Domiciliation, 2018 Singapore Asset Management Survey: The Gateway to Asset Management Opportunities in Asia and 2019 Singapore Asset Management Survey: Singapore — The Asset Management and Sustainability Center in Asia Pacific.
Source: MAS

opportunity, given that the AUM of S$4.7 trillion in Singapore as at 2020 is a small slice of the global pie which is estimated at US$103 trillion (approximately S$142 trillion)[36].

3.1. Types of fund vehicles

In the Singapore context, fund vehicles are commonly set up in the form of companies, limited partnerships and trusts. A new type of vehicle, the variable capital company, has recently been introduced and is increasingly gaining popularity among fund managers.

3.1.1. *Companies*

Companies incorporated in Singapore are governed by the Companies Act[37] and their constitution documents[38]. A Singapore incorporated company is a

---

[36] MAS, 2020 Singapore Asset Management Survey: Singapore — A Progressive and Vibrant Asset Management Centre in Asia Pacific.

[37] Cap. 50.

[38] Previously referred to as the memorandum and articles of association.

body corporate with separate legal personality from its shareholders. It may hold property under its own name and is capable of suing and being sued[39].

Singapore incorporated companies can be either a public company or a private company. Unlike a public company, a private company cannot have more than 50 shareholders[40]. The shareholders of a company, regardless whether it is public or private, have limited liability and are not personally liable for the debts and liabilities of the company. While the use of a company may help shield the shareholders from unlimited liabilities, a drawback of the corporate structure is the capital maintenance rules which make it restrictive to use the Singapore company as a fund vehicle. A company incorporated in Singapore may only distribute dividends out of profits'[41] and additional administrative procedures such as solvency tests are required prior to any repayment of capital via redemption or buyback of shares. Companies are also subject to certain reporting requirements, including disclosing the details of the shareholders of the company.

For income tax purposes, a company is subject to tax on its income at the prevailing corporate tax rate of 17% unless it qualifies for specific tax incentives[42].

3.1.2. *Limited partnerships*

The limited partnership is commonly used as a fund vehicle in many jurisdictions including Singapore. Limited partnerships in Singapore are governed by their limited partnership agreements as well as the Limited Partnerships Act[43], which came into operation in 2009.

Since the launch of the Singapore limited partnership in 2009, it has become the vehicle of choice for the setting up of private funds. Based on the latest Accounting and Corporate Regulatory Authority (ACRA) annual report, as of 31 March 2021, there are 496 limited partnerships active in

---

[39] S 19(5) of the Companies Act.
[40] S 18(1)(b) of the Companies Act.
[41] S 403 of the Companies Act.
[42] See Section 7 for more details on taxation.
[43] Cap. 163B.

Singapore, with 127 (or almost one-quarter of the total) established in year 2020[44].

At the second reading of the Limited Partnerships Bill, the then Senior Minister of State for Finance, Mrs Lim Hwee Hua, explained that the structure of the Singapore limited partnership is based on those in Delaware, Jersey as well as in the United Kingdom. Mrs Lim further added that[45]:

> The [limited partnership] is a well-established concept in other leading jurisdictions and is most commonly used in the types of businesses that focus on a single or limited term project. They are also useful in "labour-capital" partnerships, where one or more financial backers prefer to contribute money or resources while the other partner performs the actual work. The introduction of LPs [limited partnerships] will enable Singapore to better meet the diverse business needs and offer entrepreneurs and investors an additional form of business structure to choose from.

A limited partnership is a partnership consisting of at least two partners — one general partner and one limited partner. The general partner and limited partners of a limited partnership may be individuals or corporations. Unlike a company which has separate legal personality from its shareholders, a limited partnership does not have a separate legal personality from its partners. It cannot hold property under its own name, and cannot sue or be sued in its own name.

The general partner is responsible for the day-to-day management of the limited partnership and is liable for all debts and obligations of the limited partnership incurred while he is a general partner in the limited partnership[46]. In this regard, the general partner is in all major aspects in the same legal position as partners in a conventional partnership (e.g. such as having unlimited liability). In order to address the risk of having unlimited liability, the general partner is usually a company, given that companies have limited liability.

---

[44] ACRA, Annual Report 2020/21; Transformation Taking Flight.

[45] Second reading of the Limited Partnerships Bill by Mrs Lim Hwee Hua, the then Senior Minister of State for Finance, 18 November 2008.

[46] S 3(3) of the Limited Partnerships Act.

A limited partner on the other hand is not liable for the debts and obligations of the limited partnership beyond his agreed contribution[47]. This is provided that the limited partner does not take part in the management of the limited partnership[48]. Since limited partners are generally not expected to be involved in the management of the fund, the limited partnership structure accords the limited liability required by such investors who are merely investing passively into the funds.

The use of limited partnerships as a fund vehicle confers various advantages over that of a company. Firstly, limited partnerships offer flexibility in the distribution of proceeds to the partners, even in the absence of accounting profits. Secondly, where a limited partnership is established primarily as a fund for investment and the fund is managed by a licensed fund manager[49], the particulars of the limited partners and any document containing the particulars of such limited partners filed or lodged with the Registrar is not open to inspection by the public[50]. In addition, no such particulars or document and no copy or extract thereof shall be furnished to the public, or certified, by the Registrar[51]. Another advantage of using the limited partnership as a fund vehicle is that it provides limited liability to investors who participate in the limited partnership as limited partners.

A disadvantage of using a limited partnership as a fund vehicle is that it does not have separate legal personality and may not by itself be entitled to tax treaty benefits. In addition, unlike companies, it is not currently possible to list interests of a limited partnership on the Singapore Exchange.

For income tax purposes, a limited partnership is not a taxable entity and is instead treated similarly as a general partnership[52]. In this regard, the partners of the limited partnership are subject to tax on their respective

---

[47] S 3(4) of the Limited Partnerships Act.

[48] See First Schedule to the Limited Partnerships Act for a list of the acts not regarded as taking part in management of the limited partnership.

[49] Reg 12(5) of the Limited Partnerships Regulations. A 'licensed fund manager' is defined to include a person exempt from being so licensed under s 99 of the Securities and Futures Act.

[50] Regs 12(1) and (2) of the Limited Partnerships Regulations.

[51] Regs 12(1) and (2) of the Limited Partnerships Regulations.

[52] S 36C(1) of the Income Tax Act.

proportion of the partnership income, unless a specific tax incentive is applicable[53].

3.1.3. Trusts

A trust is an arrangement where the legal ownership of the assets is vested in a trustee which holds those assets in trust for the benefit of the unitholders[54]. A trust is typically constituted by a trust deed which governs the appointment/retirement of the trustee and the managers, their respective duties, the distribution or accumulation of trust income, investment powers, dealings in units and valuation[55].

The applicable legislation with regard to trusts and trustees in Singapore are the Trust Companies Act[56] and the Trustees Act[57]. A trust is largely contractual in nature and as such is fairly flexible. Similar to a limited partnership, it offers relative ease of cash repatriation even in the absence of profits.

A primary disadvantage of setting up a trust is that trusts do not have separate legal personality. In this regard, the requirement to have a trustee to hold the trust assets adds to the cost of setting up a trust. Another key disadvantage is that the concept of trusts may not be familiar to investors in certain jurisdictions.

For income tax purposes, a trust is in itself not a taxable entity[58]. Further details on the taxation of trust income are set out in Section 7.2.1.3.

3.1.4. Variable capital companies

The proposed introduction of the Variable Capital Company (VCCs) was first announced in 2016, with a view to encouraging fund managers to set

---

[53] See Section 7 for more details on taxation.

[54] For an overview of trusts, see Tang Hang Wu, 'Teaching Trust Law in the Twenty First Century' in Elise Bant and Matthew Harding (eds.), *Exploring Private Law* (Cambridge, 2010), p. 125.

[55] From a legal perspective, however, the existence of a written trust deed is not necessary to create a trust. A trust relationship may exist to the extent that there is a clear intention to create a trust.

[56] Cap. 336.

[57] Cap. 337.

[58] See Section 7 for more details on taxation.

up and domicile their funds in Singapore[59]. The objective is to strengthen Singapore's status as a full-service international fund management center, via the establishment of a full-service fund ecosystem, with the fund vehicle, fund manager, fund administrator, legal counsel, tax advisors and other service providers, all domiciled in Singapore. The introduction of the VCC is considered a game changer for Singapore's fund management industry as it will allow the country to capture value from the full fund management value chain, including product development, fund management, administration and distribution[60].

Traditionally, a significant proportion of the funds that are managed by Singapore-based fund managers are domiciled outside the country due to the flexible corporate structures available in those countries. Consequently, the economic benefits generated by these funds accrue outside Singapore[61]. With the Variable Capital Companies Act[62] coming into force in early 2020, fund managers now have additional operational flexibility in the constitution of funds in Singapore. In addition to establishing funds using the traditional vehicles such as companies, limited partnerships and trusts, funds may now also be set up as VCCs[63]. VCCs which may be used as open-ended or closed-end funds, provide a suitable corporate structure for both traditional and alternative funds[64].

---

[59] The VCC was first introduced as the open-ended investment company (OEIC) in 2016. It was later renamed the Singapore Variable Capital Company (S-VACC) in March 2017 before being known as the Variable Capital Company (VCC) from September 2018.

[60] 'Singapore's new VCC Act the main event drawing funds here,' *The Business Times*, 7 September 2020. The introduction of the VCC has also been touted as the driving force helping Singapore become the 'Luxembourg of Asia'. Luxembourg has over Euro 4.8 trillion (S$7.7 trillion) in AUM, second only to the United States. Luxembourg handles 62% of cross-border investments funds worldwide from over 70 countries, and 98 of the top 100 asset managers globally have funds domiciled in Luxembourg. See 'How VCCs will help Singapore become the Luxembourg of Asia,' *The Business Times*, 20 October 2020.

[61] As an example, fund servicing activities such as accountancy, legal, custody and tax are undertaken outside Singapore when the fund vehicles are domiciled outside Singapore.

[62] Act 44 of 2018.

[63] The VCC is similar to the open-ended investment company (OEIC) in the United Kingdom, the Irish Collective Asset-Management Vehicle (ICAV) in Ireland, the Segregated Portfolio Company (SPC) in Cayman Islands and British Virgin Islands, the Protected Cell Company (PCC) in Labuan, Malaysia and the Open-ended Fund Company (OFC) in Hong Kong, China.

[64] Traditional funds are commonly structured as open-ended funds where investors can exit their investments by redeeming their investment units or shares in the fund. Alternative funds, such as private equity and real estate funds, are typically structured as closed-end funds. Such funds have a fixed number of shares that cannot be redeemed at the election of shareholders, except in limited circumstances where permitted by the fund.

A VCC has separate legal personality and can operate as a single standalone fund or as an umbrella fund with two or more sub-funds, each holding segregated assets and liabilities. The cellular structure of the VCC allows sub-funds to be created under a single umbrella fund. Although the umbrella VCC and its sub-funds constitute a single legal entity[65], the assets of a sub-fund will not be available to satisfy the debts and obligations of another sub-fund of the same umbrella VCC[66]. This is in recognition of the fact that the investors of each sub-fund may be different and as such it will not be equitable for the assets of a particular sub-fund to be utilized in settlement of the liabilities of another sub-fund.

In this regard, a key advantage of the umbrella VCC structure is that it allows fund managers to manage multiple funds with different investment objectives, strategies and risk profiles in a single investment fund vehicle. This is notwithstanding that each sub-fund of the umbrella VCC may have different investors or shareholders. The structuring of funds as VCC with sub-funds also helps optimize their overall costs structure via economies of scale given that the sub-funds may share a board of directors and common service providers (e.g. fund manager, custodian, auditor and administrator)[67].

Notably, the VCC is designed to overcome the limitations faced by fund managers who set up funds using the traditional company structure. In this regard, the VCC, as a fund vehicle, confers a number of advantages when compared to the traditional companies, including (i) the creation of sub-fund with segregated assets and liabilities which are ring-fenced from those of other sub-funds, (ii) the ability to redeem shares at the fund's net asset value[68],

---

[65] In other words, the sub-fund of an umbrella VCC does not have separate legal personality from the umbrella VCC. Consequently, the umbrella VCC will have to contract on behalf of each of its sub-funds when entering into transactions. As a safeguard, s 30 of the Variable Capital Companies Act requires the umbrella VCC to set out the name of the sub-fund, the sub-fund's registration number and the fact that the assets and liabilities of the sub-fund are segregated.

[66] S 29 of the Variable Capital Companies Act.

[67] In comparison, the overall costs involved in the set-up of multiple funds by incorporating multiple companies, are expected to be higher (e.g. due to the multiple compliance related filings with the relevant authorities).

[68] It is common practice for funds to distribute or return money to investors by way of redeeming the shares/units/interests held by the investors. In this regard, the traditional company model poses administrative issues to the fund manager, given that there are various restrictions imposed on the redemption or buyback of shares of a company under the Companies Act.

(iii) the ability to pay dividends out of capital, (iv) no shareholder approval or solvency statement required to issue or redeem shares, (v) no requirement for the VCC's constitution and register of shareholders to be made available for public inspection[69] and (vi) the flexibility of keeping accounting books and records in accordance with any recognized international accounting standard (e.g. Singapore Financial Reporting Standards, International Financial Reporting Standards, etc.). These features of the VCC[70] makes it particularly attractive for use as a fund vehicle, as such features help lower administrative costs, facilitate flow of capital and income between investors and the fund, and better meet the different needs of investors from different parts of the world.

There are also provisions for an inward re-domiciliation regime to allow foreign structures that are equivalent to the VCC to re-domicile as a Singapore VCC[71]. Fund managers with offshore domiciled funds will therefore have the option of re-domiciling their existing funds to Singapore via Singapore's inward re-domiciliation regime[72], and co-locate both fund domiciliation and management activities in Singapore. A key benefit of re-domiciling existing funds, as opposed to setting up new funds, is that the existing funds will keep their legal personality (including corporate history and investment track record) after the re-domiciliation.

VCCs are required to be managed by a fund manager regulated or licensed by the MAS (i.e. a holder of a capital markets services licence for fund management or a registered fund management company)[73]. Certain classes of persons exempt from the requirement to hold a licence but still subject to MAS oversight, are also permitted to manage VCCs (e.g. a bank licensed under the Banking Act[74], a merchant bank approved under the MAS

---

[69] Such a feature of the VCC provides the investors with privacy, and is a key consideration of many high net worth individuals.

[70] As the name suggests, variable capital companies are able to vary their capital structure readily. Traditional companies, on the other hand, have to undergo complex capital reduction procedures to vary their capital.

[71] See Part 12 of the Variable Capital Companies Act.

[72] Part 10A of the Companies Act.

[73] S 46 of the Variable Capital Companies Act.

[74] Cap. 19.

Act[75], a finance company licensed under the Finance Companies Act[76] and a company or co-operative society licensed under the Insurance Act[77]). The requirement to have a fund manager that is regulated by MAS is to mitigate risk of abuse of the VCC structure[78]. Notably, at this point in time, real estate fund managers, family offices and certain other managers which are exempt from licensing and registration, are not permitted to use VCCs[79].

Following the official launch of the VCC framework by the MAS and the ACRA on 15 January 2020[80], a total of 78 VCCs have been established in Singapore within a 6-month period[81]. By September 2020, despite the financial crisis triggered by the COVID-19 pandemic, the number of VCCs in Singapore jumped to 109, with more than 80% of the VCCs structured as umbrella funds[82]. There were more than 160 VCCs incorporated in Singapore as at the end of 2020[83]. The take-up rate for the VCC structure is poised for further growth, as global fund managers become more familiar and more experienced with the VCC.

For income tax purposes, a VCC is treated as a company and single entity[84]. This eliminates the need to file multiple income tax returns for the sub-funds. In addition, the tax exemption schemes for funds under sections 13R and 13X (which have been re-numbered as 13O and 13U with effect from 31 December 2021) of the Income Tax Act would be granted at the

---

[75] Cap. 186.

[76] Cap. 108.

[77] Cap. 142.

[78] Given that the VCC regime is relatively new in Singapore, the MAS could be concerned with VCCs being used for illicit or fraudulent purposes.

[79] Examples include single family office which is neither a capital markets services licence holder nor a registered fund management company. In contrast, a multi-family office which is licensed by or registered with the MAS may set up and manage funds using the VCC vehicle. It is however reported that an enhancement may be in the works to tweak the VCC framework to satisfy to the strong interest among single family offices. 'Plan to tweak VCC framework to draw more single family offices,' *The Business Times*, 7 December 2020.

[80] See Press release, *MAS and ACRA Launch Variable Capital Companies Framework*, 15 January 2020 and 'Much-lauded Variable Capital Companies framework and grant scheme launched,' *The Business Times*, 16 January 2020.

[81] 'Singapore's new fund structure makes a strong start,' *The Straits Times*, 7 July 2020.

[82] 'Variable Capital Companies: The right structure at the right place, right time,' *The Edge Singapore*, 14 September 2020.

[83] 'Plan to tweak VCC framework to draw more single family offices,' *The Business Times*, 7 December 2020.

[84] See MAS Circular, *Tax Framework for Variable Capital Companies (VCC)* (FDD Cir 14/2018), 31 October 2018.

umbrella VCC level. This in turn means that for the purposes of applying for these income tax exemption schemes, the qualifying conditions and the corresponding economic commitments are to be satisfied at the level of the umbrella VCC (as opposed to the being satisfied individually by each of the underlying sub-funds)[85].

3.2. Common features of fund management arrangements

While each fund structure has its own unique features, there are certain common features applicable to many of such structures, irrespective of the type of the vehicle the fund is established as. Some of these common features are set out below.

- **Duration of the fund life:** It is common for fund vehicles to be a fixed-life investment vehicle (e.g. 7 year or 10 years, plus some number of extensions, where applicable).
- **Management fees:** The fund vehicle will pay a management fee to the fund manager for the management of the fund (e.g. 1–2% of the committed capital or AUM of the fund).
- **Distribution Waterfall:** The process by which capital/income is allocated or distributed to the various investors is typically agreed upfront (commonly referred to as the "distribution waterfall"). It is common for the waterfall to include certain preferred return. A minimum rate of return (e.g. 8%) which is typically required to be achieved before the manager can receive any carried interest or share of the profits above the preferred return (e.g. 20%).
- **Transfer of an interest in the fund:** Private equity and closed-end funds are typically not intended to be transferred or traded. Where such interests are to be transferred to another investor, prior consent from the general partner may be required.
- **Mandate:** The fund manager has significant discretion to make investments and control the affairs of the fund. However, the mandate of the fund manager is typically restricted by the type, size, or geographic focus of investments permitted, and by its duration.

---

[85] See Sections 7.2.2.2 and 7.2.2.3 for more details on the tax exemption schemes available under s 13O and 13U of the Income Tax Act.

4. Typical Fund Structures

Traditionally, fund vehicles are domiciled in offshore jurisdictions such as British Virgins Islands and Cayman Islands. The management of such funds may however vest with a fund manager based in another jurisdiction such as Singapore or elsewhere. Where the fund manager is based outside Singapore, a Singapore-based sub-manager or investment adviser may nevertheless be appointed in instances where the fund makes investment in or via Singapore.

Prior to the introduction of the VCC, the three types of vehicles commonly used by fund managers in Singapore for funds were companies, limited partnerships or trusts. However, each vehicle comes with inherent limitations[86]. For example, companies are subject to the rules set out under the Companies Act which allow dividends to be paid out of profits only, restrict the buy-back of shares to 20% and impose restrictions on capital reduction. Limited partnerships, on the other hand, do not have separate legal personality and by themselves may not be entitled to tax treaty benefits. As for trusts, such structures are not commonly used outside the United Kingdom and the Commonwealth. In this regard, significant proportion of the funds that are managed by Singapore-based fund managers are often domiciled outside the country due to the flexible vehicles available in offshore jurisdictions such as the British Virgin Islands and Cayman Islands.

The introduction of the VCC vehicle is a game changer which enabled Singapore to directly compete with these traditional offshore fund domiciliation hubs amid global pressures requiring businesses to be domiciled in jurisdictions where they have substantive operations. Singapore, which is widely recognized as a leading fund management hub with strengths in portfolio management, trading and research, is poised to become the next fund domiciliation hub and to capture value from the entire value chain.

Fund structures commonly seen in Singapore include the master–feeder structure where the feeder fund acts as an investment pooling vehicle into which investors would invest their moneys. The feeder fund would in turn invest all or substantially all its funds into a master fund (i.e. the investment holding company that would make the investments).

---

[86] 'Singapore to attract more global funds,' *The Business Times*, 24 March 2017.

4.1. Fund vehicles constituted as companies

In fund structures where the fund vehicle is constituted as a company, the investors typically invest into the fund as ordinary and/or preference shareholders. The investors may also hold debt instruments in the fund. The fund company will in turn appoint a fund manager to manage its investments in return for a fee. A diagrammatic illustration of a simplified fund structure constituted as a company is set out in Figure 1.

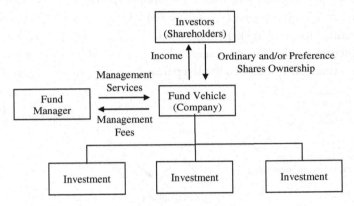

Figure 1:   Simplified company fund structure.

Where the fund is structured as a company, the constitution documents would typically set out the manner in which the company is governed (including the rights attached to the shares issued by the company, restriction on the transfer of shares, appointment and removal of directors, etc.).

4.2. Fund vehicles constituted as limited partnerships

In the limited partnership fund, the general partner may be the fund manager, a company controlled by the fund manager or a company directly owned by the key officers and/or shareholders of the fund manager[87]. The general partner of the limited partnership raises capital from investors who invest in

---

[87] As long as the general partner is ultimately owned by the key officers and/or shareholders of the fund management company, the fund management company may manage the fund as an accredited/institutional licensed fund management company or registered fund management company (as the case may be), notwithstanding that the general partner does not meet the requirements of an accredited investor or institutional investor.

the limited partnership fund as limited partners. The limited partners may also hold debt instruments in the limited partnership.

The limited partnership fund will appoint a fund manager to manage its investments in return for a fee. In this regard, the investors (who are the limited partners of the limited partnership fund) typically take a passive role and rely on the fund manager to make decisions in respect of the investments.

As limited partnerships do not have separate legal personality and are not entitled to benefits available under Singapore's network of tax treaties, it is common for a special purpose company (which has separate legal personality and is entitled to tax treaty benefits) to be interposed in the limited partnership fund structure, as a holding company. A diagrammatic illustration of a simplified fund structure constituted as a limited partnership is set out in Figure 2.

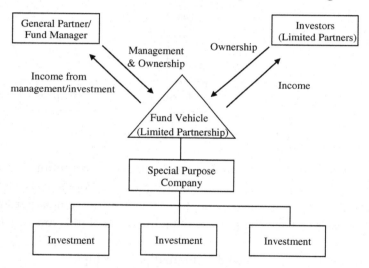

Figure 2: Simplified limited partnership fund structure.

4.3. Fund vehicles constituted as trusts

In fund structures where the fund vehicle is constituted as a trust, the investors typically invest into the fund as unitholders, with the investment assets of the trust fund held by a trustee. The unitholders may also hold debt instruments in the trust fund. The trust fund will in turn appoint a fund manager to manage its investments in return for a fee.

As trusts do not have separate legal personality and are not entitled to benefits available under Singapore's network of tax treaty, it is common for a special purpose company (which has separate legal personality and is entitled to tax treaty benefits) to be interposed in the trust fund structure, as a holding company. A diagrammatic illustration of a simplified fund structure constituted as a trust is set out in Figure 3.

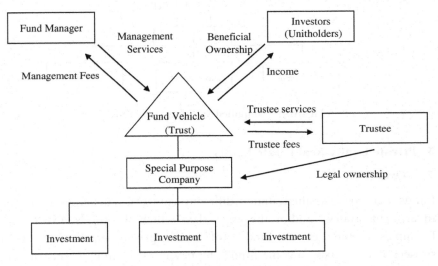

Figure 3: Simplified trust fund structure.

4.4. Fund vehicles constituted as VCCs

In fund structures where the fund vehicle is constituted as a VCC, the investors may invest into the fund via different classes of shares. The investors may also hold debt instruments in the fund.

In a VCC fund structure, the VCC may act as a standalone fund or an umbrella fund with multiple cells. Where the VCC fund has different classes of investors investing into different cells, each class of investors will typically hold different classes of shares in the VCC.

The VCC fund company will appoint a fund manager to manage its investments in return for a fee. A diagrammatic illustration of a simplified fund structure constituted as a VCC is set out in Figure 4.

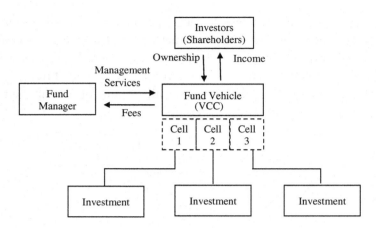

Figure 4: Simplified VCC fund structure.

5. Private Equity Real Estate Funds

5.1. Overview

Funds may be classified under different categories depending on the investment strategy and/or the asset class which the funds invest into. Examples include equity fund[88] (of which private equity fund is a subset), debt or fixed income fund[89], money market fund[90], infrastructure fund[91], real estate fund, hedge fund[92], venture capital fund[93], etc.

---

[88] Funds which primarily invest in equity instruments issued by other companies. Such equity instruments may be listed or unlisted.

[89] Funds which primarily invest in debt instruments such as bonds and similar instruments are issued by companies, government, and other organizations.

[90] Funds which primarily invest in the monetary market. Such funds are characterized by high liquidity, short-term securities and low risk profile compared to other investment funds.

[91] Funds which primarily invest in infrastructure projects and related investments.

[92] There is no statutory definition of what constitute a hedge fund in Singapore. Generally speaking, a hedge fund is understood to be a collective investment scheme which aims to achieve a high return through the use of advanced investment strategies. See Appendix 3 of the Code on Collective Investment Schemes (CIS Code), issued by the MAS, revised edition 1 July 2021. Such advanced investment strategies include market directional, corporate restructuring, convergence trading or opportunistic strategies. In assessing whether a collective investment scheme is to be regarded as hedge fund, the MAS would consider, among other aspects, the following: (i) the use of advanced investment strategies which may involve financial instruments which are not liquid, financial derivatives, concentration of investments, leverage or short selling; and (ii) the use of alternative asset classes. Hedge funds established in Singapore are commonly structured as trusts. For more details of the regulatory and tax regime applicable to hedge funds, see: Dale Gabbert and Andrew Wylie, *The Law of Hedge Funds: A Global Perspective*, 2018, Second Edition, LexisNexis.

[93] Funds which primarily invest in startup or early-stage companies. See also, Lin Lin, *Venture capital in Singapore: The way forward*, [2019] 5 Journal of Business Law 363.

Funds may also be classified as open-end or closed-end. Open-end funds are not limited by the number of units or shares which they can issue. When an investor invests into an open-end fund, more units or shares are issued; and when the investor exits the open-end fund, the open-end fund would buy back the units or shares, usually at net asset value. Closed-end funds, on the other hand, have a fixed number of units or shares. After the closing of the fund, no new investment capital flows into the fund. Investors of closed-end funds are generally not allowed to redeem or withdraw their investment during the lifetime of the fund. When the investor intends to exit his investment in the closed-end fund, he would generally have to sell or transfer his units or shares to other investors, at prices determined according to demand and supply of those units or shares. In this regard, closed-end funds (unlike open-end funds), may trade at a discount or premium to their net asset value.

Traditional funds are often structured as open-end funds, where investors can exit their investments by redeeming their investment units or shares in the fund. In contrast, alternative funds[94] (i.e. non-traditional funds), such as private equity, venture capital and real estate funds, are commonly structured as closed-end funds[95], which generally invest in illiquid assets with no readily available market for such assets.

As an example, investment in private equity funds are often closed-end, and generally made with a long-term investment horizon where profits are only realized in the long run. In contrast, open-end money market funds invest primarily in highly liquid short-term investments. Unlike money market funds where the investors can usually cash out their investments in the fund readily, investors of private equity funds are typically required to commit their capital for a minimum period of time (e.g. 3–5 years, 7–10 years, etc.)[96].

---

[94] Broadly speaking, there are two different types of alternatives. The first type involves investments in assets other than stocks, bonds and cash. Examples of such alternative investments include infrastructure, real estate and private equity. The second type involves investment strategies that go beyond traditional methods. Such alternative strategies may involve short-selling and the use of leverage. See website of BlackRock, one of the world's leading asset management firms <https://www.blackrock.com/sg/en/investment-ideas/alternative-investments-education-center/what-are-alternative-investments> (accessed 10 August 2020).

[95] Second reading of the Variable Capital Companies Bill by Ms Indranee Rajah, Second Minister for Finance, on 1 October 2018, available on the website of the Parliament of Singapore.

[96] In recent years, private equity firms such as Blackstone have raised funds that own companies for 15 years or longer, versus the typical 10-year model. Companies are staying private longer because of the

Generally speaking, closed-end funds such as private equity, venture capital and real estate funds are typically structured as limited partnerships (instead of corporate vehicles), due to the preference of global investors[97].

5.2. Private equity funds

Private equity funds are a specific category of funds which primarily invest in equities of private companies (as opposed to equities of publicly traded companies)[98]. Generally speaking, private equity funds are closed-end collective investment schemes. Such funds are usually marketed to and invested into by accredited and institutional investors.

At the inception of the fund, investors are generally required to commit a sum of capital for investment into the fund. The committed capital is drawn down during the investment term of the fund at the discretion of the fund manager, by way of a capital call. Where the fund is unable to identify suitable investment opportunities, it may not draw on the investors' commitment, and the investors may potentially invest less than expected or committed.

After acquiring a stake in the companies, private equity funds look to improve the profitability and value of the company through management changes, streamlining operations, or expansion, with the ultimate goal of exiting or selling the portfolio company for a profit. The exit may be by way of an initial public offering of the portfolio company or a sale to other interested private buyers, which may include another private equity firm.

Investors in closed-end private equity funds typically only receive returns on their investments at the end of the lifetime of the fund (generally 5–10 years) or in circumstances where the underlying investments are realized. Given the limited liquidity of the underlying investments, the capital injected by the investors are "locked-up" during the lifetime of the fund.

---

availability of capital and the ability to build their business model to prepare for the public market. See 'Private equity luring companies to stay private for longer,' *The Business Times*, 19 December 2019

[97] 'Variable capital company will boost Singapore fund sector,' *The Business Times*, 14 January 2020.

[98] For further discussion on private equity funds, see Lin Lin, *Private Equity in Singapore*, NUS Law Working Paper 2019/004, February 2019.

In terms of investment risks, the risk of loss of capital is typically higher for investment in private equity funds than investment in publicly traded companies, but lower than investment in venture capital funds. Venture capital funds which invest in companies during the earliest phases of their development, typically involve higher financial leverage.

5.3. Private equity real estate funds

Private equity real estate is a subset or specific category of private equity funds. In recent years, Singapore has become an emerging hot market for private real estate funds[99]. According to estimates by CBRE, some US$6 billion may have been deployed in Singapore from 2018 to 2020, with about US$4 billion having been invested in Singapore by private equity real estate funds between 2014 and the third quarter of 2017. The investors of real estate funds include pension funds, sovereign wealth funds and insurance companies[100].

In April 2019, CapitaLand announced that it has raised US$391.3 million for its first discretionary real estate equity fund, CapitaLand Asia Partners I (CAP I), which will invest in office buildings in Asia's key gateway cities, specifically Singapore, Beijing, Guangzhou, Shanghai, Shenzhen, Osaka and Tokyo, where CapitaLand is well established and has a proven track record as a developer–owner–operator. CAP I is CapitaLand's first discretionary private equity fund that allows CapitaLand to make full investment and asset management decisions on behalf of its capital partners. Before CAP I was announced, CapitaLand had earlier raised US$556 million in its first closing of Credo I China, the company's first discretionary real estate debt fund, in February 2019[101].

Private equity real estate funds raise capital from investors and utilize the capital to acquire and develop real estate, operate and enhance the real estate, and ultimately sell the real estate to realize a return on the

---

[99] 'Singapore an emerging hot market for private equity real estate funds,' *The Business Times*, 1 February 2018.

[100] 'AUM up 12% for top 5 Singapore property funds targeting Asia-Pacific,' *The Business Times*, 23 May 2019.

[101] 'CapitaLand's first closing of discretionary property equity fund raises US$391.3m,' *The Business Times*, 23 April 2019.

investment. Private equity real estate funds typically focus on commercial and industrial real estate, including offices, retail shops and malls, hotels, logistics facilities warehouses, etc. Such funds generally follow core, core-plus, value added, or opportunistic strategies when making investments[102]. A general description of the various categories of funds following different investment strategies are set out below[103].

- **Core strategy**: A low-leverage, low-risk strategy where the fund invests in stabilized assets with predictable cash flows (e.g. fully leased class A properties in core markets such as metropolitan or gateway cities), with the objective of securing stabilized income or yield for the long term. Leverage for core strategies typically lies in the 0–30% range. The targeted return is typically in the range of 7–10%, and the investment horizon may range from 7 to 15 years.

    An example of a fund pursuing core strategy is the closed-end private real estate fund, Allianz Real Estate Asia-Pacific Core I (AREAP Core I) jointly set up by the Allianz Group together with The National Pension Service of Korea in mid-2020[104]. The new fund, which is domiciled in Singapore, is expected to be the largest diversified closed-end core property fund in Asia Pacific and will have a fund life of 13 years, with targeted internal rate of return in line with the 7–10% range for core property funds in general. The fund, which has equity of US$2.3 billion, will pursue equity investments in Singapore, Japan, Australia, Hong Kong and China across office, logistics, multi-family residential and student housing sectors. The investment manager and general partner of the fund is Allianz Real Estate, the property investment manager within Allianz Group, a Munich-based insurer and asset manager.

- **Core plus**: The term "core plus" refers to "core" plus leverage, or leveraged core. Leverage for core plus strategies typically lies in the 30–50% range.

---

[102] 'Singapore an emerging hot market for private equity real estate funds,' *The Business Times*, 1 February 2018.

[103] It is to be noted that there is no universally agreed definition. Funds which follow similar investment strategies may well be structured differently.

[104] 'Allianz, Korean pension service set up Asia-Pac property fund,' *The Business Times*, 29 June 2020.

- **Value Added:** This is a medium-to-high-risk strategy targeted at properties with existing rental yield but seeks to grow the yield over time by making improvements to or re-positioning the property. Such strategy often involves acquiring under-leased or mis-positioned properties, improving the properties, and eventually selling them for gain. Such strategies typically involve properties which have management or operational problems, require physical improvement, and/or suffer from capital constraints. Value added strategies typically involve leverage ranging between 40% and 60%. The targeted return of value added funds could be in the range of 12–16%, with an investment horizon ranging from 3 to 7 years.
- **Opportunistic:** Such strategies follow the value-add approach, but take on significantly more risks. Opportunistic strategy is a high-risk, high-return strategy where the properties typically require a higher degree of enhancement (e.g. distressed assets). Such strategy may also involve investments in development, raw land, and niche property sectors. Opportunistic strategies typically employ leverage of up to 60% or higher. The targeted return of opportunistic funds could be in excess of 20%, with investment horizon which may range from 2 to 4 years.

Notably, there were recent reports that globally, institutional investors are starting to turn away from private equity real estate and infrastructure investments in favor of liquid funds that put their money to work faster[105]. In this regard, it was reported that private equity firms are driving up the cost of deals as they raise money faster than they can spend it, stockpiling a record US$1.26 trillion in undeployed capital as at March 2019, with about US$500 billion raised for real estate and infrastructure projects. Consequently, the earnings gap between public and private funds has been narrowing due to the amount of money pouring into private funds. Instead of waiting to deploy their capital in private funds, institutional investors are reportedly moving to mutual funds and other public vehicles that offer exposure to similar assets.

---

[105] 'Investors turning away from private equity real estate assets,' *The Business Times*, 24 April 2019.

5.4. Private equity real estate funds vs REITs vs listed real estate companies

While private real estate funds are similar to REITs and listed real estate companies in that they all invest primarily into real estate, there exist significant differences among them.

In the Singapore context, REITs are listed on a public stock exchange and raise capital from the public markets to acquire, develop, and invest in real estate. REITs are subject to governance framework and guidelines such as the Code on Collective Investment Schemes (CIS Code) which contains certain restrictions such as those concerning non-income producing real estate, development activities, borrowings and leverage. In addition, for income tax purposes, a REIT is required to distribute at least 90% of its distributable income in order to qualify for "tax transparency" treatment.

In contrast, listed real estate companies and private equity real estate funds are lightly regulated and not subject to similar guidelines and restrictions and do not enjoy the same tax benefits as REITs. Private equity real estate funds, being private investments, are the least regulated compared to listed real estate companies and REITs which are available to the general public for investment.

It is also worthwhile noting that investment in private equity real estate funds is relatively illiquid compared to investment in S-REITs and listed real estate companies[106]. The capital of the investors in private equity real estate funds is locked up for a number of years during the lifetime of the fund whereas investors in REITs and listed real estate companies generally do not have difficulty disposing of their investments.

5.5. Offer of securities

Funds are generally regarded as collective investment schemes (CIS)[107]. In Singapore, the offer of units or shares in a CIS is primarily governed

---

[106] See also: 'Stapled developer and REIT structure suggested to arrest trading discount,' *The Business Times*, 17 May 2021, which discussed the possibility of having a hybrid stapled vehicle which combines the attractive high distribution yield of a S-REIT and the riskier property development business of a listed real estate company. In that article, the stapled security comprising KLCC Property Holdings and KLCC REIT (whose assets include the Petronas Twin Tower) was cited.

[107] See definition of 'collective investment scheme' under s 2 of the Securities and Futures Act.

by the Securities and Futures Act[108], the Securities and Futures (Offers of Investments) (Collective Investment Schemes) Regulations 2005 ["Offers of Investments (CIS) Regulations"][109] and the CIS Code.

An offer of units or shares in a CIS to the general public in Singapore is required to fulfil certain key requirements. Where the CIS is constituted in Singapore, it has to be authorized by the MAS pursuant to section 286 of the Securities and Futures Act ("Authorized Scheme"). On the other hand, where the CIS is constituted outside Singapore, it has to be recognized by the MAS pursuant to section 287 of the Securities and Futures Act ("Recognized Scheme").

Any offer of units or shares in the CIS to the general public is also to be accompanied by a prospectus that is prepared in accordance with the prescribed requirements, lodged with and registered by the MAS[110]. Such prospectus is to be accompanied by a product highlight sheet that is prepared in accordance with the prescribed requirements and lodged with the MAS[111]. Some commonly relied upon exemptions from the prospectus requirements include:

- **Small offering exemption** under Section 302B of the Securities and Futures Act where the total amount raised from such offers within any 12-month period does not exceed S$5 million.
- **Private placement exemption** under section 302C of the Securities and Futures Act — where offers are not made to more than 50 persons in any 12-month period.
- **Institutional investor exemption** under section 304 of the Securities and Futures Act where the offers are made only to institutional investors.
- **Accredited investor and relevant person exemption** under section 305 of the Securities and Futures Act where the offers are made to accredited investors and other relevant persons[112]. The exemption also applies to

---

[108] Cap. 289.

[109] S 602/2005.

[110] See s 296 of the Securities and Futures Act as well as Part III and Third Schedule of the Offers of Investments (CIS) Regulations.

[111] See s 296A of the Securities and Futures Act as well as Part III and Eight Schedule of the Offers of Investments (CIS) Regulations.

[112] Defined under s 305 of the Securities and Futures Act as (a) an accredited investor, (b) a corporation the sole business of which is to hold investments and the entire share capital of which is owned by one or more individuals, each of whom is an accredited investor, (c) a trustee of a trust the sole purpose of

offers to a person who acquires the units as principal if the offer is on terms that the units may only be acquired at a consideration of not less than $200,000 for each transaction.

6. Fund Management

Fund management[113] is one of the regulated activities under the Securities and Futures Act[114]. A person who carries on a business of fund management is required to hold a capital markets services (CMS) licence for fund management[115], unless otherwise specifically exempt from holding a CMS licence[116].

In the Singapore context, fund managers are typically incorporated as private limited companies. Fund management companies seeking to be licensed or registered in Singapore must be incorporated in Singapore with a permanent physical office in Singapore[117].

From a regulatory perspective, fund management companies may broadly be categorized as licensed fund management company (LFMC), registered fund management company (RFMC) or other exempt fund management company[118].

---

which is to hold investments and each beneficiary of which is an individual who is an accredited investor; (d) an officer or equivalent person of the person making the offer (such person being an entity) or a spouse, parent, brother, sister, son or daughter of that officer or equivalent person, or (e) a spouse, parent, brother, sister, son or daughter of the person making the offer (such person being an individual).

[113] Defined in the Second Schedule to the Securities and Futures Act as managing the property of, or operating, a collective investment scheme, or undertaking on behalf of a customer (whether on a discretionary authority granted by the customer or otherwise), the management of a portfolio of capital markets products or the entry into spot foreign exchange contracts for the purpose of managing the customer's funds, but does not include real estate investment trust management.

[114] See Second Schedule to the Securities and Futures Act. Other regulated activities include dealing in capital markets products, advising on corporate finance, real estate investment trust management, product financing, providing credit rating services and providing custodial services.

[115] S 82 of the Securities and Futures Act.

[116] S 99 and Third Schedule to the Securities and Futures Act.

[117] See para 3.1 of Guidelines on licensing, registration and conduct of business for fund management companies (Guideline No: SFA 04-G05), issued by the MAS on 7 August 2012 (last revised on 25 March 2019) pursuant to s 321 of the Securities and Futures Act.

[118] For a discussion of the fund management industry in Singapore prior to the 21st century, see Ramin Cooper Maysami, *The Fund Management Industry in Singapore*, [1999] J.I.B.L 185.

6.1. Licensed fund management companies

A licensed fund management company (LFMC) is one which holds a capital markets services (CMS) licence for fund management activities. A LFMC may be (i) a licensed accredited/institutional investor fund management company (A/I LFMC) which serves "qualified investors" such as accredited/institutional investors, without restriction on the numbers or (ii) a licensed retail fund management company (Retail LFMC) which serves all types of investors (including retail investors i.e. non-accredited and non-institutional investors)[119]. More recently, a new regime was introduced on 20 October 2017 for fund management companies which manage venture capital funds offered to qualified investors[120] (VC LFMC)[121].

6.2. Registered fund management companies

A registered fund management company (RFMC) is one which is exempt from holding a CMS licence for fund management activities but is registered with the MAS[122]. A RFMC should have asset under management of no more than S\$250 million[123] and serves no more than 30 "qualified investors" of which no more than 15 are collective investment schemes, closed-end funds or limited partnerships where the limited partners comprise solely of accredited investors and/or institutional investors.

A high-level summary of the key requirements/restrictions applicable to Retail LFMC, A/I LFMCs, VC LFMC and RFMCs are set out in the Table 2.

---

[119] Retail LFMCs are subject to more stringent licensing and regulatory requirements compared to A/I LFMCs and RFMCs which are typically only offered to sophisticated and high net worth investors.

[120] See definition of 'venture capital funds' in reg 4(8) of the Securities and Futures (Licensing and Conduct of Business) Regulations (Rg. 10). Generally speaking a venture capital fund (i) invest at least 80% of committed capital in specified products that are directly issued by an unlisted business venture that has been incorporated for no more than 10 years at the time of initial investment ('qualifying investments'); (ii) invest up to 20% of committed capital in other unlisted business ventures that do not meet sub-criterion (i) above; (iii) the funds must not be continuously available for subscription, and must not be redeemable at the discretion of the investor; and (iv) the funds are offered only to accredited investors and/or institutional investors.

[121] For further discussion on the regulatory regime relating to private equity funds and their managers, see: Lin Lin, *Private Equity in Singapore*, NUS Law Working Paper 2019/004, February 2019.

[122] Registered under para 5(1)(i) of the Second Schedule to the Securities and Futures (Licensing and Conduct of Business) Regulations (Rg. 10).

[123] Para 5(7B)(d) of the Second Schedule to the Securities and Futures (Licensing and Conduct of Business) Regulations (Rg. 10).

Table 2: Summary of key requirements/restrictions applicable to Retail LFMC, A/I LFMCs, VC LFMCs and RFMCs.

	Retail LFMC	A/I LFMC	VC LFMC	RFMC
Types of Investors	All investors (including retail investors)	Accredited investors/Institutional investors	Accredited investors/Institutional investors	Accredited investors/Institutional investors
Limitation on Number of Clients	No restriction	No restriction	No restriction	30 clients (of which a maximum of 15 may be funds or limited partnerships)
Limitation on assets under Management	No restriction	No restriction	No restriction	Capped at S$250 million
Base Capital Requirement	S$500,000[a] to S$1 million[b]	S$250,000	None	S$250,000
Risk Based Capital Requirement	Financial resources are at least 120% of operational risk requirement	Financial resources are at least 120% of operational risk requirement	None	None
Chief Executive Officer (CEO)	At least 10 years of relevant experience	At least 5 years of relevant experience	No requirement on relevant experience	At least 5 years of relevant experience
Directors	At least 2 directors with 5 years of relevant experience. At least 1 Singapore resident executive director	At least 2 directors with 5 years of relevant experience. At least 1 Singapore resident executive director	At least 2 directors. No requirement on relevant experience. At least 1 Singapore resident executive director	At least 2 directors with 5 years of relevant experience. At least 1 Singapore resident executive director
Relevant Professionals[c]	At least 3 residing in Singapore with 5 years of relevant experience	At least 2 residing in Singapore with 5 years of relevant experience	At least 2 residing in Singapore. No requirement on relevant experience	At least 2 residing in Singapore with 5 years of relevant experience
Representatives[d]	At least 3 residing in Singapore	At least 2 residing in Singapore	At least 2 residing in Singapore	At least 2 residing in Singapore

| Others | A Retail LFMC or its shareholders should have at least a 5-year track record of managing funds for retail investors in a jurisdiction which has a regulatory framework that is comparable to Singapore. | The fund management company and its related corporations should also manage total assets of at least S$1 billion. |

Notes:

a Where the fund management company carries out fund management (non-CIS) on behalf of any customer other than an accredited or institutional investor.

b Where the fund management company carries out fund management in respect of any CIS offered to any investor other than an accredited or institutional investor.

c Relevant professionals would include the directors, CEO and representatives of the fund management company. If the relevant professional has sufficient experience, he/she may qualify as the relevant professional, representative and director.

d Individuals who are conducting regulated activities on behalf of a CMS licence holder or a financial institution exempted from licensing under s 99(1)(a) to (d) of the Securities and Futures Act are required to be appointed as an appointed, provisional or temporary representatives. See s 99B to s 99P of the Securities and Futures Act (and in particular, s 99B and s 99H). Representatives are individuals who conduct the regulated activity of fund management such as portfolio construction and allocation, research and advisory, business development and marketing or client servicing. They may include the directors and CEO of the fund management company. Representatives are required to meet applicable minimum entry and examination requirements as set out in the 'Notice on Minimum Entry and Examination Requirements for Representatives of Holders of Capital Markets Services licence and Exempt Financial Institutions under the Securities and Futures Act [SFA04-N09]' and any other relevant notices issued by MAS.

6.3. Other exempt fund management companies

Other persons exempt from holding a CMS licence for fund management activities include fund management companies which manage real estate funds for accredited/institutional investors as well as those which manages funds for related parties.

It is worthwhile noting that such exemptions generally restrict and limit the clientele of the fund management companies. As these exempt fund managers expand their fund management activities, they may consider going for the RFMC or LFMC status which allows them to diversify their clienteles and activities.

6.3.1. *Real estate fund managers — Immovable assets exemption*

A person who carries on business in fund management in Singapore on behalf of qualified investors where the assets managed comprise securities issued by one or more corporations or interests in bodies unincorporate, where the sole purpose of each such corporation or body unincorporate is to hold, whether directly or through another entity or trust, immovable assets, is exempt from holding a CMS licence (commonly referred to as the "immovable assets exemption")[124].

In other words, a fund manager which manages funds that invest solely in immovable assets or in securities issued by investment holding companies whose sole purpose is to invest into immovable assets and where the fund is offered only to accredited and/or institutional investors, would not be required to be registered with or licensed by MAS.

6.3.2. *Proprietary fund managers — Related corporation exemption*

A corporation which carries on business in fund management for or on behalf of any of its related corporations, is also exempt from holding a CMS

---

[124] Para 5(1)(h) of the Second Schedule to the Securities and Futures (Licensing and Conduct of Business) Regulations (Rg. 10).

licence (commonly referred to as the "related corporation exemption")[125]. Such fund managers are commonly referred to as proprietary fund managers and include family offices which manage internal funds of affluent families.

Broadly speaking, a family office is an entity which is set up to manage the financial and non-financial affairs of a family. This in particular include managing the assets of ultra-high net worth individuals or families, with a view to wealth preservation and/ or enhancement for their future generations[126]. The term "family" in this context may refer to individuals who are lineal descendants from a single ancestor as well as their spouses, ex-spouses, children, adopted children and step children[127].

Singapore, being a leading global financial services and wealth management hub, with world-class infrastructure, political stability and rule of law, is one of the preferred jurisdictions for wealthy families to set up family offices to manage their assets and investments. It is estimated that there are between 100 and 120 formalized family offices in Singapore as at year 2019[128], with another 221 family offices established in the country during year 2020[129].

Family offices may generally be classified under two broad categories — single family office (SFO) or multi-family office (MFO). SFOs are those which serve a single affluent family and is wholly owned or controlled by

---

[125] Para 5(1)(b) of the Second Schedule to the Securities and Futures (Licensing and Conduct of Business) Regulations (Rg. 10).

[126] The term 'family office' is not defined under the Securities and Futures Act.

[127] Frequently Asked Questions (FAQs) on The Licensing and Registration of Fund Management Companies published by the MAS, last updated on 17 September 2018.

[128] 'Ultra-rich family offices' investment returns hit by global uncertainties: Survey,' *The Straits Times*, 8 October 2019. According to the article, there is a strong and rising trend among Asian family offices to allocate their investments to private markets and real estate. Besides wealth management, family offices may also take on other functions for the family, including philanthropy and estate management.

[129] 'Singapore sees jump in family offices as Asia's ultra-rich set up camp,' *The Business Times*, 4 May 2021. With the robust growth of the family office sector in Singapore, the MAS announced in early 2022 that funds managed by family offices will have to meet stricter criteria to apply for tax incentives from 18 April 2022. These include new requirements on minimum fund size, AUM growth, business spending and investment professionals, among other stricter criteria. These changes seek to increase the professionalism of family offices in Singapore, and enhance the positive spillovers to the Singapore economy. See: 'MAS tightens criteria for family offices to qualify for tax incentives,' *The Business Times*, 14 April 2022.

members of the same family. On the other hand, MFOs are those which serve multiple affluent families.

Family offices which only provide services to related corporation may be exempt from obtaining licences for carrying on fund management[130] and financial advisory activities[131]. For example, where an affluent family sets up an office to manage the family's monies and hires employees to carry on such activities, no licensing or registration with the MAS is required as the SFO is essentially managing its own monies[132]. In contrast, MFOs which manage the funds of third parties are regulated and subject to the oversight of the MAS. An example of a SFO structure which could fall under the aforementioned exemption is set out in Figure 5[133]:

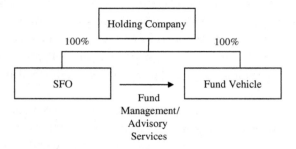

Figure 5: Simplified SFO structure.

Where an entity is in substance managing funds on behalf of a single family only but does not fall neatly within the scope of existing class licensing exemptions, it may seek licensing exemption from the MAS under section 99(1)(h) of the Securities and Futures Act.

Examples of such scenarios include cases where the fund vehicle or assets managed by the SFO are held directly by members of the family

---

[130] Exemption is available under para 5(1)(b) of the Second Schedule to the Securities and Futures (Licensing and Conduct of Business) Regulations (Rg. 10), read together with reg. 14 of Rg. 10 and section 99(1)(h) of the Securities and Futures Act.

[131] Exemption is available under the reg. 27(1)(b) of the Financial Advisers Regulations (Rg. 2) read together with s 20(1)(g) of the Financial Advisers Act.

[132] On the other hand, where the monies are managed by a third-party service provider, the third-party service provider conducting such activities would be required to hold a licence or otherwise be specifically exempt from holding a licence.

[133] Frequently Asked Questions (FAQs) on The Licensing and Registration of Fund Management Companies published by the MAS, last updated on 17 September 2018.

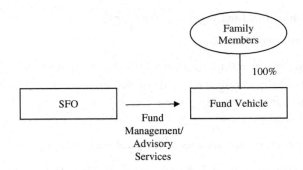

Figure 6: Fund vehicle held directly by family members.

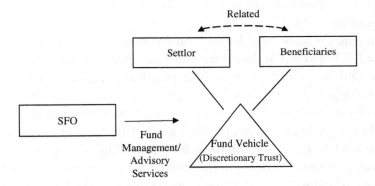

Figure 7: Fund vehicle constituted as discretionary trust.

(i.e. without the use of a common holding company) (see Figure 6) or where the assets are held under a discretionary trust with the settlor of the trust and the beneficiaries being members of the same family (see Figure 7).

7. Taxation of Fund Management Companies and Fund Vehicles

In the last section of this chapter, the taxation of fund management companies and fund vehicles will be discussed.

7.1. Taxation of fund management companies

7.1.1. *General taxation rules*

A fund management company carrying on fund management activities in Singapore would generally be taxed on the income which it derives from such activities, at the prevailing corporate income tax rate of 17%.

7.1.2. *Concessionary tax treatment for fund management companies*

A concessionary tax rate of 10% may be available if the fund management company meets the qualifying conditions, applies for the Financial Sector Incentive — Fund Management (FSI-FM) award, and the application is approved by the MAS.

Broadly speaking, in order for a fund management company to qualify for the FSI-FM award, it should have an asset under management of at least S$250 million, employ at least three investment professionals[134] and be licensed, registered or expressly exempted by the MAS from the licensing requirements to conduct fund management activities in Singapore[135].

The concessionary tax rate of 10% is granted in respect of income derived by the fund management company from providing fund management or investment advisory services to qualifying funds under the Section 13CA, Section 13R and/or Section 13X Exemption Schemes (which have since been re-numbered as Section 13D, Section 13O and section 13U respectively). These would be discussed at Section 7.2.2.

7.1.3. *Transfer pricing considerations*

In recent years, fund managers which outsource part of their work to related parties in overseas jurisdictions are subject to increasing scrutiny from tax authorities on their transfer pricing. This is especially so in light of the BEPS

---

[134] 'Professionals' refer to persons who are earning more than S$3,500 per month and must be engaged substantially in the FSI-FM qualifying activity. Such 'professionals' include to portfolio managers, research analysts, traders and any other roles as determined by MAS.

[135] See MAS Circulars, *Revisions to the Financial Sector Incentive Schemes* (Circular No: FDD Cir 06/2017), 11 May 2017 and *Extension and Refinement to the Financial Sector Incentive Schemes* (Circular No: FDD Cir 03/2013), 28 June 2013. In addition, please see Income Tax (Concessionary Rate of Tax for Financial Sector Incentive Companies) Regulations 2017 (S 239/2017).

initiative led by the OECD which had published 15 action plans, of which at least 4 are focused on transfer pricing[136].

Transfer pricing refers to the pricing of goods, services and intangibles between related parties. Singapore adopts the internationally accepted arm's length principle which requires related party transactions to be undertaken under conditions and circumstances similar to transactions between unrelated parties. The steps involved in the application of the arm's length principle include conducting a comparability analysis, identifying the most appropriate transfer pricing method and tested party, as well as determining the arm's length results[137]. In essence, the arm's length principle seeks to ensure that fair amounts of profit and tax are allocated to the jurisdictions where value creating activities are performed.

In the context of fund management, a key step in establishing a proper transfer pricing framework involves a comprehensive value chain assessment that maps out the core activities undertaken by a group of companies. Typically, core functions consist of portfolio management, trade execution, research, marketing and distribution activities while non-core functions may consist of accounting, fund administration as well as other back-end reporting activities[138].

The most appropriate transfer pricing method to be adopted in respect of each related party transaction is a question of fact. Various transfer pricing methods such as the comparable uncontrolled price method[139], the cost-plus method[140] and the profit-split method[141] may be suitable[142], depending on the specific factual matrix of the case on hand. This includes taking into

---

[136] See final reports of the OECD/G20 BEPS Project published 5 October 2015. The transfer pricing related action plans include, Actions 8 to 10: Aligning Transfer Pricing Outcomes with Value Creation, and Action 13: Transfer Pricing Documentation and Country-by-Country reporting.

[137] IRAS e-Tax Guide, *Transfer Pricing Guidelines*, Sixth Edition, 10 August 2021.

[138] See 'Managing transfer pricing risks,' *The Business Times*, 20 October 2020, for a discussion on the transfer pricing considerations.

[139] The comparable uncontrolled price method compares the price charged in a related party transaction to the price charged for similar transactions between independent parties in comparable circumstances. It is the most direct way to determine arm's length price and is generally preferred to the other methods.

[140] Under the cost plus method, a comparable gross mark-up is added to the costs of the goods or services in the related party transaction to arrive at the arm's length price of that transaction.

[141] The profit split method is based on the concept of dividing the combined profits of a transaction between related parties, in a similar way to how independent parties would under comparable circumstances.

[142] Other transfer pricing methods includes the resale price method and the transactional net margin method.

consideration whether the fund manager has full discretionary authority to undertake investment decisions, whether the fund manager sub-contracts a part of portfolio management to a sub-adviser, whether the sub-adviser has any discretionary investment decision-making capabilities, whether the sub-adviser is also involved in discretionary fund management activities of its directly managed funds (in addition to the provision of advisory services to its related parties), amongst others.

7.2. Taxation of fund vehicles

Over the years, Singapore has introduced a suite of tax incentive schemes to encourage the development of the fund management industry in Singapore and to enhance the country's attractiveness as a global hub for fund management activities. These tax exemption and concession schemes are available to Singapore-based fund managers and the funds which they managed, subject to meeting the relevant conditions. These schemes are reviewed by the authorities on a regular basis, with necessary enhancements and modifications made to the schemes to ensure that they remain relevant. In the absence of such tax exemption schemes, the income of a fund which is attributable to the discretionary fund management activities of a Singapore-based fund manager, may constitute Singapore sourced income and be taxable in Singapore.

Singapore's relatively low corporate income tax rate, comprehensive tax treaty network with more than 85 countries as well as the aforementioned tax incentive schemes have drawn many fund management companies to establish their presence in Singapore.

7.2.1. General taxation rules

The general taxation rules which are applicable under the Income Tax Act[143] in the absence of specific tax exemptions, are as set out below.

7.2.1.1. Companies and VCCs

For income tax purposes, companies and VCCs are subject to tax on their income at the prevailing corporate tax rate of 17% unless they qualify for specific tax incentives.

---

[143] Cap. 134.

To ease the compliance burden, an umbrella VCC with sub-funds will only be required to file a single corporate income tax return with the Inland Revenue Authority of Singapore (IRAS). Notwithstanding that, deductions and allowances for umbrella VCCs will be applied at the sub-fund level to determine the sub-fund's chargeable income[144].

7.2.1.2. Limited partnerships

For Singapore income tax purposes, limited partnerships are tax transparent entities. This basically means that limited partnerships do not pay any income tax; instead, the partners of a limited partnership are taxed on their respective share of income from the limited partnership. This is similar to the tax treatment accorded to general partnerships[145].

Where the limited partner of a limited partnership is an individual, his share of income from the limited partnership will be taxed based on his personal income tax rate. On the other hand, where the limited partner is a company, its share of income from the limited partnership will be taxed at the applicable corporate tax rate.

Being a tax transparent entity, limited partnerships are not entitled to the benefits available under Singapore's network of tax treaties. For this reason, a number of fund managers have set up their Singapore domiciled funds as a company instead of a limited partnership. Other fund managers opt for a master–feeder fund structure where the maser fund is set up as a Singapore tax resident company (which is entitled to the benefits available under Singapore network of tax treaty) and the feeder fund is a limited partnership.

7.2.1.3. Trusts

A trust is a vehicle constituted by a trust deed and does not have separate legal personality. Under a trust arrangement, the trustee is the legal owner of the underlying trust assets (commonly referred to as the "deposited property" in trust deeds), and the income arising from the use of the assets

---

[144] For further details on the taxation of VCCs, see: IRAS e-Tax Guide, *Tax Framework for Variable Capital Companies*, 28 August 2020.

[145] S 36C(1) of the Income Tax Act.

held under trust. In this regard, for Singapore income tax purposes, the general rule is that the income of a trust constitutes the statutory income of the trustee (and not that of the settlor or the beneficiary)[146]. The income is chargeable to tax in the hands of the trustee at the applicable corporate income tax rate.

Nevertheless, where the beneficiaries of a trust are tax resident in Singapore and entitled to a share of the income of the trust, a corresponding share of the income may be taxed in the hands of the beneficiaries[147]. Under such a scenario, the Singapore tax resident beneficiaries would also be accorded the concessions, exemptions and foreign tax credits available under the Income Tax Act, as though the beneficiaries had received the trust income directly[148]. In other words, the trust distributions received by such Singapore tax resident beneficiaries are deemed to have retained the nature of the underlying trust income for the purpose of claiming the concessions, exemptions and foreign tax credits.

It is a question of fact whether or not a beneficiary is entitled to the trust income. In this regard, the terms of the trust deed may be useful in shedding light on whether the beneficiaries of the trust are indeed entitled to the trust income. In practice, the Comptroller of Income Tax will regard the beneficiaries as being entitled to the income of the trust, where the trust income is distributed to the beneficiaries within the same year in which the trust income is derived.

The abovementioned "tax transparency" treatment does not apply in cases where (i) the income is derived by the trustee from a trade or business[149], (ii) trust income to which the beneficiaries are not entitled and (iii) trust income to which non-resident beneficiaries are entitled. In such cases, the trust income would be subject to a final tax in the hands of the trustee. Distributions subsequently made by the trustee out of such income would be capital in nature and would not be subject to any further tax in the hands of the beneficiaries.

---

[146] S 35(11) of the Income Tax Act.

[147] IRAS e-Tax Guide, *Income Tax Treatment of Trusts*, 8 October 2014.

[148] S 13Q, S 43M and S 50B of the Income Tax Act.

[149] S 43(2A)(c) and S 35(16)(c) of the Income Tax Act.

Where the trust income is to be taxed at the trustee level, the trustee is regarded as a body of persons for tax purposes. This is notwithstanding that the trustee may have legal personality in its own right (e.g. as a company or an individual). The applicable tax rate is the prevailing corporate tax rate (currently 17%)[150]. The partial tax exemption provided under section 43(6) of the Income Tax Act, would however not be granted to the trustee[151].

The overall effect of abovementioned tax treatment is that income derived through a trust would not be imposed twice — at the trustee level and again at the level of the beneficiaries.

7.2.2. *Income tax exemption for fund vehicles*

The fund vehicle tax exemption schemes currently available include the following:

(1) Tax exemption scheme for qualifying offshore funds under section 13CA (which has since been re-numbered as section 13D) of the Income Tax Act (Offshore Fund Exemption Scheme) — The exemption is available to certain qualifying non-citizen non-resident individuals, non-resident companies and trust funds where the trustee does not have a taxable presence or carry on a business in Singapore[152]; (collectively referred to as "prescribed persons").

(2) Tax exemption scheme for qualifying resident or onshore funds under section 13R (which has since been re-numbered as section 13O) of the Income Tax Act (Resident Fund Exemption Scheme) — The exemption is available to qualifying Singapore incorporated tax resident companies; and

(3) Tax exemption scheme for enhanced tier funds under section 13X (which has since been re-numbered as section 13U) of the Income Tax Act (Enhanced Tier Fund Exemption Scheme) — The exemption is available to qualifying onshore and offshore funds.

---

[150] S 43(1)(c) of the Income Tax Act.

[151] See IRAS e-Tax Guide, *Income Tax Treatment of Trusts*, 8 October 2014.

[152] Other than due to its functions as the trustee of that trust fund, or the presence of a fund manager.

The Offshore Fund Exemption Scheme is primarily designed for offshore fund vehicles (i.e. those which are established outside Singapore) whereas the Resident Fund Exemption Scheme is targeted at onshore fund vehicles (i.e. those which are established in Singapore). Both schemes are sometimes referred to as the "Basic Tier Fund Schemes" and cater to funds which are primarily invested by non-Singapore investors.

On the other hand, the Enhanced Tier Fund Exemption Scheme offers additional flexibility and does not restrict the tax residency status of the fund and that of the fund's investors. In addition, the exemption scheme is available in respect of all types of fund vehicles, including managed accounts. The Enhanced Tier Fund Exemption Scheme, however, comes with higher qualifying thresholds, including a S$50 million minimum fund size requirement and an annual S$200,000 minimum local business spending requirement. The different qualifying conditions which are attached to the respective fund vehicle tax exemption are elaborated in the subsequent sections.

Notwithstanding the different qualifying conditions attached to each of the fund vehicle tax exemption schemes (i.e. Offshore Fund Exemption Scheme/Resident Fund Exemption Scheme/Enhanced Tier Exemption Scheme, as the case may be), a common requirement is that the fund must be managed in Singapore by a Singapore-based fund manager[153]. In the absence of a Singapore-based fund manager (who is contributing to the overall economic activities in Singapore), there would have been no incentive for the Singapore Government to confer tax exemption status to the funds.

In the event that any of the qualifying conditions for any basis period is not satisfied, the fund will not be entitled to enjoy the income tax exemption of "specified income" derived from "designated investments" for the relevant basis period. Nonetheless, the fund would be entitled to income tax exemption in the subsequent period during the lifetime of the fund, where it satisfies the relevant conditions in that subsequent period.

---

[153] 'Fund manager' is defined in s 2 of the Income Tax Act as 'a company holding a capital markets services licence under the Securities and Futures Act 2001 for fund management or that is exempted under that Act from holding such a licence'. Under the Resident Fund Exemption Scheme, the fund may also be managed by a person approved or appointed by the Minister for Finance.

The scope of each fund vehicle tax exemption scheme is also the same in that the exemption is granted in respect of "specified income" arising or derived from "designated investments"[154] managed by the Singapore-based fund manager.

The list of "designated investments" includes instruments which investors commonly invest in, such as stocks and shares, debt securities, units in REITs, exchange traded funds, and registered business trusts, as well as immovable properties situated outside Singapore. The list of "designated investments" however specifically exclude[155] such stocks, shares and debt securities, which are issued by an unlisted company that is in the business of trading or holding of Singapore immovable properties.

The abovementioned exclusion however does not apply to instruments issued by companies that are in the business of property development. In other words, stocks, shares and debt securities issued by property development companies (whether such companies are listed or not) would qualify as "designated investments".

It is also to be noted that immovable properties situated in Singapore are specifically excluded from the list of "designated investments". In this regard, where a tax exempt fund invests in Singapore immovable properties (i.e. non "designated investments"), the income arising from such investments (e.g. rental income and disposal gains) would not qualify for tax exemption under the relevant fund vehicle tax exemption scheme. Such exclusion of Singapore immovable properties from the list of "designated investments" is for good policy reason, particularly given that any exemption of income arising in connection with Singapore immovable properties could have the effect of encouraging investments in immovable properties in land-scarce Singapore, which may in turn cause property prices to spiral out of control.

---

[154] For definitions of 'specified income' and 'designated investments,' please refer to Income Tax (Exemption of Income of Prescribed Persons Arising from Funds Managed by Fund Manager in Singapore) Regulations 2010 (S 6/2010).

[155] The exclusion in respect of debt securities only applies to 'non-qualifying debt securities'. 'Non-qualifying debt securities' are debt securities that do not enjoy the 'qualifying debt securities' tax status as defined under s 13(16) of the Income Tax Act. In other words, 'qualifying debt securities' issued by an unlisted company that is in the business of trading or holding of Singapore immovable properties should qualify as 'designated investments'. The term 'qualifying debt securities' is in turn defined under s 13(16) of the Income Tax Act.

While the list of "designated investments" is updated on a regular basis, the exhaustive nature of the listing means that any investments (particularly, emerging and new classes of assets) which are not specifically covered within the list of "designated investments" would not qualify for tax exemption.

The list of "specified income", on the other hand, is crafted as a "negative list"[156] which deems all streams of income as "specified income", except for a few types of income which are specifically identified as not being "specified income". The types of income which do not qualify as "specified income" generally relate to income of "tax transparent entities" (e.g. S-REITs or trusts), such as distributions made by a trustee of a real estate investment trust that is listed on the Singapore Exchange[157] as well as distributions made by a trustee of a trust which is a resident of Singapore or a permanent establishment in Singapore, unless the trust enjoys tax exemption[158]. Where a tax exempt fund received income which is not "specified income" (e.g. distribution from a REIT listed on the Singapore Exchange), the income received by the fund would be subject to Singapore income tax under the prevailing tax rate.

Where a tax exempt fund received income which is not "specified income" from "designated investments", this should not in itself disqualify the fund from enjoying tax exemption in respect of any other "specified income" which it derived from "designated investments".

The fund vehicle tax exemption schemes currently have a sunset clause with the expiry date of 31 December 2024. Prior to the expiry of the schemes, the Government would review the usefulness and relevance of the schemes and determine whether the schemes should be extended and/or refined. In any case, all funds which have been approved by the MAS for the purposes of the relevant fund vehicle tax exemption schemes as of 31 December 2024 would continue to enjoy the tax exemption after 31 December 2024, subject to them meeting the relevant conditions of the respective schemes[159].

---

[156] The 'negative list' came into operation on 17 February 2012. The objective was to simplify the list of specified income, so as to keep up with industry development and changes. With the introduction of the 'negative list', all income derived from designated investments will be regarded as 'specified income,' unless otherwise excluded.

[157] For further discussion on real estate investment trusts listed on the Singapore Exchange, please see Chapter 8.

[158] Where the tax exemption is granted under ss 13D, 13F, 13L, 13U of the Income Tax Act.

[159] See MAS circular, *Tax Incentive Schemes for Funds* (Circular No: FDD Cir 09/2019), 7 June 2019.

In addition, qualifying funds[160] that are managed or advised by Singapore-based fund managers also enjoy withholding tax exemption and Goods and Services Tax (GST) remission on expenses incurred by the fund vehicles for the purposes of their investment activities[161].

7.2.2.1. Offshore Fund Exemption Scheme

The Offshore Fund Exemption Scheme was introduced with a view to promoting the use of Singapore-based fund managers to manage funds which are domiciled outside the country (i.e. offshore funds), where such funds are substantially invested by foreign persons. Under the Offshore Fund Exemption Scheme[162], the income of a "prescribed person" arising from funds managed in Singapore by any fund manager may be exempt from income tax[163]. A "prescribed person" includes an individual, a company and a trustee of a trust fund.

To qualify as a "prescribed person", an individual must be neither a citizen of Singapore nor resident in Singapore. In addition, the individual must be the beneficial owner of the funds managed by a fund manager in Singapore.

In the case of a company, the company must not be resident in Singapore. It must not have a permanent establishment in Singapore (other than a fund manager) or carry on any business in Singapore. It must also not be a company with income which is derived from investments which have been transferred (other than by way of a sale on market terms and conditions) from a person carrying on a business in Singapore, where the

---

[160] Funds which satisfy the conditions for the tax exemption under sections 13D, 13O, 13U of the Income Tax Act throughout the relevant period.

[161] The GST remission for prescribed funds managed by prescribed fund managers in Singapore is available until 31 December 2024. See: MAS circular, *Goods and Services Tax Remission on Expenses for Prescribed Funds Managed by Prescribed Fund Managers in Singapore* (FDD Cir 11/2021), 29 November 2021. The circular provides the fixed recovery rate of 89% for 1 January 2022 to 31 December 2022.

[162] See Income Tax (Exemption of Income of Prescribed Persons arising from Funds managed by Fund Manager in Singapore) Regulations 2010 (S 6/2010) for the regulations which governs the Offshore Fund Exemption Scheme.

[163] The Offshore Fund Exemption Scheme is not available in respect of a trust that is a pension or provident fund which is approved under s 5 of the Income Tax Act, a designated unit trust as defined in s 35(14) of the Income Tax Act, a real estate investment trust as defined in s 43(10) of the Income Tax Act and a company or trust which is approved under the Enhanced Tier Fund Exemption Scheme.

income derived by that person from those investments was not, or would not have been if not for the transfer, exempt from tax. Basically, the exemption scheme should not be used as a tax shelter for income of a company which is otherwise taxable.

As regards the trustee of a trust fund, the trustee must not (i) have a permanent establishment in Singapore (other than due to its functions as the trustee of that trust fund, or the presence of a fund manager or any other person who acts on behalf of the trustee in carrying out its functions as the trustee of that trust fund) or (ii) carry on any business in Singapore (other than due to its functions as the trustee of that trust fund). It must also not be a trustee with income which is derived from investments which have been transferred to him in his capacity as a trustee of that trust fund (other than by way of a sale on market terms and conditions) from a person carrying on a business in Singapore where the income derived by that person from those investments was not, or would not have been if not for their transfer, exempt from tax. Basically, the exemption scheme should not be used as a tax shelter for trust income which is otherwise taxable.

A "qualifying investor" of a qualifying fund under the Offshore Fund Exemption Scheme includes an individual investor, a *bona fide* non-resident non-individual investor[164], a designated person[165], a fund under the Resident Fund Exemption Scheme[166], a fund under the Enhanced Tier Fund Exemption Scheme[167] and an investor (other than one falling within any of the aforementioned categories) who either alone or together with

---

[164] A *bona fide* non-resident non-individual investor is one which carries out substantial business activities for genuine commercial reasons and has not as its sole purpose the avoidance or reduction of tax. The *bona fide* entity not resident in Singapore should not have a permanent establishment in Singapore (other than a fund manager) and does not carry on a business in Singapore. Where the *bona fide* entity not resident in Singapore carries on an operation in Singapore through a permanent establishment in Singapore, the funds used by the entity to invest directly or indirectly in the qualifying fund should not be obtained from such operation.

[165] The definition of 'designated person' includes GIC Pte Ltd, certain GIC affiliates, certain approved companies wholly owned by the Minister as a corporation established under the Minister for Finance (Incorporation) Act, and statutory boards. See Income Tax (Exemption of Income of Prescribed Persons Arising from Funds Managed by Fund Manager in Singapore) Regulations 2010 (S 6/2010) for the full definition of 'designated person'.

[166] The fund must at all times during the basis period satisfies the conditions of the Resident Fund Exemption Scheme.

[167] The fund must at all times during the basis period satisfy the conditions of the Enhanced Tier Fund Exemption Scheme.

his associates[168] beneficially own on the relevant day[169] not more than the prescribed percentage[170] of the issued securities or total value (as the case may be), in the qualifying fund under the Offshore Fund Exemption Scheme[171].

Any non-qualifying investor would be liable to pay a financial penalty to the Comptroller of Income Tax. In essence, the financial penalty is designed to clawback the income tax benefits which the non-qualifying investors would otherwise have enjoyed through the Offshore Fund Exemption Scheme.

Unlike the Resident Fund Exemption Scheme and Enhanced Tier Fund Exemption Scheme, no formal application is required for the purposes of enjoying the Offshore Fund Exemption Scheme. It is also worthwhile noting that the setting up and maintenance of a fund qualifying under the Offshore Fund Exemption Scheme is relatively easy, as compared to the higher threshold requirements to be satisfied in order to qualify for the Resident Fund Exemption Scheme and Enhanced Tier Fund Exemption Schemes which are further discussed below.

7.2.2.2. Resident Fund Exemption Scheme

The Resident Fund Exemption Scheme was introduced in year 2006 to encourage the domiciliation of funds in Singapore, with a view to creating a positive spin-off effect for the fund management eco-system in Singapore. In

---

[168] Two investors of the fund under the Offshore Fund Exemption Scheme are deemed to be associates of each other if (i) at least 25% of the total value of the issued securities in one investor is beneficially owned, directly or indirectly, by the other; or (ii) at least 25% of the total value of the issued securities in each of the two investors is beneficially owned, directly or indirectly, by a third entity. The latter does not apply where an investor is an independent listed entity and does not have 25% or more shareholding in any other investor of the fund.

[169] 'Relevant day' generally refers to the last day of the fund's financial year. For the full definition of 'relevant day,' please see s 13D(9) of the Income Tax Act.

[170] The prescribed percentage is (i) 30% where the fund has less than 10 investors and (ii) 50% where the fund has at least 10 investors. This is also known as the '30/50 rule'.

[171] Unit trusts which are constituted on or after 1 April 2019 would be granted a waiver from the 30/50 rule for the first 2 years of assessment from the date of the unit trusts' constitution, provided that the unit trust is a retail unit trust [i.e. a unit trust which is included under the Central Provident Fund Investment Scheme (CPFIS) or which meets all of the following conditions: (a) the unit trust is a collective investment scheme (CIS) that is authorized under section 286 of the Securities and Futures Act and the units of which are open to public for subscription; (b) the unit trust is not a real estate investment trust (REIT) or a property trust that invests directly in Singapore immovable properties; and (c) the trustee of the unit trust is tax resident in Singapore]. See MAS Circular, *Tax Incentive Schemes for Funds* (Circular No.: FDD Cir 09/2019), 7 June 2019.

this regard, the Resident Fund Exemption Scheme[172] is available to funds set up in the form of a Singapore incorporated and tax resident[173] company[174]. Such funds are required to meet various conditions including incurring at least S$200,000 in expenses in each financial year[175], using a Singapore-based fund administrator, and being managed or advised directly by a fund management company in Singapore[176].

Other conditions imposed include the fund not serving other investment purposes apart from what it is approved for under the Resident Fund Exemption Scheme[177], as well as not deriving income from investments which have been transferred (other than by way of a sale on market terms and conditions) from a person that was previously carrying on a business in Singapore, where the income derived by that person would not have been tax-exempted if not for the transfer.

---

[172] See Income Tax (Exemption of Income of Approved Companies arising from Funds managed by Fund Manager in Singapore) Regulations 2010 (S 8/2010) for the regulations which governs the Resident Fund Exemption Scheme.

[173] A company is tax resident in Singapore if the control and management of its business is exercised in Singapore. As a general rule, the meetings of the board of directors of the fund company must be held in Singapore.

[174] The Resident Fund Exemption Scheme is available to VCCs. See MAS Circular, *Tax Framework for Variable Capital Companies (VCC)* (FDD Cir 14/2018), 31 October 2018.

[175] According to general accounting principles. With effect from 18 April 2022, stricter conditions are imposed on new applications for the Resident Fund Exemption Scheme by fund vehicles managed or advised by a family office which (i) is an exempt fund management company which manages assets for or on behalf of the family(ies) and (ii) is wholly owned or controlled by members of the same family(ies). In particular, such applicants must have a minimum fund size of $10 million at the point of application, and must be committed to increasing AUM to $20 million within a 2-year period. The family offices managing the applicant funds are also required to have at least 2 investment professionals. Furthermore, the minimum business spending requirement for such funds will be subject to a tiered framework pegged to AUM size. The required minimum business spending is set at $200,000 for funds with AUM of less than $50 million, and $1 million for funds with AUM of $100 million and above. Applicant funds are also required to invest at least 10% of their AUM or $10 million, whichever is lower, in local investments at any one point in time. Examples of 'local investments' include equities listed on the Singapore-licensed exchanges, qualifying debt securities, funds distributed by Singapore-licensed/ registered fund managers, or private equity investments into non-listed Singapore incorporated companies such as start-ups with operating businesses in Singapore. Prior to the change, there were no such stipulated conditions pertaining to minimum fund size, minimum number of investment professionals, tiered minimum business spending and minimum local investments. For the avoidance of doubt, the criteria for other applicants to qualify for the Resident Fund Exemption Scheme remain unchanged.

[176] The fund management company must hold a capital markets services licence for the regulated activity of fund management under the Securities and Futures Act, be exempt from the requirement to hold such a licence under the Securities and Futures Act, or is approved by the Minister or such other person as he may appoint.

[177] The investment objective/strategy of the fund should be within the scope of what the fund is mandated to do via its offering document (or its equivalent).

In addition, the fund must satisfy all other conditions as specified in the letter of approval issued by the MAS for the purpose of the Resident Fund Exemption Scheme.

One of the conditions typically specified in the letter of approval for the purpose of the Resident Fund Exemption Scheme is that the fund must not be a person who was previously carrying on a business in Singapore, where that business in Singapore generated income that would not have been tax-exempted. The MAS has since clarified that with effect from 19 February 2019, this would exclude income from (i) warehousing of investments[178], (ii) setting up bank accounts in anticipation of commencing operations and (iii) placement of monies in deposits or money market instruments on a temporary basis before an application for the Resident Fund Exemption Scheme is made[179].

In order for a fund to enjoy the benefits of the Resident Fund Exemption Scheme, an application would have to be made to the MAS for approval. In addition, the fund manager is required to make an annual declaration to the MAS confirming that the relevant conditions have been satisfied.

Previously, there was an additional condition that the fund must not have 100% of the value of its issued securities beneficially owned, directly or indirectly, by Singapore persons. Such a restriction has since been removed with effect from the year of assessment 2020 (i.e. financial year ending 2019). Notwithstanding the removal of the abovementioned restriction, investors of a fund under the Resident Fund Exemption Scheme, who either alone or together with their associates[180], on the relevant day[181], beneficially own issued securities of the fund, the value of which is more than the

---

[178] 'Warehousing of investments' means a fund acquiring investments at an initial stage of the fund's existence, prior to closing the fund.

[179] See MAS Circular, *Tax Incentive Schemes for Funds* (Circular No.: FDD Cir 09/2019), 7 June 2019.

[180] Two investors of the fund are deemed to be associates of each other if (i) at least 25% of the total value of the issued securities in one investor is beneficially owned, directly or indirectly, by the other; or (ii) at least 25% of the total value of the issued securities in each of the two investors is beneficially owned, directly or indirectly, by a third entity. The above does not apply where an investor is an independent listed entity and does not have 25% or more shareholding in any other investor of the fund.

[181] Relevant day refers to the last day of the fund's financial year or in the case where the fund ceases to be an approved fund within the financial year, the last day on which the fund enjoys the Resident Fund Exemption Scheme.

prescribed percentage[182], would be regarded as "non-qualifying investors" for the purposes of the scheme and would be liable to pay to the Comptroller of Income Tax a financial penalty. Such financial penalty would however not apply to the following investors: an individual, a *bona fide* entity not resident in Singapore[183], a designated person[184], another fund under the Resident Fund Exemption Scheme[185] or a fund under the Enhanced Tier Fund Exemption Scheme[186].

Similar to the Offshore Fund Exemption Scheme, the imposition of a financial penalty under the Resident Fund Exemption Scheme is designed to clawback any income tax benefits which would otherwise have been enjoyed by the non-qualifying investors.

7.2.2.3. Enhanced Tier Fund Exemption Scheme

The Enhanced Tier Fund Exemption Scheme[187] was introduced in year 2009 to further increase the attractiveness of Singapore as a fund management hub, by providing Singapore-based fund managers with greater flexibility in sourcing for investment mandates.

Unlike the then existing tax exemption schemes (i.e. Offshore Fund Exemption Scheme and Resident Fund Exemption Scheme), the then newly-introduced Enhanced Tier Fund Exemption Scheme provides considerable

---

[182] The prescribed percentage is (i) 30% where the fund has less than 10 investors and (ii) 50% where the fund has at least 10 investors. This is also known as the '30/50 rule'.

[183] The *bona fide* entity not resident in Singapore should not have a permanent establishment in Singapore (other than a fund manager) and does not carry on a business in Singapore. Where the *bona fide* entity not resident in Singapore carries on an operation in Singapore through a permanent establishment in Singapore, the funds used by the entity to invest directly or indirectly in the approved company should not be obtained from such operation.

[184] The definition of 'designated person' includes GIC Pte Ltd, certain GIC affiliates, certain approved companies wholly owned by the Minister as a corporation established under the Minister for Finance (Incorporation) Act, and statutory boards. See Income Tax (Exemption of Income of Prescribed Persons Arising from Funds Managed by Fund Manager in Singapore) Regulations 2010 (S 6/2010) for the full definition of 'designated person'.

[185] The fund must at all times during the basis period satisfy the conditions of the Resident Fund Exemption Scheme.

[186] The fund must at all times during the basis period satisfy the conditions of the Enhanced Tier Fund Exemption Scheme.

[187] See Income Tax (Exemption of Income arising from Funds managed in Singapore by Fund Manager) Regulations 2010 (S 414/2010) for the regulations which governs the Enhanced Tier Fund Exemption Scheme.

flexibility in that it does not dictate whether the funds are established offshore or onshore and does not impose any restriction on the amount of investments that a Singapore person may invest into the fund. This greatly eased the administrative burden placed on the fund managers who are otherwise required to track the investors and the interest which they hold in funds under the Offshore Fund Exemption Scheme and Resident Fund Exemption Scheme.

In addition, the Enhanced Tier Fund Exemption Scheme accords flexibility in that it is available to fund vehicles set up in any form[188]. Prior to 20 February 2018, it was only available in respect of funds set up in the form of companies, limited partnerships and trusts. The relaxation of the rules to allow fund vehicles to be set up in any form to qualify for the Enhanced Tier Fund Exemption Scheme, takes into account the fact that fund vehicles, particularly those which are set up outside Singapore, may not always be in the same legal form (i.e. companies, limited partnerships, trusts and VCCs) as those in Singapore.

Given the flexibility offered under the Enhanced Tier Fund Exemption Scheme, the qualifying conditions and thresholds are higher than those of the Offshore Fund and Resident Fund Exemption Schemes. These conditions include having a minimum fund size of S$50 million at the time of application[189], incurring at least S$200,000 of local business spending in each basis period relating to any year of assessment[190], using a Singapore-

---

[188] Including managed accounts with effect from 19 February 2019. Such a change paves the way for the Enhanced Tier Fund Exemption Scheme to be available in situations where the holder of a managed account is an entity with an active business operation.

[189] As investment performance and investor redemptions are factors external to the fund and given that these external factors will affect the ongoing fund size, the fund size condition is only required to be complied with at the point of application. The other qualifying conditions will have to be fulfilled by the fund throughout the life of the fund.

[190] According to general accounting principles. Such expenses include the following expenses paid to local entities: remuneration, management fees and other operating costs. With effect from 18 April 2022, stricter conditions are imposed on new applications for the Enhanced Tier Fund Exemption Scheme by fund vehicles managed or advised directly by a family office which (i) is an exempt fund management company which manages assets for or on behalf of the family(ies) and (ii) is wholly owned or controlled by members of the same family(ies). In particular, the family offices managing the applicant funds are also required to have at least 3 investment professionals, with at least one of them being a non-family member. Furthermore, the minimum business spending requirement for such funds will be subject to a tiered framework pegged to AUM size. The required minimum local business spending is set at $500,000 for funds with AUM of less than $100 million, and $1 million for funds with AUM of $100 million and above. Applicant funds are also required to invest at least 10% of their AUM or $10 million, whichever

based fund administrator if the fund is a company incorporated in Singapore, with its tax residence in Singapore[191], as well as being managed or advised directly by a fund management company[192] in Singapore which employs at least 3 investment professionals[193] in Singapore. The majority of the funds under the Enhanced Tier Fund Exemption Scheme should generally not have difficulty meeting the S$200,000 local business spending requirement, given that the fund management fees charged by their Singapore-based fund managers are well likely to exceed the required S$200,000 threshold, assuming fees are charged at 0.5% of the fund size of S$50 million.

In respect of the S$50 million fund size requirement, where real estate, infrastructure, private equity, debt or credit funds as well as private equity fund of funds are concerned, the condition may be satisfied by the committed capital secured by the fund. This is provided that the committed capital is legally enforceable through a contract between the investor and the fund, and the fund manager should have recourse to recover any capital committed or to take the necessary remedial action in the event the investor defaults on its commitments. In addition, the fund must demonstrate that a component of payments made to the fund manager is charged based on the committed capital (i.e. undrawn amounts included). The concession takes into account the fact that such funds typically operate on a committed capital basis.

Other qualifying conditions for the purpose of the Enhanced Tier Fund Exemption Scheme include the fund not serving other investment

is lower, in local investments at any one point in time. Examples of 'local investments' include equities listed on the Singapore-licensed exchanges, qualifying debt securities, funds distributed by Singapore-licensed/registered fund managers, or private equity investments into non-listed Singapore incorporated companies such as start-ups with operating businesses in Singapore. Prior to the change, there were no such stipulated conditions pertaining to non-family member investment professionals, tiered minimum local business spending and minimum local investments. For the avoidance of doubt, the criteria for other applicants to qualify for the Enhanced Tier Fund Exemption Scheme remain unchanged.

[191] A company is tax resident in Singapore if the control and management of its business is exercised in Singapore. As a general rule, the meetings of the board of directors of the company must be held in Singapore.

[192] The fund management company must hold a capital markets services licence for the regulated activity of fund management under the Securities and Futures Act, be exempt from the requirement to hold such a licence under the Securities and Futures Act, or is approved by the Minister or such other person as he may appoint.

[193] Investment professionals refer to portfolio managers, research analysts and traders who are earning more than S$3,500 per month and must be engaging substantially in the qualifying activity.

purposes apart from what it is approved for under the Enhanced Tier Fund Exemption Scheme,[194] as well as not concurrently enjoying other tax incentive schemes[195].

In addition, the fund must satisfy all other conditions as specified in the letter of approval issued by the MAS for the purpose of the Enhanced Tier Fund Exemption Scheme.

In recognising that most fund managers structure their portfolio holdings under one or more special purpose vehicles (SPVs) to facilitate ring-fencing of liabilities, the Enhanced Tier Fund Exemption Scheme is also available to (i) master–feeder fund structures, (ii) master-SPV fund structures as well as (iii) master–feeder–SPV fund structures where the master–feeder funds hold their investments via SPVs[196]. Funds with any of the aforementioned structures may submit a consolidated tax incentive application.

The minimum fund size for master–feeder fund structures where (i) the feeder funds invest solely in the master fund and (ii) the feeder funds do not trade, is S$50 million. On the other hand, in respect of (i) master–feeder fund structures with trading feeder funds, (ii) master–feeder–SPV fund structures with trading feeder funds and (iii) master–SPV fund structures, the minimum fund size will be the sum of the economic commitments expected from each fund entity. As an example, for a structure comprising a master fund, 2 feeder funds that trade and a SPV, the fund structure should collectively have a minimum fund size of S$200 million (i.e. S$50 million × 4) at the point of application and incur at least S$800,000 (i.e. S$200,000 × 4) in local business spending in each financial year.

---

[194] The investment objective/strategy of the fund should be within the scope of what the fund is mandated to do via its offering document (or its equivalent).

[195] Funds that are currently under the other tax incentive schemes for funds (e.g. Resident Fund Exemption Scheme) can also be considered for the Enhanced Tier Fund Exemption Scheme if they are able to meet the relevant conditions. For the purposes of this condition, any trust which enjoys or used to enjoy an approved pension or approved provident fund status under section 5 of the Income Tax Act will not be deemed as having met this condition.

[196] Under a master–SPV fund and master–feeder–SPV structure, the master fund must be a company, trust or limited partnership incorporated/constituted/registered in Singapore, as the case may be, and be regarded as a Singapore tax resident for each basis period. The SPV may be partially or wholly owned by the master fund. With effect from 19 February 2019, (i) the SPV can take on any legal form, (ii) the SPV can be partially owned by the master fund and co-investors are allowed if the co-investors are incentivized funds (i.e. funds incentivized under fund vehicle tax exemption schemes) or foreign investors, and (iii) there is no restriction on the number of tiers of SPVs that the master fund can have.

As regards master–feeder–SPV fund structures with non-trading feeder funds, the minimum fund size will be the sum of the economic commitments expected from the master fund and each of its SPVs.

In order for a fund to enjoy the benefits of the Enhanced Tier Fund Exemption Scheme, an application would have to be made to the MAS for approval. In addition, the fund manager is required to make an annual declaration to the MAS confirming that the relevant conditions have been satisfied.

Looking into the Future

Financialization of Real Estate

Real estate is known notoriously for its heterogeneity, illiquidity, immobility and even opacity as an asset class. Then two decades ago, Singapore saw the securitization of real estate in the listing of its first real estate investment trust (REIT) in CapitaMall Trust. Through such securitization, real estate has been repackaged and transformed into standardized, liquid and transparent financial assets, which are readily tradeable in the domestic and global investment markets and evaluated in terms of their risks and yields. Through the process, ownership of real estate is separated from its management and liquidity is created out of spatial fixity[1]. That was a momentous step in the convergence of the property and financial markets, or the financialization of real estate in Singapore[2].

Tokenisation of Real Estate

Almost two decades on, an emerging trend in the financialization of real estate is tokenization which will provide for further integration of the financial and property markets. The term "tokenisation" is generally used to refer to the fractionalisation of rights via the digital representation of

---

[1] See KF Cotham, 'Creating Liquidity out of Spatial Fixity: The Secondary Circuit of Capital and the Restructuring of the US Housing Finance System' in MB Aalbers (ed), *Subprime Cities: The Political Economy of Mortgage Markets*, Blackwell Publishing, 2012.

[2] See Liew Mun Leong, 'A new look for the for the real estate sector', *The Business Times*, 9 August 2002. The article by the former President and CEO of CapitaLand Ltd, was published soon after the listing of CapitaMall Trust in July 2002.

ownership of the asset or of the benefits from the asset, and usually involves distributed ledger technologies such as blockchain[3]. The tokens may then be traded on a secondary market.

In the context of real estate, the trend may refer to (i) the tokenisation of direct interests in or benefits from real estate or (ii) the tokenisation of shares in or benefits from real estate holding entities. In essence, tokenisation gives the investors a share in an underlying real estate, or a share in benefits from the underlying real estate. With such tokenisation, an investor in consideration of his monetary investment, will receive digital tokens which is generally seen as a capital markets product where the offer or issue of digital tokens is regulated under the Securities and Futures Act[4]. The fractional ownership model allows investors to own a fraction of the underlying asset or the benefits flowing from the asset, as opposed to owning the entire asset[5].

A digital token may constitute a share, a debenture, a unit in a business trust, a securities-based derivatives contract or a unit in a collective investment scheme[6]. Such a token has sometimes been referred to as a security token which may be sub-categorised into equity tokens (representing an equity claim on the issuer of the tokens) and debt tokens (representing a debt claim on the issuer)[7]. Singapore-based digital asset exchanges which issue security tokens include 1exchange, iSTOX (which has since been re-branded as ADDX) and ECXX Global.

The efficiencies of blockchain technology have been said to offer cost savings for the issuance and trading of asset-backed security tokens[8]. In Singapore, digital tokens are still at the nascent stage. In April 2021, it

---

[3] See 'The next steps in real estate: Tokenisation and fractionalisation,' *The Edge,* 25 October 2021, *Tokenized Securities & Commercial Real Estate,* MIT Digital Currency Initiative, Working Group Research Paper, 14 May 2019, *Tokenisation: the future of real estate investment?* (University of Oxford Research, January 2020) and 'Real estate tokenisation — what does it mean for investors,' *The Business Times,* 10 February 2022.

[4] See Ronald J.J. Wong, 'Digital Tokens and Market Conduct Laws,' *Law Gazette,* December 2020.

[5] See 'Straits Trading launches shareholders' club, offering fractional investment in properties,' *The Business Times,* 10 September 2021.

[6] Monetary Authority of Singapore (23 December 2019), *A Guide to Digital Token Offerings,* para 2.3.

[7] The other two types of digital tokens are (i) payment tokens which are intended as a means of payment for goods and services, and (ii) utility tokens which are intended to provide access to an application or service, e.g. cloud storage or the use of a meeting room.

[8] 'Singapore, as a top financial hub, should ride blockchain wave,' *The Business Times,* 1 October 2020.

was reported that digital securities platform iSTOX (which has since been renamed ADDX) had, for the first time, tokenised a private real estate fund — Mapletree Europe Income Trust (MERIT), a European office fund launched by Mapletree Investments — and reduced the investment ticket into the fund for 50 accredited investors. Smaller accredited investors (such as those with a net worth between $2 million and $20 million) often find it very difficult to gain access to private real estate funds because of the minimum investment amount required. iSTOX enabled that access by tokenising the assets into smaller ticket size, using blockchain and smart-contract technology to overcome manual processes in the life cycle of a security, such as custody, ownership tracking, fund earnings distribution and secondary trading[9]. The use of these tokens may also bring down costs for issuers and investors by eliminating the need for intermediaries. No doubt, we will hear more of digital tokens and there will be more to write about, in the years ahead.

Meanwhile, the Singapore tax system has to evolve to provide greater certainty on the tax treatment of the distributions of the security tokens for the greater reception of digital tokens in the market place[10]. There has to be tax neutrality in that tax treatment of the distributions from equity tokens and debt tokens should be aligned with that of the distributions from shares and bonds/notes, if investors are to switch to the digital counterparts.

---

[9] 'Part of Mapletree's first European office fund offered in digital tokens,' *The Business Times*, 7 April 2021.

[10] The Inland Revenue Authority of Singapore has issued an e-Tax Guide, *Income Tax Treatment of Digital Tokens*, Revised Edition, 9 October 2020.

Postscript

The Land Betterment Charge Act 2021 discussed in Chapter 3 has come into operation on 1 August 2022, together with the following subsidiary legislation:

(a) Land Betterment Charge (Table of Rates and Valuation Method) Regulations 2022[1];
(b) Land Betterment Charge (Concessionary Relief) Order 2022[2];
(c) Land Betterment Charge (General) Regulations 2022[3];
(d) Land Betterment Charge (Deferment) Regulations 2022[4]; and
(e) Land Betterment Charge (Compoundable Offences) Regulations 2002[5].

The Table of Rates in the Second Schedule of the Land Betterment Charge (Table of Rates and Valuation Method) Regulations, replaced the Development Charge Table in the revoked Planning (Development Charges) Rules. As discussed in Chapter 3, the land betterment charge (unlike the earlier development charge) gives a discount for the leasehold tenure of the development site. The discount table (which is the Singapore Land Authority leasehold value table[6]) appears in the Seventh Schedule to the Regulations.

With the migration of the development charge under the Planning Act 1998 to the land betterment charge under the Land Betterment Charge Act

---

[1] S 569/2022.
[2] S 570/2022.
[3] S 571/2022.
[4] S 572/2022.
[5] S 573/2022.
[6] See Table 3 in Chapter 3.

2021, the following subsidiary legislation under the Planning Act 1998 has been revoked on 1 August 2022:

(a) Planning (Hotel Concession) Rules;

(b) Planning (Development Charges) Rules;

(c) Planning (Development Charge — Exemption) Rules;

(d) Planning (Development Charge — Exemption in relation to the Historical Base Value) Rules 2008;

(e) Planning (Deferment of Payment of Development Charge by Charities) Rules 2017;

(f) Planning (Temporary Development Levy) Rules;

(g) Planning (Temporary Development Levy — Exemption) Rules; and

(h) Planning (Deferment of Payment of Temporary Development Levy by Charities) Rules 2016.

Authors' Biography

TAY HONG BENG

Hong Beng is the Head of Real Estate sector and was until September 2020, the Head of Tax at KPMG in Singapore. He has more than 30 years of experience in tax consulting for the real estate and financial services sectors and is heavily involved in advising on complex tax issues in structured transactions, merger and acquisition deals (including tax due diligence and pre-IPO restructuring), corporate restructuring, international tax planning and investment projects.

In recent years, Hong Beng has participated as a key advisor for several high-profile real estate transactions and tax disputes resolution assignments in Singapore. He is a member of KPMG's Global Real Estate Steering Committee and KPMG Singapore's Operations Committee. He is a regular speaker at tax seminars and contributed numerous articles and commentaries on current and topical tax-related issues. Hong Beng is also a Board Member of Singapore Chartered Tax Professionals.

LEUNG YEW KWONG

Yew Kwong is Principal Tax Advisor at KPMG in Singapore. He practised as a tax lawyer before joining KPMG in 2012 and argued the landmark cases of *ACC v Comptroller of Income Tax* [2011] 1 SLR 1217 (on the income tax issue of withholding tax on interest rate swap payments), *ZF v Comptroller of Income Tax* [2011] 1 SLR 1044 (on the income tax issue of workers' dormitories as plant) and *Chief Assessor v First DCS Pte Ltd* [2008] 2 SLR(R)

724 (on the property tax issue of district cooling system as qualifying machinery), amongst others.

Prior to his tax practice, Yew Kwong was with the Singapore Inland Revenue for 28 years where his last held positions were Chief Legal Officer and Chief Valuer. Yew Kwong has authored and co-authored a number of books including *Property Tax in Singapore* (Third edition, 2015, LexisNexis), *LexisNexis Annotated Statutes of Singapore: Stamp Duties Act* (2022 electronic edition) and *Development Land and Development Charge in Singapore* (Butterworths, 1987).

SEE WEI HWA

Wei Hwa is a tax partner at KPMG in Singapore with more than a decade of tax advisory and compliance experience in managing an entire spectrum of domestic and international tax issues. In his current role, Wei Hwa is focused on formulating and implementing tax strategies as well as managing and resolving tax disputes. His areas of practice include advising on the tax aspects of mergers & acquisitions, internal restructurings, initial public offerings, intellectual property planning and value chain management.

As a Singapore tax practitioner, Wei Hwa has extensive experience in managing all major aspects of income tax, stamp duty, property tax and goods and services tax. As an international tax practitioner, Wei Hwa has been significantly involved in cross-border transactions, including advising on permanent establishment risks, withholding tax exposures, BEPS developments and tax treaty interpretation.

Wei Hwa is an accredited tax advisor and chartered accountant who also holds a Master of Laws. He has written various articles and books pertaining to taxation, and also lectured at the tax academy where he taught intermediate and advanced taxation.

Index

A

Additional buyer's stamp duty, ABSD, 34, 83, 85, 86, 88–97, 100, 101, 112, 114, 163, 184, 188–192, 196, 197, 198, 199, 342, 351–357, 360, 361, 364, 396, 397, 398, 401, 410, 513
    introduction, 88–96, 351–355
    remission for housing developers, 89–93, 355–357

ABSD (Trust), 91, 354

Additional conveyance duty, ACD, 83, 84, 96–99, 101, 112, 199, 394–407, 409–417, 422, 513
    acting in concert, 409
    anti-avoidance, 411–414
    associates, 399, 406–409
    property holding entity, PHE, 84, 97–99, 199, 395–407, 410–414
    prescribed immovable property, 395, 400–404, 410, 411, 414
    rates, 410
    significant owner, 199, 396, 399–401, 405–407

B

Badges of trade, 378, 379, 389, 422, 423, 426
    capacity to hold, 389
    circumstances leading to disposal, 386–388
    frequency of similar transactions, 383, 384
    length of period of ownership, 384, 385
    mode of financing, 389
    motive, 379–383
    subject matter of realization, 383
    supplementary work carried out, 388

Banking Act, 563

Base erosion and profit shifting, 554

Borrower–Mortgagor requirement, 371

Building Control Act, 426

Building Management and Strata Management Act, 40

Business trusts, 429, 439–441, 443, 445, 447, 449, 463, 485, 509, 511, 517–549, 551, 552, 593
    Registered business trust, 511, 517, 520, 524, 528–548, 593
        responsible entity, 531, 534, 538
        sponsor, 537

trustee-manager, 531, 533–541,
  545
typical structure, 535
unitholders, 541
Business Trusts Act, 517, 526–530,
  533–536, 538–543

C
Charities Act, 501
Collective sale, 31–35, 37, 39, 41,
  43–45, 56, 183, 190, 194, 359
  collective sale order, 183, 190, 359
  consent level, 36, 37, 42, 46
  financial loss, 38
  distribution of proceeds, 38
  share value, 37–45
  SISV guidelines, 38, 44
  strata area, 38, 39, 41–45
  Strata Titles Board, 37, 43, 190
Companies Act, 347, 527, 530, 534,
  538, 556, 557, 562, 563, 566
Compulsory acquisition, 2–10, 13–17,
  20, 25–27, 31, 55, 147, 169
  betterment, 28
  (ex-gratia) compensation, 18–20,
    25, 27
  fire site, 9, 22, 24
  person interested, 30
  Pointe Gourde principle, 26
  profit rent, 30, 31
  public purpose, 7, 10, 11, 13, 14,
    16, 22, 25, 26, 28, 138
  public safety, 5
  road lines, 26, 27
  unearned increment, 22
Concept Plan, 106–108, 143
  Long Term Plan, 106, 108
  State and City Planning Project,
    106

Constitution of Singapore
  equal protection, 8, 35
Co-operative Societies Act, 501
COVID-19 (Temporary Measures) Act,
  61–67, 76, 327, 493, 533
COVID-19 pandemic, 4, 61–67, 74, 76,
  86, 93, 102, 152, 183, 184, 189, 192,
  240, 244, 326, 327, 341, 342, 354,
  356, 360, 361, 459, 486, 487, 493,
  530, 533, 534, 564
  rental relief, 4, 61, 65–67

D
Development charge, DC, 35, 52, 99,
  100, 102, 120, 123, 126–129, 131,
  134, 136–153, 156–179, 181, 209,
  442, 460, 468, 552
  Chief Valuer, 135, 136, 150, 162,
    164, 171–173, 176, 179, 181,
    188, 335
  development baseline, 32, 100,
    131, 137, 139–149
  development ceiling, 131, 139, 140
  development charge exemption,
    139, 148–150
  development charge table, 100,
    123, 131, 150–165, 171–173,
    175, 176, 179, 181
  section 39 valuation, 139, 151,
    157, 164–167
  use group, 135, 152, 156–161,
    163–165, 176
Development Guide Plan, 32, 34, 35,
  141–143
Differential premium, DP, 52, 102, 113,
  126–129, 131, 133, 134, 137, 161,
  173–177, 179–181
Due diligence work, 415, 430
  disclosure letter, 434–437

tax indemnity, 437
tax warranty, 431

F
Family office, 551, 564, 583, 584, 598, 601
Finance Companies Act, 564
Financialization of real estate, 605–607
Fiscal measures, 74
Fund management, 550–556, 560–566, 578
   licensed fund management companies, 579
   registered fund management companies, 579
   other exempt fund management companies, 582
Fund vehicle, 556
   companies, 556
   limited partnerships, 557
   trusts, 560
   variable capital companies, 560
   income tax exemption, 591
      designated investments, 592–594
      enhanced tier fund exemption scheme, 600
      offshore fund exemption scheme, 595
      resident fund exemption scheme, 597
      specified income, 592–594
   typical fund structures, 566–570

G
Givings, 1–3, 31, 34, 35, 52
   derivative giving, 1–3
   physical giving, 1–3
   regulatory giving, 1–3

Goods and Services Tax, GST, 76, 101, 236, 237, 238, 311, 312, 357, 378, 390, 391, 428, 429, 488, 489, 490, 509, 510, 511, 546, 547, 595
   self-accounting, 509, 510
   GST Act, 101, 236, 237, 311, 357, 390, 428, 429, 509, 510
   recovery of GST, 510, 511
Government Land Sales, GLS, 12, 71, 75, 85, 91, 96, 100, 104, 105, 107, 108, 109, 112, 113, 114, 163, 185, 187, 188, 189, 236, 238, 239
Good class bungalow, 105
Greater Southern Waterfront, 2, 110, 111
Guarantor–Borrower requirement, 371

H
Housing Developers (Control and Licensing) Act, 90, 187, 191, 200, 202
   Housing Developers Rules, 206, 207
   project account, 201–206, 210, 211, 264
   stakeholding money, 206–209
Housing and Development Board (HDB) flats
   build-to-order, BTO, 1–3
   lease decay, 45
   lottery effect, 2
   minimum occupation period, 2, 367, 370,
   prime location public housing model, 2, 107
   selective en bloc redevelopment scheme, SERS, 2, 31, 46
   voluntary early redevelopment scheme VERS, 45, 46

I

Income tax
  business of the making of
    investments, 248, 250–252
    same investment, 253
  capital allowances, 247, 248, 250,
    251, 299–301, 306, 307, 308,
    310, 311, 544
    business use test, 304, 305
    completeness test, 304, 305
    functional test, 302
    premises test, 304, 305
  change of intention, 121, 222–224,
    229, 235
    principle of mutuality, 231
  commencement of business, 257,
    258
  deduction, 255
    borrowing costs, 293
    capital vs revenue expenditure
      272
    diminution in value, 213
    duality of purpose, 270
    enduring benefit test, 273
    identifiable asset test, 275
    in the production of income,
      210, 213, 248, 253, 255,
      259–266, 269, 270, 272,
      285, 299, 303
    interest expense, 275
    practical and business point of
      view, 271
    purpose test, 259–261
    repair expenses, 294
    wider nexus test, 211,
      262–264
  safe harbour rule, 423–426
  single project concession, 221
Income Tax Act, 76, 77, 79, 101, 201,
  203, 208, 210, 211, 214, 215,
  218–220, 223, 225, 228, 233, 235,
  245, 247, 248, 250, 251, 255–257,
  261, 264, 271, 272, 276, 278, 285,
  286, 288, 293, 294, 299, 300, 307,
  394, 398, 423, 425, 427, 428, 431,
  441, 469, 488, 491, 494–497,
  499–507, 520, 542–545, 559, 564,
  565, 589, 590–595, 597, 603
International Organizations (Immunities
  and Privileges) Act, 501, 502, 505

J

Jurong Town Corporation, JTC, 17, 57,
  119, 125

K

Kampong Glam, 3, 23, 47–51, 122
    Sultan Hussain (Amendment) Act,
      47, 50
    Sultan Hussain Ordinance, 47–50

L

Land betterment charge, LBC, 35, 52,
  99, 100, 102, 113, 121, 125–137,
  139, 141, 150–152, 158, 161, 164,
  168, 173, 177, 179, 180–182, 223
    chargeable consent, 128–132, 134,
      135
    chargeable event, 130, 131
    concessional State title, 134
    controlled activity, 128–130, 132,
      135
    post-chargeable valuation, 131,
      132, 139
    pre-chargeable valuation, 131, 132,
      139
    table of rates, 129, 131, 132, 135,
      136, 150, 151, 158, 173, 181, 182
Land Titles (Strata) Act, 35–40, 46, 190,
  231

Leasehold value table, 177
Limited liability partnerships, 349, 350,
    398, 403–405, 407, 412, 428, 468,
    506, 547, 548
Limited Liability Partnerships Act, 468
Limited partnerships, 393, 398,
    403–405, 407, 412, 419–421,
    556–568, 572, 579, 580, 589, 601,
    603
Limited Partnerships Act, 420, 557–559
Loan tenure, 74, 191, 365–367
Loan-to-value ratio, LTV, 73, 74, 88, 90,
    191, 353, 365–367, 372

M
Macroprudential policy instruments, 73
Master Plan, 2, 20, 21, 26, 27, 29, 30,
    32, 34, 57, 69, 86, 87, 88, 94, 95,
    101–115, 117–119, 122, 123, 134,
    141–151, 158, 164–166, 168–171,
    236, 237, 391, 401, 411
    CBD Incentive Scheme, 110, 164
    Master Plan zones, 86–88, 94, 95,
        101, 111, 158
    Written Statement, 103, 109, 111,
        112, 117, 141
    Strategic Development Incentive
        scheme, 110
Minister for Finance (Incorporation)
    Act, 596, 600
Mortgage servicing ratio, 365, 367

O
Offer of securities, 576
Option to purchase, OTP, 83, 123, 343,
    354, 366, 371, 372, 399

P
Partnership Act, 420

Planning (Use Classes) Rules, 115, 116,
    126, 244
Planning Act, 29, 30, 34, 35, 87, 94,
    95, 99, 101–103, 111, 116, 121–127,
    129–131, 134, 138–140, 144,
    146–148, 151, 157, 164, 166–169,
    173–175, 223, 240, 243, 244, 328,
    391, 402
    1960 existing use, 124, 126
    material change of use, 122, 133, 244
    outline permission, 123
    pre-application consultation
        services, 122
    provisional permission, 30, 123,
        124, 151, 152, 159, 165, 175
    written permission, 30, 54, 101,
        102, 104, 116, 117, 121–126,
        130, 138–140, 151, 152, 170,
        172, 223, 240, 402
Property Market Consultative
    Committee, 71, 75, 454
Property tax, 52, 62–66, 74–76, 102,
    141, 209, 238, 240, 242, 244, 247,
    250, 268, 301, 312, 314, 315,
    317–327, 429, 476, 478
    annual value, 63, 65, 75, 238–240,
        312–320, 324, 327, 429, 478
    development land, 238
    installation of fixtures, 319
    machinery, 320
    rebates, 326
    remission, 62–66, 102
    rent-free period, 317, 318
Property Tax Act, 62, 238, 240, 268,
    312, 314, 320, 326, 429

R
REITs
    asset enhancement initiatives, 461

Code on Collective Investment
Scheme, CIS Code, 478–484,
487, 523, 527, 530, 531, 534,
540, 543, 570, 576, 577
interest coverage ratio, ICR, 484,
485, 487
limitation on sources of other
revenue, 481
limitations on borrowings and
leverage, 483
permissible investments, 480–482
real estate related assets, 441, 467,
474, 475, 479–481, 488, 527,
530
restriction on development
activities, 482, 483
valuation of the underlying real
estate, 487
exchange traded funds, 450–452,
488, 490, 491, 494, 495,
499–505, 593
mergers and consolidations, 452,
461
property manager, 458, 466, 467,
476–478
sponsor, 469
S-REIT manager, 471
trustee, 471
typical structure, 466
unitholders, 470
rental support payments, 496, 497
sub-trusts, 462, 468, 488, 491,
492, 494, 496-500, 504, 511,
532
tax transparency, 440, 447, 455,
467–469, 488–497, 499–505,
514, 520, 529, 532, 534, 541,
542, 576, 590
specified income, 491, 493–495,
497, 499–501, 503, 505

Rent control, 4, 58, 59, 61
Controlled Premises (Special
Provisions) Act, 59
designated development area, 59,
60
Golden Shoe area, 59, 60, 446,
468, 483
repeal of rent control, 4, 58
Tenants Compensation Board, 60
Residential Property Act, 70, 102,
182–184, 188, 357–359, 361–363
clearance certificate, 357–360
Controller of Residential Property,
184, 358, 359
extension charge, 102, 182, 184,
185, 360–362, 364
project completion period, PCP,
102, 183–185, 359–361
qualifying certificate, QC,
182–185, 188, 229, 357,
359–364

S
Sale and purchase agreement, 86, 97,
98, 193–196, 201, 206, 207, 343,
370, 398, 399, 414–417, 419, 431,
434
Securities and Futures Act, 99, 441,
462, 463, 478, 479, 481, 488, 524,
527, 528, 530, 534, 559, 576–578,
581, 583, 584, 592, 597, 598, 602
Seller's stamp duty, SSD, 38, 71, 74,
78–89, 101, 114, 118, 124, 372–378,
397, 398, 410, 513
industrial property, 376
relief, 377
residential property, 372
exemption/remission, 377
Stamp duty
advancement of duty point, 97

book-entry securities, 98, 99, 416, 417, 513

buyer's stamp duty, BSD, 78–80, 82, 89, 91, 189, 190, 192, 193, 196, 198, 199, 343, 344, 351, 354, 357, 361, 377, 396–398, 410, 422, 513

contingency principle, 331–337, 419

conveyance direction, 195–199

deferred consideration, 417

earn-outs, 394, 417–419

lease vs licence, 328

partnership interests, 419

scripless shares, 98, 416, 417, 548

relief from stamp duty, 344, 422

  amalgamation, 346

  associated permitted entities, 349

  reconstruction, 344–346, 348, 349, 351, 377, 422

Stamp Duties Act, 78, 79–83, 86, 89, 91, 94–97, 114, 127, 184, 189, 190, 193, 196, 277, 328, 330, 331, 333, 334, 336–339, 343–345, 347, 349, 373, 374, 394, 395, 398, 399, 401–407, 409, 411–418, 422, 547, 548

State leases

  extension, 3, 52

  topping-up premium, 56, 127, 182

Subterranean space, 4, 25, 57, 58

T

Takings, 1–4

Total debt servicing ratio, TDSR, 74, 84, 88, 191, 365, 368–371

Temporary Occupation Permit, 37, 134, 191, 197, 202–205, 258, 354, 359

Tokenization, 605–607

Trade Unions Act, 501

Trust scheme of arrangement, 452, 461–465, 524

Trustees Act, 528, 560

V

Variable Capital Companies Act, 561–563

Printed in the United States
by Baker & Taylor Publisher Services